Level 2   **TEACHER EDITION**   Units 1–6

CALIFORNIA

LANGUAGE!®Live

VOYAGER SOPRIS LEARNING™

Louisa Moats, Ed.D., Author

1 2 3 4 5   FRD   19 18 17 16 15

978-1-4916-0568-4
1-4916-0568-5
346175

Printed in the United States of America
Published and Distributed by

VOYAGER SOPRIS
LEARNING™

17855 Dallas Parkway, Suite 400 • Dallas, TX 75287 • 800 547-6747
www.voyagersopris.com

Table of Contents

Unit 1

Excerpt from *Holes*
by Louis Sachar
Text type: literature—novel

"The Science of Catching Criminals"
Text type: informational

Table of Contents

Table of Contents

Unit 5

Excerpt from *Breaking Night*
by Liz Murray
Text type: informational—memoir

"From Homeless to Harvard"
Text type: informational

Unit 6

"The Symbol of Freedom"
Text type: informational

"I Am Prepared to Die"
by Nelson Mandela
Text type: informational—speech

About the Author

Louisa Moats, Ed.D., has been a teacher, psychologist, researcher, graduate school faculty member, and author of many influential scientific journal articles, books, and policy papers on the topics of reading, spelling, language, and teacher preparation. After a first job as a neuropsychology technician, she became a teacher of students with learning and reading difficulties, earning her Master's degree at Peabody College of Vanderbilt. Later, after realizing how much more she needed to know about teaching, she earned a doctorate in Reading and Human Development from the Harvard Graduate School of Education. Dr. Moats spent the next 15 years in private practice as a licensed psychologist in Vermont, specializing in evaluation and consultation with individuals of all ages and walks of life who experienced reading, writing, and language difficulties. At that time, she trained psychology interns in the Dartmouth Medical School Department of Psychiatry. Dr. Moats spent one year as resident expert for the California Reading Initiative and four years as site director of the NICHD Early Interventions Project in Washington, DC, where she was invited to testify to Congress three times on issues of teacher preparation and reading instruction in high poverty schools. Recently, she concluded 10 years as research adviser and consultant with Voyager Sopris Learning, serving as Principle Investigator on two Small Business Innovation Research (SBIR) grants from the National Institutes of Health.

Dr. Moats was a contributing writer of the Common Core State Standards, Foundational Reading Skills, for grades K–5. In addition to the *LETRS* professional development series, Dr. Moats's books include *Speech to Print: Language Essentials for Teachers* (Brookes Publishing); *Spelling: Development, Disability, and Instruction* (Pro-Ed); *Straight Talk About Reading* (with Susan Hall, Contemporary Books), and *Basic Facts about Dyslexia*. Dr. Moats's awards include the prestigious Samuel T. and June L. Orton award from the International Dyslexia Association, for outstanding contributions to the field.

Based on the original work of Jane Fell Greene, Ed.D.

Jane Fell Greene has been at the forefront of the nation's literacy movement for many years. Prior to creating *LANGUAGE!*®, *The Comprehensive Literacy Curriculum*—used to teach reading, writing, vocabulary, grammar, spelling, and language to at-risk and ESL students since 1995 and now in its 4th edition—Dr. Greene earned credentials in and taught English, speech, and ESL at both middle and high school levels for 20 years. Subsequently, she taught undergraduate and graduate courses in reading, reading disabilities, ESL, and clinical diagnosis for another 10 years.

A tireless advocate for students who experience delays in literacy acquisition, Dr. Greene has been a frequent presenter at national and international conferences. She oversaw the *National Council of LANGUAGE! Trainers* until 2010. She has served on the Board of Directors of the International Dyslexia Association and is a Fellow of the Orton Gillingham Academy of Practitioners and Educators.

Program Contributors

Contributing Author and Developers

Anne Whitney, Ed.D., CCC-SLP
Level 2 Author; Level 1 Developer
Clinical Professor
University of Colorado
Speech, Language, Hearing Department

Sheryl Ferlito, Ed.S. (Levels 1 and 2)
Co-author of *Sortegories*
Secondary Special Education Literacy Teacher

Debra D. Coultas, M.A. (Level 1)
National Literacy Consultant and Trainer

Program Reviewers

Meagan Dorman
Adjunct Professor
Fresno State University

Gina Hernandez
Specialized Academic Instruction
Newport Mesa Unified School District

Francine Wenhardt
Coordinator, Special Education
Tustin Unified School District

Program Validation

Arlington Independent School District (Level 1)
Arlington, Texas
  Nichols Middle School

Central Unified School District (Level 1)
Fresno, California
  El Capitan Middle School
  Glacier Point Middle School
  Rio Vista Middle School

Charleston County School District (Level 2)
Middle and High Schools,
Charleston, South Carolina

Cohoes City School District (Level 2)
Cohoes, New York
  Cohoes Middle and High School

Kansas City Public Schools (Level 2)
Kansas City, Missouri
  African-Centered College Preparatory Academy
  East High School

Kent Independent School District (Level 1)
Kent, Washington
  Cedar Heights Middle School
  Northwood Middle School

New York City Department of Education (Level 2)
Cluster D75
New York, New York
  P.S. K753–School For Career Development
  P.S. M138
  P.S. M751–Manhattan School for Career
    Development
  P.S. R037
  P.S. X721–Stephen McSweeney School

Orange Unified School District (Levels 1 and 2)
Orange, California
  El Ranch Charter School
  Portola Middle School

Paulding County School District (Level 2)
Dallas, Georgia
  Dobbins Middle School
  East Paulding Middle School
  McClure Middle School

Schenectady City School District (Level 2)
Schenectady, New York
  Steinmetz Career & Leadership Academy
  Success Academy for Middle School Students

Walla Walla Public Schools (Levels 1 and 2)
Walla Walla, Washington
  Garrison Middle School

Washington Unified School District (Level 2)
Fresno, California
  Washington Union High School
  West Fresno Middle School

Program Overview

Welcome to *LANGUAGE!® Live*. This exciting program blends the best of online instruction with the important aspects of teacher-directed instruction to empower struggling learners and close the reading and writing gap. This one program with two levels creates strategic entry points and the ability to accelerate learning.

Level 1 focuses on the foundational skills that students may have missed in their earlier reading instruction and enables students to practice critical skills such as basic decoding and spelling. Level 2 enables students to hone the important literacy skills they need to not only become fluent readers, but comprehending readers. Syllable types, prefixes and suffixes, and Greek and Latin roots are critical components of Level 2. Both levels include rich comprehension, language, vocabulary, and writing components implemented through teacher-directed lessons, exposing students to complex text and collaborative discussions.

Within each level there are two components—Word Training and Text Training. The Word Training component of the program includes instruction critical to help students learn to read. The Text Training component of the program includes the instruction critical to help students comprehend what they read and write. Both components work together to provide a full English Language Arts program.

Level 1

Consonant sounds

Vowel sounds

Phoneme/grapheme mapping

Blending and reading words

Rhyming

Reading phrases and sentences

Sentence completion

Syllabification

Spelling

Fluency

Text structure

Text types

Story elements

Writing

STUDENTS BELOW GRADE LEVEL

SUCCESSFUL GRADE-LEVEL PARTICIPATION

Level 2

Syllable types
Compound words
Diphthongs
Prefixes
Suffixes
Contractions
Greek and Latin roots
Morphemes
Homophones
Fluency
Text evidence
Compare and contrast
Author's point of view
Literature
Writing

LANGUAGE! Live uses two different delivery methods. The online components provide students with the opportunity to move at their own pace. While students work online, the teacher receives reports and can make assignments at critical junctures within students' learning paths. The teacher-directed components reinforce grade-level expectations while the teacher delivers explicit instruction. This combination ensures accelerated learning, intensive instruction of foundational skills, and exposure to grade-equivalent standards, text, and vocabulary to move students to reading independence.

Program Strands

Reading proficiency occurs when word recognition becomes automatic and language comprehension becomes strategic. A student must develop the foundational skills of reading and the ability to make meaning from letters and words (and later sentences, paragraphs, and whole texts), all while acquiring content knowledge and the vocabulary and grammar knowledge necessary for language development to occur. Students must simultaneously develop the craft of effective expression—both orally and in writing.

Reading Foundational Skills

Dr. Louisa Moats's carefully developed scope and sequence helps students progress in reading from phonemic awareness to morphology. Simultaneously, irregularly spelled words are mastered in an online gaming environment. Students with gaps in encoding and decoding receive ample instruction and practice to help make meaning from letters and word parts—allowing them to focus on the comprehension of content and the building of knowledge.

Reading Comprehension

High-interest texts have been chosen to engage students in reading. Students are given tools to make meaning from complex texts and build content knowledge in the following ways:

1. Background videos provide the necessary content knowledge to make complex topics and themes more manageable.

2. Vocabulary is pretaught, further building the background knowledge necessary for comprehension.

3. Grammar and language structures are explicitly taught, allowing students to understand the complex language structures used by many authors.

4. Close reading and critical analysis of text is teacher-guided.

5. Explicit instruction explains how to engage in civil collaborative exchanges with peers as they discuss thought-provoking and relevant texts—learning from one another and deepening comprehension.

Vocabulary

Language development occurs when passage vocabulary words, chosen primarily from the lists attributed to Marzano and Coxhead, are pretaught before reading and recontextualized and reviewed throughout the unit. Based on research, vocabulary lessons are made up of an oral question and response technique that keeps students from spending valuable learning time copying definitions. Language development continues as academic vocabulary words that cover the four depth of knowledge levels are explicitly taught and reciprocally practiced. This gives students the tools to make meaning from prompts and develop the ability to critically think about text.

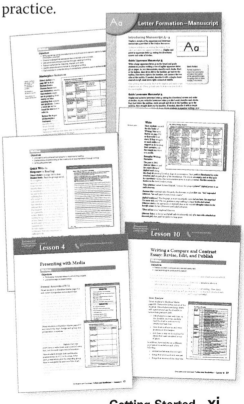

Grammar

Students further develop language through an extensive grammar strand across both levels. These lessons ensure students comprehend sentence structure when reading. Grammar skills are reinforced in the writing strand to ensure students develop an ability to effectively express themselves in writing. In addition, online practice activities offer more opportunities for recursive practice.

Writing

Through writing lessons and writing projects, students are given the tools for effective expression in the following ways:

1. Short and expanded constructed responses are written after close reading of text.

2. Handwriting is taught, practiced, and mastered.

3. Sentence and paragraph writing is developed alongside the grammar strand and practiced in both levels.

4. Process writing develops over the levels until students are using the six traits of writing consistently.

5. Research skills and mastery of technology develop as students engage in short research-based writing projects.

6. Presentation skills are explicitly taught and practiced.

7. The effective use of graphics and multimedia elements to enhance presentations is developed throughout the course of the writing projects.

Program Components

The *LANGUAGE! Live* blended program includes Word Training and Text Training. Students complete Word Training lessons and activities independently online. Text Training lessons and activities are teacher-directed with online practice.

Level 1   Level 2

Teacher Materials (Level-Specific)

Two easy-to-use Teacher Editions for the explicit instruction of comprehension, language, vocabulary, and writing:

- Part 1 (Units 1–6)
- Part 2 (Units 7–12)

LANGUAGE! Live Teacher Center, including the following:

- Dashboard
- Course Guide, providing access to the online student activities of Word Training and Text Training
- Course Resources, including a video library
- Program Planning resources
- Writing Projects
- Class settings and information
- Handwriting Supplement and Cards
- Reteach lessons
- Posters
- *ReadingScape*
- Power Pass
- Assessment tools including Content Mastery and Benchmark Assessments
- eBooks

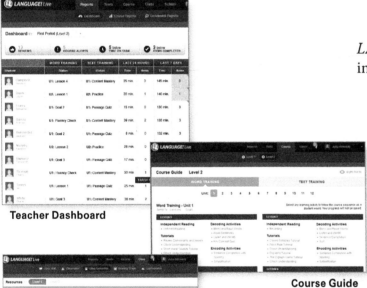

Teacher Dashboard

Course Guide

Video Library

Assignments

The blended learning components of *LANGUAGE! Live* provide meaningful opportunities for students to access content and excel in all of the critical components necessary to learn to read and read to learn. *LANGUAGE! Live* offers defined time and instruction for teachers to provide instruction to small groups of students. In addition, *LANGUAGE! Live* offers students an online component,

Level 1

Level 2

which allows them to work at their own pace. By offering different experiences in two different ways, this blended learning model allows teachers to gain important information about students and receive multiple data points to continue to make informed instructional decisions as students succeed.

Word Training Video and Activity

Student Materials (Level-Specific)

Two Student Books for the teacher-directed instruction of comprehension, language, vocabulary, and writing:

- Part 1 (Units 1–6)
- Part 2 (Units 7–12)

LANGUAGE! Live Student Center, including the following:

- Dashboard
- Class Wall
- Avatar and Student Profile
- Word Training instruction
- Sight Words game
- *ReadingScape*
- Power Pass
- Assigned Content Mastery and Benchmark Assessments
- Assigned Online Text Training Practice activities
- eBooks

Sight Words Game

Student Dashboard

Course Resources

The online **Course Resources** are organized into three areas: **Program Planning**, Text Training, and Word Training. Resources include videos, posters, and digital editions of print materials to help a teacher optimize instruction. These components can be displayed for whole class instruction or printed for extra practice, review, or homework.

Text Training

Connects Students to Text Through Teacher-Directed Instruction

Text Training connects students to text through comprehensive, engaging, teacher-directed lessons with online practice and progress monitoring opportunities assigned by the teacher.

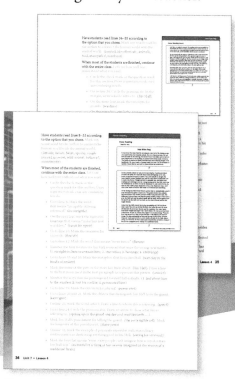

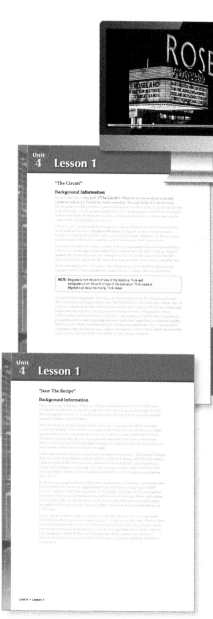

Close Reading

Students become deeply involved with the close analysis of text. Students notice the features and language of the author as they think through the details and meaning of the text.

Building Content Knowledge

Background information provided to the teacher and student through video and text promotes the comprehension of text used in each unit.

Content Mastery

These online activities are assigned by the teacher throughout the program to inform instruction of the critical content and skills taught and allow teachers to utilize the reteach lessons as needed.

ReadingScape

This online library of exciting, interactive text engages students by providing a variety of genres to build their content knowledge and stretch their reading level.

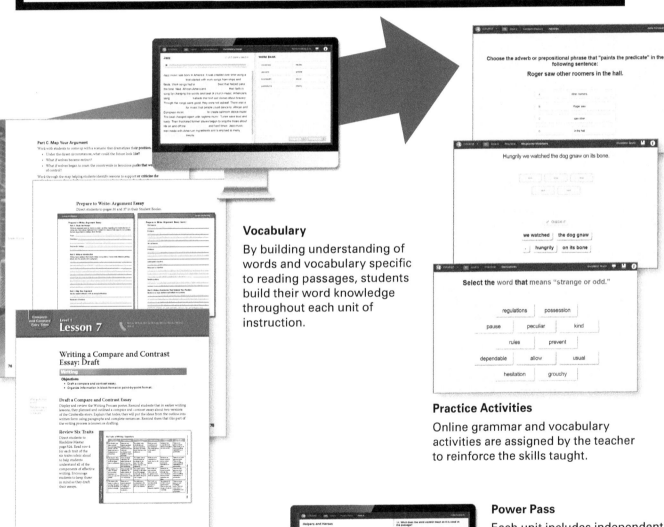

Level 1 Text Training

- Oral and teacher-supported reading comprehension
- 280L – 1000L with strong teacher support
- Instruction builds to grade-level text and vocabulary
- Close reading and evidence-based questioning
- Grammar and writing in response to text
- Collaborative discussions

Level 2 Text Training

- Instruction with grade-level text and vocabulary
- 590L – 1200L moving to independent reading
- Close reading and evidence-based questioning
- Grammar and writing projects
- Collaborative discussions

Vocabulary

By building understanding of words and vocabulary specific to reading passages, students build their word knowledge throughout each unit of instruction.

Practice Activities

Online grammar and vocabulary activities are assigned by the teacher to reinforce the skills taught.

Power Pass

Each unit includes independent text for students to read and two-part questions to answer using text evidence. These are assigned at the end of each unit by the teacher and are another opportunity to monitor progress.

Writing

Explicit lesson and writing projects are used to respond to different text types and genres through constructed response, often using the formal writing process.

Word Training

Enables Students to Learn and Practice Through Self-Paced Instruction

Word Training provides an engaging online experience so students can learn to break the code and fill in gaps they have accessing text.

Consonants and Vowels

Word Training lessons begin with the basics: phonemes and graphemes, consonants and vowels. Providing students with a solid background in foundational skills allows them to close their knowledge gaps and move on to grade-level reading.

Orthographic Patterns

Instruction provided on sound-symbol relationships, spelling patterns, and inflectional endings are the building blocks to make meaning from text.

Phoneme/Grapheme Correspondences

Unique activities such as Phoneme/Grapheme Mapping, Blend and Read Words, and Big Word Strategy teach the basics of phoneme-grapheme correspondence and syllable types. Audio feedback and recording options enhance the learning experience.

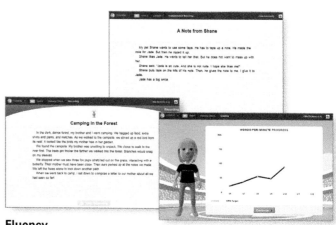

Fluency

Students improve their fluency by beginning with sounds, words, and phrases, then building to connected text in a carefully scaffolded progression. Independent reading passages and fluency checks allow students to read and record themselves multiple times to improve their fluency and track their results.

Level 1 Word Training

- Foundational skills
  - ✓ intensive instruction on English phonemes
  - ✓ in-depth study of sound-spelling correspondences
  - ✓ activities such as Blend and Read Words, Sorting, and Sentence Dictation
- Connected text
- 150L – 650L with controlled text

 Level 2 Word Training

- Word analysis
  - ✓ introduction to six syllable types
  - ✓ exposure to multisyllabic words in activities such as Word Construction and Shuffle
  - ✓ Prefixes and suffixes
  - ✓ Greek and Latin roots
- Connected text
- 250L – 900L with some controlled text

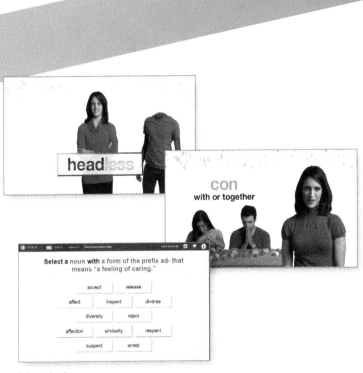

Morphology

As students move beyond basic foundational skills, prefixes and suffixes additively and cumulatively extend word knowledge.

Greek and Latin Roots

Students are taught Greek and Latin roots to make sense of words and expand their vocabulary. Word building activities reinforce the skills.

Classroom Management

To ensure a smooth facilitation of *LANGUAGE! Live* in the classroom, follow these guidelines on the checklist.

Class Grouping

Use Benchmark I assessment scores to divide class into two homogenous groups. (See cut score information on page xxxix.)

❏ Create a Level 1 group and a Level 2 group if necessary. This will ensure students are appropriately leveled and challenged during teacher-led Text Training. Homogenous grouping allows teachers to teach both levels of *LANGUAGE! Live* in one class.

❏ Identify the student-to-computer ratio. This is important to ensure students have both instruction with the teacher and time online. Knowing this will help inform the best implementation model.

    ❏ 1:1 Ratio   ❏ 2:1 Ratio   ❏ 3:1 Ratio

❏ Choose an implementation model to fit your specific schedule. There are a variety of ways to implement the program. See the following models.

90-Minute Implementation Models

Standard Model—This is the standard implementation model for daily, uninterrupted 90-minute class periods. In this model, students can work concurrently in Level 1 and Level 2, based on the results of the LRS, and can receive online and teacher-led instruction each day. Requires only one teacher.

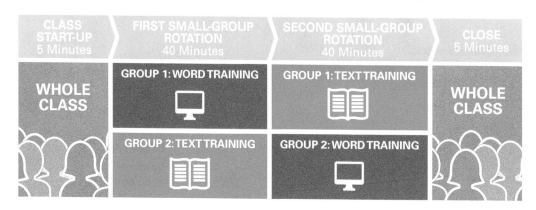

Three-Group Model—With 90 minutes of instruction, this model is organized so groups can rotate every 30 minutes. The rotation occurs between online instruction and two teacher-led instruction components. Requires a teacher and paraprofessional.

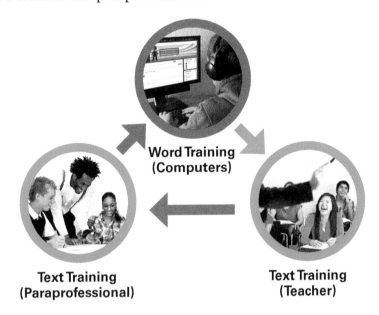

Word Training
(Computers)

Text Training
(Paraprofessional)

Text Training
(Teacher)

45-Minute Implementation Models

Split Class Model—designed for a supplemental model with a choice of Foundational and Fluency; Comprehension, Vocabulary, Language, and Writing in Response to Reading; or Writing Projects.

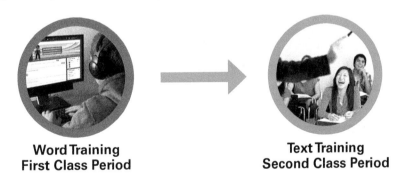

Word Training
First Class Period

Text Training
Second Class Period

General Class Arrangement

The following checklist provides some strategic planning tips for a successful integration of blended learning in a *LANGUAGE! Live* classroom.

- ❑ Arrange desks/tables in a location central to the classroom. This allows the teacher to work with students and monitor students at computers.

- ❑ Arrange computers so that the monitors face the teacher while he or she is teaching a small group and can be seen while the teacher is monitoring students.

- ❑ Ensure charging outlets are available for devices at desks (if utilized).

- ❑ Devise a system for storing and accessing headphones.

- ❑ Talk with students about the expectations of learning in a blended environment.

  - ❑ Discuss the role and expectations of students while working online.

  - ❑ Discuss the role and expectations of students while working with the teacher.

  - ❑ Discuss the etiquette of using computers.

  - ❑ Establish speaking and listening expectations.

  - ❑ Share the expectations of a learning environment with flexible grouping.

- ❑ Create a space in the classroom to hold *LANGUAGE! Live* student materials.

- ❑ Print and display the posters to benefit students.

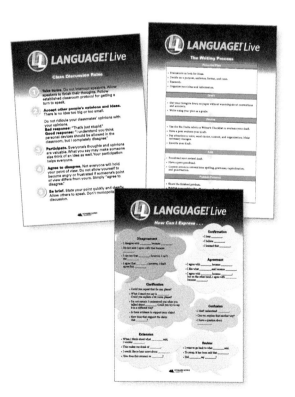

Classroom Routines

Use the checklist below to help establish classroom routines and procedures for *LANGUAGE! Live* classroom.

❏ Students know the device they will use during their computer time.
Assigning computer stations or devices to students for their work in LANGUAGE! Live *avoids confusion and ensures a smooth start to online work time.*

❏ Students understand the appropriate voice level at their designated work station (online or teacher-directed).
Students working in a blended classroom understand that the "buzz" or noise is necessary as teachers and students work together and as students work independently. Establishing the noise expectation helps promote the understanding of appropriate working voices.

❏ Students know how to adjust the volume on the computer or device.
As work stations and devices are used for a variety of tasks, students know how to adjust the volume of the computer to provide for the best online experience.

❏ Students easily access the materials needed for teacher-directed instruction.
When students either begin instruction with the teacher or transition from their computer to teacher-led instruction, they understand where materials are stored and how to access their student book.

❏ Students have easy access to the login and URL for *LANGUAGE! Live.*
It is best when http://ll.languagelive.com *is set as a bookmark or icon on each students computer or device. If the link is not working, students know where to look to find the URL needed to access* LANGUAGE! Live. *Students also should have easy access to their unique username and password.*

❏ Students working on their computer or device know the routine to troubleshoot a problem online or to request the attention of the teacher.
Establish a procedure for students working online when they encounter a technical problem. The use of "Help Cards" or flags are frequently used to quietly alert the teacher of attention needed.

❏ Students transition between online and teacher-led instruction in a quiet manner.
To utilize all of the time during the LANGUAGE! Live *class, smooth transitions between work stations are critical.*

Instructional Routine

Implementing Text Training

The following checklist highlights the components of a successful implementation of Text Training.

❏ Review the Instructional Pacing Guide (see pages xl–xli) to determine the rate to progress through each lesson. Teach the lessons as instructed, using the script explicitly or as a guide based on personal comfort level. **Important Note:** Skills progress throughout the unit(s). It is not necessary to spend additional instructional time as mastery will occur over time.

❏ Preread each unit. This will help facilitate a smooth instructional flow when teaching.

❏ Preread each text selection.

❏ Review the Unit Opener video. This is found in the Course Resources online.

Unit Opener videos

❏ Begin each unit with students by playing the Unit Opener video. This will help build background knowledge for students.

Lesson Opener

❏ Use the Lesson Openers with the whole class or post them for students to respond to online. These can be used to review skills, facilitate topic-centered thinking, connect students to the texts, and focus students on learning upon entering the classroom.

❏ Assign the online Practice Activities and Assessments as noted in the margins of the Teacher Edition.

❏ Score the constructed response portion of Power Pass and provide feedback to students.

❏ Collect student activity pages as needed for grading.

Text Training Assignments

❏ Collect data from online Practice Activities and Assessments to determine if students need extra practice on particular skills.

❏ Print Reteach activities, found in the online Course Resources and eBooks, to solidify learning and move students toward mastery.

Text Training Results

Implementing Word Training

Use this checklist as a reminder of ways to stay involved with each student's individual work in Word Training.

❑ Create an avatar and profile. This will reinforce to students that their teacher is part of their online environment.

❑ Begin the dialogue with students by posting on the Class Wall or sending messages to students welcoming them to class, posing thoughts regarding their work, or discussing text they are reading.

❑ As often as possible, review student time and tasks completed to determine whether intervention is needed to keep students moving through Word Training.

❑ Review the Gateway Goal recordings each week. Offer constructive feedback to students.

❑ Review Fluency Check recordings at the end of each unit. Review the recordings to determine if students need to redo the Fluency Check to ensure progress.

Avatar

Class Wall

Word Training Results

Gateway Goal Review

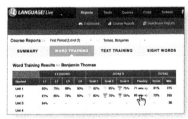

Fluency Report

Program Pacing Guide

Core Replacement: 90 minutes—180 days of instruction

Implementation: 90 minutes per day for students far below grade level

Pacing Recommendations: Level 1 (recommended) or Level 2

* Each unit implemented in three weeks to include Writing Projects and other recommended resources

Majority of the 90-minute instructional day consists of:

Week(s)	Unit	Key Instructional Pacing Routines
1	Start-Up	**Word Training:** Online lessons—45 minutes per day (includes Sight Word Game)
2–4	Unit 1	
5–7	Unit 2	**Text Training:**
8–10	Unit 3	Teacher-directed lesson—45 minutes per day
11–13	Unit 4	Writing Projects: Teacher-directed writing projects can be taught at the end of a unit or scheduled during the
14–16	Unit 5	instructional time.
17–19	Unit 6	**Other resources embedded in the daily lessons:**
20–22	Unit 7	Text Training Practice Activities: Online and assigned by the teacher
23–25	Unit 8	**Progress Monitoring:**
26–28	Unit 9	Online and assigned by the teacher at the end of each unit
29–31	Unit 10	Content Mastery
32–34	Unit 11	Power Pass
		Handwriting: Embedded in the lessons
35–36	Unit 12	*ReadingScape*: Online wide reading opportunities

Supplemental: 45 minutes to support Core Instruction

Implementation: 45 minutes per day for students who need additional support beyond their core instruction

Pacing Recommendations: Level 2 (recommended) or Level 1

- During a 45-minute supplemental block, teachers may implement Word Training and Text Training using Text Training on days 1, 3, and 5 and Word Training on days 2 and 4. (recommended)
- If students do not need explicit instruction in each domain, then teachers can provide instruction in Word Training, Text Training, or Writing Projects. Teaching students to become proficient readers and writers is a comprehensive task that requires all domains of literacy. The following instructional resources can be used to support core ELA instruction, collectively or independently, focusing on the needs of students.

Instructional Resources: 45 minutes of instruction can include the following . . .

Foundational Skills and Fluency

- Word Training online instruction and ongoing Progress Monitoring

Comprehension, Grammar, Vocabulary, and Writing in Response to Reading

- Teacher-directed Text Training lessons and online Practice activites and Progress Monitoring

Writing Projects

- Choice of eight 5- or 10-lesson Writing Projects per level

45-Minute Supplemental Instruction		
Foundational and Fluency	**Comprehension, Vocabulary, Language, Writing in Response to Reading**	**Writing Projects**
Word Training	Text Training Handwriting Writing Projects Power Pass *ReadingScape*	Informational Cause and Effect Narrative Argument Compare and Contrast Literary Analysis Career Documents Scientific Research

Opportunities for Reading

Level 1

LANGUAGE! Live texts are rich and engaging. In Level 1, students read compelling texts about topics they care about—topics such as environmental pollution, extreme weather, censorship, music, paleontology, and marine wildlife. In addition, students read a wide range of literary texts. From the genres of contemporary to classical, students are immersed in poetry, historical fiction, and mythology.

Literature

- "Austin Trip Graphic Novel"*
- "Discovery Graphic Novel"*
- "Stargazing Graphic Novel"*
- "Dolphin Talk"
- "Stuck in the Mud"*
- "Quite a Bike Ride"*
- "Canyon Song"*
- "Allergy Trip"*
- "A Whole New World"*
- "The Dragon and the Princess"*
- "Ominous Sky"*
- *The Time Machine*
- *Back to the Future*
- "Unmoved by Winds of Change"
- "Fury"
- "The Gorgon's Head"

Informational

- "Batty About Bats"
- "Africa Digs"
- "Gemini: The Twins"
- "The Big Dogs and the Rams"*
- "Jazz: The Recipe"
- "Coming Clean About Toxic Pollution"
- "Censorship"
- "Dear Congressman Whipple"
- "Whale Song"
- "OceanPlace Debate"
- "How Bugs Bug Us"
- "Sonia Sotomayor"*
- "Bugs in Medicine"
- "Hurricane!"
- "Twisting a Path of Destruction"
- "Mythological Women"

*Indicates selections in Power Pass

Firsthand and secondhand accounts illustrate differences between subjective and objective viewpoints.

Paired passages of informational text and classical mythology build deeper conceptual understanding.

Paired texts provide opportunities to experience literature in various time periods.

Real-life issues engage readers and encourage thoughtful exploration of the world around them.

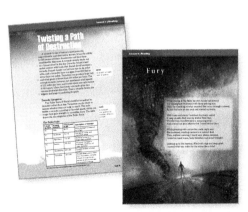

Close reading of informational and literary texts illustrates different perspectives of a topic.

Visual and audio capabilities of *ReadingScape* bring content-area learning to life. For more information on *ReadingScape*, see page xxxi.

Opportunities for Reading

Level 2

In Level 2, students continue working with texts from various genres, eras, and cultures at greater complexity. The high-interest texts by authors such as Langston Hughes, Jack London, Francisco Jiménez, Gwendolyn Brooks, Jodi Picoult, Paula Underwood, and Pearl S. Buck were carefully selected to engage students with their blend of real-world topics and literary significance.

Literature

- *Holes*
- "Thank, You M'am"
- "Tea Drobomir"*
- "If I Were in Charge of the World"
- "We Real Cool"
- *The Outsiders*
- *The Play of the Diary of Anne Frank*
- *White Fang*
- "A Wolf in Dark Glasses"*
- "The White Wolf of the Hartz Mountains"
- *Who Speaks for Wolf*
- *The Strange Case of Dr. Jekyll and Mr. Hyde Graphic Novel*
- *The Good Earth*
- *Nectar in a Sieve*
- *My Sister's Keeper*

Informational

- "Clues: What's Left Behind"*
- "From Vandal to Artist"*
- "The Science of Catching Criminals"
- "César Chávez: From Migrant Worker to Leader"*
- "StreetWise Magazine"*
- "Helpers and Heroes"*
- "Fenrir the Wolf"*
- "Wolf Society"*
- "The Circuit"
- "Must Be the Shoes"*
- "Rising Giants: The Modern Development of China and India"*
- "To Clone or Not to Clone"*
- *The Autobiography of Malcolm X*
- *Breaking Night*
- "From Homeless to Harvard"
- "The Symbol of Freedom"
- *I Am Prepared to Die*
- "Return of the Wolves"
- "The Mysterious Human Brain"
- "North High School Letter"
- "Say Yes to Free Dress!"

Diverse passages deepen content-area knowledge across disciplines.

*Indicates selections in Power Pass

Classic literature comes
alive in an exciting
graphic novel.

Real-world topics challenge
adolescent readers.

Historical and personal perspectives are
unveiled through poetry and drama.

Author biographies provide important
background and help students understand
the writer's point of view.

ReadingScape provides access
to engaging classical literature.
For more information about
ReadingScape, see page xxxi.

Power Pass

POWER PASS

Power Pass provides the opportunity for students to apply the strategies they have learned in *LANGUAGE! Live* as they read new text. Teachers can assign one of the 24 passages and the corresponding questions throughout the implementation of *LANGUAGE! Live*.

- **Passage selections include literary and informational text**, the genres required for most high-stakes assessments.

- **Text-based, two-part multiple choice questions** and short answer prompts make up each Power Pass quiz.

- **Short-answer questions** are graded online by the teacher using a predetermined scoring rubric. Students have access to the rubric to understand scoring criteria.

- Power Pass is **accessible through any device** once assigned by the teacher.

Power Pass provides additional opportunities for students to read literary and informational text. While applying strategies, students increase their knowledge of the world around them. Among the passages are biographies of Sonia Sotomayor and César Chávez, poetry, a drama set in the Grand Canyon, a personal narrative about coming to America, and an inspiring story of a vandal turned graffiti artist.

ReadingScape

Visual and audio capabilities of *ReadingScape* bring content-area learning to life.

READINGSCAPE

ReadingScape is an **online, interactive library** containing literary and informational texts divided into three levels for student self-selection. Students continue their reading experiences by choosing from these engaging online texts.

The **visual, audio, and interactive capabilities** encourage more wide reading by even the most reluctant adolescents. Biographies include Junot Díaz, Margaret Chan, Venus Williams, and Steve Wozniak. Informational texts allow readers to investigate the mysteries of the human body, Tasmanian devils, giant squid, and bugs used in medicine. Students can read about the emergence of Dubai as a global city or the mysterious disappearance of a Native American city 1,000 years ago. Selections allow students to go back in time to read about the great pyramid in Chichen Itza, to uncover the secrets of a frozen Inca mummy, or to understand the influences of ancient Roman architecture on our structures today.

The diverse selections in *ReadingScape* allow students to read classic tales of Mu-Lan and Molly Pitcher, as well as international folktales such as "Lon Po Po" and "The Maiden Who Loved a Fish." For a change of pace, students may read classics such as "The Legend of Sleepy Hollow" and "The Tell-Tale Heart," or choose from a collection of nail-biting ghost stories. Additional contemporary literature options include stories about an unusual service animal, cultural perspectives, and life in the tropics.

Writing Connection

Writing and Speaking and Listening

The development of language skills is a prerequisite to becoming a participating member of society. When a learner struggles to develop the skills necessary to speak, read, and write fluently and confidently, he or she becomes frustrated and often unmotivated. Concurrently, learners who do not develop the necessary skills to listen carefully and analyze what they hear will become reluctant to participate in discussions and increasingly more isolated. In short, language skills are a necessity for students' success.

Through reading the texts in *LANGUAGE! Live*, students have a chance to develop culturally, emotionally, intellectually, and socially. The texts enable students to acquire knowledge and to build on what they already know. However, these developments will mean little if students fail to develop means of expression simultaneously.

LANGUAGE! Live arms students with the tools necessary not only to read and write fluently and proficiently, but also to speak fluently and listen carefully and critically. These skills are imperative so that they can communicate their ideas and thoughts to others, and through speech, others can communicate with them.

Throughout the Text Training units, students engage in meaningful collaborative exchanges through the following:

- Adherence to established Classroom Discussion Rules
- Use of collegial discussion stems
- Engaging topics of discussion relevant to their lives

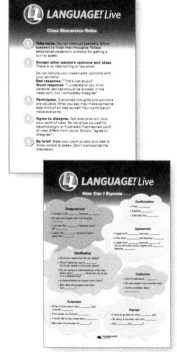

The two main components of writing development are transcription and composition. For most learners, transcription (spelling and handwriting) develops first. However, for many struggling students, the lack of development in transcription further delays the development in composition (articulating ideas and structuring them in speech and writing). Composition depends on proficiency in transcription. Students who can spell and write quickly and legibly because of their knowledge of phonics, morphology, and orthography can effectively articulate complex ideas and thoughts in writing.

Through Word Training (online) and the use of the Handwriting Lessons, students achieve proficiency in transcription, which will enable them to achieve proficiency in composition.

Effective composition involves articulating and communicating ideas, then organizing them coherently for a reader. This requires development of ideas, awareness of the purpose and audience, and a well-developed knowledge of vocabulary, grammar, and conventions. Through Text Training lessons and the Writing Projects, students achieve proficiency in composition.

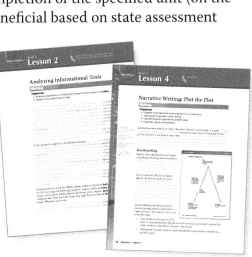

Writing Projects

Eight major Writing Projects per level were developed to not only increase student proficiency in writing, but also increase comfort and proficiency in speaking and listening skills. Individual writing projects can be printed from the online Course Resources.

- Students will work to master objectives, not only in writing within the specific genres, but also in analysis of text, grammar essentials, peer collaboration, speaking and listening, research, use of technology, and presentation.

- Each Writing Project incorporates a student presentation, multimedia development, and/or artistic project to accompany the writing.

- Teacher-directed Writing Projects can be administered periodically during the course of a Text Training unit or at the completion of the specified unit (on the Unit Plan page) or as the teacher deems beneficial based on state assessment calendars.

Writing Projects

Level 1	Students will . . .	Level 2	Students will . . .
Basic Paragraph (5 days) Focus: Basic Paragraph Structure and Introduction to the Writing Process	• write narrative, opinion, and informational paragraphs in response to multicultural works of art. • begin developing presentation skills by delivering a short opinion speech.	**Informational** Focus: Basic Essay Structure	• analyze the varying text structures and features of informational text. • become familiar with all stages of the writing process as they work collaboratively and independently to develop an informational essay on a topic directly affecting their lives. • publish a magazine article.
Shared Scientific Research Focus: Basic Essay Structure; Group Collaboration; Understanding Audience	• analyze informational texts about various diets. • conduct a week-long diet experiment and write an informational report about the findings. • plan and deliver a multimedia presentation tailored to a specific audience.	**Narrative** Focus: Character Development; Plot Development; Using Dialogue to Convey Information	• write a short story. • go through the process of a writer attempting to become published. • publish their stories in a book.

Level 1	Students will . . .	Level 2	Students will . . .
Problem and Solution Focus: Various Structures of Informational Writing	• analyze the structure of informational texts and become familiar with their purposes. • compare and contrast informational texts on the same topic, delivered in differing structures. • use research and writing skills to identify and explain a problem that affects them as well as a possible solution.	**Compare and Contrast Fiction and Nonfiction** Focus: Analysis of How Writers of Fiction Use and Alter History	• read and analyze a fictional portrayal of 9/11. • conduct research and present findings about the events of 9/11. • become familiar with two structures of compare and contrast writing. • compare and contrast a fictional portrayal of an event with a factual portrayal and analyze the fiction author's use of historical facts.
Firsthand and Secondhand Accounts Focus: Analysis of Firsthand and Secondhand Accounts to Distinguish Fact from Fiction	• compare and contrast the information provided in two firsthand accounts, a piece of artwork, and a secondhand account of a historical occurrence. • write a firsthand account of an event. • conduct research and write a secondhand account of the same event. • publish a news report.	**Argument** Focus: Developing and Supporting Opinions; Multimedia Presentations	• read and analyze two argumentative texts in opposition of the same topic. • evaluate the impact of multimedia elements of a presentation. • identify bias and fallacies in argumentative writing. • write and publish an argument regarding a school issue. • deliver a multimedia persuasive presentation.

Writing Projects (cont.)

Level 1	Students will . . .	Level 2	Students will . . .
Compare and Contrast Fairy Tale Focus: Analysis of Different Versions of a Fairy Tale	• read two versions of a fairy tale from different cultures and determine similarities and differences. • compare classic fairy tales to a poetic contemporary version of the same tale. • create an artistic rendering of fairy tales. • expand upon speaking and listening skills through the presentation of essays and works of art.	**Compare and Contrast Thematic Literature** (5 Days) Focus: The Approach to Similar Themes by Multiple Authors	• read a fairy tale and an excerpt from a drama from different cultures and determine similarities and differences in their approaches to a shared theme. • compare classic literature to contemporary literature with a shared theme. • increase familiarity with the structures of compare and contrast writing. • reference and cite literary works in a compare and contrast writing. • create and publish an artistic rendering to accompany their interpretations of the thematic approach.
Thematic Literature Focus: Literary Genres; Theme; Character Development; Plot Development	• read fables and determine the themes. • use a chosen class theme to write a work of literature in their chosen genre. • compare and contrast each author's approach to the same theme.	**Literary Analysis** Focus: The Approach to Similar Themes across Ancient Texts from Various Cultures	• read and analyze ancient Sumerian, Indian, and Hebrew texts with shared themes. • analyze a piece of contemporary literature and the writer's approach to a shared theme from ancient religious works. • write a literary analysis using ancient and contemporary texts. • create and present an artistic rendering of an ancient theme that has been adapted to modern times.

Level 1	Students will . . .	Level 2	Students will . . .
Argument Focus: Developing and Supporting Opinions; Multimedia Presentations	• read and evaluate two argumentative texts in opposition of the same topic. • evaluate the impact of multimedia elements of a presentation. • identify bias and fallacies in argumentative writing. • write and publish an argument regarding a school issue. • deliver a multimedia persuasive presentation.	**Cause and Effect** Focus: Causes and Effects; Writing Process	• evaluate the structure and purpose of an informational text. • use all steps in the writing process to write about an issue and either its causes or its effects. • publish writing and provide feedback to other writers.
Career Documents (5 days) Focus: Completing a Job Application; Writing a Formal Letter	• research careers and choose one to focus on. • complete a job application. • write a letter of interest in a formal style.	**Career Documents** (5 Days) Focus: Developing a Résumé; Writing a Formal Letter	• research careers and choose one to focus on. • evaluate the pros and cons of different style of résumés. • develop a résumé for a chosen job/career. • write a cover letter to accompany their résumé using a formal style.

Assessment Overview

LANGUAGE! Live is designed for students who read and write below grade level and need a program that places them at their instructional level and accelerates them to grade-level expectations. *LANGUAGE! Live's* assessment system includes reliable, effective tools and measures of reading achievement to provide the highest quality of assessment information for placing students and monitoring their progress.

Benchmark Assessments are administered, completed, and scored online. These assessments make recommendations for entry and exit points as well as student growth throughout the school year.

- **Progress Assessment of Reading (PAR)**
- **Test of Silent Contextual Reading Fluency (TOSCRF)**
- **Test of Written Spelling, Fourth Edition (TWS-4)**

End-of-Unit Progress Monitoring provides a diagnostic assessment of critical skills at the completion of each self-paced Word Training unit online and each teacher-led Text Training unit. Text Training progress monitoring activities are assigned online by the teacher.

Word Training

- **Say Sounds, Read Words, and Read Passages** assess students' cumulative progress and track progress.
- **Fluency Checks** provide cumulative review of skills at the end of each unit with individualized remediation.

Text Training

- **Content Mastery** provides a quick diagnostic of key skills taught in the unit. Reteach lessons located in the online Course Resources provide additional instruction.

Ongoing Progress Monitoring can be done daily during the teacher-led Text Training lessons. There are many opportunities to maximize instruction by providing online support and reteaching as necessary, including:

- **Close Reading opportunities**
- **Writing Projects**
- **Student writing samples**
- **Vocabulary and Grammar practice activities**
- **Power Pass**

How to Monitor Students' Progress Online:

- **Log in daily** to check student progress and review student lessons.
- Check the **Dashboard** to monitor students' time on task.
- Go to **Course Reports** to see class and individual student reports.
- Go to **Tools** to assign Text Training activities and **review** online assessments.

Placement Recommendations

Entry Recommendations

The following recommendations can be used to place your students in the program. Detailed exit and placement recommendations for current *LANGUAGE! Live* students are included in the Assessment section in the Program Guide.

- Identify students as being potential candidates for *LANGUAGE! Live* based on existing district data and teacher recommendations.
- Once these students have been identified, use an existing Lexile® score or administer the Benchmark 1 PAR Assessments to obtain a Lexile score.
- Use the chart below to determine placement using the Lexile score. Placement is based on time of year, grade level, and Lexile.
- For assistance in using the PAR for placement purposes, please e-mail **support@voyagersopris.com**.

Spring Grade Level	Spring Lexile	Fall Grade Level	Fall Lexile	*LANGUAGE! Live* Placement
4	< 325	5	< 405	Level 1 Unit 1
	325–625		405–690	Level 1 Unit 5
5	< 345	6	< 370	Level 1 Unit 1
	345–465		370–475	Level 1 Unit 5
	470–670		480–695	Level 2 Unit 1
	675–740		700–770	Level 2 Unit 7
6	< 415	7	< 460	Level 1 Unit 1
	415–520		460–575	Level 1 Unit 5
	525–735		580–785	Level 2 Unit 1
	740–805		790–855	Level 2 Unit 7
7	< 505	8	< 490	Level 1 Unit 1
	505–615		490–605	Level 1 Unit 5
	620–820		610–835	Level 2 Unit 1
	825–885		840–905	Level 2 Unit 7

Text Training—Daily Lesson Pacing

Teachers of all experience levels can successfully teach and implement the comprehensive curriculum of *LANGUAGE! Live* through the use of detailed lesson support.

Each level of *LANGUAGE! Live* is divided into 12 units. Lessons that support these units are taught online and through teacher-directed lessons.

Students complete Word Training lessons online as these components cover the foundational reading skills students need, such as Phonics and Word Analysis. **Text Training** lessons are teacher-directed lessons focusing on Reading Comprehension, Vocabulary, Grammar, and Writing. Additional online activities practice and reinforce the teacher-directed instruction. Other components such as Power Pass, Handwriting, and Writing Projects can also be used to provide a rich English Language Arts learning experience for students.

Every lesson offers a set routine. The following chart illustrates the **Text Training** lesson structure and the approximate amount of time allocated for each section. Adjustments can be made to fit multiple scheduling needs.

LANGUAGE! Live Instructional Design—Level 1

	Lesson 1	Lesson 2	Lesson 3	Lesson 4	Lesson 5	Lesson 6	Lesson 7	Lesson 8	Lesson 9	Lesson 10	Online Support
Reading (Units 1–6)	30–40 min		30–35 min	30 min	30 min		40 min	5 min		5–10 min	Power Pass 20–30 min
Reading (Units 7–12)	30–40 min	5–10 min (once in a while)	20–25 min	30–35 min	45 min		40 min	45 min	10–15 min	5–10 min	Power Pass 20–30 min
Vocabulary	5–10 min	10 min	10–15 min		5–10 min	20 min	5 min	15 min	20 min		Text Training Practice Activities Content Mastery 20–30 min
Grammar		30 min		15 min		10–15 min		20 min	25 min		Text Training Practice Activities Content Mastery 45–60 min
Writing with Handwriting		10 min				5–10 min		10 min		30–45 min	Power Pass Constructed Responses 15–20 min
Other Resources	**Writing Projects** Basic Paragraph; Shared Scientific Research; Problem and Solution; Firsthand and Secondhand Accounts; Compare and Contrast Fairy Tales; Thematic Literature; Argument; Career Documents										
	ReadingScape										

LANGUAGE! *Live* Instructional Design—Level 2

	Lesson 1	Lesson 2	Lesson 3	Lesson 4	Lesson 5	Lesson 6	Lesson 7	Lesson 8	Lesson 9	Lesson 10	Online Support
Reading	35 min		45 min	40–45 min	10 min	35 min	40 min	45 min	40–45 min	5–10 min	Power Pass 20–30 min
Vocabulary	5–10 min	5 min		5 min	5 min	5–10 min	5 min		5 min	5 min	Text Training Practice Activities / Content Mastery / 20–30 min
Grammar (embedded in Writing)		30–35 min									Text Training Practice Activities / Content Mastery / 45–60 min
Writing with Handwriting		10–15 min			30 min					30–45 min	Power Pass Constructed Responses / 15–20 min
Other Resources	**Writing Projects** Informational, Cause and Effect, Narrative, Argument, Compare and Contrast Thematic Literature, Compare and Contrast Fiction and Nonfiction, Literary Analysis, Career Documents										
	ReadingScape										

Unit at a Glance

The Unit Plan shows how the instructional design strategically weaves all the English Language Arts strands into a cohesive 10-lesson cycle.

A The text references provide a quick glance at the text selections and text types read in the unit.

B The colored headings under the lesson headers correlate to the ELA strands taught within each lesson.

C The objectives and skills taught within a literacy strand are part of the overall learning progression across each lesson. (Pages are referenced when the number of objectives exceed the limit.)

D Word Study and fluency elements taught online are listed within each Unit Plan, although students may work at their own pace on these activities. The Grammar and Vocabulary Practice activities, as well as the Content Mastery assessments, are included to inform the teacher what he or she will assign online for student completion.

E A suggested Writing Project can be implemented with the corresponding unit, or at another time. Students are instructed in grammar, sentences structure, process writing, research, and presentation skills.

Unit 8 Unit Plan

Instructional Texts:
"The White Wolf of the Hartz Mountains"
by Captain Frederick Marryat
A Text type: literature—short story

Who Speaks for Wolf
by Paula Underwood
Text type: literature—learning story

LANGUAGE! Live Online
D

Grammar Practice
- Use relative pronouns correctly.
- Use relative adverbs correctly.
- Distinguish between contractions and possessives.
- Use commas and semicolons correctly in sentences.
- Distinguish between independent and dependent clauses.
- Use indefinite pronouns correctly.
- Identify and correct vague and incorrect pronoun usage.
- Use conjunctions correctly.

Vocabulary Practice
- Determine the meaning of derivations of words.
- Increase depth of word knowledge through the use of analogies.

Content Mastery
- Demonstrate an understanding of . . .
  - word meaning by answering questions and using words in sentences.
  - relative pronouns and relative clauses.
  - apostrophe usage.

Word Study
- Blend, read, spell, and divide multisyllabic words with stable final syllable -cle.
- Add inflectional endings to words ending in -le.
- Identify homophones.
- Read connected text to build fluency.

Lesson 1

Reading
- Determine and discuss the topic of a text.
- Determine and discuss the author's purpose.
- Use text features to preview text.

Vocabulary
- Evaluate word knowledge.
- Determine the meaning of key passage vocabulary.

Reading
- Read a short story.
- Monitor comprehension during text reading.
- Identify first-person point of view.

Lesson 6

Reading
- Determine and discuss the topic of a text.
- Determine and discuss the author's purpose.
- Use text features to preview text.

Vocabulary
- Evaluate word knowledge.
- Determine the meaning of key passage vocabulary.

Reading
- Read a legend.
- Monitor comprehension during text reading.
- Determine the point of view of literary text.
- Identify shifts in point of view.

B

E **Writing Project: Compare and C
Thematic Litera**

		Lesson 3	Lesson 4	Lesson 5
vocabulary. contractions ns. their ctly. elative clauses ct inappropriate and mood. s to create ation when at contain		**Reading** • Establish a purpose for rereading literary text. • Use critical thinking skills to write responses to prompts about text. • Support written answers with evidence from text. • Cite evidence in support of a particular point.	**Vocabulary** • Review key passage vocabulary. **Reading** • Read literature with purpose and understanding. • Answer questions to demonstrate comprehension of text. • Monitor comprehension of text during reading. • Identify text evidence that supports inferences. • Determine the impact of word choice. • Analyze how dialogue or incidents reveal aspects of a character. • Determine how differences in character point of view create suspense. • Identify leading questions and their intended purpose. • Identify shifts in mood. • Identify common religious or mythological themes in texts. *See pg. 118 for additional lesson objectives.*	**Vocabulary** • Review key passage vocabulary. **Writing** • Write an analysis of the use of foreshadowing in "The White Wolf of the Hartz Mountains." • Identify how an author's choice of words is used to create suspense. **Reading** • Self-correct as comprehension of text deepens. • Engage in class discussion. • Identify the enduring understandings from a piece of text. • Objectively summarize literary text. • Determine the theme of a story. • Determine how the theme is developed over the course of a text. • Analyze the effect characters have on the theme. • Identify the author's point of view. • Identify common conventions of a tale.

		Lesson 8	Lesson 9	Lesson 10
e vocabulary. rize literary text. of a story. s and their topics. espond to g skills to write ts about text. swers with text		**Reading** • Establish a purpose for revisiting literature. • Listen to an audio version of a text. • Use information from text and media to answer questions. • Compare and contrast the experience of reading a story with listening to an audio version of the story. • Use critical thinking skills to write responses to prompts about text. • Support written answers with evidence. • Recognize a shift in character point of view. • Write objective summaries. • Evaluate the impact of an audio performance of a text.	**Vocabulary** • Review key passage vocabulary. **Reading** • Read literature with purpose and understanding. • Answer questions to demonstrate comprehension of text. • Identify and explain explicit details from text. • Monitor comprehension of text during reading. • Determine the impact of word choice, poetic style, and repetition. • Determine the meaning of proverbs, adages, and aphorisms. • Identify shifts in point of view. • Identify the use of the interrogative and conditional moods. • Identify foreshadowing in literature. *See pg. 171 for additional lesson objectives.*	**Vocabulary** • Review key passage vocabulary. **Writing** • Use multiple texts to write coherently. • Use a process to write. • Write a compare/contrast essay on cultural views of wolves. • Compare and contrast the treatment of similar topics in stories from different cultures. *See pg. 189 for additional lesson objectives.* **Reading** • Self-correct as comprehension of text deepens. • Answer questions to demonstrate comprehension of text *See pg. 194 for additional lesson objectives.*

Unit at a Glance (cont.)

The carefully crafted lessons provide clear guidance and support for effective instruction.

A The California Common Core State Standards for English Language Arts addressed in each lesson are listed for reference and planning.

B The Lesson Opener provides several prompts to begin the class with either a collaborative conversation about previous learning or a check for understanding of previously taught concepts and skills. The prompts can be presented either online or as class discussion.

C The colored headings and objectives show the ELA strand and learning objective for that specific portion of the lesson.

D Passage Vocabulary is introduced and reviewed multiple times for students to internalize the word meanings.

E Annotated student materials are pictured at point of use to support planning and provide a real-time resource.

F Scripted lessons make it easier to plan and implement instruction.

G Margin notes alert the teacher when assignments or assessments should be released online for students to complete during computer time.

Unit 8 **Lesson 7** **A** RL.1.2; RL SL.3.6; L.

Lesson Opener

Before the lesson, choose one of the following activitie on the *LANGUAGE! Live* Class Wall online.

B
- *Write a summary sentence about the lesson the Pe*
- *Make a list of adjectives describing Wolf after the*
- *Identify the following as a phrase or a clause.*
  - *the white wolf's brother*
  - *who lived outside*
  - *running fast through the woods*
  - *she felt alive once more*
  - *a wolf in disguise*
  - *was looking at me with hatred*

Vocabulary

C **Objective**
- Review key passage vocabulary.

Review Passage Vocabulary

Direct students to page 74 in their Student Books. Us following questions to review the vocabulary words ir *Speaks for Wolf*. Have students answer each question the vocabulary word or indicating its meaning in a co sentence.

- Wolf stares at the fire and the boy watches Wolf *immobile*. Are they moving? (No; if they are im they are perfectly still.) Why does Wolf's behav the boy *immobile*? (It makes him immobile bec: fascinated; Wolf doesn't seem afraid of anything

- Grandfather sings the story of the shared histor Wolf and the people. One of the people was kno Wolf's Brother. People who *sought* what would g knowledge of Wolf would go to Wolf's Brother.) **D** place where they lived, what did they *seek*? (The

- The People chose a new place without being *cou* they ask Wolf's Brother his opinion? (No; if they counseling, they chose it without getting his opi learned of the new choice, what did he *counsel* h counseled them to choose a different place beca coexist with Wolf in the place they had chosen.)

- Once they learned Wolf's Brother's opinion, did choice? Why or why not? (No, they did not reco started the work of settling in the new place.) As caused them to begin to *reconsider*? (They bega began to disappear and when Wolf began to wall

- The women started putting out food for Wolf at the edge of the village, but what soon became *apparent*? (It soon became apparent that this would be too big a drain on the food supply.) What else made the problems with this plan *apparent*? (The problems with this plan became more apparent when Wolf grew bolder and began coming into the village to look for food.)

- What strategy did the men *devise* in response? (They devised a strategy to protect the village by standing guard and driving Wolf away if needed.) This strategy used up all their energy. What other plan did they *devise* but not put into action? (They devised but did not follow through with a plan to kill all the wolves.)

- What did the People realize would happen to them if they followed such a *course*? (They realized that if they followed such a course, they would become Wolf Killers, people who took other creatures' lives to sustain their own.) What did one of the Elders realize about the *course* Wolf's Brother had recommended? (He realized that the course Wolf's Brother had recommended was the wiser course—that in the end, it would have required less time and energy.)

F · When Grandfather pauses in his story, how does he *maintain* the rhythm of the chant? (He maintains rhythm by tapping his knee in time.) When he resumes the story, he tells how the people realized their mistake and vowed to *maintain* a new way of life. What new way of life do they vow to *maintain*? (They vow to maintain a way of life in which they thoroughly discuss any new decision and think through all the possible ways energy might flow through each course of action.)

- When the new People came on wooden ships, did they *cherish* Wolf as Grandfather's people had learned to do? (No, they did not cherish Wolf; they did not understand that he was their brother.) How do Grandfather's people show that they *cherish* the new People, even though the new People are foolish? (They show they cherish the new People by giving them time to learn and by maintaining hope that they will change as they grow strong.)

- The story ends by pointing out an *omission* in the conversation between Grandfather's people and the new People. What is this *omission*? (The omission is that nobody seems to be speaking for Wolf.) Think of Wolf as a symbol of nature. What *omissions* or actions in our day and age show that nobody is speaking for Wolf? (Possible responses: We are using nature and killing parts of it for our own advancement. We pass few laws to protect nature. We fail to control pollution in many forms. We build on any open space without thinking of the consequences for other species. All of these omissions or forms of neglect show that nobody is speaking for Wolf.)

 G

Assign online practice by opening the Tools menu, then selecting Assignments. Be sure to select the correct class from the drop-down menu.

E

Unit at a Glance *(cont.)*

A The reading strand builds comprehension through explicit systematic instruction of academic vocabulary to ask and answer questions.

B Students are asked to provide evidence-based responses to develop conceptual understanding and strategic thinking. This carefully crafted learning progression teaches the key strategies needed to be successful on high-stakes assessments.

Direct students to page 41 in their Student Books or have them tear out the extra copy of the excerpt from the back of their book.

Note: To minimize flipping back and forth between the pages, a copy of each text has been included in the back of the Student Books. Encourage students to tear this out and use it when working on activities that require the use of the text.

Choose an option for reading text. Have students read the text according to the option that you chose.

> Options for reading text:
> - Teacher read-aloud
> - Teacher-led or student-led choral read
> - Paired read or independent read with bold vocabulary words read aloud

Passage Comprehension

Write the words *clarify, present, prove,* and *synthesize* on the board. Have students read the words aloud with you.

Direct students to pages 14 and 15 in their Student Books. It is critical to understand what the question is asking and how to answer it. Today, we will review four direction words used in prompts.

Have students review the words on the board in the chart on pages 14 and 15. Check for understanding by requesting an oral response to the following questions.

- If the prompt asks you to *clarify,* the response requires you to . . . (explain it so that it is easy to understand).
- If the prompt asks you to *present,* the response requires you to . . . (deliver information).
- If the prompt asks you to *prove,* the response requires you to . . . (give evidence to show that it is true).
- If the prompt asks you to *synthesize,* the response requires you to . . . (combine information in a logical way).

Direct students to pages 59–61 in their Student Books.

Let's practice answering questions written as prompts that require critical thinking.

Model

Listen as I model the first one for you.

B

> 1. Clarify the narrator's intuition about his siblings' deaths. Provide text evidence.

According to the chart, if the prompt asks me to *clarify,* I need to explain it so that it is easily understood.

Now, I need to turn the prompt into a question to confirm my understanding. But first, I need to figure out what *intuition* is because I am not familiar with the term. **Have a student look up the definition in a dictionary and share it with the class.**

Now that I know *intuition* means "something that is known or believed without proof," I will ask myself a basic question using the question word *what.* What did the narrator suspect that Christina was involved in?

Next, I need to look for text evidence. The text says " . . . our stepmother was in some way connected with my brother's death," and "I could not help thinking that my stepmother was implicated in both their deaths, although I could not explain it."

Write the answer on the board. Have students write the answer on their page as well as the text evidence.

> *The narrator believed that Christina was connected to his siblings' deaths, but he could not explain the connection.*

Guided Practice

> 2. Synthesize and present the information that leads to the narrator's intuition regarding his siblings' deaths.

If the prompt asks you to *synthesize,* what should you do? (combine information in a logical way) And what do we do when we present? (deliver information) Let's turn the prompt into a question to confirm our understanding. If we change this to a question, what would it be? (What led to the narrator's intuition about Christina?)

Let's begin by framing our answer with some sentence starters. **Write the following sentence starters on the board.**

114   Unit 8 • Lesson 3

Unit 8 • Lesson

C A strong grammar strand directly linked to the writing strand builds knowledge of language, which allows students to effectively express themselves in writing.

D Strategies and skills are explicitly taught using teacher modeling, guided practice, and student application.

E Requiring students to write their responses provides the handwriting practice students need to become more fluent writers.

Guided Practice

Read the instructions aloud, and guide students in the completion of each sentence.

C **Relative Pronouns and Relative Clauses**

We know that a relative pronoun begins a relative clause. A relative clause modifies or describes a noun or noun phrase. Sometimes it gives extra, nonessential information, and sometimes it gives essential (restrictive) information. Remember, commas set off the nonrestrictive or nonessential relative clauses—the ones that aren't necessary to understand the sentence.

Direct students to page 53 in their Student Books. Read the instructions aloud.

We actually have three steps to follow in order to complete this activity. What is the first step? (Circle the relative pronoun.) What is the second step? (Underline the relative clause.) What is the third step? (Draw an arrow from the relative clause to the noun or noun phrase it is describing.)

D Model

Listen to the example: *The curse, which had already claimed the lives of Marcella and Caesar, haunted my thoughts.*

My first step is to find and circle the relative pronoun. The relative pronoun *which* has been used in this sentence, so I need to circle it. My second step is to identify and underline the relative clause. *Which had already claimed the lives of Marcella and Caesar* is the clause. It has a verb, *claimed*, and a subject. In this case, the subject is the pronoun *which*. *Which* is a pronoun used to take the place of the noun *curse*. This part of the sentence is underlined. My last step is to figure out what *which had already claimed the lives of Marcella and Caesar* is referencing. What claimed their lives? The curse claimed their lives, so an arrow is drawn from the clause back to *curse*. Is the relative clause essential? (no)

Guided Practice

Listen as I read #1: *My father offered the young lady, whose name was Christina, his bed and he would remain at the fire, sitting up with her father.*

What's our first step? (to find and circle the relative pronoun) What relative pronoun has been used in this sentence? (whose) Circle *whose*. What is the second step? (to identify and underline the relative clause) What words follow *whose* and complete the clause? (name was Christina) What is the clause you will underline? (*whose name*

Unit 8 • Lesson 2 **105**

Independent Practice

Have partners complete items 5–8. After all students are finished, review their answers as a class. Provide correction and affirmative feedback as appropriate.

Writing

Objectives
- Use relative clauses to create complex sentences.
- Use correct punctuation when writing sentences that contain relative clauses.

Using Relative Clauses

Understanding the job of relative clauses enables us to use them to create more variety in our sentence structure. Often, two short sentences can be effectively combined by creating a relative clause out of one of the sentences. Combining two simple sentences into one complex sentence helps a writer eliminate wordiness and redundancy in writing. We have done this with coordinating conjunctions (and, but, or, so), but they don't always work.

Direct students to page 58 in their Student Books. Read the instructions aloud. You have been given a relative pronoun to use in the new sentence. When combining the sentences, you must have one clause that can stand alone. What kind of clause can stand alone? (independent clause) Sentences that contain an independent clause and a dependent clause are called complex sentences.

E

Model

Listen as I read the example: *The wolf howled under our window. The wolf disappeared quickly.* We must use the relative pronoun *that* to join the two clauses and form a new complex sentence. I will think about how the sentences are related before I determine an effective way to combine them. If I think about the adjective questions, I can more readily determine how the two sentences are connected. Which wolf disappeared? The wolf that howled under our window is the wolf that disappeared. Using that question, I can combine the sentences to create: *The wolf that howled under our window disappeared quickly.* Only sentences that have a redundant *who* or *what* will work when trying to create a relative clause. When you are revising your writing, look for sentences that have the same subject, direct object, or object of the preposition. Those will be sentences that are candidates for this kind of combining.

Unit 8 • Lesson 2 **111**

Unit at a Glance (cont.)

A Teachers guide students through a close reading of every text.

B Students analyze text to prepare for writing.

C Students analyze sentence and paragraph structure for meaning.

D Students determine the meaning and intent of an author's language.

E Students determine the meaning of punctuation. Students identify and understand an author's use of literary devices.

F Students identify and understand an author's use of literary devices.

A

B **Have students read lines 13–40 according to** the option that you chose.
Pay attention to the descriptions of Christina. Mark the ways that she is beast-like when in human form. (mouth, although somewhat large; brilliant teeth; restless; sly; cruelty in her eyes)

When most of the students are finished, continue with the entire class.
Let's see how well you understood what you read.

- Circle the check mark or the question mark for this section. Draw a question mark over any confusing words.
- Go to line 16. Mark the word that means "a yellowish color." (flaxen)
- In the same sentence, mark the simile that describes the female's hair. Circle the words being compared. (hair; mirror)
- Go to line 23. Mark the adverb that means "in a friendly way." (kindly) Circle the common adverb suffix. (-ly)

C
- Go to line 24. Mark the transition phrase that changes directions and means "in contrast." (on the contrary)
- In the second paragraph, mark the indication that the children had a different point of view than the father. (made us children afraid; approached her with fear and trembling; Marcella would not come near her) In the margin, write why the author included this information. What mood is he trying to create? (suspense)
- In the fourth paragraph, mark the adjectives that tell why the children were unable to sleep. (bewildered; curious)
- Go to line 32. In the margin, write a synonym for *bewildered*. (confused)
- On line 33, mark the word that is similar to *cried* but indicates that the action was loud and convulsive. (sobbed)

D **Expanding Instruction:**
Figurative language can be difficult for students with a limited vocabulary to understand. Therefore, it is important to increase students' lexicons by pointing out connotations of words within text. Words with similar definitions (denotations) often have variations in associations or specificities. These nuances in meaning must be pointed out in an effort to expand students' vocabulary and help them comprehend the impact and meaning behind the author's word choice. Have students identify other variations of the word *cried* and identify how the meanings change.

Unit 8 • Lesson 4 **121**

- Go to lines 34 and 35. Mark the example of personification. (Our curious ears were ready to catch the slightest whisper.)
- Go to line 37. Mark the word with the base word *converse*. (conversation)
- Mark the evidence in this section that Marcella had a sense that something wasn't right about Christina. (Marcella would not come near her; trembled and sobbed the whole night)

Have students read lines 41–62 according to the option that you chose.

When most of the students are finished, continue with the entire class.
Let's see how well you understood what you read.

- Circle the check mark or the question mark for this section. Draw a question mark over any confusing words.
- Go to line 41. Mark the words that tell who Christina is. (hunter's daughter)

E
- Go to line 47. Mark the punctuation used to indicate a pause for emphasis. (em dash)
- On the same line, mark the adverb that indicates something unexpected. (even)
- On the same line, mark the conjunction that means "however" and indicates a change in direction. (but)
- Go to line 52. Mark the man who performed the marriage of Marcella's father. (hunter)

F
- Go to line 55. Mark the foreshadowing words in the marriage vows. (that my hand shall never be raised against her to harm her)
- Go to line 56. Mark the synonym for *revenge*. (vengeance)
- Go to line 57. Number the revengeful acts in the marriage vows. (1. perish; 2. flesh be torn; 3. bones fade in the wilderness)
- Go to line 61. Mark the synonym for *control*. (restrain)
- Go to line 62. Mark the action of Christina's father. (rode away)
- Mark the evidence in this section that Marcella had a sense that something wasn't right about Christina. (the child burst into tears and sobbed as if her heart would break; even Marcella; could not restrain herself and burst into tears)

122 Unit 8 • Lesson 4

G Students write in response to reading in every unit. Teachers guide them as they transition from a simple summary to an essay as they develop effective written expression through process writing.

H Exemplar writings are provided for teachers to use with students who need examples and extra support.

I Students evaluate self or peer writing and make necessary edits before submitting for review.

J Scoring rubrics are provided for teacher evaluation of student writing.

K All necessary examples and questions to give students 10 to 12 exposures to vocabulary throughout the unit are provided.

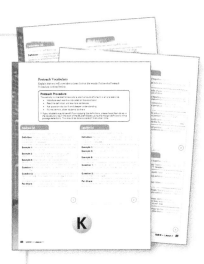

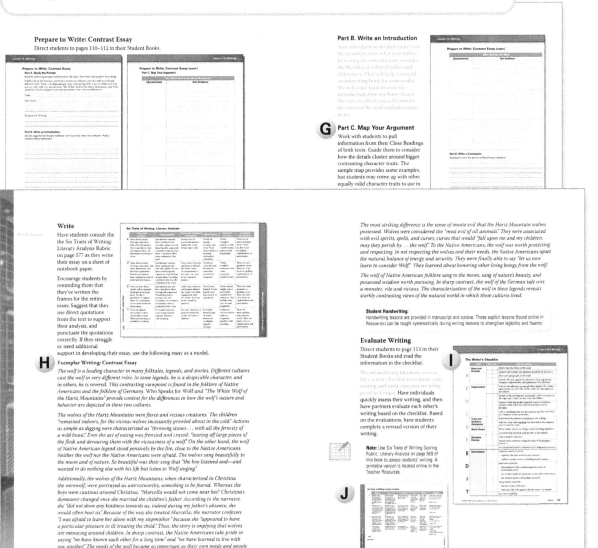

The purpose of the Start-Up Unit is to establish classroom procedures and expectations during the implementation of *LANGUAGE!® Live* in your classroom. You and your students will familiarize yourselves with the Text Training and Word Training components as well as take care of the non-instructional elements of the program. But, above all else, the Start-Up Unit will empower your students to improve their reading and writing proficiency through the use of engaging videos.

Preparation

Before beginning the Start-Up:

- Walk through the Program Guide for a comprehensive overview of the *LANGUAGE! Live* program and its unique features.
- To locate the Program Guide online, first log in to *LANGUAGE! Live*, then select Tools at the top of the screen. Next, select Course Resources. Then, click on the Program Planning tab.
- Establish groups and rotations. Students who are reading at a Lexile® level below 450 should be assigned to Level 1. Students who are reading at a Lexile level above 450 should be assigned to Level 2.
- Design your personal avatar and complete your profile. Students will be able to see your avatar while they are working online. Follow the instructions on pages 8–10 of PowerPoint 1, Welcome to *LANGUAGE! Live*.
- Set up your audio visual equipment to project videos, found online in the Program Planning tab, Start-Up section, for Days 1 and 2.
- Secure the use of computers as well as headphones with microphones for each student in the class for Day 3 of the Start-Up. After that, the number of computers/headphones needed is based on your rotation. If you have two groups, you will have a 1:2 computer/headphone to student ratio, but computers/headphones will be needed every day. If you have one group, you will have a 1:1 computer/headphone to student ratio, but computers/headphones will only be needed every other day.

 Materials   **Classroom Materials**

- *Start-Up Video 1: Introduction to LANGUAGE! Live*
- *Class Discussion Rules poster*
- *Collegial Discussion poster*
- *Start-Up Video 2: Getting Familiar*
- *PowerPoint 1, Welcome to LANGUAGE! Live*
- *Start-Up Video 3: Training and Performance*

- *Start-Up Video 4: The Brain*
- *LANGUAGE! Live Student Books*
- *Usernames and passwords (found online through Tools, Class Settings, Roster)*
- *Start-Up Video 5: The History of English*
- *Start-Up Video 6: Phonemes Primer*

- *Computers*

 Instructional Resources

- *Unit 1 Background Information (assign as homework at the end of Lesson 3)*

Lesson 1

SL.5.1b; SL.5.1c; SL.5.1d; SL.3.2; SL.6.2; SL.7.2

Objectives
- Determine the main idea of a video.
- Determine correct navigation of online environment.
- Engage in collaborative discussions.

Program Introduction

Welcome students to *LANGUAGE!® Live*. Explain to students that they will be exploring and learning about a new program that will help them become better readers.

Start-Up Video 1: Introduction to LANGUAGE! Live

Have students watch Start-Up Video 1: Introduction to *LANGUAGE! Live*. This video is located online in the Course Resources. Select the Tools menu, then the Course Resources menu. You will see a tab for Program Planning. The video is located in the Start-Up section. You will find all the other videos for the Start-Up here as well.

Class Discussion Rules poster

Collegial Discussion poster

After viewing the video, read aloud the Rules for Discussion from the poster you have posted in your room. Explain that students will follow these rules when engaging in any collaborative discussion. Then, direct them to page 382 in their Student Books. Explain that this page is a sort of "cheat sheet" for how to express themselves during discussions.

Once the rules have been established, encourage a brief discussion about the video.

Use the following prompts to encourage discussion:

- What is something new you learned from this video?
- Why are words so important?
- Why is reading important?
- What do you find intriguing about this program?

To help facilitate class discussion, use the following bullet points as a guide.

- Encourage students with a limited concept of the importance of reading to ask for further explanation from peers.

- Provide opportunities for students to explain their ideas by ensuring students follow the rules for class discussion.

- Suggest students refer to the collegial discussion sentence frames in the back of their Student Books.

- Encourage speakers to link comments to the remarks of others in an effort to keep the focus of the discussion and create cohesion, even when their comments are contradictory.

Introduce Online Navigation

Start-Up Video 2: Getting Familiar

PowerPoint 1, Welcome to LANGUAGE! Live

Have students watch Start-Up Video 2: Getting Familiar. Explain and demonstrate navigation of the online program using pages 1–7 of the PowerPoint 1, Welcome to *LANGUAGE! Live*. This PowerPoint is located online in the Course Resources under the Program Planning tab, Start-Up section as well. Use the teacher text provided with each slide, adapting as needed for your own delivery. Explain that this is an overview of the program, and assure students that they will have plenty of time to go online and explore the features soon.

After the presentation, ask students the following questions:

- What is the Homepage?
- What is a Notification?
- What is the Leaderboard?

Establish Routines

Based on your chosen setup and implementation plan (see Program Guide), briefly discuss the following that apply to your specific classroom:

- Instructional components
- Daily schedule or rotation with *LANGUAGE! Live* Word Training and *LANGUAGE! Live* Text Training components (Post information in your classroom to show the schedule or rotation.)
- Classroom expectations and rules

Explain that classroom time will be divided between the online component, called Word Training, and the print component, called Text Training. Word Training includes tutorial videos by experts and peers; activities involving sounds, letter combinations, and word parts; and passage reading and recording. Text Training includes text analysis, vocabulary, grammar, and writing. Students will spend time reading and analyzing passages and completing activities while interacting with one another and the teacher.

If you are new to *LANGUAGE! Live*, take some time to browse through the Teacher's Edition and familiarize yourself with the lesson layout, content, and expectations. Then, login to the online environment and familiarize yourself with the following:

- Where to set up your class usernames and passwords
- Where to release Benchmark Tests
- Where to access the Program Overview and Start-Up videos
- Where to find the Program Guide
- Where to access the Teacher Editions and Student Editions for use with whiteboards or tablets
- Where to access Text Training Unit Opener Videos and audio/video support for selected texts
- Where to post assignments or comments to your class
- Where to find an overview of each unit of Word Study
- Where to view student time and tasks completed
- Where to review student Gateway recordings
- Where to review and score student Fluency Checks
- Where to assign Practice Activities (grammar and vocabulary), Content Mastery, and Power Pass
- Where to score constructed responses from Power Pass
- Where to find the scores for the online Practice Activities and assessments to determine if students need extra practice on particular skills or elements
- Where to find Reteach activities
- Where to access Writing Projects, Writing Scoring Rubrics, Writing Anchor Papers, and Progress Monitoring Across the Six Traits of Writing charts
- Where to find Handwriting

Lesson 2

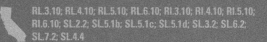

RL.3.10; RL.4.10; RL.5.10; RL.6.10; RI.3.10; RI.4.10; RI.5.10; RI.6.10; SL.2.2; SL.5.1b; SL.5.1c; SL.5.1d; SL.3.2; SL.6.2; SL.7.2; SL.4.4

Objectives

- Determine the main idea of a video.
- Deliver a personal narrative about an experience.
- Engage in collaborative discussions.
- Establish goals.

Understanding the Training Metaphor

Explain that students will continue learning more about what they can expect in *LANGUAGE! Live.*

Now, we will begin by watching more videos about *LANGUAGE! Live.*

Start-Up Video 3: Training and Performance

Start-Up Video 4: The Brain

Have students watch Start-Up Video 3: Training and Performance and Start-Up Video 4: The Brain.

Remind students of the Classroom Discussion Rules. Discuss the ideas covered in the video. Use the following prompts to encourage discussion:

- Why is training important?

- What are some things you have trained for, either in school or in your personal life?

- What is one new thing you learned about the human brain?

- What goes on in your brain when you read?

Presenting Personal Experiences

It can be helpful for students to consider experiences in other areas of life to understand the value of the skills they will learn in *LANGUAGE! Live.*

Establish small groups. Have students spend time in thought and discussion. Remind them of the Class Discussion Rules.

Tell your group about a time you learned how to do something new.

Tell your group about a time you struggled with something but worked at it until you improved.

Direct students to page S1 in their Student Books. Read aloud the prompt and instructions. Have students choose one of the topics and write some notes that will help them with their short presentation.

When groups have finished, have each student deliver his or her narrative to the class. Each presentation should be 1–2 minutes.

After students have delivered their narratives, relate their stories to the goal of *LANGUAGE! Live*, learning to read better.

Have students make connections between the times they struggled at something and then improved or times they learned how to do something new. Help them to see the parallels between their previous experiences and the new experiences they will have with *LANGUAGE! Live*.

One way to get the most out of this class and *LANGUAGE! Live* is to set goals. A goal is something that you are trying to do or achieve.

Have students return to their groups. Remind them of the Class Discussion Rules. Have students discuss the importance of reading and what they hope to achieve by the end of this school year.

Personal Narrative

You will present a short narrative to the class about a memorable experience. Choose one of the following topics:

- A time you learned how to do something new
- A time you struggled and then improved

Write what you remember about the event. Include the context surrounding the event (when, where, and what came before to lead to it). Identify why the event was memorable and important. How did it impact you?

Start-Up S1

Direct them to page S2 in their Student Books. Have students think of two goals that they hope to achieve from using *LANGUAGE! Live.*

Examples might include improving reading comprehension, not only in classwork and books, but also in text messages, hall posters, or road signs. Maybe you have a specific book you would like to read. Maybe you want to perform better in science or social studies. Maybe you want to improve your chances of getting into college or getting a job. Or, maybe you simply want to get out of this class and have more freedom to choose classes you enjoy.

Have students write their goals on the page.

Now, let's think about the steps you will take to meet these goals and how to monitor whether you are on track.

Discuss making an effort, using class time, and working online at home and how this work will be reflected on the student Dashboard through achievements. Explain the importance of working hard and taking the class seriously. Then, have students complete the page.

If you have students submit their goals, they can be used for accountability purposes during the course of the program.

Personal Goals

Record two goals for this class, the steps you will take to meet the goals, and how you will monitor your achievements.

Goal 1:			
Step 1:		How I will monitor:	
Step 2:		How I will monitor:	
Step 3:		How I will monitor:	
Goal 2:			
Step 1:		How I will monitor:	
Step 2:		How I will monitor:	
Step 3:		How I will monitor:	

S2 *LANGUAGE! Live*

Lesson 3

SL.2.2; SL.5.1b; SL.5.1c; SL.5.1d; SL.3.2; SL.6.2; SL.7.2

Objectives

- Answer questions to set up an online profile.
- Design a personal Avatar as a representation of self.
- Answer questions about information learned.
- Agree to follow rules for online engagement.

Students will be logging in to the *LANGUAGE! Live* system today. Prior to them logging in, post one of the following assignments for students to respond to.

> *Describe LANGUAGE! Live using one word.*
>
> *What is one thing you learned from the videos?*

Introduce Avatars and Profiles

PowerPoint 1, Welcome to LANGUAGE! Live

Usernames and passwords (These can be posted in Student Books before starting class.)

We have been learning about the *LANGUAGE! Live* program. We have talked about the importance of reading, shared our experiences, and established goals for the school year. Today, we will go online and make an avatar.

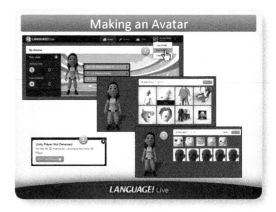

Explain the concepts of avatars and profiles to students using pages 8–10 of the PowerPoint 1, Welcome to *LANGUAGE! Live*. Use the teacher text provided with each slide, adapting as needed for your own delivery. Depending on your classroom setup and the needs of your students, it may be helpful to demonstrate the steps of making a profile and avatar while projecting your computer screen to students.

Create Avatars and Profiles

LANGUAGE! Live Student Books

Usernames and passwords (These can be posted in Student Books before starting class.)

Computers

Direct students to page S3 in their Student Books. Explain that this is a "cheat sheet" for the online program. If you haven't already done so, distribute usernames and passwords to students. Explain to students that they should keep their usernames and passwords safe. It is important that they do not lose or share this information. All students' online activity will be tracked by the *LANGUAGE! Live* system.

Instruct students to log in. Have them complete their avatars and profiles online. Provide assistance and answer questions as needed. Allow students to share their avatars with the class.

Posting

Have students explore the communication options available in *LANGUAGE! Live*. Ask students to post on the class wall.

Remind students that their comments will be visible not only to you, but to the entire class.

Explain that they will receive points for completion of this assignment.

Class Wall and Feedback

Netiquette

As we are working online in *LANGUAGE! Live*, we need to follow certain rules so that everything runs smoothly.

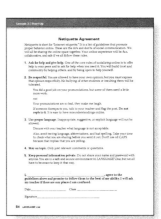

- Direct students to the Netiquette Agreement on page S4 of their Student Books. Explain the definition of netiquette, and instruct students to follow along as you read the information.

- Engage students in a discussion of appropriate and inappropriate online behavior using the prompts given. Encourage students to answer as honestly as possible.

- Be sure to make clear what behavior will and will not be tolerated in class.

- Emphasize to students that in or out of school, the *LANGUAGE! Live* program is school property, and teachers and administrators have access to all student accounts.

Have students sign the Netiquette Agreement and return it to you.

Learning About Our Language

We are almost ready to begin our lessons. Before we do, let's watch two more videos about English. We will learn just how English came to be, and then we'll learn about how sounds are created and represented by letters in way that's like a code. *LANGUAGE! Live* will help you to decode words and ultimately become a better reader.

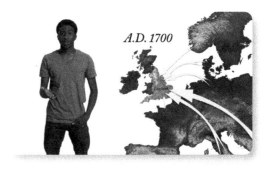

A.D. 1700

Start-Up Video 5: The History of English

Start-Up Video 6: Phonemes Primer

Have students watch Start-Up Video 5: The History of English and Start-Up Video 6: Phonemes Primer.

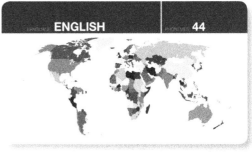

ENGLISH   44

After students have created their avatars and profiles, watched the videos, and explored the program, discuss students' experience.

- What have you learned about *LANGUAGE! Live*?
- What is your favorite part of the program?

Note: You and your students will begin with Lesson 1 in Word Training and Text Training during the next class period. Before that, complete the following:

- Choose a Lesson Opener from Lesson 1 (Teacher's Edition page 4) and post the Lesson Opener online or write it on the board for students to respond to at the beginning of the next class period.

- Set up audio visual equipment to play the Unit 1 Text Training video.

Unit Big Ideas

- To what degree is our destiny within our control?
- Is punishment a pathway to rehabilitation and reformation?
- Is punishment always just?
- How does science influence crime and punishment?

Instructional Texts

Excerpt from *Holes* by Louis Sachar
Text type: literature—novel

"The Science of Catching Criminals"
Text type: informational

Materials

- *Unit 1 video (Crime and Punishment)*
- *Class Discussion Rules poster—display in classroom*
- *Collegial Discussion poster—display in classroom*
- *Vocabulary Rating Scale poster—display in classroom*
- *Masterpiece Sentences poster—display in classroom*
- *Six Traits of Writing Scoring Rubric: Basic (print as needed)*

Optional
- *Unit 1 Background Information*
- *Progress Monitoring Across the Six Traits scales (one per trait for each student, to be used with Lesson 10 of each unit)*

Classroom Materials

- *Colored index cards*
- *Highlighters or colored pencils*
- *Notebook paper*

Optional
- *Feature film:* Holes

Instructional Resources

- *Unit 1 Reteach*
- *Handwriting Lessons*
- *Unit 2 Background Information (assign as homework at the end of the unit)*

Instructional Texts:
Excerpt from *Holes*
by Louis Sachar
Text type: literature

"The Science of Catching Criminals"
Text type: informational

LANGUAGE! *Live* Online

Grammar Practice
- Identify nouns and verbs in sentences.
- Distinguish between action verbs and linking verbs.
- Use plural nouns correctly.
- Use past and present tense verbs correctly.
- Use pronouns correctly.

Vocabulary Practice
- Determine the meaning of derivations of words.

Content Mastery
- Demonstrate an understanding of . . .
  - word meaning by answering questions and using words in sentences.
  - nouns and verbs.
  - pronouns.
  - past and present tense verbs.

Word Study
- Blend, read, and spell words with short vowels; digraphs and inflectional endings; and long vowels and silent -e.
- Read connected text to build fluency.

Lesson 1

Reading
- Determine and discuss the topic of a text.
- Determine and discuss the author's purpose.
- Use text features to preview text.

Vocabulary
- Evaluate word knowledge.
- Determine the meaning of key passage vocabulary.

Reading
- Read an excerpt from a novel.
- Monitor comprehension during text reading.
- Make and verify predictions about what will happen next in a story.

Lesson 2

Vocabulary
- Review key passage vocabulary.

Grammar
- Identify the purpose and function of nouns.
- Identify the purpose and function of pronouns.
- Identify the purpose and function of verbs.
- Distinguish between action verbs and linking verbs.

Writing
- Write simple sentences.
- Identify the structure of a sentence.
- Edit sentences for punctuation and capitalization.

Lesson 6

Reading
- Determine and discuss the topic of a text.
- Determine and discuss the author's purpose.
- Use text features to preview text.
- Distinguish between features of literary and informational text.

Vocabulary
- Evaluate word knowledge.
- Determine the meaning of key passage vocabulary.

Reading
- Read informational text.
- Monitor comprehension during text reading.
- Summarize text.

Lesson 7

Vocabulary
- Review key passage vocabulary.

Grammar
- Use possessive nouns correctly.
- Identify the function and purpose of the apostrophe.
- Identify the function and purpose of verb tenses.
- Distinguish between past and present tense verbs.

Writing
- Write simple sentences.
- Identify the structure of a sentence.
- Identify the simple subject of a sentence.
- Identify the simple predicate of a sentence.
- Use subject-verb agreement in writing.

Lesson 3	Lesson 4	Lesson 5
Reading	**Vocabulary**	**Vocabulary**
• Establish a purpose for rereading literary text.	• Review key passage vocabulary.	• Review key passage vocabulary.
• Demonstrate an understanding of how to ask questions and answer them appropriately.	**Reading**	**Writing**
	• Read with purpose and understanding.	• Self-correct as comprehension of text deepens.
• Use complete sentences and text evidence to answer questions.	• Answer questions to demonstrate comprehension of text.	• Use text to write coherent paragraphs in response to reading.
• Use critical thinking skills to write responses to prompts about text.	• Identify and explain explicit details from text.	• Identify the setting of a story.
• Support written answers with text evidence.	• Monitor comprehension of text during reading.	• Analyze character point of view.
	• Demonstrate understanding of words by relating them to their synonyms.	**Reading**
		• Answer questions to demonstrate comprehension of text.
	• Connect pronouns to their antecedents.	• Engage in class discussion.
	• Identify the setting of a story.	• Identify the enduring understandings from a piece of text.
	• Determine how the setting affects the characters.	• Compare text and film.
	• Identify the protagonist and antagonist of a story.	

Lesson 8	Lesson 9	Lesson 10
Reading	**Vocabulary**	**Vocabulary**
• Establish a purpose for rereading informational text.	• Review key passage vocabulary.	• Review key passage vocabulary.
• Demonstrate an understanding of how to ask questions and answer them appropriately.	**Reading**	**Writing**
	• Read informational text.	• Demonstrate an understanding of writing prompts.
• Use complete sentences and text evidence to answer questions.	• Read with purpose and understanding.	• Orally retell key information from an informational text.
• Use critical thinking skills to write responses to prompts about text.	• Answer questions to demonstrate comprehension of text.	• Write a topic sentence.
• Support written answers with text evidence.	• Identify and explain explicit details from text.	• Use correct capitalization and quotation marks in titles.
	• Monitor comprehension during text reading.	• Write a summary.
	• Determine how each section of text contributes to the whole.	• Use a rubric to guide and evaluate writing.
		Reading
		• Answer questions to demonstrate comprehension of text.
		• Engage in class discussion.
		• Identify the enduring understandings from a piece of text.
		• Self-correct as comprehension of text deepens.

Lesson 1

RL.3.1; RL.1.10; RL.1.10a; RL.4.10; RI.1.10a; SL.1.2; SL.5.1.b; SL.5.1.c; SL.5.1.d; L.3.5.b; L.6.6

Lesson Opener

Before the lesson, choose one of the following activities to write on the board or post on the *LANGUAGE! Live* Class Wall online.

- *Describe your avatar.*
- *Write two sentences about why it is important to learn to read.*
- *Write two sentences about the kind of food you like, naming a few of your favorites.*

Reading

Objectives

- Determine and discuss the topic of a text.
- Determine and discuss the author's purpose.
- Use text features to preview text.

Passage Introduction

Direct students to page 1 in their Student Books. Discuss the content focus.

Content Focus

crime and punishment

What do you think you will read about in this passage? (Answers will vary.)

What happens to people who commit a crime? (go to prison; pay a fine)

Type of Text

literature

There are different types of texts, or reading selections. The text we will read today belongs to a category called literature. Say *literature*. (literature) Literature consists of stories, poems, dramas, and creatively written prose.

The text we will read today is a story. It comes from a longer work of fiction called a novel. A work of fiction is one in which events, characters, and details are made up, or not true. This story is told by a narrator in third-person point of view. That means he or she is outside the story. Is a fictional work made up or based on real life? (made up) So will today's text contain real people or made-up characters? (made-up characters)

Lesson 1 | Reading

Let's Focus: Excerpt from *Holes*

Content Focus	Type of Text
crime and punishment	literature—novel

Author's Name Louis Sachar

Author's Purpose to entertain

Big Ideas
Consider the following Big Idea questions. Write your answer for each question.

To what degree is our destiny within our control? Explain your answer.

_____

_____

Is punishment a pathway to rehabilitation and reformation? Explain your answer.

_____

_____

Narrative Preview Checklist: the excerpt from *Holes* on pages 3–6.
- ☐ Title: What clue does it provide about the passage?
- ☐ Pictures: What additional information is added here?
- ☐ Margin Information: What vocabulary is important to understand this story?

Enduring Understandings
After reading the text . . .

_____

_____

_____

_____

_____

_____

Unit 1   **1**

Author's Purpose

Have students glance at the text. Who is the author of *Holes*? (Louis Sachar) **Have students write it on the page.** That means that he wrote the book. The author's purpose is the reason that he or she wrote the text. Authors write for different purposes. They write to entertain, to persuade, or to inform or teach. Knowing an author's purpose can help a reader better understand a text. Was *Holes* written to inform or entertain? (entertain) Will the author teach you something or entertain you? (entertain) **Have students write the answer on the page in their Student Books.** Have you read any other piece of literature in which the author's purpose was to entertain? Turn and tell your neighbor the title of the last fiction book that you read. If you like the chapter we are about to read, you should consider reading the entire book, followed by the sequel, or continuation, *Small Steps*.

Play the Unit 1 Text Training video found in the Teacher Resources online.

Before we read the excerpt from *Holes*, we will watch a short video to help build our background knowledge. **Play the Unit 1 Text Training video. Have partners discuss the main points the videographer was trying to make and what evidence was provided to support the points.**

> **Note:** Additional Background Information about juvenile correctional facilities in the United States can be found in the Teacher Resources online. Choose the Text Training tab, and then select Unit 1. The Background Information will be in the first section.

Print the Class Discussion Rules poster and the Collegial Discussion poster found in the Teacher Resources online and post where students can easily see them.

Read aloud the Rules for Discussion and explain that students will follow these rules when engaging in any collaborative discussion. Then, direct them to page 381 in their Student Books. Explain that this page is a sort of "cheat sheet" of how to express themselves during discussions. Read the Big Idea questions aloud.

Big Ideas

To what degree is our destiny within our control?

Is punishment a pathway to rehabilitation and reformation?

As a class, consider the two Big Idea questions.

- Encourage students with limited knowledge of the terms *destiny*, *rehabilitation*, and *reformation* to ask for further explanation from peers.

- Provide opportunities for students to explain their ideas and answers to the Big Idea questions in light of the discussion by ensuring students follow the rules for class discussion, which can be printed in poster form from the Teacher Resources online.

- Suggest students refer to the Collegial Discussion sentence frames in the back of their books.

- Encourage speakers to link comments to the remarks of others to keep the focus of the discussion and create cohesion, even when their comments are in disagreement.

After discussing each question, have students write an answer. We'll come back to these questions after we finish reading *Holes*. You can add to your answers as you gain information and perspective.

Preview

Read the Narrative Preview Checklist on page 1. Follow the Preview Procedure outlined below.

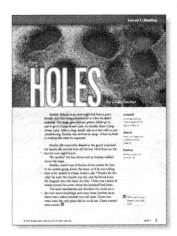

Preview Procedure
- Group students with partners or in triads.
- Have students count off as 1s or 2s. The 1s will become the student leaders. If working with triads, the third students become 3s.
- The student leaders will preview the text in addition to managing the checklist and pacing.
- The 2s and 3s will preview the text with 1s.
- Direct 1s to open their Student Books to page 1 and 2s and 3s to open their Student Books to page 3. This allows students to look at a few different pages at one time without turning back and forth.

What is the title? (*Holes*) What clue does the title provide about the passage? **Provide sharing time.** Let's look to see what additional information the pictures provide. What picture do you see behind the title, *Holes*? (holes in the dry ground) What is the next picture that you see? (sunflower seeds) What tool is pictured at the bottom of the next page? (a shovel) What creature is pictured on the next page? (yellow lizard) What do you know about lizards? What do you wonder? **Provide wait time.** I wonder if this is a fictional lizard or if they really exist. I wonder what they eat. I wonder if these yellow lizards are safe.

Objectives
- Evaluate word knowledge.
- Determine the meaning of key passage vocabulary.

Rate Vocabulary Knowledge

Direct students to page 2 in their Student Books. Another important component to becoming a proficient reader and writer is vocabulary. Put very simply, vocabulary is word meaning. Knowing what words mean will help you understand what you read. The more words you know, the easier reading will become.

Let's take a look at the vocabulary words from the *Holes* excerpt, the first passage we will read. The words are listed in the first column. The part of speech is in the second column. I'm going to read each one aloud, and you will repeat it, then write it in the third column. Then, you will rate your knowledge of the word.

If you are familiar with the word and can use it correctly in a sentence, give yourself a 3. If you are familiar with the word but not sure if you know the correct meaning, give yourself a 2. If you have heard the word before but aren't sure how to use it, give yourself a 1. If you can't pronounce the word or have never heard the word before, give yourself a 0. The points are not a grade; they are just there to help you know which words you need to focus on. By the end of this unit, you should be able to change all your ratings to a 3—that's the goal.

Lesson 1 | Vocabulary

Key Passage Vocabulary: Excerpt from *Holes*

Read each word. Write the word in column 3. Then, circle a number to rate your knowledge of the word.

Vocabulary	Part of Speech	Write the Word	Knowledge Rating
commit	(v)	commit	0 1 2 3
dazed	(adj)	dazed	0 1 2 3
barren	(adj)	barren	0 1 2 3
juvenile	(adj)	juvenile	0 1 2 3
declare	(v)	declare	0 1 2 3
premises	(n)	premises	0 1 2 3
aware	(adj)	aware	0 1 2 3
consist	(v)	consist	0 1 2 3
avoid	(v)	avoid	0 1 2 3
vast	(adj)	vast	0 1 2 3

Vocabulary Rating Scale

0—I have never heard the word before.

1—I have heard the word, but I'm not sure how to use it.

2—I am familiar with the word, but I'm not sure if I know the correct meaning.

3—I know the meaning of the word and can use it correctly in a sentence.

Read each word aloud. Have students repeat it, write the word, and rate it. Then, have volunteers who rated a word *2* or *3* use the word in an oral sentence.

Preteach Vocabulary

Let's take a closer look at the words. Provide definitions and examples as indicated on the word cards. Ask questions to clarify and deepen understanding. If time permits, allow students to share.

> ### Preteach Procedure
> This activity is intended to take only a short amount of time. It is an oral exercise.
> - Introduce each word as indicated on the word card.
> - Read the definition and example sentences.
> - Ask questions to clarify and deepen understanding.
> - If time permits, allow students to share.
>
> * If your students would benefit from copying the definitions, please have them do so in the vocabulary log in the back of the Student Books using the margin definitions in the passage selections. This should be done outside of instruction time.

commit (v)

Let's read the first word together. *Commit.*

Definition: *Commit* means "to do something that is against the law or harmful." What means "to do something that is against the law or harmful"? (commit)

Example 1: People sometimes *commit* theft if they are hungry enough.

Example 2: If a player *commits* too many fouls, he or she has to leave the game.

Example 3: If you *commit* a parking error, you may not pass the driving test.

Question 1: Does a person *commit* a sneeze? Yes or no? (no)

Question 2: When Vera stole lipstick, did she *commit* a crime? Yes or no? (yes)

Pair Share: Turn to your partner and tell about a crime that was *committed* on a TV show you recently watched.

dazed (adj)

Let's read the next word together. *Dazed.*

Definition: *Dazed* means "very confused and unable to think clearly." What means "very confused and unable to think clearly"? (dazed)

Example 1: A roller coaster ride can leave you feeling *dazed* and dizzy.

Example 2: Some people feel *dazed* when they walk out of a dark theater into the blinding light.

Example 3: My kitten looked *dazed* after it ran into a wall.

Question 1: Could getting bumped on the head leave you feeling *dazed*? Yes or no? (yes)

Question 2: If a person is struggling with homework, is it possible he is *dazed*? Yes or no? (yes)

Pair Share: Turn to your partner and tell about a time you or a friend were *dazed*.

barren (adj)

Let's read the next word together. *Barren*.

Definition: *Barren* means "without plant or animal life." What means "without plant or animal life"? (barren)

Example 1: The *barren* desert landscape offers little shade.

Example 2: Some people go camping in *barren* areas so allergies won't bother them.

Example 3: The arctic region is *barren* and cold.

Question 1: Is the rain forest *barren*? Yes or no? (no)

Question 2: Is the moon *barren*? Yes or no? (yes)

Pair Share: Turn to your partner and tell about a movie or story that takes place in a *barren* setting.

(3)

juvenile (adj)

Let's read the next word together. *Juvenile*.

Definition: *Juvenile* means "related to a person under 18 years of age." What means "related to a person under 18 years of age"? (juvenile)

Example 1: *Juvenile* crime is down in recent years.

Example 2: A 16-year-old car thief would likely be sent to a *juvenile* detention center.

Example 3: The school board invited two *juvenile* citizens to give their opinions about the dress code.

Question 1: Is a grandfather a *juvenile* member of the family? Yes or no? (no)

Question 2: Could a *juvenile* coaching staff be made up of teenagers? Yes or no? (yes)

Pair Share: Turn to your partner and describe the perfect *juvenile* vacation resort.

(4)

declare (v)

Let's read the next word together. *Declare*.

Definition: *Declare* means "to state something in a firm or official way." What means "to state something in a firm or official way"? (declare)

Example 1: The seniors *declared* the first row of parking spots to be theirs.

Example 2: Officials *declare* the winner at the end of a tournament.

Example 3: A man *declared* his love for his girlfriend by proposing to her on the radio.

Question 1: The principal announced her retirement over the intercom. Did she *declare* her retirement? Yes or no? (yes)

Question 2: If you think a thought in your mind, have you *declared* it? Yes or no? (no)

Pair Share: Turn to your partner and *declare* him or her the Best Human Being Alive.

(5)

premises (n)

Let's read the next word together. *Premises*.

Definition: *Premises* are the land and buildings owned by a person or company. What means "the land and buildings owned by a person or company"? (premises)

Example 1: You may not smoke on the *premises* of many restaurants.

Example 2: My mother is allergic to cats and does not want them on her *premises*.

Example 3: A fence marks the *premises* of my aunt's ranch.

Question 1: Are classes held on the school *premises*? Yes or no? (yes)

Question 2: Would you find a concession stand on the *premises* of a ballpark? Yes or no? (yes)

Pair Share: Turn to your partner and describe the *premises* of the elementary school you attended.

(6)

aware (adj)

Let's read the next word together. *Aware*.

Definition: *Aware* means "knowing something exists or is happening." What means "knowing something exists or is happening"? (aware)

Example 1: When I saw the dark clouds, I became *aware* of the coming storm.

Example 2: She is *aware* that the new boy likes her but wishes he would say so.

Example 3: We are *aware* that satellites are in the sky even though we can't see them.

Question 1: When your stomach growls, are you *aware* of your hunger? Yes or no? (yes)

Question 2: When a baby is born, is he or she *aware* of the hospital rules? Yes or no? (no)

Pair Share: Turn to your partner and tell about the moment you became *aware* of something that made you happy.

(7)

consist (v)

Let's read the next word together. *Consist*.

Definition: *Consist* means "to be made up of." What means "to be made up of"? (consist)

Example 1: The fine arts *consist* of theater, dance, and music.

Example 2: The sport of baseball *consists* of throwing, batting, running, and catching.

Example 3: My lunch will *consist* of a sandwich, an apple, and pretzels.

Question 1: Does the solar system *consist* of planets orbiting the sun? Yes or no? (yes)

Question 2: Does a garden *consist* of streets and buildings? Yes or no? (no)

Pair Share: Turn to your partner and tell what your favorite outfit *consists* of.

(8)

avoid (v)

Let's read the next word together. *Avoid*.

Definition: *Avoid* means "to stay away from something or someone." What means "to stay away from something or someone"? (avoid)

Example 1: I *avoid* people when they are sick.

Example 2: People with fair skin usually try to *avoid* the sun to keep from getting burned.

Example 3: My dog hides behind the couch to *avoid* his bath.

Question 1: Should an athlete in training *avoid* sugary snacks? Yes or no? (yes)

Question 2: Do you try to *avoid* your best friends? Yes or no? (no)

Pair Share: Turn to your partner and tell about a food you *avoid*.

(9)

vast (adj)

Let's read the last word together. *Vast*.

Definition: *Vast* means "extremely large." What means "extremely large"? (vast)

Example 1: It took us over an hour to walk through the *vast* furniture store.

Example 2: Finding my car in a *vast* parking lot is always a challenge.

Example 3: When I look out at the *vast* ocean, I imagine very distant shores.

Question 1: Is outer space *vast*? Yes or no? (yes)

Question 2: Is the tip of a pencil *vast*? Yes or no? (no)

Pair Share: Turn to your partner and tell how you would feel in the middle of a *vast* desert.

(10)

Reading

Objectives
- Read an excerpt from a novel.
- Monitor comprehension during text reading.
- Make and verify predictions about what will happen next in a story.

Excerpt from *Holes*

Direct students to page 3 in their Student Books.

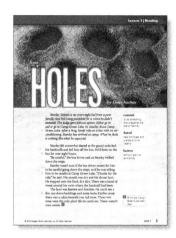

Now that we have pondered the big ideas and previewed some vocabulary we will see in the text, it's time to read. Good readers keep their eyes on text while forming mental pictures in their mind's eye. I will read the first page to model the reading behaviors of a good reader. While I read aloud, your eyes should be on text. Follow along using your writing utensil as a pointer.

Where are your eyes? **(on text)** Where is your pencil? **(following along, word for word)** What will you be thinking about while I read? **(forming a mental picture)** Before I read, notice the difference between the font used in the introduction and the font used in the rest of the story. What is this font called? **(italics)** Why is the first paragraph in italics? **(It is providing background information so that we can understand the story better.)**

Read lines 1–23 aloud.

SE p. 3, paragraphs 1–5

*Stanley Yelnats is an overweight kid from a poor family. And he's being punished for a crime he didn't **commit**. The judge gave him an option: Either go to jail or go to Camp Green Lake. So Stanley chose Camp Green Lake. After a long, lonely ride on a bus with no air-conditioning, Stanley has arrived at camp. What he finds is nothing like what he expected.*

Stanley felt somewhat **dazed** as the guard unlocked his handcuffs and led him off the bus. He'd been on the bus for over eight hours.

"Be careful," the bus driver said as Stanley walked down the steps.

Stanley wasn't sure if the bus driver meant for him to be careful going down the steps, or if he was telling him to be careful at Camp Green Lake. "Thanks for the ride," he said. His mouth was dry and his throat hurt. He stepped onto the hard, dry dirt. There was a band of sweat around his wrist where the handcuff had been.

The land was **barren** and desolate. He could see a few run-down buildings and some tents. Farther away there was a cabin beneath two tall trees. Those two trees were the only plant life he could see. There weren't even weeds.

What do you notice at the end of the fifth paragraph? (a number) Good readers pause to stop and think while reading. They reflect on what they read before continuing. Sometimes when good readers stop and think, they make a mental prediction about what will happen next. Sometimes, good readers ask themselves questions while reading. **Have students read the question in the margin that corresponds to the number.** (1. What did Camp Green Lake look like?)

Model a think-aloud for students, focusing on the setting. While reading, I'm imagining the setting—where the story takes place—in my mind's eye. Using the pictures of the holes at the top of page as my backdrop, I see dry, hard dirt. I see two or three old buildings that are not kept up. I see tents and two tall trees. Try to form that image in your mind.

As you continue reading the text, I want you to stop at the numbers and read the corresponding questions. This will help you with comprehension.

Guiding Students Toward Independent Reading

It is important that your students read as much and as often as they can. Assign texts that meet the needs of your students, based on your observations and data. This is a good opportunity to stretch your students. If students become frustrated, scaffold the reading with paired reading, choral reading, or a read-aloud.

Options for reading text:

- Teacher read-aloud
- Teacher-led or student-led choral read
- Paired read or independent read

Choose an option for reading the remainder of the text. Have students read according to the option that you chose. If you choose to read the text aloud or chorally, use the text below and stop to ask questions and have students answer them.

SE p. 4, paragraphs 1–3

The guard led Stanley to a small building. A sign in front said, YOU ARE ENTERING CAMP GREEN LAKE **JUVENILE** CORRECTIONAL FACILITY. Next to it was another sign which **declared** that it was a violation of the Texas Penal Code to bring guns, explosives, weapons, drugs, or alcohol onto the **premises**.

As Stanley read the sign he couldn't help but think, *Well, duh!*

The guard led Stanley into the building, where he felt the welcome relief of air-conditioning.

2. Why is Stanley happy to enter the building?

SE p. 4, paragraphs 4–5

A man was sitting with his feet up on a desk. He turned his head when Stanley and the guard entered, but otherwise didn't move. Even though he was inside, he wore sunglasses and a cowboy hat. He also held a can of soda, and the sight of it made Stanley even more **aware** of his own thirst.

He waited while the bus guard gave the man some papers to sign.

3. Who do you think the new character is?

SE p. 4, paragraphs 6–9

"That's a lot of sunflower seeds," the bus guard said.

Stanley noticed a burlap sack filled with sunflower seeds on the floor next to the desk.

"I quit smoking last month," said the man in the cowboy hat. He had a tattoo of a rattlesnake on his arm, and as he signed his name, the snake's rattle seemed to wiggle. "I used to smoke a pack a day. Now I eat a sack of these every week."

The guard laughed.

4. Why did the guard laugh?

SE p. 4, paragraphs 10–12

There must have been a small refrigerator behind his desk, because the man in the cowboy hat produced two more cans of soda. For a second Stanley hoped that one might be for him, but the man gave one to the guard and said the other was for the driver.

"Nine hours here, and now nine hours back," the guard grumbled. "What a day."

Stanley thought about the long, miserable bus ride and felt a little sorry for the guard and the bus driver.

5. Why does Stanley feel sorry for the guard and bus driver?

SE p. 4, paragraphs 13–14

The man in the cowboy hat spit sunflower seed shells into a wastepaper basket. Then he walked around the desk to Stanley. "My name is Mr. Sir," he said. "Whenever you speak to me you must call me by my name, is that clear?"

Stanley hesitated. "Uh, yes, Mr. Sir," he said, though he couldn't imagine that was really the man's name.

SE p. 5, paragraph 1

"You're not in the Girl Scouts anymore," Mr. Sir said.

6. What kind of comment is this?

*SE p. 5,
paragraphs 2–6*

Stanley had to remove his clothes in front of Mr. Sir, who made sure he wasn't hiding anything. He was then given two sets of clothes and a towel. Each set **consisted** of a long-sleeve orange jumpsuit, an orange T-shirt, and yellow socks. Stanley wasn't sure if the socks had been yellow originally.

He was also given white sneakers, an orange cap, and a canteen made of heavy plastic, which unfortunately was empty. The cap had a piece of cloth sewn on the back of it, for neck protection.

Stanley got dressed. The clothes smelled like soap.

Mr. Sir told him he should wear one set to work in and one set for relaxation. Laundry was done every three days. On that day his work clothes would be washed. Then the other set would become his work clothes, and he would get clean clothes to wear while resting.

"You are to dig one hole each day, including Saturdays and Sundays. Each hole must be five feet deep and five feet across in every direction. Your shovel is your measuring stick. Breakfast is served at 4:30."

7. Predict the purpose of digging the holes.

*SE p. 5,
paragraphs 7–14*

Stanley must have looked surprised, because Mr. Sir went on to explain that they started early to **avoid** the hottest part of the day. "No one is going to baby-sit you," he added. "The longer it takes you to dig, the longer you will be out in the sun. If you dig up anything interesting, you are to report it to me or any other counselor. When you finish, the rest of the day is yours."

Stanley nodded to show he understood.

"This isn't a Girl Scout camp," said Mr. Sir.

He checked Stanley's backpack and allowed him to keep it. Then he led Stanley outside into the blazing heat.

"Take a good look around you," Mr. Sir said. "What do you see?"

Stanley looked out across the **vast** wasteland. The air seemed thick with heat and dirt. "Not much," he said, then hastily added, "Mr. Sir."

Mr. Sir laughed. "You see any guard towers?"

"No."

SE p. 6, paragraph 1

"How about an electric fence?"

*p. 6,
paragraphs 2–5*

"No, Mr. Sir."

"There's no fence at all, is there?"

"No, Mr. Sir."

"You want to run away?" Mr. Sir asked him.

8. Why does Mr. Sir ask these questions?

*p. 6,
paragraphs 6–9*

Stanley looked back at him, unsure what he meant.

"If you want to run away, go ahead, start running. I'm not going to stop you."

Stanley didn't know what kind of game Mr. Sir was playing.

"I see you're looking at my gun. Don't worry. I'm not going to shoot you." He tapped his holster. "This is for yellow-spotted lizards. I wouldn't waste a bullet on you."

9. How is Mr. Sir making Stanley feel?

*p. 6,
paragraphs 10–15*

"I'm not going to run away," Stanley said.

"Good thinking," said Mr. Sir. "Nobody runs away from here. We don't need a fence. Know why? Because we've got the only water for a hundred miles. You want to run away? You'll be buzzard food in three days."

Stanley could see some kids dressed in orange and carrying shovels dragging themselves toward the tents.

"You thirsty?" asked Mr. Sir.

"Yes, Mr. Sir," Stanley said gratefully.

"Well, you better get used to it. You're going to be thirsty for the next eighteen months."

For confirmation of engagement, take 30 seconds to have students share a prediction with their partner about what could happen next. Have volunteers share predictions with the class. Encourage students to read the book or watch the movie to verify their predictions.

Note: Author information is included at the end of each piece of authentic literature in the Student Books. Because it is not necessary for completion of the unit, it is not included here. However, your students may find it interesting and helpful.

Lesson Opener

Before the lesson, choose one of the following activities to write on the board or post on the *LANGUAGE! Live* Class Wall online.

- *Write one or two sentences that summarize the excerpt from* Holes.
- *Write one sentence describing Stanley and one sentence describing Mr. Sir.*
- *Describe a camp that you would like to go to.*

Vocabulary

Objective

- Review key passage vocabulary.

Review Passage Vocabulary

Direct students to page 2 in their Student Books. Use the following questions to review the vocabulary words from the *Holes* excerpt. Have students answer each question using the vocabulary word or indicating its meaning in a complete sentence.

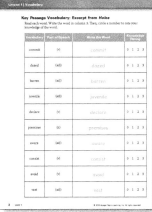

- What crime did Stanley *commit*? (He didn't commit a crime.) How could Stanley or another camper *commit* an offense while at Camp Green Lake? (They could commit an offense by bringing weapons, drugs, or alcohol into the camp; by not calling Mr. Sir "sir"; or by not digging.)

- Why did Stanley feel *dazed* when he got off the bus? (Stanley felt dazed because the bus ride was so long and hot.) What about the camp itself might leave a person feeling *dazed*? (The bleak landscape, the heat, and the strangeness of everything could make a person feel dazed.)

- What makes the land around the camp *barren*? (The land around the camp is barren because it has little plant or animal life.) Is Camp Green Lake a good name for such a *barren* place? Why or why not? (No, it is not a good name for such a barren place because nothing is green or living there.)

- Camp Green Lake is a *juvenile* detention center. How old are the people sent to a *juvenile* center? (People sent to a juvenile center are under 18.) Who in this classroom could not be sent to a *juvenile* center? (The teacher could not be sent to a juvenile center.)

- What does the sign in front of the building *declare*? (It declares that no weapons, drugs, or alcohol are allowed.) What does Mr. Sir *declare* to Stanley several times? (He declares that this is not a Girl Scout camp.)

- What can be found on the *premises* of Camp Green Lake? (A few rundown buildings, a cabin, and two tall trees can be found on the camp premises.) Are the *premises* marked by a fence or in any other way? (No, the premises are not marked.)

- When he sees Mr. Sir's soda, what does Stanley become *aware* of? (Stanley becomes aware of his own thirst.) When Mr. Sir tells Stanley to try to run away if he wants to, what else does Stanley become *aware* of? (He becomes aware of the fact that there's no way out.)

- What does a Green Lake camper's clothing set *consist* of? (It consists of an orange jumpsuit, an orange T-shirt, and yellow socks.) What activities does a camper's day *consist* of? (A camper's day consists of eating breakfast and then digging a hole.)

- The campers start digging very early in the morning. What does digging early help them *avoid*? (Digging early helps them avoid the hottest part of the day.) If you were Stanley, what else might you try to *avoid* at Camp Green Lake? (I might try to avoid making Mr. Sir mad.)

- Why is Camp Green Lake described as a "*vast* wasteland"? (It is described as a "vast wasteland" because it is huge and there is nothing there.) How would being in a *vast* wasteland make you feel? (Being in a vast wasteland would make me feel lonely and scared.)

Grammar

Objectives
- Identify the purpose and function of nouns.
- Identify the purpose and function of pronouns.
- Identify the purpose and function of verbs.
- Distinguish between action verbs and linking verbs.

Nouns

Words in our language fit into categories. One category is nouns. A noun is a naming word. It answers the *who* or *what* question. It names people, places, things, and ideas. Think about the excerpt from *Holes* that you read and give me some nouns from the selection. **Write student responses on the board. Prompt students to generate examples of common, proper, singular, and plural nouns.** (Possible responses: Stanley, guard, Mr. Sir, hat, sunglasses, seeds, Camp Green Lake, bus, shovel, jumpsuit, backpack, trees, holes, driver, dirt, campers, drink)

Review the list of nouns and have students determine if each noun answers the *who* or the *what*. Then, have them determine if it names a person, place, thing, or idea.

Nouns can be considered common nouns or proper nouns. A common noun names a *general* person, place, or thing. What does a common noun name? (a general person, place, or thing) A proper noun names a *specific* person, place, or thing. What does a proper noun name? (a specific person, place, or thing) Proper nouns come with a hint because they begin with a capital letter. Let's sort these nouns as to whether they are common or proper nouns.

Draw two columns on the board, labeled *common nouns* and *proper nouns*. Sort the nouns generated into the two columns.

Sort based on possible responses above:

common: guard, hat, sunglasses, seeds, bus, shovel, jumpsuit, backpack, trees, holes, driver, dirt, campers, drink

proper: Stanley, Mr. Sir, Camp Green Lake

Another way to look at nouns is whether they name one or more than one person, place, or thing. *Singular* means "one," and *plural* means "more than one." Let's take one more look at our list of nouns and determine if they are singular or plural nouns.

Draw two columns on the board, labeled *singular nouns* and *plural nouns*. Sort the nouns generated into the two columns.

Sort based on possible responses above:

singular: Stanley, Mr. Sir, Camp Green Lake, guard, hat, bus, shovel, jumpsuit, backpack, driver, dirt, drink

plural: sunglasses, seeds, trees, holes, campers

Direct students to page 7 in their Student Books and read the instructions for Part A aloud.

Model

Listen as I read the first sentence and look for all of the nouns.

Stanley wasn't sure if the bus driver meant for him to be careful going down the steps, or if he was telling him to be careful at Camp Green Lake.

Let's find the obvious nouns. I know *Stanley* is the main character's name, so I will circle it. *Bus* is a thing, but because it is followed by the word *driver*, in this case, it is acting as an adjective—describing the noun *driver*. Any time you see two nouns next to each other in a sentence and they are not separated by a comma, it is likely that the first noun is describing the second noun. OK, so I know that *driver* is another person, so I will circle it. I also see the word *steps,* and I

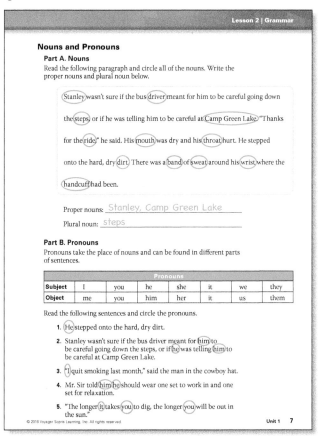

know they are a thing, so I will circle it. The sentence also includes the name of a place, *Camp Green Lake*, so I will circle it. After identifying all of the easily identifiable nouns, we can look at the remaining words and ask ourselves if they answer the *who* or the *what* question. **Have students do this and identify any other words that answer the *who* or the *what*.** (him, he) Though these are pronouns, some students may identify them as nouns. Accept these responses and explain the difference in the upcoming section.

Guided Practice

Read the remaining sentences and guide students in finding the nouns. As you read the sentences, remember nouns can show up in all parts of a sentence.

Once completed, guide students in identifying the proper nouns and the plural noun.

Pronouns

Another category of words is closely related to nouns. In fact, these words can take the place of a noun. They are called pronouns. What are they called? (pronouns) What do they do? (take the place of nouns) Pronouns replace nouns to help us speak and write more efficiently and to eliminate the need to repeat the same word over and over again.

Write the following sentences on the board and read them aloud.

> *The man in the cowboy hat spit sunflower seed shells into a wastepaper basket. Then he walked around the desk to Stanley.*

In the second sentence, *he* is a pronoun. It answers the *who* question. Who walked around the desk? (the man in the cowboy hat) *He* is the pronoun that replaced "the man in the cowboy hat." Using a pronoun prevented the author from repeatedly using "the man in the cowboy hat" every time the character is referenced.

Direct students to Part B on the page. Look at the list of pronouns in the chart. They should look very familiar. These are words you use all of the time. **Read the list together.** This list does not contain all of the different pronouns, but it does contain some basic pronouns. **Read the instructions for the activity.**

Model

Let's look at the first sentence: *He stepped onto the hard, dry dirt.* I see the word *he* in the box and in the sentence. I know it's a pronoun, so I'll circle it. When we read sentences in isolation, we can't always tell what the pronoun is replacing. In this case, we know *he* is replacing *Stanley.*

Guided Practice

Read the next sentence and guide students in identifying the pronouns.

Independent Practice

Have students identify the pronouns in the remaining sentences. Review the answers as a class.

Action Verbs

We know that nouns answer the *who* or *what* questions in sentences. Let's focus on the words that answer the *what did they do* question. We'll turn our attention to another major category of words: verbs. One job verbs do is show action. Let's think about what happened in the story—about what the characters did. Stanley rode the bus. *Rode* is an action verb. It answers the question *What did Stanley do?* What else happened in the story?

Have students generate other actions from the text. (Possible answers: stepped, sweated, sat, spit, chewed, changed, dressed, looked, answered, said, stood)

Let's see if you can find the verbs in some sentences taken from the text. **Direct students to Part A of page 8 in their Student Books and read aloud the instructions.**

Model

Listen as I read the first sentence: *He stepped onto the hard, dry dirt.*

I ask myself *What did he do?* He stepped. I will underline *stepped* because it's a verb.

Guided Practice

Listen to the second sentence: *He checked Stanley's backpack and allowed him to keep it.* What did he do? (He checked.) What else did he do? (He allowed.) In this sentence, the character did two actions: *checked* and *allowed.* You need to underline both verbs.

Independent Practice

Have students identify the action verbs in the remaining sentences. Review the answers as a class.

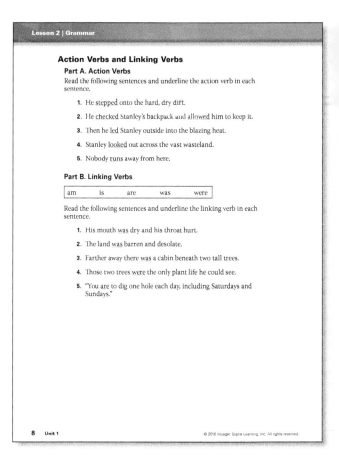

Linking Verbs

Not all verbs are action verbs. Some verbs work to connect the noun to the rest of the sentence. They are called linking verbs because they link or connect sentence parts. What do you call verbs that link or connect sentence parts? (linking verbs) Why are they called linking verbs? (because they link or connect sentence parts) Forms of the verb *be* are common linking verbs.

Write the forms of *be* on the board: *am, is, are, was, were.*

You use these verb forms frequently in your everyday speech. You also encounter them frequently in print. **Explain that *am*, *is*, and *are* are present tense verbs and that *was* and *were* are past tense verbs.**

Write the following sentence frame on the board and read it aloud.

> *Stanley is _____.*

Stanley is the noun. *Is* serves as the verb. Let's use this sentence frame to describe Stanley. That means Stanley isn't doing an action. The verb *is* will just connect the noun to the adjective. Turn to your partner and use the sentence frame to describe Stanley. (possible answers: thirsty, hot, not guilty, lonely, jealous, confused)

Now, let's use the same sentence frame to tell where Stanley is. Again, that means that he is not doing anything. The verb *is* will just connect the noun to the rest of the sentence. Turn to your partner and use the sentence frame to tell where Stanley is. (possible answers: at Camp Green Lake, on the bus, in juvenile detention, in the office, in the desert)

Let's look at some sentences taken from the text and identify the linking verbs. **Direct students to Part B and read the instructions aloud.**

Model

Listen as I read the first sentence: *His mouth was dry and his throat hurt.*

Mouth is a noun that answers the *what* question, so I have to ask myself: *What did it do?* It didn't do anything. I see the word *was* and the describing word *dry.* The word *was* is connecting, or linking, *mouth* and *dry.* It's a linking verb, so I'll underline it. I may not be finished with this sentence because of the *and.* I keep reading and find another noun, *throat.* Did it do anything? Yes, it hurt. That shows action, so it is not a linking verb. I will not underline it.

Guided Practice

Listen as I read the second sentence: *The land was barren and desolate.* What is the noun? (land) What did the land do? (It didn't do anything.) We see two words that describe the land. What are they? (barren and desolate) We have a verb that links *land* with *barren and desolate.* What is the linking verb? (was) Underline it.

Independent Practice

Have students identify the linking verbs in the remaining sentences. Review the answers as a class.

Objectives

- Write simple sentences.
- Identify the structure of a sentence.
- Edit sentences for punctuation and capitalization.

Masterpiece Sentences

Print the Masterpiece Sentences poster found in the Teacher Resources online and display where students can easily see it.

Let's use what we've learned about nouns and verbs. Sentences can be divided into two parts: the subject and the predicate. The subject is the part of the sentence that answers the *who* or the *what*. The predicate is the part of the sentence that answers the *what did they do* question—no matter how much detail is in the sentence.

I am going to introduce you to a process for writing basic sentences and then expanding them. It's called Masterpiece Sentences. In each stage, we will expand our base sentence by answering questions about the noun and verb that will make the subject and predicate grow.

Write the following sentences on the board:

The man chewed sunflower seeds.

Instead of smoking, the lone irritable man who had an icy stare constantly chewed sunflower seeds in his office.

The process will help us transform simple sentences like *The man chewed sunflower seeds.* into Masterpiece Sentences like *Instead of smoking, the lone irritable man who had an icy stare constantly chewed sunflower seeds in his office.* Direct students to page 9 in their Student Books and read the stages aloud. Demonstrate the process by following the chart on the next page.

Prepare subject- and predicate-colored index cards.

Display sentence parts written on index cards as an example for each stage of the sentence-writing process. Be sure to follow the process on the next page and ask the questions at each stage.

Subject-colored index cards:	Predicate-colored index cards:
The man	*chewed*
mean-looking	*sunflower seeds*
grouchy	*instead of smoking*
lone	*in his office*
irritable	*constantly*
who had an icy stare	

Masterpiece Sentences: A Six-Stage Process

Stage	Process	Questions to Answer	Display on index cards
Stage 1: Prepare Your Canvas	Choose a noun for the subject.	Subject: Who or what did it?	The man
	Choose a verb for the predicate.	Predicate: What did the subject do?	chewed
		What did the subject do it to?	sunflower seeds

Display index cards: The man chewed sunflower seeds.

Stage	Process	Questions to Answer	Display on index cards
Stage 2: Paint Your Predicate	Tell more about what happened.	When?	instead of smoking
		Where?	in his office
		How?	constantly
Stage 3: Move Your Predicate Painters	Move the predicate painters to create a different sentence structure.		*Demonstrate moving cards to make the sentence sound better.*

Display index cards: The man chewed sunflower seeds instead of smoking in his office constantly.

Move index cards: Instead of smoking, the man constantly chewed sunflower seeds in his office.

Stage	Process	Questions to Answer	Display on index cards
Stage 4: Paint Your Subject	Tell more about the subject.	Which one?	mean-looking
		What kind?	grouchy
		How many?	lone

Display index cards: Instead of smoking, the lone, grouchy, mean-looking man constantly chewed sunflower seeds in his office.

Stage	Process	Questions to Answer	Display on index cards
Stage 5: Paint Your Words	Select words or phrases in your sentence and replace them with more descriptive words or phrases.		*Demonstrate the removal of* grouchy *and* mean-looking.

Replace grouchy *and* mean-looking *index cards: Instead of smoking, the lone irritable man who had an icy stare constantly chewed sunflower seeds in his office.*

Stage	Process	Questions to Answer	Display on index cards
Stage 6: Finishing Touches	Finalize sentence structure; check spelling and punctuation.		

Today, you will only be working with Stage 1, but I wanted you to see the entire process. We will use the painter questions often as we examine the rules that govern our language.

Stage 1

Direct students to the bottom of the page and read the instructions aloud.

Provide assistance if students struggle. When students have finished, have volunteers share their sentences.

Capitalization and Punctuation

The rules that govern the way we write our language are called conventions. What are conventions? (rules for writing) We always capitalize the first word in a sentence. Other words within the sentence might be capitalized, but the first word is always capitalized. What do we do to the first word in a sentence? (capitalize it) We also always end a sentence with a period, a question mark, or an exclamation mark. The sentences you wrote using the Masterpiece Sentence strategy were statements. They should end with a period. What punctuation mark do you put at the end of a statement? (period)

Masterpiece Sentences: A Six-Stage Process

Stage	Process	Questions to Answer	Examples
Stage 1: Prepare Your Canvas	Choose a noun for the subject. Choose a verb for the predicate.	**Subject.** Who or what did it? **Predicate.** What did the subject do? What did the subject do it to?	The man chewed sunflower seeds
Stage 2: Paint Your Predicate	Tell more about what happened.	When? Where? How?	instead of smoking in his office constantly
Stage 3: Move Your Predicate Painters	Move the predicate painters to create a different sentence structure.		Instead of smoking, the man constantly chewed sunflower seeds in his office.
Stage 4: Paint Your Subject	Tell more about the subject.	Which one? What kind? How many?	mean-looking grouchy lone
Stage 5: Paint Your Words	Select words or phrases in your sentence and replace them with more descriptive words or phrases.		Instead of smoking, the lone, ~~grouchy~~, ~~mean-looking~~ man constantly chewed sunflower seeds in his office.
Stage 6: Finishing Touches	Finalize sentence structure; check spelling and punctuation.		Instead of smoking, the lone, irritable man who had an icy stare constantly chewed sunflower seeds in his office.

Stage 1

Answers will vary.

Use the following questions to create simple sentences about the characters in *Holes*.

Who did it?	What did they do?	Sentence
Stanley	walked	Stanley walked.
The guard	laughed	The guard laughed.

Who did it?	What did they do?	What did they do it to?	Sentence
Stanley	rode	the bus	Stanley rode the bus.
The boys	dug	holes	The boys dug holes.

Unit 1   9

Direct students to page 10 in their Student Books and read the instructions.

Model

Let's look at the example sentence. Notice the first word was not capitalized, so there are three lines underneath the *b* and a capital *B* written above the word. The next error is one of capitalizing a word that shouldn't be capitalized. *Bus* is a common noun, so it shouldn't be capitalized. A slash mark has been drawn through the *B* in *Bus* and a lowercase *b* has been written above it. What kind of noun is *Stanley*? (proper noun) We know that proper nouns have to be capitalized. Three lines were drawn below the *s* and a capital *S* was written above it. Finally, there is no end punctuation mark. A circle with a period in it was placed at the end to show the need for a period.

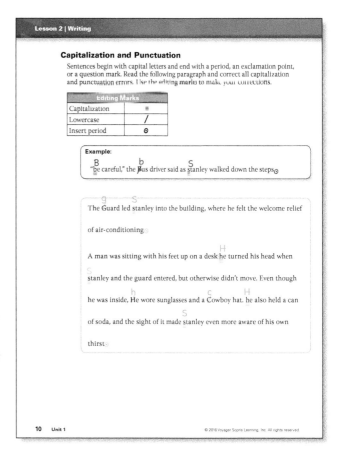

Independent Practice

Listen as I read the excerpt. When I finish, you will work with your partner to correct all of the mistakes. Remember to look for unnecessary capital letters as well as missing capital letters.

Have partners correct the mistakes in the paragraph. Monitor student progress after the first two sentences. If students struggle, complete the activity as a class. Review the answers as a class.

Lesson Opener

Before the lesson, choose one of the following activities to write on the board or post on the *LANGUAGE! Live* Class Wall online.

- *Write one sentence about yourself, one sentence about me, one sentence about a friend, one sentence about a group of people you know, and another sentence about our class. Then, rewrite each sentence using a pronoun.*
- *Write two sentences that follow this pattern: who or what? + what did they do? + what did they do it to?*
- *Why is the desert a tough place to spend time? Explain your answer.*

Reading

Objectives

- Establish a purpose for rereading literary text.
- Demonstrate an understanding of how to ask questions and answer them appropriately.
- Use complete sentences and text evidence to answer questions.
- Use critical thinking skills to write responses to prompts about text.
- Support written answers with text evidence.

Reading for a Purpose: Excerpt from *Holes*

We are going to read the excerpt from *Holes* again. Sometimes it is helpful to give yourself a purpose for reading. Our purpose for this read is to help us answer questions about the text.

Direct students to page 11 in their Student Books. Have students read the questions aloud with you.

1. Who is the juvenile camp resident? (Who)

2. What is Camp Green Lake Juvenile Correctional Facility? (What)

3. Where is Camp Green Lake? (Where)

4. When does Stanley get to leave the Camp Green Lake premises? (When)

Now, it is time to reread the text.

Direct students to page 3 in their Student Books or have them tear out the excerpt from the back of their book.

Lesson 3 | Reading

Critical Understandings: Question Words
How to Answer Questions

Question Words	How to Answer
If the question asks . . .	Your answer must include . . .
Who	information about a person or group
What	an action or name of a thing
When	a specific time, date, or event
Where	a general location or specific place

Respond to each question using complete sentences. Refer to the chart above to determine how to respond to each question.

1. Who is the juvenile camp resident?
   Stanley Yelnats, an overweight kid from a poor family, who was found guilty of a crime he didn't commit, is the juvenile camp resident of Camp Green Lake.

2. What is Camp Green Lake Juvenile Correctional Facility?
   Camp Green Lake Juvenile Correctional Facility is a prison-like camp where young people dig holes as punishment.

3. Where is Camp Green Lake?
   Camp Green Lake is in Texas.

4. When does Stanley get to leave the Camp Green Lake premises?
   Stanley gets to leave the Camp Green Lake premises after 18 months.

Unit 1   11

Note: To minimize flipping back and forth between the pages, a copy of each text has been included in the back of the Student Books. Encourage students to tear this out and use it when working on activities that require the use of the text.

Choose an option for rereading text. Have students read the text according to the option that you chose.

> Options for reading text:
> - Teacher read-aloud
> - Teacher-led or student-led choral read
> - Paired read or independent read with bold vocabulary words read aloud

Critical Understandings

In school, you are often asked questions. This is how teachers determine whether you are learning and whether they have taught something well. If you are unable to answer the question, they know that you didn't learn the information.

It is critical to understand what the question is asking and how to answer it. Let's continue our work with question words.

Write the question words *who*, *what*, *when*, and *where* on the board. Have students read the words aloud with you.

Direct students to page 11 in their Student Books. Have them read the chart with their partner.

Chart Reading Procedure

- Group students with partners or in triads.
- Have students count off as 1s or 2s. The 1s will become the student leaders. If working with triads, the third students become 3s.
- The student leaders will read the left column (Question Words) in addition to managing the time and turn-taking if working with a triad.
- The 2s will explain the right column of the chart (How to Answer). If working in triads, 2s and 3s will take turns explaining the right column.
- Students should follow along with their pencil eraser while others are explaining the chart.
- Students should work from left to right, top to bottom in order to benefit from this activity.
- Attempt to give all students a chance to be a student leader as you move through the lessons.

Critical Understandings: Question Words

How to Answer Questions

Question Words	How to Answer
If the question asks . . .	Your answer must include . . .
Who	information about a person or group
What	an action or name of a thing
When	a specific time, date, or event
Where	a general location or specific place

Respond to each question using complete sentences. Refer to the chart above to determine how to respond to each question.

1. Who is the juvenile camp resident?

   Stanley Yelnats, an overweight kid from a poor family, who was found guilty of a crime he didn't commit, is the juvenile camp resident of Camp Green Lake.

2. What is Camp Green Lake Juvenile Correctional Facility?

   Camp Green Lake Juvenile Correctional Facility is a prison-like camp where young people dig holes as punishment.

3. Where is Camp Green Lake?

   Camp Green Lake is in Texas.

4. When does Stanley get to leave the Camp Green Lake premises?

   Stanley gets to leave the Camp Green Lake premises after 18 months.

Unit 1   **11**

Check for understanding by asking the following questions:

- If the question asks *who*, your answer must include what? (information about a person or group)
- If the question asks *what*, your answer must include what? (an action or name of a thing)
- If the question asks *when*, your answer must include what? (a specific time, date, or event)
- If the question asks *where*, your answer must include what? (a general location or a specific place)

Model

Let's practice answering questions. Listen as I model the first one for you.

1. Who is the juvenile camp resident?

Looking at the chart, because the question is a *who* question, I know the answer will be a person. We will put part of the question in our answer, but let's start with the name, *Stanley Yelnats*. I know that Stanley Yelnats is the camp resident, but I want to tell more about *who* he really is. Next, I can go back into the text to find information about his character. While I write my answer on the board, look at the introduction of the text and let me know if I have a good explanation of who Stanley is.

Write the following answer on the board:

> *Stanley Yelnats, an overweight kid from a poor family, who was found guilty of a crime he didn't commit, is the juvenile camp resident of Camp Green Lake.*

Let's check for accuracy. Do I have a person in my answer? Yes, Stanley. How about the mechanics of a sentence? Have I used correct punctuation and capitalization? I have capitalized Stanley's name and the name of the camp. I have a period at the end of my sentence. I am finished.

Please write the answer on the page.

Guided Practice

> 2. What is Camp Green Lake Juvenile Correctional Facility?

If the question asks *what*, our answer must include an action or name of a thing. In this case, we have the name of a thing and we have to tell what it is. Start by putting part of the question in your answer. **Have a volunteer orally provide a sentence starter.**

Write the following sentence frame on the board:

> *Camp Green Lake Juvenile Correctional Facility is* _____.

Next, we have to remember or figure out what all these words mean.

What does *juvenile* mean? (young person)

What is a correctional facility? Let's look at the word *correctional*. What is the base word? (correct) Next, let's look at the word *facility*. A facility is a place designed for a specific use. Let's put the words together: correctional facility. A juvenile correctional facility is a place to correct young people, or a prison for young people.

Finish answering the question and add some details from the text. Have volunteers orally provide the details for the answer. Complete the answer on the board.

> *Camp Green Lake Juvenile Correctional Facility is a prison-like camp where young people dig holes as punishment.*

Independent Practice

Now, it's your turn to answer questions. Read the two remaining questions and answer them in complete sentences. Use the chart to determine how to answer each question. Be sure to use part of the question in your answer.

Have students respond to the remaining questions. For students who need more assistance, provide the following sentence starters.

> Sentence starters:
>
> 3. *Camp Green Lake is* _____.
>
> 4. *Stanley gets to leave the Camp Green Lake premises* _____.

Lesson Opener

Before the lesson, choose one of the following activities to write on the board or post on the *LANGUAGE! Live* Class Wall online.

- *Use* am, is, are, was, *and* were *in sentences about your best friend.*
- *Write three sentences about what you did last night. Identify the nouns and verbs in each sentence.*
- *Write two questions about Camp Green Lake. Use the question words* what *and* where.

Reading

Objectives
- Read with purpose and understanding.
- Answer questions to demonstrate comprehension of text.
- Identify and explain explicit details from text.
- Monitor comprehension of text during reading.
- Demonstrate understanding of words by relating them to their synonyms.
- Connect pronouns to their antecedents.
- Identify the setting of a story.
- Determine how the setting affects the characters.
- Identify the protagonist and antagonist of a story.

Close Reading of the Excerpt from *Holes*

Highlighters or colored pencils

Let's reread the excerpt from *Holes* one more time. I will provide specific instructions on how to mark the text that will help you with comprehension.

Have students get out a highlighter or colored pencil.

Direct students to pages 12–15 in their Student Books.

Draw a rectangle around the title, *Holes*.

Circle the part of the text that serves as an introduction.

Next, we will read the vocabulary words aloud. Automatic recognition of words allows your brain to access the meaning of the words more quickly. After confirming the pronunciation of each word, we will recall its meaning and use the word in a sentence.

- What's the first bold vocabulary word? (**commit**) *Commit* means "to do something that is against the law or harmful." Stanley was sent to Camp Green Lake because some people thought he *committed* a crime. **Have partners use the word in a sentence.**

- What's the next bold vocabulary word? (**dazed**) *Dazed* means "very confused and unable to think clearly." Stanley was *dazed* by all Mr. Sir told him but was too nervous to ask questions. **Have partners use the word in a sentence.**

- What's the next bold vocabulary word? (**barren**) *Barren* means "without plant or animal life." Camp Green Lake is in the middle of a *barren* desert. **Have partners use the word in a sentence.**

- What's the next bold vocabulary word? (juvenile) *Juvenile* means "related to a person under 18 years of age." Stanley is a *juvenile* offender, so he was sent to camp with other kids his age instead of prison. **Have partners use the word in a sentence.**

- What's the next bold vocabulary word? (declared) *Declared* means "stated something in a firm or official way." Mr. Sir *declared* that Camp Green Lake wasn't a Girl Scout camp multiple times. **Have partners use the word in a sentence.**

- What's the next bold vocabulary word? (premises) *Premises* are the land and buildings owned by a person or company. No fence surrounds the *premises* of Camp Green Lake because escapees wouldn't survive the desert. **Have partners use the word in a sentence.**

- What's the next bold vocabulary word? (aware) *Aware* means "knowing something exists or is happening." Stanley quickly became *aware* that Mr. Sir wasn't going to help him get settled. **Have partners use the word in a sentence.**

- What's the next bold vocabulary word? (consisted) *Consisted* means "made up of." Stanley's day *consisted* of nothing but eating, sleeping, and digging. **Have partners use the word in a sentence.**

- What's the next bold vocabulary word? (avoid) *Avoid* means "to stay away from something or someone." Stanley would not be able to *avoid* the heat at Camp Green Lake. **Have partners use the word in a sentence.**

- What's the last bold vocabulary word? (vast) *Vast* means "extremely large." Stanley wondered how many holes would cover the *vast* campgrounds by the end of the summer. **Have partners use the word in a sentence.**

Talk with a partner about any vocabulary word that is still confusing for you to read or understand.

You will read the excerpt from *Holes* a small section at a time. After each section, you will monitor your understanding by circling the check mark if you understand the text or the question mark if you don't understand the text. I also want you to draw a question mark over any confusing words, phrases, or sentences.

> Options for reading text:
> - Teacher read-aloud
> - Teacher-led or student-led choral read
> - Paired read or independent read with bold vocabulary words read aloud

Choose an option for reading text. Have students read lines 1–17 according to the option that you chose. As you read, mark any words or phrases that have to do with the setting of the story. The setting tells about the time and place that the story happened. What does the setting tell? (time and place) The setting provides answers to the questions *where* and *when*.

When most of the students are finished, continue with the entire class. Let's see how well you understood what you read.

- Circle the check mark or the question mark for this section. Draw a question mark over any confusing words.

- Go to line 3. Number Stanley's two options or choices. (1. Go to jail; 2. Go to Camp Green Lake)

- Go to line 5. Mark the word that means the same as *entered*. (arrived) Words with the same or similar meanings are called *synonyms*.

- On the same line, mark the synonym for *assumed*. (expected)

- Go to line 7. Mark the duration of the bus ride. (over eight hours) On the previous line, mark the word that shows how this event affected Stanley. (dazed)

- Go to lines 11–13. Mark the phrases that describe Stanley's condition. (mouth was dry, throat hurt, band of sweat around his wrist)

- If you haven't already done so, mark the words that relate to the setting. (hard, dry dirt; barren and desolate; few run-down buildings and some tents; two trees) Based on Stanley's condition, what else can we assume about the setting at Camp Green Lake? (it is hot)

- Go to line 14. Mark the synonym for *deserted*. (desolate)

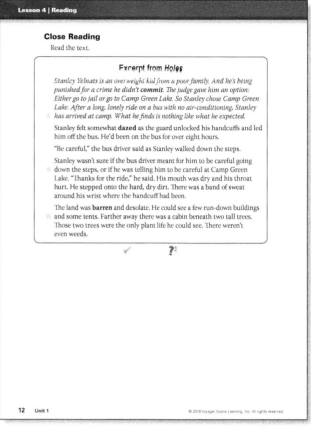

Lesson 4 | Reading

Close Reading

Read the text.

Excerpt from Holes

*Stanley Yelnats is an overweight kid from a poor family. And he's being punished for a crime he didn't **commit**. The judge gave him an option: Either go to jail or go to Camp Green Lake. So Stanley chose Camp Green*
5 *Lake. After a long, lonely ride on a bus with no air-conditioning, Stanley has arrived at camp. What he finds is nothing like what he expected.*

Stanley felt somewhat **dazed** as the guard unlocked his handcuffs and led him off the bus. He'd been on the bus for over eight hours.

"Be careful," the bus driver said as Stanley walked down the steps.

Stanley wasn't sure if the bus driver meant for him to be careful going
10 down the steps, or if he was telling him to be careful at Camp Green Lake. "Thanks for the ride," he said. His mouth was dry and his throat hurt. He stepped onto the hard, dry dirt. There was a band of sweat around his wrist where the handcuff had been.

The land was **barren** and desolate. He could see a few run-down buildings
15 and some tents. Farther away there was a cabin beneath two tall trees. Those two trees were the only plant life he could see. There weren't even weeds.

Have students read lines 18–50 according to the option that you chose. As you read, mark any words or phrases that have to do with the setting of the story.

When most of the students are finished, continue with the entire class. Let's see how well you understood what you read.

- Circle the check mark or the question mark for this section. Draw a question mark over any confusing words.

- If you haven't done so already, mark the text that is related to the setting. **(small building; A sign on the front said, YOU ARE ENTERING CAMP GREEN LAKE JUVENILE CORRECTIONAL FACILITY; air-conditioning in building)**

- Go to line 18. Find the noun that means "display that informs" and mark it with an *N*. **(sign)**

- Go to line 21. Mark the word that means "a breaking of the law." **(violation)**

- On the same line, mark the synonym for *bombs*. **(explosives)**

- Go to line 24. Mark the word that means "change for the better." **(relief)**

- Skim lines 26–29. Mark the words and phrases that describe Mr. Sir. **(feet up on the desk, sunglasses, cowboy hat, held a can of soda)**

- Go to line 30. Find the verb that means "write your signature" and mark it with a *V*. **(sign) Point out the noun usage they marked in line 18.**

- Go to line 34. Mark a reason that the man might be irritable. **(quit smoking last month)**

- Go to line 35. Mark what is on the man's arm. **(tattoo of a rattlesnake)**

- Go to line 37. Circle the word *these*. Draw an arrow to the noun that *these* represents. **(sunflower seeds)**

- Go to line 40. Mark the word that means "presented." **(produced)**

- Go to line 41. Circle the word *one*. Draw a line to what it represents. **(cans of soda)**

- Go to lines 45 and 46. Mark the phrase that describes how Stanley feels. **(miserable, a little sorry for the guard and the bus driver)**

- Go to line 48. Mark the man's name. **(Mr. Sir)**

- Mark the comment that indicates Mr. Sir is strict. **(Whenever you speak to me you must call me by my name, is that clear?)**

- Reread the quote that you just marked. Circle the phrase that means "do you understand?" **(is that clear?)**

Close Reading (*cont.*)

The guard led Stanley to a small building. A sign in front said, YOU ARE ENTERING CAMP GREEN LAKE **JUVENILE** CORRECTIONAL FACILITY. Next to it was another sign which stated that it was a violation of the Texas Penal Code to bring guns, explosives, weapons, drugs, or alcohol onto the **premises**

As Stanley read the sign he couldn't help but think, *Well, duh!*

The guard led Stanley into the building, where he felt the welcome relief of air-conditioning.

A man was sitting with his feet up on a desk. He turned his head when Stanley and the guard entered, but otherwise didn't move. Even though he was inside, he wore sunglasses and a cowboy hat. He also held a can of soda, and the sight of it made Stanley even more **aware** of his own thirst.

He waited while the bus guard gave the man some papers to sign.

"That's a lot of sunflower seeds," the bus guard said.

Stanley noticed a burlap sack filled with sunflower seeds on the floor next to the desk.

"I quit smoking last month," said the man in the cowboy hat. He had a tattoo of a rattlesnake on his arm, and as he signed his name, the snake's rattle seemed to wiggle. "I used to smoke a pack a day. Now I eat a sack of these every week."

The guard laughed.

There must have been a small refrigerator behind his desk, because the man in the cowboy hat produced two more cans of soda. For a second Stanley hoped that one might be for him, but the man gave one to the guard and said the other was for the driver.

"Nine hours here, and now nine hours back," the guard grumbled. "What a day."

Stanley thought about the long, miserable bus ride and felt a little sorry for the guard and the bus driver.

The man in the cowboy hat spit sunflower seed shells into a wastepaper basket. Then he walked around the desk to Stanley. "My name is Mr. Sir," he said. "Whenever you speak to me you must call me by my name, is that clear?"

Unit 1 **13**

Have students read lines 51–79 according to the option that you chose. *As you read, mark any words or phrases that have to do with the setting of the story.*

When most of the students are finished, continue with the entire class. *Let's see how well you understood what you read.*

- Circle the check mark or the question mark for this section. Draw a question mark over any confusing words.

- Go to line 51. Mark the synonym for *paused*. (hesitated)

- On the same line, mark the comment that has a cautious tone. (Uh, yes, Mr. Sir)

- Go to line 53. Mark the evidence that Mr. Sir is sarcastic. (You're not in the Girl Scouts anymore.)

- Mark what Stanley had to do that likely embarrassed him. (Stanley had to remove his clothes in front of Mr. Sir.)

- Go to line 58. Mark the synonym for *in the first place*. (originally)

- Go to line 60. Mark the synonym for *sadly*. (unfortunately)

- On the same line, mark what was unfortunate about the canteen. (empty)

- Go to line 61. Mark the synonym for *safety*. (protection)

- Go to line 64. Circle the number word that tells how many days Stanley must wear his work clothes. (three)

- Go to line 67. Mark the word that means "hollow space dug out of the ground." (hole) In the margin, write how many days of the week Stanley will be digging holes. (7)

- Circle the approximate length of Stanley's shovel. (five feet)

- Highlight the repeated sarcastic comment. (This isn't a Girl Scout camp.)

- Go to line 78. Mark what Mr. Sir checked. (backpack)

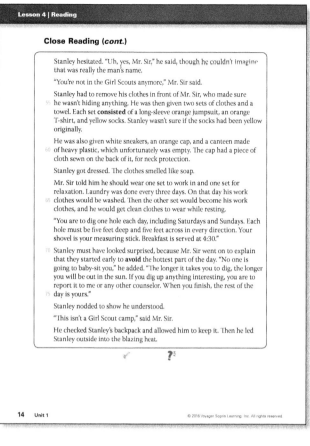

Close Reading (*cont.*)

Stanley hesitated. "Uh, yes, Mr. Sir," he said, though he couldn't imagine that was really the man's name.

"You're not in the Girl Scouts anymore," Mr. Sir said.

Stanley had to remove his clothes in front of Mr. Sir, who made sure he wasn't hiding anything. He was then given two sets of clothes and a towel. Each set **consisted** of a long-sleeve orange jumpsuit, an orange T-shirt, and yellow socks. Stanley wasn't sure if the socks had been yellow originally.

He was also given white sneakers, an orange cap, and a canteen made of heavy plastic, which unfortunately was empty. The cap had a piece of cloth sewn on the back of it, for neck protection.

Stanley got dressed. The clothes smelled like soap.

Mr. Sir told him he should wear one set to work in and one set for relaxation. Laundry was done every three days. On that day his work clothes would be washed. Then the other set would become his work clothes, and he would get clean clothes to wear while resting.

"You are to dig one hole each day, including Saturdays and Sundays. Each hole must be five feet deep and five feet across in every direction. Your shovel is your measuring stick. Breakfast is served at 4:30."

Stanley must have looked surprised, because Mr. Sir went on to explain that they started early to **avoid** the hottest part of the day. "No one is going to baby-sit you," he added. "The longer it takes you to dig, the longer you will be out in the sun. If you dig up anything interesting, you are to report it to me or any other counselor. When you finish, the rest of the day is yours."

Stanley nodded to show he understood.

"This isn't a Girl Scout camp," said Mr. Sir.

He checked Stanley's backpack and allowed him to keep it. Then he led Stanley outside into the blazing heat.

14 Unit 1

Have students read lines 80–106 according to the option that you chose. As you read, mark any words or phrases that have to do with the setting of the story.

When most of the students are finished, continue with the entire class. Let's see how well you understood what you read.

- Circle the check mark or the question mark for this section. Draw a question mark over any confusing words.

- Go to line 81. If you haven't already done so, mark the words that relate to the setting. (**vast wasteland**)

- Go to line 82. Mark the synonym for *quickly*. (**hastily**)

- Go to line 87. If you haven't already done so, mark the words that relate to the setting. (**no fence at all**)

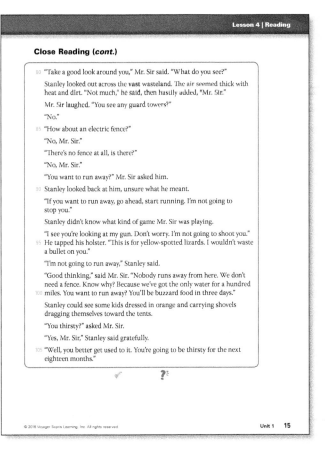

- Go to line 95. Mark the word that means "case for a pistol." (**holster**)

- On the same line, mark the dangerous animal. (**yellow-spotted lizards**)

- Go to lines 99 and 100. If you haven't already done so, mark the words that relate to the setting. (**the only water for a hundred miles**)

- Go to line 100. Mark the name of a bird that eats decaying flesh. (**buzzard**)

- Go to line 102. Mark the evidence that the campers are unhappy. (**dragging themselves**)

- Go to line 105. An *idiom* is a saying that is used in a particular place or time. The group of words cannot be taken literally because the dictionary definitions of the individual words do not apply. Mark the idiom that means "that's how things are" or "accept it." (**get used to it**)

- On the same line, mark one condition Stanley will have for 18 months. (**thirsty**) How does the setting relate to this condition? (**the hot, dry weather causes the thirst**)

- Many stories contain a main character who is the "good" person in the story, called the protagonist, as well as a secondary character who is the "bad" person, or antagonist. *Holes* is one of these stories. Find the name of each and label them. (**Stanley: protagonist; Mr. Sir: antagonist**)

Have partners compare text markings and correct any errors.

Lesson Opener

Before the lesson, choose one of the following activities to write on the board or post on the *LANGUAGE! Live* Class Wall online.

- *Write two sentences about Camp Green Lake. Use a present tense linking verb in the first sentence and a past tense linking verb in the second sentence. Then, write two sentences about regular prison. Use action verbs in each sentence.*
- *Dress your avatar as though he or she is going to spend the day digging holes at Camp Green Lake. Describe his or her outfit and your reason for choosing the specific items.*
- *Write four sentences with at least two vocabulary words in each. Show you know the meanings. (commit, dazed, barren, juvenile, declare, premises, aware, consist, avoid, vast)*

Vocabulary

Objective

- Review key passage vocabulary.

Recontextualize Passage Vocabulary

Direct students to page 2 in their Student Books. Use the following questions to review the vocabulary words from the excerpt from *Holes.*

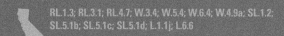

- Would you find a kitchen on the *premises* of a restaurant? (yes) Is there a skyscraper on the school *premises*? (no) What are the land and buildings owned by someone called? (premises)

- Are you likely to find adults attending a *juvenile* camp? (no) What would you call a court that hears cases related to people under 18? (juvenile court)

- Is a cruise ship built to travel *vast* distances? (yes) Is a pond *vast*? (no) What word describes an ocean, *vast* or *small*? (vast)

- If you were blindfolded and spun around and around, would it make you feel *dazed*? (yes) If I am confused and unable to think clearly, what am I? (dazed)

- Is it a good idea to *avoid* an angry bear? (yes) Is it a good idea to *avoid* fruits and vegetables? (no) If I am trying to stay away from a pushy salesman, what am I trying to do? (avoid him)

- Are you *aware* of the person next to you? (yes) Are you *aware* of the temperature in London, England, right now? (no) If you know something exists or is happening, what are you? (aware of it)

- Does dinner usually *consist* of pancakes and bacon? (no) Does a talent show *consist* of different acts? (yes) If something is made up of blocks, does it *persist* of blocks? (no) It what? (consists of blocks)

- Is a forest that is home to dozens of animal species *barren*? (no) Is land consumed by a forest fire *barren*? (yes) What is an area that has no plant or animal life called? (barren)

- If I break into your home, am I *committing* a crime? (yes) If I stop at a red light in my car, am I *committing* a violent act? (no) A basketball player whacks another player on the arm as she shoots. What has the first player done? (committed a foul)

- *Declare* your name in a formal voice. (My name is ____.) What does a judge *declare* at the end of a trial? (guilt or innocence) To state something in a firm or official way is to do what? (declare it)

Writing

Objectives
- Self-correct as comprehension of text deepens.
- Use text to write coherent paragraphs in response to reading.
- Identify the setting of a story.
- Analyze character point of view.

Revisit Critical Understandings: Question Words

Direct students back to page 11 in their Student Books. Have students review their answers and make any necessary changes. Then, have partners share their answers and collaborate to revise and strengthen them.

Stories take place in a certain time and place. The time and place are referred to as a story's setting. Let's revisit your Critical Understandings questions one more time to determine which questions were related to the setting. Is question one related to the setting? (no) How about question two? (yes) What about question three? (yes) How about question four? (no) Questions two and three were related to the setting.

In Lesson 4, you highlighted text that related to the setting of *Holes*. Let's review the text that you highlighted to see if it answers the question *where* or *when*. What question does the setting answer? (where or when)

Review Close Reading answers related to setting.

Quick Write in Response to Reading

Direct students to page 16 in their Student Books and read the instructions. Have you ever received a letter in the mail? If most students raise their hands, have them turn and talk to their partner about how it made them feel. Have you ever written a letter? People stay in touch with each other in a variety of ways, but very few are as permanent and personal as a card or a letter. You will write a letter from Stanley's point of view.

Have students write the letter. When students finish, have them share their letter with their partner.

Review the use of a comma in greetings and closings of letters.

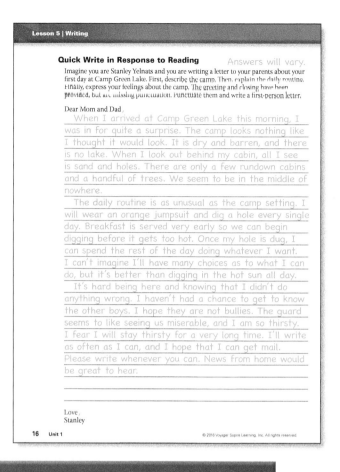

Reading

Objectives

- Answer questions to demonstrate comprehension of text.
- Engage in class discussion.
- Identify the enduring understandings from a piece of text.
- Compare text and film.

Enduring Understandings

Direct students back to page 1 in their Student Books. Reread the Big Idea questions.

To what degree is our destiny within our control?

Is punishment a pathway to rehabilitation and reformation?

Generate a class discussion about the questions and the answers students came up with in Lesson 1. Have them consider whether their answers have changed after reading the text.

Use the following talking points to foster conversation. Refer to the Class Discussion Rules poster and have students use the Collegial Discussion sentence frames on page 382 of their Student Books.

- Stanley Yelnats believed that his life was cursed and that, no matter how hard he tried, bad things were going to keep happening to him. He believed that this is how he ended up at Camp Green Lake for a crime he didn't commit. Do curses exist? Does luck exist? Is your life already planned out, or are you in control of your destiny?

- We know that prisons vary across the nation and that they are often violent places. Yet, prisons and other types of treatment facilities are intended to reform criminals. How likely is it that reform occurs? Can people really change?

What we read should make us think. Use our discussion and your thoughts about the text to determine what you will "walk away with." Has it made you think about a personal experience or someone you know? Has your perspective or opinion on a specific topic changed? Do you have any lingering thoughts or questions? Write these ideas as your enduring understandings. What will you take with you from this text? Discuss the enduring understandings with the class. Then, have students write their enduring understandings from the unit.

Have students consider why the author wrote the passage and whether he was successful.

Comparing Film and Print (Optional Activity)

Though we don't recommend watching the entire movie *Holes* in class, watching the excerpt that coincides with the text can be a wonderful learning experience. If you choose to show the excerpt in class, have students compare the experiences.

Ask the following questions to foster conversation:

1. Which version was more entertaining?

2. Which version was easier to understand?

3. What did you get from the film that you did not get from your reading?

4. How did seeing the characters and hearing their voices impact your experience?

5. Did you "hear" or "see" anything differently when you read it? Did the characters look different in your mind?

6. In what ways was the film different from the book, and in what ways did the director stay true to the story? Cite a specific example from the text that is different from the film.

Lesson 6

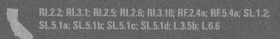

RI.2.2; RI.3.1; RI.2.5; RI.2.6; RI.3.10; RF.2.4a; RF.5.4a; SL.1.2;
SL.5.1a; SL.5.1b; SL.5.1c; SL.5.1d; L.3.5b; L.6.6

Lesson Opener

Before the lesson, choose one of the following activities to write on the board or post on the *LANGUAGE! Live* Class Wall online.

- *What is your opinion of Mr. Sir? Use complete sentences.*
- *In sentence form, give three reasons why a person might be falsely accused of a crime. Then, explain how you would feel if it happened to you.*
- *Write two sentences about Stanley. Use a linking verb in the first sentence and an action verb in the second sentence. Repeat the process with a sentence about Mr. Sir.*

Reading

Objectives

- Determine and discuss the topic of a text.
- Determine and discuss the author's purpose.
- Use text features to preview text.
- Distinguish between features of literary and informational text.

Passage Introduction

Direct students to page 17 in their Student Books. Discuss the content focus.

Content Focus

crime and punishment

What do you think you will read about in this passage? (Answers will vary.)

What do you know about forensics? What TV shows or books involve forensics? (*CSI, Forensic Files, Body of Proof, Cold Case Files, The First 48, The Investigators*)

Type of Text

informational

You have learned that there are different types of texts or reading selections. *Holes* belongs to a category called literature. Say *literature*. (literature) Literature consists of stories, poems, dramas, and creatively written prose. *Holes* is fiction, or not real. The text we will read today, "The Science of Catching Criminals," is nonfiction, or not fiction. It is informational. Say *informational*. (informational) That means it provides information, or facts. Is a nonfiction work made up or based on real life? (based on real life) So will today's text contain real people or made-up characters? (real people)

> **Lesson 6 | Reading**
>
> **Let's Focus: "The Science of Catching Criminals"**
>
> | **Content Focus** | **Type of Text** |
> |---|---|
> | crime and punishment | informational |
>
> **Author's Name** _unknown_
>
> **Author's Purpose** _to inform_
>
> **Big Ideas**
> Consider the following Big Idea questions. Write your answer for each question.
>
> Is punishment always just?
>
> _____
>
> _____
>
> How does science influence crime and punishment?
>
> _____
>
> _____
>
> **Informational Preview Checklist:** "The Science of Catching Criminals" on pages 19 and 20.
> ☐ Title: What clue does it provide about the passage?
> ☐ Pictures and Captions: What additional information is added here?
> ☐ Headings: What topics will this text include?
> ☐ Margin Information: What vocabulary is important to understand this text?
> ☐ Maps, Charts, and Graphs: Are additional visuals present that will help me understand?
>
> **Enduring Understandings**
> After reading the text . . .
>
> _____
>
> _____
>
> _____
>
> _____
>
> _____
>
> _____
>
> _____
>
> © 2016 Voyager Sopris Learning, Inc. All rights reserved.   Unit 1   17

Author's Purpose

Have students glance at the text. Who is the author of the text? (unknown) This text is the type of text you would read in a textbook. The information is factual, but there isn't an author's name attributed to it. It likely means that someone was paid to write this text for a publishing company but isn't necessarily considered an "author." The author's purpose is the reason that he or she wrote the text. Authors write for different purposes. They write to entertain, to persuade, or to inform or teach. Knowing an author's purpose can help a reader better understand a text. *Holes* was written to entertain us. "The Science of Catching Criminals" was written to inform or teach. Was "The Science of Catching Criminals" written to inform or entertain? (inform) Will the author teach you something or entertain you? (teach) **Have students write the answer on the page in their Student Books.** Have you read any other text in which the author's purpose was to teach? Turn and tell your neighbor the title of the last nonfiction text that you read.

Background Information

Many words in the English language came from other languages. The origin of the word *forensic* comes from the Latin word *forensis*, which means "belonging to debate or public discussion." The modern definition of *forensic* means "belonging to or used in courts, or to public discussion or debate." *Forensic science* is science used in public, in a court, or in the justice system. Any science used for the purposes of the law is a forensic science.

Read the Big Idea questions aloud.

Big Ideas

Is punishment always just?

How does science influence crime and punishment?

Class Discussion Rules poster

Collegial Discussion poster

As a class, consider the two Big Idea questions.

- Encourage students with limited knowledge of forensics and the legal system to ask for further explanation from peers.

- Provide opportunities for students to explain their ideas and answers to the Big Idea questions in light of the discussion by ensuring students follow the rules for class discussion, which can be printed in poster form from the Teacher Resources online.

- Suggest students refer to the Collegial Discussion sentence frames in the back of their books.

- Encourage speakers to link comments to the remarks of others to keep the focus of the discussion and create cohesion, even when their comments are in disagreement.

After discussing each question, have students write an answer. We'll come back to these questions after we finish reading "The Science of Catching Criminals." You can add to your answers as you gain information and perspective.

Preview

Read the Informational Preview Checklist on page 17. Follow the Preview Procedure outlined below.

Preview Procedure

- Group students with partners or in triads.
- Have students count off as 1s or 2s. The 1s will become the student leaders. If working with triads, the third students become 3s.
- The student leaders will preview the text in addition to managing the checklist and pacing.
- The 2s and 3s will preview the text with 1s.
- Direct 1s to open their Student Books to page 17 and 2s and 3s to open their Student Books to page 19. This allows students to look at a few different pages at one time without turning back and forth.

What is the title? ("The Science of Catching Criminals") What clue does the title provide about the passage? (The title is similar to the definition of *forensics*.) Let's look to see what additional information the pictures provide. What picture do you see behind the title? (a fingerprint; double helix) What do you know about fingerprints? (Each one of us has a different or unique fingerprint.) What is pictured on the bottom of the page? (forensic tools) What is pictured on the next page? (a scientist in a laboratory) Let's read the headings together. Ready? Put your pencil pointer on the first heading. Read it with me. (At the Crime Scene) Next heading? (Back at the Lab) Last heading? (The Power of Forensic Science)

Let's take a moment and compare the text features of a nonfiction text like "The Science of Catching Criminals" with the format of a fiction text like *Holes*. What do you notice? **Write students' observations on the board.**

Example:

Fiction	Both	Nonfiction
Nonscientific words	New vocabulary words	May require more time to learn vocabulary
Pictures may include setting, characters	Pictures	Charts, graphs, captions
No headings		Headings
Quotation marks, characters talking		Facts, talking about real people

Vocabulary

Objectives

- Evaluate word knowledge.
- Determine the meaning of key passage vocabulary.

Rate Vocabulary Knowledge

Direct students to page 18 in their Student Books. We are about to read a passage titled "The Science of Catching Criminals." Before we read, let's review the vocabulary words for this passage. I'm going to read each word aloud, and you will repeat it and write the word in the third column. Then, you will rate your knowledge of the word. Display the Vocabulary Rating Scale poster or write the information on the board. Review the meaning of each rating.

Lesson 6 | Vocabulary

Key Passage Vocabulary: "The Science of Catching Criminals"

Read each word. Write the word in column 3. Then, circle a number to rate your knowledge of the word.

Vocabulary	Part of Speech	Write the Word	Knowledge Rating
evidence	(n)	evidence	0 1 2 3
fiber	(n)	fiber	0 1 2 3
innocence	(n)	innocence	0 1 2 3
convict	(v)	convict	0 1 2 3
trace	(n)	trace	0 1 2 3
preserve	(v)	preserve	0 1 2 3
identify	(v)	identify	0 1 2 3
unique	(adj)	unique	0 1 2 3
suspect	(n)	suspect	0 1 2 3
witness	(n)	witness	0 1 2 3

18   Unit 1

Vocabulary Rating Scale

0—I have never heard the word before.

1—I have heard the word, but I'm not sure how to use it.

2—I am familiar with the word, but I'm not sure if I know the correct meaning.

3—I know the meaning of the word and can use it correctly in a sentence.

The points are not a grade; they are just there to help you know which words you need to focus on. By the end of this unit, you should be able to change all your ratings to a 3—that's the goal.

Read each word aloud. Have students repeat it, write it, and rate it. Then, have volunteers who rated a word *2* or *3* use the word in an oral sentence.

Preteach Vocabulary

Let's take a closer look at the words. Provide definitions and examples as indicated on the word cards. Ask questions to clarify and deepen understanding. If time permits, allow students to share.

Preteach Procedure

This activity is intended to take only a short amount of time, so make it an oral exercise.

- Introduce each word as indicated on the word card.
- Read the definition and example sentences.
- Ask questions to clarify and deepen understanding.
- If time permits, allow students to share.

* If your students would benefit from copying the definitions, please have them do so in the vocabulary log in the back of the Student Books using the margin definitions in the passage selections. This should be done outside of instruction time.

---

evidence (n)

Let's read the first word together. *Evidence.*

Definition: *Evidence* is proof—something that shows another thing happened or is true. What is proof, or something that shows another thing happened or is true? (evidence)

Example 1: Crumbs on the counter are *evidence* of a late-night snack.

Example 2: I got an e-mail that contains *evidence* that my brother and sister aren't getting along.

Example 3: To be hired, you must provide *evidence* that you can handle the job.

Question 1: Are footprints on the carpet *evidence* that someone was in the room? Yes or no? (yes)

Question 2: I have a gut feeling that it will rain. Is this *evidence* that it will rain? Yes or no? (no)

Pair Share: Turn to your partner and tell what the *evidence* in your backpack says about you.

(1)

fiber (n)

Let's read the next word together. *Fiber.*

Definition: A *fiber* is a thin thread. What is a thin thread? (a fiber)

Example 1: Clothing is made of thousands of *fibers* woven together.

Example 2: Some socks are made of man-made *fibers*, not real cotton.

Example 3: Native Americans used plant *fibers* to make baskets, nets, and belts.

Question 1: Is the sheet on your bed made of *fibers*? Yes or no? (yes)

Question 2: Is water made of *fibers*? Yes or no? (no)

Pair Share: Turn to your partner and name two things made of *fibers*.

(2)

innocence (n)

Let's read the next word together. *Innocence*.

Definition: *Innocence* means "the state of not being guilty." What is the state of not being guilty called? (innocence)

Example 1: *Innocence* should not be punished.

Example 2: My cat licked her paws with an expression of *innocence*, but the dead bird suggested that she was guilty.

Example 3: The jury doubted the man's *innocence* after seeing his fingerprints on the weapon.

Question 1: Is a cheater in a state of *innocence*? Yes or no? (no)

Question 2: Would a person want to hide his or her *innocence* during a murder investigation? Yes or no? (no)

Pair Share: Turn to your partner and make a facial expression that shows *innocence*.

③

convict (v)

Let's read the next word together. *Convict*.

Definition: *Convict* means "to find someone guilty in a court of law." What means "find someone guilty in a court of law"? (convict)

Example 1: At the end of the trial, the jury *convicted* the man accused of murder.

Example 2: I was *convicted* of running the red light because there was camera evidence.

Example 3: In a mystery novel I read, the wrong person was *convicted* of the crime.

Question 1: If you break a law, can you be *convicted*? Yes or no? (yes)

Question 2: If you are late to school, can you be *convicted*? Yes or no? (no)

Pair Share: Turn to your partner and tell about a movie or TV show in which someone is *convicted* of a crime he or she didn't commit.

④

trace (n)

Let's read the next word together. *Trace*.

Definition: *Trace* means "a small sign that someone or something was present." What means "a small sign that someone or something was present"? (trace)

Example 1: By noon, the sun had melted the last *trace* of snow.

Example 2: There is no *trace* of a pet living in this school.

Example 3: At the end of a movie I recently watched, the whole town disappeared without a *trace*.

Question 1: There is only one drop of water left in the pool. Is there a *trace* of water in the pool? Yes or no? (yes)

Question 2: The garden is overflowing with flowers. Does it have a *trace* of flowers? Yes or no? (no)

Pair Share: It is thousands of years in the future. Cars no longer exist. Turn to your partner and tell what *traces* of cars might be found.

⑤

preserve (v)

Let's read the next word together. *Preserve*.

Definition: *Preserve* means "to keep something the way it is." What means "to keep something the way it is"? (preserve)

Example 1: My mother *preserved* my sister's bedroom even after she moved to her own apartment.

Example 2: To *preserve* a work of art, store it in a cool, dry place.

Example 3: Please help *preserve* the beauty of the school premises; don't litter.

Question 1: Can you *preserve* food by freezing it? Yes or no? (yes)

Question 2: If workers tear down an old building, are they *preserving* it? Yes or no? (no)

Pair Share: Turn to your partner and tell about a place in your town or city that you hope will always be *preserved*.

⑥

identify (v)

Let's read the next word together. *Identify.*

Definition: *Identify* means "to recognize; to match with a person or name." What means "to match with a person or name"? (identify)

Example 1: I can *identify* my grandma in a crowd by her very large hat.

Example 2: This morning I saw a beautiful bird, but I cannot *identify* its species.

Example 3: Your eyes can *identify* you as a member of your family.

Question 1: Can most people *identify* the color red? Yes or no? (yes)

Question 2: Can you *identify* the most recent star scientists have discovered by looking at the sky? Yes or no? (no)

Pair Share: Turn to your partner and tell one way you can *identify* him or her.

unique (adj)

Let's read the next word together. *Unique.*

Definition: *Unique* means "one of a kind; different from all others." What means "one of a kind; different from all others"? (unique)

Example 1: Each person's way of sneezing is *unique.*

Example 2: The inhabitants of a tiny island in the Pacific Ocean have their own *unique* language.

Example 3: I listened to a band perform music that is a *unique* blend of jazz and country.

Question 1: Is brown hair *unique*? Yes or no? (no)

Question 2: Is each person's signature *unique*? Yes or no? (yes)

Pair Share: Turn to your partner and name one *unique* thing about yourself.

suspect (n)

Let's read the next word together. *Suspect.*

Definition: A *suspect* is a person who police think may be guilty of a crime. What word means "a person who may be guilty of a crime"? (suspect)

Example 1: The *suspect* is being held at the police station until the trial.

Example 2: Sometimes people become a *suspect* of a crime because they were in the wrong place at the wrong time.

Example 3: The *suspect* claims to have been sleeping when the crime was committed.

Question 1: Is a *suspect* known to be guilty? Yes or no? (no)

Question 2: Should a *suspect* be careful with his words or actions? Yes or no? (yes)

Pair Share: Turn to your partner and tell why you would not want to be a *suspect.*

witness (n)

Let's read the last word together. *Witness.*

Definition: *Witness* means "a person who saw something happen." A person who saw something happen is a what? (witness)

Example 1: Some *witnesses* write down the details of the incident so they won't forget them.

Example 2: I am often a *witness* to students treating each other inconsiderately, and it upsets me.

Example 3: If I could go back in history, I would want to be a *witness* to Rosa Parks's famous bus ride.

Question 1: If you are a *witness* of an act of kindness, do you see it or do it? (see it)

Question 2: Does a *witness* have to be present when the event happens? Yes or no? (yes)

Pair Share: Turn to your partner and tell about something amazing you have *witnessed.*

Objectives

- Read informational text.
- Monitor comprehension during text reading.
- Summarize text.

"The Science of Catching Criminals"

Direct students to page 19 in their Student Books.

Now, it's time to read. Pay attention to the nonfiction text features while you read.

Guiding Students Toward Independent Reading

It is important that your students read as much and as often as they can. Assign texts that meet the needs of your students, based on your observations and data. This is a good opportunity to stretch your students. If students become frustrated, scaffold the reading with paired reading, choral reading, or a read-aloud.

Options for reading text:

- Teacher read-aloud
- Teacher-led or student-led choral read
- Paired read or independent read

Choose an option for reading text. Students read according to the option that you chose. Review the purpose of the numbered squares in the text (monitor comprehension while reading by stopping periodically to ensure understanding of small portions of text) and prompt students to stop periodically to check comprehension. If you choose to read the text aloud or chorally, use the text on the following pages and stop to ask questions and have students answer them.

SE p. 19, paragraphs 1–2

In courts of law, the tiniest piece of **evidence** can bring a criminal to justice. Something as small as a **fiber** can connect a thief to a burglary. The science used to show a person's guilt or **innocence** is called forensics. A forensic team is made up of different people. Some work at the crime scene itself. Others work in labs to study the evidence. All of them have the same goal: to use evidence to catch and **convict** a criminal.

At the Crime Scene

Anyone who commits a crime leaves evidence behind. He or she may try to clean up, but usually some **trace** remains. It could be a fingerprint or a shoe print. It might be a bit of blood or skin. It may be a hair or thread.

1. How can trace evidence lead to conviction of a criminal?

SE p. 19, paragraph 3

For this reason, a forensic investigation starts at the crime scene. First, police investigators **preserve** the scene. They seal it off to make sure nobody changes it. Then, they gather evidence. Because evidence can be very small, the investigators must be very careful. They use special tools to scan every inch. They place tiny samples in clean containers. Even dust, pollen, or seeds can help break a case. The examiners try not to overlook anything.

Back at the Lab

SE p. 20, paragraphs 1–2

Once collected, the evidence is sent to a special lab. There, forensic scientists study it closely. They put it under microscopes. They run tests on it. They learn what it is made of and where it came from. If a piece of evidence is from a human body, the scientists can **identify** its DNA.

All living things have DNA. It is in every cell of a person's body. It tells the cells how to grow. When blood, skin, or hair is left at a crime scene, the person's DNA is left there too. Each person's DNA is **unique**, just like a fingerprint. If the DNA in a piece of evidence matches the DNA in a blood sample from a **suspect**, it can be evidence of guilt. If it doesn't, it can be evidence of innocence.

2. Where can DNA be found?

The Power of Forensic Science

SE p. 20, paragraphs 3–4

Whether it's a speck of fuzz or human blood, forensic evidence can make or break a case. Here are a couple of examples.

In 1982, orange fibers were found on the body of a murder victim in Ohio. Forensic scientists concluded that they were carpet fibers from a van. Later, a woman was kidnapped by a man named Robert Anthony Buell, but she escaped and reported him to the police. Investigators learned that Buell had a van with orange carpeting. They took samples of the fibers for analysis. The fibers from the van carpet matched the fibers on the victim. Buell was proven guilty.

3. What trace evidence was used to convict Buell?

SE p. 20, paragraphs 5–6

In another famous case, four men were convicted of a murder in Illinois. This crime happened before DNA testing could be done. The ruling was based on the report of a **witness** who said she had seen the crime. The men were sentenced to a very long time in prison. Two were put on Death Row. Later, the witness confessed that her report had been a lie. By this time, DNA testing had been developed. It was used to show that the Ford Heights Four were innocent and that another man was guilty.

Thanks to forensic science, justice was served.

4. The Ford Heights Four spent many years in prison and thought they were going to be killed. How would you feel if you were wrongly convicted of a terrible crime?

For confirmation of engagement, have students share two facts about forensic science.

Summarize with IVF Topic Sentences

When students have finished reading, direct them to page 21 in their Student Books. Good readers can share a summary about what they read using concise words rather than going on and on with a string of details. The IVF Topic Sentence provides a format that is an effective way to begin a summary paragraph.

Model

First, let's identify the heading of the first section and record it in the first column. Next, we need to choose a strong verb from our word bank. Let's choose the verb *explains*. Finally, we need to finish our thought. Let's try to use at least one vocabulary word in our response. Write the following sentence on the board as you read it aloud.

> *At the Crime Scene explains how trace evidence is found and preserved at the crime scene.*

Summarize with IVF Topic Sentences   Answers will vary.
Write an IVF Topic Sentence for each section of the text and the text as a whole.

I (Identify the item)	V (select Verb)	F (Finish your thought)
At the Crime Scene	explains	how trace evidence is found and preserved at the crime scene.
Back at the Lab	provides	information about how forensic scientists use trace evidence and DNA to convict criminals.
The Power of Forensic Science	teaches	about the role of trace evidence and DNA in proving the guilt of one man and the innocence of another.
"The Science of Catching Criminals"	tells	how forensic science is used to solve crimes.

Verb Bank

explains	tells	shows	provides	presents
describes	gives	compares	lists	teaches

Unit 1   **21**

Guided Practice

Let's focus on just the second section, Back at the Lab. What do we do first? (Identify the item.) Write the heading in the box. What's the next step? (Choose a strong verb.) We need to choose a different verb this time. Have volunteers select a verb and finish the thought as you write the sentence on the board.

> *Back at the Lab provides information about how forensic scientists use trace evidence and DNA to convict criminals.*

Independent Practice

Have students write the IVF sentence for the final section. Review the answers as a class, then have students write the final IVF sentence about the whole text. Circulate around the room suggesting edits as needed.

Lesson Opener

Before the lesson, choose one of the following activities to write on the board or post on the *LANGUAGE! Live* Class Wall online.

- *Write a summary sentence about what we did in class yesterday.*
- *Write two sentences about the techniques forensic scientists use to match evidence to a suspect.*
- *List five nouns that would fit in this category: Things that are trace evidence.*

Vocabulary

Objective
- Review key passage vocabulary.

Review Passage Vocabulary

Direct students to page 18 in their Student Books. Use the following questions to review the vocabulary words from "The Science of Catching Criminals." Have students answer each question using the vocabulary word or indicating its meaning in a complete sentence.

- If someone's *innocence* is proved, is he or she guilty? (No; if a person's innocence is proved, he or she is not guilty.) Think of the passage title. What can help prove *innocence*? (Science can help prove innocence.)

- How much *evidence* can show a person's guilt? (A very small bit of evidence can show a person's guilt.) What are some examples of crime scene *evidence*? (Hair, blood, skin, and fingerprints are examples of evidence.)

- Are *fibers* too small to prove a person's guilt? (No, even a fiber can show a person's guilt.) What kind of *fiber* helped catch kidnapper Robert Anthony Buell? (A carpet fiber helped catch the kidnapper.)

- Does a criminal usually take all *traces* with him? (No, a criminal usually leaves traces behind.) What does a *trace* show? (A trace shows that someone or something was present.) Can a *trace* be used as evidence? (Yes, a trace can be used as evidence.)

- When investigators *preserve* a crime scene, what do they do to it? (When they preserve a crime scene, they keep it the way they found it.) Why is it important to *preserve* the scene? (It is important to preserve the scene so investigators can look for clues and take samples.)

- If clues and samples help *convict* a criminal, the criminal has been found what? (A convicted person has been found guilty.) Is a person *convicted* in a court of law or outside it? (A person is convicted in a court of law.)

- What makes a fingerprint *unique*? (It is unique because it is different from all others.) Is your DNA *unique,* or does it match the DNA of others? (DNA is unique.)

- If the DNA in a blood sample is *identified,* it has been what? (DNA that is identified has been recognized as belonging to a certain person.) How can criminals be *identified*? (They can be identified by fingerprints, DNA, looks, etc.)

- A *suspect* is a person who what? (A suspect is a person who police think may be guilty of a crime.) How can the DNA in a blood sample help show a *suspect's* guilt? (If the DNA in the blood sample matches the suspect's DNA, he or she is probably guilty.)

- If you are a *witness* to a crime, what have you done? (If you are a witness to a crime, you have seen it happen.) Why can't a couch or a carpet be a *witness* to a crime? (A couch or a carpet cannot be a witness to a crime because they cannot see.)

Grammar

Objectives
- Use possessive nouns correctly.
- Identify the function and purpose of the apostrophe.
- Identify the function and purpose of verb tenses.
- Distinguish between past and present tense verbs.

Possessive Nouns

We have learned about nouns in previous lessons. Think about what we learned about types or forms of nouns.

Write *common* and *proper* on the board. Have students read the words chorally. Then, have them generate examples of both kinds of nouns from "The Science of Catching Criminals."

Possible responses:

Common: scientist, investigators, police, crime, criminals, fibers

Proper: DNA, Ohio, Illinois, Robert Anthony Buell, Death Row, Ford Heights Four

Write *singular* and *plural* on the board. Have students read the words chorally. Then, have them generate examples of singular nouns from "The Science of Catching Criminals," then change them to their plural forms. (Possible answers: scientist-scientists; investigator-investigators; criminal-criminals; crime-crimes; van-vans; fingerprint-fingerprints)

To build on our knowledge of nouns, let's talk about how we show that something belongs to someone. We use a specific punctuation mark to show ownership.

Direct students to page 22 in their Student Books and read the information about possessive nouns including the examples for singular and plural possessive nouns.

Apostrophe is a weird word. Say it with me: apostrophe. What is the name of the punctuation mark we use to show possession? (apostrophe) *Apostrophes are tricky because they have different uses and meanings. Apostrophes can also signal missing letters when two or more words are combined in a contraction. What makes apostrophes so tricky?* (They have different uses and meanings.)

Model

Now, we'll read some sentences from "The Science of Catching Criminals" and Holes. **Read the instructions for Part A and the first sentence.** *As he signed his name, the snake's rattle on his tattoo seemed to wiggle.*

I see a word with an apostrophe, but I have to check to make sure it's being used to create a possessive noun. Snake's rattle makes me think the rattle belongs to the snake, so it sounds like a possessive noun. I will underline it. Next, I have to determine if it's singular or plural. If I cover up the 's, the word snake is left. Covering up the 's lets us see what word was there before the apostrophe was added. Snake is singular, so I will write an S above the word.

Guided Practice

Listen as I read the second sentence. He checked Stanley's backpack and allowed him to keep it. Again, I see a word with an apostrophe. What word has an apostrophe? (Stanley's) *The sentence is making reference to Stanley's what?* (backpack) *The backpack belongs to Stanley, so underline Stanley's. What do we have to do next?* (determine if it's singular or plural) *Yes, so we cover up the 's and what's left?* (Stanley) *Is Stanley singular or plural?* (singular) *Write an S above the word.*

Independent Practice

Have students identify the possessive nouns in the remaining sentences. Review the answers as a class. If students struggled with *killers'* as a plural possessive noun, remind them to cover up only the apostrophe because they need to know what was there before the apostrophe was added. When they do, they will see *killers* and then identify it as a plural noun because it ends in -s.

Understanding possessive nouns will improve your reading comprehension. It can also improve your writing. Sometimes awkward phrases can be replaced with possessive nouns to improve the flow of your writing.

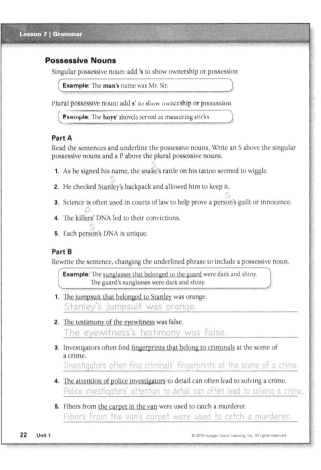

Possessive Nouns

Singular possessive noun: add **'s** to show ownership or possession

Example: The **man's** name was Mr. Sir.

Plural possessive noun: add **s'** to show ownership or possession

Example: The **boys'** shovels served as measuring sticks

Part A
Read the sentences and underline the possessive nouns. Write an S above the singular possessive nouns and a P above the plural possessive nouns.

1. As he signed his name, the snake's rattle on his tattoo seemed to wiggle.
2. He checked Stanley's backpack and allowed him to keep it.
3. Science is often used in courts of law to help prove a person's guilt or innocence.
4. The killers' DNA led to their convictions.
5. Each person's DNA is unique.

Part B
Rewrite the sentence, changing the underlined phrase to include a possessive noun.

Example: The sunglasses that belonged to the guard were dark and shiny.
The guard's sunglasses were dark and shiny.

1. The jumpsuit that belonged to Stanley was orange.
Stanley's jumpsuit was orange.
2. The testimony of the eyewitness was false.
The eyewitness's testimony was false.
3. Investigators often find fingerprints that belong to criminals at the scene of a crime.
Investigators often find criminals' fingerprints at the scene of a crime.
4. The attention of police investigators to detail can often lead to solving a crime.
Police investigators' attention to detail can often lead to solving a crime.
5. Fibers from the carpet in the van were used to catch a murderer.
Fibers from the van's carpet were used to catch a murderer.

Direct students to Part B and read the instructions.

Guided Practice

Read the first sentence and guide students through the same question sequence as the
example sentence. Repeat the process with sentences 2 and 3.

Independent Practice

Have students rewrite the remaining sentences. Review the answers as a class.

Verbs

Action

Let's quickly review what we learned about verbs in previous lessons. Verbs can serve
two functions in a sentence. They can show action, and they can link the subject to the
rest of the sentence. Police investigated the scene. What did they do? (**investigated**)
Forensic scientists solved crimes. What did they do? (**solved**)

Linking

With linking verbs, there is no action. Linking verbs usually tell us more about the
subject. *Forensic science is important.* What is the linking verb? (**is**) The sentence tells
us about the value of forensic science. The crime was a mystery. What is the linking
verb? (**was**) What two things are being linked? (**crime and mystery**)

Tense

Both action and linking verbs convey time. *Tense* is another word for *time*. What is
another word for *time*? (**tense**) When we refer to things happening at this time or
in the present, we use the present tense. What tense means "now" or "at this time"?
(**present tense**)

When we refer to things that have already happened, we use the past tense. What
tense do we use to talk about things that have already happened? (**past tense**) You
use these two different tenses frequently when you speak, and you see them when you
read. Good readers pay attention to verb tense to help them clarify meaning and track
the sequence of events.

Draw two columns on the board and label them *present tense* and *past tense*.

Write these sentences under *present tense*:

> *Police look for clues.*
>
> *Scientists test for DNA.*
>
> *Investigators are careful.*
>
> *I am scared of being kidnapped.*

In the first sentence, the verb *look* is in the present tense. It means they do it now. To make *look* past tense, we add -ed. **Write *Police looked for clues.* under *past tense.*** Now it means they did it before.

In the next sentence, the verb *test* is in the present tense. It means scientists do it now. They have not finished. How do we make *test* past tense? (add -ed) **Write *Scientists tested for DNA.* under *past tense.***

For regular action verbs, we add an -ed to express the past tense. What do we add to a regular action verb to express the past tense? (-ed)

Look at the third sentence. What is the verb? (are) Is it an action verb or a linking verb? (linking verb) Linking verbs don't follow the same pattern as regular action verbs. **Write *Investigators were careful.* under *past tense.*** The past tense of *are* is *were*.

Look at the fourth sentence. What is the verb? (am) Is it an action verb or a linking verb? (linking verb) What do we need to change *am* to to make it past tense? (was) **Write *I was scared of being kidnapped.* under *past tense.*** The past tense of *am* is *was*. *Was* is also the past tense of *is*.

Direct students to page 23 in their Student Books and read the instructions.

Model

Follow along as I read the example: *Forensic science was essential in solving the crime.* The first thing I have to do is underline the verb. Forensic science did what? It didn't do anything. The sentence tells me more about forensic science, so *was* is linking the subject to the rest of the sentence. I'll underline *was*. Now, I have to determine if it's present tense or past tense. Let me read the sentence again to look for clues about time. Linking verbs are irregular, and *was* is the past tense of *is*. So, I will write *was* in the past tense column of the chart.

Guided Practice

Listen as I read the first sentence: *Investigators carefully preserve the crime scene.* Who or what is the

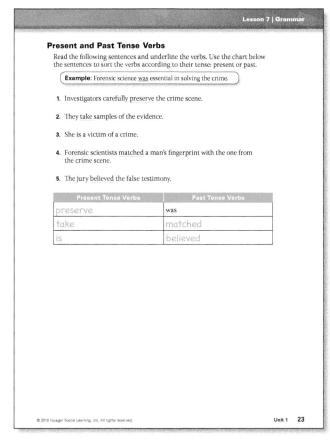

Present and Past Tense Verbs

Read the following sentences and underline the verbs. Use the chart below the sentences to sort the verbs according to their tense: present or past.

> **Example:** Forensic science <u>was</u> essential in solving the crime.

1. Investigators carefully <u>preserve</u> the crime scene.

2. They <u>take</u> samples of the evidence.

3. She <u>is</u> a victim of a crime.

4. Forensic scientists <u>matched</u> a man's fingerprint with the one from the crime scene.

5. The jury <u>believed</u> the false testimony.

Present Tense Verbs	Past Tense Verbs
preserve	was
take	matched
is	believed

Unit 1   23

sentence about? (investigators) What do they do? (preserve) *Preserve* is the verb. Is it an action or a linking verb? (action) What do we do next? (Underline the verb.) Now, we have to determine if it's present or past tense. Is there an -ed on the end? (no) Because we were able to answer the *what do they do?* question, we know it is an action verb that doesn't end in -ed. It must be present tense, so what's the last step? (Write *preserve* in the present tense column.)

Independent Practice

Have students find and sort the verbs in the remaining sentences. Review the answers as a class.

Writing

Objectives

- Write simple sentences.
- Identify the structure of a sentence.
- Identify the simple subject of a sentence.
- Identify the simple predicate of a sentence.
- Use subject-verb agreement in writing.

Masterpiece Sentences

In a previous lesson, I introduced you to a sentence writing process called Masterpiece Sentences. Today, you will continue working on building basic sentences, using the questions in Stage 1.

Direct students to page 24 in their Student Books and read the instructions. Remind students to look at the Process Chart on page 9 if they need more support. Have students write a sentence for each picture. Then, have volunteers share their sentences. Encourage students to listen for similarities and differences between volunteers' sentences.

Simple Subject and Simple Predicate

The sentences you have just created are base sentences. Stage 1 questions help us build the core of a sentence: the simple subject and the simple predicate. When we read text, the sentences often have more than one noun and sometimes they have more than one verb. It's our job as readers to determine the main noun or subject and the main verb or predicate. We must do this to make sure we understand the meaning of the sentence.

Have students generate a sentence about something you have done on the board. Encourage them to be descriptive about you and your actions. Guide them in identifying the main noun and the main verb. Then, explain that this is the simple subject and simple predicate.

Example:

On Friday, Mrs. Jones loudly told us to stop playing around.

Simple Subject: Mrs. Jones

Simple Predicate: told

Direct students to Part A of page 25 in their Student Books and read the instructions.

What am I looking for? (the simple subject and the simple predicate) What part of speech is the simple subject? (noun) What part of speech is the simple predicate? (verb)

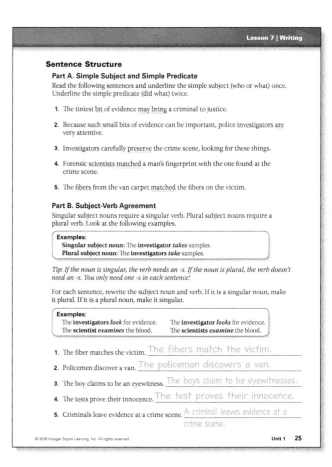

Model

Let's look at the first sentence. **Read the first sentence:** *The tiniest bit of evidence may bring a criminal to justice.* Who or what is this sentence about? It is about a bit of evidence, so the simple subject would be *bit*. I need to underline it once. What does *bit* do? It may bring a criminal to justice, so the simple predicate is *may bring*. I need to underline it twice. All of the other details in the sentence help paint a more complete picture, but the base sentence is *bit may bring*.

Guided Practice

Let's look at the next sentence. *Because such small bits of evidence can be important, police investigators are very attentive.* Who or what is this sentence about? (police investigators) So, what is the simple subject? (investigators) Underline it once. What do investigators do? (nothing) So there is no action verb. What is the sentence saying about the investigators? (They are very attentive.) What is the linking verb? (are) What is the simple predicate? (are) Underline it twice. **Convey the importance of the clause that begins the sentence and point out the comma.**

Complete the activity as a whole group, and continue to ask clarifying questions to help students properly identify the simple subject and the simple predicate.

Subject-Verb Agreement

We have spent a great deal of time on nouns and verbs. One of the trickiest things about our language is how nouns and verbs work together. Singular nouns have to be paired with singular verbs, and plural nouns have to be paired with plural verbs. The idea of singular and plural nouns should be familiar, but the term *singular and plural verbs* is probably not familiar.

Direct students to Part B and read the information on subject-verb agreement.

Take a moment and read the tip in italics.

Read the instructions for the activity.

Model

Let's look at the examples. Listen as I read the first sentence: *The investigators look for evidence.* Who? Investigators. So *investigators* is the subject and it's a plural noun. What do they do? They look. So *look* is the predicate. To rewrite the new sentence, I need to make it a singular noun. *The investigator . . .* Is it *look* or *looks*? Because there is no -s on *investigator*, there must be one on *look*. *The investigator looks for evidence.* An -s has to be added to the verb because I need one -s when working with regular nouns and verbs.

The next sentence is *The scientist examines the blood.* Who? Scientist. *Scientist* is the subject and it's a singular noun. Notice *examines* has an -s. To rewrite this sentence, I need to make the subject plural, so I add an -s to *scientist* and leave it off of *examine*. Remember only one -s is needed. *The scientists examine the blood.*

Guided Practice

Let's look at the first sentence: *The fiber matches the victim.* Who or what? (fiber) *Fiber* is the subject. Is it singular or plural? (singular) Our new sentence needs what kind of subject noun? (plural) What does the fiber do? (matches) What is the new sentence? (The fibers match the victim.) Did you remember you only needed one -s? Point out that because *match* ends in *tch*, we add -es to make it plural.

Independent Practice

Have students rewrite the remaining sentences. Review the answers as a class.

When students have finished, write the following sentence frame on the board.

Mia and Jaxon _____ books about forensic science.

Have a volunteer complete the present tense sentence with the correct form of *read*. Point out that in this case, neither noun has -s, but the subject is plural because there is more than one person, and therefore the verb doesn't need an -s.

Assign online practice by opening the Tools menu, then selecting Assignments. Be sure to select the correct class from the drop-down menu.

Lesson Opener

Before the lesson, choose one of the following activities to write on the board or post on the *LANGUAGE! Live* Class Wall online.

- *Complete each sentence with an action verb, paying close attention to subject-verb agreement.*

  Scientists _____ the evidence.

  The investigators _____ the crime scene.

  The criminal _____ trace evidence.

  Stanley _____ a drink of water.

- *List five verbs that would fit in this category: Jobs of the forensic scientist.*

- *What do you think the Ford Heights Four did when they were released? Use complete sentences.*

Reading

Objectives

- Establish a purpose for rereading informational text.
- Demonstrate an understanding of how to ask questions and answer them appropriately.
- Use complete sentences and text evidence to answer questions.
- Use critical thinking skills to write responses to prompts about text.
- Support written answers with text evidence.

Reading for a Purpose: "The Science of Catching Criminals"

Let's read "The Science of Catching Criminals" again. Let's read some questions to provide a purpose for rereading the text.

Direct students to page 26 in their Student Books. Have them read the questions aloud with you.

1. What examples of trace evidence are used to solve crimes?

2. When is DNA better evidence than an eyewitness?

3. Who is similar to Stanley Yelnats?

4. When did the Ford Heights Four become different from Stanley Yelnats?

> Options for reading text.
>
> - Teacher read-aloud
>
> - Teacher-led or student-led choral read
>
> - Paired read or independent read with bold vocabulary words read aloud

Direct students to page 19 in their Student Books or have them tear out the extra copy of "The Science of Catching Criminals" from the back of their book.

Note: To minimize flipping back and forth between the pages, a copy of each text has been included in the back of the Student Books. Encourage students to tear this out and use it when working on activities that require the use of the text.

Have students read "The Science of Catching Criminals."

Passage Comprehension

We are required to ask and answer a variety of questions at different levels of difficulty. We talked about the word *evidence* as it relates to forensic science. How do we use evidence to confirm our understanding of text? (We can locate evidence in the text to prove our answer.) Evidence from text can be a single word, a phrase, or a group of sentences.

It is critical to understand what a question is asking and how to answer it. Today, we will review four question words. We will become masters at answering these types of questions.

Write the question words *who, what, when,* and *where* on the board. Have students read the words aloud with you. Direct students to page 26 in their Student Books. Have them review the chart. Check for understanding by requesting an oral response to the following questions.

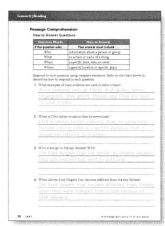

- If the question asks *who,* your answer must include what? (information about a person or group)

- If the question asks *what,* your answer must include what? (an action or name of a thing)

- If the question asks *when,* your answer must include what? (a specific time, date, or event)

- If the question asks *where,* your answer must include what? (a general location or a specific place)

Guided Practice

Let's practice answering questions. Listen as I model the first one for you.

1. What examples of trace evidence are used to solve crimes?

Looking at the chart, because the question is a *what* question, I know the answer will require the name of something. Let's circle the question word *what*. Next, let's underline words in the question that we can use in our answer. (trace evidence used to solve crimes) How shall we start our answer? (Trace evidence such as . . .) Next, I can use information in the text to provide the best answer. **Have students finish the sentence with their partner.** (fibers, dust, pollen, seeds, fingerprints, shoe prints, thread, DNA)

Write the following answer on the board:

> *Trace evidence such as fibers, dust, pollen, seeds, fingerprints, shoe prints, thread, and DNA are used to solve crimes.*

Let's check for accuracy. Did I answer the *what* question with the names of things? (yes) How about the mechanics of my sentence? Have I used correct punctuation and capitalization? Did I capitalize the first word and put a period at the end of my sentence?

Have students write the answer on the page.

Independent Practice

Work with your partner to answer the next question. Follow the same procedure that we did for number one.

- Skim headings to determine which section of the text can be used as evidence for your answer.
- Locate evidence for your answer.
- Combine words in the question with evidence in the text to write complete sentences.

Have partners answer the remaining questions with text evidence. For students who need more assistance, provide the following sentence starters.

> Sentence starters:
>
> 2. *DNA is _____ better than an eyewitness. Humans _____.*
>
>   *DNA is _____.*
>
> 3. *The Ford Heights Four are similar to Stanley because _____.*
>
> 4. *The Ford Heights Four became different from Stanley when _____.*

Lesson Opener

Before the lesson, choose one of the following activities to write on the board or post on the *LANGUAGE! Live* Class Wall online.

- *Identify the simple subject and the simple predicate in the following sentences:*
  The brilliant scientist examined the dead body for evidence.
  The forgetful thief planned a bank robbery on Thanksgiving.
- *Someone in class has stolen the teacher's money. Write five* what *questions you would ask the suspects.*
- *Write five sentences about forensic science. Identify the nouns and verbs in each sentence.*

Reading

Objectives

- Read informational text.
- Read with purpose and understanding.
- Answer questions to demonstrate comprehension of text.
- Identify and explain explicit details from text.
- Monitor comprehension during text reading.
- Determine how each section of text contributes to the whole.

Close Reading of "The Science of Catching Criminals"

highlighters or colored pencils

Let's reread "The Science of Catching Criminals." I will provide specific instructions on how to mark the text to help with comprehension.

Have students get out a highlighter or colored pencil.

Direct students to pages 27–29 in their Student Books.

Please mark your text according to my instructions.

- Draw a rectangle around the title, "The Science of Catching Criminals."

- Circle each heading: At the Crime Scene, Back at the Lab, The Power of Forensic Science.

Next, we will read the vocabulary words aloud.

- What's the first bold vocabulary word? (evidence) *Evidence* is proof— something that shows another thing happened or is true. Police found a glove at the scene of the crime that was used as *evidence* to convict the killer. Have partners use the word in a sentence.

- What's the next bold vocabulary word? (fiber) A *fiber* is a thin thread. Carpets and clothing leave behind *fibers* that police use as evidence. Have partners use the word in a sentence.

- What's the next bold vocabulary word? (innocence) *Innocence* means "the state of not being guilty." DNA can prove someone's guilt or *innocence.* Have partners use the word in a sentence.

- What's the next bold vocabulary word? (convict) *Convict* means "to find someone guilty in a court of law." Criminals are *convicted* of a crime based on evidence. **Have partners use the word in a sentence.**

- What's the next bold vocabulary word? (trace) *Trace* means "a small sign that someone or something was present." Though the criminal cleaned up the blood, *trace* amounts were left on the carpet. **Have partners use the word in a sentence.**

- What's the next bold vocabulary word? (preserve) *Preserve* means "to keep something the way it is." Forensic scientists *preserve* crime scenes until they have finished their examination. **Have partners use the word in a sentence.**

- What's the next bold vocabulary word? (identify) *Identify* means "to recognize; to match with a person or name." The police were able to *identify* the criminal because of the fingerprint he left on the glass. **Have partners use the word in a sentence.**

- What's the next bold vocabulary word? (unique) *Unique* means "one of a kind; different from all others." Everyone's fingerprint and DNA are *unique*. **Have partners use the word in a sentence.**

- What's the next bold vocabulary word? (suspect) A *suspect* is a person who police think may be guilty of a crime. The *suspect* was not allowed to leave the country until the end of the trial. **Have partners use the word in a sentence.**

- What's the last bold vocabulary word? (witness) *Witness* means "a person who saw something happen." The *witness* of the crime wasn't able to positively identify the criminal, but the DNA did. **Have partners use the word in a sentence.**

Talk with a partner about any vocabulary word that is still confusing for you to read or understand.

You will read the text, "The Science of Catching Criminals," one section at a time. After each section, you will monitor your understanding by circling the check marks or the question marks. Please be sure to draw a question mark over any confusing words, phrases, or sentences.

> Options for rereading text.
> - Teacher read-aloud
> - Teacher-led or student-led choral read
> - Paired read or independent read with bold vocabulary words read aloud

Choose an option for reading text. Have students read the introduction according to the option that you chose. As you read, mark any words or phrases that provide examples of different types of evidence. What will you mark? (examples of evidence)

When most of the students are finished, continue with the entire class. Let's see how well you understood what you read.

- Circle the check mark or the question mark for this section. Draw a question mark over any confusing words.

- Go to line 1. Mark where forensics is used. (courts of law)

- Go to line 2. If you haven't already done so, mark the evidence. (fiber)

- Go to line 4. Number the two places that forensic scientists work. (1. crime scene; 2. labs)

- Go to lines 5 and 6. Mark the job of forensic scientists. (use evidence to catch and convict a criminal)

Close Reading

Read the text.

"The Science of Catching Criminals"

In courts of law, the tiniest piece of **evidence** can bring a criminal to justice. Something as small as a **fiber** can connect a thief to a burglary. The science used to show a person's guilt or **innocence** is called forensics. A forensic team is made up of different people. Some work at the crime scene itself. Others work in labs
5 to study the evidence. All of them have the same goal: to use evidence to catch and **convict** a criminal.

At the Crime Scene

Anyone who commits a crime leaves evidence behind. He or she may try to clean up, but usually some **trace** remains. It could be a fingerprint or a shoe print. It might be a bit of blood or skin. It may be a hair or thread.
10 For this reason, a forensic investigation starts at the crime scene. First, police investigators **preserve** the scene. They seal it off to make sure nobody changes it. Then, they gather evidence. Because evidence can be very small, the investigators must be very careful. They use special tools to scan every inch. They place tiny samples in clean containers. Even dust, pollen, or seeds can help break a case.
15 The examiners try not to overlook anything.

Unit 1 **27**

Have students read At the Crime Scene according to the option that you chose.
As you read, mark any words or phrases that provide examples of different types of evidence.

When most of the students are finished, continue with the entire class.
Let's see how well you understood what you read.

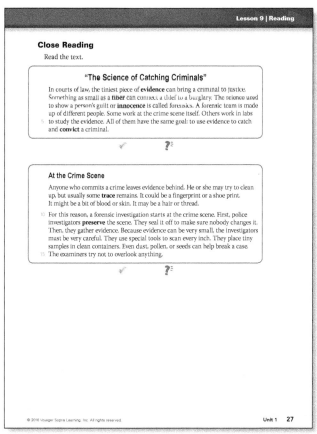

Close Reading

Read the text.

"The Science of Catching Criminals"

In courts of law, the tiniest piece of **evidence** can bring a criminal to justice. Something as small as a **fiber** can connect a thief to a burglary. The science used to show a person's guilt or **innocence** is called forensics. A forensic team is made up of different people. Some work at the crime scene itself. Others work in labs
5 to study the evidence. All of them have the same goal: to use evidence to catch and **convict** a criminal.

At the Crime Scene

Anyone who commits a crime leaves evidence behind. He or she may try to clean up, but usually some **trace** remains. It could be a fingerprint or a shoe print. It might be a bit of blood or skin. It may be a hair or thread.
10 For this reason, a forensic investigation starts at the crime scene. First, police investigators **preserve** the scene. They seal it off to make sure nobody changes it. Then, they gather evidence. Because evidence can be very small, the investigators must be very careful. They use special tools to scan every inch. They place tiny samples in clean containers. Even dust, pollen, or seeds can help break a case.
15 The examiners try not to overlook anything.

- Circle the check mark or the question mark for this section. Draw a question mark over any confusing words.

- Go to the first paragraph. If you haven't already done so, mark examples of trace evidence. **(fingerprint, shoe print, blood, skin, hair, thread)**

- In the same paragraph, circle the word *it* three times. Draw an arrow to connect each pronoun to the word it represents. **(trace)**

- Go to the second paragraph. Number the steps taken by police investigators. **(1. preserve the scene; 2. gather evidence; 3. scan every inch; 4. place tiny samples in clean containers)**

- Go to line 11. Mark the way a crime scene is preserved. **(seal it off)**

- Go to line 14. Mark the verb that means *solve*. **(break)**

- On the same line, if you haven't already done so, mark examples of "small bits of evidence." **(dust, pollen, seeds)**

- In the second paragraph, circle each occurrence of the word *they*. Draw an arrow to indicate who *they* refers to. **(investigators)**

- In the last sentence, mark the word being used to replace *investigators*. **(examiners)** Use the root word to determine a synonym for *investigate*. Write both verbs in the margin with an equal sign between them. **(investigate = examine)**

- The title of the text is "The Science of Catching Criminals." This particular section is titled At the Crime Scene. How does this section connect to the title? Write the answer at the bottom of the page. **(This section explains the scientific steps taken at the place the criminal committed the crime.)**

Have students read Back at the Lab according to the option that you chose. As you read, mark any words or phrases that provide examples of different types of evidence.

When most of the students are finished, continue with the entire class. Let's see how well you understood what you read.

- Circle the check mark or the question mark for this section. Draw a question mark over any confusing words.

- Go to line 17. Mark the tools used to look at evidence in the lab. (microscopes)

- Go to line 18. Mark what a scientist can learn about evidence from studying it. (what it is made of and where it came from)

- Go to line 19. Mark what can be identified if evidence comes from the human body. (DNA)

- Go to line 21. If you haven't already done so, mark the evidence. (blood, skin, hair)

- Go to line 24. Mark the two words that function as antonyms, or have opposite meanings. (guilt, innocence)

- Go to line 20. Circle the word *DNA*. Skim that paragraph. Mark all words and phrases that help define DNA and what it is used for. (all living things, in every cell, tells the cells how to grow, blood, skin, hair, unique, evidence of guilt, evidence of innocence)

- Use context from the entire paragraph to define DNA. (DNA is an important molecule in all living things that tells cells how to grow. DNA is unique to each person and can be found in every cell. DNA can be used to determine guilt or innocence.)

- Provide examples of evidence that includes DNA. (blood, skin, hair)

- The title of the text is "The Science of Catching Criminals." This particular section is titled Back at the Lab. How does this section connect to the title? Write the answer at the bottom of the page. (This section explains how what scientists do at the lab can be used to convict criminals.)

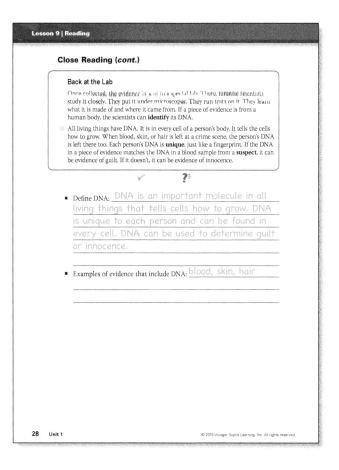

Have students read The Power of Forensic Science according to the option that you chose. As you read, mark any words or phrases that provide examples of different types of evidence.

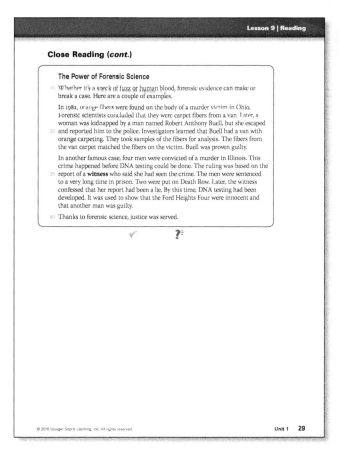

- Circle the check mark or the question mark for this section. Draw a question mark over any confusing words.

- Go to line 25. If you haven't already done so, mark the examples of trace evidence. (fuzz, human blood)

- Go to line 27. If you haven't already done so, mark the evidence. (orange fibers)

- Go to line 28. If you haven't already done so, mark the evidence. (carpet fibers)

- In the same line, circle the transition word that means "after 1982." (Later)

- Go to lines 29 and 30. Number the actions of Buell's victim. (1. escaped; 2. reported)

- Go to line 31. Mark the word that means "close study." (analysis)

- Go to line 33. Mark the word whose base word is *convict*. (convicted)

- Go to line 36. Circle the transition word that means "after conviction." (Later)

- Mark the word in the same sentence that means "admitted to being at fault." (confessed)

- Go to lines 37 and 38. Mark the event that saved the Ford Heights Four. (DNA testing had been developed.)

- Go to line 40. Mark the word that means "fair treatment." (justice)

- The title of the text is "The Science of Catching Criminals." This particular section is titled The Power of Forensic Science. How does this section connect to the title? Write the answer at the bottom of the page. (This section provides examples in which forensic science was used to catch a murderer and free others.)

Have partners compare text markings and correct any errors.

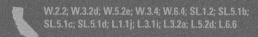
Lesson Opener

Before the lesson, choose one of the following activities to write on the board or post on the *LANGUAGE! Live* Class Wall online.

- *Dress your avatar as though he or she were a forensic scientist going to the scene of a murder. Describe his or her outfit and your reason for choosing the specific items.*
- *Write five sentences about criminal cases you are familiar with. Identify the simple subject and the simple predicate in each sentence.*
- *Write three sentences with at least two vocabulary words in each. Show you know the meanings. (innocence, evidence, fiber, trace, preserve, convict, unique, identify, suspect, witness)*

Vocabulary

Objective
- Review key passage vocabulary.

Recontextualize Passage Vocabulary

Direct students to page 18 in their Student Books. Use the following questions to review the vocabulary words from "The Science of Catching Criminals."

- How could you *preserve* your hairstyle on a very windy day? **(stay indoors)** Where could you *preserve* some ice cubes? **(in the freezer)** If you *preserve* something, what do you do to it? **(keep it the same)**

- Is each human being *unique*? **(yes)** Is your textbook *unique*? **(no)** If I lose a *unique* ring, could I find another one like it? **(no)**

- Were you a *witness* to the moon landing? **(no)** Were you a *witness* of people walking in the hallway this morning? **(yes)** If a friend tells you about a dream she had, are you a *witness* to the dream? **(no)**

- Is *innocence* the state of being guilty? **(no)** If someone accused you of sleeping during class, how would you show your *innocence*? **(by repeating what was discussed)** If you showed your *innocence*, would you be guilty of sleeping in class? **(no)**

- Is a jacket made up of *fibers*? **(yes)** Is sand made up of *fibers*? **(no)** Is a *fiber* more like a very tiny string, or a very tiny ball? **(a very tiny string)**

- If you are *convicted*, you are found to be what? **(guilty)** Is a person usually *convicted* in a hospital? **(no)** Is a person *convicted* in a church? **(no)** Is a person *convicted* in a court of law? **(yes)**

- Can a birthmark *identify* you? **(yes)** Can you *identify* all the countries in the world? **(no)** Can you *identify* your best friend's voice? **(yes)** When you *identify* something, do you recognize it, or does it stay a mystery? **(You recognize it.)**

- I have an apple. Is the apple *evidence* that I own an apple tree? **(no)** Is the apple *evidence* that there is an apple tree somewhere? **(yes)** What does *evidence* show? **(that something is true or happened)**

- Is there a *trace* of dirt on the floor? **(yes)** Is there a *trace* of volcanic ash on the floor? **(no)** Is a large amount of something a *trace*? **(no)**

- A *suspect* is thought to be possibly what? **(guilty)** Can a *suspect* be found innocent? **(yes)** If I am thought to be guilty of rudeness, am I a *suspect*? **(no)** A *suspect* is possibly guilty of what? **(a crime)**

Writing

Objectives

- Demonstrate an understanding of writing prompts.
- Orally retell key information from an informational text.
- Write a topic sentence.
- Use correct capitalization and quotation marks in titles.
- Write a summary.
- Use a rubric to guide and evaluate writing.

Six Traits of Effective Writing

Direct students to page 30 in their Student Books. Read aloud the six traits of writing and explain to students that as they progress through the program, they will learn to write effectively using all the traits. For now, they will focus on the basics of writing.

This unit's focus is on sentence fluency. In the description, it mentions varied sentence use and avoiding run-on sentences. Because those elements haven't been taught, we will focus our attention on avoiding sentence fragments. As you write your summary, be sure to use complete sentences that answer both the *who* or *what did it* and the *what did they do* questions. Remember, a sentence begins with a capital letter and ends with punctuation.

Eventually, sentence fluency will mean more than writing in complete sentences, but for this unit, that will be our focus.

Lesson 10 | Writing

Six Traits of Effective Writing

Trait	What does this mean?
Ideas and Content	• The writing meets the expectations of the assignment and answers the prompt. • The writing starts and ends in an interesting way. • Important ideas are fully developed, with enough elaborations and relevant details. • The content is strong, accurate, detailed, interesting, and appropriate to the audience.
Organization	• The purpose of the writing is clearly stated in the introduction. • Ideas are presented in a clear order (which aligns with the plan), with varied transitions to connect them? • For narrative writing: There is a clear beginning, middle, and end. • For informational and argumentative writing: There is a clear introduction, body, and conclusion. • Varied transitions connect ideas, facilitating the flow.
Voice and Audience Awareness	• The voice and style are appropriate to the purpose and audience? • The information is presented in the right tone and mood for the purpose and audience?
Word Choice	• Rich, interesting, and precise words are used. • Word choice is appropriate for the topic and audience.
Sentence Fluency	• Sentences are varied in structure and length. • There are no sentence fragments or run-on sentences.
Conventions	• The text doesn't contain errors in capitalization, usage, punctuation, or spelling. • Paragraphs are properly formatted.

Prepare to Write: Summary Paragraph

Direct students to pages 31 and 32 in their Student Books.

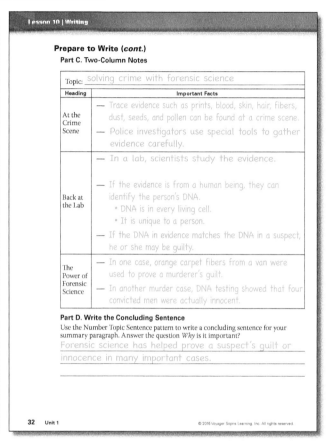

Lesson 10 | Writing

Prepare to Write. Summary Paragraph

Part A. Study the Prompt

Read the prompt and circle the topic. Underline the instructions.

Write a paragraph that summarizes the text "The Science of Catching Criminals." Make sure to include examples in your paragraph.

Part B. Write the Topic Sentence

Write an IVF topic sentence for your summary paragraph.

"The Science of Catching Criminals" reveals the value of forensic science in solving crimes.

© 2016 Voyager Sopris Learning, Inc. All rights reserved.   Unit 1   31

Lesson 10 | Writing

Prepare to Write (cont.)

Part C. Two-Column Notes

Topic: solving crime with forensic science

Heading	Important Facts
At the Crime Scene	— Trace evidence such as prints, blood, skin, hair, fibers, dust, seeds, and pollen can be found at a crime scene. — Police investigators use special tools to gather evidence carefully.
Back at the Lab	— In a lab, scientists study the evidence. — If the evidence is from a human being, they can identify the person's DNA. • DNA is in every living cell. • It is unique to a person. — If the DNA in evidence matches the DNA in a suspect, he or she may be guilty.
The Power of Forensic Science	— In one case, orange carpet fibers from a van were used to prove a murderer's guilt. — In another murder case, DNA testing showed that four convicted men were actually innocent.

Part D. Write the Concluding Sentence

Use the Number Topic Sentence pattern to write a concluding sentence for your summary paragraph. Answer the question *Why* is it important?

Forensic science has helped prove a suspect's guilt or innocence in many important cases.

32   Unit 1   © 2016 Voyager Sopris Learning, Inc. All rights reserved.

Part A. Study the Prompt

Read the instructions for Part A and the prompt aloud. The first thing we need to do is circle the topic. What is the topic? ("The Science of Catching Criminals") Now, let's underline the instructions. What is the first thing you need to underline? (Write a paragraph that **summarizes**) Are there any other instructions? (Yes, include examples.)

Part C. Two-Column Notes

We will come back to Part B and write the topic sentence after we have written some notes from the text. As you take notes, keep in mind our focus is to summarize. For a concise summary, we need to consider the big ideas from the text and find a way to condense the important information into one paragraph. **Direct students to Part C.** Let's complete the notes together, thinking about the important facts. When we consider the topic, let's think beyond the title. What is the passage about? (using science to solve crimes; solving crime with forensic science) **Have students write the topic.** The chart is organized according to headings. Let's work together to pull important facts from the text. We will then use the notes to summarize the text. **Direct students to the Close Reading on pages 27–29 of their Student Books.**

What is the first heading? (At the Crime Scene) Let's look for important facts in that section. What can be found at a crime scene? (evidence) What are some examples of trace evidence? (prints, blood, skin, hair, fibers, dust, seeds, pollen) How can we say this in a sentence? Use your own words. (Trace evidence such as prints, blood, skin, etc. can be found at a crime scene.) Write this sentence under Important Facts.

Who gathers the evidence? (police investigators) What do they use? (special tools) Are they careless or careful? (careful) How can we say all of this in a sentence? Use your own words. (Police investigators use special tools to gather evidence carefully.) Write that under Important Facts.

Let's move on to the next heading. What is it? (Back at the Lab) Let's look there for some important facts. Where does the evidence go? (to a special lab) What happens to it there? (Scientists run tests on it.) What can they learn? (what it is made of and where it came from) How can we say all this in a sentence, using our own words? (In a lab, scientists study the evidence to determine what it is made of and where it came from.) Write this under Important Facts. **Pause.** If the evidence is from a human, what can the scientists do? (identify DNA) Write this under Important Facts.

What is the next paragraph about? (DNA) What does DNA do? (tells cells how to grow) Where is it found? (in every cell) How is it like a fingerprint? (It is unique.) How does it help catch a criminal? (If it matches the DNA in a suspect's blood, it may prove the person's guilt.) Write three important facts about DNA under Important Facts in your own words.

What is the last heading? (The Power of Forensic Science) How many cases does this section describe? (two) What happened in the first case? (Orange carpet fibers from a van were used to prove a murderer's guilt.) Write this under Important Facts. **Pause.** What happened in the second case? (Four men were convicted of murder, but DNA testing later showed they were innocent.) Write this under Important Facts. Remember to use your own words. What do both cases have in common? (Forensic science brought justice.)

> **Note:** If students are having a hard time generating responses, provide clues and assistance in formulating these quick notes. The focus of the assignment is to write a good summary, so facts have been intentionally dropped into the teacher talk to help students move forward with the writing assignment. This scaffolding will fade as students become more proficient with their writing skills.

Topic Sentences: IVF and Number Sentences

Now that we've made some notes for our writing assignment, let's turn our attention to writing the topic sentence. **Direct students to page 33 in their Student Books.**

Earlier in this unit, you had the opportunity to practice writing IVF sentences. You wrote them to help you focus on the content of each section of the text. Let's review what the initials stand for. What does the *I* stand for? **(identify)** What does the *V* stand for? **(verb)** Finally, what does the *F* stand for? **(finish the thought)** Think about how you can write your own IVF statement to serve as a topic sentence for the summary paragraph. Look at the example sentence provided: *An article in the newspaper explained the suspicious circumstances surrounding the actor's death.* What is the source of information? **(a newspaper article)**

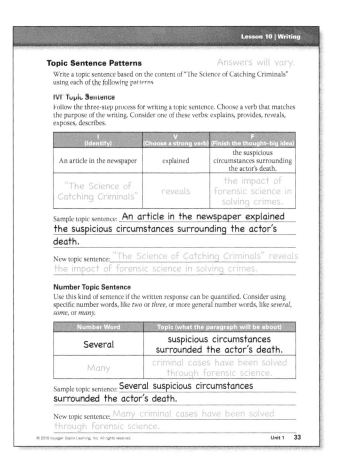

What is the verb? **(explained)** Notice the writer didn't choose a verb like *told* or *said*. Weak verbs won't hook a reader and that's what we want to do. Remember, verbs are the workhorses in a sentence, and in a topic sentence, the verb really helps us set the tone. What's the big idea in the article? **(the suspicious circumstances surrounding the actor's death)** That is how they finish the thought. Think about these three elements as you write your topic sentence.

Part B. Write the Topic Sentence

Solicit some ideas from the class orally for the I, V, and F. Remind students that they have a list of verbs from which they can choose and to look at the prompt if they need help with the big idea. Point out the use of capital letters on words over three letters and quotation marks when writing the title of an article. Then, give them a few minutes to write a topic sentence. Circulate around the room and monitor student progress. If students are struggling, provide a model sentence for them to use. Have volunteers share their topic sentences. Direct them back to page 31 in their Student Books and have them write their sentence in Part B.

Part D. Write the Concluding Sentence

Direct students back to page 33 in their Student Books. Any pattern that we examine for writing a topic sentence can also be used to help us end our paragraph. Good writers use topic sentences to help readers know what they can expect in a paragraph, and they also restate the topic sentence to help "wrap up" a paragraph. The concluding sentence gives writers a chance to emphasize why the information is important. Let's work on writing a Number Topic Sentence that we can use to restate our IVF topic sentence. It will become our concluding sentence.

Read the information about Number Topic Sentence. Then, read the example sentence.

Notice the number word isn't always an actual number. Here the example sentence uses *several*. The topic is still suspicious circumstances surrounding the actor's death. Read the sample topic sentence. Do you see how it nicely wraps up a summary of an article about the investigation of the actor's death? It provides a pattern that helps us vary our sentence structure while restating the focus of the paragraph. Use this pattern to restate your topic sentence about forensic science. What number words do you think would work for this paragraph? **(many, some)** We might have a hard time with a specific number. What about the topic? How can we identify the topic without using the name of the text? **(the role of forensic science in solving crimes; contributions of forensic science to solving crimes)** **Remind students to look at the prompt to determine the topic.**

Have students write a number topic sentence. If students are struggling, provide a model sentence for them to use. Have volunteers share their sentences. Direct them back to page 32 in their Student Books and have them write their sentence in Part D.

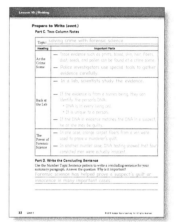

Write

Like a set of bookends, you have the sentences that will frame your summary paragraph. Look over your two-column notes. Read each one to yourself.

- If it's a complete sentence, does it make sense? Did you leave out any important words? If so, add them.

- If it isn't a complete sentence, what words could you add to make it complete? Remember, a sentence has a subject and a verb. When you say it out loud, it makes sense and sounds like a complete idea.

Give students time to look over their notes. Then, have students read their notes aloud to a partner. Ask your partner if your sentences sound complete and make sense. If not, work together to fix them.

When partners are finished working on their sentence, have students get out a clean sheet of notebook paper. Now it's time to write your summary paragraph. Begin your summary paragraph by writing your topic sentence from the middle of page 31. Because you are writing a paragraph, be sure to indent the first line. When you indent, you leave a space. **Show an example if necessary.**

You have the beginning of your paragraph. Next, you need to write the body of your paragraph. The body is all the sentences in the middle. Where do you think these sentences will come from? **(the two-column chart)** Yes. Because you took notes for each section of the text, in order, you can use your notes in the same order. You can write your sentences for each category, one after the other, to create the body of your paragraph. String your sentences together instead of starting each new sentence on a new line. **Monitor students as they work, providing guidance as needed.**

Once students have written the body of their paragraph, direct them to add their concluding sentence from the bottom of page 32.

Some students may need to be pulled into a small group and receive more support in getting their thoughts down on paper.

Exemplar Writing: Summary Paragraph:

"The Science of Catching Criminals" reveals the value of forensic science in solving crimes. Forensic science is the science used to show a person's guilt or innocence. Its goal is to use evidence to catch a criminal. Trace evidence such as prints, blood, skin, hair, fibers, dust, and other particles can be found at a crime scene. Police investigators use special tools to gather the evidence carefully. Then, in a lab, scientists study the evidence. If the evidence is from a human being, they can identify the person's DNA. DNA is in every living cell. It is unique to a person. If the DNA in evidence matches a suspect's, he or she may be guilty. In one case, carpet fibers from a van were used to prove a murderer's guilt. In another, DNA testing showed that four men convicted of murder were innocent. Many criminal cases have been solved through forensic science.

Student Handwriting:

Handwriting lessons are provided in manuscript and cursive. These explicit lessons (found online in Resources) can be taught systematically during writing lessons to strengthen legibility and fluency.

When students have completed their summaries, have them evaluate their writing using the Writer's Checklist on page 34. This can be done independently or by a peer.

Note: Because paragraph structure has not been taught yet, students' summary paragraphs may or may not be broken into paragraphs. Accept paragraphs, such as the sample, that are overly informative with very little structure.

Note: Use Six Traits of Writing Scoring Rubric: Basic on page 564 of this book to assess students' writing. A printable version is located online in the Teacher Resources.

Lesson 10 | Writing

The Writer's Checklist

	Trait	Yes	No	Did the writer . . .?
R	Ideas and Content			focus all sentences on the topic
E				provide supporting details for the topic sentence
V	Organization			write a topic sentence
I				tell things in an order that makes sense
S				write a concluding sentence
E	Voice and Audience Awareness			think about the audience and purpose for writing
	Word Choice			try to find a unique way to say things
	Sentence Fluency			write complete sentences
	Conventions			capitalize words correctly:
				capitalize the first word of each sentence
E				capitalize proper nouns, including people's names
D				punctuate correctly:
I				put a period or question mark at the end of each sentence
				use grammar correctly:
T				use the correct verb tense
				make sure the verb agrees with the subject in number
				use correct spelling

34   Unit 1

© 2016 Voyager Sopris Learning, Inc. All rights reserved

Six Traits of Writing: Basic

Objectives

- Answer questions to demonstrate comprehension of text.
- Engage in class discussion.
- Identify the enduring understandings from a piece of text.
- Self-correct as comprehension of text deepens.

Revisit Passage Comprehension

Direct students to page 26 in their Student Books. Have students review their answers and make any necessary changes. Then, have partners share their answers and collaborate to perfect them.

Enduring Understandings

Direct students back to page 17 in their Student Books. Reread the Big Idea questions.

Is punishment always just?

How does science influence crime and punishment?

Generate a class discussion about the questions and the answers students came up with in Lesson 6. Have them consider whether their answers have changed any after reading the text.

Use the following talking points to foster conversation. Refer to the Class Discussion Rules poster and have students use the Collegial Discussion sentence frames on page 382 of their Students Books.

- Occasionally, innocent people are punished. And many people believe that some crimes are just. Are there crimes that shouldn't be punished? Are there punishments that are too harsh or too easy for the crimes?

What we read should make us think. Use our discussion and your thoughts about the text to determine what you will "walk away with." Has the text made you think about a personal experience or someone you know? Has your perspective or opinion of crime and punishment changed? Do you have any lingering thoughts or questions? Write these ideas as your enduring understandings. What will you take with you from this text?

Discuss the enduring understandings with the class. Then, have students write their enduring understandings from the unit.

Have students consider why the author wrote the passage and whether he or she was successful.

End-of-Unit Online Assessments

Monitor students' progress in the unit by utilizing online assessments. Students should prioritize these assessments over successive Word Training units.

- Assign Unit 1 Content Mastery quizzes to assess skills taught in this unit.
- Assign Power Pass to assess reading comprehension skills in a standardized test format.

All assessments can be assigned online by opening the Tools menu, then selecting Assignments. Be sure to select the correct class and unit from the drop-down menu.

Reteach

Based on students' performance in Content Mastery, extra practice may be needed.

- If student scores fall at 60 percent or below, reteach the content to small groups.
- If student scores fall between 61–79 percent, reinforce the skills by assigning the student reteach activity pages as homework.

Reteach lessons can be found online on the Course Reports page for each unit.

Comprehension Building

Background knowledge is a key component of reading comprehension. It is important for students to develop knowledge of a topic prior to class discussion and reading of complex text.

Print Unit 2 Background Information from the online Resources and assign as homework for students to read. Encourage students to come to class prepared for discussion.

Unit Big Ideas

- Can a brief, chance encounter make a lasting impact?
- Do people always need to be punished for their crimes?
- Are we in control of our lives?
- To what degree do the choices we make as teens affect our futures?

Instructional Texts

"Thank You, M'am" by Langston Hughes
  Text type: literature—short story

"If I Were in Charge of the World" by Judith Viorst
  Text type: literature—poetry

"We Real Cool" by Gwendolyn Brooks
  Text type: literature—poetry

 Materials

- *Unit 2 video (The Great Migration)*
- *"We Real Cool" audio file*
- *Critical Understandings posters—display in classroom*
- *Six Traits of Writing Scoring Rubric: Basic (print as needed)*

Optional
- *Unit 2 Background Information*
- *Progress Monitoring Across the Six Traits scales*

Classroom Materials

- *Highlighters or colored pencils*
- *Notebook paper*

 Instructional Resources

- *Unit 2 Reteach*
- *Handwriting Lessons*

- *Unit 3 Background Information (assign as homework at the end of the unit)*
- *Writing Project: Informational*

- *Progress Monitoring Across the Six Traits scales (one per trait for each student, to be used with Writing Projects)*

Instructional Texts:

"Thank You, M'am"
by Langston Hughes

Text type: literature—short story

"If I Were in Charge of the World"
by Judith Viorst

Text type: literature—poetry

"We Real Cool"
by Gwendolyn Brooks

Text type: literature—poetry

LANGUAGE! Live Online

Grammar Practice
- Use proper capitalization and punctuation in a sentence.
- Use plural and possessive nouns correctly.
- Distinguish between action verbs and linking verbs.
- Use adverbs correctly.
- Use prepositions correctly.
- Use pronouns correctly.

Vocabulary Practice
- Determine the correct usage of multiple-meaning words.

Content Mastery
- Demonstrate an understanding of . . .
  - word meaning by answering questions and using words in sentences.
  - pronouns and their antecedents.
  - the purpose of adverbs and prepositional phrases.
  - preposition meaning and usage.

Word Study
- Blend, read, and spell words with consonant blends; r-controlled vowels; vowel teams and diphthongs; and soft -c and soft -g.
- Read connected text to build fluency.

Lesson 1

Reading
- Determine and discuss the topic of a text.
- Determine and discuss the author's purpose.
- Use text features to preview text.

Vocabulary
- Evaluate word knowledge.
- Determine the meaning of key passage vocabulary.

Reading
- Read a short story.
- Monitor comprehension during text reading.
- Analyze the interactions of story elements in a short story.
- Distinguish between standard and nonstandard English.

See pg. 87 for additional lesson objectives.

Lesson 2

Vocabulary
- Review key passage vocabulary.

Grammar
- Understand the function and purpose of nouns.
- Distinguish between types of nouns.
- Understand the function and purpose of pronouns.
- Distinguish between types of pronouns.
- Understand the function and purpose of verbs.

See pg. 96 for additional lesson objectives.

Writing
- Use adverbs and prepositional phrases correctly in sentence writing.
- Produce, expand, and rearrange complete sentences.

Lesson 6

Reading
- Determine and discuss the topic of a text.
- Determine and discuss the author's purpose.
- Use text features to preview text.

Vocabulary
- Evaluate word knowledge.
- Determine the meaning of key passage vocabulary.

Reading
- Read poetry.
- Monitor comprehension during text reading.
- Compare a poem with its audio production.
- Identify the point of view in poetry.
- Use word choice to determine the tone of a poem.
- Determine the function of subjunctive verbs.
- Summarize poetry.

Lesson 7

Vocabulary
- Review key passage vocabulary.

Writing
- Understand the function and purpose of prepositions and prepositional phrases.
- Use prepositions correctly.
- Use adverbs and prepositional phrases correctly in sentence writing.
- Produce, expand, and rearrange complete sentences.
- Use commas to set off prepositional phrases.

Grammar
- Identify the function and purpose of pronouns.
- Use pronouns correctly.
- Use pronouns to determine author's point of view.

Reading
- Identify the structure and form of poetry.
- Analyze the impact of word choice, graphical elements, and rhyme in poetry.

Writing Project: Informational

Lesson 3

Reading

- Establish a purpose for rereading literary text.
- Demonstrate an understanding of how to ask questions and answer them appropriately.
- Use critical thinking skills to write responses to prompts about text.
- Support written answers with text evidence.
- Identify how a character changes over time.
- Determine the meaning of figurative language in text.

Lesson 4

Vocabulary

- Review key passage vocabulary.

Reading

- Read literary text with purpose and understanding.
- Answer questions to demonstrate comprehension of text.
- Identify and explain explicit details from text.
- Monitor comprehension of text during reading.
- Determine the meaning of figurative language in text.
- Match pronouns to their antecedents.
- Distinguish between standard and nonstandard English.
- Compare and contrast the experiences of characters in stories.

Lesson 5

Vocabulary

- Review key passage vocabulary.

Writing

- Analyze literary characters.
- Use descriptive words in writing.
- Write in response to text.

Reading

- Self-correct as comprehension of text deepens.
- Answer questions to demonstrate comprehension of text.
- Engage in class discussion.
- Identify the enduring understandings from a piece of text.

Lesson 8

Reading

- Read poetry.
- Monitor comprehension during text reading.
- Use critical thinking skills to write responses to prompts about text.
- Support written answers with text evidence.

Lesson 9

Vocabulary

- Review key passage vocabulary.

Reading

- Read poetry with purpose and understanding.
- Answer questions to demonstrate comprehension of text.
- Identify and explain explicit details from text.
- Monitor comprehension during text reading.
- Identify the purpose of the literary epigraph.
- Identify the impact of alliterations in poetry.

Lesson 10

Vocabulary

- Review key passage vocabulary.

Writing

- Analyze word choice in writing.
- Use exemplar text to write poetry.
- Use a process to write.
- Recite poetry.

Reading

- Self-correct as comprehension of text deepens.
- Answer questions to demonstrate comprehension of text.
- Engage in class discussion.
- Identify the enduring understandings from a piece of text.

Lesson Opener

Before the lesson, choose one of the following activities to write on the board or post on the *LANGUAGE! Live* Class Wall online.

- *Write a sentence about a crime that is just. Rewrite the sentence using a pronoun.*
- *Describe a time when someone helped you.*
- *Write three sentences about a time you helped someone and received nothing in return. Identify the nouns and verbs in each sentence.*

Reading

Objectives

- Determine and discuss the topic of a text.
- Determine and discuss the author's purpose.
- Use text features to preview text.

Passage Introduction

Direct students to page 35 in their Student Books. Discuss the content focus.

Content Focus

forgiveness; empowerment

What do you think this story will be about? (Answers will vary.)

Have you ever been forgiven for a mistake that you made? Have you ever felt empowered to be a better person after making a mistake or being forgiven? **Provide sharing time.**

Type of Text

literature

In Unit 1, we read a chapter from the fiction novel *Holes*. A chapter is part of a larger piece of literature. Today, we are going to read another type of literature called a short story. "Thank You, M'am" is not part of a larger piece of literature. It is one story in a book of stories. Each story can stand alone. This story is told by a narrator in third-person point of view. That means that the person telling the story is not a character in the story. The narrator is outside the story. Where is the narrator? (outside the story)

Unit
2

Lesson 1 | Reading

Let's Focus: "Thank You, M'am"

Content Focus
forgiveness; empowerment

Type of Text
literature—short story

Author's Name Langston Hughes **Author's Purpose** to entertain; to teach a lesson

Big Ideas
Consider the following Big Idea questions. Write your answer for each question.

Can a brief, chance encounter make a lasting impact?

_____

_____

Do people always need to be punished for their crimes?

_____

_____

Narrative Preview Checklist: "Thank You, M'am" on pages 37–41.

☐ Title: What clue does it provide about the passage?

☐ Pictures: What additional information is added here?

☐ Margin Information: What vocabulary is important to understand this story?

Enduring Understandings
After reading the text . . .

_____

_____

_____

_____

_____

© 2018 Voyager Sopris Learning, Inc. All rights reserved.   Unit 2   35

Author's Purpose

Have students glance at the first page of the text. Who is the author of the story? (Langston Hughes) The author's purpose is the reason that he or she wrote the text. Authors write for different purposes. They write to entertain, to persuade, or to inform or teach. Knowing an author's purpose can help a reader better understand a text. "Thank You, Ma'm" was written to entertain us. Have students write the answers on the page. Sometimes, authors teach a moral through storytelling. A moral is an ethical message. A moral teaches us a life lesson. What does a moral teach? (a life lesson)

Play the Unit 2 Text Training video found in the Teacher Resources online.

Before we read "Thank You, M'am," we will watch a short video to help build our background knowledge. Play the Unit 2 Text Training video. Have partners discuss the main points the videographer was trying to make and what evidence was provided to support the points.

Note: Additional Background Information about the Harlem Renaissance can be found in the Teacher Resources online. Choose the Text Training tab, and then select Unit 2. The Background Information will be in the first section.

Direct students to page 35 in their Student Books. Read the Big Idea questions aloud.

Big Ideas

Can a brief, chance encounter make a lasting impact?

Do people always need to be punished for their crimes?

As a class, consider the two Big Idea questions.

- Encourage students with limited understanding of the concept of chance to ask for further explanation from peers.

- Have students reflect on the Background Information for the unit and ask clarifying questions when needed.

- Provide opportunities for students to explain their ideas and answers to the Big Idea questions in light of the discussion by ensuring students follow the rules for class discussion, which can be printed in poster form from the Teacher Resources online.

- Suggest students refer to the Collegial Discussion sentence frames in the back of their books.

- Encourage speakers to link comments to the remarks of others to keep the focus of the discussion and create cohesion, even when their comments are in disagreement.

After discussing each question, have students write an answer. We'll come back to these questions after we finish reading the story. You can add to your answers as you gain information and perspective.

Preview

Read the Narrative Preview Checklist on page 35. Follow the Preview Procedure outlined below.

> ### Preview Procedure
> - Group students with partners or in triads.
> - Have students count off as 1s or 2s. The 1s will become the student leaders. If working with triads, the third students become 3s.
> - The student leaders will preview the text in addition to managing the checklist and pacing.
> - The 2s and 3s will preview the text with 1s.
> - Direct 1s to open their Student Books to page 35 and 2s and 3s to open their Student Books to page 37. This allows students to look at a few different pages at one time without turning back and forth.

If it is necessary, guide students in a short preview using the following talking points. What is the title? ("Thank You, M'am") What clue does the title provide about the passage? Provide sharing time. Who do we call M'am? (a respected lady or woman; *M'am* is short for *madam*.) Let's look to see what additional information the illustrations provide. What do you see? (a black woman; a young boy trying to steal her purse; an urban neighborhood; the boy looks thoughtful at the end)

Objectives
- Evaluate word knowledge.
- Determine the meaning of key passage vocabulary.

Rate Vocabulary Knowledge

Direct students to page 36 in their Student Books. Let's take a look at the vocabulary words from "Thank You, M'am," the first text we will read in this unit. I am going to say each word aloud. You will repeat the word and write it in the third column. Then, you will rate your knowledge of the word. Display the Vocabulary Rating Scale poster or write the information on the board. Review the meaning of each rating.

Key Passage Vocabulary: "Thank You, M'am"

Read each word. Write the word in column 3. Then, circle a number to rate your knowledge of the word.

Vocabulary	Part of Speech	Write the Word	Knowledge Rating
balance	(n)	balance	0 1 2 3
permit	(v)	permit	0 1 2 3
release	(v)	release	0 1 2 3
frail	(adj)	frail	0 1 2 3
furnished	(adj)	furnished	0 1 2 3
suede	(n)	suede	0 1 2 3
presentable	(adj)	presentable	0 1 2 3
embarrass	(v)	embarrass	0 1 2 3
latch	(v)	latch	0 1 2 3
stoop	(n)	stoop	0 1 2 3

36   Unit 2

© 2016 Voyager Sopris Learning, Inc. All rights reserved.

Vocabulary Rating Scale

0—I have never heard the word before.

1—I have heard the word, but I'm not sure how to use it.

2—I am familiar with the word, but I'm not sure if I know the correct meaning.

3—I know the meaning of the word and can use it correctly in a sentence.

Remember, the points are there to help you know which words you need to focus on. By the end of this unit, you should be able to change all your ratings to a 3—that's the goal.

Read each word aloud and have students repeat it, write it, and rate it. Then, have volunteers who rated a word *2* or *3* use the word in an oral sentence.

Preteach Vocabulary

Explain that you will now take a closer look at the words. Follow the Preteach Procedure outlined below.

Preteach Procedure

This activity is intended to take only a short amount of time, so make it an oral exercise.

- Introduce each word as indicated on the word card.
- Read the definition and example sentences.
- Ask questions to clarify and deepen understanding.
- If time permits, allow students to share.

* If your students would benefit from copying the definitions, please have them do so in the vocabulary log in the back of the Student Books using the margin definitions in the passage selections. This should be done outside of instruction time.

---

balance (n)

Let's read the first word together. *Balance*.

Definition: *Balance* means "the ability to stay steady and not fall." What means "the ability to stay steady and not fall"? (balance)

Example 1: I tripped, lost my *balance*, and fell.

Example 2: I am amazed that models and dancers can keep their *balance* in such high heels.

Example 3: Some people use a cane to keep their *balance*.

Question 1: Is it hard to keep your *balance* when dizzy? Yes or no? (yes)

Question 2: Is it easy to keep your *balance* when lying down? Yes or no? (yes)

Pair Share: Turn to your partner and tell about a time you lost your *balance*.

(1)

permit (v)

Let's read the next word together. *Permit*.

Definition: *Permit* means "to allow." What means "to allow"? (permit)

Example 1: During passing periods and lunch, you are *permitted* to use your phone.

Example 2: If it is an emergency, most teachers will *permit* you to use the restroom during class.

Example 3: I *permit* my children to have one soda per week.

Question 1: Would your parents *permit* you to miss a week of school for relaxation purposes? Yes or no? (no)

Question 2: Will you be *permitted* into a concert without a ticket? Yes or no? (no)

Pair Share: Turn to your partner and tell what you wish your parents would *permit* you to do, but they won't.

(2)

release (v)

Let's read the next word together. *Release.*

Definition: *Release* means "to let go of; to set free." What means "to let go of; to set free"? (release)

Example 1: If you *release* a balloon, it will float away.

Example 2: Some people want to *release* zoo animals from their cages.

Example 3: After they are *released*, prisoners must get used to being free again.

Question 1: Are students *released* from school at the end of the day? Yes or no? (yes)

Question 2: Is it sometimes hard to *release* hurt feelings? Yes or no? (yes)

Pair Share: Turn to your partner and tell about a time you were *released* from an unpleasant task or duty.

(3)

frail (adj)

Let's read the next word together. *Frail.*

Definition: *Frail* means "weak and easily broken." What means "weak and easily broken"? (frail)

Example 1: Older people are sometimes thin and *frail*.

Example 2: If you have *frail* bones, they are prone to fractures.

Example 3: A *frail* tree will likely snap on a windy day.

Question 1: Is a *frail* person healthy and strong? Yes or no? (no)

Question 2: Could a *frail* person win a boxing match? Yes or no? (no)

Pair Share: Turn to your partner and describe a person you know who is *frail*.

(4)

furnished (adj)

Let's read the next word together. *Furnished.*

Definition: *Furnished* means "having furniture, appliances, or basic supplies." What means "having furniture, appliances, or basic supplies"? (furnished)

Example 1: People who do not own furniture can rent a *furnished* apartment.

Example 2: Some hotel rooms are nicely *furnished*; others have a bed only.

Example 3: The soldiers' *furnished* barracks contained bunk beds and sinks.

Question 1: Is this a *furnished* classroom? Yes or no? (yes)

Question 2: Does a *furnished* kitchen have dishes, pots, and pans? Yes or no? (yes)

Pair Share: Turn to your partner and describe your idea of an amazingly *furnished* hangout room.

(5)

suede (n)

Let's read the next word together. *Suede.*

Definition: *Suede* is soft, velvety leather. What is soft, velvety leather called? (suede)

Example 1: *Suede* boots keep your feet warm on a cold day.

Example 2: Items made of *suede* should be cleaned and brushed every so often.

Example 3: *Suede* pajamas would be hot and uncomfortable.

Question 1: Is *suede* rough and hard? Yes or no? (no)

Question 2: Could a hat be made of *suede*? Yes or no? (yes)

Pair Share: Turn to your partner and tell what accessory you would like to have in *suede*.

(6)

presentable (adj)

Let's read the next word together. *Presentable*.

Definition: If something is *presentable*, it is fit to appear in public. What means "fit to appear in public"? (presentable)

Example 1: Many people do not feel *presentable* when they get out of bed in the morning.

Example 2: I like to paint, but my paintings would not be *presentable* in a museum.

Example 3: People in bathing suits are not *presentable* in a fancy restaurant.

Question 1: If you are *presentable*, are you clean? Yes or no? (yes)

Question 2: Would you want to look *presentable* when meeting someone you admire? Yes or no? (yes)

Pair Share: Turn to your partner and tell three things that make a person look *presentable*, in your opinion.

(7)

embarrass (v)

Let's read the next word together. *Embarrass*.

Definition: *Embarrass* means "to make someone uncomfortable or ashamed." What means "to make someone uncomfortable or ashamed"? (embarrass)

Example 1: It *embarrasses* some people to be praised in front of others.

Example 2: If you *embarrass* a friend, you should quickly apologize.

Example 3: I have a friend who tries to *embarrass* me by causing a scene in restaurants.

Question 1: Does it *embarrass* some people to sing in public? Yes or no? (yes)

Question 2: Does it *embarrass* you to drink water? Yes or no? (no)

Pair Share: Turn to your partner and tell about something that *embarrassed* you when you were younger.

(8)

latch (v)

Let's read the next word together. *Latch*.

Definition: *Latch* means "to grip; to fasten onto." What means "to grip; to fasten onto"? (latch)

Example 1: Bear cubs *latch* onto each other when they are playing.

Example 2: Small children sometimes *latch* onto a parent when they are afraid.

Example 3: It is easy to build towers with small plastic building blocks that *latch* onto each other.

Question 1: Does a train car *latch* onto the tracks? Yes or no? (yes)

Question 2: Do raindrops *latch* onto a windowpane? Yes or no? (no)

Pair Share: Turn to your partner and tell whether you have anything *latched* onto your backpack.

(9)

stoop (n)

Let's read the last word together. *Stoop*.

Definition: A *stoop* is a small porch. What is a small porch called? (a stoop)

Example 1: Some people like to sit on their *stoop* on warm evenings.

Example 2: You often find potted plants on a *stoop*.

Example 3: If a house is raised, you may climb steps to reach its *stoop*.

Question 1: Is a *stoop* inside? Yes or no? (no)

Question 2: Is there a door on one side of a *stoop*? Yes or no? (yes)

Pair Share: Turn to your partner and tell whether your home has a *stoop*. If it does, tell what can be found on it.

(10)

Objectives
- Read a short story.
- Monitor comprehension during text reading.
- Analyze the interactions of story elements in a short story.
- Distinguish between standard and nonstandard English.
- Determine the impact of the author's word choice on the story.
- Make and verify predictions about what will happen next in a story.

"Thank You, M'am"

Direct students to page 37 in their Student Books.

Now that we are familiar with the vocabulary words, it's time to read. You will be reading a story with characters. One way to pay attention to the characters is to keep track of the dialogue, or who is talking. Dialogue is noted with quotation marks. **Write a sample on the board.** Please skim the text and find the first piece of dialogue noted with quotation marks. Does the first paragraph include dialogue? **(no)** How do you know? **(no quotation marks)** How about the second paragraph? **("Pick up my pocketbook, boy, and give it here.")** Who is talking? **(the woman)** How can you tell? **(the words *After that the woman said*, plus quotation marks)** Tell your partner the next piece of dialogue. **("Now ain't you ashamed of yourself?")** Who is talking? **(the woman)** How can you tell? **(the words *Then she said*)** Find the next piece of dialogue. Who is talking now? **(the boy)** What did he say? **("Yes'm")** What does that mean? **(yes, M'am)** What is *M'am* short for? **(madam)**

I will read the first paragraph to model the reading behaviors of a good reader. While I read aloud, your eyes should be on the text. Follow along using your writing utensil as a pointer.

Read the first paragraph aloud.

SE p. 37, paragraph 1

> She was a large woman with a large purse that had everything in it but a hammer and nails. It had a long strap, and she carried it slung across her shoulder. It was about eleven o'clock at night, dark, and she was walking alone, when a boy ran up behind her and tried to snatch her purse. The strap broke with the single tug the boy gave it from behind. But the boy's weight and the weight of the purse combined caused him to lose his **balance**. Instead of taking off full blast as he had hoped, the boy fell on his back on the sidewalk, and his legs flew up. The large woman simply turned around and kicked him right square in his blue-jeaned sitter. Then she reached down, picked the boy up by his shirtfront, and shook him until his teeth rattled.

What do you notice at the end of this paragraph? (a number) I want you to stop and think while reading, which is why the numbers are there. Sometimes it is helpful to make a prediction about will happen next. **Have students read the question in the margin that corresponds to the number.** (1. What do you think the woman will do next?) Let me model thinking after reading this first paragraph. I predict that the large woman will yell at him very loudly so that others gather and help her. I will check my prediction after the next section to see if it was accurate. What do you think will happen? **Have volunteers share their predictions.** Don't stop long enough to let your mind wander away from the text. This should be a brief pause to gather your thoughts.

Guiding Students Toward Independent Reading

It is important that your students read as much as and as often as they can. Assign readings that meet the needs of your students, based on your observations and data. This is a good opportunity to stretch your students. If students become frustrated, scaffold the reading with paired reading, choral reading, or a read-aloud.

Options for reading text:

- Teacher read-aloud
- Teacher-led or student-led choral read
- Paired read or independent read

Choose an option for reading the remainder of the text. Have students read according to the option that you chose. If you choose to read the text aloud or chorally, use the text on the following pages and stop to ask questions and have students answer them.

SE p. 37,
paragraphs 2–6

After that the woman said, "Pick up my pocketbook, boy, and give it here."

She still held him tightly. But she bent down enough to **permit** him to stoop and pick up her purse. Then she said, "Now ain't you ashamed of yourself?"

Firmly gripped by his shirtfront, the boy said, "Yes'm."

The woman said, "What did you want to do it for?"

The boy said, "I didn't aim to."

She said, "You a lie!"

SE p. 38,
paragraphs 1–8

By that time two or three people passed, stopped, turned to look, and some stood watching.

"If I turn you loose, will you run?" asked the woman.

"Yes'm," said the boy.

"Then I won't turn you loose," said the woman. She did not **release** him.

"Lady, I'm sorry," whispered the boy.

"Um-hum! Your face is dirty. I got a great mind to wash your face for you. Ain't you got nobody home to tell you to wash your face?"

"No'm," said the boy.

"Then it will get washed this evening," said the large woman, starting up the street, dragging the frightened boy behind her.

Clearly my prediction wasn't accurate because the woman didn't need anyone's help.

2. Where is the woman taking the boy?

SE p. 38,
paragraphs 9–14

He looked as if he were fourteen or fifteen, **frail** and willow-wild, in tennis shoes and blue jeans.

The woman said, "You ought to be my son. I would teach you right from wrong. Least I can do right now is to wash your face. Are you hungry?"

"No'm," said the being-dragged boy. "I just want you to turn me loose."

"Was I bothering *you* when I turned that corner?" asked the woman.

"No'm."

"But you put yourself in contact with *me*," said the woman. "If you think that that contact is not going to last awhile, you got another thought coming. When I get through with you, sir, you are going to remember Mrs. Luella Bates Washington Jones."

3. Why does Mrs. Jones want the boy to remember her?

SE p. 38,
paragraphs 15–17

Sweat popped out on the boy's face and he began to struggle. Mrs. Jones stopped, jerked him around in front of her, put a half-nelson about his neck, and continued to drag him up the street. When she got to her door, she dragged the boy inside, down a hall, and into a large kitchenette-**furnished** room at the rear of the house. She switched on the light and left the door open. The boy could hear other roomers laughing and talking in the large house. Some of their doors were open, too, so he knew he and the woman were not alone. The woman still had him by the neck in the middle of her room.

She said, "What is your name?"

"Roger," answered the boy.

SE p. 39, paragraph 1

"Then, Roger, you go to that sink and wash your face," said the woman, whereupon she turned him loose—at last. Roger looked at the door—looked at the woman—looked at the door—*and went to the sink*.

4. Why didn't Roger run?

SE p. 39,
paragraphs 2–7

"Let the water run until it gets warm," she said. "Here's a clean towel."

"You gonna take me to jail?" asked the boy, bending over the sink.

"Not with that face, I would not take you nowhere," said the woman. "Here I am trying to get home to cook me a bite to eat, and you snatch my pocketbook! Maybe you ain't been to your supper either, late as it be. Have you?"

"There's nobody home at my house," said the boy.

"Then we'll eat," said the woman, "I believe you're hungry—or been hungry—to try to snatch my pocketbook!"

"I wanted a pair of blue **suede** shoes," said the boy.

5. Was Roger stealing to get something he wants or something he needs?

SE p. 39,
paragraphs 8–11

"Well, you didn't have to snatch *my* pocketbook to get some suede shoes," said Mrs. Luella Bates Washington Jones. "You could of asked me."

"M'am?"

The water dripping from his face, the boy looked at her. There was a long pause. A very long pause. After he had dried his face and not knowing what else to do dried it again, the boy turned around, wondering what next. The door was open. He could make a dash for it down the hall. He could run, run, run, run, *run*!

The woman was sitting on the daybed. After a while she said, "I were young once and I wanted things I could not get."

6. What is Mrs. Jones trying to do?

E p. 39,
aragraphs 12–13

There was another long pause. The boy's mouth opened. Then he frowned, not knowing he frowned.

The woman said, "Um-hum! You thought I was going to say *but*, didn't you? You thought I was going to say, *but I didn't snatch people's pocketbooks*. Well, I wasn't going to say that." Pause. Silence. "I have done things, too, which I would not tell you, son—neither tell God, if He didn't already know. Everybody's got something in common. So you set down while I fix us something to eat. You might run that comb through your hair so you will look **presentable**."

E p. 40, paragraph 1

In another corner of the room behind a screen was a gas plate and an icebox. Mrs. Jones got up and went behind the screen. The woman did not watch the boy to see if he was going to run now, nor did she watch her purse, which she left behind her on the daybed. But the boy took care to sit on the far side of the room, away from the purse, where he thought she could easily see him out of the corner of her eye if she wanted to. He did not trust the woman *not* to trust him. And he did not want to be mistrusted now.

7. Reread the last two sentences. What does this mean?

SE p. 40,
paragraphs 2–6

"Do you need somebody to go to the store," asked the boy, "maybe to get some milk or something?"

"Don't believe I do," said the woman, "unless you just want sweet milk yourself. I was going to make cocoa out of this canned milk I got here."

"That will be fine," said the boy.

She heated some lima beans and ham she had in the icebox, made the cocoa, and set the table. The woman did not ask the boy anything about where he lived, or his folks, or anything else that would **embarrass** him. Instead, as they ate, she told him about her job in a hotel beauty shop that stayed open late, what the work was like, and how all kinds of women came in and out, blondes, red-heads, and Spanish. Then she cut him a half of her ten-cent cake.

"Eat some more, son," she said.

8. Why is Mrs. Jones being so nice to someone who tried to steal from her?

SE p. 40, paragraphs 7–9

When they were finished eating, she got up and said, "Now, here, take this ten dollars and buy yourself some blue suede shoes. And next time, do not make the mistake of **latching** onto *my* pocketbook *nor nobody else's* because shoes come by devilish like that will burn your feet. I got to get my rest now. But from here on in, son, I hope you will behave yourself."

She led him down the hall to the front door and opened it. "Goodnight! Behave yourself, boy!" she said, looking out into the street as he went down the steps.

The boy wanted to say something else other than "Thank you, m'am" to Mrs. Luella Bates Washington Jones, but although his lips moved, he couldn't even say that as he turned at the foot of the barren **stoop** and looked up at the large woman in the door. Then she shut the door.

9. Is this how the story should have ended?

For confirmation of engagement, take 30 seconds to have students share one prediction with their partner about what could happen next. Have volunteers share predictions with the class.

Author's Choice of Language

Ask students what they notice about the language in the text.

Do the characters use standard English, like we are taught in school, or nonstandard English, like some people use in informal settings? (nonstandard) **Have students provide an example from the text.** Clearly, the author knows how to use standard English because it is used throughout the story. It is only the dialogue that is nonstandard. Why would the author do this? (to help the reader understand the characters and the setting)

Story Elements

Draw a simple story map like the one on the next page on the board.

Discuss story elements with students, then lead them in completing the story map for "Thank You, M'am."

Setting: Time and place of story
Characters: People, animals, or things that interact in the story
Initiating Event: Problem that starts the story
Conflict: Plot or sequence of events
Climax: Turning point
Resolution: The solution to the problem
Conclusion: The situation at story's end

Story Map

Story Title "Thank You, M'am"

Introduction

Setting

11 p.m.; city; apartment

_____

_____

Characters

Roger; Mrs. Luella Bates
Washington Jones

_____

Conflict (rising action)

Climax!

Mrs. Jones grabs Roger into a
full-nelson and drags him to her
apartment.

_____

_____

_____

Roger admits he will run if released.

_____

_____

Roger struggles to get free.

_____

_____

Initiating Event

Roger snatches Mrs. Jones's
pocketbook; she kicks Roger
in the behind.

_____

_____

Resolution

Mrs. Jones gives Roger ten dollars for
him to get some blue suede shoes.

_____

_____

Conclusion

Roger leaves the room trying to say
thank you to Mrs. Jones before she
shuts the door.

_____

_____

Lesson Opener

Before the lesson, choose one of the following activities to write on the board or post on the *LANGUAGE! Live* Class Wall online.

- *Describe the setting in "Thank You, M'am."*
- *Identify the nouns, verbs, and pronouns in the following sentences.*
    Roger wanted a pair of blue suede shoes but didn't have the money to buy them.
    She wanted to trust him not to run but didn't know him well enough yet.
- *Write sentences with* release *and* embarrass, *using them as past-tense verbs.*

Vocabulary

Objective

- Review key passage vocabulary.

Review Passage Vocabulary

Direct students to page 36 in their Student Books. Use the following questions to review the vocabulary words from "Thank You, M'am." Have students answer each question using the vocabulary word or indicating its meaning in a complete sentence.

- What causes Roger to lose his *balance*? (His own weight and the weight of the purse cause him to lose his balance.) If he had kept his *balance*, what did he plan to do? (If he had kept his balance, he planned to run off with Mrs. Jones's purse.)

- What does Mrs. Jones *permit* Roger to do once they are in the house? (She permits him to eat and wash his face.) Is it easy or hard for her to *permit* him to move about her apartment? Why? (It is hard. She has no idea if she can trust him or not, so permitting him to move about near her purse must be difficult.)

- Mrs. Jones asks Roger what he will do if she *releases* him. What does he say? (He admits he will run away.) When does she finally *release* him? (She releases him only when they have reached the room where she lives.)

- Which of the two characters is more *frail*, Roger or Mrs. Jones? (Roger is the more frail of the two.) Does Mrs. Jones make Roger more *frail*, or does she strengthen him in some way? (She does not make him more frail. She strengthens him by feeding him and by teaching him a lesson.)

- What is Mrs. Jones's apartment *furnished* with? (It is furnished with a kitchenette, including an icebox and a gas stove, and a daybed.) What does Roger hope to *furnish* himself with? (He hopes to furnish himself with a pair of blue suede shoes.)

- How would a pair of blue *suede* shoes feel? (They would feel soft and velvety.) Why do you think *suede* shoes might be attractive to Roger? (He probably does not have many nice things. His life is hard, and the shoes are soft and luxurious and were stylish at the time.)

- What does Mrs. Jones tell Roger to do to make himself *presentable*? (She tells him to wash his face and comb his hair.) At work, how does Mrs. Jones help make other people *presentable*? (She does women's hair in a hotel beauty shop.)

- What kinds of questions would *embarrass* Roger? (Questions about where he lives and questions about his parents would embarrass Roger.) Why might such questions *embarrass* him? (Such questions might embarrass him because he probably doesn't live in a very nice place and his parents don't seem to take care of him.)

- After his time with Mrs. Jones, do you think Roger will try to *latch* onto another woman's pocketbook? Why or why not? (No; he has learned that latching onto and stealing someone else's belongings is wrong.) What does Mrs. Jones hope Roger does *latch* onto? (She hopes that Roger latches onto an honest and respectable way of living.)

- Where is the front *stoop* in relation to Mrs. Jones's room? (The front stoop is down the hall and outside the front door.) Why does Roger think of Mrs. Jones's *stoop* as "barren"? Remember, we learned the meaning of *barren* in Unit 1. It means "without plant or animal life." (Roger thinks of the stoop as barren because it is empty compared to Mrs. Jones's home.)

Objectives

- Understand the function and purpose of nouns.
- Distinguish between types of nouns.
- Understand the function and purpose of pronouns.
- Distinguish between types of pronouns.
- Identify the antecedent of pronouns.
- Understand the function and purpose of verbs.
- Distinguish between types of verbs.
- Understand the function and purpose of adverbs.
- Understand the function and purpose of prepositional phrases.

Nouns

It's important to understand the jobs that words do in sentences. What kind of words answer the *who* or *what* question? (nouns)

Direct students to page 42 in their Student Books.

Concrete vs. Abstract

Nouns can be categorized several different ways. The first two columns show one way to sort nouns. They can either be concrete nouns or abstract nouns. Read the words under Concrete with me: *stoop, beans, purse.*

Read the words under Abstract with me: *balance, goodness, intelligence.* What is the difference between a concrete and an abstract noun? Turn and talk about it with your partner. Think of one more example of each type of noun. **Provide sharing time. Have students share their nouns and what distinguishes a concrete noun from an abstract noun. Answers should revolve around how concrete nouns can be seen, touched, or held; whereas abstract nouns cannot be seen, touched, or held.**

Common vs. Proper

Nouns can also be categorized as either common or proper. Read the common nouns in the chart with me: *justice, beans, purse. Beans* and *purse* are common nouns that are also concrete nouns. *Justice* is a common noun, but it can't be seen or touched— so what is it? (abstract) Now, look at the list of proper nouns and tell me what distinguishes them from common nouns. (They name specific people, places, and things and they begin with capital letters.)

Nouns

Job: Naming words that answer the *who* or *what* questions

Types of Nouns			
Concrete	**Abstract**	**Common**	**Proper**
stoop	balance	justice	Federal Bureau of Investigation
beans	goodness	beans	Alabama
purse	intelligence	purse	Nike

		Inflectional Ending	Examples
Singular	one	none	• book • table • chair
			• glass • patch • fox
			• child • goose • woman
Plural	more than one	-s	• books • tables • chairs
		-es	• glasses • patches • foxes
		irregular	• children • geese • women
Possessive	ownership	's (singular)	• book's page • glass's edge • table's leg • patch's pattern • chair's cushion • fox's den
		' (plural)	• books' pages • glasses' edges • tables' legs • patches' patterns • chairs' cushions • foxes' tails
		's (plural irregular)	• children's toys • women's clothes • geese's feathers

42   Unit 2

Singular, Plural, and Possessive

Nouns can also be classified as singular or plural. Let's review using the examples in the chart. **Read each singular noun and ask students for the plural form. Point out the different inflectional endings used to make nouns plural.** The first row of singular nouns just requires an -s to make them plural. The second row of nouns requires an -es to make them plural, whereas the third row represents irregular spellings.

We also studied how to make nouns show ownership or possession. How do you make a singular noun possessive? (Add an 's to make it possessive.) How do you make a regular plural noun possessive? (Just add an apostrophe.) Work with your partner to create three sentences using the examples of possessive nouns in the chart: singular, plural, and irregular. **Have students share their sentences.**

Tell students that the chart can be used as a reference.

Pronouns

We recently learned about words that can act like nouns in a sentence. What words take the place of nouns? (pronouns)

Direct students to page 43 in their Student Books. Read the Types of Pronouns chart aloud.

Understanding pronoun usage is essential for reading comprehension. Knowing what or who a pronoun is referencing can dramatically affect your ability to understand what you read. Because nouns have different functions in a sentence, the pronouns that we can use instead of nouns are also different. We choose the pronoun based on the job the noun would be doing in the sentence. Today, we're going to take a closer look at three types of pronouns. The chart is missing some information that needs to be added.

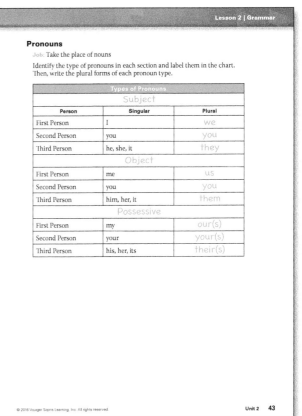

Subject Pronouns

Examples of the first type of pronoun are listed. Listen to an example for each pronoun.

- First person: I am walking to my friend's house.

- Second person: You should come along.

- Third person: She is standing on the sidewalk. What is the job of the pronoun in each sentence? In each sentence, it provides the main *who* for the sentence, or the subject. Because they answer the main *who* or *what* question, they are the subject pronouns. Label the first group of pronouns as *Subject* pronouns in the chart.

We'll work together to figure out the plural subject pronouns. First-person plural refers to a group that includes me. How would I refer to a group that includes me? Maybe Martha, Sam, Jennifer, Bill, and I are going to the movies. What pronoun could be used to fill in the blank: _____ are going to the movies? (We) We are going to the movies. *We* includes everyone, as well as me. Write *we* in the chart as the first-person plural pronoun. Turn to your partner and use the pronoun *we* in a sentence. **Have students turn and talk briefly.**

If I were talking to the group, but not a part of it, I could say "You are going to the movies." *You* is considered a pronoun that can mean one person or a group of people. In other words, it can be singular or plural. Because we want to use it to mean a group of people, think of a sentence that could be directed to the entire class. **Have volunteers share sentences using *you* as a plural pronoun.**

Third-person pronouns are used to talk about someone that you are not talking directly to or about something other than a person. Imagine you are talking about Martha, Sam, Jennifer, and Bill going to the movies. Fill in the blank: _____ are going to the movies. (They) They are going to the movies. **After students fill in their charts, have them work with their partners to use *they* in a sentence. Offer an example using items such as pencils and pens.**

Object Pronouns

Let's look at the examples for the next type of pronouns. Read them with me: *me, you, him, her, it*. Turn to your partner and think of a sentence with the word *me*. **Have students turn and talk briefly and have volunteers share their sentences.** (Possible answers: She gave me the money. She opened the door for me. My dad picked my sister and me up from school.)

What question does *me* answer in each of these sentences? Is it the *who* or is it the *did to who* question? (It answers the *did to who* question.) These pronouns are not functioning as the subject. As part of the predicate, they are working with the verb or possibly a preposition as an object, so label the second group *Object* pronouns. **Have students fill in the plural forms of the object pronouns, then use each form in sentences with their partners or the whole class.** Do you see any pronouns that function as subject and object pronouns? (Yes, *you* and *it* are on both lists.) This makes it very important to understand how the pronoun is being used and what noun it is referencing. It's easy to get confused when pronouns are overused.

Possessive Pronouns

Let's look at the final group of pronouns in the chart. Read them with me: *my, your, his, her, its.* Listen. "My dog is very friendly. Is your house close to the mall? His books are on the floor." In each sentence, the pronouns are doing the same job. What information are they providing? (They show ownership or possession.) In each sentence, the pronoun tells us whose things we are referencing. How do we make nouns possessive or show ownership? (Add an *'s* or just an apostrophe.) An apostrophe helps us recognize possessive nouns, but they are not used with pronouns. We have to look for different forms of the pronouns to help us recognize possession or ownership. **Guide students in filling in the plural possessive pronouns, and make sure their chart is completely filled in and each type of pronoun is labeled. Point out the double usage of *her* as both an object pronoun and possessive pronoun.**

Tell students that the chart can be used as a reference.

Direct students to page 44 in their Student Books. Have them follow along as you read the instructions.

Model

Read the first sentence: *She was a large woman with a large purse that had everything in it but a hammer and nails.* The first pronoun is *she. She* is the woman, so I'll write *the woman* in the parentheses. The other underlined pronoun in this sentence is *it.* What has everything in it? The purse has everything in it, so *it* must mean the purse. Write *purse* in the parentheses.

Read the sentence one more time using the nouns instead of the pronouns as a way to model double-checking your response.

Guided Practice

Read the next sentence and guide students in identifying and replacing the pronouns.

Independent Practice

Have students identify and replace the pronouns in the remaining sentences. Review the answers as a class.

Verbs

Direct students to page 45 in their
Student Books.

Now, let's work with words that have
a different job. What kind of words
answer the *what did they do* question?
(verbs) To have a complete sentence,
we need a noun and a verb. So let's
consider what we already know about
verbs.

Like nouns, there are different types
of verbs. In the preceding unit, we
worked with two types of verbs. What
were they? (action and linking verbs)
What do action verbs tell us? (They
describe actions that characters do.)
Think about "Thank You, M'am." What
were some of the actions taken by
Mrs. Jones and Roger? **Write student
responses on the board.** (Possible
answers: grabbed, fell, shook, dragged,
ate, talked, sat)

What is the other type of verb we
examined in the preceding unit?
(linking verbs) What is their job?
(Their job is to connect or link the subject to a word or words in the predicate.) Give
some examples of linking verbs. **Write student responses on the board.** (Possible
answers: is, are, was, were, am)

We also learned that verbs can help us establish time. What is another word for *time*?
(tense) We worked with two different times or tenses: the past and the present. Look
at the two examples for regular verbs and tell me how a verb shows past tense. (We
add -ed to make a verb show past tense.) What kind of endings can signal a present
tense verb? (Present tense verbs can end with nothing, -s, or -es.)

Irregular verbs do not follow the pattern and neither do linking verbs. We just have to
remember the correct forms.

Read the instructions for the activity and model the completion of the examples.

Guided Practice

Guide students in completion of the first sentence.

Independent Practice

Have students complete the activity. Review the answers as a class.

Verbs

Action Verbs: Describe actions that we can see and some that we cannot see
Linking Verbs: Connect or link the subject to a word or group of words in
the predicate
Verb Tense: Signals time

Verbs	Yesterday	Today	Tomorrow
	Past	Present	Future
regular verbs	walked	walk(s)	
	matched	match(es)	
irregular verbs	sat	sit(s)	
linking verbs	was/were	am/is/are	

Underline the verb in each of the following sentences. Place check marks in
the chart to identify each verb as action or linking and present or past tense.

Sentence	Type		Tense	
	Action	Linking	Present	Past
Ex: She is a large woman.		✓	✓	
She heated lima beans and ham on her stove.	✓			✓
1. There was another long pause.		✓		✓
2. The boy's mouth opened.	✓			✓
3. Then he frowned.	✓			✓
4. Mrs. Jones got up and went behind the screen.	✓			✓
5. "Now, here, take this ten dollars and buy yourself some blue suede shoes."	✓		✓	

Unit 2   45

Adverbs

Certain words help "paint" the verbs so we have a clearer image of the action. They add information by answering the *when*, *where*, and *how* questions. Because these words "add to the verb," we call them adverbs.

Write *adverb* on the board, underlining *ad* and then *verb*.

What do we call words that describe or add information about the verb? (adverbs) What are some of the questions they answer? (when, where, and how) This additional information allows us to visualize the action more accurately and vividly. Adverbs typically end in -ly. **Have students generate some examples of words that end in -ly that describe the way a person moves.** (Possible responses: quickly, slowly, gracefully, carefully, carelessly, sneakily)

However, not all adverbs end in -ly. **On the board, write a list of common adverbs without an -ly ending and challenge students to use them in a sentence.**

Examples: almost, always, down, fast, hard, here, in, long, now, often, out, quite, rather, so, then, there, too, up, very, well, everywhere

> **Note:** The adverbs *too* and *very* modify only adjectives and other adverbs: very funny, too old

Write the following sentence on the board.

Devon drives.

Have students answer the *when*, *where*, and *how* questions. After each question is answered, rewrite the sentence. Then, challenge students to arrange the answers to create a coherent sentence that answers all three questions.

Possible Answers:

When: Devon drives now.

Where: Devon drives everywhere.

How: Devon drives carefully.

Combination Sentence: Now, Devon drives everywhere carefully.

Let's examine some sentences from the text and determine what kind of information has been added to the verb.

Direct students to page 46 in their Student Books. Read the instructions aloud.

In each sentence, the verb has been underlined, and in each sentence there is additional information about the verb. The information answers the *when, where,* or *how* question.

Guided Practice

Guide students in determining the adverb in the first two sentences.

Independent Practice

Have students answer the questions in the remaining sentences, then put the adverbs in the chart. Review the answers as a class.

When we read, we use adverbs to visualize the action more vividly as we read. When we write, we use adverbs to paint these vivid images.

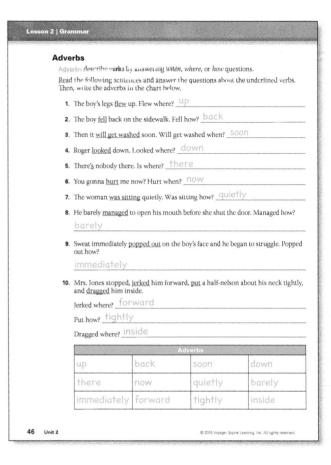

Prepositions and Prepositional Phrases

Adverbs answer the *when, where,* and *how* questions. So do prepositional phrases. Prepositional phrases begin with little words that work very hard in sentences. They are called prepositions.

Prepositions are small words that show the position or relationship between words in a sentence.

Write the following sentence on the board:

Roger is at the table.

Read the sentence aloud and underline *at.* What does the word *at* tell us about Roger and the table? It tells us where Roger is. Where is he? (at the table) In this sentence, the word *at* shows the position or relationship between words in the sentence. What are these words called? (prepositions)

Write the word *preposition* on the board and underline *position.*

Its name contains a powerful hint about its job. Do you see the word *position* in the name? I can change the position or relationship by changing the preposition. Replace *at* with the following prepositions:

> *on*
>
> *above*
>
> *by*
>
> *under*
>
> *behind*

Read the sentence with each preposition. With each new sentence, ask students how the preposition changed Roger's relationship to the table.

I'm going to give you a "cue sentence" that I want you to use whenever you're trying to decide if a word is a preposition or if you are trying to think of a preposition.

Write the following sentence frame on the board:

The rabbit hopped _____ the log.

Write the following prepositions on the board:

at

on

by

under

behind

Write these nonexamples on the board:

car

fast

slowly

ran

Read the sentence aloud using a preposition from the list. Then, use a nonexample. Explain why the nonexamples don't work.

Now, you try it. Work with your partner to find at least two words other than these that work in the sentence. If the word works, it is a preposition.

Have volunteers share their prepositions. (over, onto, into, near, toward, from, around, etc.)

A prepositional phrase is a group of words that tells *where, when,* or *how.* It begins with a preposition and always includes a noun. Look again at the sentence on the board. *Roger is at the table. At the table* is the prepositional phrase. It begins with a preposition. What preposition does it begin with? **(at)** The word *table* is a naming word. What do we call a naming word? **(a noun)**

Let's look at the other sentences about the rabbit. What kind of a word does this sentence end in? **(a noun)** Prepositional phrases end in a naming word. Knowing this can help us find prepositional phrases and know what they are saying.

Direct students to page 47 in their Student Books. Read the common prepositions and instructions aloud.

Model

Look at the example sentence: *Sweat appeared on the boy's face.*

I see the word *on*, which I know is a preposition. On what? On the boy's face. So I'm going to circle the preposition *on* and then underline *on the boy's face.* What was on the boy's face? Sweat was on the boy's face. *On* is telling me the position of the sweat and the boy's face. The sweat isn't under his face or by his face. It is *on* his face. I'm going to draw an arrow from *face* to *sweat.*

Guided Practice

Guide students in completion of the first two sentences.

Independent Practice

Have students identify the prepositions and connect the words in the remaining sentences. Review the answers as a class.

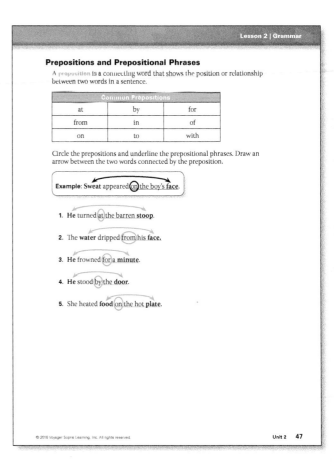

Prepositions and Prepositional Phrases

A preposition is a connecting word that shows the position or relationship between two words in a sentence.

Common Prepositions		
at	by	for
from	in	of
on	to	with

Circle the prepositions and underline the prepositional phrases. Draw an arrow between the two words connected by the preposition.

Example: Sweat appeared on the boy's face.

1. He turned at the barren **stoop.**

2. The **water** dripped from his **face.**

3. He frowned for a **minute.**

4. He stood by the **door.**

5. She heated **food** on the hot **plate.**

Unit 2   47

Objectives
- Use adverbs and prepositional phrases correctly in sentence writing.
- Produce, expand, and rearrange complete sentences.

Masterpiece Sentences: Predicate Painters

Let's consider another sentence from the text.

Write the following sentence on the board.

The woman still had him by the neck in the middle of her room.

What is the verb? (had) Let's see what information has been added to the verb. What question does *still* answer? (when) What question does *by the neck* answer? (where or how) Students could say it tells how she was holding him as well as where she was holding him. What question does *in the middle of her room* answer? (where) Have students distinguish between adverbs and prepositional phrases.

Direct students to page 48 in their Student Books. Read the instructions aloud. Have partners paint the predicate in each sentence by answering each question and then writing the new sentence. When you write your new sentence, remember to capitalize the first word and include an end punctuation mark.

Note: In the provided answers, predicate painters have been moved around, which is the next step in the process. If students have not developed their sentence writing skills, they will likely place their predicate painters consecutively in the sentences. This will be corrected in an upcoming lesson.

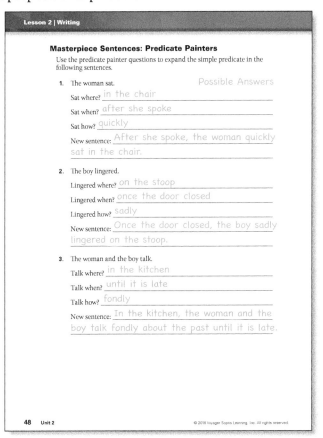

Lesson 2 | Writing

Masterpiece Sentences: Predicate Painters
Use the predicate painter questions to expand the simple predicate in the following sentences.

Possible Answers

1. The woman sat.
   Sat where? in the chair
   Sat when? after she spoke
   Sat how? quickly
   New sentence: After she spoke, the woman quickly sat in the chair.

2. The boy lingered.
   Lingered where? on the stoop
   Lingered when? once the door closed
   Lingered how? sadly
   New sentence: Once the door closed, the boy sadly lingered on the stoop.

3. The woman and the boy talk.
   Talk where? in the kitchen
   Talk when? until it is late
   Talk how? fondly
   New sentence: In the kitchen, the woman and the boy talk fondly about the past until it is late.

48   Unit 2   © 2016 Voyager Sopris Learning, Inc. All rights reserved.

Lesson Opener

Before the lesson, choose one of the following activities to write on the board or post on the *LANGUAGE! Live* Class Wall online.

- *Expand the following base sentences by adding at least one predicate painter.*
  The large woman yelled.
  The thief walked.
- *What would you have done differently if you were Roger? How would the story have ended?*
- *Write sentences with* latch *and* manage *as past-tense verbs.*

Reading

Objectives

- Establish a purpose for rereading literary text.
- Demonstrate an understanding of how to ask questions and answer them appropriately.
- Use critical thinking skills to write responses to prompts about text.
- Support written answers with text evidence.
- Identify how a character changes over time.
- Determine the meaning of figurative language in text.

Reading for a Purpose: "Thank You, M'am"

We are going to read "Thank you, M'am" again. Our purpose for this read is to help us answer questions about the text.

Direct students to page 49 in their Student Books. Have them read the questions aloud with you.

1. Why does Roger make contact with Mrs. Jones?

2. Why does Mrs. Jones feed Roger and have him clean himself up?

3. How does Mrs. Jones feel about stealing? Use the following quote to inform your answer: "shoes come by devilish like that will burn your feet."

4. How did Roger's character change over time? Provide evidence for your answer.

Critical Understandings: Question Words
How to Answer Questions

Question Words	How to Answer
If the question asks . . .	Your answer must include . . .
Why	a reason or explanation
How	the way something is done

Respond using complete sentences. Use the chart above to help you.

1. Why does Roger make contact with Mrs. Jones?
   Roger makes contact with Mrs. Jones so he can steal enough money to buy a pair of blue suede shoes.

2. Why does Mrs. Jones feed Roger and have him clean himself up?
   Mrs. Jones feeds Roger and has him clean himself up because she notices that he is dirty and hungry and thinks that is why he was stealing from her.

3. How does Mrs. Jones feel about stealing? Use the following quote to inform your answer: "shoes come by devilish like that will burn your feet."
   Mrs. Jones feels that stealing will come back to get you. "Shoes come by devilish like that will burn your feet" means that if you acquire shoes through stealing, negative things will happen as payback.

4. How did Roger's character change over time? Provide evidence for your answer.
   Roger's character changed over time from dishonest to honest. For example, Roger was dishonest when he attempted to steal Mrs. Jones's purse and said that he didn't mean to steal her purse. Roger was honest when he didn't run away or steal her purse when he had a second chance.

Direct students to page 37 in their Student Books or have them tear out the extra copy of "Thank You, M'am" from the back of their book.

Note: To minimize flipping back and forth between the pages, a copy of each text has been included in the back of the Student Books. Encourage students to tear this out and use it when working on activities that require the use of the text.

Have students reread the text in triads with expression. Before reading in triads, students should choose a role: narrator, Roger, or Mrs. Jones. Model how to read sentences that end with question marks and exclamation points. Remind students to be prepared to answer the prompts after reading.

Note: Divide students into triads. Students can self-select roles or be assigned parts according to data. For example, the most fluent student could be the narrator. Roger's sections could be assigned to the most dysfluent reader. The third person would read dialogue related to Mrs. Jones. If necessary, have students highlight the different parts of the story. They choose one color for Roger and a different color for Mrs. Jones. Students should highlight dialogue spoken by Mrs. Jones in one color and highlight dialogue spoken by Roger in a different color. The text related to the narrator is left unhighlighted.

Critical Understandings: Question Words *why, how*

It is critical to understand how to answer different types of questions. Today, we will look at two question words. We will become familiar with these question words and learn how to answer these types of questions.

Write the question words *why* and *how* on the board. Have students read the words aloud with you.

Direct students to page 49 in their Student Books. Have them read the chart with their partner.

Chart Reading Procedure
- Group students with partners or in triads.
- Have students count off as 1s or 2s. The 1s will become the student leaders. If working with triads, the third students become 3s.
- The student leaders will read the left column (Question Words) in addition to managing the time and turn-taking if working with a triad.
- The 2s will explain the right column of the chart (How to Answer). If working in triads, 2s and 3s will take turns explaining the right column.
- Students should follow along with their pencil eraser while others are explaining the chart.
- Students should work from left to right, top to bottom in order to benefit from this activity.
- Attempt to give all students a chance to be a student leader as you move through the lessons.

Check for understanding by requesting an oral response to the following questions.

- If the question asks *why*, your answer must include what? (a reason or explanation)
- If the question asks *how*, your answer must include what? (the way something is done)

Model

Direct students to the questions. Let's practice answering questions. Listen as I model the first one for you.

1. Why does Roger make contact with Mrs. Jones?

The question word is *why*, so we know the answer must include a reason or an explanation. The first contact Roger makes with Mrs. Jones is an attempt to steal her purse. So, we need to know why he tried to steal her purse. I remember that she thought he was hungry, but he admits that he wanted a pair of blue suede shoes. So, the answer to the question would be:

Roger makes contact with Mrs. Jones so he can steal enough money to buy a pair of blue suede shoes.

While I write my answer on the board, look at the text and point to the evidence. **Have students write the answer on the page and tell you where the evidence in the text can be found.**

Critical Understandings: Question Words

How to Answer Questions

Question Words	How to Answer
If the question asks . . .	Your answer must include . . .
Why	a reason or explanation
How	the way something is done

Respond using complete sentences. Use the chart above to help you.

1. Why does Roger make contact with Mrs. Jones?
   Roger makes contact with Mrs. Jones so he can steal enough money to buy a pair of blue suede shoes.

2. Why does Mrs. Jones feed Roger and have him clean himself up?
   Mrs. Jones feeds Roger and has him clean himself up because she notices that he is dirty and hungry and thinks that is why he was stealing from her.

3. How does Mrs. Jones feel about stealing? Use the following quote to inform your answer: "shoes come by devilish like that will burn your feet."
   Mrs. Jones feels that stealing will come back to get you. "Shoes come by devilish like that will burn your feet" means that if you acquire shoes through stealing, negative things will happen as payback.

4. How did Roger's character change over time? Provide evidence for your answer.
   Roger's character changed over time from dishonest to honest. For example, Roger was dishonest when he attempted to steal Mrs. Jones's purse and said that he didn't mean to steal her purse. Roger was honest when he didn't run away or steal her purse when he had a second chance.

Unit 2   49

Guided Practice

2. Why does Mrs. Jones feed Roger and have him clean himself up?

The next question word is also *why*. What does the answer need to include? (a reason or explanation) Because the story is not written from the point of view of Mrs. Jones, it doesn't say explicitly why she fed Roger and had him clean himself up. But, we can look at the dialogue to infer why she feeds him. **Have students find examples of dialogue that help explain why she fed him and had him clean himself up.** ("Um-hum! And your face is dirty. I got a great mind to wash your face for you. Ain't you got nobody home to tell you to wash your face?"; "Then we'll eat," said the woman, "I believe you're hungry—or been hungry—to try to snatch my pocketbook.") Think about the dialogue and determine what Mrs. Jones thinks. **Provide wait time. Have volunteers share answers.** (She thinks he is dirty and hungry because nobody is home to take care of him. This is why he is trying to steal from her.)

Write the following sentence starter on the board and have students complete it on their page.

Mrs. Jones feeds Roger and has him clean himself up because _____.

Independent Practice

Have students respond to the remaining prompts. For students who need more assistance, provide the following sentence starters.

Sentence starters:

3. *Mrs. Jones feels that stealing _____.*

   "Shoes come by devilish like that will burn your feet" means _____.

4. *Roger's character changed over time from _____.*

   For example, Roger was dishonest when _____.

   Roger was honest when _____.

Lesson Opener

Before the lesson, choose one of the following activities to write on the board or post on the *LANGUAGE! Live* Class Wall online.

- *Write two sentences about Roger and Mrs. Jones using the object pronouns* him *and* her.
- *Dress your avatar as though you were Roger the day after meeting Mrs. Jones. Explain your choices.*
- *Expand the simple sentences by adding two predicate painters.*
    The weary woman sat.
    The hungry boy walked.

Reading

Objectives

- Read literary text with purpose and understanding.
- Answer questions to demonstrate comprehension of text.
- Identify and explain explicit details from text.
- Monitor comprehension of text during reading.
- Determine the meaning of figurative language in text.
- Match pronouns to their antecedents.
- Distinguish between standard and nonstandard English.
- Compare and contrast the experiences of characters in stories.

Close Reading of "Thank You, M'am"

Highlighters or colored pencils

Let's reread "Thank You, M'am." I will provide specific instructions on how to mark the text that will help with comprehension.

Have students get out a highlighter or colored pencil.

Direct students to pages 50–54 in their Student Books.

Draw a rectangle around the title, "Thank You, M'am."

Next, we will read the vocabulary words aloud.

- What's the first bold vocabulary word? (balance) *Balance* means "the ability to stay steady and not fall." Roger fell when he lost his *balance.* **Have partners use the word in a sentence.**

- What's the next word? (permit) *Permit* means "to allow." Though he tried to steal from her, Mrs. Jones *permitted* the boy to sit alone in her apartment near her pocketbook. **Have partners use the word in a sentence.**

- What's the next vocabulary word? (release) *Release* means "to let go of; to set free." You cannot be *released* early from school without an adult. **Have partners use the word in a sentence.**

- Next word? (frail) *Frail* means "weak and easily broken." Roger is likely *frail* because he doesn't have enough to eat. **Have partners use the word in a sentence.**

- Let's continue. (furnished) *Furnished* means "having furniture, appliances, or basic supplies." Roger's home is not *furnished* with food for him to eat. **Have partners use the word in a sentence.**

- Next word? (suede) *Suede* is soft, velvety leather. *Suede* is less common in clothing because it is difficult to clean. **Have partners use the word in a sentence.**

- Let's continue. (presentable) *Presentable* means "fit to appear in public." Roger didn't look *presentable* because nobody was home to make sure he bathed. **Have partners use the word in a sentence.**

- Next word? (embarrass) *Embarrass* means "to make someone uncomfortable or ashamed." Mrs. Jones was careful not to *embarrass* Roger about his background. **Have partners use the word in a sentence.**

- Let's continue. (latching) *Latching* means "gripping; fastening onto." Roger *latched* onto Mrs. Jones's purse, then Mrs. Jones *latched* onto him. **Have partners use the word in a sentence.**

- Last word. (stoop) A *stoop* is a small porch. Roger stood outside the door on the *stoop.* **Have partners use the word in a sentence.**

Talk with a partner about any vocabulary word that is still confusing for you to read or understand.

You will read "Thank You, M'am" a small section at a time. After each section, you will monitor your understanding by circling the check mark if you understand the text or the question mark if you don't understand the text. I also want you to draw a question mark over any confusing words, phrases, or sentences.

Options for reading text:
- Teacher read-aloud
- Teacher-led or student-led choral read
- Paired read or independent read with bold vocabulary words read aloud

---

Choose an option for reading text. Have students read lines 1–19 according to the option that you chose. As you read, mark the descriptions of the characters—both physical descriptions and personality traits.

When most of the students are finished, continue with the entire class. Let's see how well you understood what you read.

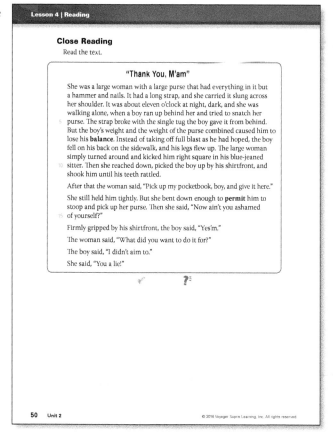

Close Reading
Read the text.

"Thank You, M'am"

She was a large woman with a large purse that had everything in it but a hammer and nails. It had a long strap, and she carried it slung across her shoulder. It was about eleven o'clock at night, dark, and she was walking alone, when a boy ran up behind her and tried to snatch her
5   purse. The strap broke with the single tug the boy gave it from behind. But the boy's weight and the weight of the purse combined caused him to lose his **balance**. Instead of taking off full blast as he had hoped, the boy fell on his back on the sidewalk, and his legs flew up. The large woman simply turned around and kicked him right square in his blue-jeaned
10 sitter. Then she reached down, picked the boy up by his shirtfront, and shook him until his teeth rattled.

After that the woman said, "Pick up my pocketbook, boy, and give it here."

She still held him tightly. But she bent down enough to **permit** him to stoop and pick up her purse. Then she said, "Now ain't you ashamed
15 of yourself?"

Firmly gripped by his shirtfront, the boy said, "Yes'm."

The woman said, "What did you want to do it for?"

The boy said, "I didn't aim to."

She said, "You a lie!"

- Circle the check mark or the question mark for this section. Draw a question mark over any confusing words.

- What character information did you mark about the woman? (large woman)

- Go to lines 1 and 2. Mark the figurative language used to indicate that there were many different things in the purse. (everything in it but a hammer and nails)

- On line 2, mark the pronoun *it* twice. Draw an arrow from the word *it* to the noun that it refers to. (purse)

- Go to line 4. Mark the synonym for *grab*. (snatch)

- Go to line 5. Mark the word that means the opposite of *in front of*. (behind)

- Go to line 6. Number two reasons that the boy lost his balance. (1. boy's weight; 2. weight of the purse)

- Go to lines 9 and 10. Mark the phrase that means "behind" or "butt." (blue-jeaned sitter)

- Go to line 11. Mark the phrase that tells how hard the woman shook the boy. (shook him until his teeth rattled)

- Go to line 12. Mark the synonym for *purse*. (pocketbook)

- Go to line 13. Mark the synonym for *allow*. (permit)

- On the next line, mark the word that is spelled the same as one of our vocabulary words but has a different meaning. (stoop) In the margin, write a synonym for the word as it is used here. (bend)

- Go to line 14. Mark the nonstandard word for *aren't*. (ain't)

- On the same line, mark the antonym or opposite of *proud*. (ashamed)

- Go to line 16. Mark the nonstandard word for *Yes, M'am*. (Yes'm)

- Go to line 18. Mark the phrase that means "mean to" or "intend to." (aim to)

- Go to line 19. Edit the nonstandard sentence "You a lie!" (insert *are*; change *lie* to *liar*)

Have students read lines 20–41 according to the option that you chose. As you read, mark the descriptions of the characters—both physical descriptions and personality traits.

When most of the students are finished, continue with the entire class. Let's see how well you understood what you read.

- Circle the check mark or the question mark for this section. Draw a question mark over any confusing words.

- What character information did you mark about the boy? (sorry; face is dirty; frightened; fourteen or fifteen; frail)

- Though it isn't written in words, what do you know about Mrs. Jones? (caring; strong) Write the descriptions in the margin and highlight them.

- Go to line 22. Mark the phrase that means "let you go." (turn you loose)

- Go to line 26. Mark the phrase that means "should." (got a great mind to)

- Go to line 27. Edit the nonstandard sentence part "Ain't you got nobody home" (Delete *ain't you got nobody*; replace with *isn't anyone*)

- Go to line 28. Mark the nonstandard word for *No, M'am.* (No'm)

- Go to line 30. Mark the adjective that describes the boy. (frightened)

- Go to line 31. Mark the word that means "weak and thin." (willow-wild)

- Go to line 33. Mark the phrase that means "should." (ought to be)

- Go to line 38. Mark the word that means "physical touch." Mark it with a one. (contact 1)

- Go to line 39. Mark the word that means "interaction." Mark it with a two. (contact 2)

- Go to line 40. Circle the word that indicates that Mrs. Jones has a strict tone. (sir)

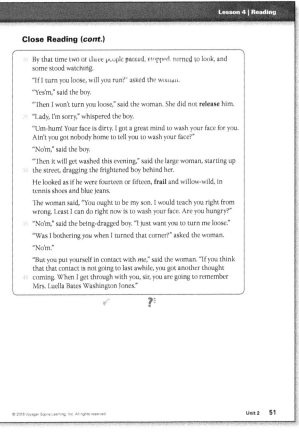

Close Reading (*cont.*)

20 By that time two or three people passed, stopped, turned to look, and some stood watching.

"If I turn you loose, will you run?" asked the woman.

"Yes'm," said the boy.

"Then I won't turn you loose," said the woman. She did not **release** him.

25 "Lady, I'm sorry," whispered the boy.

"Um-hum! Your face is dirty. I got a great mind to wash your face for you. Ain't you got nobody home to tell you to wash your face?"

"No'm," said the boy.

"Then it will get washed this evening," said the large woman, starting up 30 the street, dragging the frightened boy behind her.

He looked as if he were fourteen or fifteen, **frail** and willow-wild, in tennis shoes and blue jeans.

The woman said, "You ought to be my son. I would teach you right from wrong. Least I can do right now is to wash your face. Are you hungry?"

35 "No'm," said the being-dragged boy. "I just want you to turn me loose."

"Was I bothering *you* when I turned that corner?" asked the woman.

"No'm."

"But you put yourself in contact with *me*," said the woman. "If you think that that contact is not going to last awhile, you got another thought 40 coming. When I get through with you, sir, you are going to remember Mrs. Luella Bates Washington Jones."

Unit 2 **51**

Have students read lines 42–73 according to the option that you chose. As you read, mark the descriptions of the characters—both physical descriptions and personality traits.

When most of the students are finished, continue with the entire class. Let's see how well you understood what you read.

- Circle the check mark or the question mark for this section. Draw a question mark over any confusing words.

- What character information did you mark about the boy? (there's nobody home at my house)

- Though it isn't written in words, what do you know about Mrs. Jones? (lives alone; hungry) Write the descriptions in the margin and highlight them.

- Mark the evidence that suggests Mrs. Jones trusts Roger. (left the door open; turned him loose) Write *trusting* in the margin.

- Go to line 43. Mark the word that represents her arm hooked under his shoulder and around the back of his neck. (half-nelson)

- Go to line 47. Mark the word that means "residents." (roomers)

- Go to line 54. Mark the transition word that means "so." (whereupon)

- On the same line, mark the phrase that means "finally." (at last)

- Go to line 57. Edit "you gonna" using standard English. (Are you going to)

- Go to line 60. Edit "late as it be" using standard English. (late as it is)

- Go to line 67. Edit "could of" using standard English. (could have)

Close Reading (*cont.*)

Sweat popped out on the boy's face and he began to struggle. Mrs. Jones stopped, jerked him around in front of her, put a half-nelson about his neck, and continued to drag him up the street. When she got to her door, she dragged the boy inside, down a hall, and into a large kitchenette-**furnished** room at the rear of the house. She switched on the light and left the door open. The boy could hear other roomers laughing and talking in the large house. Some of their doors were open, too, so he knew he and the woman were not alone. The woman still had him by the neck in the middle of her room.

She said, "What is your name?"

"Roger," answered the boy.

"Then, Roger, you go to that sink and wash your face," said the woman, whereupon she turned him loose—at last. Roger looked at the door— looked at the woman—looked at the door—*and went to the sink.*

"Let the water run until it gets warm," she said. "Here's a clean towel."

"You gonna take me to jail?" asked the boy, bending over the sink.

"Not with that face, I would not take you nowhere," said the woman. "Here I am trying to get home to cook me a bite to eat, and you snatch my pocketbook! Maybe you ain't been to your supper either, late as it be. Have you?"

"There's nobody home at my house," said the boy.

"Then we'll eat," said the woman, "I believe you're hungry—or been hungry—to try to snatch my pocketbook!"

"I wanted a pair of blue **suede** shoes," said the boy.

"Well, you didn't have to snatch *my* pocketbook to get some suede shoes," said Mrs. Luella Bates Washington Jones. "You could of asked me."

"M'am?"

The water dripping from his face, the boy looked at her. There was a long pause. A very long pause. After he had dried his face and not knowing what else to do, dried it again, the boy turned around, wondering what next. The door was open. He could make a dash for it down the hall. He could run, run, run, run, *run!*

✓   ?

Have students read lines 74–104 according to the option that you chose. As you read, mark the descriptions of the characters—both physical descriptions and personality traits.

When most of the students are finished, continue with the entire class. Let's see how well you understood what you read.

- Circle the check mark or the question mark for this section. Draw a question mark over any confusing words.

- What character information did you mark about Mrs. Jones? **(done things she wouldn't tell Roger or God; worked at hotel beauty shop; worked late; didn't want to embarrass Roger)**

- Mark the evidence that suggests Roger likes Mrs. Jones. **(sat where she could easily see him; did not want to be mistrusted; offered to go to the store)**

- Mark the evidence that suggests Mrs. Jones trusts Roger. **(offered the use of her comb; did not watch the boy; did not watch her purse)**

- Go to line 83. Mark the idiom that means "comb one's hair quickly." **(run that comb through your hair)**

- Go to line 85. Mark the device that Mrs. Jones uses instead of a stove. **(gas plate)**

- On the next line, mark the synonym for *refrigerator*. **(icebox)**

- Go to line 90. Mark the idiom that means "at a glance." **(out of the corner of her eye)**

- Go to line 92. Mark the word that means "not trusted." **(mistrusted)** Circle the prefix *mis-*. *Mis-* means "not."

- Go to line 101. Mark the phrase that tells where Mrs. Jones was coming from when Roger attempted to steal her purse. **(hotel beauty shop)**

- Estimate the closing time of the beauty shop. Annotate the time in the margin. **(11:00 p.m.)**

Close Reading (*cont.*)

The woman was sitting on the daybed. After a while she said, "I were young once and I wanted things I could not get."

There was another long pause. The boy's mouth opened. Then he frowned, not knowing he frowned.

The woman said, "Um-hum! You thought I was going to say *but*, didn't you? You thought I was going to say, *but I didn't snatch people's pocketbooks.* Well, I wasn't going to say that." Pause. Silence. "I have done things, too, which I would not tell you, son—neither tell God, if He didn't already know. Everybody's got something in common. So you set down while I fix us something to eat. You might run that comb through your hair so you will look **presentable**."

In another corner of the room behind a screen was a gas plate and an icebox. Mrs. Jones got up and went behind the screen. The woman did not watch the boy to see if he was going to run now, nor did she watch her purse, which she left behind her on the daybed. But the boy took care to sit on the far side of the room, away from the purse, where he thought she could easily see him out of the corner of her eye if she wanted to. He did not trust the woman *not* to trust him. And he did not want to be mistrusted now.

"Do you need somebody to go to the store," asked the boy, "maybe to get some milk or something?"

"Don't believe I do," said the woman, "unless you just want sweet milk yourself. I was going to make cocoa out of this canned milk I got here."

"That will be fine," said the boy.

She heated some lima beans and ham she had in the icebox, made the cocoa, and set the table. The woman did not ask the boy anything about where he lived, or his folks, or anything else that would **embarrass** him. Instead, as they ate, she told him about her job in a hotel beauty shop that stayed open late, what the work was like, and how all kinds of women came in and out, blondes, red-heads, and Spanish. Then she cut him a half of her ten-cent cake.

Unit 2   53

Have students read from line 105 to the end according to the option that you chose. As you read, mark the descriptions of the characters—both physical descriptions and personality traits.

When most of the students are finished, continue with the entire class. Let's see how well you understood what you read.

- Circle the check mark or the question mark for this section. Draw a question mark over any confusing words.

- Though it isn't written in words, what do you know about Mrs. Jones? (kind; generous; superstitious) Write the descriptions in the margin and highlight them.

- Though it isn't written in words, what do you know about Roger? (shy; grateful) Write the descriptions in the margin and highlight them.

- Go to line 105. Mark the word that represents Roger. (son)

- Go to line 109. Mark "come by devilish like that." Draw an arrow from *that* to what it refers to in the line above. (latching onto my pocketbook) What does that mean? (stealing) Write it in the margin.

- Go to line 110. Mark the phrase that means "from now on." (from here on in)

- Go to line 113. Mark the word that represents Roger. (boy)

- Go to line 117. Mark the word *that*. Draw an arrow from *that* to what it refers to. (say "Thank you, ma'am")

Have partners compare text markings and correct any errors.

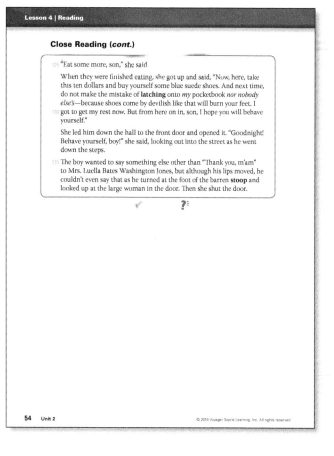

Character Analysis

Though characters often share adventures during a story, their experiences are markedly different. Let's talk about what each character experienced to determine how the outcomes for each character are the same and how they are different.

When Mrs. Luella Bates Washington Jones left work, what was she likely planning to do? (go home and eat, relax, then go to bed) When Roger saw Mrs. Jones, what did he think was going to happen? (he was going to steal her purse, run off, and buy blue suede shoes) How did Mrs. Jones likely view the encounter with Roger? (a nuisance) Now, let's think about their entire adventure together. What kind of experience was this for Roger? (a good experience; he experienced love and compassion and still got the money he was after) What kind of experience was this for Mrs. Jones? (the opportunity for company; a teaching opportunity; the ability to affect the life of someone less fortunate)

As you can see, the experiences of characters in the same series of events can be different. Keep that in mind as you read stories.

Lesson Opener

Before the lesson, choose one of the following activities to write on the board or post on the *LANGUAGE! Live* Class Wall online.

- *Write a sentence that follows each pattern:*

  When? + who or what? + what did he do? + what did he do it to? + how?

  Where? + who or what? + what did it do? + what did he do it to? + when?

  When? + where? + who or what? + what did he do? + how

- *Create a list of words that describe Roger. Create a list of words that describe Mrs. Jones. If there are any character traits they share, circle them.*

- *Write four sentences with at least two vocabulary words in each. Show you know the meanings. (latch, embarrass, release, permit, suede, balance, stoop, furnished, presentable, frail)*

Vocabulary

Objective

- Review key passage vocabulary.

Recontextualize Passage Vocabulary

Direct students to page 36 in their Student Books. Use the following questions to review the vocabulary words from "Thank You, M'am."

- Is a baby bird *frail*? (yes) Are football players usually *frail*? (no) What word describes a thin, sickly child—*healthy* or *frail*? (frail)

- If I grab a life preserver in rough water and do not let go, have I *latched* onto it? (yes) If I toss a flying disk to my dog, have I *latched* onto it? (no) Will the dog *latch* onto it? (yes) If you keep hold of your friend's arm in a crowded place, what have you done? (latched onto him or her)

- Are airplanes made of *suede*? (no) Can jackets be made of *suede*? (yes) Would you rather have a *suede* belt or a *suede* bathing suit? (Answers will vary.) Why is *suede* appealing? (It is soft and warm.)

- After a muddy camping trip with no running water, are you *presentable*? (no) After you shower and put on fresh clothes, are you *presentable*? (yes) If you are to receive an award at a special ceremony, how should you look? (presentable)

- If your mom allowed you to attend the school dance, were you *permitted* to do it? (yes) If I show up to the Super Bowl without a ticket, will I be *permitted* to enter? (no) You need to get your project out of your locker or you will fail. What do I need to do? (permit me to go get it)

- Is it hard to keep your *balance* on a one-wheeled cycle? (yes) It is hard to keep your *balance* on a wide, flat floor? (no) If I spin around 20 times, what might I lose? (your balance)

- If a person feels comfortable and is having a good time, is she being *embarrassed*? (no) If you forgot your lines in a play, would it *embarrass* you? (yes) If someone makes you feel uncomfortable and self-conscious, what is that person doing? (embarrassing me)

- If a house has a very large, covered patio, does it have a *stoop*? (no) Might a delivery person leave a package on a *stoop*? (yes) If I am sitting on the top step of my small porch, where am I sitting? (on the stoop)

- Does a *furnished* room have furniture in it? (yes) Do tents come *furnished* with bathrooms? (no) If a lake cabin has cots, a table and chairs, and a kitchenette, what is it? (furnished)

- Is it easy to *release* a hot pan or plate? (yes) Is it easy to *release* a ball of sticky dough? (no) If I am trying to let go of bad feelings, what am I trying to do? (release them)

Writing

Objectives
- Analyze literary characters.
- Use descriptive words in writing.
- Write in response to text.

Quick Write in Response to Reading

Part A. Paint the Subject

Direct students to Part A of page 55 in their Student Books. To prepare for your writing assignment, I want you to start thinking about how you would describe Mrs. Luella Bates Washington Jones. What are some words that describe "M'am?" Think quietly and write down traits or characteristics of this character. **Have every student share one trait they wrote down.** I think of words like *compassionate, concerned, strong-willed, determined, caring,* and *hard-working*.

Note: If students need more support, complete the activity with the whole class brainstorming traits. Write the traits on the board and have students copy them.

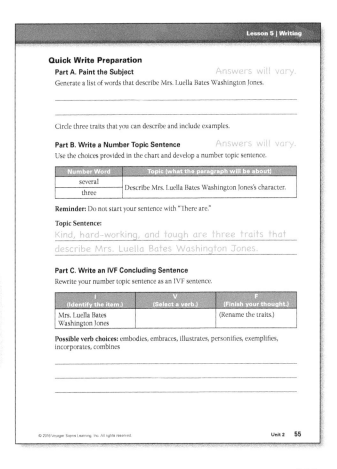

Lesson 5 | Writing

Quick Write Preparation

Part A. Paint the Subject   Answers will vary.
Generate a list of words that describe Mrs. Luella Bates Washington Jones.

Circle three traits that you can describe and include examples.

Part B. Write a Number Topic Sentence   Answers will vary.
Use the choices provided in the chart and develop a number topic sentence.

Number Word	Topic (what the paragraph will be about)
several	
three	Describe Mrs. Luella Bates Washington Jones's character.

Reminder: Do not start your sentence with "There are."

Topic Sentence:
Kind, hard-working, and tough are three traits that
describe Mrs. Luella Bates Washington Jones.

Part C. Write an IVF Concluding Sentence
Rewrite your number topic sentence as an IVF sentence.

I (Identify the item.)	V (Select a verb.)	F (Finish your thought.)
Mrs. Luella Bates Washington Jones		(Rename the traits.)

Possible verb choices: embodies, embraces, illustrates, personifies, exemplifies, incorporates, combines

Unit 2   55

Now, looking at your list of traits, choose three traits. Make sure you can provide an example from the text to support your choice of traits.

Part B. Write a Number Topic Sentence

Direct students to Part B. **Read the instructions for writing a number topic sentence, including the reminder.** Try starting your sentence with the three traits you've identified. Then, decide if you want to use the specific number word *three* or a word like *several*. Finally, write your topic sentence. **Provide a model sentence if students struggle.**

Part C. Write an IVF Concluding Sentence

Direct students to Part C. I want you to restate your number topic sentence as an IVF statement. Who are we writing about, or what is our *I*? (Mrs. Luella Bates Washington Jones) If you are struggling to think of a strong verb to use, choose one from the list below the chart. **Read the verbs aloud.** To finish the thought, restate or rename the traits you've chosen. **Have students write their sentences. Provide a model sentence if they struggle.**

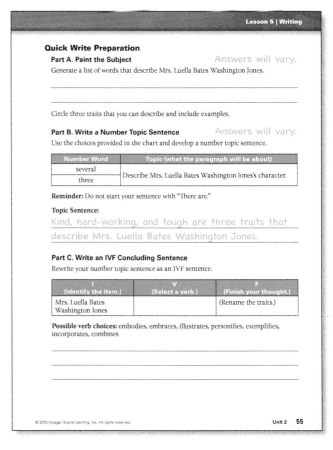

Direct students to page 56 in their Student Books and read the instructions for writing a descriptive paragraph aloud. Students should pull up their topic sentence and concluding sentence as a frame for their paragraph.

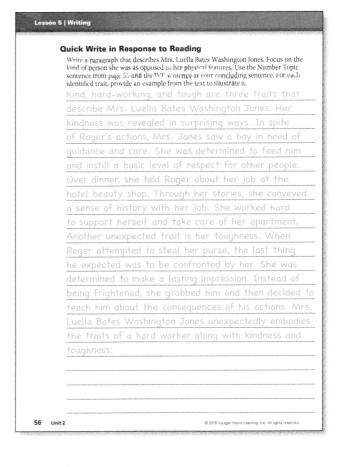

Reading

Objectives

- Self-correct as comprehension of text deepens.
- Answer questions to demonstrate comprehension of text.
- Engage in class discussion.
- Identify the enduring understandings from a piece of text.

Revisit Critical Understandings

Direct students back to page 49 in their Student Books. Have them review their answers and make any necessary changes. Then, have partners share their answers and collaborate to perfect them.

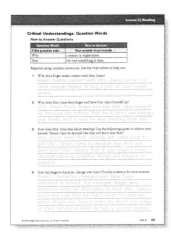

Enduring Understandings

Direct students back to page 35 in their Student Books. Reread the Big Idea questions.

Can a brief, chance encounter make a lasting impact?

Do people always need to be punished for their crimes?

Generate a class discussion about the questions and the answers students came up with in Lesson 1. Have them consider whether their answers have changed after reading the text.

Use the following talking points to foster conversation. Refer to the Class Discussion Rules poster and have students use the Collegial Discussion sentence frames on page 382 of their Student Books.

- People often come into our lives by chance. Sometimes, people associate these chance encounters with a spiritual happening—something out of their control. How long would the encounter have to be to foster genuine change?

- First impressions are important but don't always tell the whole story. Sometimes, we allow ourselves to unfairly pass judgments on people after a brief introduction.

- Is it possible that there are valid reasons for committing a crime? And, are forgiveness and love a deterrent to crime . . . or is punishment the only solution?

What we read should make us think. Use our discussion and your thoughts about the text to determine what you will "walk away with." Has it made you think about a personal experience or someone you know? Has your perspective or opinion on a specific topic changed? Do you have any lingering thoughts or questions? Write these ideas as your enduring understandings. What will you take with you from this text?

Discuss the enduring understandings with the class. Then, have students write their enduring understandings from the unit.

Have students consider why the author wrote the passage and whether he was successful.

Lesson 6

RL.4.6; RL.5.6; RL.7.5; RL.4.7; RL.1.10; RL.5.10; RF.5.4b;
SL.1.2; SL.5.1a; SL.5.1b; SL.5.1c; SL.5.1d; L.5.3b; L.3.4d;
L.3.5b; L.6.4c; L.6.6

Lesson Opener

Before the lesson, choose one of the following activities to write on the board or post on the *LANGUAGE! Live* Class Wall online.

- *Rewrite the sentences using plural pronouns:*
  - *I like to ride roller coasters.*
  - *He is waiting for the bus.*
  - *You are working in the yard.*
- *Make these nouns plural possessives and use them in sentences:*
  - *boy, shoe, stoop, student*
- *Imagine you are Roger and you run into Mrs. Jones on the street a year after you met. Describe the encounter. Would she recognize you? What would you tell her about yourself? What would you ask her?*

Reading

Objectives

- Determine and discuss the topic of a text.
- Determine and discuss the author's purpose.
- Use text features to preview text.

Passage Introduction

Direct students to page 57 in their Student Books. Discuss the content focus.

Content Focus
empowerment

We are about to read some poetry. Keep an open mind about poetry. A good attitude will help you understand this genre of literature. Poetry has the potential to make you think deeply and learn about the power of words. What do you think the poems will be about?

Type of Text
literature—poetry

Literature is divided into categories or genres. Say *genres*. **(genres)** "Thank You, M'am" belongs to the short story genre. The texts we will read today, "If I Were in Charge of the World" and "We Real Cool," belong to the poetry genre.

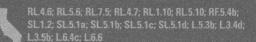

Lesson 6 | Reading

Let's Focus: "If I Were in Charge of the World"/"We Real Cool"

Content Focus	Type of Text
empowerment	literature—poetry

Authors' Names _Judith Viorst; Gwendolyn Brooks_

Authors' Purposes _to entertain; to teach a lesson_

Big Ideas
Consider the following Big Idea questions. Write your answer for each question.

Are we in control of our lives? Why or why not?

_____

_____

To what degree do the choices we make as teens affect our futures? Explain.

_____

_____

Poetry Preview Checklist: "If I Were in Charge of the World" and "We Real Cool" on pages 59 and 60.

☐ Title: What clue does it provide about the poem?

☐ Pictures: What additional information is added here?

☐ Margin Information: What vocabulary is important to understand this poem?

☐ Form: What do you notice about the poem's length, shape, layout, punctuation?

Enduring Understandings
After reading the poems . . .

_____

_____

_____

_____

_____

_____

Unit 2   57

Author's Purpose

Have students glance at the poems. Who is the author of "If I Were in Charge of the World"? (Judith Viorst) Who is the author of "We Real Cool"? (Gwendolyn Brooks) The author's purpose is the reason that he or she wrote the text. Authors write for different purposes. Poets write to entertain, express their thoughts, and make us think. Knowing an author's purpose can help you understand a text better. What do you know about poetry? Do all poems rhyme? (no) Do you have any favorite poems? **Provide sharing time.** Have you ever attempted to write poetry? **Provide sharing time.**

Have students write the answers on the page.

> **Note:** Determine if students need Background Information pertaining to public education and truancy. This can be found in the Teacher Resources online. Choose the Text Training tab, and then select Unit 2. The Background Information will be in the first section.

Read the Big Idea questions aloud.

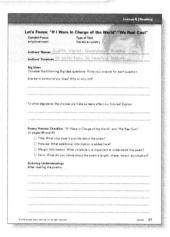

Big Ideas

Are we in control of our lives? Why or why not?

To what degree do the choices we make as teens affect our futures? Explain.

As a class, consider the two Big Idea questions.

- Encourage students with limited knowledge of juvenile rights and parental rights to ask for further explanation from peers.

- Have students reflect on the Background Information for the unit and ask clarifying questions when needed.

- Provide opportunities for students to explain their ideas and answers to the Big Idea questions in light of the discussion by ensuring students follow the rules for class discussion, which can be printed in poster form from the Teacher Resources online.

- Suggest students refer to the Collegial Discussion sentence frames in the back of their books.

- Encourage speakers to link comments to the remarks of others to keep the focus of the discussion and create cohesion, even when their comments are in disagreement.

After discussing each question, have students write an answer. We'll come back to these questions after we finish reading the poems. You can add to your answers as you gain information and perspective.

Preview

Read the Poetry Preview Checklist on page 57. Follow the Preview Procedure outlined below.

> ## Preview Procedure
> - Group students with partners or in triads.
> - Have students count off as 1s or 2s. The 1s will become the student leaders. If working with triads, the third students become 3s.
> - The student leaders will preview the text in addition to managing the checklist and pacing.
> - The 2s and 3s will preview the text with 1s.
> - Direct 1s to open their Student Books to page 57 and 2s and 3s to open their Student Books to pages 59 and 60. This allows students to look at a few different pages at one time without turning back and forth.

If it is necessary, guide students in a short preview using the following talking points. What is the title of the first poem? ("If I Were in Charge of the World") What clue does the title provide about the passage? (Someone wants to change the world.) Let's look to see what additional information the pictures provide. (about a young boy) What do you notice about the poem's form? (It is four stanzas long. The last two are longer than the first two. Proper punctuation is used.) What is the title of the next poem? ("We Real Cool") What clue does the title provide about the passage? (nonstandard English) Let's look to see what additional information the pictures provide. (The setting is at a pool hall.) What do you notice about the poem's form? (It also has four stanzas or paragraphs, but each one is only two sentences. Each sentence is only three words. Each line ends with *We*.)

Vocabulary

Objectives
- Evaluate word knowledge.
- Determine the meaning of key passage vocabulary.

Rate Vocabulary Knowledge

Direct students to page 58 in their Student Books. We are about to read two poems, "If I Were in Charge of the World" and "We Real Cool." Before we read, let's take a look at the vocabulary words we will come across in these poems. Remind students that as you read each word in the first column aloud, they will write the word in the third column and then rate their knowledge of it in the fourth. Display the Vocabulary Rating Scale poster or write the information on the board. Review the meaning of each rating.

Vocabulary Rating Scale

0—I have never heard the word before.

1—I have heard the word, but I'm not sure how to use it.

2—I am familiar with the word, but I'm not sure if I know the correct meaning.

3—I know the meaning of the word and can use it correctly in a sentence.

Key Passage Vocabulary: "If I Were in Charge of the World" and "We Real Cool"

Read each word. Write the word in column 3. Then, circle a number to rate your knowledge of the word.

Vocabulary	Part of Speech	Write the Word	Knowledge Rating
charge	(n)	charge	0 1 2 3
cancel	(v)	cancel	0 1 2 3
allergy	(n)	allergy	0 1 2 3
healthy	(adj)	healthy	0 1 2 3
lonely	(adj)	lonely	0 1 2 3
punch	(v)	punch	0 1 2 3
allow	(v)	allow	0 1 2 3
lurk	(v)	lurk	0 1 2 3
straight	(adv)	straight	0 1 2 3
sin	(n)	sin	0 1 2 3

The points are not a grade; they are just there to help you know which words you need to focus on. By the end of this unit, you should be able to change all your ratings to a 3—that's the goal.

Read each word aloud. Have students repeat it, write the word, and rate the word. Then, have volunteers who rated a word *2* or *3* use the word in an oral sentence.

Preteach Vocabulary

Let's take a closer look at the words. Follow the Preteach Procedure below.

Preteach Procedure

This activity is intended to take only a short amount of time, so make it an oral exercise.

- Introduce each word as indicated on the word card.
- Read the definition and example sentences.
- Ask questions to clarify and deepen understanding.
- If time permits, allow students to share.

* If your students would benefit from copying the definitions, please have them do so in the vocabulary log in the back of the Student Books using the margin definitions in the passage selections. This should be done outside of instruction time.

charge (n)

Let's read the first word together. *Charge.*

Definition: *Charge* means "the responsibility of managing or controlling something." What is the responsibility of managing or controlling something? (charge)

Example 1: It would be nice if students would take *charge* of keeping the campus looking nice.

Example 2: I am in *charge* of making dinner at my house. Who is in *charge* of making dinner at your house?

Example 3: Congress has the *charge* of making laws.

Question 1: If you are in *charge* of something, are you the boss? Yes or no? (yes)

Question 2: Can you be in *charge* of a person? Yes or no? (yes)

Pair Share: Turn to your partner and describe one event in school that you would like to be in *charge* of planning.

(1)

cancel (v)

Let's read the next word together. *Cancel.*

Definition: *Cancel* means "to stop something from happening or existing." What word means "to stop something from happening"? (cancel)

Example 1: If you get sick, you might have to *cancel* some plans.

Example 2: When it rains, baseball games can be *canceled.*

Example 3: A restaurant may *cancel* your reservation if you do not show up on time.

Question 1: A test you are dreading gets *canceled.* Are you glad? Yes or no? (yes)

Question 2: If you *cancel* a food order, will you receive the food? Yes or no? (no)

Pair Share: Turn to your partner and tell about an upcoming event you hope gets *canceled.*

(2)

allergy (n)

Let's read the next word together. *Allergy.*

Definition. If you have an *allergy*, you get sick when you eat, breathe, or touch something that doesn't bother most other people. What means "an illness from eating, breathing, or touching something"? (allergy)

Example 1: If you have a peanut *allergy*, you will get sick if you eat peanut butter.

Example 2: Some people take shots to help manage their *allergies.*

Example 3: My child has a cat *allergy*, so I cannot adopt a kitten.

Question 1: If you get sick whenever you eat shrimp, could you have an *allergy*? Yes or no? (yes)

Question 2: If oak pollen makes you sneeze, could a medicine made for *allergies* help? Yes or no? (yes)

Pair Share: Turn to your partner and tell whether you have an *allergy*, and if so, what its effects are.

(3)

healthy (adj)

Let's read the next word together. *Healthy.*

Definition: *Healthy* means "in a good state or condition." What means "in a good state or condition"? (healthy)

Example 1: Someone who exercises every day is *healthier* than someone who doesn't.

Example 2: A young, energetic child is *healthy*, but an old person with medical problems is unhealthy.

Example 3: If you have a goldfish and it dies, it was likely not *healthy.*

Question 1: Is a person who eats fresh fruit *healthier* than one who eats fruit-flavored candy? Yes or no? (yes)

Question 2: Is a blooming rose bush *healthy*? Yes or no? (yes)

Pair Share: Turn to your partner and name two things you could do to make yourself *healthier.*

lonely (adj)

Let's read the next word together. *Lonely.*

Definition: *Lonely* means "sad from being without the company of others." Sad from being without the company of others is what? (lonely)

Example 1: When I get home from work, I am *lonely* until my family gets home.

Example 2: My grandmother lives alone. She was *lonely*, so we bought her a dog.

Example 3: When I feel *lonely*, I turn on the television so there are voices in the room.

Question 1: Would you likely feel *lonely* in a crowd of friends? Yes or no? (no)

Question 2: Is feeling *lonely* a good feeling? Yes or no? (no)

Pair Share: Turn to your partner and tell about a time you felt *lonely.*

(5)

punch (v)

Let's read the next word together. *Punch.*

Definition: *Punch* means "to hit hard with a fist." What means "to hit hard with a fist"? (punch)

Example 1: Boxers *punch* a large stuffed bag during practice.

Example 2: If you *punch* someone's arm, he or she might get a bruise.

Example 3: I always shut my eyes when one character *punches* another in a movie.

Question 1: If you *punch* a brick wall, will it hurt your hand? Yes or no? (yes)

Question 2: If you *punch* your friend, will he or she punch you back? Yes or no? (Answers will vary.)

Pair Share: Turn to your partner and tell why *punching* someone is not a good way to solve a disagreement.

(6)

allow (v)

Let's read the next word together. *Allow.*

Definition: *Allow* means "to let something happen." What means "to let something happen"? (allow)

Example 1: When I was young, my parents did not *allow* me to stay up late.

Example 2: If you raise your hand, I will *allow* you to speak.

Example 3: By opening a window, you *allow* air to flow into the room.

Question 1: Does a cast *allow* a broken arm to move? Yes or no? (no)

Question 2: Would a strict parent *allow* a child to watch R-rated movies? Yes or no? (no)

Pair Share: Should laws *allow* 14-year-olds to drive? Turn to your partner and share your opinion.

(7)

lurk (v)

Let's read the next word together. *Lurk.*

Definition: *Lurk* means "to wait in secret, to hang out where you shouldn't be." What means "to wait in secret or to hang out where you shouldn't be"? (lurk)

Example 1: If you *lurk* at the back of a store, the manager might grow suspicious.

Example 2: In old houses, it sometimes feels as if a ghost *lurks* around every corner.

Example 3: You should not *lurk* in the school hallways after hours.

Question 1: If you leave a movie theater right after the movie is over, are you *lurking*? Yes or no? (no)

Question 2: If you hang out in the alley behind the theater late at night, are you *lurking*? Yes or no? (yes)

Pair Share: Turn to your partner and describe a scene in a horror movie in which someone is *lurking*. You can make up the scene.

(8)

straight (adv)

Let's read the next word together. *Straight.*

Definition: *Straight* means "in a firm and direct way." What word means "in a firm and direct way"? (straight)

Example 1: Tell me *straight*: do you like my outfit?

Example 2: Don't hesitate; just dive *straight* into the cold water.

Example 3: The basketball hit me *straight* in the face.

Question 1: If you hit a pool ball *straight*, are you a good shot? Yes or no? (yes)

Question 2: If you walk *straight* into the classroom, do you hesitate? Yes or no? (no)

Pair Share: Turn to your partner and tell whether you would march *straight* to the principal's office if you were called, and why.

(9)

sin (n)

Let's read the last word together. *Sin.*

Definition: A *sin* is an offense against religious or moral law. What is an offense against religious or moral law? (sin)

Example 1: Lying is a *sin*, but many people do this to make people feel good, such as by saying "I like your new haircut."

Example 2: In "Thank You, M'am," Roger tried to commit the *sin* of stealing.

Example 3: People who don't consider themselves to be religious still typically follow a moral code to avoid *sins*.

Question 1: If you say "please" and "thank you," are you *sinning*? Yes or no? (no)

Question 2: Is a *sin* considered wrong? Yes or no? (yes)

Pair Share: Turn to your partner and tell a *sin* that you witnessed on TV this week.

(10)

Objectives

- Read poetry.
- Monitor comprehension during text reading.
- Compare a poem with its audio production.
- Identify the point of view in poetry.
- Use word choice to determine the tone of a poem.
- Determine the function of subjunctive verbs.
- Summarize poetry.

"If I Were in Charge of the World" and "We Real Cool"

Direct students to pages 59 and 60 in their Student Books.

Now it's time to read. When reading, you should be thinking about the meaning of the text and the poet's word choice and use of rhyme. Reading poetry out loud can help you hear the rhythm. Reading multiple times can increase your understanding of the poem and the author's intent.

Guiding Students Toward Independent Reading

It is important that your students read as much as and as often as they can. Assign readings that meet the needs of your students, based on your observations and data. This is a good opportunity to stretch your students. If students become frustrated, scaffold the reading with paired reading, choral reading, or a read-aloud.

Options for reading text:

- Teacher read-aloud
- Teacher-led or student-led choral read
- Paired read or independent read

Choose an option for reading text. Students read both poems according to the option that you chose.

After the initial read, have students read the poems aloud with a partner. Read the poetry reading tips aloud.

Tips for Reading Poetry Out Loud

Many people do not have experience reading poetry out loud. Some people think it is an art form. Have you ever heard a great song sung poorly? How would that impact your opinion of the song? Singing is to song as reading is to poetry. The way the poem is read is as important as the way a song is sung.

Billy Collins, former Poet Laureate, provides pointers about the oral recitation of poetry.

1. Read the poem slowly. Set the pace by pausing for a few seconds between the title and the poem's first line.

2. Read in a normal, relaxed tone of voice. Speak clearly and slowly. Let the words of the poem do their work.

3. Pause only where there is punctuation, not at the end of every line.

4. Read accurately and fluently; look up unfamiliar or hard-to-pronounce words in the dictionary.

SE p. 59

If I Were in Charge of the World

If I were in **charge** of the world
I'd **cancel** oatmeal,
Monday mornings,
Allergy shots, and also
Sara Steinberg.

If I were in charge of the world
There'd be brighter night lights,
Healthier hamsters, and
Basketball baskets forty-eight inches lower.

If I were in charge of the world
You wouldn't have **lonely**.
You wouldn't have clean.
You wouldn't have bedtimes.
Or "Don't **punch** your sister."
You wouldn't even have sisters.

If I were in charge of the world
A chocolate sundae with whipped cream and nuts
    would be a vegetable.
All 007 movies would be G.
And a person who sometimes forgot to brush,
And sometimes forgot to flush,
Would still be **allowed** to be
In charge of the world.

We Real Cool

THE POOL PLAYERS. SEVEN AT THE GOLDEN SHOVEL.

We real cool. We
Left school. We

Lurk late. We
Strike **straight**. We

Sing **sin**. We
Thin gin. We

Jazz June. We
Die soon.

*"We Real Cool"
audio file*

Note: The audio version of "We Real Cool" can be found online in the Teacher Resources. Because beat poetry needs to be read in a specific way for effect, it is beneficial to play an audio performance after students' initial read.

"If I Were in Charge of the World"

"If I Were in Charge of the World" is a first-person narrative. Who is telling the narrative? (a child under 13 years old) How do you know? (night lights; G-rated movies) This poem is told by a narrator in first-person point of view. That means that the person telling the story is the character in the poem. The narrator is inside the poem. Where is the narrator? (inside the poem)

What does the narrator like? What does the narrator dislike? (The narrator likes chocolate sundaes, Secret Agent James Bond, sleeping with night lights on, hamsters, and basketball. The narrator doesn't like oatmeal, Monday mornings, allergy shots, Sara Steinberg, going to bed early, the dark, vegetables, his sister, bathing, or brushing his teeth every day.)

Note: The use of *Were* in the title of the poem may confuse students based on the lesson on past tense linking/helping verbs. Explain to students that when a sentence starts with a dependent clause beginning with *if* and expressing a condition that does not exist, the subjunctive verb *were* is used.

"We Real Cool"

"We Real Cool" is also a first-person narrative told by one of the seven pool players that dropped out of school. How do you know? (*We* includes the narrator.) Is the narrator inside or outside of the poem? (inside)

What is the tone in the beginning of the poem? (The tone starts out upbeat, full of bravado.)

When does the tone change? (last line of play) The tone quickly changes to solemn when referring to death.

What is the narrator's point of view on authority in each poem? (Both narrators dislike authority, but Viorst's narrator acknowledges the need for rules like trying to eat vegetables, brushing one's teeth, and following the rules of standard English. On the other hand, Brooks's narrator shows no value for rules and conventions, as represented by short sentences, nonstandard English, staying up late, and skipping school.)

Comparing Audio with Print

If you played the audio version of "We Real Cool," generate a class discussion about the differences between hearing the poem and reading the poem. Ask the following questions to foster conversation:

1. Which version was more entertaining?

2. Which version was easier to understand?

3. What did you get from the audio version that you did not get from your reading?

Summarize with IVF Topic Sentences

Direct students to page 62 in their Student Books.

An effective strategy for monitoring your comprehension is to share a summary about what you read using concise words rather than going on and on with a string of details. The IVF Topic Sentence provides a format that is an effective way to begin a summary. First, let's identify the title of the first poem and record it in the first column. Next, I will choose a strong verb from the verb bank. I'll choose the verb *presents*. Finally, we need to finish the thought.

Have volunteers finish the thought. Write the sentence on the board.

I Identify the Item.	V Select a Verb.	F Finish Your Thought.
"If I Were in Charge of the World"	presents	changes that a child would make if he had the authority.
"We Real Cool"	describes	the trouble teens get in when they drop of out of school.

Have partners write an IVF Topic Sentence for each poem.

When most partners have finished, collect one sentence per partner. Share summary sentences with the entire group to begin a class discussion about their immediate impression of each poem. Invite students to make suggestions for edits that include mechanics and word choice, such as spelling, punctuation, correct use of quotation marks, and a variety of strong verbs. Encourage students to fix their own mistakes.

Unit 2
Lesson 7

RL.5.2; RL.2.4; RL.3.5; RL.4.6; RL.6.5; RL.6.6; RL.7.4; RL.7.5;
RL.8.5; RL.6.9; L.1.1d; L.1.1j; L.2.1e; L.2.1f; L.3.1a; L.3.1i;
L.5.2b; L.6.6

Lesson Opener

Before the lesson, choose one of the following activities to write on the board or post on the *LANGUAGE! Live* Class Wall online.

- *Write an IVF summary sentence about two movies you like.*
- *Replace "the purse" in both sentences with a pronoun. Identify whether it is the subject of the sentence or the object of the sentence.*

    The purse had a long strap.

    She carried the purse slung across her shoulder.

- *Write two sentences with* latch, *using it as a noun in one sentence and a verb in another.*

Vocabulary

Objective

- Review key passage vocabulary.

Review Passage Vocabulary

Direct students to page 58 in their Student Books. Use the following questions to review the vocabulary words from "If I Were in Charge of the World" and "We Real Cool." Have students answer each question using the vocabulary word or indicating its meaning in a complete sentence.

- The speaker of "If I Were in Charge of the World" wants to *cancel* oatmeal. Does he like oatmeal? (No; if you want to cancel oatmeal, you do not want it to exist.) What else does he want to *cancel*? (He also wants to cancel Monday mornings.)

- Does the speaker of "If I Were in Charge of the World" have *allergies*? (Yes, the speaker has allergies.) How do you know? (He wants to cancel allergy shots too, and he wouldn't need the shots if he didn't have allergies.)

- The speaker wishes for "*healthier* hamsters." What might have happened to his hamsters? (His hamsters might have gotten sick and died because they weren't healthy.) What can a *healthy* hamster do that an unhealthy hamster cannot? (A healthy hamster can run on a wheel, burrow, and play.)

- Who asks the speaker not to *punch* his sister? (It is probably his mother or father who asks him not to punch his sister.) Would his sister like being *punched*? Why or why not? (No, his sister would not like being punched because it hurts to be hit hard with someone's fist.)

- The speaker wishes to be in *charge* of the world. Would life be different if the speaker were in *charge*? (Yes, the world would be very different if the speaker were in charge.) Would sundaes be eaten if he were in charge of the world? (Yes, sundaes would be eaten regularly if he were in charge.)

- The speaker no longer wants to feel *lonely*. What would make the speaker feel less *lonely*? (He would feel less lonely if he were surrounded by friends.) Based on his age, when do you think the speaker feels *lonely*? (The speaker probably feels lonely at night when he is trying to sleep.)

- Is the speaker *allowed* to stay up past his bedtime? How do you know? (No, he is not allowed to stay up past his bedtime because he wishes there were no bedtimes.) Is the speaker *allowed* to watch movies made for grown-ups? How do you know? (He is not allowed to watch movies made for grown-ups because he wishes all 007 movies were rated G.)

- In "We Real Cool," when do the speakers *lurk*? (They lurk late.) Where should the speakers be, instead of *lurking*? (They should be at home instead of lurking.)

- What do the speakers say they do *straight*? (They say they strike straight.) What are they *striking*? (They are pool players, so they are probably striking pool balls—but they also sound rough and may be striking people.)

- The seven pool players sing about what? (They sing about sin.) What is the topic of their "songs"? (Their "songs" are about things they have done wrong.) In this usage, what does *singing* mean? (*Singing* means "bragging" in this usage.) Why would they brag about their *sins*? (They would brag to look cool.)

Objectives

- Understand the function and purpose of prepositions and prepositional phrases.
- Use prepositions correctly.
- Use adverbs and prepositional phrases correctly in sentence writing.
- Produce, expand, and rearrange complete sentences.
- Use commas to set off prepositional phrases.

Using Commas in Masterpiece Sentences

What type of words add to the verb? (adverbs) We learned to paint the predicate, or the verb, by answering what questions? (when, where, and how) This can be done with adverbs or prepositional phrases.

Moving predicate painters around in your sentence is a great way to create variety in sentence structure. When you move a predicate painter phrase to the beginning of a sentence, it becomes an introductory element and has to be set off from the rest of the sentence with a comma. The comma separates the extra information about the predicate from the subject part of the sentence. For readers, it's a cue to pause and consider the information the phrase provides. It's important to realize that commas are not randomly placed. They help us group words together that belong together. **Direct students to page 63 in their Student Books and read the instructions aloud.**

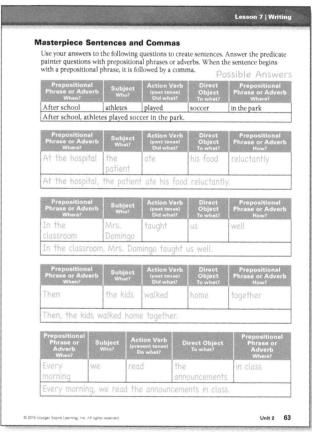

Guided Practice

Let's look at the sample sentence. The prepositional phrase *after school* has been placed at the beginning of the sentence. What's the subject of the sentence? (athletes) What's the action verb? (played) What tense is the verb? (past tense) What did they play? (They played soccer.) *Soccer* is receiving the action, so it's called the direct object. Do we know where they played soccer? (Yes, they played soccer in the park.) When I write the complete sentence, I have to remember to add a comma at the end of the adverb phrase *after school*. It needs to be separated from the subject part of the sentence.

Independent Practice

Have students write sentences that match the remaining patterns. Make sure you add the necessary punctuation to each sentence. Have volunteers share their sentences with the class. Correct as needed.

Note: If students are struggling, keep the class together and walk through each sentence encouraging students to brainstorm options and then choose from all of the ideas.

Grammar

Objectives
- Identify the function and purpose of pronouns.
- Use pronouns correctly.
- Use pronouns to determine author's point of view.

Pronouns and Point of View

What words take the place of nouns? (pronouns) Using pronouns makes our speech and writing more efficient because we use them instead of repeatedly using the nouns they replace. Pronouns also help establish point of view within a piece of text.

Direct students to page 64 in their Student Books and reference the chart. What are the first-person pronouns? (I, we, me, us, my, our, mine, ours) This list includes more than just subject and object pronouns. Which first-person pronouns are subject pronouns? (I, we) Which ones are object pronouns? (me, us) Which ones are possessive pronouns? (my, mine, our, ours) When does a narrator or author use first person? (when he is writing about himself) What are the second-person pronouns? (you, your, yours) The pronoun *you* can refer to one person or more than one and functions as the subject and object pronoun. When does a narrator or storyteller use second person? (when a narrator is writing to explain something to someone) Let's take a look at third-person pronouns. The list is quite long compared to the other categories. What are the subject pronouns? (she, he, it, they) What are the object pronouns? (her, him, it, them) Which ones are possessive pronouns? (her, hers, his, its, their, theirs) When would a narrator use third person? (when writing about a person, place, thing, or idea)

Lesson 7 | Grammar

Pronouns and Point of View

The position of the narrator in relation to other people and events in the story is called point of view. The point of view is often described in terms of first person, second person, or third person.

Person	Pronoun forms		Used when the narrator is . . .
First Person	I we me us my our mine ours		writing about him- or herself
Second Person	you your yours		writing to explain something to someone
Third Person	she he it they her him it them hers his its their theirs		writing about a person, place, thing, or idea

"Thank You, M'am"

Point of View _Third person_

Pronouns to Prove It: _she, it, him, his, he, her_

"If I Were in Charge of the World"

Point of View _First person_

Pronouns to Prove It: _I_

"We Real Cool"

Point of View _First person_

Pronouns to Prove It: _we_

64   Unit 2   © 2016 Voyager Sopris Learning, Inc. All rights reserved.

Point out the pronouns *mine, ours, yours, hers,* and *theirs.* Explain to students that we use these pronouns when the object that they possess does not follow the pronoun in the sentence.

Examples: That is my blanket. That blanket is mine. It is mine.

That is her car. That car is hers. It is hers.

Direct students to "Thank You, M'am" and then each poem, or have them tear them out of the back of the book.

Let's take a look at the three text selections in this unit and determine the point of view in each one. We will focus on the pronouns to determine the point of view. **Have students identify the point of view, then have them cite pronoun usage to support the chosen point of view. Have students write the information on the page.**

Assign online practice by opening the Tools menu, then selecting Assignments. Be sure to select the correct class from the drop-down menu.

Reading

Objectives
- Identify the structure and form of poetry.
- Analyze the impact of word choice, graphical elements, and rhyme in poetry.

Elements of Poetry

We read the poems "If I Were in Charge of the World" and "We Real Cool" in the last lesson. Now we'll have the chance to look at their form and content. What is poetry? **Have volunteers share ideas.** Poetry is literature written in verse. Poets write stories that rhyme or have rhythm. Not all poems rhyme; some create rhythm through alliteration. Listen: *Pete the poet picks particular patterns.* What did you notice? (Most words start with the /p/ sound.) Alliteration is when you use words that have the same sound in the beginning. Say *alliteration.* (alliteration) Some poems don't have rhyme or rhythm. Poems without much rhyme or rhythm are called free verse. What are poems called that don't have much rhyme or rhythm? (free verse)

Many poems have distinctive signs or elements. Let's take a look at six elements, or characteristics, of poetry.

Direct students to page 65 in their Student Books and reference the six elements of poetry.

Theme: A poem has a message, or theme. What would you say is the overall message in "If I Were in Charge of the World"? (childhood concerns, empowerment) How about "We Real Cool"? (hopelessness, rebellion against society)

Imagery: Imagery is another element in poetry. The words in a poem are typically chosen to create a vivid picture in the reader's mind, one that will help communicate the theme. Choose one of the poems that we read. Tell your neighbor about the image that you have created in your mind's eye about that poem. **Provide sharing time.**

Mood: A poet strives to choose words that will create a certain mood or feeling. Some poems are dark and melancholy, while others are light and playful. What kind of mood do you think the poet tried to create in "If I Were in Charge of the World"? (light, playful, empowering, constructive) How about "We Real Cool"? (dark, loss of hope, destructive)

Melody: Many song lyrics would qualify as poetry. The arrangement of words, unusual sentence or phrase structure, and rhyme contribute to the sense of rhythm or melody. Which poem uses rhyme patterns to create a sense of melody? ("We Real Cool") Some say that "We Real Cool" reads like the lyrics of a jazz song. It is an example of beat poetry. This kind of poetry is meant to be read aloud. What rhyming pairs are in "We Real Cool"? (cool/school; late/straight; sin/gin; June/soon)

Meter: In more sophisticated poems, such as sonnets, the poet consciously chooses words to build a certain number of syllables and units of stress. Meter, or a set pattern of stressed and unstressed syllables, is another way poets create rhythm. What do you notice about the number of syllables of each word in "We Real Cool" by Gwendolyn Brooks? (Each word has one syllable.)

Form: Form refers to the physical structure of the poem. Some poems have set forms whereas others do not. A poem with a set form would have a certain number of lines, a certain meter, and a certain rhyme scheme that contributes to its meaning. A poem without a set form might have varying line lengths and no rhyme at all. Compare the physical structure of both poems. Discuss observations with your partner. ("If I Were in Charge of the World" starts with the same line at the beginning of each stanza, which is the same as the title. Each verse has varying line lengths. "We Real Cool" has three-word sentences of one-syllable words. The first sentence is the same as the title. Each line ends with the beginning of the next sentence: *We*. Both poems are four

Elements of Poetry

Theme	Thought is the element that contains the poem's message. One component of thought is the theme, which is often stated as a universal truth—unlimited by time and space.
Imagery	Imagery refers to the poem's creation of mental pictures, or images, for the reader. Metaphor, simile, and personification are examples of techniques that poets use to create imagery.
Mood	Poems evoke emotions and set an atmosphere or a tone for the reader. This element is called mood.
Melody	Melody is the element created by a poet's use of sound. Alliteration, rhyme, assonance, consonance, and onomatopoeia are examples of devices used to create melody in poetry.
Meter	Patterns of stressed and unstressed syllables in a poem create meter or poetic rhythm.
Form	Form is the element that defines the poem's actual structure. Examples of poetic forms include quatrain, sonnet, blank verse, limerick, ballad, and free (open) verse.

Complete the chart below based on the poem "If I Were in Charge of the World."

"If I Were in Charge of the World"	
Theme	Being in charge; having the ability to change rules and expectations
Imagery	Achieved through unusual twists, like canceling oatmeal or an unpleasant person like Sara Steinberg; brighter night lights; chocolate sundae being a vegetable; common objects easily imagined in reader's mind
Mood	Humorous—achieved through whimsical ideas, but very pertinent to a child
Melody	Repeating the first line in every stanza; within each stanza is a sense of rhythm unique to that stanza

Unit 2   65

verses, but "We Real Cool" only has two lines per verse. "We Real Cool" has a set form; "If I Were in Charge of the World" does not. It is free verse.)

Let's apply the first four traits to the poem "If I Were in Charge of the World." Listen as I reread the poem and think about the message within the poem. What does the poet want us to take away from the poem? **Read the poem.**

SE p. 59

If I Were in Charge of the World

If I were in **charge** of the world
I'd **cancel** oatmeal,
Monday mornings,
Allergy shots, and also
Sara Steinberg.

If I were in charge of the world
There'd be brighter night lights,
Healthier hamsters, and
Basketball baskets forty-eight inches lower.

If I were in charge of the world
You wouldn't have **lonely**.
You wouldn't have clean.
You wouldn't have bedtimes.
Or "Don't **punch** your sister."
You wouldn't even have sisters.

If I were in charge of the world
A chocolate sundae with whipped cream and nuts
    would be a vegetable.
All 007 movies would be G.
And a person who sometimes forgot to brush,
And sometimes forgot to flush,
Would still be **allowed** to be
In charge of the world.

Have volunteers share their ideas. (Possible ideas: being in charge; having the ability to change rules and expectations.) **Offer ideas if students are struggling to identify the message. Have students write ideas in the chart.**

Think about imagery. The poet doesn't use a tremendous number of adjectives or descriptors and yet creates vivid imagery. How does she do that? (Possible answers: unique ideas like canceling oatmeal or an unpleasant person; brighter night lights; chocolate sundae as a vegetable. Objects are easily imagined in the reader's mind.)

What is the mood of the poem? Is it serious, gloomy, humorous? (humorous—ideas are lighthearted, doing no harm to anyone else)

How does the poet create a sense of rhythm or melody in the poem? (Possible answers: First line of every stanza is the same; within each stanza the lines have a similar sound or cadence.)

Understanding the elements of poetry can help us read and interpret a poem the way the author intended.

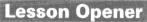
Lesson 8

RL.1.3; RL.1.10; RL.4.1; RL.5.10; RL.6.6

Lesson Opener

Before the lesson, choose one of the following activities to write on the board or post on the *LANGUAGE! Live* Class Wall online.

- *Combine these two sentences to make one sentence:*
  Sarah studied for her test yesterday afternoon.
  Sarah studied for her test in the library.
- *Write sentences with* release, *using it as a noun and as a verb.*
- *How would the world be different if you were in charge?*

Reading

Objectives

- Read poetry.
- Monitor comprehension during text reading.
- Use critical thinking skills to write responses to prompts about text.
- Support written answers with text evidence.

Reading for a Purpose: "If I Were in Charge of the World" and "We Real Cool"

Let's reread both poems. Our purpose for this read is to help us answer questions about the text.

Direct students to page 67 in their Student Books. Have students read the prompts aloud with you.

1. Use context to determine who the poems are about.

2. Empowerment and hopelessness are antonyms. Explain how these terms relate to each poem as well as the short story "Thank You, M'am."

3. Describe the setting in the poem "We Real Cool."

4. Explain how the choices that the pool players make will affect their lives.

5. Tell the things the narrator of "If I Were in Charge of the World" dislikes.

Notice that the "questions" you will be answering don't have question marks.

Lesson 8 | Reading

Passage Comprehension

Read the prompts and respond using complete sentences. Use the chart on page 66 to determine how to respond.

1. Use context to determine who the poems are about.
   "If I Were in Charge of the World" is about a child who wishes he had more control over his life. "We Real Cool" is about seven troubled teens who spend the day playing pool, bragging about things they've done wrong, and doing illegal acts instead of going to school.

2. Empowerment and hopelessness are antonyms. Explain how these terms relate to each poem as well as the short story "Thank You, M'am."
   "If I Were in Charge of the World" is about a child feeling empowered to change the world so that he has more control over his life. "We Real Cool" is about teens who felt hopeless in school so they tried to empower themselves in a negative way by rebelling against society. In "Thank You, M'am," Roger started out feeling that he needed to steal in order to get what he wanted out of life. At the end, Roger felt empowered to do the right thing in the future, thanks to Mrs. Jones.

3. Describe the setting in the poem "We Real Cool."
   "We Real Cool" takes place late at night at a pool hall called the Golden Shovel.

4. Explain how the choices that the pool players make will affect their lives.
   The bad choices made by the pool players, such as leaving school, adding water to alcohol, bragging about breaking the rules, and staying out late, will eventually lead to an early death.

5. Tell the things the narrator of "If I Were in Charge of the World" dislikes.
   The narrator of "If I Were in Charge of the World" dislikes oatmeal, Monday mornings, feeling lonely, being clean, going to bed early, and sisters.

Unit 2   **67**

That's because they are prompts instead of questions. We will learn how to answer these types of questions after we reread the poems.

> Choose an option for rereading text.
> - Teacher read-aloud
> - Teacher-led or student-led choral read
> - Paired read or independent read
> - Individual or paired read-aloud

Direct students to pages 59 and 60 in their Student Books or have them tear out the extra copies of the poems from the back of their book.

Note: To minimize flipping back and forth between the pages, a copy of each text has been included in the back of the Student Books. Encourage students to tear this out and use it when working on activities that require the use of the text.

Have students reread the poems.

Print the Critical
Understandings
posters found in the
Teacher Resources
online and display
where students can
easily see it.

Critical Understandings: Direction Words *describe, explain, tell, use*

In this class and in others, you are often asked questions at a variety of difficulty levels.

Some are in the form of questions, and some are in the form of prompts. Prompts are statements that require a constructed response, which can range from a list to a complete sentence to a paragraph or an essay.

Write the words *describe, explain, tell,* and *use* on the board. Have students read the words aloud with you. Direct students to page 66 in their Student Books. It is critical to understand what the question is asking and how to answer it. Today, we will look at four direction words used in prompts. You will become familiar with these direction words and learn how to answer different types of questions.

Have students read about the four words on the chart on page 66 with their partner. They should only focus on the direction words on the board.

Chart Reading Procedure

- Group students with partners or in triads.
- Have students count off as 1s or 2s. The 1s will become the student leaders. If working with triads, the third students become 3s.
- The student leaders will read the left column (Prompt) in addition to managing the time and turn-taking if working with a triad.
- The 2s will explain the middle column of the chart (How to Respond). If working in triads, 2s and 3s take turns explaining the middle column.
- The 1s read the model in the right column (Model), and 2s and 3s restate the model as a question.
- All students should follow along with their pencil eraser while others are explaining the chart.
- Students must work from left to right, top to bottom in order to benefit from this activity.

Check for understanding by requesting an oral response to the following questions.

- If the prompt asks you to *describe*, the response requires you to . . . (state detailed information about a topic).
- If the prompt asks you to *explain*, the response requires you to . . . (express understanding of an idea or concept).
- If the prompt asks you to *tell*, the response requires you to . . . (say or write specific information).
- If the prompt asks you to *use*, the response requires you to . . . (apply information or a procedure).

Passage Comprehension

Direct students to page 67 in their Student Books. Let's practice answering questions that are written as prompts. Remember to use the chart as reference.

Model

Listen as I model the first one for you.

> 1. Use context to determine who the poems are about.

According to the chart, if the prompt asks you to *use*, you should apply information or a procedure. In this case, we are applying our knowledge of context (the text surrounding a word or group of words). Let's restate the prompt using a basic question word. Who are the poems about? How will I start my answer?

Write the following sentence starters on the board.

"If I Were in Charge of the World" is about _____.

"We Real Cool" is about _____.

There is a picture of a young boy on the page, and it talks about G-rated movies and 007, so I think "If I Were in Charge of the World" is about a young boy. **Write the answer on the board.**

The text says that "We Real Cool" is about seven pool players, so I will use that to write my answer. But, I also know more about the pool players from the context of the poem. I know they are high-school dropouts and troublemakers. I will add that to my answer. **Write the answer on the board. Have students write the answer on the page.**

Passage Comprehension

Read the prompts and respond using complete sentences. Use the chart on page 66 to determine how to respond.

1. Use context to determine who the poems are about.
   "If I Were in Charge of the World" is about a child who wishes he had more control over his life. "We Real Cool" is about seven troubled teens who spend the day playing pool, bragging about things they've done wrong, and doing illegal acts instead of going to school.

2. Empowerment and hopelessness are antonyms. Explain how these terms relate to each poem as well as the short story "Thank You, M'am."
   "If I Were in Charge of the World" is about a child feeling empowered to change the world so that he has more control over his life. "We Real Cool" is about teens who felt hopeless in school so they tried to empower themselves in a negative way by rebelling against society. In "Thank You, M'am," Roger started out feeling that he needed to steal in order to get what he wanted out of life. At the end, Roger felt empowered to do the right thing in the future, thanks to Mrs. Jones.

3. Describe the setting in the poem "We Real Cool."
   "We Real Cool" takes place late at night at a pool hall called the Golden Shovel.

4. Explain how the choices that the pool players make will affect their lives.
   The bad choices made by the pool players, such as leaving school, adding water to alcohol, bragging about breaking the rules, and staying out late, will eventually lead to an early death.

5. Tell the things the narrator of "If I Were in Charge of the World" dislikes.
   The narrator of "If I Were in Charge of the World" dislikes oatmeal, Monday mornings, feeling lonely, being clean, going to bed early, and sisters.

Unit 2   67

Guided Practice

> 2. Empowerment and hopelessness are antonyms. Explain how these terms relate to each poem as well as the short story "Thank You, M'am."

How should we respond according to the chart? (If the prompt asks you to *explain*, the response requires you to express understanding of an idea or concept.) Now, turn the prompt into a question to confirm your understanding. Tell your partner the question. (How do empowerment and hopelessness play out in the three different text selections?) When you feel empowered, you feel that you can take action to make a difference for yourself or someone else. In contrast, when you feel hopeless, you don't think your actions or the actions of others can make much of a difference. Let's apply these ideas to the three pieces of text listed in the question. Now, answer the question. Provide the following sentence starters and have a volunteer complete the sentences.

"If I Were in Charge of the World" is about _____.

"We Real Cool" is about _____.

In "Thank You, M'am," Roger started out feeling _____.
At the end, Roger felt _____ *thanks to Mrs. Jones.*

Independent Practice

Have partners respond to the remaining prompts with text evidence. For students who need more assistance, provide the alternative questions and sentence starters.

Alternative questions and sentence starters:

3. When and where does "We Real Cool" take place?

"We Real Cool" takes place _____.

4. How will the choices that the pool players make affect their lives?

The bad choices made by the pool players, such as _____,

will eventually lead to _____.

5. What does the narrator of "If I Were in Charge of the World" dislike?

The narrator of "If I Were in Charge of the World" dislikes _____, _____,

_____, _____, _____, *and* _____.

Lesson Opener

Before the lesson, choose one of the following activities to write on the board or post on the *LANGUAGE! Live* Class Wall online.

- *Rewrite the sentences by moving the predicate painters.*

    Ralph watched the football game at the stadium last night.

    Sam painted the cabinets in the kitchen carefully last weekend.

- *Use predicate painters to write five sentences about your favorite things to do. Indicate where, when, and how you do them.*

- *In the poem "We Real Cool," it is evident that the boys are proud of being "bad" and often talk about it. Many teenagers are drawn to people who break the rules. Why is this true? Explain your answer.*

Reading

Objectives

- Read poetry with purpose and understanding.
- Answer questions to demonstrate comprehension of text.
- Identify and explain explicit details from text.
- Monitor comprehension during text reading.
- Identify the purpose of the literary epigraph.
- Identify the impact of alliterations in poetry.

Close Reading of "If I Were in Charge of the World"

Let's reread "If I Were in Charge of the World."

Highlighters or colored pencils

Have students get out a highlighter or colored pencil.

Direct students to page 68 in their Student Books. Please mark your text according to my instructions.

Draw a rectangle around the title.

Next, we will read the vocabulary words aloud.

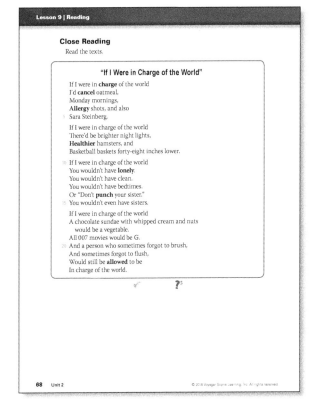

- What's the first bold vocabulary word? (charge) *Charge* is the responsibility of managing or controlling something. The principal is in *charge* of the school. The narrator of the poem wants to be in *charge* of the world. **Have partners use the word in a sentence.**

- What's the next bold vocabulary word? (cancel) *Cancel* means "to stop something from happening or existing." There are things the boy wants to *cancel* because he doesn't like them. **Have partners use the word in a sentence.**

- What's the next vocabulary word? (allergy) *Allergy* means "an illness from eating, breathing, or touching something." Some people have an *allergy* to nuts. **Have partners use the word in a sentence.**

- Let's continue. (healthier) *Healthier* means "in a better state or condition." Vegetables are *healthier* than sundaes. **Have partners use the word in a sentence.**

- Next word? (lonely) *Lonely* means "sad from being without the company of others." When the boy is *lonely*, he wishes there were people around to talk to him. **Have partners use the word in a sentence.**

- Next word? (punch) *Punch* means "to hit hard with a fist." When he *punches* his sister, he gets in trouble. **Have partners use the word in a sentence.**

- Last word. (allowed) *Allowed* means "let something happen." People should be *allowed* to cancel oatmeal if they don't like it. **Have partners use the word in a sentence.**

Talk with a partner about any vocabulary word that is still confusing for you to read or understand.

As you read "If I Were in Charge of the World," you will monitor your understanding by circling the check mark or the question mark. Please be sure to draw a question mark over any confusing words, phrases, or sentences.

Options for rereading text.

- Teacher read-aloud
- Teacher-led or student-led choral read
- Paired read or independent read with bold vocabulary words read aloud

Choose an option for reading text. Have students read the poem according to the option that you chose.

While reading, mark things and activities that the narrator likes. If you finish before others, read the poem again.

When most of the students are finished, continue with the entire class. Let's see how well you understood the first poem.

- Circle the check mark or the question mark for this poem. Draw a question mark over any confusing words.
- Go to line 1. Circle the word that indicates that this isn't really happening. (If)
- Go to line 2. Mark the contraction that means "I would." (I'd)
- Go to the second stanza, which is like a paragraph. Let's check your marks. If you haven't done so already, mark what the narrator likes in that stanza. (night lights, hamsters, basketball)
- Go to line 7. Mark the contraction that means "there would." (there'd)
- Go to line 11. Mark the phrase that proves he likes to be around other people. (wouldn't have lonely)
- Go to line 12. Mark the contraction that means "would not." (wouldn't)
- Go to line 14. Mark the contraction that means "do not." (Don't)
- Go to the last stanza, which is like a paragraph. Let's check your marks. If you haven't done so already, mark what the narrator likes in that stanza. (chocolate sundae with whipped cream and nuts, 007 movies)
- Go to line 20. Mark the word that means "once in a while." (sometimes)
- Go to lines 20 and 21. Circle the rhyming words. (brush/flush)

Close Reading of "We Real Cool"

Now, let's reread "We Real Cool."

Direct students to page 69 in their Student Books. Please mark your text according to my instructions.

Draw a rectangle around the title.

Next, we will read the vocabulary words aloud.

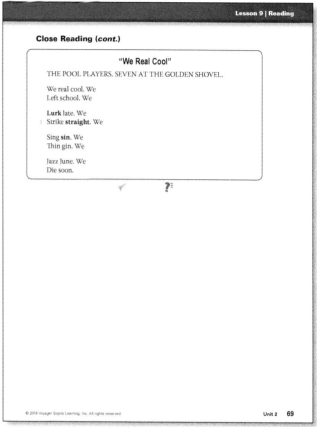

Close Reading (*cont.*)

"We Real Cool"

THE POOL PLAYERS. SEVEN AT THE GOLDEN SHOVEL.

We real cool. We
Left school. We

Lurk late. We
Strike **straight**. We

Sing **sin**. We
Thin gin. We

Jazz June. We
Die soon.

- First word? (lurk) *Lurk* means "to wait in secret; to hang out where you shouldn't be." Roger must have *lurked* until he saw Mrs. Jones coming. **Have partners use the word in a sentence.**

- Let's continue. (straight) *Straight* means "in a firm and direct way." They go *straight* to the Golden Shovel when they wake up in the afternoon. **Have partners use the word in a sentence.**

- Last word. (sin) *Sin* is an offense against religious or moral law. I wonder what *sins* the pool players participate in—stealing and killing? **Have partners use the word in a sentence.**

Have students read the poem according to the option that you chose.

While reading, highlight the bad things the pool players do. What are you going to highlight? (the bad things they do) If you finish before others, read the poem again.

When most of the students are finished, continue with the entire class. Let's see how well you understood the second poem.

- Circle the check mark or the question mark for this poem. Draw a question mark over any confusing words.

- Go to the title. Edit the title using standard English. (insert *are* and change *real* to *really*)

- Go to the epigraph. The epigraph is used to set up what you are about to read. It can be a quote or a phrase. Read the epigraph out loud. Star the word that represents a lucky number. (seven)

- Mark the word in the epigraph that implies death and burial. (shovel)

- Go to line 2. Mark the repeated word that indicates that the narrator is one of the seven pool players. (We)

- Go to line 4. Circle the alliteration. Authors use alliteration when they choose words with the same initial sound. (Lurk late)

Have partners compare text markings and correct any errors.

Explanation of Poem: To be shared at your discretion, after students have read the poem. The poem is about a group of boys who are contemptuous of the establishment. The nonstandard English is an indication that they want to distance themselves from everything proper and established.

Pool players. Seven at the Golden Shovel. (Seven signifies luck, golden signifies the carefree spirit of youth, and shovel is foreshadowing of death/burial.)

We real cool. We
Left school. We

Lurk late. We (stay out late, which is associated with illegal activity)
Strike straight. We (commit crimes correctly so they won't be caught)

Sing sin. We (brag about the bad things they have done)
Thin gin. We (dilute alcohol for selling . . . make more money)

Jazz June. We (June is the establishment . . . or what society tells them is right. Because jazz was originally a rebellious style of music, this means that they are rebelling against the establishment.)
Die soon.

Lesson Opener

Before the lesson, choose one of the following activities to write on the board or post on the *LANGUAGE! Live* Class Wall online.

- *Write four sentences with at least two vocabulary words in each. Show you know the meanings. (cancel, allergy, healthy, punch, allow, lurk, straight, charge, sin, lonely)*
- *Add two predicate painters to each of the following sentences:*
    The boy wrote a story.
    The boys left school.
- *Dress your avatar as though you were going to hang out with the seven pool players. Explain your choices.*

    or

    Dress your avatar as though you were in charge of the world and made the rules. Explain the avatar's clothing and what he or she would be doing today.

Vocabulary

Objective
- Review key passage vocabulary.

Recontextualize Passage Vocabulary

Direct students to page 58 in their Student Books. Use the following questions to review the vocabulary words from "If I Were in Charge of the World" and "We Real Cool."

- If you *cancel* a party, is it going to happen? (No; if you cancel a party, it isn't going to happen.) If your library card gets *canceled*, can you check out a book? (No, you cannot check out a book with a canceled card.) If you can't go to your dentist appointment, what should you do? (cancel it)

- If I sneeze in a dusty room, do I have a dust *allergy*? (Yes, sneezing around dust means you have a dust allergy.) How does a person feel when her *allergies* are flaring up? (When a person's allergies are flaring up, she feels sick or has other symptoms.) If you break out in a rash when you use a certain soap, what do you have? (an allergy)

- Who is *healthier*, a person who smokes or a person who doesn't smoke? (A person who doesn't smoke is healthier.) How could a person who smokes get *healthier*? (The person could get healthier by not smoking.) I am going to start walking two miles a day. Will I be *healthier* or less healthy? (healthier)

- Could I *punch* you with my pinkie finger? (no) What would happen if you *punched* a pile of straw? (If you punched a pile of straw, your fist would go into it.) When a boxer hits an opponent, what has he done? (punched the opponent)

- Would you likely feel *lonely* at a party? (no) Is it possible to feel *lonely* when you are home by yourself? (yes) When you feel sad from being without the company of others, what are you? (lonely)

- Are you *allowed* to vote? (no) Would you *allow* your best friend to insult you? (no) If you let someone go ahead of you in line, what are you doing? (You are allowing him or her to cut.)

- Might a shark *lurk* in shallow waters? (yes) Might an obsessed fan *lurk* near a movie star's home? (yes) If you wanted to meet someone who goes to the library every day at lunch, what could you do? (lurk in the library)

- If I tell you the truth *straight*, do I get right to the point? (yes) If you're very tired, could you go *straight* to sleep? (yes) What is the best way to remove an adhesive bandage? (pull it straight off)

- If you witness a murder, have you witnessed a *sin*? (yes) Are many people in prison guilty of *sinning*? (yes) An offense against religious or moral law is what? (a sin)

- Are teachers in *charge* of their classrooms? (yes) Are students in *charge* of their education? (yes) The responsibility of managing or controlling something is what? (charge)

Writing

Objectives
- Analyze word choice in writing.
- Use exemplar text to write poetry.
- Use a process to write.
- Recite poetry.

Six Traits of Effective Writing

Direct students back to page 30 from Unit 1 in their Student Books. Reread the Six Traits of Effective Writing.

In the last unit, we focused on sentence fluency. Our focus was on writing complete sentences. Using what we have learned in Masterpiece Sentences, we now have the ability to vary our sentence use because we have the tools to expand our sentences. However, we will not focus on that in this unit because we will not be writing in complete sentences.

Because we are writing poetry, our focus for this unit will be word choice. We will try to find our own way of saying things—not just saying things exactly as we read them. We will also focus on our descriptive language through the use of adjectives, adverbs, and prepositional phrases.

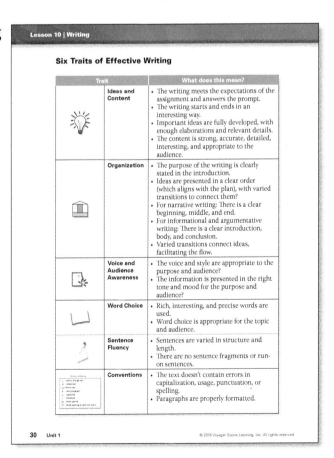

Prepare to Write: Poetry

Direct students to page 70 in their Student Books.

Part A. Study the Prompt

Read the instructions for Part A and the prompt. Guide students to fill in the directions and purpose for writing.

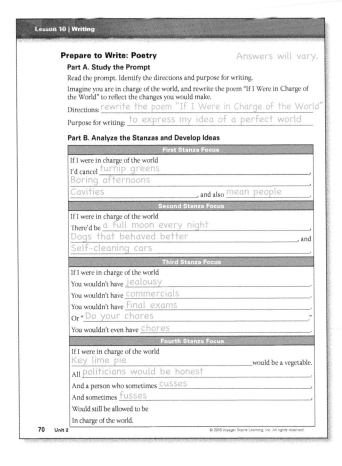

Part B. Analyze the Stanzas and Develop Ideas

Listen as I read the poem and then we'll tackle rewriting the poem, one stanza at a time. Read the poem. Direct students to Part B.

If I Were in Charge of the World

If I were in **charge** of the world
I'd **cancel** oatmeal,
Monday mornings,
Allergy shots, and also
Sara Steinberg.

If I were in charge of the world
There'd be brighter night lights,
Healthier hamsters, and
Basketball baskets forty-eight inches lower.

If I were in charge of the world
You wouldn't have **lonely**.
You wouldn't have clean.
You wouldn't have bedtimes.
Or "Don't **punch** your sister."
You wouldn't even have sisters.

If I were in charge of the world
A chocolate sundae with whipped cream and nuts
    would be a vegetable.
All 007 movies would be G.
And a person who sometimes forgot to brush,
And sometimes forgot to flush,
Would still be **allowed** to be
In charge of the world.

The first stanza focuses on things the narrator would like to cancel. What are some things you would like to cancel? Some things that I don't like are turnip greens, boring afternoons, cavities, and mean people. Share some ideas with your partner and then write down at least four things you'd like to cancel. Give students a few minutes to brainstorm things they'd like to cancel and then write them in the chart.

The second stanza is not about canceling things but improving things. What are some things you like and would want to improve? I love a full moon, well-behaved dogs, and clean cars. Share some ideas with your partner and then write down at least three things you'd like to improve. Give students a few minutes to brainstorm things they'd like to improve and then write them in the chart.

The third stanza focuses again on things he wouldn't have in his world. I wouldn't have jealousy, commercials on TV, final exams, or chores. What are some things you wouldn't have if you had that kind of power? Talk about it with your partner and jot down at least five things. **Give students a few minutes to brainstorm things they wouldn't have and then write them in their chart.**

The final stanza ends on a positive note, with wishful thinking. Wouldn't it be nice if you could eat your favorite dessert and you'd be "eating your vegetables"? I'd love permission to eat more key lime pie, and I'd love it if all politicians told the truth, and that it would be okay if I accidentally cuss or sometimes fuss. Notice in a few places, the poet incorporated rhyme. Write down four things that you would like to see. **Give students a few minutes to brainstorm things they'd like to see and then write them in the chart.**

Write and Recite

Notebook paper

You've done the hard part by generating ideas for your poem. Take a few minutes now and write your poem. Remember to follow the poem's format. **Give students some time to write their own versions of "If I Were in Charge of the World," monitoring progress and offering help with spelling and formatting. Once students have completed their poems, have them recite their poems to the class.**

Exemplar Writing: Poem

If I were in charge of the world
I'd cancel turnip greens,
Boring afternoons,
Cavities, and also
Mean people.

If I were in charge of the world
There'd be a full moon every night,
Dogs that behaved better, and
Self-cleaning cars.

If I were in charge of the world
You wouldn't have jealousy.
You wouldn't have commercials.
You wouldn't have final exams.
Or "Do your chores."
You wouldn't even have chores.

If I were in charge of the world
Key lime pie would be a vegetable.
All politicians would be honest.
And a person who sometimes cusses,
And sometimes fusses,
Would still be allowed to be
In charge of the world.

Student Handwriting:
Handwriting lessons are provided in manuscript and cursive. These explicit lessons (found online in Resources) can be taught systematically during writing lessons to strengthen legibility and fluency.

- Self-correct as comprehension of text deepens.
- Answer questions to demonstrate comprehension of text.
- Engage in class discussion.
- Identify the enduring understandings from a piece of text.

Revisit Passage Comprehension

Direct students to page 67 in their Student Books. Have students review their answers and make any necessary changes. Then, have partners share their answers and collaborate to perfect them.

Enduring Understandings

Direct students back to page 57 in their Student Books. Reread the Big Idea questions.

Are we in control of our lives? Why or why not?

To what degree do the choices we make as teens affect our futures? Explain.

Generate a class discussion about the questions and the answers students came up with in Lesson 6. Have them consider whether their answers have changed any after reading the text.

Use the following talking points to foster conversation. Refer to the Class Discussion Rules poster and have students use the Collegial Discussion sentence frames on page 382 of their Student Books.

- Teens often live in the "now." Thinking about the future is an ability that develops with maturity. But, do the choices we make as teens affect our future in big ways? What about things we post on social media, classes we decide not to work hard at, and choices we make about friends? Can these choices really affect us twenty or thirty years from now?

- As teens, we often feel like other people make decisions and rules that affect us, and we have very little say in our lives. Is this true?

- What about religious beliefs? How much free will do we have? Are there aspects of our lives that are out of our control? What do you think?

What we read should make us think. Use our discussion and your thoughts about the text to determine what you will "walk away with." Has it made you think about a personal experience or someone you know? Has your perspective or opinion on a specific topic changed? Do you have any lingering thoughts or questions? Write these ideas as your enduring understandings. What will you take with you from this text?

Discuss the enduring understandings with the class. Then, have students write their enduring understandings from the unit.

Have students consider why the authors wrote the poems and whether they were successful.

Progress Monitoring

End-of-Unit Online Assessments

Monitor students' progress in the unit by utilizing online assessments. Students should prioritize these assessments over successive Word Training units.

- Assign Unit 2 Content Mastery quizzes to assess skills taught in this unit.
- Assign Power Pass to assess reading comprehension skills in a standardized test format.

All assessments can be assigned online by opening the Tools menu, then selecting Assignments. Be sure to select the correct class and unit from the drop-down menu.

Reteach

Based on students' performance in Content Mastery, extra practice may be needed.

- If student scores fall at 60 percent or below, reteach the content to small groups.
- If student scores fall between 61–79 percent, reinforce the skills by assigning the student reteach activity pages as homework.

Reteach lessons can be found online on the Course Reports page for each unit.

Comprehension Building

Background knowledge is a key component of reading comprehension. It is important for students to develop knowledge of a topic prior to class discussion and reading of complex text.

Print Unit 3 Background Information from the online Resources and assign as homework for students to read. Encourage students to come to class prepared for discussion.

Unit Big Ideas

- Do people have an innate need to fit in?
- What is the effect of hatred between social groups?
- Are all people really good at heart?
- Are people a product of their beliefs or a product of their circumstances?

Instructional Texts

Excerpt from *The Outsiders* by S.E. Hinton

Text type: literature—novel

Excerpt from *The Play of the Diary of Anne Frank* by Frances Goodrich and Albert Hackett

Text type: literature—drama

Materials

- *Unit 3 video (Outsiders)*
- *"The Play of the Diary of Anne Frank" audio file*
- *Steps for Paragraph Writing poster—display in classroom*
- *Six Traits of Writing Scoring Rubric: Basic (print as needed)*

Optional

- *Unit 2 Background Information*
- *Progress Monitoring Across the Six Traits scales*

Classroom Materials

- *Highlighters or colored pencils*
- *Notebook paper*

Optional

- *Feature film:* The Outsiders

Instructional Resources

- *Unit 2 Reteach*
- *Handwriting Lessons*
- *Unit 4 Background Information (assign as homework at the end of the unit)*

Instructional Texts:

Excerpt from *The Outsiders*

by S.E. Hinton

Text type: literature—novel

Excerpt from *The Play of the Diary of Anne Frank*

by Frances Goodrich and Albert Hackett

Text type: literature—drama

LANGUAGE! Live Online

Grammar Practice

- Identify the subject and predicate of a sentence.
- Use singular and plural nouns, adjectives, prepositional phrases, and pronouns correctly.
- Distinguish between formal and informal language.

Vocabulary Practice

- Distinguish between commonly confused words.
- Determine the meaning of derivations of words.
- Use synonyms and antonyms to increase vocabulary knowledge.

Content Mastery

- Demonstrate an understanding of . . .
  - word meaning by answering questions and using words in sentences.
  - adjective use, including comparatives and superlatives.
  - complete predicate and complete subject.

Word Study

- Blend, read, and spell multisyllabic closed syllable words and compound words.
- Determine syllable stress in multisyllabic words.
- Divide multisyllabic closed syllable words with doubled consonants.
- Read connected text to build fluency.

Lesson 1

Reading

- Determine and discuss the topic of a text.
- Determine and discuss the author's purpose.
- Use text features to preview text.

Vocabulary

- Evaluate word knowledge.
- Determine the meaning of key passage vocabulary.

Reading

- Read literary text.
- Monitor comprehension during text reading.
- Analyze the interactions of story elements in a novel.
- Analyze the plot development in a novel.
- Make and verify predictions about what will happen next in a story.

Lesson 2

Vocabulary

- Review key passage vocabulary.
- Identify and define compound words.

Grammar

- Identify the function and purpose of adjectives.
- Use commas correctly when writing consecutive adjectives in sentences.
- Use adjectives to make comparisons.
- Identify the function and purpose of comparatives and superlatives.

Writing

- Use adjectives and adverbs correctly in sentence writing.
- Produce, expand, and rearrange complete sentences.
- Identify the complete subject of a sentence.
- Identify the complete predicate of a sentence.
- Identify the function and purpose of quotation marks in literature.

Lesson 6

Reading

- Determine and discuss the topic of a text.
- Determine and discuss the author's purpose.
- Use text features to preview text.
- Determine the meaning of multiple-meaning words.

Vocabulary

- Evaluate word knowledge.
- Determine the meaning of key passage vocabulary.

Reading

- Read a drama.
- Monitor comprehension during text reading.

Lesson 7

Vocabulary

- Review key passage vocabulary.

Writing

- Read a series of sentences.
- Identify the structure of a paragraph.
- Analyze how a particular sentence fits into the meaning and structure of a paragraph.

Reading

- Identify the structure and form of a drama.
- Analyze how a drama's structure contributes to its meaning.
- Answer questions about text.
- Support written answers with text evidence.
- Determine the meaning of idioms and phrases while reading.
- Distinguish between firsthand accounts and secondhand accounts.
- Identify the differences in an original work and the fictional adaptation of it.
- Compare and contrast a fictional portrayal of events and a historical account of the same event.

* See pg. 240 for additional lesson objectives.

Lesson 3

Reading

- Establish a purpose for rereading literary text.
- Demonstrate an understanding of how to ask questions and answer them appropriately.
- Use critical thinking skills to write responses to prompts about text.
- Support written answers with text evidence.
- Objectively summarize literary text.

Lesson 4

Vocabulary

- Review key passage vocabulary.

Reading

- Read with purpose and understanding.
- Answer questions to demonstrate comprehension of text.
- Identify and explain explicit details from text.
- Monitor comprehension of text during reading.
- Connect pronouns to their antecedents.
- Distinguish between formal and informal language.
- Use context to determine the meaning of words.
- Analyze dialogue to determine the setting.
- Determine the meaning of novel words.

See pg. 196 for additional lesson objectives.

Lesson 5

Vocabulary

- Review key passage vocabulary.

Writing

- Write in response to reading.
- Analyze a literary character.
- Compare self to literary character.

Reading

- Self-correct as comprehension of text deepens.
- Answer questions to demonstrate comprehension of text.
- Engage in class discussion.
- Identify the enduring understandings from a piece of text.
- Identify elements of a story, including climax and resolution.
- Identify the plot of a drama and how characters respond to change.
- Analyze the interaction of story elements.
- Compare text with a filmed version.

Lesson 8

Reading

- Establish a purpose for rereading dramatic literature.
- Demonstrate an understanding of how to ask questions and answer them appropriately.
- Use critical thinking skills to write responses to prompts about text.
- Support written answers with text evidence.
- Compare and contrast the experience of reading a play and listening to a dramatized audio production.
- Objectively summarize text.
- Identify flashbacks in literature and determine their purpose.
- Compare interactions among characters in multiple texts.
- Determine the purpose of stage directions in a drama.
- Determine the meaning of regional vocabulary.

Lesson 9

Vocabulary

- Review key passage vocabulary.

Reading

- Read a play with purpose and understanding.
- Answer questions to demonstrate comprehension of text.
- Identify and explain explicit details from text.
- Monitor comprehension during text reading.
- Identify allusions in text.
- Connect pronouns to their antecedents.
- Use synonyms and antonyms to increase depth of word knowledge.
- Identify the setting of a play.
- Use context to determine word knowledge.
- Analyze how a story's events affect the characters' actions.
- Determine the meaning of foreign word usage.

See pg. 253 for additional lesson objectives.

Lesson 10

Vocabulary

- Review key passage vocabulary.

Writing

- Write an explanatory paragraph that proves a position.
- Use a process to write.
- Connect text to life experiences to write coherently.
- Use a rubric to guide and assess writing.

Reading

- Self-correct as comprehension of text deepens.
- Answer questions to demonstrate comprehension of text.
- Engage in class discussion.
- Identify the enduring understandings from a piece of text.

Lesson Opener

Before the lesson, choose one of the following activities to write on the board or post on the *LANGUAGE! Live* Class Wall online.

- *Describe a time when you felt like you didn't belong.*
- *Write two sentences about the importance of family. Identify the nouns and verbs in each sentence.*
- *Write two sentences describing something you did for a friend. Identify the adverbs and prepositional phrases in each sentence.*

Reading

Objectives

- Determine and discuss the topic of a text.
- Determine and discuss the author's purpose.
- Use text features to preview text.

Passage Introduction

Direct students to page 71 in their Student Books. Discuss the content focus.

Content Focus
friendship; belonging

What do you think this story will be about? (Answers will vary.)

Do you have friends that feel like family members? Have you ever felt like you didn't fit in or didn't belong? Have partners discuss.

If necessary, write the following sentence frames on the board for students to use during discussion:

My friends _____ feel like family because _____ .

I feel like I don't belong when _____ .

I felt like I didn't belong when _____ .

Type of Text
literature

In Unit 1, we read an excerpt, or part, from the literary text *Holes*. Now, we are going to read an excerpt from another piece of literature, *The Outsiders*. *The Outsiders* is a novel, or a rather long fiction story. A narrator in first-person point of view tells this

---

Unit
3

Lesson 1 | Reading

Let's Focus: Excerpt from *The Outsiders*

Content Focus
friendship; belonging

Type of Text
literature—novel

Author's Name S.E. Hinton   **Author's Purpose** to entertain

Big Ideas
Consider the following Big Idea questions. Write your answer for each question.

Do people have an innate need to fit in? Why or why not?

_____

_____

What is the effect of hatred between social groups?

_____

_____

Narrative Preview Checklist: the excerpt from *The Outsiders* on pages 74–81.

☐ Title: What clue does it provide about the passage?

☐ Pictures: What additional information is added here?

☐ Margin Information: What vocabulary is important to understand this story?

Enduring Understandings
After reading the text . . .

_____

_____

_____

_____

_____

Unit 3   71

story. That means that the narrator, or person telling the story, is a character in the story. Where is the narrator? (inside the story)

Author's Purpose

Have students glance at the text. Who is the author of this novel? (S.E. Hinton) The author's purpose is the reason that he or she wrote the text. Authors write for different purposes. They write to entertain, to persuade, or to inform, or to teach. Knowing an author's purpose can help a reader understand a text better. *The Outsiders* was written to entertain us. This book was also written to express frustration with different cliques, or social groups, at the author's high school.

Have students write the answers on the page.

Before we read the excerpt from *The Outsiders*, we will watch a short video to help build our background knowledge. **Play the Unit 3 Text Training video. Have partners discuss the main points the videographer was trying to make and what evidence was provided to support the points.**

Play the Unit 3 Text Training video found in the Teacher Resources online.

> **Note:** Additional Background Information about youth subcultures in the 1950s and 1960s can be found in the Teacher Resources online. Choose the Text Training tab, and then select Unit 3. The Background Information will be in the first section.

Read the Big Idea questions aloud.

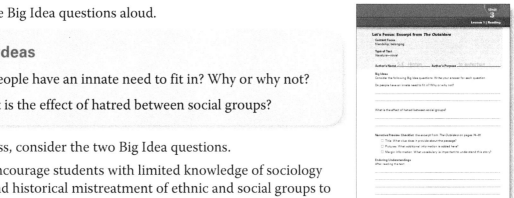

Big Ideas

Do people have an innate need to fit in? Why or why not?

What is the effect of hatred between social groups?

As a class, consider the two Big Idea questions.

- Encourage students with limited knowledge of sociology and historical mistreatment of ethnic and social groups to ask for further explanation from peers.

- Have students reflect on the Background Information for the unit and ask clarifying questions when needed.

- Provide opportunities for students to explain their ideas and answers to the Big Idea questions in light of the discussion by ensuring students follow the rules for class discussion, which can be printed in poster form from the Teacher Resources online.

- Suggest students refer to the Collegial Discussion sentence frames in the back of their books.

- Encourage speakers to link comments to the remarks of others to keep the focus of the discussion and create cohesion, even when their comments are in disagreement.

After discussing each question, have students write an answer. If students struggle, define *innate* as "something in a person naturally—not learned." We'll come back to these questions after we finish reading the story. You can add to your answers as you gain information and perspective.

Preview

Read the Narrative Preview Checklist on page 71. Follow the Preview Procedure outlined below.

Preview Procedure

- Group students with partners or in triads.
- Have students count off as 1s or 2s. The 1s will become the student leaders. If working with triads, the third students become 3s.
- The student leaders will preview the text in addition to managing the checklist and pacing.
- The 2s and 3s will preview the text with 1s.
- Direct 1s to open their Student Books to page 71 and 2s and 3s to open their Student Books to page 74. This allows students to look at a few different pages at one time without turning back and forth.

If it is necessary, guide students in a short preview using the talking points below.
What is the title? (*The Outsiders*) What clue does the title provide about the passage? (Answers will vary.) Who are the outsiders? (the guys in the picture) Let's look to see what additional information the pictures provide. Who is pictured near the title? (seven guys) What are they wearing? (They are wearing leather jackets, T-shirts, flannel shirts, and jeans.) What else do you notice? (Answers will vary.) Scan through the remaining pictures. What do you notice about the facial expressions? (no smiles) What does that tell you about the story? (Answers will vary.)

Objectives

- Evaluate word knowledge.
- Determine the meaning of key passage vocabulary.

Rate Vocabulary Knowledge

Direct students to page 72 in their Student Books. Let's take a look at the vocabulary words from the first text we will read in this unit. I am going to say each word aloud. You will repeat the word and write it in the third column. Then, you will rate your knowledge of the word. Display the Vocabulary Rating Scale poster or write the information on the board. Review the meaning of each rating.

Vocabulary Rating Scale

0—I have never heard the word before.

1—I have heard the word, but I'm not sure how to use it.

2—I am familiar with the word, but I'm not sure if I know the correct meaning.

3—I know the meaning of the word and can use it correctly in a sentence.

Key Passage Vocabulary: Excerpt from *The Outsiders*

Read each word. Write the word in column 3. Then, circle a number to rate your knowledge of the word.

Vocabulary	Part of Speech	Write the Word	Rate the Word
falter	(v)	falter	0 1 2 3
abruptly	(adv)	abruptly	0 1 2 3
resemblance	(n)	resemblance	0 1 2 3
deserve	(v)	deserve	0 1 2 3
ornery	(adj)	ornery	0 1 2 3
casual	(adj)	casual	0 1 2 3
possession	(n)	possession	0 1 2 3
hesitation	(n)	hesitation	0 1 2 3
strict	(adj)	strict	0 1 2 3
deny	(v)	deny	0 1 2 3

72   Unit 3   © 2016 Voyager Sopris Learning, Inc. All rights reserved.

Remember, the points are there to help you know which words you need to focus on. By the end of this unit, you should be able to change all your ratings to a 3—that's the goal.

Read each word aloud and have students repeat it, write it, and rate it. Then, have volunteers who rated a word *2* or *3* use the word in an oral sentence.

Preteach Vocabulary

Explain that you will now take a closer look at the words. Follow the Preteach Procedure outlined below.

Preteach Procedure

This activity is intended to take only a short amount of time, so make it an oral exercise.

- Introduce each word as indicated on the word card.
- Read the definition and example sentences.
- Ask questions to clarify and deepen understanding.
- If time permits, allow students to share.

* If your students would benefit from copying the definitions, please have them do so in the vocabulary log in the back of the Student Books using the margin definitions in the passage selections. This should be done outside of instruction time.

falter (v)

Let's read the first word together. *Falter*.

Definition: *Falter* means "to fade off or stumble; to lose confidence." What means "to fade off or stumble; to lose confidence"? (falter)

Example 1: Many people feel nervous and *falter* when they are trying to express deep feelings.

Example 2: If I don't prepare note cards, I *falter* when speaking in public.

Example 3: Someone who is just learning to read may *falter* when he or she comes across a new word.

Question 1: When speaking a new language in a foreign country, might a person *falter*? Yes or no? (yes)

Question 2: If you change your mind about something mid-sentence, might you *falter*? Yes or no? (yes)

Pair Share: Turn to your partner and name a situation in which you would not want to *falter*.

(1)

abruptly (adv)

Let's read the next word together. *Abruptly*.

Definition: *Abruptly* means "in a sudden or unexpected way." What means "in a sudden or unexpected way"? (abruptly)

Example 1: If you stop *abruptly* on a busy sidewalk, the person behind you might bump into you.

Example 2: It startles me when a siren or alarm goes off *abruptly*.

Example 3: When the TV show ended *abruptly*, many of its fans were upset.

Question 1: Does a flower grow *abruptly*? Yes or no? (no)

Question 2: Do people sometimes sneeze *abruptly*? Yes or no? (yes)

Pair Share: Turn to your partner and tell about a time your mood changed *abruptly*.

(2)

resemblance (n)

Let's read the next word together. *Resemblance.*

Definition: A *resemblance* is a similarity, or likeness, between two things. What means "a similarity, or likeness, between two things"? (resemblance)

Example 1: There is a strong physical *resemblance* between my grandmother and me.

Example 2: Have you ever noticed the *resemblance* between some dog owners and their dogs?

Example 3: German settlers were drawn to a certain part of Texas by the *resemblance* between it and their homeland.

Question 1: Is there often a *resemblance* between the children in a family? Yes or no? (yes)

Question 2: Is there a *resemblance* between this classroom and the one next door? Yes or no? (yes)

Pair Share: Turn to your partner and tell whether there is a *resemblance* between you and someone in your family. Explain the *resemblance.*

③

deserve (v)

Let's read the next word together. *Deserve.*

Definition: *Deserve* means "to earn something by your words or actions." What means "to earn something by your words or actions"? (deserve)

Example 1: When you work hard during the week, you *deserve* to sleep in on Saturday.

Example 2: If I ask a rude question, I *deserve* a rude response.

Example 3: The person with the fewest absences *deserves* the attendance award.

Question 1: Does a child who misbehaves *deserve* a time-out? Yes or no? (yes)

Question 2: Does a kind, gentle person *deserve* an insult? Yes or no? (no)

Pair Share: Turn to your partner and tell about a time you felt you *deserved* something but did not receive it.

④

ornery (adj)

Let's read the next word together. *Ornery.*

Definition: *Ornery* means "grouchy and bad-tempered." What means "grouchy and bad-tempered"? (ornery)

Example 1: *Ornery* people are difficult to be around.

Example 2: My *ornery* neighbor complains about everyone's yards and pets.

Example 3: Small children can get *ornery* when they are tired.

Question 1: Could long-term illness or pain cause a person to be *ornery*? Yes or no? (yes)

Question 2: Do *ornery* people smile very often? Yes or no? (no)

Pair Share: It is a rainy day. Turn to your partner and tell what an *ornery* person might say about this. Then, tell what a person who isn't *ornery* might say.

⑤

casual (adj)

Let's read the next word together. *Casual.*

Definition: *Casual* means "relaxed; laid back." What means "relaxed; laid back"? (casual)

Example 1: It was hard for me to be *casual* about final exams in college; I took them very seriously.

Example 2: A *casual* greeting from a young soldier might offend a high-ranking officer.

Example 3: Your prom date might not enjoy dinner at a *casual* restaurant.

Question 1: Can you speak in a *casual* way with your best friends? Yes or no? (yes)

Question 2: Do you wear *casual* dress or formal dress to school? (casual)

Pair Share: Turn to your partner and tell whether you would prefer a *casual* dance or a formal one, and why.

⑥

possession (n)

Let's read the next word together. *Possession.*

Definition: A *possession* is something owned. What word means "something owned"? (possession)

Example 1: Old family photos are a treasured *possession* for many people.

Example 2: If I had to leave my home in a hurry, I would take _____. It is my most prized *possession.*

Example 3: In some communities, people have no *possessions*; instead, everything is shared.

Question 1: Could a cloud ever be a *possession*? Yes or no? (no)

Question 2: When people are treated like a *possession*, are they being respected for who they really are? Yes or no? (no)

Pair Share: Turn to your partner and tell about your most prized *possession.*

(7)

hesitation (n)

Let's read the next word together. *Hesitation.*

Definition: A *hesitation* is a delay or a pause. What word means "a delay or a pause"? (hesitation)

Example 1: When I was offered this job, I accepted it without *hesitation.*

Example 2: If the jury members agree without *hesitation*, they come to a verdict right away.

Example 3: After a brief *hesitation* during my sophomore year in college, I decided to become a teacher.

Question 1: Could a brief *hesitation* at the starting block cause an Olympic runner to lose a race? Yes or no? (yes)

Question 2: Can you state your name without *hesitation*? Yes or no? (yes)

Pair Share: Turn to your partner and tell about a decision you made with *hesitation.* Explain why you *hesitated.*

(8)

strict (adj)

Let's read the next word together. *Strict.*

Definition: *Strict* means "firm; having many rules and expecting to be obeyed." What means "having many rules and expecting to be obeyed"? (strict)

Example 1: My *strict* Aunt Martha would never let us jump on the bed.

Example 2: Parents are sometimes *strict* because they want to keep their children safe.

Example 3: A *strict* coach might want his players in bed by nine at night and on the field by six in the morning.

Question 1: Is a music teacher who requires two hours of daily practice *strict*? Yes or no? (yes)

Question 2: What does a *strict* parent say more often, yes or no? (no)

Pair Share: Turn to your partner and name something an adult you know is *strict* about.

(9)

deny (v)

Let's read the last word together. *Deny.*

Definition: To *deny* something is to say it isn't true. What means "to say something isn't true"? (deny)

Example 1: Many criminals *deny* that they are guilty.

Example 2: You cannot *deny* the fact that it is daytime.

Example 3: A spy is trained to *deny* having important information.

Question 1: Is a well-known fact hard to *deny*? Yes or no? (yes)

Question 2: Would you *deny* that two plus two equals seven? Yes or no? (yes)

Pair Share: Turn to your partner and tell about a time someone accused you of something and you *denied* it.

(10)

Objectives
- Read literary text.
- Monitor comprehension during text reading.
- Analyze the interactions of story elements in a novel.
- Analyze the plot development in a novel.
- Make and verify predictions about what will happen next in a story.

Excerpt from *The Outsiders*

Direct students to page 73 in their Student Books.

Prior to reading the text, review the story map to prepare students for the chapter they are about to read. Offer a brief explanation of the story elements if needed.

Setting: Time and place of story

Characters: People, animals, or things that interact in the story

Initiating Event: Problem that starts the story

Conflict: Plot or sequence of events

Climax: Turning point

Resolution: The solution to the problem

Conclusion: The situation at story's end

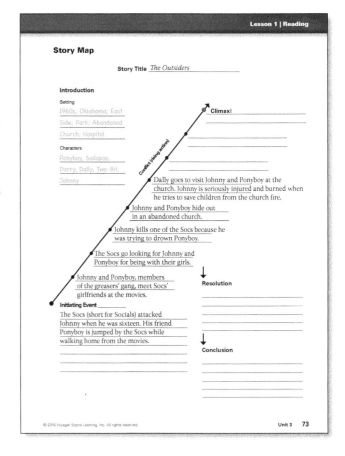

Direct students to page 74 in their Student Books.

Now that we have previewed vocabulary and identified what has happened in the previous chapters, it's time to read. Pay attention to the setting and the characters. One way to pay attention to the characters is to keep track of the dialogue, or who is talking. Dialogue is noted with quotation marks. How is dialogue noted? (with quotation marks)

I will read the first paragraph to model the reading behaviors of a good reader. While I read aloud, your eyes should be on text. Follow along using your writing utensil as a pointer.

Read the introduction aloud.

SE p. 74, paragraph 1

> *No one ever said life was easy. But Ponyboy is pretty sure that he's got things figured out. He knows that he can count on his brothers, Darry and Sodapop. And he knows that he can count on his friends—true friends who would do anything for him, like Johnny and Two-Bit. And when it comes to the Socs—a vicious gang of rich kids who enjoy beating up on the "greasers" like him and his friends—he knows that he can count on them for trouble. But one night someone takes things too far, and Ponyboy's world is turned upside down . . .*

Note: *Soc* is short for *social* and is pronounced sōsh.

What do you notice at the end of this paragraph? **(a number)** Good readers pause to stop and think while reading. They reflect on what they read before reading on. Sometimes, when good readers stop and think, they make a mental prediction about will happen next. Sometimes, good readers ask themselves questions while reading. **Have students read the corresponding question aloud.** (1. What do you think will happen to Ponyboy?) Let me model thinking after reading this first paragraph. I predict that something bad is going to happen to one of Ponyboy's brothers or friends. **Have volunteers share predictions.** Don't stop long enough to let your mind wander away from the text. This should be a brief pause to gather your thoughts.

Guiding Students Toward Independent Reading

It is important that your students read as much and as often as they can. Assign readings that meet the needs of your students, based on your observations and data. This is a good opportunity to stretch your students. If students become frustrated, scaffold the reading with paired reading, choral reading, or a read-aloud.

Options for reading text:

- Teacher read-aloud
- Teacher-led or student-led choral read
- Paired read or independent read

Choose an option for reading the remainder of the text. Have students read according to the option that you chose.

Note: If you think your students will struggle to keep track of the characters, write the following on the board:

Ponyboy - narrator
Johnny - in critical condition in hospital
Dally - also in hospital, not as injured
Two-Bit - visits hospital with Ponyboy
Darry - Ponyboy's oldest brother
Sodapop - Ponyboy's brother

SE p. 74,
paragraphs 2–4

The nurses wouldn't let us see Johnny. He was in critical condition. No visitors. But Two-Bit wouldn't take no for an answer. That was his buddy in there and he aimed to see him. We both begged and pleaded, but we were getting nowhere until the doctor found out what was going on.

"Let them go in," he said to the nurse. "He's been asking for them. It can't hurt now."

page break

Two-Bit didn't notice the expression in his voice. It's true, I thought numbly, he is dying. We went in, practically on tiptoe, because the quietness of the hospital scared us. Johnny was lying still, with his eyes | closed, but when Two-Bit said, "Hey, Johnnykid," he opened them and looked at us, trying to grin. "Hey, y'all."

SE p. 75,
paragraphs 1–6

The nurse, who was pulling the shades open, smiled and said, "So he can talk after all."

Two-Bit looked around. "They treatin' you okay, kid?"

"Don't . . ."—Johnny gasped—"don't let me put enough grease on my hair."

"Don't talk," Two-Bit said, pulling up a chair, "just listen. We'll bring you some hair grease next time. We're havin' the big rumble tonight."

Johnny's huge black eyes widened a little, but he didn't say anything.

"It's too bad you and Dally can't be in it. It's the first big rumble we've had—not countin' the time we whipped Shepard's outfit."

2. Why can't Johnny and Dally be in the rumble?

*SE p. 75,
paragraphs 7–17*

"He came by," Johnny said.

"Tim Shepard?"

Johnny nodded. "Came to see Dally."

Tim and Dallas had always been buddies.

"Did you know you got your name in the paper for being a hero?"

Johnny almost grinned as he nodded. "Tuff enough," he managed, and by the way his eyes were glowing, I figured Southern gentlemen had nothing on Johnny Cade.

I could see that even a few words were tiring him out; he was as pale as the pillow and looked awful. Two-Bit pretended not to notice.

"You want anything besides hair grease, kid?"

Johnny barely nodded. "The book"—he looked at me—"can you get another one?"

Two-Bit looked at me too. I hadn't told him about *Gone with the Wind*.

"He wants a copy of *Gone with the Wind* so I can read it to him," I explained. "You want to run down to the drugstore and get one?"

3. Why does Johnny want Ponyboy to read to him?

SE p. 75,
paragraphs 18–20

"Okay," Two-Bit said cheerfully. "Don't y'all run off."

I sat down in Two-Bit's chair and tried to think of something to say. "Dally's gonna be okay," I said finally. "And Darry and me, we're okay now."

page break

I knew Johnny understood what I meant. We had always been close buddies, and those lonely days in the | church strengthened our friendship. He tried to smile again, and then suddenly went white and closed his eyes tight.

SE p. 76,
paragraphs 1–8

"Johnny!" I said, alarmed. "Are you okay?"

He nodded, keeping his eyes closed. "Yeah, it just hurts sometimes. It usually don't . . . I can't feel anything below the middle of my back . . ."

He lay breathing heavily for a moment. "I'm pretty bad off, ain't I, Pony?"

"You'll be okay," I said with fake cheerfulness. "You gotta be. We couldn't get along without you."

The truth of that last statement hit me. We couldn't get along without him. We needed Johnny as much as he needed the gang. And for the same reason.

"I won't be able to walk again," Johnny started, then **faltered**. "Not even on crutches. Busted my back."

"You'll be okay," I repeated firmly. Don't start crying, I commanded myself, don't start crying, you'll scare Johnny.

"You want to know something, Ponyboy? I'm scared stiff. I used to talk about killing myself . . ." He drew a quivering breath. "I don't want to die now. It ain't long enough. Sixteen years ain't long enough. I wouldn't mind it so much if there wasn't so much stuff I ain't done yet and so many things I ain't seen. It's not fair. You know what? That time we were in Windrixville was the only time I've been away from our neighborhood."

4. Why does Johnny want to live?

SE p. 76, paragraphs 9–11

"You ain't gonna die," I said, trying to hold my voice down. "And don't get juiced up, because the doc won't let us see you no more if you do."

Sixteen years on the streets and you can learn a lot. But all the wrong things, not the things you want to learn. Sixteen years on the streets and you see a lot. But all the wrong sights, not the sights you want to see.

Johnny closed his eyes and rested quietly for a minute. Years of living on the East Side teaches you how to shut off your emotions. If you didn't, you would explode. You learn to cool it.

5. What likely happens on the East Side that makes them have to shut off their emotions?

SE p. 77, paragraphs 1–2

A nurse appeared in the doorway. "Johnny," she said quietly, "your mother's here to see you."

Johnny opened his eyes. At first they were wide with surprise, then they darkened. "I don't want to see her," he said firmly.

6. What kind of relationship does Johnny have with his mother?

E p. 77,
paragraphs 3–9

"She's your mother."

"I said I don't want to see her." His voice was rising. "She's probably come to tell me about all the trouble I'm causing her and about how glad her and the old man'll be when I'm dead. Well, tell her to leave me alone. For once"—his voice broke—"for once just to leave me alone." He was struggling to sit up, but he suddenly gasped, went whiter than the pillowcase, and passed out cold.

The nurse hurried me out the door. "I was afraid of something like this if he saw anyone."

I ran into Two-Bit, who was coming in.

"You can't see him now," the nurse said, so Two-Bit handed her the book. "Make sure he can see it when he comes around." She took it and closed the door behind her. Two-Bit stood and looked at the door a long time. "I wish it was any one of us except Johnny," he said, and his voice was serious for once. "We could get along without anyone but Johnny."

Turning **abruptly**, he said, "Let's go see Dallas."

As we walked out into the hall, we saw Johnny's mother. I knew her. She was a little woman, with straight black hair and big black eyes like Johnny's. But that was as far as the **resemblance** went. Johnnycake's eyes were fearful and sensitive; hers were cheap and hard. As we passed her she was saying, "But I have a right to see him. He's my son. After all the trouble his father and I've gone to raise him, this is our reward! He'd rather see those no-count hoodlums than his own folks . . ." She saw us and gave us such a look of hatred that I almost backed up. "It was your fault. Always running around in the middle of the night getting jailed and heaven knows what else . . ." I thought she was going to cuss us out. I really did.

7. Who does Johnny's mom blame for his condition?

SE p. 78, paragraph 1

Two-Bit's eyes got narrow and I was afraid he was going to start something. I don't like to hear women get sworn at, even if they **deserve** it. "No wonder he hates your guts," Two-Bit snapped. He was going to tell her off real good, but I shoved him along. I felt sick. No wonder Johnny didn't want to see her. No wonder he stayed overnight at Two-Bit's or at our house, and slept in the vacant lot in good weather. I remembered my mother . . . beautiful and golden, like Soda, and wise and firm, like Darry.

8. What can you speculate about Ponyboy's mother?

SE p. 78, paragraphs 2–12

"Oh, lordy!" There was a catch in Two-Bit's voice and he was closer to tears than I'd ever seen him. "He has to live with that."

We hurried to the elevator to get to the next floor. I hoped the nurse would have enough sense not to let Johnny's mother see him. It would kill him.

Dally was arguing with one of the nurses when we came in. He grinned at us. "Man, am I glad to see you! These——hospital people won't let me smoke, and I want out!"

We sat down, grinning at each other. Dally was his usual mean, **ornery** self. He was okay.

"Shepard came by to see me a while ago."

"That's what Johnny said. What'd he want?"

"Said he saw my picture in the paper and couldn't believe it didn't have 'Wanted Dead or Alive' under it. He mostly came to rub it in about the rumble. Man, I hate not bein' in that."

Only last week Tim Shepard had cracked three of Dally's ribs. But Dally and Tim Shepard had always been buddies; no matter how they fought, they were two of a kind, and they knew it.

Dally was grinning at me. "Kid, you scared the devil outa me the other day. I thought I'd killed you."

"Me?" I said, puzzled. "Why?"

"When you jumped out of the church. I meant to hit you just hard enough to knock you down and put out the fire, but when you dropped like a ton of lead I thought I'd aimed too high and broke your neck." He thought for a minute. "I'm glad I didn't, though."

9. What happened at the church?

SE p. 79,
paragraphs 1–4

"I'll bet," I said with a grin. I'd never liked Dally—but then, for the first time, I felt like he was my buddy. And all because he was glad he hadn't killed me.

Dally looked out the window. "Uh . . ."—he sounded very **casual**—"how's the kid?"

"We just left him," Two-Bit said, and I could tell that he was debating whether to tell Dally the truth or not. "I don't know about stuff like this . . . but . . . well, he seemed pretty bad to me. He passed out cold before we left him."

Dally's jaw line went white as he swore between clenched teeth.

10. How does Dally feel about Johnny's condition?

SE p. 79,
paragraphs 5–8

"Two-Bit, you still got that fancy black-handled switch?"

"Yeah."

"Give it here."

Two-Bit reached into his back pocket for his prize **possession**. It was a jet-handled switchblade, ten inches long, that would flash open at a mere breath. It was the reward of two hours of walking aimlessly around a hardware store to divert suspicion. He kept it razor sharp. As far as I knew, he had never pulled it on anyone; he used his plain pocketknife when he needed a blade. But it was his showpiece, his pride and joy—every time he ran into a new hood he pulled it out and showed off with it. Dally knew how much that knife meant to Two-Bit, and if he needed a blade bad enough to ask for it, well, he needed a blade. That was all there was to it. Two-Bit handed it over to Dally without a moment's **hesitation**.

11. Speculate why Dally wanted the knife.

SE p. 79,
paragraphs 9–11

"We gotta win that fight tonight," Dally said. His voice was hard. "We gotta get even with the Socs. For Johnny."

He put the switch under his pillow and lay back, staring at the ceiling. We left. We knew better than to talk to Dally when his eyes were blazing and he was in a mood like that.

We decided to catch a bus home. I just didn't feel much like walking or trying to hitch a ride. Two-Bit left me sitting on the bench at the bus stop while he went to a gas station to buy some cigarettes. I was kind of sick to my stomach and sort of groggy. I was nearly asleep | when I felt someone's hand on my forehead. I almost jumped out of my skin. Two-Bit was looking down at me worriedly. "You feel okay? You're awful hot."

page break

SE p. 80,
paragraphs 1–4

"I'm all right," I said, and when he looked at me as if he didn't believe me, I got a little panicky. "Don't tell Darry, okay? Come on, Two-Bit, be a buddy. I'll be well by tonight. I'll take a bunch of aspirins."

"All right," Two-Bit said reluctantly. "But Darry'll kill me if you're really sick and go ahead and fight anyway."

"I'm okay," I said, getting a little angry. "And if you keep your mouth shut, Darry won't know a thing."

"You know somethin'?" Two-Bit said as we were riding home on the bus. "You'd think you could get away with murder, living with your big brother and all, but Darry's **stricter** with you than your folks were, ain't he?"

12. Who does Ponyboy live with?

SE p. 80,
paragraphs 5–8

"Yeah," I said, "but they'd raised two boys before me. Darry hasn't."

"You know, the only thing that keeps Darry from bein' a Soc is us."

"I know," I said. I had known it for a long time. In spite of not having much money, the only reason Darry couldn't be a Soc was us. The gang. Me and Soda. Darry was too smart to be a greaser. I don't know how I knew, I just did. And I was kind of sorry.

I was silent most of the way home. I was thinking about the rumble. I had a sick feeling in my stomach and it wasn't from being ill. It was the same kind of helplessness I'd felt that night Darry yelled at me for going to sleep in the lot. I had the same deathly fear that something was going to happen that none of us could stop. As we got off the bus I finally said it. "Tonight—I don't like it one bit."

13. What does Ponyboy think about the rumble?

SE p. 80,
paragraphs 9–11

Two-Bit pretended not to understand. "I never knew you to play chicken in a rumble before. Not even when you was a little kid."

I knew he was trying to make me mad, but I took the bait anyway. "I ain't chicken, Two-Bit Mathews, and you know it," I said angrily. "Ain't I a Curtis, same as Soda and Darry?"

Two-Bit couldn't **deny** this, so I went on: "I mean, I got an awful feeling something's gonna happen."

SE p. 81,
paragraphs 1–2

"Somethin' is gonna happen. We're gonna stomp the Socs' guts, that's what."

Two-Bit knew what I meant, but doggedly pretended not to. He seemed to feel that if you said something was all right, it immediately was, no matter what. He's been that way all his life, and I don't expect he'll change. Sodapop would have understood, and we would have tried to figure it out together, but Two-Bit just ain't Soda. Not by a long shot.

For confirmation of engagement, take 30 seconds to have students share whether their prediction at the beginning of the text was accurate and one prediction about the upcoming rumble. Have volunteers share predictions with the class.

Lesson Opener

Before the lesson, choose one of the following activities to write on the board or post on the *LANGUAGE! Live* Class Wall online.

- *Describe a relationship you have with a friend. How does that friend impact your life?*
- *Write one sentence explaining something good about your best friend. Write one sentence explaining something bad about your best friend. Use a prepositional phrase in each sentence.*
- *Write five questions you would ask a new student to determine if you will become friends.*

Vocabulary

Objectives

- Review key passage vocabulary.
- Identify and define compound words.

Review Passage Vocabulary

Direct students to page 72 in their Student Books. Use the following questions to review the vocabulary words in the excerpt from *The Outsiders*. Have students answer each question using the vocabulary word or indicating its meaning in a complete sentence.

- Why does Johnny *falter* as he talks about his injuries? (He falters, or stumbles over his words, because he is scared.) Does Ponyboy *falter* when he tells Johnny he'll be okay? Why or why not? (No, Ponyboy doesn't falter. He speaks firmly in order to reassure Johnny.)

- When Two-Bit turns around *abruptly*, how does he turn around? (When he turns abruptly, he turns in a sudden or unexpected way.) Why does the nurse *abruptly* shoo the boys from Johnny's room? (She abruptly shoos them from his room because he has just passed out.)

- What is Johnny's *resemblance* to his mother? (His straight black hair and big black eyes give him a resemblance to his mother.) Why does Ponyboy say the *resemblance* ends there? (He says the resemblance ends there because her eyes are "cheap and hard" and Johnny's are "fearful and sensitive.")

- What does Ponyboy say Johnny's mother *deserves*? (He admits she deserves to be sworn at.) Would Ponyboy say that Johnny *deserves* his mother? (No, Ponyboy would say Johnny deserves, or has earned, a better mother.)

- Why does Ponyboy describe Dally as *ornery*? (He describes Dally as ornery because Dally is grouchy and bad-tempered.) How might being *ornery* help a greaser? (Being ornery would help a greaser intimidate his enemies.)

- Dally asks Ponyboy and Two-Bit about Johnny in a *casual* voice. Why do you think he uses a *casual* voice? (He uses a casual voice to mask his fear and concern. He also wants to be seen as "cool.") When Two-Bit explains what bad shape Johnny is in, does Dally continue to act *casual*? (No, his attitude does not stay casual. He gets wound up. He clenches his teeth and swears.)

- What is Two-Bit's prize *possession*? (His prize possession is his jet-handled switchblade.) How did the switchblade come to be Two-Bit's *possession*? (He stole it from a hardware store.) So, is it actually his *possession*? (No, it isn't really his possession; he doesn't legally own it.)

- Why is Ponyboy surprised that Two-Bit hands Dally the blade without a moment's *hesitation*? (Ponyboy is surprised that Two-Bit hands over the blade without hesitation because he values it so much; it is his "pride and joy.") Does Two-Bit pause to think? (No, he doesn't pause to think.) Why does Two-Bit hand it over without *hesitation*? (He hands it over without hesitation because he trusts Dally.)

- What does Two-Bit mean when he says Darry is *stricter* with Ponyboy than their parents were? (Two-Bit means that Darry has many rules and expects to be obeyed.) How does Ponyboy seem to feel about Darry being so *strict*? (Ponyboy understands that Darry is strict because he loves him and wants to protect him.)

- Two-Bit can't *deny* that Ponyboy is a Curtis. If he did *deny* this, what would he say? (If he denied it, he would say, "Ponyboy is not a Curtis.") Does Two-Bit *deny* that "something's gonna happen" at the rumble? (No, he does not deny this. He says that something is going to happen—the greasers are going to stomp the Socs.) What feeling is Two-Bit really trying to *deny*? (He is trying to deny Ponyboy's fear—and his own.)

Vocabulary Concept: Compound Words

Words are in relationship with each other, just as people are. You might behave one way with a parent or teacher and another way with a friend. Words do the same thing. Their meaning can change and grow in relation to other words.

Explain that a word made up of two smaller words is called a *compound word*. Use the word *backpack* to guide students in determining that it is "a pack you wear on your back."

Write the following words on the board:

> *overnight*
>
> *tiptoe*
>
> *gentlemen*
>
> *drugstore*
>
> *doorway*

Have volunteers draw a line to separate each compound word into two smaller words. Then, guide students in piecing the words together to determine a definition.

Direct students to page 82 in their Student Books and read the instructions.

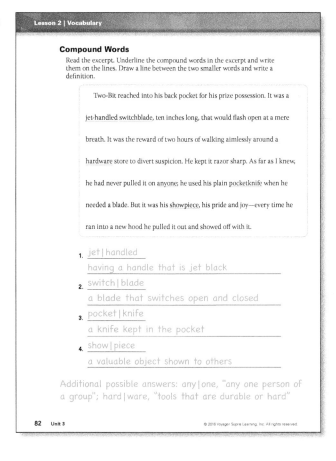

Read the paragraph aloud. Give students time to complete the activity. Review students' answers as a class, or have partners review their answers together and correct any errors.

> Two-Bit reached into his back pocket for his prize possession. It was a jet-handled switchblade, ten inches long, that would flash open at a mere breath. It was the reward of two hours of walking aimlessly around a hardware store to divert suspicion. He kept it razor sharp. As far as I knew, he had never pulled it on anyone; he used his plain pocketknife when he needed a blade. But it was his showpiece, his pride and joy—every time he ran into a new hood he pulled it out and showed off with it.

Grammar

Objectives
- Identify the function and purpose of adjectives.
- Use commas correctly when writing consecutive adjectives in sentences.
- Use adjectives to make comparisons.
- Identify the function and purpose of comparatives and superlatives.

Adjectives

We have talked about different ways to categorize words. Thinking about the questions that words answer helps us put words into certain categories. What category of words answers the *who* or *what* question? (nouns) What category of words answers the *did what* question? (verbs) What category of words "paint" the verb and answer the *when, where,* or *how* questions? (adverbs) We have used these questions to help us write and comprehend sentences.

What about words that describe nouns? Words that describe nouns can be placed into a category as well. We often describe people, places, and things using adjectives.

Have partners make a list of adjectives to describe each other. Remind them to be kind.

Adjectives answer the *which one, what kind,* or *how many* questions. What words answer the *which one, what kind,* or *how many* questions? (adjectives)

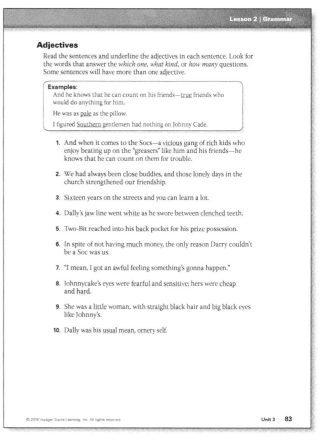

Write the following sentences on the board:

> *Ponyboy fondly remembered the <u>childhood</u> friend.* (Which one?)
>
> *Two-Bit carried a <u>fancy</u> switchblade.* (What kind?)
>
> *The <u>three</u> brothers lived together alone.* (How many?)

Have students identify the question being answered with the underlined words.

Direct students to page 83 in their Student Books and read the instructions aloud.

Model

Listen as I model the examples. *And he knows that he can count on his friends—true friends who would do anything for him.* I am looking for words that describe the *who* or *what* in a sentence. Do I know what kind of friends Ponyboy is talking about? Yes, they are true friends, so I underline *true.*

He was as pale as the pillow. What do I know about the subject? I know he was pale, so I underline *pale.*

I figured Southern gentlemen had nothing on Johnny Cade. What kind of gentlemen? Southern gentlemen, so I underline *Southern.*

Guided Practice

Let's look at the first sentence. We have to keep an eye out for our nouns and ask ourselves if the sentence provides any descriptive words related to the *who* or *what.* Read the first sentence. Do we know anything about what kind of gang? (yes, **vicious**) Underline *vicious.* Do we know anything about what kind of kids? (yes, **rich**) Underline *rich.* Do we know anything about any of the other naming words or nouns in the sentence? (**no**)

Independent Practice

Have students identify the adjectives in the remaining sentences. Review the answers as a class.

Adjectives and Commas

Sometimes, we use more than one adjective to describe someone or something. Coordinate adjectives are equal modifiers and must be separated by a comma or conjunction in a sentence.

Write the following sentence on the board:

> *Johnnycake's eyes were fearful and sensitive; hers were cheap and hard.*

Notice that there are two adjectives describing Johnny's eyes and two adjectives describing his mom's eyes. Both sets are separated by the word *and.* Both *fearful* and *sensitive* are of equal importance and if we switch the order of the adjectives, it doesn't change the meaning. This is also true for *cheap* and *hard.* **Repeat the sentence switching the order of both sets of adjectives.**

Write the following sentence on the board:

> *Dally was his usual mean, ornery self.*

In this sentence, there are three adjectives. Let's focus first on the two adjectives separated by a comma. Because they are separated by a comma, what kind of adjectives must they be? (coordinate) This means they are of equal importance in the sentence and that we could switch the order and it wouldn't matter. Try it.

Now, let's look at the first adjective, *usual*. Notice that this adjective is not separated from *mean* with a comma or a conjunction, so that means it is not of equal importance. In this particular sentence, *mean* and *ornery* are describing Dally, and *usual* is needed to describe how often he is mean and ornery. Therefore, we can't switch the order of the adjectives.

Let's look at one more sentence.

Write the following sentence on the board:

> *She was a little woman, with straight black hair and big black eyes like Johnny's.*

Let's look at the two adjectives that modify *hair* and the two adjectives that modify *eyes*. Switch the order and see if it means the same thing. In this sentence, *straight* is describing her black hair and *big* is describing her black eyes. Therefore, they are not of equal importance and, thus, not coordinate adjectives. Remember, not all consecutive adjectives must be separated by a comma because they are not equal modifiers, which means that one adjective is actually describing the already modified noun.

Adjectives that Compare

Direct students to page 84 in their Student Books.

Write the following sentences on the board and read them aloud.

- *"You'd think you could get away with murder, living with your big brother and all, but Darry's stricter with you than your folks were, ain't he?"*

- *There was a catch in Two-Bit's voice and he was closer to tears than I'd ever seen him.*

A comparison is being made in the first sentence. Darry, Ponyboy's brother, is being compared to Ponyboy's parents. Not only do we know that Darry is strict, but we also know that he is stricter than his parents.

When we compare two things by describing them, often we can add -er to express the comparison.

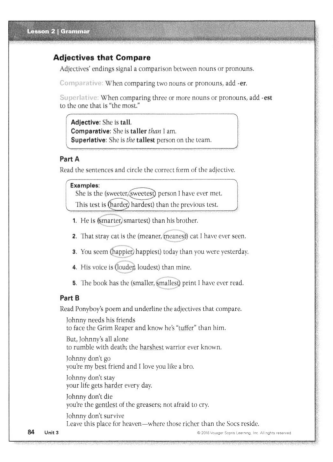

What's being compared in the second sentence? (Two-Bit's states of sadness) Two-Bit is close to crying. When I read that, I see a boy whose eyes may be watering or turning red and with a sad expression on his face. I also know Ponyboy has never seen him cry, but he has seen him close to tears before. However, this moment he is "more close" or *closer* to crying than the times before.

Writers use comparisons to create rich images drawing on what the reader already knows. We can add endings to many adjectives to create these rich images.

Read the definitions and examples of comparative and superlative adjectives.

Model

Direct students to Part A. Listen: *She is the _____ person I have ever met.* I have to choose between *sweeter* and *sweetest*. To make the right choice, I have to determine if I am comparing her with one other person or to a group of people. *Sweetest* is the correct choice because the sentence compares her with everyone else I have ever met.

Listen: *This test is _____ than the previous test.* I have to choose between *harder* and *hardest*. Again, to make the right choice, I have to determine if I am comparing this test with one other test or with all of the other tests I have taken. *Harder* is the correct choice because I am comparing it with one other test, the previous test. Here's a tip that will help most of the time. When using -est, *the* usually comes before the adjective. When using -er, the sentence usually contains the word *than*.

Guided Practice

Read the sentences in Part A and give students time to make their choices. Have students respond chorally and correct as needed.

Independent Practice

Have partners complete Part B. Review the answers as a class. Have volunteers explain what is being compared in each stanza.

Stanza 1: Johnny and the Grim Reaper

Stanza 2: death and all other warriors

Stanza 3: Johnny and all Ponyboy's friends

Stanza 4: Johnny's life one day and his life the next day

Stanza 5: Johnny and all other greasers

Stanza 6: Socs and those who are in heaven

Objectives

- Use adjectives and adverbs correctly in sentence writing.
- Produce, expand, and rearrange complete sentences.
- Identify the complete subject of a sentence.
- Identify the complete predicate of a sentence.
- Identify the function and purpose of quotation marks in literature.

Masterpiece Sentences: Stage 4—Painting the Subject

We have worked on painting the predicate by answering the *when*, *where*, and *how* questions. In this lesson, we will focus on adding details to the subject of the sentence. We paint the *who* or *what* by answering the *what kind, which one*, and *how many* questions. Like the predicate painters, we can answer these questions with single words or with phrases. Using prepositions and prepositional phrases helps us avoid a string of single describing words.

Direct students to page 85 in their Student Books and read the instructions aloud.

Guided Practice

Guide students through answering the questions for each picture. Then, direct them to write their expanded sentence below the starting sentence. As students complete each sentence, have volunteers share their new sentences.

Note: Though relative clauses have not been taught, accept them as responses if students offer them. For example: Five good friends who are looking forward to summer break pose for a picture.

Masterpiece Sentences: Stages 1–4

Direct students to page 86 in their Student Books and read the instructions aloud.

Let's put everything you know about painting predicates and subjects together. Use the picture and complete the chart to write your new sentence.

If students struggle to generate ideas, offer them suggestions. Guide students through each stage to ensure they are writing their ideas on paper.

Complete Subject and Complete Predicate

Write the following sentences on the board, leaving off the underlines. They are variations of the Masterpiece Sentences.

- *Five good friends with smiles on their faces posed for a picture.*

- *A sad teenager with a great deal on his mind needed a friend.*

- *Two brave warriors with swords in hand battled.*

Let's work together to identify the simple subject and the simple predicate in each sentence. Read the first sentence. Who or what is this sentence about? (friends) *I'm going to underline the word friends once. What did the friends do?* (posed) *They posed, so I'm going to underline posed twice. Do we know anything about the friends? Yes, we know how many, what kind, and which ones. All of these describing words paint the subject and create the complete subject. I'm going to extend my single line to include all of these painters. What about posed? Do we know anything else about what they did? We know they posed for a picture. I'm going to extend my double line to include the predicate painters. All of the words that tell us more about the verb make up the complete predicate.*

Read through the other two sentences and repeat the process of first finding the simple subject and simple predicate. Then, walk through identifying the complete subject and predicate. Using the words *subject painters* and *predicate painters* helps students see the connection between masterpiece sentence development and sentence elements.

Look back at the sentences you wrote on page 85 and underline the complete subject once and the complete predicate twice. To confirm understanding, have volunteers share their sentences and how they marked their complete subjects and complete predicates.

To solidify understanding, write the following sentence without underlines on the board and have partners determine the complete subject and the complete predicate:

After school, five tough boys with fighting on their minds waited anxiously in the park.

What is the complete subject? (five tough boys with fighting on their minds) What is the complete predicate? (After school, waited anxiously in the park) Help students see that *after school* is a predicate painter and part of the complete predicate, even though it is at the beginning of the sentence.

Have students identify the complete subject and the complete predicate in their masterpiece sentence on page 86. Have volunteers share their sentences and how they identified their complete subjects and complete predicates.

Spotlight on Punctuation: Dialogue

Direct students to part A on page 87 in their Student Books.

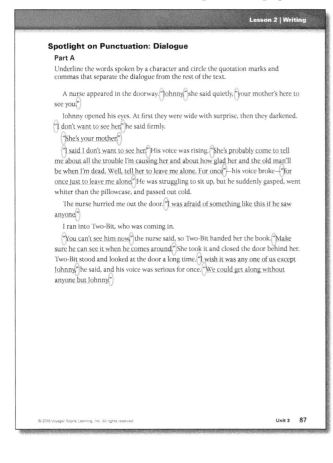

Follow along as I read the following excerpt from the text. Pay close attention to the punctuation marks used to show when characters are speaking.

A nurse appeared in the doorway. "Johnny," she said quietly, "your mother's here to see you."

Johnny opened his eyes. At first they were wide with surprise, then they darkened. "I don't want to see her," he said firmly.

"She's your mother."

"I said I don't want to see her." His voice was rising. "She's probably come to tell me about all the trouble I'm causing her and about how glad her and the old man'll be when I'm dead. Well, tell her to leave me alone. For once"—his voice broke—"for once just to leave me alone." He was struggling to sit up, but he suddenly gasped, went whiter than the pillowcase, and passed out cold.

The nurse hurried me out the door. "I was afraid of something like this if he saw anyone."

I ran into Two-Bit, who was coming in.

"You can't see him now," the nurse said, so Two-Bit handed her the book. "Make sure he can see it when he comes around." She took it and closed the door behind her. Two-Bit stood and looked at the door a long time. "I wish it was any one of us except Johnny," he said, and his voice was serious for once. "We could get along without anyone but Johnny."

What are the first words spoken by the nurse? (Johnny, your mother's here to see you.) Did you notice the quotation marks that are placed in front of the first word and after the last word spoken? A comma is used to separate the words spoken from the words that identify the speaker. Notice that the comma falls inside the quotation marks. Read the instructions for the activity and guide students to identify the spoken words as well as the punctuation marks used for dialogue.

Then, direct them to part B on page 88 and have them sort the dialogue under the correct speaker.

Lesson Opener

Before the lesson, choose one of the following activities to write on the board or post on the *LANGUAGE! Live* Class Wall online.

- *What would you have done if you were Ponyboy and thought that something bad was going to happen at the rumble? Would you have gone?*
- *Explain a rumble that you have witnessed or taken part in. Use adverbs and adjectives in your description.*
- *Write five sentences containing compound words.*

Reading

Objectives

- Establish a purpose for reading literary text.
- Demonstrate an understanding of how to ask questions and answer them appropriately.
- Use critical thinking skills to write responses to prompts about text.
- Support written answers with text evidence.
- Objectively summarize literary text.

Reading for a Purpose: Excerpt from *The Outsiders*

We are going to reread the excerpt from *The Outsiders*. Let's read the questions to provide a purpose for rereading the text.

Direct students to page 89 in their Student Books. Have them read the prompts aloud with you.

1. Describe Ponyboy's family.

2. Tell the names of the greasers.

3. Use context to determine the meaning of this quote: "We couldn't get along without him. We needed Johnny as much as he needed the gang. And for the same reason."

4. Explain Johnny's reaction to his mother's visit.

5. Describe how Johnny fits the stereotype of gang members.

6. Explain how greasers and Socs are different and alike.

Direct students to page 74 in their Student Books or have them tear out the extra copy of the excerpt from the back of their book.

Note: To minimize flipping back and forth between the pages, a copy of each text has been included in the back of the Student Books. Encourage students to tear this out and use it when working on activities that require the use of the text.

In Lesson 1, we discussed the dialogue, or who is talking. How is dialogue marked in text? (Dialogue is noted with quotation marks.)

Dialogue starts in the third paragraph. A paragraph usually includes the dialogue of only one character, but that isn't always the case. Read lines 119–125 to yourself. Determine who is talking. Look up when you are finished. **Provide wait time.** Who is *him* in the first sentence? (Johnny) Who is saying this? (the nurse) Who is *he* in the second sentence? (Johnny) Who is saying this? (Two-Bit) It is important to identify the speaker and also match pronouns to the nouns they represent.

Choose an option for reading text. Have students read the text according to the option that you chose.

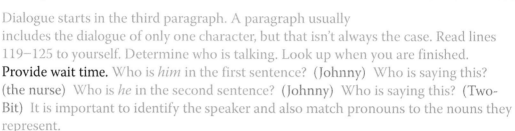

Options for reading text:
- Teacher read-aloud
- Teacher-led or student-led choral read
- Paired read or independent read with bold vocabulary words read aloud

Passage Comprehension

We are going to check our comprehension of the passage by answering questions. Remember, questions consist of a variety of difficulty levels. Some are in the form of questions and some are in the form of prompts. Prompts are statements that require a constructed response, which can range from a list to a complete sentence to a paragraph or an essay.

Write the words *describe, explain, tell,* and *use* on the board. Have students read the words aloud with you. Direct students to page 66 in their Student Books. It is critical to understand what the question is asking and how to answer it. Today, we will review four direction words used in prompts. You will become more familiar with these question words and learn how to answer different types of questions.

Have students review the words in the chart on page 66. Check for understanding by requesting an oral response to the following questions. Let's review.

- If the prompt asks you to *describe*, the response requires you to . . . (state detailed information about a topic).

- If the prompt asks you to *explain*, the response requires you to . . . (express understanding of an idea or concept).

- If the prompt asks you to *tell*, the response requires you to . . . (say or write specific information).

- If the prompt asks you to *use*, the response requires you to . . . (apply information or a procedure).

Model

Direct students to page 89 in their Student Books. Let's practice answering questions that are written as prompts. Listen as I model the first one for you.

> ## 1. Describe Ponyboy's family.

How will we start our answer? According to the chart, if the prompt asks me to *describe*, I know I need to state detailed information about a topic.

Now, we need to turn the prompt into a question to confirm our understanding. The question would be *What is Ponyboy's family like?* I remember that Ponyboy lives with his brothers Darry and Sodapop, but I can't remember why or what they are like. I need to return to the text and find out the details because that is what I need to provide. On page 78, Ponyboy says, "I remembered my mother . . . beautiful and golden, like Soda, and wise and firm, like Darry." Then, on page 80, Two-Bit tells Ponyboy "You'd think you could get away with murder, living with your big brother and all, but Darry's stricter with you than your folks were, ain't he?" and Ponyboy says, "Darry was too smart to be a greaser." "I ain't chicken, Two-Bit Mathews, and you know it," I said angrily. "Ain't I a Curtis, same as Soda and Darry?"

On the last page, Ponyboy says "Sodapop would have understood."

Now, I can combine all of those things to describe the family. First of all, I know that Ponyboy lives with Darry and Sodapop because his parents are dead. This is an inference because Two-Bit uses the past tense *were* and Ponyboy *remembers* his mom. Now, I need to describe Darry and Sodapop because they are his family. I know that Darry is smart and strict (or wise and firm). I know that Sodapop is beautiful and understanding. I also know that Ponyboy explains that he is not chicken because he is like his brothers. That means they are brave. So, let me formulate my answer.

Ponyboy's family consists of only his brothers because his parents are dead. Darry is the oldest and is smart and strict. Sodapop is beautiful and understanding. Both brothers are brave in a fight.

Passage Comprehension

Use evidence from the text to respond to the prompts using complete sentences. Refer to the chart on page 66 to determine how to respond.

1. Describe Ponyboy's family.
   Ponyboy's family consists of only his brothers because his parents are dead. Darry is the oldest and is smart and strict. Sodapop is beautiful and understanding. Both brothers are brave in a fight.

2. Tell the names of the greasers.
   Ponyboy, Sodapop, Darry, Two-Bit, Johnny, and Dally are the greasers.

3. Use context to determine the meaning of this quote: "We couldn't get along without him. We needed Johnny as much as he needed the gang. And for the same reason."
   The quote means that Johnny needs the greasers because they are more supportive of him than his own family. The greasers need Johnny to give them purpose and meaning in their lives. Protecting Johnny justifies their violent actions.

4. Explain Johnny's reaction to his mother's visit.
   At first, Johnny is surprised that his mom came to visit. Surprise quickly turns to anger because she is bitter, doesn't like his friends, and thinks he causes too much trouble for her.

5. Describe how Johnny fits the stereotype of gang members.
   Johnny fits the stereotype of gang members because he is poor, abused, and comes from a troubled home. Because Johnny doesn't feel like he belongs at home, he looks for a sense of belonging with the greasers.

6. Explain how greasers and Socs are different and alike.
   Greasers and Socs are alike because they are both gangs that use violence to solve problems. Greasers and Socs are different because greasers are poor, mostly uneducated, and live on the east side of town. Socs are rich, educated, and live on the west side of town.

Unit 3 **89**

Guided Practice

2. Tell the names of the greasers.

If the prompt asks you to *tell*, what should you do? (say or write specific information)
Now, we need to turn the prompt into a question to confirm our understanding. If
we change this into a question, what would it be? (Who are the greasers?) So we
are simply stating the names of the greasers. Who do you remember from the text?
(Johnny, Ponyboy, Sodapop, Darry, Dally, Two-Bit) **If students struggle, refer them
back to the text.**

Provide the following sentence frame if necessary.

_____, _____, _____, _____, _____, *and* _____
are greasers.

Independent Practice

Have students use text evidence to respond to the remaining questions. For students who
need more assistance, provide the following alternative questions and sentence starters.

> Alternative questions and sentence starters:
>
> 3. What does "We couldn't get along without him. We needed Johnny as much as
>   he needed the gang. And for the same reason." mean?
>
>   *The quote means* _____.
>
> 4. How did Johnny react to his mother's visit?
>
>   *Johnny's reaction was* _____.
>
>   *For example,* _____.
>
>   *In addition,* _____.
>
> 5. How does Johnny fit with your perception of gang members?
>
>   *Johnny fits the stereotype of gang members because* _____.
>
>   *For example,* _____.
>
>   *Also,* _____.
>
> 6. How are greasers and Socs alike? How are greasers and Socs different?
>
>   *Greasers are Socs are alike because* _____.
>
>   *Greasers and Socs are different because* _____.

Summarization

After reading text like this, we often form opinions of the characters. For instance, an
opinion might be "Johnny's mom was mean and didn't love him." Sometimes, it is hard
to keep those opinions from popping up when we talk or write about the text. When
we summarize text, it is important to write an objective summary—one free from our
own opinions.

Turn to your partner and summarize the text objectively. Then, switch.

Lesson 4

RL.1.3; RL.3.1; RL.4.1; RL.4.10; RF.3.3a; RF.2.4a; RF.2.4c;
RF.5.4a; RF.5.4c; L.3.3b; L.5.3b; L.1.4a; L.4.5c; L.6.4a

Lesson Opener

Before the lesson, choose one of the following activities to write on the board or post on the *LANGUAGE! Live* Class Wall online.

- *Dress your avatar as though he or she were Ponyboy the day after the rumble. Explain your choices.*
- *Create two new compound words to describe something you like to do . . . two things at once.*
- *Make a list of adjectives describing Two-Bit.*

Reading

Objectives

- Read with purpose and understanding.
- Answer questions to demonstrate comprehension of text.
- Identify and explain explicit details from text.
- Monitor comprehension of text during reading.
- Connect pronouns to their antecedents.
- Distinguish between formal and informal language.
- Use context to determine the meaning of words.
- Analyze dialogue to determine the setting.
- Determine the meaning of novel words.
- Use details in text to determine character traits.
- Identify literary irony and sarcasm.
- Determine the meaning of figurative language.
- Determine the purpose of punctuation.
- Determine the purpose of consecutive modifiers.

Close Reading of an Excerpt from *The Outsiders*

Highlighters or colored pencils

Let's reread the excerpt from *The Outsiders*. I will provide specific instructions on how to mark the text that will help with comprehension.

Have students get out a highlighter or colored pencil.

Direct students to pages 90–96 in their Student Books.

Draw a rectangle around the title, *The Outsiders*.

Star the paragraph that serves as an introduction to this chapter of the novel.

Now, let's read the vocabulary words aloud.

- What's the first bold vocabulary word? (faltered) *Faltered* means "faded off or stumbled; lost confidence." His smile *faltered* when he saw his test grade. **Have partners use the word in a sentence.**
- What's the next vocabulary word? (abruptly) *Abruptly* means "in a sudden or unexpected way." The bus stopped *abruptly*. **Have partners use the word in a sentence.**
- Next word? (resemblance) *Resemblance* means "a similarity, or likeness, between two things." There is a strong *resemblance* between my dad and me. **Have partners use the word in a sentence.**

- Let's continue. (deserve) *Deserve* means "to earn something by your words or actions." If you don't study, you *deserve* the grade you get. **Have partners use the word in a sentence.**

- Next word? (ornery) *Ornery* means "grouchy and bad-tempered." Sometimes I feel *ornery* when I haven't eaten. **Have partners use the word in a sentence.**

- Let's continue. (casual) *Casual* means "relaxed; laid back." I thought that the dance was going to be more *casual.* **Have partners use the word in a sentence.**

- Next word? (possession) *Possession* means "something owned." The police dogs are looking for illegal *possession* of drugs. **Have partners use the word in a sentence.**

- Let's continue. (hesitation) *Hesitation* means "a delay or a pause." After some *hesitation,* my teacher allowed gum chewing. **Have partners use the word in a sentence.**

- Next word? (stricter) *Stricter* means "firmer; having more rules expected to be obeyed than others." School rules are *stricter* than rules at home. **Have partners use the word in a sentence.**

- Last word. (deny) *Deny* means "to say something isn't true." The suspect will *deny* that he was involved. **Have partners use the word in a sentence.**

Talk with a partner about any vocabulary word that is still confusing for you to read or understand.

You will read the excerpt from *The Outsiders* a small section at a time. After each section, you will monitor your understanding by circling the check mark if you understand the text or the question mark if you don't understand the text. I also want you to draw a question mark over any confusing words, phrases, or sentences.

> Options for reading text:
> - Teacher read-aloud
> - Teacher-led or student-led choral read
> - Paired read or independent read with bold vocabulary words read aloud

Choose an option for reading text. Have students read lines 1–20 according to the option that you chose. Choose a character: Ponyboy, Johnny, or Dally. As you read, mark the descriptions of your chosen character—both physical descriptions and personality traits.

When most of the students are finished, continue with the entire class. Let's see how well you understood what you read.

- Circle the check mark or the question mark for this section. Draw a question mark over any confusing words.

- Circle the names of the people who are most important to Ponyboy. (Darry, Sodapop, Johnny, and Two-Bit)

- Go to line 5. Mark the synonym for *violent*. (vicious)

- On the same line, mark the gang whose symbol is greased-back hair. (greasers)

- Go to line 8. Mark the phrase that means "extremely ill; at risk of death." (critical condition)

- In the second paragraph, circle the pronouns used that indicate that the story is written in first person. (us, we, we)

- Go to lines 15 and 16. Mark the description of the setting. (quietness of the hospital)

- Go to line 18. Mark the spoken contraction used to make you think that the story takes place in the south. (y'all)

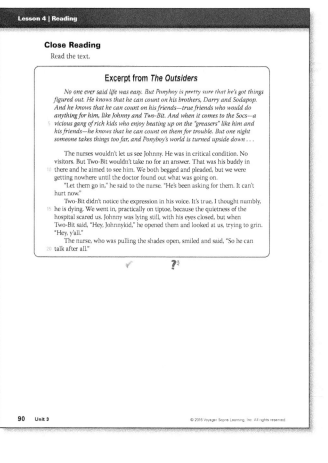

Close Reading

Read the text.

Excerpt from *The Outsiders*

No one ever said life was easy. But Ponyboy is pretty sure that he's got things figured out. He knows that he can count on his brothers, Darry and Sodapop. And he knows that he can count on his friends—true friends who would do anything for him, like Johnny and Two-Bit. And when it comes to the Socs—a [5] *vicious gang of rich kids who enjoy beating up on the "greasers" like him and his friends—he knows that he can count on them for trouble. But one night someone takes things too far, and Ponyboy's world is turned upside down . . .*

The nurses wouldn't let us see Johnny. He was in critical condition. No visitors. But Two-Bit wouldn't take no for an answer. That was his buddy in [10] there and he aimed to see him. We both begged and pleaded, but we were getting nowhere until the doctor found out what was going on.

"Let them go in," he said to the nurse. "He's been asking for them. It can't hurt now."

Two-Bit didn't notice the expression in his voice. It's true, I thought numbly, [15] he is dying. We went in, practically on tiptoe, because the quietness of the hospital scared us. Johnny was lying still, with his eyes closed, but when Two-Bit said, "Hey, Johnnykid," he opened them and looked at us, trying to grin. "Hey, y'all."

The nurse, who was pulling the shades open, smiled and said, "So he can [20] talk after all."

✓   ?

Have students read lines 21–57 according to the option that you chose. As you read, mark the descriptions of your chosen character—both physical descriptions and personality traits.

When most of the students are finished, continue with the entire class. Let's see how well you understood what you read.

Close Reading (cont.)

Two-Bit looked around. "They treatin' you okay, kid?"

"Th—" "—Johnny gasped. "don't let me put enough grease on my hair"

"Don't talk." Two-Bit said, pulling up a chair, "just listen. We'll bring you some hair grease next time. We're havin' the big rumble tonight."

25 Johnny's huge black eyes widened a little, but he didn't say anything.

"It's too bad you and Dally can't be in it. It's the first big rumble we've had—not countin' the time we whipped Shepard's outfit."

"He came by," Johnny said.

"Tim Shepard?"

30 Johnny nodded. "Came to see Dally."

Tim and Dallas had always been buddies.

"Did you know you got your name in the paper for being a hero?"

Johnny almost grinned as he nodded. "Tuff enough," he managed, and by the way his eyes were glowing, I figured Southern gentlemen had nothing on

35 Johnny Cade.

I could see that even a few words were tiring him out; he was as pale as the pillow and looked awful. Two-Bit pretended not to notice.

"You want anything besides hair grease, kid?"

Johnny barely nodded. "The book"—he looked at me—"can you get another

40 one?"

Two-Bit looked at me too. I hadn't told him about *Gone with the Wind*.

"He wants a copy of *Gone with the Wind* so I can read it to him," I explained. "You want to run down to the drugstore and get one?"

"Okay," Two-Bit said cheerfully. "Don't y'all run off."

45 I sat down in Two-Bit's chair and tried to think of something to say. "Dally's gonna be okay," I said finally. "And Darry and me, we're okay now."

I knew Johnny understood what I meant. We had always been close buddies, and those lonely days in the church strengthened our friendship. He tried to smile again, and then suddenly went white and closed his eyes tight.

50 "Johnny!" I said, alarmed. "Are you okay?"

He nodded, keeping his eyes closed. "Yeah, it just hurts sometimes. It usually don't . . . I can't feel anything below the middle of my back . . ."

He lay breathing heavily for a moment. "I'm pretty bad off, ain't I, Pony?"

"You'll be okay," I said with fake cheerfulness. "You gotta be. We couldn't get

55 along without you."

The truth of that last statement hit me. We couldn't get along without him. We needed Johnny as much as he needed the gang. And for the same reason.

✓   ?

Unit 3   91

- Circle the check mark or the question mark for this section. Draw a question mark over any confusing words.

- Go to line 22. Mark the information that explains why the group is called "greasers." **(don't let me put enough grease on my hair)**

- Go to line 24. Mark the word that means "fight." **(rumble)**

- Go to line 27. Mark the word that means "group of people." **(outfit)**

- Go to line 31. Mark Dally's real name. **(Dallas)**

- Go to line 33. Mark the word that sounds like a synonym for *strong* and means "cool." **(tuff)**

- Go to lines 34 and 35. Mark the statements that indicate Johnny was proud and good. **(eyes were glowing, Southern gentlemen had nothing on Johnny Cade)**

- Go to line 42. Mark the information that proves that Ponyboy is educated, but his friend is not. **("He wants a copy of *Gone with the Wind* so I can read it to him.")**

- Go to line 44. Mark the words that prove that Two-Bit is fun-loving and happy. **(Don't y'all run off; said cheerfully)**

- Go to line 46. Mark the sentence that proves that Ponyboy has been fighting with his brother Darry. **(And Darry and me, we're okay now.)**

- Go to line 48. Mark the words that indicate where Johnny and Ponyboy had been before Johnny was put in the hospital. **(lonely days in the church)**

- Go to line 50. Mark the word that means "anxiously aware of danger." **(alarmed)**

- Go to line 53. Mark the nickname that Johnny uses for Ponyboy. **(Pony)**

- Go to line 54. Edit the nonstandard sentence "You gotta be". **(Delete *gotta*; replace with *have got to*.)** *Gotta* is an example of a colloquial word typically used when we speak. "I gotta go to the store after work." It is a sort of contraction for the words *have got to*. When we are writing, we typically don't use it. In this case, the author used *gotta* in the dialogue to make it sound like natural speaking. "You have got to be." would sound stuffy as a spoken sentence.

Have students read lines 58–75 according to the option that you chose. As you read, mark the descriptions of your chosen character—both physical descriptions and personality traits.

When most of the students are finished, continue with the entire class. Let's see how well you understood what you read.

- Circle the check mark or the question mark for this section. Draw a question mark over any confusing words.

- Go to line 61. Mark the words that prove that Ponyboy is sensitive. (**don't start crying, you'll scare Johnny**)

- Go to line 63. Mark the phrase that means "took a fearful, shaking breath." (**drew a quivering breath**)

- On the same line, mark the irony of Johnny's condition. (**I don't want to die now.**)

- Go to line 64. Circle Johnny's age. (**sixteen**)

- In the same paragraph, mark the slang contraction used multiple times. (**ain't**) Replace each one with the correct contraction. (**isn't, isn't, haven't, haven't**) In the next paragraph, do the same. (**aren't**)

- Go to line 70. Mark the phrase that explains how they live. (**on the streets**)

- Go to line 74. Mark the words that explain why the greasers were described as cold and heartless. (**shut off your emotions**)

- On the same line, circle the synonym for *feelings*. (**emotions**)

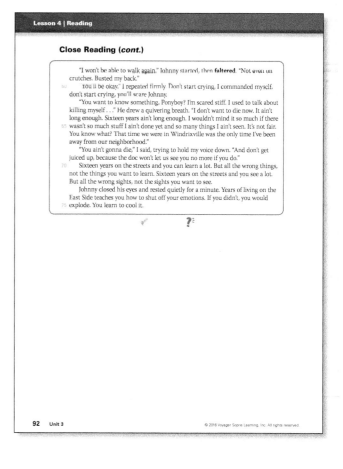

Close Reading (*cont.*)

"I won't be able to walk again," Johnny started, then **faltered**. "Not even on crutches. Busted my back."

60 "You'll be okay," I repeated firmly. Don't start crying, I commanded myself, don't start crying, you'll scare Johnny.

"You want to know something, Ponyboy? I'm scared stiff. I used to talk about killing myself . . ." He drew a quivering breath. "I don't want to die now. It ain't long enough. Sixteen years ain't long enough. I wouldn't mind it so much if there

65 wasn't so much stuff I ain't done yet and so many things I ain't seen. It's not fair. You know what? That time we were in Windrixville was the only time I've been away from our neighborhood."

"You ain't gonna die," I said, trying to hold my voice down. "And don't get juiced up, because the doc won't let us see you no more if you do."

70 Sixteen years on the streets and you can learn a lot. But all the wrong things, not the things you want to learn. Sixteen years on the streets and you see a lot. But all the wrong sights, not the sights you want to see.

Johnny closed his eyes and rested quietly for a minute. Years of living on the East Side teaches you how to shut off your emotions. If you didn't, you would

75 explode. You learn to cool it.

Have students read lines 76–113 according to the option that you chose.

As you read, mark the descriptions of your chosen character—both physical descriptions and personality traits.

When most of the students are finished, continue with the entire class.

Let's see how well you understood what you read.

- Circle the check mark or the question mark for this section. Draw a question mark over any confusing words.

- Go to lines 78 and 79. Mark the evidence that Johnny isn't sure how to react to his mother's visit. (At first they were wide with surprise, then they darkened.)

- Go to line 85. Mark the figurative language that means "pale." (went whiter than the pillowcase)

- Go to line 90. Mark the phrase that means "wakes up." (comes around)

- In the same paragraph, mark the evidence that proves that Two-Bit and Ponyboy feel the same way about Johnny. (We could get along without anyone but Johnny.)

- Go to line 100. Mark the word that means "people who engage in violence." (hoodlums)

- In the next paragraph, mark the evidence that suggests Ponyboy's respect for women. (I don't like to hear women get sworn at, even if they deserve it.)

- Go to line 108. Mark evidence of Johnny's feelings toward his mother. (No wonder Johnny didn't want to see her.)

- Go to line 109. Circle the antonym for *occupied.* (vacant)

- Go to lines 110 and 111. Mark evidence of Ponyboy's feelings toward his mother. (beautiful and golden; wise and firm) Circle the verb purposely used by the author to help the reader understand something about Ponyboy's family. (remembered)

Close Reading (*cont.*)

A nurse appeared in the doorway. "Johnny," she said quietly, "your mother's here to see you."

Johnny opened his eyes. At first they were wide with surprise, then they darkened. "I don't want to see her," he said firmly.

80 "She's your mother."

"I said I don't want to see her." His voice was rising. "She's probably come to tell me about all the trouble I'm causing her and about how glad her and the old man'll be when I'm dead. Well, tell her to leave me alone. For once"—his voice broke—"for once just to leave me alone." He was struggling to sit up, but he

85 suddenly gasped, went whiter than the pillowcase, and passed out cold.

The nurse hurried me out the door. "I was afraid of something like this if he saw anyone."

I ran into Two-Bit, who was coming in.

"You can't see him now," the nurse said, so Two-Bit handed her the book.

90 "Make sure he can see it when he comes around." She took it and closed the door behind her. Two-Bit stood and looked at the door a long time. "I wish it was any one of us except Johnny," he said, and his voice was serious for once. "We could get along without anyone but Johnny."

Turning **abruptly**, he said, "Let's go see Dallas."

95 As we walked out into the hall, we saw Johnny's mother. I knew her. She was a little woman, with straight black hair and big black eyes like Johnny's. But that was as far as the **resemblance** went. Johnnycake's eyes were fearful and sensitive; hers were cheap and hard. As we passed her she was saying, "But I have a right to see him. He's my son. After all the trouble his father and I've gone to raise

100 him, this is our reward! He'd rather see those no-count hoodlums than his own folks . . ." She saw us and gave us such a look of hatred that I almost backed up. "It was your fault. Always running around in the middle of the night getting jailed and heaven knows what else . . ." I thought she was going to cuss us out. I really did.

105 Two-Bit's eyes got narrow and I was afraid he was going to start something. I don't like to hear women get sworn at, even if they **deserve** it. "No wonder he hates your guts," Two-Bit snapped. He was going to tell her off real good, but I shoved him along. I felt sick. No wonder Johnny didn't want to see her. No wonder he stayed overnight at Two-Bit's or at our house, and slept in the vacant

110 lot in good weather. I remembered my mother . . . beautiful and golden, like Soda, and wise and firm, like Darry.

"Oh, lordy!" There was a catch in Two-Bit's voice and he was closer to tears than I'd ever seen him. "He has to live with that."

✓   ?

Unit 3   93

Have students read lines 114–137 according to the option that you chose. As you read, mark the descriptions of your chosen character—both physical descriptions and personality traits.

When most of the students are finished, continue with the entire class. Let's see how well you understood what you read.

- Circle the check mark or the question mark for this section. Draw a question mark over any confusing words.

- Go to line 115. Mark the pronoun *it*. Draw an arrow to what *it* is referencing. (let Johnny's mother see him)

- Go to line 117. Mark the punctuation used to show a hesitation. (——) This is probably because Dally really wanted to call them something else but had to find nicer words.

- Go to line 119. Mark the words that describe Dally's personality. (his usual mean, ornery self)

- Go to line 129. Edit the spoken colloquial word *outa* using standard English for writing. (out of)

- Mark the proof that Dally and Pony were involved in an act of bravery. (he saw my picture in the paper; you jumped out of the church; put out the fire)

- Go to line 133. Mark the proof that Dally saved Ponyboy's life. (knock you down and put out the fire)

- Go to line 136. Mark the sarcastic comment. (I'll bet.)

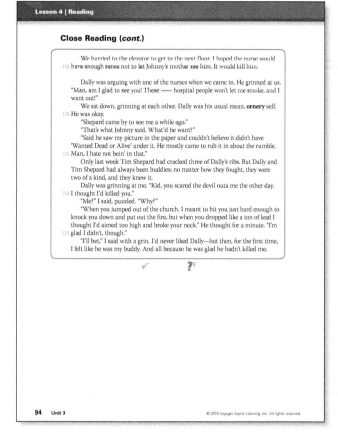

Close Reading (*cont.*)

We hurried to the elevator to get to the next floor. I hoped the nurse would
115 have enough sense not to let Johnny's mother see him. It would kill him.

Dally was arguing with one of the nurses when we came in. He grinned at us.
"Man, am I glad to see you! These —— hospital people won't let me smoke, and I
want out!"
We sat down, grinning at each other. Dally was his usual mean, **ornery** self.
120 He was okay.
"Shepard came by to see me a while ago."
"That's what Johnny said. What'd he want?"
"Said he saw my picture in the paper and couldn't believe it didn't have
'Wanted Dead or Alive' under it. He mostly came to rub it in about the rumble.
125 Man, I hate not bein' in that."
Only last week Tim Shepard had cracked three of Dally's ribs. But Dally and
Tim Shepard had always been buddies; no matter how they fought, they were
two of a kind, and they knew it.
Dally was grinning at me. "Kid, you scared the devil outa me the other day.
130 I thought I'd killed you."
"Me?" I said, puzzled. "Why?"
"When you jumped out of the church. I meant to hit you just hard enough to
knock you down and put out the fire, but when you dropped like a ton of lead I
thought I'd aimed too high and broke your neck." He thought for a minute. "I'm
135 glad I didn't, though."
"I'll bet," I said with a grin. I'd never liked Dally—but then, for the first time,
I felt like he was my buddy. And all because he was glad he hadn't killed me.

Have students read lines 138–160 according to the option that you chose. As you read, mark the descriptions of your chosen character—both physical descriptions and personality traits.

When most of the students are finished, continue with the entire class. Let's see how well you understood what you read.

- Circle the check mark or the question mark for this section. Draw a question mark over any confusing words.

- Go to line 140. Mark the word that means "trying to decide." (debating)

- Go to the paragraph after the dialogue. Mark the evidence that suggests that Two-Bit stole the switchblade. (It was the reward of two hours of walking aimlessly around a hardware store to divert suspicion.)

- Circle the synonym for *distract*. (divert)

- Go to lines 150 and 151. Mark the evidence that suggests that Two-Bit isn't much of a fighter. (he had never pulled it on anyone)

- Go to line 152. Mark the compound word that means "piece that he wants to show." (showpiece)

- On the same line, mark the word used to mean a kid similar to them. (hood)

- Mark the evidence that suggests that Dally is trustworthy. (Two-Bit handed it over to Dally without a moment's hesitation.)

- Go to line 156. Circle the pronoun that Dally uses when he speaks about the rumble. (we) Write what you think that means in the margin. (Dally is leaving the hospital.)

- Go to the last paragraph. Mark the evidence that indicates that Dally is a little bit crazy. (We knew better than to talk to Dally when his eyes were blazing and he was in a mood like that.)

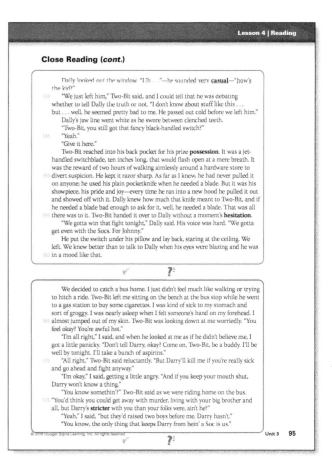

Close Reading (*cont.*)

Dally looked out the window. "Uh . . . "—he sounded very **casual**—"how's the kid?"

140 "We just left him," Two-Bit said, and I could tell that he was debating whether to tell Dally the truth or not. "I don't know about stuff like this . . . but . . . well, he seemed pretty bad to me. He passed out cold before we left him."

Dally's jaw line went white as he swore between clenched teeth.

"Two-Bit, you still got that fancy black-handled switch?"

145 "Yeah."

"Give it here."

Two-Bit reached into his back pocket for his prize **possession**. It was a jet-handled switchblade, ten inches long, that would flash open at a mere breath. It was the reward of two hours of walking aimlessly around a hardware store to 150 divert suspicion. He kept it razor sharp. As far as I knew, he had never pulled it on anyone; he used his plain pocketknife when he needed a blade. But it was his showpiece, his pride and joy—every time he ran into a new hood he pulled it out and showed off with it. Dally knew how much that knife meant to Two-Bit, and if he needed a blade bad enough to ask for it, well, he needed a blade. That was all 155 there was to it. Two-Bit handed it over to Dally without a moment's **hesitation**.

"We gotta win that fight tonight," Dally said. His voice was hard. "We gotta get even with the Socs. For Johnny."

He put the switch under his pillow and lay back, staring at the ceiling. We left. We knew better than to talk to Dally when his eyes were blazing and he was 160 in a mood like that.

✓   ?

We decided to catch a bus home. I just didn't feel much like walking or trying to hitch a ride. Two-Bit left me sitting on the bench at the bus stop while he went to a gas station to buy some cigarettes. I was kind of sick to my stomach and sort of groggy. I was nearly asleep when I felt someone's hand on my forehead. I 165 almost jumped out of my skin. Two-Bit was looking down at me worriedly. "You feel okay? You're awful hot."

"I'm all right," I said, and when he looked at me as if he didn't believe me, I got a little panicky. "Don't tell Darry, okay? Come on, Two-Bit, be a buddy. I'll be well by tonight. I'll take a bunch of aspirins."

170 "All right," Two-Bit said reluctantly. "But Darry'll kill me if you're really sick and go ahead and fight anyway."

"I'm okay," I said, getting a little angry. "And if you keep your mouth shut, Darry won't know a thing."

"You know somethin'?" Two-Bit said as we were riding home on the bus. 175 "You'd think you could get away with murder, living with your big brother and all, but Darry's **stricter** with you than your folks were, ain't he?"

"Yeah," I said, "but they'd raised two boys before me. Darry hasn't."

"You know, the only thing that keeps Darry from bein' a Soc is us."

✓   ?   Unit 3   **95**

Have students read lines 161–178 according to the option that you chose. As you read, mark the descriptions of your chosen character—both physical descriptions and personality traits.

When most of the students are finished, continue with the entire class. Let's see how well you understood what you read.

- Circle the check mark or the question mark for this section. Draw a question mark over any confusing words.

- Go to line 165. Mark the adverb that means "with anxiety or worry." Circle the suffix. (worriedly, -ly)

- On the next line, mark the two consecutive modifiers. (awful; hot) Draw an arrow from each modifier to connect it to what it is describing. (hot-you; awful-hot) *Hot* is an adjective describing *you* and *awful* is an adverb answering *how hot*.

- Go to line 170. Mark the adverb that means "with hesitation." Circle the suffix. (reluctantly, -ly)

- Mark the evidence that proves that Darry is protective of Ponyboy. (But Darry'll kill me if you're really sick and go ahead and fight anyway.)

- Go to line 176. Circle the two people who are being compared. (Darry, folks)

- On the last line, mark what keeps Darry from being a Soc. (us) Based on who said this, write who *us* represents in the margin. (greasers)

Close Reading (cont.)

Dally looked out the window. "Uh . . ."—he sounded very **casual**—"how's the kid?"

140 "We just left him," Two-Bit said, and I could tell that he was debating whether to tell Dally the truth or not. "I don't know about stuff like this . . . but . . . well, he seemed pretty bad to me. He passed out cold before we left him."

Dally's jaw line went white as he swore between clenched teeth.

"Two-Bit, you still got that fancy black-handled switch?"

145 "Yeah."

"Give it here."

Two-Bit reached into his back pocket for his prize **possession**. It was a jet-handled switchblade, ten inches long, that would flash open at a mere breath. It was the reward of two hours of walking aimlessly around a hardware store to 150 divert suspicion. He kept it razor sharp. As far as I knew, he had never pulled it on anyone; he used his plain pocketknife when he needed a blade. But it was his showpiece, his pride and joy—every time he ran into a new hood he pulled it out and showed off with it. Dally knew how much that knife meant to Two-Bit, and if he needed a blade bad enough to ask for it, well, he needed a blade. That was all 155 there was to it. Two-Bit handed it over to Dally without a moment's **hesitation**.

"We gotta win that fight tonight," Dally said. His voice was hard. "We gotta get even with the Socs. For Johnny."

He put the switch under his pillow and lay back, staring at the ceiling. We left. We knew better than to talk to Dally when his eyes were blazing and he was 160 in a mood like that.

 ?

We decided to catch a bus home. I just didn't feel much like walking or trying to hitch a ride. Two-Bit left me sitting on the bench at the bus stop while he went to a gas station to buy some cigarettes. I was kind of sick to my stomach and sort of groggy. I was nearly asleep when I felt someone's hand on my forehead. I 165 almost jumped out of my skin. Two-Bit was looking down at me worriedly. "You feel okay? You're awful hot."

"I'm all right," I said, and when he looked at me as if he didn't believe me, I got a little panicky. "Don't tell Darry, okay? Come on, Two-Bit, be a buddy. I'll be well by tonight. I'll take a bunch of aspirins."

170 "All right," Two-Bit said reluctantly. "But Darry'll kill me if you're really sick and go ahead and fight anyway."

"I'm okay," I said, getting a little angry. "And if you keep your mouth shut, Darry won't know a thing."

"You know somethin'?" Two-Bit said as we were riding home on the bus. 175 "You'd think you could get away with murder, living with your big brother and all, but Darry's **stricter** with you than your folks were, ain't he?"

"Yeah," I said, "but they'd raised two boys before me. Darry hasn't."

"You know, the only thing that keeps Darry from bein' a Soc is us."

Unit 3 95

Have students read from line 179 to the end according to the option that you chose. As you read, mark the descriptions of your chosen character—both physical descriptions and personality traits.

When most of the students are finished, continue with the entire class. Let's see how well you understood what you read.

- Circle the check mark or the question mark for this section. Draw a question mark over any confusing words.

- Go to line 179. Mark the phrase used to indicate being poor had no effect. (In spite of)

- Go to line 181. Mark the proof that the typical greaser has little education. (Darry was too smart to be a greaser.)

- Go to line 182. Mark the consecutive modifiers. (kind of; sorry) Draw an arrow from each modifier to connect it to what it is describing. (sorry-I; kind of-sorry) *Sorry* is an adjective describing *I* and *kind of* is an adverbial phrase answering *how sorry.*

- In the second paragraph, number the reasons that Ponyboy is sick to his stomach. (1. helplessness; 2. deathly fear)

- In the third paragraph, mark the evidence that proves that Ponyboy is not a coward. (I never knew you to play chicken in a rumble before.)

- Mark the evidence that proves that Ponyboy has been in a gang since he was very young. (Not even when you was a little kid.)

- Go to line 191. Mark the figurative language that means "to fall for a trick and allow someone to get you to do something." (took the bait)

- In the last paragraph, mark the evidence that Two-Bit is an optimist and definitely not a realist. (Two-Bit knew what I meant, but doggedly pretended not to. He seemed to feel that if you said something was all right, it immediately was, no matter what.)

- Circle the adverb that means "tried really hard." Circle the suffix. (doggedly, -ly)

Have partners compare text markings and correct any errors.

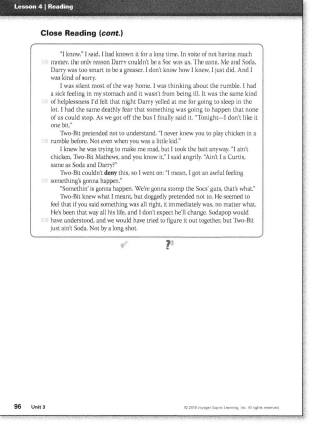

Close Reading (*cont.*)

"I know," I said. I had known it for a long time. In spite of not having much money, the only reason Darry couldn't be a Soc was us. The gang. Me and Soda. Darry was too smart to be a greaser. I don't know how I knew, I just did. And I was kind of sorry.

I was silent most of the way home. I was thinking about the rumble. I had a sick feeling in my stomach and it wasn't from being ill. It was the same kind of helplessness I'd felt that night Darry yelled at me for going to sleep in the lot. I had the same deathly fear that something was going to happen that none of us could stop. As we got off the bus I finally said it. "Tonight—I don't like it one bit."

Two-Bit pretended not to understand. "I never knew you to play chicken in a rumble before. Not even when you was a little kid."

I knew he was trying to make me mad, but I took the bait anyway. "I ain't chicken, Two-Bit Mathews, and you know it," I said angrily. "Ain't I a Curtis, same as Soda and Darry?"

Two-Bit couldn't **deny** this, so I went on: "I mean, I got an awful feeling something's gonna happen."

"Somethin' is gonna happen. We're gonna stomp the Socs' guts, that's what."

Two-Bit knew what I meant, but doggedly pretended not to. He seemed to feel that if you said something was all right, it immediately was, no matter what. He's been that way all his life, and I don't expect he'll change. Sodapop would have understood, and we would have tried to figure it out together, but Two-Bit just ain't Soda. Not by a long shot.

Unit 3

Lesson 5

RL.1.3; RL.3.3; RL.4.1; RL.4.7; RL.6.3; RL.7.3; W.2.10; W.4.10;
W.5.9b; W.6.10; W.8.10; SL.5.1b; SL.5.1c; SL.5.1d; L.6.6

Lesson Opener

Before the lesson, choose one of the following activities to write on the board or post on the *LANGUAGE! Live* Class Wall online.

- *Write four sentences with at least two vocabulary words in each. Show you know the meanings. (falter, abruptly, resemblance, deserve, ornery, casual, possession, hesitation, strict, deny)*
- *Create a list of adjectives that describe Ponyboy. Create a list of adjectives that describe Johnny. If there are any character traits they share, circle them.*
- *Make a prediction: What will happen at the rumble? Use adjectives, adverbs, and prepositional phrases in your prediction.*

Vocabulary

Objective

- Review key passage vocabulary.

Recontextualize Passage Vocabulary

Direct students to page 72 in their Student Books. Use the following questions to review the vocabulary words in the excerpt from *The Outsiders*.

- Could a student *falter* while reciting a poem? (yes) Is a professional actor likely to *falter*? (no) What might you do if you were asking someone out on a date and got nervous? (falter)

- If my hair *abruptly* turned another color, would it happen instantly? (yes) Does a year pass *abruptly*? (no) If a rainstorm came out of nowhere, would it begin slowly or *abruptly*? (abruptly)

- Is there a *resemblance* between a pigeon and a palm tree? (no) Is there a *resemblance* between twins? (yes) If you look a lot like your grandmother, what is there between the two of you? (a resemblance)

- Does the team who wins a tournament *deserve* a trophy? (yes) If you work hard in school, do you *deserve* good grades? (yes) You stay out past curfew and get grounded. Why is this fair? (because you deserve it)

- Could being tired and hungry make someone *ornery*? (yes) Would finding twenty dollars make you *ornery*? (no) If your brother snaps at you when you say "Good morning," what kind of mood is he in? (an ornery one)

- Is a skating party *casual*? (yes) Is a wedding? (no) If you wear jeans and a T-shirt to a school dance, what kind of dance is it? (a casual one)

- Is the ocean anyone's *possession*? (no) Is your backpack your *possession*? (yes) If I buy a car, it becomes my what? (possession)

- Would most people parachute out of an airplane without *hesitation*? (no) If a food smells bad, will there be a *hesitation* before you try it? (yes) You are being asked the winning question on a game show. You can only answer once. What will there be before you respond? (a hesitation)

- If a parent never lets a child watch TV, is the parent *strict*? (yes) If a teacher lets students sleep during a lesson, is she *strict*? (no) A teenager is never allowed to stay up past nine. Her parents are what? (strict)

- If you *deny* that you left dirty dishes in the sink, are you saying you left them there? (no) If you *deny* that the sun will set this evening, are you saying it will go down? (no) If I say you could be a movie star and you say "No, way," what are you doing? (denying it)

Writing

Objectives

- Use text to write coherent paragraphs in response to reading.
- Analyze a literary character.
- Compare self to literary character.

Quick Write in Response to Reading

Direct students to pages 97 and 98 in their Student Books and read the instructions aloud. Introduce the prewriting strategy of choosing a character and using the graphic to map out traits, evidence, and connections to self. Model this process if necessary.

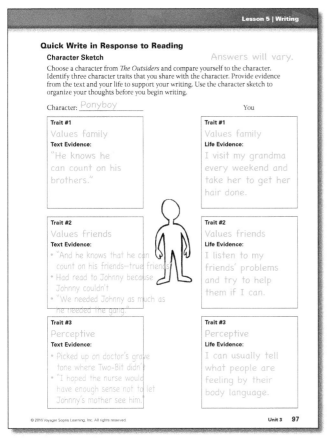

Note: The example response has been broken into paragraphs. Paragraphing is desirable, and you may encourage your students to write in that manner. However, if your students aren't able to do it, it will be taught in later units.

Reading

Objectives
- Self-correct as comprehension of text deepens.
- Answer questions to demonstrate comprehension of text.
- Engage in class discussion.
- Identify the enduring understandings from a piece of text.
- Identify elements of a story, including climax and resolution.
- Identify the plot of a drama and how characters respond to change.
- Analyze the interaction of story elements.
- Compare text with a filmed version.

Revisit Passage Comprehension

Direct students to page 89 in their Student Books. Have students review their answers and make any necessary changes. Then, have partners share their answers and collaborate to perfect them.

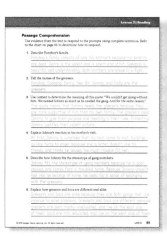

Enduring Understandings

Direct students back to page 71 in their Student Books. Reread the Big Idea questions.

Do people have an innate need to fit in?

What is the effect of hatred between social groups?

Generate a class discussion about the questions and answers students came up with in Lesson 1. Have them consider whether their answers have changed after reading the text.

Use the following talking points to foster conversation. Refer to the Class Discussion Rules poster and have students use the Collegial Discussion sentence frames on page 382 of their Student Books.

- People are more alike than different. Everyone wants a family to love them and friends to like them. There are many circumstances out of our control, such as color of skin, height, intelligence, talents, socioeconomic status, where we live, who is in our family, and cultural beliefs and traditions. Is it possible for these things to create limitations, problems, or undeserved praise?

- Snap judgments affect everyone involved. Judging people too quickly is dangerous. People who appear to be outsiders likely don't choose to be left out.

What we read should make us think. Use our discussion and your thoughts about the text to determine what you will "walk away with." Has it made you think about a personal experience or someone you know? Has your perspective or opinion on a specific topic changed? Do you have any lingering thoughts or questions? Write these ideas as your enduring understandings. What will you take with you from this text?

Discuss the enduring understandings with the class. Then, have students write their enduring understandings from the unit.

Have students consider why the author wrote the passage and whether she was successful.

Story Elements and Plot Development

Direct students back to page 73 in their Student Books. Have students review the story map. Then, have them add to the rising action, complete the setting and characters, and predict what they think the climax and resolution will be. Offer brief explanations of the story elements if students struggle.

All of the elements of a good story interact with each other and affect each other. The development of one character affects the development of another character. For instance, what did we learn about Darry in the excerpt that affects the personalities of Soda and Ponyboy? (Darry is strict, which probably has led to Soda being fun-loving and laid back. Darry's sacrifices for his brothers have made them desire to impress him and seek his approval.) What do we know about the setting that affects the characters? (They live in poverty, across the track from those who are wealthy. This likely makes them "fighters" by nature and causes them to lean on each other for support as well as dislike those on the other side.)

The development of the plot affects everything in a story. Why does the setting change from the abandoned church to the hospital in the chapter that we read? (Johnny and Dally were hurt in a fire.) How does Johnny change after the incident in the church? (Johnny becomes scared and begins thinking seriously about the possibility of death. He loses the fighting spirit.) How does the possibility of losing Johnny affect the other characters? (Two-Bit becomes more angry than fun-loving; Dally wants to seek vengeance; Ponyboy becomes fearful and cautious—doesn't want to lose anybody else in a stupid fight.)

It is important to pay attention to how each element of a story affects the others.

Comparing Film with Print (Optional Activity)

Though we don't recommend watching the entire movie *The Outsiders*, watching the excerpt that coincides with the text can be a wonderful learning experience. If you choose to show the excerpt in class, have students compare the experiences.

Ask the following questions to foster conversation:

1. Which version was more entertaining?

2. Which version was easier to understand?

3. What did you get from the film that you did not get from your reading?

4. How did seeing the characters and hearing their voices impact your experience?

5. Did you "hear" or "see" anything differently when you read it? Did the characters look different in your mind?

6. In what ways was the film different from the book, and in what ways did the director stay true to the story?

Lesson Opener

Before the lesson, choose one of the following activities to write on the board or post on the *LANGUAGE! Live* Class Wall online.

- *Imagine you are Ponyboy, and Johnny's mother insists on taking him home. What would you do?*
- *Describe a time when you hid from someone. Why did you hide? What happened when you came out of hiding?*
- *Write one sentence about a family member. Write one sentence about another family member. Use an adverb or prepositional phrase in each sentence.*

Reading

Objectives

- Determine and discuss the topic of a text.
- Determine and discuss the author's purpose.
- Use text features to preview text.
- Determine the meaning of multiple-meaning words.

Passage Introduction

Direct students to page 99 in their Student Books. Discuss the content focus.

Content Focus

family; ostracism

We are about to read a famous play, or drama, about the *Diary of Anne Frank*. It is a play about a family who is ostracized, or banished, from society and hides in order to stay alive.

Before we get started, let's talk about the multiple meanings of two words: *play* and *drama*. *Play* can be a noun or a verb. If you play video games, *play* is a verb—an action that means "take part in." *Play* can also be a noun, which is a piece of writing performed in a theater, on the radio, or on television. Similarly, *drama* has multiple meanings. Turn and tell your neighbor what *drama* means to you. While students are sharing, write the following sentences on the board:

The Outsiders *is a novel full of drama.*

The Play of the Diary of Anne Frank *is a drama based on a real diary.*

Lesson 6 | Reading

Let's Focus: Excerpt from *The Play of the Diary of Anne Frank*

Content Focus
family; ostracism

Type of Text
literature—drama (based on a true story)

Authors' Names _Frances Goodrich and Albert Hackett; Anne Frank_

Authors' Purpose _entertainment; self-expression; to teach a lesson_

Big Ideas
Consider the following Big Idea questions. Write your answer for each question.

Are all people really good at heart?

_____

_____

Are people a product of their beliefs or a product of their circumstances?

_____

_____

Drama Preview Checklist: the excerpt from *The Play of the Diary of Anne Frank* on pages 101–118.

- ☐ Title: What clue does it provide about the play?
- ☐ Pictures: What additional information is added here?
- ☐ Features: What other text features do you notice?
  - ○ How many acts?
  - ○ How many scenes?
  - ○ How many characters?

Enduring Understandings
After reading the play . . .

_____

_____

_____

_____

_____

Unit 3 **99**

Tell your partner about the meaning of *drama* in both sentences. **Provide talk time.** Switch roles. Share a sentence that uses *play* as a noun and another sentence that uses *play* as a verb.

A *drama* is a serious play or movie. *Drama* can also mean "an exciting situation or a situation with intense conflict." The excitement of drama can be good or bad. *Drama* can have a negative connotation if it is ongoing or upsetting.

Type of Text
literature—drama (based on a true story)

You have learned that literature is divided into categories, or genres. Say *genres*. (genres) Dramas, or plays, are a genre of literature. This play, however, is based on a diary, which is considered informational text. A drama is a form of writing intended for a performance. It has cast members, or a list of characters. It shows what each character says, line by line. In a drama, the characters talk to one another, not the reader. What are the characters called in a drama? (cast members) Who do the cast members talk to? (one another) A drama also tells what the character does through the use of stage directions. How are stage directions used? (Stage directions are used to inform the characters' actions.) *The Play of the Diary of Anne Frank* is based on a true story. It is an adaptation of what a young girl wrote in her diary.

Author's Purpose

Have students glance at the text. Who are the authors of the play and the diary it was based on? (Frances Goodrich and Albert Hackett; Anne Frank) The author's purpose is the reason that he or she wrote the text. Authors write for different purposes. Anne Frank did not intend to have this diary published. Her purpose for writing was to express private thoughts about what it was like being a teenage girl ostracized from society. Anne's father decided to publish the diary after her death to inform others about Jewish suffering during the Holocaust. Then, Frances Goodrich and Albert Hackett adapted her work into a play.

Have students write the answers on the page.

Have you ever read or written in a diary? **Provide sharing time.**

Anne Frank wrote a private diary that went public. Have you ever written something private that went public? **Provide sharing time. If needed, guide the discussion with the following.** Have you ever used social media such as Facebook or Twitter as a public diary? What other forms of media allow you to express personal thoughts?

> **Note:** Determine if students need Background Information pertaining to Anne Frank and the Holocaust. This can be found in the Teacher Resources online. Choose the Text Training tab, and then select Unit 3. The Background Information will be in the first section.

Read the Big Idea questions aloud.

Big Ideas

Are all people really good at heart?

Are people a product of their beliefs or a product of their circumstances?

As a class, consider the two Big Idea questions.

- Encourage students with limited understanding of the terms *product* and *circumstances* to ask for further explanation from peers.

- Have students reflect on the Background Information for the unit and ask clarifying questions when needed.

- Provide opportunities for students to explain their ideas and answers to the Big Idea questions in light of the discussion by ensuring students follow the rules for class discussion, which can be printed in poster form from the Teacher Resources online.

- Suggest students refer to the Collegial Discussion sentence frames in the back of their books.

- Encourage speakers to link comments to the remarks of others to keep the focus of the discussion and create cohesion, even when their comments are in disagreement.

After discussing each question, have students write an answer. We'll come back to these questions after we finish reading the acts from the play. You can add to your answers as you gain information and perspective.

Preview

Read the Drama Preview Checklist on page 99. Follow the Preview Procedure outlined below.

Preview Procedure

- Group students with partners or in triads.
- Have students count off as 1s or 2s. The 1s will become the student leaders. If working with triads, the third students become 3s.
- The student leaders will preview the text in addition to managing the checklist and pacing.
- The 2s and 3s will preview the text with 1s.
- Direct 1s to open their Student Books to page 99 and 2s and 3s to open their Student Books to page 101. This allows students to look at a few different pages at one time without turning back and forth.

If it is necessary, guide students in a short preview using the talking points below.
What is the title of the play? (*The Play of the Diary of Anne Frank*) Let's look to see what additional information the pictures provide. Point to the picture that looks like an apartment. Read the caption with me. (The spice warehouse that enclosed

the secret annex) What is an annex? (An annex is a room or attic that extends a building.) Apparently this was a secret, so that must mean they were in hiding. Go to page 104. What hid the door to the secret annex? (a bookcase) How do you know? (the caption) Read the caption with me. (A replica of the bookcase that hid the door to the secret annex) What is a replica? (a copy) Find the yellow star that was worn on Jewish people's clothing. **Explain that the word on the star is _Jew_ in Dutch.** Brainstorm a caption for that picture with your neighbor. **Have volunteers share their captions.**

Vocabulary

Objectives
- Evaluate word knowledge.
- Determine the meaning of key passage vocabulary.

Rate Vocabulary Knowledge

Direct students to page 100 in their Student Books. We are about to read an excerpt from a play titled _The Play of the Diary of Anne Frank_. Before we read, let's take a look at the vocabulary words that appear in this selection. Remind students that as you read each word in the first column aloud, they will write the word in the third column and then rate their knowledge of it in the fourth. Display the Vocabulary Rating Scale poster or write the information on the board. Review the meaning of each rating.

Vocabulary Rating Scale

0—I have never heard the word before.

1—I have heard the word, but I'm not sure how to use it.

2—I am familiar with the word, but I'm not sure if I know the correct meaning.

3—I know the meaning of the word and can use it correctly in a sentence.

The points are not a grade; they are just there to help you know which words you need to focus on. By the end of this unit, you should be able to change all your ratings to a 3—that's the goal.

Read each word aloud. Have students repeat it, write it, and rate it. Then, have volunteers who rated a word _2_ or _3_ use the word in an oral sentence.

Preteach Vocabulary

Let's take a closer look at the words. Provide definitions and examples as indicated on the word cards. Ask questions to clarify and deepen understanding. If time permits, allow students to share.

> ## Preteach Procedure
> This activity is intended to take only a short amount of time, so make it an oral exercise.
> - Introduce each word as indicated on the word card.
> - Read the definition and example sentences.
> - Ask questions to clarify and deepen understanding.
> - If time permits, allow students to share.
>
> * If your students would benefit from copying the definitions, please have them do so in the vocabulary log in the back of the Student Books using the margin definitions in the passage selections. This should be done outside of instruction time.

awkward (adj)

Let's read the first word together. Awkward.

Definition: *Awkward* means "uncomfortable; not sure what to do or say." What word means "uncomfortable; not sure what to do or say"? (awkward)

Example 1: If you show up at someone's house for a party and learn that the party isn't until tomorrow, you might feel *awkward.*

Example 2: I sometimes feel *awkward* working in small groups with people I don't know well.

Example 3: My brother was an *awkward* child, but now he is comfortable around others.

Question 1: If a person feels *awkward* in crowds, does he or she seek them out? Yes or no? (no)

Question 2: Is a good basketball player *awkward* on the court? Yes or no? (no)

Pair Share: Turn to your partner and tell about a time you felt *awkward.*

conspicuous (adj)

Let's read the next word together. Conspicuous.

Definition: *Conspicuous* means "easily seen." What means "easily seen"? (conspicuous)

Example 1: Wearing a winter coat to the swimming pool would make you *conspicuous.*

Example 2: In books, heroes sometimes have a *conspicuous* scar on their face.

Example 3: Hot pink hair is *conspicuous* in a room full of brown-haired people.

Question 1: If you took a dance class with a group of four-year-olds, would you be *conspicuous*? Yes or no? (yes)

Question 2: Is a single snowflake among thousands of other snowflakes *conspicuous*? Yes or no? (no)

Pair Share: Turn to your partner and describe something displayed in a *conspicuous* place in your bedroom or home.

(1)

(2)

indicate (v)

Let's read the next word together. *Indicate.*

Definition: To *indicate* is to signal something with a movement or gesture. What means "to signal something with a movement or gesture"? (indicate)

Example 1: In class, I might *indicate* that it's your turn to speak by pointing at you.

Example 2: A baseball umpire *indicates* an out with a raised fist.

Example 3: My phone *indicates* that I have a call or text by vibrating.

Question 1: If people were screaming and running away, would that *indicate* that something bad has happened? Yes or no? (yes)

Question 2: Would you *indicate* joy and excitement by frowning? Yes or no? (no)

Pair Share: A family member wants your spot on the couch. Turn to your partner and demonstrate how you would *indicate* your refusal to budge.

(3)

dependable (adj)

Let's read the next word together. *Dependable.*

Definition: *Dependable* means "trustworthy; able to be counted on or relied on." What means "trustworthy; able to be counted on or relied on"? (dependable)

Example 1: A *dependable* employee shows up for work every day.

Example 2: A *dependable* alarm clock always goes off at the right time.

Example 3: My landlord is *dependable*; he always responds immediately if there's a problem.

Question 1: Is a car *dependable* if it sometimes doesn't start? Yes or no? (no)

Question 2: If the mail comes at the same time every day, is the mail carrier *dependable*? Yes or no? (yes)

Pair Share: Turn to your partner and tell what makes a *dependable* friend.

(4)

leisure (n)

Let's read the next word together. *Leisure.*

Definition: *Leisure* is time when you are not working or busy with tasks. What means "time when you are not working or busy with tasks"? (leisure)

Example 1: If I were rich, I'd still want to work; a life of *leisure* might get boring after a while.

Example 2: As a teacher, I enjoy my *leisure* in the summertime and on breaks.

Example 3: There is little time for *leisure* when you own your own restaurant.

Question 1: If you can watch a movie at your *leisure*, can you watch it when you aren't busy? Yes or no? (yes)

Question 2: For farmers, is harvest time a time of *leisure*? Yes or no? (no)

Pair Share: Turn to your partner and describe what you do at your *leisure* on the weekend.

(5)

regulations (n)

Let's read the next word together. *Regulations.*

Definition: *Regulations* are rules set by people in power to control how things are done. What are rules set by people in power to control how things are done? (regulations)

Example 1: In our state, certain *regulations* help keep pollution levels down.

Example 2: According to school board *regulations*, you must attend school a certain number of days a year.

Example 3: During a drought, city *regulations* state that you may only run sprinklers on certain days of the week.

Question 1: Do traffic *regulations* help keep people safe? Yes or no? (yes)

Question 2: Are *regulations* the same as suggestions or pointers? Yes or no? (no)

Pair Share: Turn to your partner and tell what *regulations* you would pass if you were king or queen of the world.

(6)

interval (n)

Let's read the next word together. *Interval*.

Definition: An *interval* is a period of time between two dates or events. What means "a period of time between two dates or events"? (interval)

Example 1: After a half-time *interval* of 10 minutes, basketball players return to the court.

Example 2: In large bicycle races, groups of cyclists cross the starting line in *intervals*.

Example 3: In the *interval* between winter break and spring break, I plant my spring garden.

Question 1: Do we have an *interval* between classes? Yes or no? (yes)

Question 2: Is the *interval* between lunch and dinner more than five minutes? Yes or no? (yes)

Pair Share: You just ran a mile in PE. After what *interval* will you be ready to run another mile? Tell your partner.

(7)

garment (n)

Let's read the next word together. *Garment*.

Definition: A *garment* is an item of clothing. What means "an item of clothing"? (garment)

Example 1: A factory might produce thousands of *garments*, such as shirts or pants, a day.

Example 2: Some people enjoy hunting for hats, jackets, and other vintage *garments* at thrift shops.

Example 3: On warm days, you don't need to wear an outer *garment*.

Question 1: Is a suitcase a *garment*? Yes or no? (no)

Question 2: Do you put *garments* in a suitcase? Yes or no? (yes)

Pair Share: Turn to your partner and tell how old, worn-out *garments* might be recycled.

(8)

concentrate (v)

Let's read the next word together. *Concentrate*.

Definition: *Concentrate* means "to give all your attention to something." What word means "to give all your attention to something"? (concentrate)

Example 1: I have to *concentrate* to work an algebra problem correctly.

Example 2: If you don't *concentrate* during a complicated movie, you might get confused.

Example 3: For some people, it is hard to *concentrate* on homework when loud music is playing.

Question 1: Do you have to *concentrate* to have a dream? Yes or no? (no)

Question 2: Can you put out a fire out by *concentrating* on it? Yes or no? (no)

Pair Share: Take turns telling your partner a series of eight numbers. *Concentrate* on the numbers and then recite them.

(9)

peculiar (adj)

Let's read the last word together. *Peculiar*.

Definition: *Peculiar* means "strange; odd." What means "strange; odd"? (peculiar)

Example 1: Eating a salad for breakfast is *peculiar*.

Example 2: My cat has the *peculiar* habit of sleeping in the bathroom sink.

Example 3: In the 1990s, the *peculiar* trend of skipping to class became popular on college campuses.

Question 1: Is it *peculiar* to say hello to a friend? Yes or no? (no)

Question 2: Is it *peculiar* to greet a stranger with a hug? Yes or no? (yes)

Pair Share: You have just landed on a distant planet. Tell your partner what makes the creatures that live there *peculiar*.

(10)

Objectives

- Read a drama.
- Monitor comprehension during text reading.

Excerpt from *The Play of the Diary of Anne Frank*

Direct students to page 101 in their Student Books.

Now it's time to read. Try to visualize what is happening on the stage while reading.

Guiding Students Toward Independent Reading

It is important that your students read as much and as often as they can. Assign readings that meet the needs of your students, based on your observations and data. This is a good opportunity to stretch your students. If students become frustrated, scaffold the reading with paired reading, choral reading, or a read-aloud.

Options for reading text:

- Teacher read-aloud
- Teacher-led or student-led choral read
- Paired read or independent read

Choose an option for reading text. Students read according to the option that you chose. Review the purpose of the numbered squares in the text and prompt students to stop periodically to check comprehension.

from *The Play of the Diary of Anne Frank*

List of Characters

(in the order of their appearance)

Mr. Frank	*Pronunciation*: Frahnk
Miep Gies	*Pronunciation*: Meep
Mrs. Van Daan	*Pronunciation*: Petronella, Pet-row-nell'-ah
Mr. Van Daan	*Pronunciation*: Fahn Dahn
Peter Van Daan	*Pronunciation*: Pay'-ter
Mrs. Frank	*Pronunciation*: Edith, Ae'-dith
Margot Frank	*Pronunciation*: Mar'-gott
Anne Frank	*Pronunciation*: Ah'-nah
Mr. Kraler	*Pronunciation*: Krah'-ler

ACT ONE

Scene One

SE p. 101

The top floors of a warehouse in Amsterdam, Holland. November 1945. Late afternoon.

MR FRANK enters. He is weak and ill and is making a supreme effort at self-control. His clothes are threadbare. He carries a small rucksack. A scarf catches his eye. He takes it down, puts it around his neck, then wanders towards the couch, but stops as he sees the glove. He picks it up. Suddenly all control is gone. He breaks down and weeps. MIEP GIES *enters up the stairs. She is a Dutch girl of about twenty-two, pregnant now. She is compassionate and protective in her attitude towards* MR FRANK. *She has been a stenographer and secretary in his business. She has her coat and hat on, ready to go home. A small silver cross hangs at her throat.*

1. What does the cross tell you about Miep?

SE p. 101

MIEP	Are you all right, Mr. Frank?
MR FRANK	(*quickly controlling himself*) Yes, Miep, yes.

SE p. 102

MIEP	Everyone in the office has gone home—it's after six. Don't stay up here, Mr. Frank. What's the use of torturing yourself like this?
MR FRANK	I've come to say good-bye—I'm leaving here, Miep.
MIEP	What do you mean? Where are you going? Where?
MR FRANK	I don't know yet. I haven't decided.
MIEP	Mr. Frank, you can't leave here. This is your home. Amsterdam is your home. Your business is here, waiting for you. You're needed here. Now that the war is over, there are things that . . .
MR FRANK	I can't stay in Amsterdam, Miep. It has too many memories for me. Everywhere there's something —the house we lived in—the school—the street organ playing out there. I'm not the person you used to know, Miep. I'm a bitter old man. Forgive me. I shouldn't speak to you like this—after all that you did for us—the suffering . . .
MIEP	No. No. It wasn't suffering. You can't say we suffered.
MR FRANK	I know what you went through, you and Mr. Kraler. I'll remember it as long as I live. Come, Miep. (*He remembers his rucksack, crosses below the table to the couch and picks up his rucksack.*)
MIEP	Mr. Frank, did you see? There are some of your papers here. (*She takes a bundle of papers from the shelves, then crosses below the table to* MR FRANK.) We found them in a heap of rubbish on the floor after—after you left.
MR FRANK	Burn them. (*He opens his rucksack and puts the glove in it.*)
MIEP	But, Mr. Frank, there are letters, notes . . .
MR FRANK	Burn them. All of them.
MIEP	Burn this? (*She hands him a worn, velour-covered book.*)

2. What does Miep know that Mr. Frank does not?

SE p. 103

MR FRANK (*quietly*) Anne's diary. (*He opens the diary and reads.*) 'Monday, the sixth of July, nineteen hundred and forty-two.' (*To* MIEP.) Nineteen hundred and forty-two. Is it possible, Miep? Only three years ago. (*He reads.*) 'Dear Diary, since you and I are going to be great friends, I will start by telling you about myself. My name is Anne Frank. I am thirteen years old. I was born in Germany the twelfth of June, nineteen twenty-nine. As my family is Jewish, we emigrated to Holland when Hitler came to power.'

3. Why did the Franks leave Germany when Hitler came to power?

SE p. 103

MR FRANK
ANNE'S VOICE } (*together*)
'My father started a business, importing spice and herbs. Things went well for us until nineteen forty. Then the War came and the Dutch—(*He turns the page.*) defeat, followed by the arrival of the Germans. Then things got very bad for the Jews.'

(MR FRANK'S *voice dies out as* ANNE'S VOICE *grows stronger.*)

4. What is happening on stage here?

SE p. 103

ANNE You could not do this and you could not do that. They forced father out of his business. We had to wear yellow stars. I had to turn in my bike. I couldn't go to a Dutch school any more. I couldn't go to the cinema, or ride in an automobile, or even on a streetcar, and a million other things. But somehow we children still managed to have fun. Yesterday, father told me we were going into hiding. Where, he wouldn't say. At five o'clock this morning mother woke me and told me to hurry and get dressed. I was to put on as many clothes as I could. It would look too suspicious if we walked along carrying suitcases. It wasn't until we were on our way that I learned where we were going. Our hiding place was to be upstairs in the building where father used to have his business. Three other people were coming in with us—the Van Daans and their son Peter. Father knew the Van Daans but we had never met them.

(*The sound of distant ships' sirens is heard.*)

Scene Two

Early morning. July 1942.

The three members of the VAN DAAN *family are waiting for the* FRANKS *to arrive.* MR VAN DAAN *is smoking a cigarette and watching his wife with a nervous eye. His overcoat and suit are expensive and well-cut.* MRS VAN DAAN *is sitting on the couch. She is a pretty woman in her early forties and is clutching her possessions: a hat-box, a handbag and an attractive straw carry-all.* PETER VAN DAAN *is standing at the window in the room. He is a shy,* **awkward** *boy of sixteen. He wears a cap, a short overcoat, and long Dutch trousers, like 'plus fours'. All the* VAN DAANs *have the* **conspicuous** *yellow Star of David on the left breast of their clothing.*

MRS V.DAAN	Something's happened to them. I know it.
MR V.DAAN	Now, Kerli!
MRS V.DAAN	Mr. Frank said they'd be here at seven o'clock. He said . . .
MR V.DAAN	They have two miles to walk. You can't expect . . .
MRS V.DAAN	They've been picked up.
	(*The door below opens.*)
	That's what happened. They've been taken.

5. Who does Mrs. Van Daan think has taken the Franks?

E p. 104

(MR VAN DAAN *indicates* that he hears someone coming.)

MR V.DAAN You see?

(MR FRANK *comes up the stairwell from below.*)

MR FRANK Mrs. Van Daan, Mr. Van Daan. (*He shakes hands with them. He moves to* PETER *and shakes his hand.*) There were too many of the Green Police on the streets—we had to take the long way round.

E p. 105

(MIEP, *not pregnant now,* MARGOT, MR KRALER, *and* MRS FRANK *come up the stairs.* MARGOT *is eighteen, beautiful, quiet and shy. She carries a leatherette hold-all and a large brown paper bag, which she puts on the table.* KRALER *is a Dutchman,* **dependable** *and kindly. He wears a hearing aid in his ear and carries two brief-cases.* MRS FRANK *is a young mother, gently bred and reserved. She, like* MR FRANK, *has a slight German accent. She carries a leatherette shopping bag and her handbag. We see the Star of David conspicuous on the* FRANKS' *clothing.* KRALER *acknowledges the* VAN DAANS, *moves to the shelves and checks their contents.* MIEP *empties her straw bag of the clothes it contains and piles them on the table.*)

MRS FRANK Anne?

(ANNE FRANK *comes quickly up the stairs. She is thirteen, quick in her movements, interested in everything and mercurial in her emotions. She wears a cape, long wool socks and carries a school bag.*)

MR FRANK My wife, Edith. Mr. and Mrs. Van Daan.

(MRS FRANK *shakes* MR VAN DAAN'S *hand, then hurries across to shake hands with* MRS VAN DAAN. *She then moves to the sink and inspects it.*)

Their son, Peter—my daughters, Margot and Anne.

6. How many people will be living in the annex?

SE p. 105

(ANNE *gives a polite little curtsy as she shakes* MR VAN DAAN'S *hand. She puts her bag on the left end of the table then immediately starts off on a tour of investigation of her new home, going upstairs to the attic room.*)

SE p. 106

KRALER	I'm sorry there is still so much confusion.
MR FRANK	Please. Don't think of it. After all, we'll have plenty of **leisure** to arrange everything ourselves.
MIEP	(*indicating the sink cupboard*) We put the stores of food you sent in here. (*She crosses to the shelves.*) Your drugs are here— soap, linen, here.
MRS FRANK	Thank you, Miep.
MIEP	I made up the beds—the way Mr. Frank and Mr. Kraler said. Forgive me. I have to hurry. I've got to go to the other side of town to get some ration books for you.
MRS V.DAAN	Ration books? If they see our names on ration books, they'll know we're here.

KRALER
MIEP } (*together*)

There isn't anything . . .

Don't worry. Your names won't be on them. (*As she hurries out.*) I'll be up later.

MR FRANK	Thank you, Miep.

7. Who is helping the Franks hide?

SE p. 106

(MIEP *exits down the stairwell.*)

MRS FRANK It's illegal, then, the ration books? We've never done anything illegal.

MR FRANK We won't be living exactly according to **regulations** here.

KRALER This isn't the black market, Mrs. Frank. This is what we call the white market—helping all of the hundreds and hundreds who are hiding out in Amsterdam.

(*The carillon is heard playing the quarter hour before eight. KRALER looks at his watch. ANNE comes down from the attic, stops at the window and looks out through the curtains.*)

ANNE It's the Westertoren.

SE p. 107

KRALER I must go. I must be out of here and downstairs in the office before the workmen get here. Miep or I, or both of us, will be up each day to bring you food and news and find out what your needs are. Tomorrow I'll get you a better bolt for the door at the foot of the stairs. It needs a bolt that you can throw yourself and open only at our signal. (*To MR FRANK.*) Oh— you'll tell them about the noise?

MR FRANK I'll tell them.

KRALER Good-bye, then, for the moment. I'll come up again, after the workmen leave.

MR FRANK (*shaking KRALER'S hand*) Good-bye, Mr. Kraler.

MRS FRANK (*shaking KRALER'S hand*) How can we thank you?

KRALER I never thought I'd live to see the day when a man like Mr. Frank would have to go into hiding. When you think . . .

(KRALER *breaks off and exits down the stairs.* MR FRANK *follows him down the stairs and bolts the door after him. In the* **interval** *before he returns,* PETER *goes to* MARGOT, *gives a stiff bow and shakes hands with her.* ANNE *watches, and as they complete their greeting, moves to* PETER *and holds out her hand.* PETER *does not see her and turns away.* MR FRANK *comes up the stairs.*)

MRS FRANK What did he mean, about the noise?

MR FRANK First, let's take off some of these clothes.

8. Why do the Franks have so many clothes on?

SE p. 107

(ANNE *moves below the table, stands with her back to the audience, removes her cape and beret and puts them on the pile of clothes on the table. They all start to take off* **garment** *after garment. On each of their coats, sweaters, blouses, suits and dresses is another yellow Star of David. MR and MRS FRANK are under-dressed quite simply. The others wear several things, sweaters, extra dresses, bathrobes, aprons, etc. MRS FRANK takes off her gloves, carefully folding them before putting them away.*)

SE p. 108

MR V.DAAN It's a wonder we weren't arrested, walking along the streets—Petronella with a fur coat in July—and that cat of Peter's crying all the way.

ANNE (*removing a pair of panties*) A cat?

MRS FRANK (*shocked*) Anne, please!

ANNE It's all right. I've got on three more (*She removes two more pairs of panties. Finally, as they finish removing their surplus clothing, they settle down.*)

MR FRANK Now. About the noise. While the men are in the building below, we must have complete quiet. Every sound can be heard down there, not only in the workrooms, but in the offices, too. The men come about eight-thirty, and leave at about five-thirty. So, to be perfectly safe, from eight in the morning until six in the evening we must move only when it is necessary and then in stockinged feet. We must not speak above a whisper. We must not run any water. We cannot use the sink, or even, forgive me, the WC. The pipes go down through the workrooms. It would be heard. No rubbish . . .

(*The sound of marching feet is heard.* MR FRANK, *followed by* ANNE, *peers out of the window. Satisfied that the marching feet are going away, he returns and continues.*)

No rubbish must ever be thrown out which might reveal that someone is living here—not even a potato paring. We must burn everything in the stove at night. This is the way we must live until it is over, if we are to survive.

9. What can't the Franks and Van Daans do from 8:00 to 6:00?

SE p. 108

(*There is a pause.* MARGOT *accidentally drops the nightgown she is taking off.* PETER *jumps to pick it up for her.*)

SE p. 109

MRS FRANK   Until it is over.

MR FRANK   After six we can move about—we can talk and laugh and have our supper and read and play games—just as we would at home. (*He looks at his watch.*) And now I think it would be wise if we all went to our rooms, and were settled before eight o'clock. Mrs. Van Daan, you and your husband will go upstairs. I regret that there's no place up there for Peter. But he will be here near us. This will be our common room, where we'll meet to talk and eat and read, like one family.

MRS V.DAAN   And where do you and Mrs. Frank sleep?

MR FRANK   This room is also our bedroom.

(MRS VAN DAAN *rises in protest.*)

MRS V.DAAN and
MR V.DAAN } (*together*)   That isn't right. We'll sleep here and you take the room upstairs. It's your place.

MR FRANK   Please. I've thought this out for weeks. It's the best arrangement. The only arrangement.

(MR VAN DAAN *starts to load his arms with the clothes he and his wife have taken off and thrown across the couch.*)

MRS V.DAAN   (*shaking* MR FRANK'S *hand*) Never, never can we thank you. (*She moves to* MRS FRANK *and shakes her hand.*) I don't know what would have happened to us, if it hadn't been for Mr. Frank.

MR FRANK   You don't know how your husband helped me when I came to this country—knowing no-one—not able to speak the language. I can never repay him for that. May I help you with your things?

10. Why does Mr. Frank offer to help hide the Van Daans?

SE p. 109

MR V.DAAN No. No. (*He picks up the carton and moves towards the attic stairs. To* MRS VAN DAAN) Come along, liefje.

SE p. 110

MRS V.DAAN You'll be all right, Peter? You're not afraid?

PETER (*embarrassed*) Please, Mother. (*He picks up his gear.* MRS FRANK *goes to the head of the stairwell and stares thoughtfully down.* MR *and* MRS VAN DAAN *go upstairs.*)

MR FRANK You, too, must have some rest, Edith. You didn't close your eyes last night. Nor you, Margot.

ANNE I slept, Father. Wasn't that funny? I knew it was the last night in my own bed, and yet I slept soundly.

MR FRANK I'm glad, Anne. Now you'll be able to help me straighten things in here. (*To* MRS FRANK *and* MARGOT.) Come with me— you and Margot rest in this room for the time being.

E p. 110

MRS FRANK	You're sure? I could help, really. And Anne hasn't had her milk.
MR FRANK	I'll give it to her. (*He crosses to the table and picks up the piles of clothes.*) Anne, Peter—it's best that you take off your shoes now, before you forget. (*He leads the way to the room, goes in and switches on the pendant light. MARGOT goes into the room.* ANNE *and* PETER *remove their shoes.*)
MRS FRANK	You're sure you're not tired, Anne?
ANNE	I feel fine. I'm going to help father.
MRS FRANK	Peter, I'm glad you are to be with us.
PETER	Yes, Mrs. Frank.
	(*MRS FRANK goes into the room and closes the door. During the following scene* MR FRANK *helps* MARGOT *to hang up clothes.* PETER *takes his cat out of its case.*)

E p. 111

ANNE	What's your cat's name?
PETER	'Mouschi'.
ANNE	Mouschi! Mouschi! Mouschi! (*She picks up the cat.*) I love cats. I have one—a darling little cat. But they made me leave her behind. I left some food and a note for the neighbors to take care of her—I'm going to miss her terribly. What is yours? A him or a her?
PETER	He's a tom. He doesn't like strangers. (*He takes the cat from ANNE, and puts it back in its carrier.*)

11. How are Peter and his cat alike?

SE p. 111

ANNE	Then I'll have to stop being a stranger, won't I? Is he fixed?
PETER	Huh?
ANNE	Did you have him altered?
PETER	No.
ANNE	Oh, you ought to—to keep him from fighting. Where did you go to school?
PETER	Jewish Secondary.
ANNE	But that's where Margot and I go. I never saw you around.
PETER	I used to see you—sometimes.
ANNE	You did?
PETER	In the school yard. You were always in the middle of a bunch of kids. (*He takes a penknife from his pocket.*)

12. What do we know about Anne?

SE p. 111

SE p. 112

ANNE	Why didn't you ever come over?
PETER	I'm sort of a lone wolf. (*He starts to rip off his Star of David.*)
ANNE	What are you doing?
PETER	Taking it off.
ANNE	But you can't do that. (*She grabs his hands and stops him.*) They'll arrest you if you go out without your star.
PETER	(*pulling away*) Who's going out? (*He crosses to the stove, lifts the lid and throws the star into the stove.*)

13. What does Peter realize that Anne doesn't quite understand?

SE p. 112

ANNE   Why, of course. You're right. Of course we don't need them any more. (*She takes* PETER'S *knife and removes her star.* PETER *waits for her star to throw it away.*)

I wonder what our friends will think when we don't show up today?

PETER   I didn't have any dates with anyone.

ANNE   (*concentrating on her star*) Oh, I did. I had a date with Jopie this afternoon to go and play ping-pong at her house. Do you know Jopie de Waal?

PETER   No.

ANNE   Jopie's my best friend. I wonder what she'll think when she telephones and there's no answer? Probably she'll go over to the house—I wonder what she'll think—we left everything as if we'd suddenly been called away—breakfast dishes in the sink—beds not made . . . (*As she pulls off her star, the cloth underneath shows clearly the colour and form of the star.*) Look! It's still there. What're you going to do with yours?

PETER   Burn it. (*He moves to the stove and holds out his hand for* ANNE'S *star.* ANNE *starts to give the star to* PETER, *but cannot.*)

SE p. 113

ANNE   It's funny. I can't throw it away. I don't know why.

PETER   You can't throw . . . ? Something they branded you with? That they made you wear so they could spit on you?

ANNE   I know. I know. But after all, it is the Star of David, isn't it?

14. Would you have been able to burn something that was a symbol of your faith?

SE p. 113

(*The* VAN DAANS *have arranged their things, have put their clothes in the wardrobe and are sitting on the bed, fanning themselves.*)

PETER Maybe it's different for a girl.

(ANNE *puts her star in her school bag.*)

MR FRANK Forgive me, Peter. Now, let me see. We must find a bed for your cat. I'm glad you brought your cat. Anne was feeling so badly about hers.

(*He sees a small worn wash-tub and pulls it from the top shelf.*)

Here we are. Will it be comfortable in that?

PETER Thanks.

MR FRANK And here is your room. But I warn you, Peter, you can't grow any more. Not an inch, or you'll have to sleep with your feet out of the skylight. Are you hungry?

PETER No.

MR FRANK We have some bread and butter.

PETER No, thank you.

MR FRANK (*with a friendly pat on* PETER'S *shoulder*) You can have it for luncheon, then. And tonight we will have a real supper—our first supper together.

SE p. 114

PETER Thanks. Thanks. (*He goes into his room.* MR FRANK *closes the door after* PETER, *then sits and removes his shoes.*)

MR FRANK That's a nice boy, Peter.

ANNE He's awfully shy, isn't he?

MR FRANK You'll like him, I know.

ANNE I certainly hope so, since he's the only boy I'm likely to see for months and months.

15. How long does Anne think she will have to hide?

SE p. 114

MR FRANK   Anne, there's a box there. Will you open it?

(*The sound of children playing is heard from the street below. MR FRANK goes to the sink and pours a glass of milk from the thermos bottle.*)

ANNE   You know the way I'm going to think of it here? I'm going to think of it as a boarding-house. A very **peculiar** Summer boarding-house, like the one that we . . . (*She breaks off as she looks in the box.*) Father! Father! My film stars. I was wondering where they were—and Queen Wilhelmina. How wonderful!

MR FRANK   There's something more. Go on. Look further.

(ANNE *digs deeper into the box and brings out a velour-covered book. She examines it in delighted silence for a moment, then opens the cover slowly, and looks up at* MR FRANK *with shining eyes.*)

ANNE   A diary! (*She throws her arms around him.*) I've never had a diary. And I've always longed for one. (*She rushes to the table and looks for a pencil.*) Pencil, pencil, pencil, pencil. (*She darts across to the stair-well and starts down the stairs.*) I'm going down to the office to get a pencil.

SE p. 115

MR FRANK   Anne! No! (*He strides to* ANNE *and catches her arm.* MRS FRANK *aware of the sudden movement and sounds, sits up. After a moment she rises, goes to the window and looks out, then returns and sits on the bed.*)

ANNE   (*startled*) But there's no-one in the building now.

MR FRANK   It doesn't matter. I don't want you ever to go beyond that door.

ANNE   (*sobered*) Never? Not even at night time, when everyone is gone? Or on Sundays? Can't I go down to listen to the radio?

MR FRANK   Never. I am sorry, Anneke. It isn't safe. No, you must never go beyond that door.

ANNE   I see. (*For the first time she realizes what 'going into hiding' means.*)

16. What does "going into hiding" actually mean?

SE p. 115

MR FRANK It'll be hard, I know. But always remember this, Anneke. There are no walls, there are no bolts, no locks that anyone can put on your mind. Miep will bring us books. We will read history, poetry, mythology. (*He gives* ANNE *the glass of milk.*) Here's your milk.

(MR FRANK *puts his arm about* ANNE, *and crosses with her to the couch, where they sit side by side.*)

As a matter of fact, between us, Annie, being here has certain advantages for you. For instance you remember the battle you had with your mother the other day on the subject of goloshes? You said you'd rather die than wear goloshes. But in the end you had to wear them. Well now, you see for as long as we are here, you will never have to wear goloshes. Isn't that good? And the coat that you inherited from Margot—

(ANNE *makes a wry face.*)

—you won't have to wear that. And the piano. You won't have to practice on the piano. I tell you, this is going to be a fine life for you.

17. How is Mr. Frank trying to ease Anne's panic?

SE p. 116

(ANNE'S *panic is gone.* PETER *appears in the doorway of his room, with a saucer in one hand and the cat in the other.*)

PETER I—I—I thought I'd better get some water for Mouschi before . . .

MR FRANK Of course.

E p. 116

(*The carillon begins its melody and strikes eight. As it does so,* MR FRANK *motions for* PETER *and* ANNE *to be quiet, tiptoes to the window in the rear wall and peers down.* MR VAN DAAN *rises and moves to the head of the attic stairs.* MR FRANK *puts his finger to his lips, indicating to* ANNE *and* PETER *that they must be silent, then steps down towards* PETER *indicating he can draw no water.* PETER *starts back to his room.* ANNE *rises and crosses below the table to* PETER. MR FRANK *crosses quietly towards the girls' room. As* PETER *reaches the door of his room a board creaks under his foot. The three are frozen for a minute in fear.* ANNE *then continues over to* PETER *on tiptoe and pours some milk in the saucer.* PETER *squats on the floor, putting the milk down before the cat and encouraging him to drink.* MR FRANK *crosses to them, gives* ANNE *his fountain pen, then crosses to the girls' room, goes inside, sits on the bed and puts a comforting arm around* MRS FRANK. ANNE *squats for a moment beside* PETER, *watching the cat, then opens her diary and writes. All are silent and motionless, except* MR VAN DAAN *who returns to* MRS VAN DAAN *and fans her with a newspaper. The Westertoren finishes tolling the hour. As* ANNE *begins to write, her voice is heard faintly at first, then with growing strength.*)

SE p. 117

ANNE I expect I should be describing what it feels like to go into hiding. But I really don't know yet, myself. I only know it's funny never to be able to go outdoors—never to breathe fresh air—never to run and shout and jump. It's the silence in the night that frightens me most. Every time I hear a creak in the house, or a step on the street outside, I'm sure they're coming for us. The days aren't so bad. At least we know that Miep and Mr. Kraler are down there below us in the office. Our protectors, we call them. I asked father what would happen to them if the Nazis found out they were hiding us. Pim said that they would suffer the same fate that we would. Imagine! They know this and yet when they come up here, they're always cheerful and gay as if there were nothing in the world to bother them. Friday, the twenty-first of August, nineteen forty-two. Today I'm going to tell you our general news. Mother is unbearable. She insists on treating me like a baby, which I loathe. Otherwise things are going better. The weather is . . .

18. Why is Anne amazed by Miep and Mr. Kraler?

For confirmation of engagement, take 30 seconds to have students share one thing they learned about Anne Frank and her hiding place.

Lesson Opener

Before the lesson, choose one of the following activities to write on the board or post on the *LANGUAGE! Live* Class Wall online.

- *Write a summary sentence about Anne Frank's situation in the play.*
- *Make a list of adjectives describing Anne.*
- *Write five sentences explaining what you would do during a day that you could not go anywhere or make any noise. Use adverbs, adjectives, and prepositional phrases in the sentences.*

Vocabulary

Objective

- Review key passage vocabulary.

Review Passage Vocabulary

Direct students to page 100 in their Student Books. Use the following questions to review the vocabulary words in the excerpt from *The Play of the Diary of Anne Frank*. Have students answer each question using the vocabulary word or indicating its meaning in a complete sentence.

- What makes Peter Van Daan *awkward*? (He is awkward because he does not seem comfortable around others.) Would you describe Anne as *awkward*? (No, Anne is not awkward; she is easygoing and likes to interact with others.)

- What *conspicuous* symbol do the Van Daans have on the chest of their clothing? (A conspicuous yellow star is attached to each item of clothing.) Do the Van Daans and the Franks hope to be *conspicuous* in their hiding place? (No, they do not hope to be conspicuous; they hope not to be discovered.)

- When Mr. Frank gives Anne the diary, how does she *indicate* that she loves it? (She indicates that she loves the diary by smiling at him, throwing her arms around him, and immediately searching for a pencil.) When Anne heads downstairs to find a pencil, how does Mr. Frank *indicate* that she shouldn't? (He indicates that she shouldn't go downstairs by grabbing her arm.)

- What makes Miep and Mr. Kraler *dependable*? (They are helping hide the Van Daans and the Franks in the space above the office.) If Mr. Kraler turned the families in to the authorities, would he be *dependable*? (No, he would not be dependable; he would be untrustworthy.)

- Will the Franks and the Van Daans be at their *leisure* in the apartment? Why or why not? (Yes, they will be at their leisure because they cannot go to work or to school.) Do you think such *leisure* would be enjoyable? Why or why not? (Possible answer: Such leisure might be enjoyable for a time, but it would soon become boring and frustrating because of their lack of freedom.)

- What *regulations* control how people get food during wartime? (Ration book regulations control how they get food.) How does Mrs. Frank feel about breaking *regulations*? Why? (She feels worried about breaking regulations because the Franks have never done anything illegal before.)

- At what *intervals* does Mr. Kraler plan to visit the families? (He plans to visit them at one-day intervals.) During what *interval* each day must the families be absolutely quiet? (They must be absolutely quiet during the interval of 8:30 and 5:30—when the office workers arrive and when they leave.)

- When the Franks take off *garment* after *garment*, what are they doing? (When they take off garment after garment, they are removing the coats, sweaters, shirts, and other clothes they are wearing.) Why have they worn so many *garments* in layers? (They have layered their garments so they wouldn't have to carry suitcases.) Would carrying suitcases have made them *conspicuous*? (Yes, carrying suitcases would have made them conspicuous, or easily spotted.)

- When Anne *concentrates* on her star, what is she doing to it? (When she concentrates on her star, she is focusing her attention on it.) Do you think someone like Anne would have to *concentrate* in order to stay quiet for eight hours straight? Why or why not? (Yes, someone like Anne would have to concentrate to stay quiet because she is naturally talkative and active.)

- Anne tries to think of their hiding place as a *peculiar* summer boarding house, or vacation house. What would make such a vacation house *peculiar*? (It would be peculiar because you wouldn't be able to leave it or to relax and enjoy yourself in it, either.) Why might the Franks' situation seem *peculiar* to Americans today? (It might seem peculiar because we enjoy so many freedoms, unlike European Jews in the 1940s.)

Assign online practice by opening the Tools menu, then selecting Assignments. Be sure to select the correct class from the drop-down menu.

Writing

Objectives
- Read a series of sentences.
- Identify the structure of a paragraph.
- Analyze how a particular sentence fits into the meaning and structure of a paragraph.

Parts of a Paragraph

Print the Steps for Paragraph Writing poster found in the Teacher Resources online and display where students can easily see it.

We have learned that sentences have parts and that understanding the parts of a sentence can help us understand the meaning of the sentence. What are the two basic parts of a sentence? **(the subject and the predicate)** Paragraphs also have a structure, and knowing that structure can strengthen our ability to understand the meaning of the related sentences that make up the paragraph.

When we write, we want our writing to be informative and interesting. We need to develop a main idea by including key details and elaborations. We will use a paragraph on the benefits of exercise to uncover four of the basic building blocks found in a well-written paragraph.

Direct students to Part A on page 119 in their Student Books. Have them follow along as you introduce the parts of a paragraph.

Model

Let's start by looking for the topic sentence or the big idea of the paragraph. Then, we will identify the supporting details, or facts that support the topic sentence. Transition words help a writer or a reader move through the supporting details, so we'll circle the transition words. Paragraphs are expanded through elaborations—examples, explanations or evidence. We'll look for information related to each supporting detail. A well-written conclusion will restate the topic sentence or big idea of the paragraph. What are the four building blocks of a well-written paragraph? (a topic sentence, supporting details, elaborations, and a conclusion)

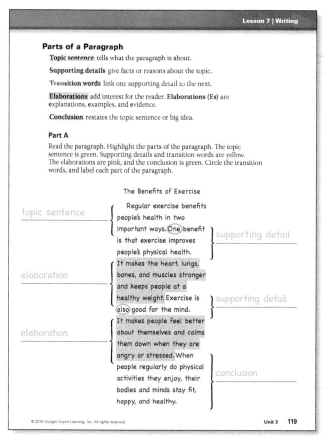

Guided Practice

Read the instructions for the activity. Read the first sentence of the paragraph aloud and have students highlight it green. Identify it as the topic sentence. If this is the topic sentence, what will it tell us? (the big idea of the paragraph) What is this paragraph about? (It is about the benefits of regular exercise.)

Read the second sentence aloud and have students highlight it yellow. Identify it as a supporting detail. If this is a supporting detail, what must it do? (It must provide a fact or facts that support the topic.) How does this sentence support the topic? (It is talking about one of the benefits of exercise.)

Notice the sentence contains the word *one*. It indicates this is the first supporting detail. Number words often work as transition words in paragraphs. How are we supposed to mark our transitions? (circle them) Other words can also help readers and writers transition from one idea to the next. Words like *another*, *also*, and *in addition* are examples of other transition words that may be used to help the flow of a paragraph.

Read the third sentence aloud. Is this a new supporting detail, or is it related to how exercise improves health? (It is related to how exercise improves health.) This must be an elaboration. It tells us how exercise can improve someone's health. How do we mark our elaborations? (Highlight them in pink.) Highlight this sentence pink.

Independent Practice

Read the remaining sentences, one at a time. Ask students to consider the role of each sentence, then mark it appropriately. Then, model how to properly label the parts of the paragraph.

Let's read another paragraph and apply what we learned about building a solid paragraph. Several of your writing prompts in the previous units have called for you to write an expository paragraph in response to the text. The next paragraph is a response to the writing prompt from Unit 2. **Direct students to Part B on page 120 in their Student Books and read the instructions aloud.**

Read the paragraph about Mrs. Luella Bates Washington Jones aloud to the class. Work with your partner to highlight the topic sentence green, supporting details yellow, and elaborations pink. Look for transition words that help move the reader through the supporting details, and circle them.

Circulate as students work on the paragraph, providing support as needed. If students seem to struggle, pull the class back together and go through the paragraph with the class. After students complete the assignment, review the correct highlighting of the sentences within the paragraph.

Parts of a Paragraph (*cont.*)

Part B

Identify the elements within the paragraph. Highlight the topic sentence and concluding sentence green, the supporting details yellow, and the elaborations pink. Circle any transition words.

Kind, hard-working, and tough are three traits that describe Mrs. Luella Bates Washington Jones. Her kindness is revealed in surprising ways. In spite of Roger's actions, Mrs. Jones sees a boy in need of guidance and care. She is determined to feed him and instill a basic level of respect for other people. She also works hard to support herself and take care of her apartment. The apartment is clean and tidy. Over dinner, she tells Roger about her job at the hotel beauty shop. Through her stories, she conveys a sense of history with her job. Another unexpected trait is her toughness. When Roger attempted to steal her purse, the last thing he expected was to be confronted by her. She was determined to make a lasting impression. Instead of being frightened, she knocked him down and then decided to teach him about the consequences of his actions. Mrs. Luella Bates Washington Jones unexpectedly embodies the traits of a hard worker along with kindness and toughness.

Reading

Objectives

- Identify the structure and form of a drama.
- Analyze how a drama's structure contributes to its meaning.
- Answer questions about text.
- Support written answers with text evidence.
- Determine the meaning of idioms and phrases while reading.
- Distinguish between firsthand accounts and secondhand accounts.
- Identify the differences in an original work and the fictional adaptation of it.
- Compare and contrast a fictional portrayal of events and a historical account of the same event.
- Analyze how an author transforms source material from a printed work.

Elements of Drama

Direct students to page 121 in their Student Books.

We read an excerpt from *The Play of the Diary of Anne Frank* in the last lesson. Now, we'll have the chance to look at its form and content. We will also compare the text features of a drama with a novel, like *The Outsiders*. What is a drama? (A drama is a production of a play.) Novels and dramas have similar features, such as plot, characters, dialogue, and symbols. Whereas novels are written by authors, plays are written by playwrights. What is a playwright? (A playwright is someone who writes a play.)

Many dramas have distinctive text features. Playwrights use specific text features to guide the people who direct and act in a play.

Acts: Like a chapter in a novel, an act is one of the main parts of a play.

Elements of a Drama

Acts	An act is one of the main parts of a play.
Scenes	Acts are made up of scenes or episodes that occur in the same location. One act can have many scenes.
Flashbacks	A flashback is a literary device used when a scene changes the chronology of events to an event back in the past.
Characters	Characters in a play are called the cast members. In a play, characters' names are written in bold font or style to tell who performs the dialogue or actions.
Stage Directions	The information set in parentheses tells stage directions. Information in parentheses is not read aloud by the actors. The stage directions tell what happens before the actors speak, or tell about a change in the stage set. These references tell the actors what to do, how to do it, or how to say the words.
Symbols	In a play, the playwright doesn't have to describe a symbol because he or she can show it (such as the Star of David worn by the Jews). Characters often explain the significance of the symbols through their dialogue with other characters.

Read the text features of a novel. Write the corresponding element of a drama. The first one is done for you.

Novel: *The Outsiders*	Drama or play: *The Play of the Diary of Anne Frank*
author	playwright
chapters	acts
plot: telling thoughts through actions	plot: showing thoughts through dialogue and actions
episodes	scenes
characters	cast
dialogue is read	dialogue is acted out
quotation marks show who is talking	bold names show who is talking
symbol: description of greased hair	symbol: image of yellow Star of David

Unit 3   **121**

Scenes: Acts are made up of scenes, or episodes that occur in the same location. One act can have many scenes. In *The Play of the Dairy of Anne Frank,* you have read the first two scenes of Act One. What are acts made up of? (scenes) Where does each scene occur? (Scenes occur in the same location.)

Flashback: A flashback is a literary device used when a scene changes the chronology of events to an event back in the past. A flashback can occur in a novel or a play. Find an example of a flashback in *The Play of the Diary of Anne Frank.* (Scene Two occurs earlier in time than Scene One.)

Characters: Characters in a play are called the cast members. Who makes up the cast? (Characters in the play make up the cast.) In a novel, quotation marks are used to show who is talking. In a play, characters' names are written in bold font or all caps to tell who performs the dialogue or actions. How can we tell who is talking in a play? (Bold font or all caps tells who is talking in a play.)

Stage directions: Unlike novels, plays have references set off by parentheses. The information set off by parentheses tells stage directions. Information in parentheses is not read aloud. Point to the first parenthetical reference in the play. (quickly controlling himself) Parenthetical references tell what happens before the actors speak, or tell about a change in the stage set. These references in parentheses tell the actors what to do, how to do it, or how to say the words. What does the first parenthetical reference show? (what to do)

Explain that the introduction to each scene is in italics, just like the introductions to the chapters they've been reading, and that stage directions are often included in the introductions.

Symbols: *The Outsiders* used greased hair to symbolize the greasers. The author told the reader about the significance of their greased hair. In a play, the playwright might show you the symbol, such as the Star of David worn by the Jews, rather than describe it in words. Characters might explain the significance of the symbols through their dialogue with other characters.

For direct application of this information, complete the activity in your Student Book to confirm your understanding of the text features related to dramas. **When students are finished, discuss the answers as a class.**

Direct students attention to the final speaking part of Anne.

Who is Anne speaking to? (herself; her diary; audience) Notice the stage directions just before this happens. It mentions that all the other characters are silent and motionless. It is as though everything and everyone stops while Anne speaks. When the rest of a scene fades out and one speaker is sharing his or her thoughts, this is called a soliloquy. A soliloquy is a long, usually serious, speech that a character in a play makes to an audience and that reveals the character's thoughts. In this particular case, Anne is also writing her thoughts in her diary, but the intention is for the audience to know what her thoughts are. **Have partners discuss why the playwright wants the audience to know what Anne is thinking.** Soliloquies occur in many plays to allow the audience to to understand characters better and to experience something through a first-person point of view, rather than a third person. Knowing what Anne is thinking is an important aspect of this play. Without that, audience members wouldn't quite understand both the attempted "normalcy" of their lives and the fear they were living with.

Critical Understandings: Direction Words *compare, define, interpret, report*

Remember, prompts are directions that require a constructed response, which can range from a list to a complete sentence to a paragraph or an essay. We can take prompts and turn them into questions to help us understand what type of response is required. Let me show you how that is done using some new direction words.

Write the words *compare, define, interpret,* and *report* on the board. Have students read the words aloud. Direct students to page 66 in their Student Books. It is critical to understand what the question is asking and how to answer it. Today, we will look at four direction words used in prompts.

Have students read about the four words in the chart with their partner.

Chart Reading Procedure

- Group students with partners or in triads.
- Have students count off as 1s or 2s. The 1s will become the student leaders. If working with triads, the third students become 3s.
- The student leaders will read the left column (Prompt) in addition to managing the time and turn-taking if working with a triad.
- The 2s will explain the middle column of the chart (How to Respond). If working in triads, 2s and 3s take turns explaining the middle column.
- The 1s read the model in the right column (Model), and 2s and 3s restate the model as a question.
- All students should follow along with their pencil eraser while others are explaining the chart.
- Students must work from left to right, top to bottom in order to benefit from this activity.

Critical Understandings: Direction Words

Prompt	How to Respond	Model
If the prompt asks you to . . .	The response requires you to . . .	For example . . .
Analyze	break down and evaluate or draw conclusions about the information	**Analyze** the development of the text's central idea.
Assess	decide on the value, impact, or accuracy	**Assess** the level of pressure in an arranged marriage.
Compare	state the similarities between two or more things	**Compare** novels and dramas.
Contrast	state the differences between two or more things	**Contrast** a biography with an autobiography.
Create	make or produce something	**Create** a timeline of events.
Define	tell or write the meaning or definition	**Define** the unknown word using context clues.
Delineate	show or list evidence, claims, ideas, reasons, or events	**Delineate** the evidence in the text.
Describe	state detailed information about a topic	**Describe** the relationship between the plot and character development.
Determine	find out, verify, decide	**Determine** the main idea.
Distinguish	recognize or explain the differences	**Distinguish** between facts and opinions.
Evaluate	think carefully to make a judgment; form a critical opinion of	**Evaluate** the ANC's plan for change.
Explain	express understanding of an idea or concept	**Explain** how the author develops the narrator's point of view.
Identify	say or write what it is	**Identify** the character's motive.
Infer	provide a logical answer using evidence and prior knowledge	Use information from the text to **infer** the value of education.
Interpret	make sense of or assign meaning to something	**Interpret** the quote to confirm your understanding.
Paraphrase	say or write it using different words	**Paraphrase** the main idea.
Report	Tell or write about a topic	**Report** the main events of the setting.
Summarize	tell the most important ideas or concepts	**Summarize** the key details of the passage.
Tell	say or write specific information	**Tell** the date that the poem was written.
Use	apply information or a procedure	**Use** text features to identify the topic.

66   Unit 2

Check for understanding by requesting an oral response to the following questions.

- If the prompt asks you to *compare*, the response requires you to . . . (state similarities between two or more things).
- If the prompt asks you to *define*, the response requires you to . . . (tell or write the meaning or definition).
- If the prompt asks you to *interpret*, the response requires you to . . . (make sense or assign meaning to something).
- If the prompt asks you to *report*, the response requires you to . . . (tell or write about a topic).

Direct students to page 122 in their Student Books.

Let's read some prompts about a small section of the play with these new direction words.

1. Define the idiom "catches his eye."

2. Report how Mr. Frank is feeling.

3. Compare Miep Gies and Mrs. Jones from "Thank You, M'am."

4. Interpret the meaning of the phrase "all control is gone."

Listen as I read an excerpt from *The Play of the Diary of Anne Frank.* We will use this excerpt to practice responding to prompts by turning them into questions.

Lesson 7 | Reading

Critical Understandings: Direction Words
Read the prompts and respond using complete sentences. Refer to the chart on page 66 to determine how to respond. Provide text evidence when requested.

1. Define the idiom "catches his eye."
"Catches his eye" means attracts his attention.

2. Report how Mr. Frank is feeling.
Mr. Frank is feeling fragile and ill.

3. Compare Miep Gies and Mrs. Jones from "Thank You, M'am."
Miep and Mrs. Jones are both kind and motherly.

4. Interpret the meaning of the phrase "all control is gone." Provide text evidence.
"All control is gone" means that Mr. Frank gets emotional.

Text Evidence: "He breaks down and weeps."

122   Unit 3   © 2016 Voyager Sopris Learning, Inc. All rights reserved.

MR FRANK *enters. He is weak and ill and is making a supreme effort at self-control. His clothes are threadbare. He carries a small rucksack. A scarf catches his eye. He takes it down, puts it around his neck, then wanders towards the couch, but stops as he sees the glove. He picks it up. Suddenly all control is gone. He breaks down and weeps.* MIEP GIES *enters up the stairs. She is a Dutch girl of about twenty-two, pregnant now. She is compassionate and protective in her attitude towards* MR FRANK. *She has been a stenographer and secretary in his business. She has her coat and hat on, ready to go home. A small silver cross hangs at her throat.*

Model

Let's practice answering questions that are written as prompts. Remember to use the chart on page 66 as a reference. Listen as I model the first one for you.

> 1. Define the idiom "catches his eye."

Because the prompt is asking me to *define*, I know that I will need to write the meaning. Now, I will turn the prompt into a question to confirm understanding. What does the idiom "catches his eye" mean? Because I know that an idiom doesn't mean exactly what it says, I can use context to figure out the answer.

Write the following sentence starter on the board.

> *"Catches his eye" means* _____.

In the text following the phrase, it says *"He takes it down, puts it around his neck."* Based on this context, I will determine what "catches his eye" means. Since he takes the scarf down, he obviously had to have seen it. Because the idiom uses *eye* in it, I would assume that "catches his eye" means that he saw it or noticed it. **Complete the answer on the board.**

Guided Practice

Let's move on to the next prompt.

> 2. Report how Mr. Frank is feeling.

Tell your partner how to respond according to the chart. (If the prompt asks you to *report*, the response requires you to tell or write about the topic.) Turn the prompt into a question to confirm understanding. (How is Mr. Frank feeling?) **While providing partner time, write the sentence starter on the board:**

> *Mr. Frank is feeling* _____.

Have volunteers complete the sentence using evidence from the text.

> 3. Compare Miep Gies and Mrs. Jones from "Thank You, M'am."

Tell your partner how to respond according to the chart. (If the prompt asks you to *compare*, the response requires you to state the similarities between two or more things.) Turn the prompt into a question to confirm understanding. (How are Miep and Mrs. Jones alike?) **While providing partner time, write the following sentence starter on the board:**

> *Miep and Mrs. Jones are both* _____.

Have volunteers complete the sentence using evidence from the text.

4. Interpret the meaning of the phrase "all control is gone."

Tell your partner how to respond according to the chart. (If the prompt asks you to *interpret*, the response requires you to make sense of or assign meaning to something.) Turn the prompt into a question to confirm understanding. (What does "all control is gone" mean?) While providing partner time, write the sentence starter on the board:

"All control is gone" means _____.

Have volunteers complete the sentence, then provide evidence from the text.

An Author's Creative License

We read *The Play of the Diary of Anne Frank*. Playwrights, as well as directors and producers, often take creative license when adapting a work to be performed for an audience. This means they may change parts of the story to be more entertaining, even if these things didn't really happen. This play was adapted from a diary written by a teenage girl in the 1940s. A diary is an example of a primary source or firsthand account. It is written by someone who was present during the events being described. Do you think the playwrights took creative license when turning the diary into a play? Think of how you would describe something in a diary. How entertaining do you think it would be to read? **Have students discuss how transitioning from a diary to a screenplay might be problematic.**

Listen as I read an excerpt from one of the first entries in Anne Frank's actual diary that the play was based on.

Sunday, 14 June, 1942

On Friday, June 12th, I woke up at six o'clock and no wonder; it was my birthday. But of course I was not allowed to get up at that hour, so I had to control my curiosity until a quarter to seven. Then I could bear it no longer, and went to the dining room, where I received a warm welcome from Moorjte (the cat).

Soon after seven I went to Mummy and Daddy and then to the sitting room to undo my presents. The first to greet me was *you*, possibly the nicest of all . . .

Generate a class discussion about the one major difference in this excerpt and the play. Have students discuss the possible reasons that the playwrights would have made this change.

According to the play, Anne was given the diary while at the annex on Friday, the 21st of August, 1942. The playwrights likely changed the date and location to avoid having to develop a scene of Anne's former residence for very little use. Also, the playwrights needed to incorporate Anne's desire to go downstairs for something simple, such as a pen, with the lesson from her father that they must never leave the annex. The impact of this fact is much greater as it is written than it would be if we just read it in the diary entry.

Direct students to page 123 in their Student Books. Read the instructions aloud. Have partners read the excerpt and discuss the major differences between the diary and the play.

Review the differences as a class, then discuss the author's possible reasons for making the changes.

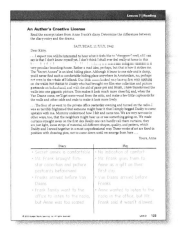

Lesson 8

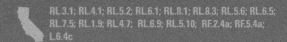

RL.3.1; RL.4.1; RL.5.2; RL.6.1; RL.8.1; RL.8.3; RL.5.6; RL.6.5;
RL.7.5; RL.1.9; RL.4.7; RL.6.9; RL.5.10; RF.2.4a; RF.5.4a;
L.6.4c

Lesson Opener

Before the lesson, choose one of the following activities to write on the board or post on the *LANGUAGE! Live* Class Wall online.

- *How would you feel if you were forced to wear something every day to indicate that you were inferior to other people?*
- *Write the dialogue of a conversation you think Anne might have with her captors on the day she was taken. Format the dialogue like a drama.*
- *Elaborate one or more of these simple sentences, using the steps in Masterpiece Sentences.*

  Anne and Peter played a game.

  Anne was afraid.

  Margot did not speak.

  The Franks moved.

Reading

Objectives

- Establish a purpose for rereading dramatic literature.
- Demonstrate an understanding of how to ask questions and answer them appropriately.
- Use critical thinking skills to write responses to prompts about text.
- Support written answers with text evidence.
- Compare and contrast the experience of reading a play and listening to a dramatized audio production.
- Objectively summarize text.
- Identify flashbacks in literature and determine their purpose.
- Compare interactions among characters in multiple texts.
- Determine the purpose of stage directions in a drama.
- Determine the meaning of regional vocabulary.

Reading for a Purpose: Excerpt from *The Play of the Diary of Anne Frank*

For our second read of the play, we are going to listen to a dramatic performance of the play. Pay close attention to the recording and follow along in your book.

You will use the text and recording to respond to prompts about the play. This will demonstrate your understanding of the text. Let's preview the prompts to provide a purpose for listening to the drama. You should recognize the direction words that we practiced in the preceding lesson.

Direct students to pages 124 and 125 in their Student Books. Have students read the prompts aloud with you.

1. Define *flashback*. Explain how this chronological text structure contributes to the development of the plot.

2. Report how the playwrights used stage directions to change point of view.

3. Compare Otto Frank's relationship with the Van Daans and Darry's relationship with Ponyboy and Sodapop.

4. Interpret the change in Anne's tone when she realizes what it means to be in hiding.

5. List words and phrases that were used in another location or time period. Define them using a dictionary.

6. Examine Anne's quote "We all live with the objective of being happy; our lives are all different and yet the same." Describe how Anne Frank and Ponyboy are both outsiders.

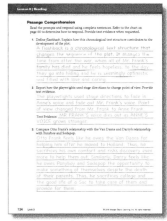

Play The Play of the Diary of Anne Frank *audio file found in the Teacher Resources online.*

Play the audio version of the excerpt from *The Play of the Diary of Anne Frank*, which can be found online in the Teacher Resources.

Direct students to page 101 in their Student Books or have them tear out the extra copies of the play from the back of their book.

Note: To minimize flipping back and forth between the pages, a copy of each text has been included in the back of the Student Books. Encourage students to tear this out and use it when working on activities that require the use of the text.

Have students follow along as they listen to the play.

Passage Comprehension

Write the words *compare, define, interpret,* and *report* on the board. Have students read the words aloud with you. Direct students to page 66 in their Student Books and have them review the information about the four words in the chart.

Check for understanding by requesting an oral response to the following questions.

- If the prompt asks you to *compare,* the response requires you to . . . (state similarities between two or more things).

- If the prompt asks you to *define,* the response requires you to . . . (tell or write the meaning or definition).

- If the prompt asks you to *interpret,* the response requires you to . . . (make sense or assign meaning to something).

- If the prompt asks you to *report,* the response requires you to . . . (tell or write about a topic).

Critical Understandings: Direction Words

Prompt	How to Respond	Model
If the prompt asks you to . . .	The response requires you to . . .	For example . . .
Analyze	break down and evaluate or draw conclusions about the information	**Analyze** the development of the text's central idea.
Assess	decide on the value, impact, or accuracy	**Assess** the level of pressure in an arranged marriage.
Compare	state the similarities between two or more things	**Compare** novels and dramas.
Contrast	state the differences between two or more things	**Contrast** a biography with an autobiography.
Create	make or produce something	**Create** a timeline of events.
Define	tell or write the meaning or definition	**Define** the unknown word using context clues.
Delineate	show or list evidence, claims, ideas, reasons, or events	**Delineate** the evidence in the text.
Describe	state detailed information about a topic	**Describe** the relationship between the plot and character development.
Determine	find out, verify, decide	**Determine** the main idea.
Distinguish	recognize or explain the differences	**Distinguish** between facts and opinions.
Evaluate	think carefully to make a judgment; form a critical opinion of	**Evaluate** the ANC's plan for change.
Explain	express understanding of an idea or concept	**Explain** how the author develops the narrator's point of view.
Identify	say or write what it is	**Identify** the character's motive.
Infer	provide a logical answer using evidence and prior knowledge	Use information from the text to **infer** the value of education.
Interpret	make sense of or assign meaning to something	**Interpret** the quote to confirm your understanding.
Paraphrase	say or write it using different words	**Paraphrase** the main idea.
Report	Tell or write about a topic	**Report** the main events of the setting.
Summarize	tell the most important ideas or concepts	**Summarize** the key details of the passage.
Tell	say or write specific information	**Tell** the date that the poem was written.
Use	apply information or a procedure	**Use** text features to identify the topic.

66   Unit 2

Direct students to pages 124 and 125 in their Student Books.

Passage Comprehension

Read the prompts and respond using complete sentences. Refer to the chart on page 66 to determine how to respond. Provide text evidence when requested.

1. Define *flashback*. Explain how this chronological text structure contributes to the development of the plot.

A flashback is a chronological text structure that changes the sequence of the plot. It changes the time from after the war, when all of Mr. Frank's family has died and he feels hopeless, to the day they go into hiding and he is seemingly optimistic and filled with love and caring.

2. Report how the playwrights used stage directions to change point of view. Provide text evidence.

The playwrights used stage directions to fade in Anne's voice and fade out Mr. Frank's voice. Point of view changed from Mr. Frank to Anne Frank.

Text Evidence: MR FRANK'S voice dies out as ANNE'S VOICE grows stronger.

3. Compare Otto Frank's relationship with the Van Daans and Darry's relationship with Ponyboy and Sodapop.

Otto Frank feels like he owes the Van Daans for helping him after he moved to Holland. Thus, he sacrifices his own comfort and risks discovery even more to help them out. Similarly, Darry feels like he owes Ponyboy and Sodapop the opportunity to make something of themselves despite the death of their parents. Thus, he sacrifices college and the good life of a Soc to take care of them and provide for them.

Passage Comprehension (cont.)

4. Interpret the change in Anne's tone when she realizes what it means to be in hiding. Provide text evidence.

When in hiding, Anne's tone changes to indicate her transition from playful, to panicked, and then eventually calm again.

Text Evidence: "You know the way I'm going to think of it here? I'm going to think of it as a boarding-house. A very peculiar Summer boarding-house, like the one that we . . ." "Never? Not even at night time, when everyone is gone? Or on Sundays? Can't I go down to listen to the radio?"; MR FRANK *puts his arm about* ANNE . . . ANNE'S *panic is gone*

5. List words and phrases that were used in another location or time period. Define them using a dictionary.

Answers will vary. Some may include:
1. Green Police—Nazi police, who wore green uniforms
2. Carillon—stationary bells that hung in a tower
3. Rucksack—type of backpack

6. Examine Anne's quote "We all live with the objective of being happy; our lives are all different and yet the same." Describe how Anne Frank and Ponyboy are both outsiders.

Anne Frank and Ponyboy are both outsiders because they were ostracized due to prejudices. During the Holocaust, Anne and her family were ostracized and forced to be outsiders because their religious beliefs were disliked by political leaders. As a result, they went into hiding to avoid violence and were not able to continue living life with freedom. Ponyboy was also an outsider. Unlike Anne Frank, Ponyboy lived on the poor side of town, which also attracted prejudice and violence. If left alone, Anne Frank and Ponyboy would probably have led happy lives with a focus on family and friends.

Let's practice answering questions that are written as prompts. Remember to use the chart on page 66 as reference.

Model

Listen as I model the first one for you.

1. Define *flashback*. Explain how this chronological text structure contributes to the development of the plot.

Because the prompt is asking me to *define*, I know that I will need to write the meaning. Now, I will turn the prompt into a question to confirm understanding. What is a *flashback*? How does a flashback change the plot? I can also use part of the question in my answer.

Write the following sentence starter on the board.

A flashback is _____ that changes the sequence of the plot by _____.

We learned that a flashback is a literary device used when a scene changes the chronology of events to an event in the past. It changes the sequence of the plot. In this particular play, I know it starts out in 1945, then jumps to 1942 because the stage directions provide the setting in each scene. This flashback contributes to the plot by changing the time from after the war, when all of Mr. Frank's family has died and he feels hopeless, to the day they go into hiding and he is optimistic and filled with love and caring.

Complete the answer on the board and have students write it on the page.

Guided Practice

2. Report how the playwrights used stage directions to change point of view. Provide text evidence.

How will I start my answer? Tell your partner how to respond according to the chart. (If the prompt asks you to *report*, the response requires you to tell or write about the topic.) Turn the prompt into a question to confirm understanding. (How do the playwrights use stage directions to change the point of view?) Now, answer the question. **Provide the following sentence starters and have a volunteer complete the sentences.**

The playwrights used stage directions to _____.

Point of view changed from _____.

Independent Practice

Have partners respond to the remaining prompts with text evidence. For students who need more assistance, provide the following alternative questions and sentence starters.

Alternative questions and sentence starters:

3. How is Otto Frank's relationship with the Van Daans similar to Darry's relationship with Ponyboy and Sodapop?

   Otto Frank feels like _____ the Van Daans _____. Thus, he _____. Similarly, Darry feels like _____ Ponyboy and Sodapop _____. Thus, he _____.

4. What is the significance of the change in Anne's tone when she realizes for the first time what it means to be in hiding? Provide text evidence.

   When in hiding, Anne's tone changes to indicate _____.

5. What words confuse you because they sound like they are from a different time or a faraway place? Make a list. Define listed words using a dictionary.

6. How are Anne Frank and Ponyboy both outsiders? Use the quote to help you.

   Anne Frank and Ponyboy are both outsiders because _____.

Possible words and definitions from the play that can be defined in #5.

1. Green Police—Nazi police, who wore green uniforms

2. carillon—stationary bells that hung in a tower

3. rucksack—type of backpack

4. ration books—books of stamps given to ensure even distribution of staple items needed to live on

5. WC—water closet or bathroom

6. hold-all—cloth traveling case or bag

7. beret—hat

8. rubbish—trash

9. paring—vegetable peel

10. pendant light—overhead light

11. Westertoren—clock that chimes every 15 minutes

Comparing Audio and Print

Generate a class discussion about the differences between hearing the drama and reading the drama. If you listened to "We Real Cool" in Unit 2 prior to reading, have students compare the difference between hearing literature performed before reading and hearing it after reading.

Ask the following questions to foster conversation:

1. Which version was more entertaining?

2. Which version was easier to understand?

3. What did you get from the audio version that you did not get from your reading?

4. How did hearing different voices for each character impact your experience?

5. Did you "hear" anything differently when you read it?

Have partners discuss the impact of "hearing" the play. Then, have them summarize the excerpt. Remind students to keep their summaries objective, or free from personal opinion.

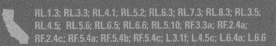

RL.1.3; RL.3.3; RL.4.1; RL.5.2; RL.6.3; RL.7.3; RL.8.3; RL.3.5;
RL.4.5; RL.5.6; RL.6.5; RL.6.6; RL.5.10; RF.3.3a; RF.2.4a;
RF.2.4c; RF.5.4a; RF.5.4b; RF.5.4c; L.3.1f; L.4.5c; L.6.4a; L.6.6

Lesson Opener

Before the lesson, choose one of the following activities to write on the board or post on the *LANGUAGE! Live* Class Wall online.

- *In the play, it is clear that the Nazis hate a group of people. Why does this happen and how can it be avoided?*
- *Make a list of adjectives describing Mr. Frank on the first day in hiding. Make a list of adjectives describing Mr. Frank after the war.*
- *Write five sentences about the courage of Miep. Use adjectives, adverbs, and prepositional phrases.*

Reading

Objectives

- Read a play with purpose and understanding.
- Answer questions to demonstrate comprehension of text.
- Identify and explain explicit details from text.
- Monitor comprehension during text reading.
- Identify allusions in text.
- Connect pronouns to their antecedents.
- Use synonyms and antonyms to increase depth of word knowledge.
- Identify the setting of a play.
- Use context to determine word knowledge.
- Analyze how a story's events affect the characters' actions.
- Determine the meaning of foreign word usage.
- Analyze the way in which an author develops a character.
- Analyze character point of view and how it is affected by the plot development.
- Distinguish personal point of view from that of the characters.
- Identify coordinate adjectives.
- Use elements of a drama to illustrate a set.

Close Reading of the Excerpt from *The Play of the Diary of Anne Frank*

highlighters or colored pencils

Let's reread the excerpt from *The Play of the Diary of Anne Frank*. I will provide specific instructions on how to mark the text to help with comprehension.

Have students get out a highlighter or colored pencil.

Direct students to page 126 in their Student Books.

Please mark your text according to my instructions.

Draw a rectangle around the title.

Draw a circle around the act number and the two scene numbers.

Now, let's read the vocabulary words aloud.

- What's the first bold vocabulary word? (awkward) *Awkward* means "uncomfortable; not sure what to do or say." I felt *awkward* wearing the dressing gown at my doctor appointment. **Have partners use the word in a sentence.**

- What's the next vocabulary word? (conspicuous) *Conspicuous* means "easily seen." *Her multicolor hair was* conspicuous. **Have partners use the word in a sentence.**

- Let's continue. (indicates) *Indicates* means "signals something with a movement or gesture." *Thumbs up* indicates *that you understand.* **Have partners use the word in a sentence.**

- Next word? (dependable) *Dependable* means "trustworthy; able to be counted on or relied on." *If you are* dependable, *you may get assigned more hours at work.* **Have partners use the word in a sentence.**

- Next word? (leisure) *Leisure* means "time when you are not working or busy with tasks." *Read a book at your* leisure. **Have partners use the word in a sentence.**

- Let's continue. (regulations) *Regulations* are rules set by people in power to control how things are done. *Regulations require teens to attend school.* **Have partners use the word in a sentence.**

- Next word? (interval) An *interval* is a period of time between two dates or events. *There is a short* interval *between classes in which students commute and communicate.* **Have partners use the word in a sentence.**

- Next word? (garment) *Garment* means "an item of clothing." *Your* garments *must adhere to the school dress code.* **Have partners use the word in a sentence.**

- Next word? (concentrating) *Concentrating* means "giving all your attention to something." *If you are* concentrating *on me, you are less likely to be distracted by your gadgets.* **Have partners use the word in a sentence.**

- Let's continue. (peculiar) *Peculiar* means "strange; odd." *The substitute teacher was acting* peculiar. **Have partners use the word in a sentence.**

Talk with a partner about any vocabulary word that is still confusing for you to read or understand.

As you read the excerpt from the play, you will monitor your understanding by circling the check marks or the question marks. Please be sure to draw a question mark over any confusing words, phrases, or sentences.

> Options for rereading text.
> - Teacher read-aloud
> - Teacher-led or student-led choral read
> - Paired read or independent read with bold vocabulary words read aloud
> - Students read the play theatrically according to characters.
>   Characters from Scene One: MIEP, MR. FRANK, ANNE
>   Characters from Scene Two: MIEP, MR. FRANK, ANNE, PETER
>   Minor characters from Scene Two: MRS. FRANK, MRS. VAN DAAN, MR. VAN DAAN, KRALER, MARGOT (doesn't speak)

Choose an option for reading text. Have students read lines 1–27 according to the option that you chose.

While reading, record a happy face in the margin when Mr. Frank is feeling hopeful. Draw a sad face in the margin when he is feeling hopeless or disagrees with what is happening to the Jewish people. What are you going to mark with a happy face? (when Mr. Frank is feeling hopeful) What are you going to mark with a sad face? (when Mr. Frank is feeling hopeless or unhappy with what is happening) If you finish before others, find a partner who is finished to compare happy and sad faces.

When most of the students are finished, continue with the entire class. Let's see how well you understood the section.

- Circle the check mark or the question mark for this section. Draw a question mark over any confusing words.

- Go to line 1. Circle the words that indicate the setting. (Amsterdam, Holland; November 1945)

- Go to line 4. Mark the word that means "worn out." (threadbare)

- Go to line 11. Mark what Miep is wearing other than a coat and hat. (small silver cross) This is an example of an author's use of allusion. It isn't written in explicit words, but what is the author alluding to with this detail? Make an inference and write your answer in the margin. (Miep is a Christian.)

- Go to line 13. Mark the stage directions that are not meant to be read aloud. Circle the parentheses. (quickly controlling himself)

- Mark the evidence that Mr. Frank is a lost soul. (I don't know yet. I haven't decided.)

- Mark the evidence that Mr. Frank doesn't want to remember anything. (I can't stay in Amsterdam; It has too many memories.)

- Go to lines 25 and 26. Circle the pronoun *you* twice. Draw an arrow to the noun that *you* is referring to. (Miep)

Close Reading

Read the text.

Excerpt from *The Play of the Diary of Anne Frank*

ACT ONE

Scene One

The top floors of a warehouse in Amsterdam, Holland. November 1945. Late afternoon.

MR FRANK enters. He is weak and ill and is making a supreme effort at self-control. His clothes are threadbare. He carries a small rucksack. A scarf catches his eye. He takes it down, puts it around his neck, then wanders towards the couch, but stops as he sees the glove. He picks it up. Suddenly all control is gone. He breaks down and weeps. MIEP GIES enters up the stairs. She is a Dutch girl of about twenty-two, pregnant now. She is compassionate and protective in her attitude towards MR FRANK. She has been a stenographer and secretary in his business. She has her coat and hat on, ready to go home. A small silver cross hangs at her throat.

MIEP   Are you all right, Mr. Frank?

MR FRANK   *(quickly controlling himself)* Yes, Miep, yes.

MIEP   Everyone in the office has gone home—it's after six. Don't stay up here, Mr. Frank. What's the use of torturing yourself like this?

MR FRANK   I've come to say good-bye—I'm leaving here, Miep.

MIEP   What do you mean? Where are you going? Where?

MR FRANK   I don't know yet. I haven't decided.

MIEP   Mr. Frank, you can't leave here. This is your home. Amsterdam is your home. Your business is here, waiting for you. You're needed here. Now that the war is over, there are things that . . .

MR FRANK   I can't stay in Amsterdam, Miep. It has too many memories for me. Everywhere there's something—the house we lived in—the school—the street organ playing out there. I'm not the person you used to know, Miep. I'm a bitter old man. Forgive me. I shouldn't speak to you like this—after all that you did for us—the suffering . . .

MIEP   No. No. It wasn't suffering. You can't say we suffered.

Have students read lines 28–63 according to the option that you chose.

When most of the students are finished, continue with the entire class. Let's see how well you understood the next section.

- Circle the check mark or the question mark for this section. Draw a question mark over any confusing words.

- Go to line 33. Mark the synonym for *garbage.* (rubbish)

- Go to line 36. Mark the evidence that Mr. Frank doesn't want to remember anything. (Burn them. All of them.)

- Go to line 38. Mark what Miep gives Mr. Frank. (Anne's diary)

- Go to lines 39–43. Circle the words that indicate time. (July, nineteen hundred and forty-two, three years ago, thirteen years old, twelfth of June, nineteen twenty-nine) Mark how long it has been since they began living in the annex. (three years)

- Go to line 44. Mark the word that means "left their own country long term." (emigrated)

- Go to line 45. Mark the word that means "bringing in goods from another country to sell." (importing)

- Go to lines 51–53. Number the ways that Anne's life changed because of Hitler. (1. wear yellow stars. 2. I had to turn in my bike. 3. I couldn't go to a Dutch school any more. 4. I couldn't go to the cinema 5. or ride in an automobile or even on a streetcar)

- Go to line 51. Mark the symbol used to ostracize the Jewish people. (yellow stars)

- Go to line 52. Mark the word that means "movie theater." (cinema)

- Go to line 61. Mark the people joining the Frank family in hiding. (the Van Daans; their son Peter)

Close Reading (*cont.*)

MR FRANK I know what you went through, you and Mr. Kraler. I'll remember it as long
30   as I live. Come, Miep. *(He remembers his rucksack, crosses below the table to the couch and picks up his rucksack.)*

MIEP Mr. Frank, did you see? There are some of your papers here. *(She takes a bundle of papers from the shelves, then crosses below the table to MR FRANK.)* We found them in a heap of rubbish on the floor after—after you left.

MR FRANK Burn them. *(He opens his rucksack and puts the glove in it.)*

35 MIEP But, Mr. Frank, there are letters, notes . . .

MR FRANK Burn them. All of them.

MIEP Burn this? *(She hands him a worn, velour-covered book.)*

MR FRANK *(quietly)* Anne's diary. *(He opens the diary and reads.)* 'Monday, the sixth of July, nineteen hundred and forty-two.' *(To MIEP.)* Nineteen hundred and
40   forty-two. Is it possible, Miep? Only three years ago. *(He reads.)* 'Dear Diary, since you and I are going to be great friends, I will start by telling you about myself. My name is Anne Frank. I am thirteen years old. I was born in Germany the twelfth of June, nineteen twenty-nine. As my family is Jewish, we emigrated to Holland when Hitler came to power.'

45 MR FRANK }*(together)* 'My father started a business, importing spice and herbs. Things
    ANNE'S VOICE }   went well for us until nineteen forty. Then the War came and the Dutch—*(He turns the page.)* defeat, followed by the arrival of the Germans. Then things got very bad for the Jews.'

(MR FRANK'S voice dies out as ANNE'S VOICE grows stronger.)

50 ANNE You could not do this and you could not do that. They forced father out of his business. We had to wear yellow stars. I had to turn in my bike. I couldn't go to a Dutch school any more. I couldn't go to the cinema, or ride in an automobile, or even on a streetcar, and a million other things. But somehow we children still managed to have fun. Yesterday, father told me we were
55   going into hiding. Where, he wouldn't say. At five o'clock this morning mother woke me and told me to hurry and get dressed. I was to put on as many clothes as I could. It would look too suspicious if we walked along carrying suitcases. It wasn't until we were on our way that I learned where we were going. Our hiding place was to be upstairs in the building where
60   father used to have his business. Three other people were coming in with us—the Van Daans and their son Peter. Father knew the Van Daans but we had never met them.

(The sound of distant ships' sirens is heard.)

Unit 3   **127**

Have students read lines 64–86 according to the option that you chose.

When most of the students are finished, continue with the entire class. Let's see how well you understood the next section.

- Circle the check mark or the question mark for this section. Draw a question mark over any confusing words.

- Go to line 64. Circle the words that indicate the setting. **(Early morning, July 1942)**

- Go to line 67. Mark the author's allusion used to "explain" that the Van Daans are not poor. **(expensive and well-cut)**

- Go to line 69. Mark the synonym for *belongings*. **(possessions)**

- Go to lines 74 and 76. In the margin, write a word to describe Mrs. Van Daan. **(anxious)** We learned that story elements affect each other. This is not likely a normal personality trait of Mrs. Van Daan, but is caused by the events in the story. Under your previous answer, write the cause of her personality change. **(fear that the plan will not work out because the Franks did not make it)**

- Go to line 77. Mark the distance that the Franks had to walk wearing layers of clothing. **(two miles)**

- Mark the reason the Franks were running late. **(too many of the Green Police on the streets)** In the margin, write who the Green Police work for. **(Hitler)**

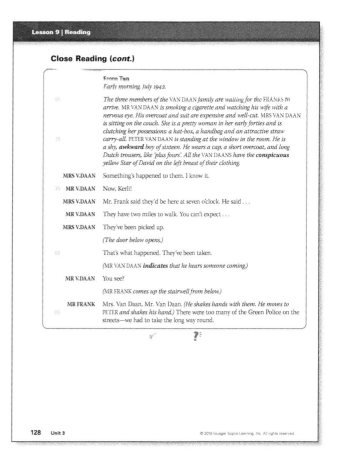

Have students read lines 87–116 according to the option that you chose.

When most of the students are finished, continue with the entire class. Let's see how well you understood the next section.

- Circle the check mark or the question mark for this section. Draw a question mark over any confusing words.

- Go to line 88. Mark evidence that Margot is not outgoing. (shy)

- Go to line 99. Mark the word that means "unpredictable." (mercurial)

- On the same line, mark the word that means "feelings." (emotions)

- Go to lines 115 and 116. Mark the phrase that means "books of stamps used to trade for essential items during scarce times." (ration books)

Close Reading (*cont.*)

90		*(MIEP, not pregnant now, MARGOT, MR KRALER, and MRS FRANK come up the stairs. MARGOT is eighteen, beautiful, quiet and shy. She carries a leatherette hold-all and a large brown paper bag, which she puts on the table. KRALER is a Dutchman, **dependable** and kindly. He wears a hearing aid in his ear and carries two brief-cases. MRS FRANK is a young mother, gently bred and reserved. She, like MR FRANK, has a slight German accent. She carries a leatherette shopping bag and her handbag. We see the Star of David conspicuous on the FRANKS' clothing. KRALER acknowledges the VAN DAANS, moves to the shelves and checks their contents. MIEP empties her straw bag of the clothes it contains and piles them on the table.)*
	MRS FRANK	Anne?
100		*(ANNE FRANK comes quickly up the stairs. She is thirteen, quick in her movements, interested in everything and mercurial in her emotions. She wears a cape, long wool socks and carries a school bag.)*
	MR FRANK	My wife, Edith. Mr. and Mrs. Van Daan.
		(MRS FRANK shakes MR VAN DAAN'S hand, then hurries across to shake hands with MRS VAN DAAN. She then moves to the sink and inspects it.)
		Their son, Peter—my daughters, Margot and Anne.
105		*(ANNE gives a polite little curtsy as she shakes MR VAN DAAN'S hand. She puts her bag on the left end of the table then immediately starts off on a tour of investigation of her new home, going upstairs to the attic room.)*
	KRALER	I'm sorry there is still so much confusion.
110	MR FRANK	Please. Don't think of it. After all, we'll have plenty of **leisure** to arrange everything ourselves.
	MIEP	*(indicating the sink cupboard)* We put the stores of food you sent in here. *(She crosses to the shelves.)* Your drugs are here—soap, linen, here.
	MRS FRANK	Thank you, Miep.
115	MIEP	I made up the beds—the way Mr. Frank and Mr. Kraler said. Forgive me. I have to hurry. I've got to go to the other side of town to get some ration books for you.

✓   ?

Unit 3   **129**

Have students read lines 117–141 according to the option that you chose.

When most of the students are finished, continue with the entire class. Let's see how well you understood the next section.

- Circle the check mark or the question mark for this section. Draw a question mark over any confusing words.

- Reread lines 123–125. Mark the word that explains the kind of activities the Franks will be engaging in. **(illegal)** Is this a normal way of living for the Franks? **(no)** In the margin, write the events that have caused them to change who they are. **(living in hiding from the Nazis)**

- Go to line 125. Mark the illegal way to buy scarce items without ration stamps. **(black market)**

- Go to line 128. Mark the word that means "bells." **(carillon)**

- Go to line 132. Mark where Kraler works. **(downstairs in the office)**

- Go to line 134. Mark the things that Miep and Kraler will bring them. **(food and news)**

- Go to line 136. Mark the only time they will open the door. **(at our signal)**

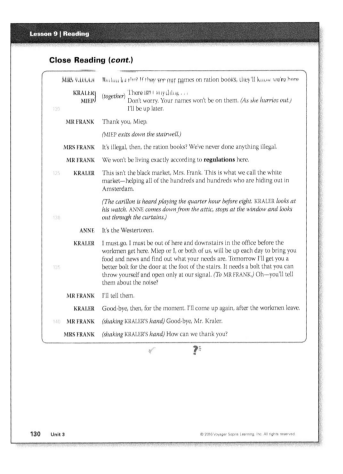

Have students read lines 142–177 according to the option that you chose.

When most of the students are finished, continue with the entire class. Let's see how well you understood the next section.

- Circle the check mark or the question mark for this section. Draw a question mark over any confusing words.

- Mark the evidence that Kraler does not agree with Hitler. **(I never thought I'd live to see the day when a man like Mr. Frank would have to go into hiding.)**

- Go to lines 152–156. Circle the garments. **(cape, beret, coats, sweaters, blouses, suits, dresses, sweaters, bathrobes, aprons, gloves)**

- Go to line 159. Mark the evidence that Mrs. Van Daan is materialistic. **(fur coat in July)**

- Go to line 163. Mark the synonym for *excess*. **(surplus)**

- Go to lines 168 and 169. Mark the phrase that means "shoeless." **(stockinged feet)**

- Go to line 170. Mark the abbreviation for "water closet" or "bathroom." **(WC)**

- Mark all the things they cannot do during the day. **(not speak above a whisper; not run any water; not use the sink or WC; no rubbish)**

- Mark what frightens Mr. Frank. **(sound of marching feet)** In the margin, write who the marching feet likely belong to. **(Green Police, SS, Nazis)**

- Go to lines 175 and 176. Mark why they can't throw out any trash. **(might reveal that someone is living there)**

- Go to line 176. Mark the word that means "vegetable skin." **(paring)**

- Go to line 177. Circle the pronoun *it*. What does *it* refer to? Write your answer in the margin. **(Holocaust, violence against Jews, war)**

Close Reading (cont.)

KRALER I never thought I'd live to see the day when a man like Mr. Frank would have to go into hiding. When you think . . .

(KRALER breaks off and exits down the stairs. MR FRANK follows him down the
145 *stairs and bolts the door after him. In the interval before he returns, PETER goes to MARGOT, gives a stiff bow and shakes hands with her. ANNE watches, and as they complete their greeting, moves to PETER and holds out her hand. PETER does not see her and turns away. MR FRANK comes up the stairs.)*

MRS FRANK What did he mean, about the noise?

150 **MR FRANK** First, let's take off some of these clothes.

*(ANNE moves below the table, stands with her back to the audience, removes her cape and beret and puts them on the pile of clothes on the table. They all start to take off **garment** after garment. On each of their coats, sweaters,*
155 *blouses, suits and dresses is another yellow Star of David. MR and MRS FRANK are under-dressed quite simply. The others wear several things, sweaters, extra dresses, bathrobes, aprons, etc. MRS FRANK takes off her gloves, carefully folding them before putting them away.)*

MR V. DAAN It's a wonder we weren't arrested, walking along the streets—Petronella with a fur coat in July—and that cat of Peter's crying all the way.

160 **ANNE** *(removing a pair of panties)* A cat?

MRS FRANK *(shocked)* Anne, please!

ANNE It's all right. I've got on three more *(She removes two more pairs of panties. Finally, as they finish removing their surplus clothing, they settle down.)*

MR FRANK Now. About the noise. While the men are in the building below, we must
165 have complete quiet. Every sound can be heard down there, not only in the workrooms, but in the offices, too. The men come about eight-thirty, and leave at about five-thirty. So, to be perfectly safe, from eight in the morning until six in the evening we must move only when it is necessary and then in stockinged feet. We must not speak above a whisper. We must not run any water. We
170 cannot use the sink, or even, forgive me, the WC. The pipes go down through the workrooms. It would be heard. No rubbish . . .

(The sound of marching feet is heard. MR FRANK, followed by ANNE, peers out of the window. Satisfied that the marching feet are going away, he returns and continues.)

175 No rubbish must ever be thrown out which might reveal that someone is living here—not even a potato paring. We must burn everything in the stove at night. This is the way we must live until it is over, if we are to survive.

Unit 3 **131**

Have students read lines 178–199 according to the option that you chose.

When most of the students are finished, continue with the entire class. Let's see how well you understood the next section.

- Circle the check mark or the question mark for this section. Draw a question mark over any confusing words.

- Mark what they can do after six that indicates they are hopeful. (talk, laugh, have our supper, read, play games) Mark the language used to make them feel like it will be normal. (just as we would at home)

- Go to line 187. Mark the words used by Mr. Frank to let the Van Daans know that they are of equal importance. (like one family)

- Go to line 190. Mark the body language that shows disagreement. (rises in protest)

- Go to line 197. Mark the body language that shows that Mrs. Van Daan appreciates Mr. Frank. (shaking Mr. Frank's hand)

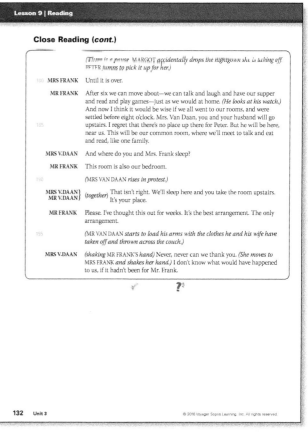

Have students read lines 200–224 according to the option that you chose.

When most of the students are finished, continue with the entire class. Let's see how well you understood the next section.

- Circle the check mark or the question mark for this section. Draw a question mark over any confusing words.

- Mark why Mr. Frank helps the Van Daans. **(your husband helped me when I came to this country)**

- Go to line 204. Mark the foreign word that must be a term of endearment like *sweetheart* or *dear*. **(liefje)**

- Go to line 209. Mark Mrs. Frank's first name. **(Edith)**

- Go to line 212. Mark the adverb that describes that Anne slept well. Circle the suffix. **(soundly, -ly)**

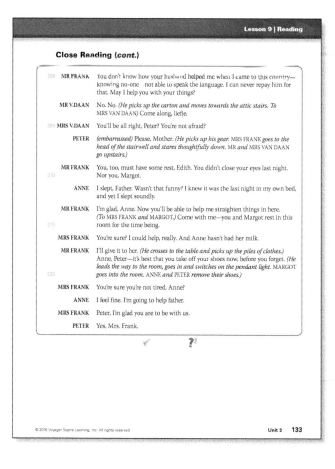

Have students read lines 225–248 according to the option that you chose.

When most of the students are finished, continue with the entire class. Let's see how well you understood the next section.

- Circle the check mark or the question mark for this section. Draw a question mark over any confusing words.

- Go to line 231. Mark the consecutive adjectives. (darling; little) Are they of the same importance and therefore coordinate? (no)

- Go to line 233. Mark the pronouns that show gender. Write *boy* or *girl* to confirm understanding. (him = boy; her = girl)

- Go to line 234. Mark the word that means "male cat." (tom)

- Go to line 241. Mark the evidence that Peter went to a segregated school for Jewish students. (Jewish Secondary)

- Mark the evidence that suggests Anne was popular in school. (in the middle of a bunch of kids)

- Go to line 248. Mark evidence that Peter is not outgoing. (lone wolf)

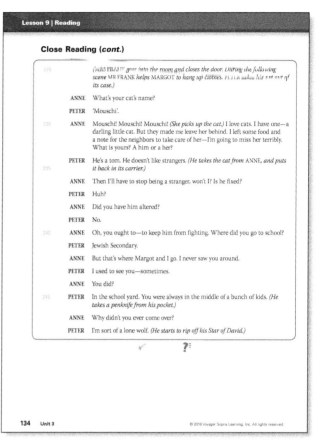

Close Reading (*cont.*)

225 (ANNE FRANK goes into the room and closes the door. During the following scene MR FRANK helps MARGOT to hang up clothes. PETER takes his cat out of its case.)

ANNE   What's your cat's name?

PETER   'Mouschi'.

230 ANNE   Mouschi! Mouschi! Mouschi! *(She picks up the cat.)* I love cats. I have one—a darling little cat. But they made me leave her behind. I left some food and a note for the neighbors to take care of her—I'm going to miss her terribly. What is yours? A him or a her?

PETER   He's a tom. He doesn't like strangers. *(He takes the cat from* ANNE, *and puts it back in its carrier.)*

235 ANNE   Then I'll have to stop being a stranger, won't I? Is he fixed?

PETER   Huh?

ANNE   Did you have him altered?

PETER   No.

240 ANNE   Oh, you ought to—to keep him from fighting. Where did you go to school?

PETER   Jewish Secondary.

ANNE   But that's where Margot and I go. I never saw you around.

PETER   I used to see you—sometimes.

ANNE   You did?

245 PETER   In the school yard. You were always in the middle of a bunch of kids. *(He takes a penknife from his pocket.)*

ANNE   Why didn't you ever come over?

PETER   I'm sort of a lone wolf. *(He starts to rip off his Star of David.)*

✓   ?

Have students read lines 249–274 according to the option that you chose.

When most of the students are finished, continue with the entire class. Let's see how well you understood the next section.

- Circle the check mark or the question mark for this section. Draw a question mark over any confusing words.

- Go to line 250. Circle the pronoun *it*. Replace it with a proper noun. **(Star of David)**

- Go to line 251. Mark what would have happened to a Jew not wearing the Star of David. **(arrest)**

- Mark the phrase that suggests that the Franks are trying to deceive the Nazis. **(left everything as if we'd suddenly been called away)**

- Go to line 272. Mark the word that means "identified." **(branded)**

- Mark how the Nazis treated the Jews. **(they could spit on you)** Do you think this is literal language or figurative language? Write your answer in the margin. **(figurative language)**

Close Reading (*cont.*)

	ANNE	What are you doing?
250	PETER	Taking it off.
	ANNE	But you can't do that. *(She grabs his hands and stops him.)* They'll arrest you if you go out without your star.
	PETER	*(pulling away)* Who's going out? *(He crosses to the stove, lifts the lid and throws the star into the stove.)*
255	ANNE	Why, of course. You're right. Of course we don't need them any more. *(She takes PETER'S knife and removes her star. PETER waits for her star to throw it away.)*
		I wonder what our friends will think when we don't show up today?
	PETER	I didn't have any dates with anyone.
260	ANNE	*(concentrating on her star)* Oh, I did. I had a date with Jopie this afternoon to go and play ping-pong at her house. Do you know Jopie de Waal?
	PETER	No.
265	ANNE	Jopie's my best friend. I wonder what she'll think when she telephones and there's no answer? Probably she'll go over to the house—I wonder what she'll think—we left everything as if we'd suddenly been called away—breakfast dishes in the sink—beds not made . . . *(As she pulls off her star, the cloth underneath shows clearly the colour and form of the star.)* Look! It's still there. What're you going to do with yours?
270	PETER	Burn it. *(He moves to the stove and holds out his hand for ANNE'S star. ANNE starts to give the star to PETER, but cannot.)*
	ANNE	It's funny. I can't throw it away. I don't know why.
	PETER	You can't throw . . . ? Something they branded you with? That they made you wear so they could spit on you?
	ANNE	I know. I know. But after all, it is the Star of David, isn't it?

✓   ?

Unit 3   **135**

Have students read lines 275–298 according to the option that you chose.

When most of the students are finished, continue with the entire class.

Let's see how well you understood the next section.

- Circle the check mark or the question mark for this section. Draw a question mark over any confusing words.

- Go to line 276. Mark the synonym for *closet*. (wardrobe)

- Go to line 280. Find the possessive pronouns. (your, hers) Replace *hers* with a noun phrase. (her cat)

- Go to line 282. Circle the word *that*. Draw an arrow to indicate what *that* refers to. (wash-tub)

- Go to line 290. Mark evidence that Mr. Frank is kind. (friendly pat)

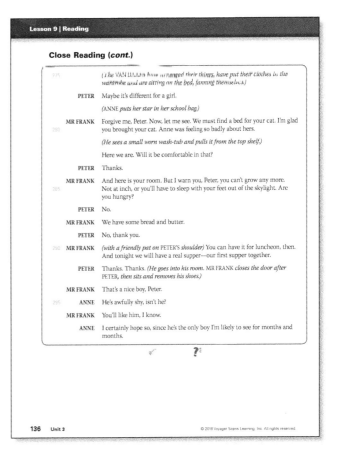

Have students read lines 299–323 according to the option that you chose.

When most of the students are finished, continue with the entire class. Let's see how well you understood the next section.

- Circle the check mark or the question mark for this section. Draw a question mark over any confusing words.

- Go to lines 302 and 303. Mark the evidence that Anne is keeping a positive point of view during a horrible situation. (I am going to think of it as a boarding-house.) Picture yourself in Anne's situation. How would your point of view be different? Would you be able to remain positive in her situation? (Answers will vary.)

Lesson 9 | Reading

Close Reading (cont.)

MR FRANK	Anne, there's a box there. Will you open it?
	(The sound of children playing is heard from the street below. MR FRANK goes to the sink and pours a glass of milk from the thermos bottle.)
ANNE	You know the way I'm going to think of it here? I'm going to think of it as a boarding-house. A very **peculiar** Summer boarding-house, like the one that we . . . *(She breaks off as she looks in the box.)* Father! Father! My film stars. I was wondering where they were—and Queen Wilhelmina. How wonderful!
MR FRANK	There's something more. Go on. Look further.
	(ANNE digs deeper into the box and brings out a velour-covered book. She examines it in delighted silence for a moment, then opens the cover slowly, and looks up at MR FRANK with shining eyes.)
ANNE	A diary! *(She throws her arms around him.)* I've never had a diary. And I've always longed for one. *(She rushes to the table and looks for a pencil.)* Pencil, pencil, pencil, pencil. *(She darts across to the stair-well and starts down the stairs.)* I'm going down to the office to get a pencil.
MR FRANK	Anne! No! *(He strides to ANNE and catches her arm. MRS FRANK aware of the sudden movement and sounds, sits up. After a moment she rises, goes to the window and looks out, then returns and sits on the bed.)*
ANNE	*(startled)* But there's no-one in the building now.
MR FRANK	It doesn't matter. I don't want you ever to go beyond that door.
ANNE	*(sobered)* Never? Not even at night time, when everyone is gone? Or on Sundays? Can't I go down to listen to the radio?
MR FRANK	Never. I am sorry, Anneke. It isn't safe. No, you must never go beyond that door.
ANNE	I see. *(For the first time she realizes what 'going into hiding' means.)*

Expanding Instruction:
When students are able to understand a character's point of view, they are more able to connect with the text and the characters. They can then make a distinction between their personal point of view and that of the characters in the story. Be sure to first guide them to identify a character's point of view and how it changes prior to having them identify their personal point of view.

- Go to line 305. Mark the Queen of the Netherlands in the late 1800s. (Queen Wilhelmina)

- Go to line 307. Circle the word *book*. Draw an arrow to the noun that renames this book. (diary)

- Go to line 312. Mark the synonym for *runs*. (darts)

- Go to line 319. Mark the adjective used to describe Anne. (sobered) Up to this point, Anne has been full of life and excited about the new adventure. What happens that sobers her and makes her turn serious and quiet? (She is told she can never leave the annex.) The author has used this incident to create a drastic change in Anne's point of view. She no longer sees "going into hiding" as a fun "camp-like" experience. Her point of view of the situation has become grave.

- Go to line 320. Mark what Anne wants to do downstairs. (listen to the radio)

Have students read lines 324–342 according to the option that you chose.

When most of the students are finished, continue with the entire class. Let's see how well you understood the next section.

- Circle the check mark or the question mark for this section. Draw a question mark over any confusing words.

- Go to line 325. Mark the body part that cannot be locked up. (your mind)

- Go to line 330. Circle the word *advantages*. Mark each advantage with a star. (never have to wear galoshes, never have to wear that coat from Margot, won't have to practice on the piano)

- Go to line 336. Mark the word that means "in mocking humor." (wry)

- Go to line 341. Mark the evidence that Peter feels bad about interrupting. (I—I—I)

Close Reading (*cont.*)

MR FRANK   It'll be hard, I know. But always remember this, Anneke. There are no walls, there are no bolts, no locks that anyone can put on your mind. Miep will bring us books. We will read history, poetry, mythology. *(He gives* ANNE *the glass of milk.)* Here's your milk.

(MR FRANK puts his arm about ANNE, *and crosses with her to the couch, where they sit side by side.)*

As a matter of fact, between us, Annie, being here has certain advantages for you. For instance you remember the battle you had with your mother the other day on the subject of goloshes? You said you'd rather die than wear goloshes. But in the end you had to wear them. Well now, you see for as long as we are here, you will never have to wear goloshes. Isn't that good? And the coat that you inherited from Margot—

(ANNE makes a wry face.)

—you won't have to wear that. And the piano. You won't have to practice on the piano. I tell you, this is going to be a fine life for you.

(ANNE'S panic is gone. PETER *appears in the doorway of his room, with a saucer in one hand and the cat in the other.)*

PETER   I—I—I thought I'd better get some water for Mouschi before . . .

MR FRANK   Of course.

Have students read from line 343 to the end according to the option that you chose.

When most of the students are finished, continue with the entire class. Let's see how well you understood the next section.

- Circle the check mark or the question mark for this section. Draw a question mark over any confusing words.

- Go to line 354. What does Mr. Frank give Anne that enables her to document their stay in the annex? (his fountain pen)

- Go to line 363. Mark what Anne will miss about the outdoors. (fresh air, run, shout, jump)

- On lines 364 and 365, Anne's point of view of the situation seems to shift yet again. What is Anne's point of view of living in the annex at this point? (fearful)

- Mark the evidence that Anne is living in fear. (Every time I hear a creak in the house, or a step on the street outside, I'm sure they're coming for us.)

- Go to line 368. Circle the word *father*. Draw an arrow to his nickname. (Pim)

- Go to line 369. Mark the synonym for *outcome*. (fate)

- Go to lines 371 and 372. Circle the text related to time. Write the date in the margin. (twenty-first of August, nineteen forty-two, 8-21-42)

- Go to line 373. Mark the synonym for *awful*. (unbearable)

- On the same line, mark the synonym for *hate*. (loathe)

Have partners compare text markings and correct any errors.

Understanding Setting

All the scenery, furniture, and props the audience sees at a production of a play make up the set design. The set designer's job is to create an environment onstage based on the stage directions written in the play, as well as the text written in the dialogue. Set designers begin the process with a rough sketch. You are going to pretend you are a set designer and draw your rough sketch of the set. Use information in the stage directions, as well as information in the dialogue, to help with your design of the annex that the Franks and the Van Daans shared. The details are very important.

To ensure students have read for details, have them draw a sketch of the set design for *The Play of the Diary of Anne Frank*. Display the designs for students to critique for attention to detail, not artistic ability.

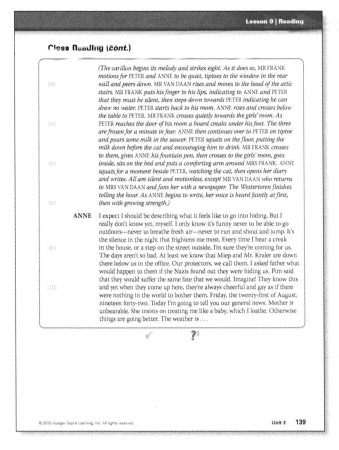

Unit 3

Lesson 10

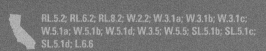

RL.5.2; RL.6.2; RL.8.2; W.2.2; W.3.1a; W.3.1b; W.3.1c;
W.5.1a; W.5.1b; W.5.1d; W.3.5; W.5.5; SL.5.1b; SL.5.1c;
SL.5.1d; L.6.6

Lesson Opener

Before the lesson, choose one of the following activities to write on the board or post on the *LANGUAGE! Live* Class Wall online.

- *Write four sentences with at least two vocabulary words in each. Show you know the meanings. (awkward, conspicuous, indicate, dependable, leisure, regulations, interval, garment, concentrate, peculiar)*

- *Dress your avatar as though you were going to live in an annex for several months without the ability to leave the building. Explain your choices.*

- *Knowing you would be severely punished if caught, would you be willing to stand up for a group of people who were being mistreated? Why or why not?*

Vocabulary

Objective

- Review key passage vocabulary.

Recontextualize Passage Vocabulary

Direct students to page 100 in their Student Books. Use the following questions to review the vocabulary words in the excerpt from *The Play of the Diary of Anne Frank*.

- Is a bus that is always late *dependable*? (no) If you were crossing the desert, would you want a *dependable* source of water? (yes) If you take groceries to your elderly neighbor every Saturday morning, what are you? (dependable)

- If you are shy and *awkward*, would you enjoy your first day at a new school? (no) Is an *awkward* person usually the life of a party? (no) If a football player were asked to dance in a ballet, how might he feel? (awkward)

- If I wore bunny ears to school, would I be *conspicuous*? (yes) Are soldiers wearing camouflage at a battle site *conspicuous*? (no) All the houses on a street are brown, but one is painted neon green. What is it? (conspicuous)

- On a summer day when you have no plans, are you at *leisure*? (yes) When you are at *leisure*, are you getting a lot of work done? (no) If you enjoy "down time" every evening, what kind of time is it? (leisure time)

- Do *regulations* let you do whatever you want? (no) Can *regulations* help create safe conditions? (yes) Can *regulations* be unfair? (yes) If you were the mayor and wanted to improve water quality in your town, what could you pass or suggest? (regulations)

- Are you allowed to wear *garments* to school? (yes) Can *garments* protect you from the cold? (yes) What are shirts, pants, and socks? (garments)

- If I hold my finger to my lips, what am I *indicating*? (that we should be quiet) How do fans at a sports event *indicate* excitement when their team scores? (jumping up, fist-pumping, and cheering) If I point to a person whose hand is raised, what am I doing? (indicating that he or she may speak)

- Does an *interval* have to be very short? (no) What is the *interval* of time between New Year's Eve and New Year's Day? (one day) If you are measuring the amount of time between thunderclaps, what are you measuring? (the interval between them)

- Do you have to *concentrate* to tell someone your name? (no) If you are at a very loud concert, do you have to *concentrate* to hear what your friend is saying? (yes) What is it best to do during a test? (concentrate)

Writing

Objectives
- Write an explanatory paragraph that proves a position.
- Use a process to write.
- Connect text to life experiences to write coherently.
- Use a rubric to guide and assess writing.

Six Traits of Effective Writing

Direct students back to page 30 from Unit 1 in their Student Books. Reread the Six Traits of Effective Writing.

In previous units, we have focused on sentence fluency and word choice. Our focus was on writing complete sentences, then on writing with descriptive language. Using what we have learned in Masterpiece Sentences, we will now begin to vary our sentence use by painting the predicate and painting the subject. While doing this, we will continue to use descriptive language and change the wording to put it in our own words—not the words of the author.

Our writing focus for this unit will be organization *and* conventions. We will try to order our sentences clearly and coherently, as well as ensure we use proper transition words in our writing. On top of that, we will focus our attention on grammar, punctuation, and spelling. We will make sure our verb agrees with our subject, we punctuate correctly within and at the end of sentences, and that we spell words correctly.

Prepare to Write: Explanatory Paragraph

Direct students to pages 140 and 141 in their Student Books and introduce the writing assignment.

Part A. Study the Prompt

Read the instructions for Part A and the prompt.

The instructions tell you to do three things after reading the prompt. What is the first thing? (identify the topic) What is the topic? (Possible answers: Mr. Frank's outlook on life; Mr. Frank's sadness; Mr. Frank's state of mind)

What's the second thing you need to do? (identify the directions) What are the directions? (to write a paragraph that contains specific details that reveal Mr. Frank's emotional state)

What is the third thing you are asked to consider? (purpose for writing) What is the goal or purpose of this writing assignment? (Possible answers: to examine a character's motivation and emotions by considering descriptive details; analyze the character's motivation)

Part B. Introduce Position Topic Sentence

For this writing assignment, you are going to learn how to write a different kind of topic sentence. It is called a Position Topic Sentence. **Read the words in the chart in Part B aloud and explain that the words are used to begin a position topic sentence.** We will come back to write a topic sentence that follows this pattern after we've taken some notes and practiced writing this type of sentence.

Lesson 10 | Writing

Prepare to Write: Explanatory Paragraph

Part A. Study the Prompt

Read the prompt. Identify the topic, directions, and purpose for writing.

The war is over, and Mr. Frank is no longer in hiding. Write a paragraph that explains why Mr. Frank seems to have lost his will to live. Choose several details from the text that reveal his state of mind.

Topic: Mr. Frank's state of mind

Directions: write a paragraph that cites examples to support conclusions about a character

Purpose for writing: examine the character's motivation and emotional state through descriptive details

Part B. Introduce Position Topic Sentence

Starting Words or Phrases					
If	After	Since	Before	So that	Because
Whenever	As long as	In order that	Even though	Although	Wherever
Unless	While	When	Even	As if	As soon as
As	Where	Though	Even if	Until	

Part C. Write Position Topic Sentence — Answers will vary.

Use a word or phrase from the chart in Part B to develop a position topic sentence.

Occasion (event/circumstance): Mr. Frank has physically survived the war.

Position (prove/explain): He has lost his will to live.

Topic Sentence: Even though Mr. Frank has physically survived the war, he seems to have lost his will to live.

140   Unit 3   © 2018 Voyager Sopris Learning, Inc. All rights reserved.

Part D. Prove the Position

Direct students to Part D. For this writing assignment, you have to cite details from the text that support your statement about Mr. Frank's state of mind. The author doesn't come out and say that Mr. Frank is depressed or has no will to live. Instead, the author describes the facial expressions, movements, and actions that reveal his sadness. Let's think about three elements that contribute to our knowledge of this character. First, let's consider what he has lost. The simple reality of his situation could help explain his emotional state. Who or what has he lost? (Answers should include: his wife, Edith; both daughters, Margot and Anne; his friends; all of his possessions) How would you feel if you survived a tragic event, but none of your loved ones did? Encourage students to share responses. What else do we learn about Mr. Frank as the play begins? Describe his physical appearance. (Answers should include: weak, ill, threadbare clothes, and very emotional) What conclusions do you draw when you see someone who looks like Mr. Frank? (Responses should include depression, overwhelming pain, a lack of caring about self) What specific behaviors does Mr. Frank exhibit? (Answers should include: weeping when he picks up a glove, telling Miep he's leaving Amsterdam, he doesn't know what he's going to do, wants to burn all of the paper including Anne's diary) Have students complete the chart. As you write the body of your paragraph, use these three categories to document your conclusions about Mr. Frank's will to live.

> **Note:** Explain that publishing Anne's diary was a way for Mr. Frank to regain a sense of purpose in his life and bring some good from the tragic Holocaust.

Prepare to Write: Explanatory Paragraph (*cont.*)

Part D Prove the Position   Answers will vary.

Losses	Physical Appearance	Behaviors
Edith, his wife	Weak and ill	Begins to weep when he picks up a glove
Anne, his daughter	Threadbare clothes	Leaving Amsterdam— painful memories
Margot, his daughter	Very emotional	Admits he has no plan
All of his possessions		Wants to burn all papers/ memories

Part E. Write Concluding Sentence   Answers will vary.

Develop a concluding sentence by restating the topic sentence. Restate the occasion and position by choosing another word or phrase from the box in Part B.
Because his grief is so complete, Mr. Frank struggles to find a purpose for living.

Passage Retell

Now that we've taken some notes and discussed them, I want you to do a little "oral rehearsal." Turn to your partner and present the information in your chart orally. Use your notes to present the information, but add descriptive words you want to use when you write. Give each other feedback on the way the ideas have been developed and particularly on the use of descriptive language.

Position Topic Sentences

Now that you've developed your thoughts and orally rehearsed your paragraph, let's turn our attention back to writing a topic sentence. We will practice writing some general position statements before you write the topic sentence for your paragraph. **Direct students to page 142 in their Student Books and read the instructions aloud. Read the example.** This type of topic sentence works well when you want to share an opinion or take a position regarding a topic or event. In the example, we start by saying how we enjoy taking vacations; however, one vacation is more special than all of the others. The position or consequence helps us choose the right word to start our sentence. Listen as I substitute different starting words for *While* and see if they make any sense. **Use *if, after, before,* and *although* and have students decide if they make sense. The only one that makes sense is *although*.**

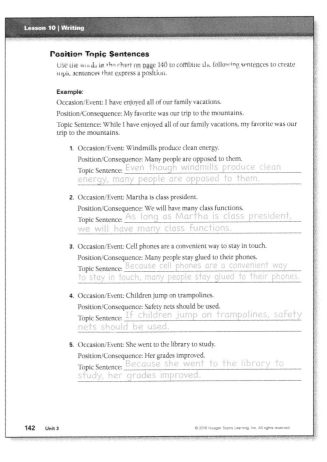

Model

Listen as I read the first one and see if you choose the same word I choose. **Model the process with the first one. Explain that the second sentence creates an exception. Have volunteers share other starters that would work and correct as needed.** You would think that people would typically support something that creates clean energy, but windmills are controversial. Notice also how we write the sentence. Adding the starting word or phrase creates an incomplete sentence. It needs something more to finish the thought, so we have to use a comma to separate the first part of the sentence from the part of the sentence that "completes the thought." The words following the comma create a complete sentence. They could stand alone and make sense.

Guided Practice

Guide students in completion of the second sentence. Discuss the word choice, and reinforce the way the sentence is written.

Independent Practice

Have partners complete the activity. Review the answers as a class. Affirm student choices that differ from the model response but still make sense. Stress the idea that there are often multiple ways to begin the topic sentences.

Part C. Write Position Topic Sentence

Direct students back to Part C of page 140. Read the instructions aloud, and orient students to the format that has been created. What is the event or circumstance that we are writing about? (Mr. Frank has survived the war; the war is over.) Have students write the occasion on the page. Encourage them to write a complete sentence. What is the position? (He has lost his will to live.) Generate a class discussion about the fact that Mr. Frank survived the horror of the Holocaust, but now that he is safe and the war is over, he does not want to live. Identify this as irony and explain the concept to students. Ask them what the difference is between Johnny and Mr. Frank.

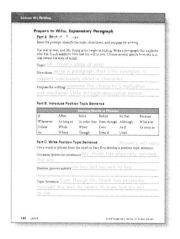

Explain that sometimes they will choose their position, but for this writing prompt, it was given to them. Have students write the position on the page. Encourage them to write a complete sentence. Now, you need to combine the two ideas. Consider the word or phrase that works best to join the two ideas and write the new combined sentence. This is your topic sentence. If students struggle, share the model occasion, position, and topic sentence for students to use.

Part E. Write Concluding Sentence

Now, you will think of a way to restate your topic sentence so it can serve as your concluding sentence. Direct students to Part E and read the instructions aloud. Think of how else you may frame your thoughts about Mr. Frank. Try rearranging the sentence and using synonyms. You should basically say the same thing your topic sentence said—just in a different way.

Turn to your partner and share your ideas about a concluding sentence and then commit your thoughts to paper.

Write

Notebook paper

Have students write their paragraph on a sheet of notebook paper. Remind students that they have their first and last sentences written. Encourage them to review their notes and consider their "oral rehearsal" as they begin to write the body of their paragraph. Remind them to include evidence from the text to support their conclusions about Mr. Frank. Have students consult the Six Traits of Writing: Basic rubric on page 389 as they write their paragraph. If they struggle or

Six Traits of Writing: Basic

	Ideas and Content	Organization	Voice and Audience Awareness	Word Choice	Sentence Fluency	Language Conventions
4	Focuses on the topic. Main idea (topic sentence) is clear and well supported with details and elaboration (examples, evidence, and explanations).	Topic sentence clearly states main idea. Ideas are clear and logically organized. Contains concluding sentence.	The words have a strong sense of person and purpose. Brings topic to life.	Words are specific to the content, accurate, and vivid. Word choice enhances meaning and the reader's enjoyment.	Writes complete sentences and varies sentence structure.	There are no grammar errors. There are few or no errors in spelling, capitalization, or punctuation.
3	Mostly focuses on the topic. Sentences supporting the main idea (topic sentence) may be general rather than detailed and specific.	Topic sentence states main idea. Organization mostly clear and logical. May contain concluding sentence.	The words have some sense of person and purpose.	Words are correctly used but may be somewhat general and unspecific.	Writes complete sentences and attempts to use expanded sentences.	There are no major grammar errors. There are few errors in spelling, capitalization, or punctuation.
2	Main idea (topic sentence) is unclear and/or lacks sufficient support.	Structure may not be entirely clear or logical. Paragraph may seem more like a list and/or be hard to follow.	The words have little sense of person and purpose.	Words may be used inaccurately or repetitively.	Writes mostly simple and/or awkwardly constructed sentences. May include some run-ons and fragments.	There are a few grammar errors. There are a few errors in spelling, capitalization, or punctuation.
1	Does not address prompt and/or lacks a topic sentence. Supporting details are absent or do not relate to topic.	No evident structure. Lack of organization seriously interferes with meaning.	The words have no sense of person or purpose. No sense of audience.	Extremely limited range of words. Restricted vocabulary impedes message.	Numerous run-ons and/or fragments interfere with meaning.	There are many grammar and/or spelling errors. There are many errors in capitalization and punctuation.

need additional support in developing their paragraph, use the following paragraph as a model.

Exemplar Writing: Explanatory Paragraph

Even though Mr. Frank has physically survived the war, he seems to have lost his will to live. He has lost the people most dear to him. His wife and his two daughters are no longer with him. His home and his possessions are also lost to him. He sits alone on the couch in threadbare clothing that reveals a lack of money and common necessities for living. Weakened and ill, he is weighed down by his emotions. Just below the surface, his grief is quickly exposed by items that spark memories. Picking up a glove causes him to weep. He knows he must leave Amsterdam, but he has no idea of where he will go. Even though his business in Amsterdam is waiting for him to return, he pushes it aside. He wants all of the papers burned until Miep shows him Anne's diary. Remembering the day he gave it to her, he is overwhelmed with memories and loss. Because his grief is so complete, Mr. Frank struggles to find a purpose for living.

Student Handwriting:
Handwriting lessons are provided in manuscript and cursive. These explicit lessons (found online in Resources) can be taught systematically during writing lessons to strengthen legibility and fluency.

Evaluate Writing

Direct students to page 143 in their Student Books. Good writers have tools that help them improve their writing. This checklist will help you evaluate your writing before submitting it to be graded. **Have individuals quickly assess their writing, then have partners evaluate each other's writing based on the checklist.**

Note: Use Six Traits of Writing Scoring Rubric: Basic on page 564 of this book to assess students' writing. A printable version is located online in the Teacher Resources.

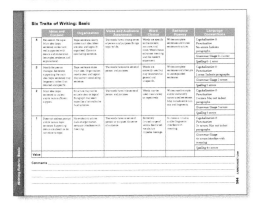

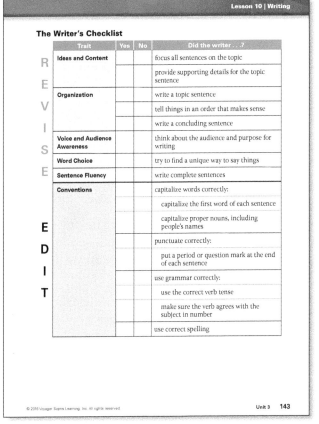

Objectives

- Self-correct as comprehension of text deepens.
- Answer questions to demonstrate comprehension of text.
- Engage in class discussion.
- Identify the enduring understandings from a piece of text.

Revisit Passage Comprehension

Direct students back to page 124 in their Student Books. Have students review their answers and make any necessary changes. Then, have partners share their answers and collaborate to perfect them.

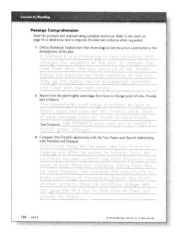

Enduring Understandings

Direct students back to page 99 in their Student Books. Reread the Big Idea questions.

Are all people really good at heart?

Are people a product of their beliefs or a product of their circumstances?

Generate a class discussion about the questions and the answers students came up with before reading. Have them consider whether their answers have changed after reading the text.

Use the following talking points to foster conversation. Refer to the Class Discussion Rules poster and have students use the Collegial Discussion sentence frames on page 382 of their Student Books.

- Often, we give in to peer pressure. We do something because others are doing it or because it is what is expected of us—even if it doesn't reflect our ideas and beliefs. The unpopular decisions and choices we make are the most difficult ones to make. When is it acceptable to "go against the grain" and do things solely based on what is in our hearts? What if the world was filled with only people who did what was expected—or what they were told? Would you like to live in a world without people like Miep Gies or Kraler?

- To what degree are we victims of circumstance? Do our beliefs and feelings change based on the time and circumstances? After the American Civil War and World War II, many people confessed that while they didn't necessarily agree with the reasons for the war, they believed in the leaders who led them into war, and so they followed along. Could that happen to you?

What we read should make us think. You should be able to make links between Anne Frank and Ponyboy. Think about the social groups that defined their identities. Was the treatment they received because of their social status fair? Was it really "who" they were? Use our discussion and your thoughts about the text to determine what you will "walk away with." Has it made you think about a personal experience or someone you know? Has your perspective or opinion on a specific topic changed? Do you have any lingering thoughts or questions? Write these ideas as your enduring understandings. What will you take with you from this text?

Discuss the enduring understandings with the class. Then, have students write their enduring understandings from the unit.

Have students consider why the authors wrote the passage and whether they were successful.

Progress Monitoring

End-of-Unit Online Assessments

Monitor students' progress in the unit by utilizing online assessments. Students should prioritize these assessments over successive Word Training units.

- Assign Unit 3 Content Mastery quizzes to assess skills taught in this unit.
- Assign Power Pass to assess reading comprehension skills in a standardized test format.

All assessments can be assigned online by opening the Tools menu, then selecting Assignments. Be sure to select the correct class and unit from the drop-down menu.

Reteach

Based on students' performance in Content Mastery, extra practice may be needed.

- If student scores fall at 60 percent or below, reteach the content to small groups.
- If student scores fall between 61–79 percent, reinforce the skills by assigning the student reteach activity pages as homework.

Reteach lessons can be found online on the Course Reports page for each unit.

Comprehension Building

Background knowledge is a key component of reading comprehension. It is important for students to develop knowledge of a topic prior to class discussion and reading of complex text.

Print Unit 4 Background Information from the online Resources and assign as homework for students to read. Encourage students to come to class prepared for discussion.

Unit Big Ideas

- Is the American Dream a possibility for everyone?
- What are the negative effects of a transient lifestyle?
- Is education the passport to the future?
- Is code-switching necessary?

Instructional Texts

"The Circuit" by Francisco Jiménez

Text type: informational—autobiography

Excerpt from *The Autobiography of Malcolm X* by Malcolm X, Alex Haley

Text type: informational—autobiography

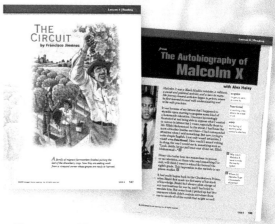

Materials

- *Unit 4 video, Part A (Immigration)*
- *Unit 4 video, Part B (Education)*
- *Six Traits of Writing Scoring Rubric: Basic (print as needed)*

Optional
- *Unit 4 Background Information*
- *Online dictionary*
- *Progress Monitoring Across the Six Traits scales*

Classroom Materials

- *Highlighters or colored pencils*
- *Notebook paper*
- *Thesauruses*

Instructional Resources

- *Unit 4 Reteach*
- *Handwriting Lessons*
- *Writing Project: Narrative*
- *Progress Monitoring Across the Six Traits scales*

Instructional Texts:

"The Circuit"

by Francisco Jiménez

Text type: informational—autobiography

Excerpt from *The Autobiography of Malcolm X*

by Malcolm X, Alex Haley

Text type: informational—autobiography

LANGUAGE! Live Online

Grammar Practice

- Identify the function of words in sentences.
- Use comparatives and superlatives correctly.
- Distinguish between formal and informal language.
- Use prepositional phrases correctly.
- Use modifiers correctly and recognize when they are misplaced.
- Use punctuation correctly within consecutive adjectives.

Vocabulary Practice

- Determine the meaning of derivations of words.

Content Mastery

- Demonstrate an understanding of . . .
  - word meaning by answering questions and using words in sentences.
  - the use of linking verbs.
  - the use of helping verbs.
  - past and present tense verbs.

Word Study

- Blend, read, and spell multisyllabic words with r-controlled vowels; words with prefixes dis-, un-, in-, non-, inter-, and under- contractions with am, is, and are; and words with digraphs.
- Read connected text to build fluency.

Lesson 1

Reading

- Determine and discuss the topic of a text.
- Determine and discuss the author's purpose.
- Use text features to preview text.

Vocabulary

- Evaluate word knowledge.
- Determine the meaning of key passage vocabulary.

Reading

- Read an autobiographical short story.
- Monitor comprehension during text reading.
- Identify the structure used to organize text.

Lesson 2

Vocabulary

- Review key passage vocabulary.

Grammar

- Identify verb tenses and use them to clarify meaning.
- Identify the function and purpose of linking verbs.
- Identify the function and purpose of helping verbs.

Writing

- Identify the subject and predicate of a sentence.
- Use adjectives and adverbs correctly in sentence writing.
- Produce, expand, and rearrange complete sentences for clarity and style.
- Refine word choice in sentences.

Lesson 6

Reading

- Determine and discuss the topic of a text.
- Determine and discuss the author's purpose.
- Use text features to preview text.

Vocabulary

- Evaluate word knowledge.
- Determine the meaning of key passage vocabulary.

Reading

- Read autobiographical text.
- Monitor comprehension during text reading.

Lesson 7

Vocabulary

- Review key passage vocabulary.

Reading

- Objectively summarize text.
- Identify multiple main ideas of a text.
- Determine the central idea of a text.
- Analyze texts from different cultures and the approach to a similar central idea or theme.
- Determine how to respond to prompts.
- Answer questions about text.

Writing

- Identify the function and purpose of transition words in writing.
- Use academic vocabulary to signal logical relationships.

Writing Project: Narrative

Lesson 3	Lesson 4	Lesson 5
Reading • Objectively summarize text. • Identify multiple main ideas of a text. • Determine the central idea of a text. • Establish a purpose for rereading autobiographical text. • Use critical thinking skills to write responses to prompts about text. • Support written answers with text evidence. • Explain how the values and beliefs of characters are affected by the historical and cultural setting.	**Vocabulary** • Review key passage vocabulary. **Reading** • Read autobiographical text with purpose and understanding. • Answer questions to demonstrate comprehension of text. • Identify and explain explicit details from text. • Monitor comprehension of text during reading. • Determine the meaning of idioms in text. • Identify the use of personification in text. • Identify first-person literary point of view. • Determine the meaning of foreign words used in literature. • Make inferences regarding the feelings and actions of characters in a story.	**Vocabulary** • Review key passage vocabulary **Writing** • Use text to write coherent paragraphs in response to reading. • Make inferences to determine a character's feelings. **Reading** • Self-correct as comprehension of text deepens. • Answer questions to demonstrate comprehension of text. • Engage in class discussion. • Identify the enduring understandings from a piece of text.

Lesson 8	Lesson 9	Lesson 10
Reading • Establish a purpose for rereading autobiographical text. • Use critical thinking skills to write responses to prompts about text. • Support written answers with text evidence. • Explain how the values and beliefs of characters are affected by the historical and cultural setting.	**Vocabulary** • Review key passage vocabulary. **Reading** • Read an autobiography with purpose and understanding. • Answer questions to demonstrate comprehension of text. • Identify and explain explicit details from text. • Monitor comprehension of text during reading. • Identify words with novel meanings in text and determine the meaning. • Identify the purpose of modifiers in text. • Recognize misplaced modifiers and determine the better placement. • Identify unnecessary words used for emphasis. • Identify the use of verb moods in literature. • Identify the meaning and purpose of conjunctive adverbs.	**Vocabulary** • Review key passage vocabulary. **Writing** • Write in response to text. • Take notes on an informational text. • Use transition words in writing. • Orally retell key information from an informational text. • Write a time-order paragraph. • Use a rubric to guide and assess writing. **Reading** • Self-correct as comprehension of text deepens. • Answer questions to demonstrate comprehension of text. • Engage in class discussion. • Identify the enduring understandings from a piece of text.

Unit
4 · Lesson 1

RRL.2.7; RI.2.2; RI.4.1; RI.2.6; RI.4.5; RI.1.10a; RI.3.10;
RF.2.4a; RF.5.4a; SL.1.2; SL.5.1a; SL.5.1b; SL.5.1c; SL.5.1d;
L.3.5b; L.6.4b; L.6.6

Lesson Opener

Before the lesson, choose one of the following activities to write on the board or post on the *LANGUAGE! Live* Class Wall online.

* *Describe a time when you were disappointed.*
* *Write two sentences about the need for money. Identify the complete subject and the complete predicate.*
* *Write two sentences describing a family member who works hard. Mark the adjectives.*

Reading

Objectives

* Determine and discuss the topic of a text.
* Determine and discuss the author's purpose.
* Use text features to preview text.

Passage Introduction

Direct students to page 145 in their Student Books. Discuss the content focus of the unit.

Content Focus

pursuit of happiness; the value of education

What do you think this story will be about? (Answers will vary.)

Type of Text

informational—autobiography

Text can be divided into two categories: informational and literary. In Unit 3, we read two scenes of *The Play of the Diary of Anne Frank*. We are going to read an excerpt from an autobiographical novel. Autobiographies and biographies are both nonfiction. They both share history about a person's life. Let's talk more about the meanings of two words: *autobiography* and *biography*. How are these words related? Let's look at the parts of the words to determine the meaning. The words parts were borrowed from the Greek language.

Let's Focus: "The Circuit"

Content Focus
pursuit of happiness; the value of education

Type of Text
informational—autobiography; short story

Author's Name Francisco Jiménez

Author's Purpose to teach others about migrant workers

Big Ideas
Consider the following Big Idea questions. Write your answer for each question.

Is the American Dream a possibility for everyone? Explain.

What are the negative effects of a transient lifestyle?

Autobiography Preview Checklist: "The Circuit" on pages 147–153.
☐ Title: What clue does it provide about the passage?
☐ Pictures: What additional information is added here?
☐ Margin Information: What vocabulary is important to understand this story?

Enduring Understandings
After reading the text . . .

Write the following on the board:

> *bio: life*
>
> *graph: to write*
>
> *auto: self*

If *bio* means "life" and *graph* means "to write," we can determine the meaning of *biography* by connecting these definitions. *Biography* means "to write about life." A *biography* is a written account of the life of a person. Now, if I add *auto* to the beginning of the word, who do you think is doing the writing? (**self**) A writer who writes about him- or herself is writing an *autobiography*. He or she is like a painter who paints a self-portrait or a teenager who takes a "selfie." Many people consider autobiographies to be subjective, or not entirely based on facts. Why do you think that is? (**The authors don't want to include the bad stuff.**) What would you include in your personal autobiography for others to read? **Have partners share ideas.**

The author of the "The Circuit" wrote about specific events or periods in his life. This type of writing can also be called a memoir because it is not about the whole life, like an autobiography. "The Circuit" is part of a larger novel with the same title. In this case, every chapter in the book tells a story that can stand alone, making them short stories (like "Thank You, M'am").

The short story "The Circuit," based on the life of the author, is written in first person. A narrator in first-person point of view tells this story. That means that the narrator, or person telling the story, is a character in the story. Where is the narrator? (**inside the story**) Is this a true story? (**yes**)

Author's Purpose

Have students glance at the text. Who is the author of the story? (Francisco Jiménez) The author's purpose is the reason that he or she wrote the text. Authors write for different purposes. They write to entertain, to persuade, or to inform or teach. Knowing an author's purpose can help a reader understand a text better. "The Circuit" was written to inform others about the conditions and times in which the person lived. "The Circuit" was written to provide insight about migrant workers who move from place to place to find work to make a better life for themselves and family members. The author wants to teach others to appreciate and value all cultures.

Have students write the answers on the page.

lay the Unit 4 Text raining video, Part A und in the Teacher esources online.

Before we read "The Circuit," we will watch a short video to help build our background knowledge. **Play the Unit 4 Text Training video, Part A. Have partners discuss the main points the videographer was trying to make and what evidence was provided to support the points.**

> **Note:** Additional Background Information about immigration can be found in the Teacher Resources online. Choose the Text Training tab, and then select Unit 4. The Background Information will be in the first section.

Direct students to page 145 in their Student Books. Read the Big Idea questions aloud.

Big Ideas

Is the American Dream a possibility for everyone? Explain.

What are the negative effects of a transient lifestyle?

Collegial Discussion poster

Class Discussion Rules poster

As a class, consider the two Big Idea questions.

- Encourage students with limited knowledge of the "American Dream" and the term *transient* to ask for further explanation from peers.

- Have students reflect on the Background Information for the unit and ask clarifying questions when needed.

- Provide opportunities for students to explain their ideas and answers to the Big Idea questions in light of the discussion by ensuring students follow the rules for class discussion, which can be printed in poster form from the Teacher Resources online.

- Suggest students refer to the Collegial Discussion sentence frames in the back of their books.

- Encourage speakers to link comments to the remarks of others to keep the focus of the discussion and create cohesion, even when their comments are in disagreement.

After discussing each question, have students write an answer. We'll come back to these questions after we finish reading the text. You can add to your answers as you gain information and perspective.

Preview

Read aloud the Autobiography Preview Checklist on page 145. Have students preview the text using the Preview Procedure outlined below.

> ### Preview Procedure
> - Group students with partners or in triads.
> - Have students count off as 1s or 2s. The 1s will become the student leaders. If working with triads, the third students become 3s.
> - The student leaders will preview the text in addition to managing the checklist and pacing.
> - The 2s and 3s will preview the text with 1s.
> - Direct 1s to open their Student Books to page 145 and 2s and 3s to open their Student Books to page 147. This allows students to look at a few different pages at one time without turning back and forth.

If it is necessary, guide students in a short preview using the following talking points. What is the title? ("The Circuit") What clue does the title provide about the passage? (Answers will vary.) Describe the graphic on the title page. (dad and two school-age students picking grapes in the vineyard) Let's look to see what additional information the pictures provide. What is pictured in the margins? (grapevines) What are grapes used for? (wine, juice, jelly, snacks) Describe the picture on page 152. (A student is looking at a trumpet with wide eyes while his teacher watches from a distance.)

Vocabulary

Objectives
- Evaluate word knowledge.
- Determine the meaning of key passage vocabulary.

Rate Vocabulary Knowledge

Direct students to page 146 in their Student Books. Let's take a look at the vocabulary words from "The Circuit." I am going to say each word aloud. You will repeat the word and write it in the third column. Then, you will rate your knowledge of the word. Display the Vocabulary Rating Scale poster or write the information on the board. Review the meaning of each rating.

Lesson 1 | Vocabulary

Key Passage Vocabulary: "The Circuit"

Read each word. Write it in column 3. Then, circle a number to rate your knowledge of the word.

Vocabulary	Part of Speech	Write the Word	Rate the Word
exchange	(v)	exchange	0 1 2 3
populated	(adj)	populated	0 1 2 3
motionless	(adj)	motionless	0 1 2 3
drone	(n)	drone	0 1 2 3
design	(n)	design	0 1 2 3
instinctively	(adv)	instinctively	0 1 2 3
murmur	(v)	murmur	0 1 2 3
savor	(v)	savor	0 1 2 3
introduce	(v)	introduce	0 1 2 3
enthusiastically	(adv)	enthusiastically	0 1 2 3

146   Unit 4   © 2016 Voyager Sopris Learning, Inc. All rights reserved.

Vocabulary Rating Scale

0—I have never heard the word before.

1—I have heard the word, but I'm not sure how to use it.

2—I am familiar with the word, but I'm not sure if I know the correct meaning.

3—I know the meaning of the word and can use it correctly in a sentence.

Remember, the points are there to help you know which words you need to focus on. By the end of this unit, you should be able to change all your ratings to a 3. That's the goal.

Read each word aloud and have students repeat it, write it, and rate it. Then, have volunteers who rated a word *2* or *3* use the word in an oral sentence.

Preteach Vocabulary

Explain that you will now take a closer look at the words. Follow the Preteach Procedure outlined below.

Preteach Procedure

This activity is intended to take only a short amount of time, so make it an oral exercise.

- Introduce each word as indicated on the word card.
- Read the definition and example sentences.
- Ask questions to clarify and deepen understanding.
- If time permits, allow students to share.

* If your students would benefit from copying the definitions, please have them do so in the vocabulary log in the back of the Student Books using the margin definitions in the passage selections. This should be done outside of instruction time.

exchange (v)

Let's read the first word together. *Exchange.*

Definition: *Exchange* means "to trade; to give one thing for another." What means "to trade; to give one thing for another"? (exchange)

Example 1: If two people *exchange* phone numbers, they can keep in touch.

Example 2: If you buy a shirt that doesn't fit, you can *exchange* it for one that does.

Example 3: I do not like to hear people *exchange* insults with each other.

Question 1: Do friends sometimes *exchange* fashion tips? Yes or no? (yes)

Question 2: Would you *exchange* belly scratches with your dog? Yes or no? (no)

Pair Share: Turn to your partner and tell about a gift that you *exchanged* or wanted to *exchange*, and why.

populated (adj)

Let's read the next word together. *Populated.*

Definition: *Populated* means "lived in; filled with." What means "lived in; filled with"? (populated)

Example 1: A wooded mountain might be *populated* by bears.

Example 2: A remote island may be *populated* only by fishermen and their families.

Example 3: On summer evenings, our backyard is *populated* by fireflies.

Question 1: Is a zoo *populated* with animals? Yes or no? (yes)

Question 2: Is the moon *populated*? Yes or no? (no)

Pair Share: Turn to your partner and tell what the ocean is *populated* with.

motionless (adj)

Let's read the next word together. *Motionless.*

Definition: If something is *motionless*, it is still and not moving. What word means "still; not moving"? (motionless)

Example 1: A statue sitting on a shelf is *motionless*.

Example 2: In freeze tag, you must remain *motionless* after you are tagged.

Example 3: It is soothing to watch river water flowing over *motionless* rocks.

Question 1: On a windy day, are the branches of a tree *motionless*? Yes or no? (no)

Question 2: Is a car in a parked position *motionless*? Yes or no? (yes)

Pair Share: Turn to your partner and name three *motionless* objects in this room.

(3)

drone (n)

Let's read the next word together. *Drone.*

Definition: A *drone* is a low, humming noise. What word means "a low, humming noise"? (drone)

Example 1: If you live near an airport, you hear the constant *drone* of airplanes overhead.

Example 2: The *drone* of traffic on the highway is not as noticeable at night.

Example 3: The sound of a tornado is a low *drone* like a passing train.

Question 1: Would you hear a *drone* near a beehive? Yes or no? (yes)

Question 2: Do clouds floating in the sky produce a *drone*? Yes or no? (no)

Pair Share: Turn to your partner and imitate the *drone* of a machine or appliance.

(4)

design (n)

Let's read the next word together. *Design.*

Definition: A *design* is a pattern or drawing. What word means "a pattern or drawing"? (design)

Example 1: I like *designs* with bright colors and sharp lines.

Example 2: People who doodle draw *designs* while they talk or think.

Example 3: Notebooks sometimes have a swirly *design* on the cover.

Question 1: Is there a *design* on your backpack? Yes or no? (Answers will vary.)

Question 2: Is it best to have a *design* before beginning a sewing project? Yes or no? (yes)

Pair Share: Turn to your partner and describe a *design* you would like to see on the ceiling of this room.

(5)

instinctively (adv)

Let's read the next word together. *Instinctively.*

Definition: *Instinctively* means "without thinking; in a natural or automatic way." What means "without thinking; in a natural or automatic way"? (instinctively)

Example 1: If you touch something hot, you pull your hand away *instinctively*.

Example 2: People sneeze *instinctively*; you can't decide to do it.

Example 3: Cats *instinctively* bathe themselves, but dogs do not.

Question 1: In very bright light, do you *instinctively* squint your eyes? Yes or no? (yes)

Question 2: Could you *instinctively* speak a language you hadn't learned? Yes or no? (no)

Pair Share: Turn to your partner and tell what you do *instinctively* if you have an itch. Then, name something else you do *instinctively*.

(6)

murmur (v)

Let's read the next word together. *Murmur.*

Definition: To *murmur* is to speak softly. What means "to speak softly"? (murmur)

Example 1: I have a hard time hearing people who *murmur.*

Example 2: If you are an actor, you have to learn to speak loudly rather than *murmur.*

Example 3: Two friends who *murmur* between themselves can make a third friend feel left out.

Question 1: Do people with a very sore throat sometimes *murmur*? Yes or no? (yes)

Question 2: If someone stomped on your toe, would you *murmur*? Yes or no? (no)

Pair Share: Turn to your partner and *murmur* the alphabet.

(7)

savor (v)

Let's read the next word together. *Savor.*

Definition: If you *savor* something, you enjoy it deeply. What word means "to enjoy something deeply"? (savor)

Example 1: I *savor* cold lemonade in the summertime.

Example 2: People who are introverts *savor* being alone.

Example 3: If you *savor* someone's company, you enjoy being with him or her.

Question 1: Do most people *savor* a visit to the dentist? Yes or no? (no)

Question 2: Do some people *savor* sleeping late on the weekend? Yes or no? (yes)

Pair Share: Turn to your partner and tell about a memory you *savor.*

(8)

introduce (v)

Let's read the next word together. *Introduce.*

Definition: *Introduce* means "to present one person to another person or to a group." What means "to present one person to another person or to a group"? (introduce)

Example 1: The host of a game show usually *introduces* the contestants.

Example 2: As a teacher, it would be my job to *introduce* a new student to the rest of you.

Example 3: People who are shy have a hard time *introducing* themselves to others.

Question 1: Could you *introduce* two strangers you do not know? Yes or no? (no)

Question 2: Do you *introduce* yourself to your family every evening? Yes or no? (no)

Pair Share: Turn to your partner and tell them how you would like to be *introduced* to someone.

(9)

enthusiastically (adv)

Let's read the last word together. *Enthusiastically.*

Definition: *Enthusiastically* means "with great energy and excitement." What means "with great energy and excitement"? (enthusiastically)

Example 1: Many people do not take out the trash *enthusiastically.*

Example 2: When he sees me with the leash and the ball, my dog responds *enthusiastically.*

Example 3: Saying "hello" to someone *enthusiastically* can help to brighten their day.

Question 1: Would you respond *enthusiastically* to a canceled science quiz? Yes or no? (yes)

Question 2: If you approach a task *enthusiastically*, do you complain about it? Yes or no? (no)

Pair Share: Turn to your partner and introduce yourself *enthusiastically.*

(10)

Objectives
- Read an autobiographical short story.
- Monitor comprehension during text reading.
- Identify the structure used to organize text.

"The Circuit"
Direct students to page 147 in their Student Books.

Chronological Text Structure
Now that we have previewed vocabulary, it's time to read. It is important to pay attention to the structure that the author uses to organize a text. The structure of "The Circuit" is chronological. Say *chronological.* (chronological) A chronological text structure uses time sequences. One way to pay attention to time is to watch for transition words and phrases related to time. How is time noted? (with transition words) Let's look at page 148 and hunt for transition words or phrases that tell time. **Provide wait time. Have volunteers share their findings.** (at sunset, when we got there, that night, early next morning, around nine o'clock) Where did you find the transitions that tell about time? (at the beginning of paragraphs)

Choose a student to read the italicized introduction aloud. Explain that the italic print provides a brief synopsis of the events that lead up to the part we are about to read.

Guiding Students Toward Independent Reading

It is important that your students read as much and as often as they can. Assign readings that meet the needs of your students, based on your observations and data. This is a good opportunity to stretch your students. If students become frustrated, scaffold the reading with paired reading, choral reading, or a read-aloud.

Options for reading text:
- Teacher read-aloud
- Teacher-led or student-led choral read
- Paired read or independent read

Choose an option for reading the remainder of the text. Have students read according to the option that you chose. Point out the italicized words within the story and explain that they are Spanish words or phrases used by the author.

Remind students to pause at the numbers and consider the questions.

If you choose to read the text aloud or chorally, use the text on the following pages and stop to ask questions and have students answer them.

"The Circuit"

SE p. 147, paragraph 1

A family of migrant farmworkers finished picking the last of the strawberry crop. Now they are seeking work from a vineyard owner whose grapes are ready to harvest.

SE p. 148, paragraphs 1–2

At sunset we drove into a labor camp near Fresno. Since Papá did not speak English, Mamá asked the camp foreman if he needed any more workers. "We don't need no more," said the foreman, scratching his head. "Check with Sullivan down the road. Can't miss him. He lives in a big white house with a fence around it."

When we got there, Mamá walked up to the house. She went through a white gate, past a row of rose bushes, up the stairs to the front door. She rang the doorbell. The porch light went on and a tall husky man came out. They **exchanged** a few words. After the man went in, Mamá clasped hands and hurried back to the car. "We have work! Mr. Sullivan said we can stay there the whole season," she said, gasping and pointing to an old garage near the stables.

1. Why is Mamá excited about an old garage?

SE p. 148, paragraphs 3–4

The garage was worn out by the years. It had no windows. The walls, eaten by termites, strained to support the roof full of holes. The dirt floor, **populated** by earthworms, looked like a gray road map.

That night, by the light of a kerosene lamp, we unpacked and cleaned our new home. Roberto swept away the loose dirt, leaving the hard ground. Papá plugged the holes in the walls with old newspapers and tin can tops. Mamá fed my little brothers and sisters. Papá and Roberto then brought in the mattress and placed it on the far corner of the garage. "Mamá, you and the little ones sleep on the mattress. Roberto, Panchito, and I will sleep outside under the trees," Papá said.

2. What is the narrator's name?

SE p. 148,
paragraphs 5–6

Early next morning, Mr. Sullivan showed us where his crop was, and after breakfast, Papá, Roberto, and I headed for the vineyard to pick.

page break

Around nine o'clock, the temperature had risen to almost one hundred degrees. I was completely soaked in sweat, and my mouth felt as if I had been | chewing on a handkerchief. I walked over to the end of the row, picked up the jug of water we had brought, and began drinking. "Don't drink too much; you'll get sick," Roberto shouted. No sooner had he said that than I felt sick to my stomach. I dropped to my knees and let the jug roll off my hands. I remained **motionless** with my eyes glued on the hot sandy ground. All I could hear was the **drone** of insects. Slowly I began to recover. I poured water over my face and neck and watched the black mud run down my arms and hit the ground.

SE p. 149, paragraph 1

I still felt a little dizzy when we took a break to eat lunch. It was past two o'clock and we sat underneath a large walnut tree that was on the side of the road. While we ate, Papá jotted down the number of boxes we had picked. Roberto drew **designs** on the ground with a stick. Suddenly I noticed Papá's face turn pale as he looked down the road. "Here comes the school bus," he whispered loudly in alarm. **Instinctively**, Roberto and I ran and hid in the vineyards. We did not want to get in trouble for not going to school. The yellow bus stopped in front of Mr. Sullivan's house. Two neatly dressed boys about my age got off. They carried books under their arms. After they crossed the street, the bus drove away. Roberto and I came out from hiding and joined Papá. "*Tienen que tener cuidado,*" he warned us.

3. Why didn't the boys go to school?

SE p. 149, paragraph 2

After lunch, we went back to work. The sun kept beating down. The buzzing insects, the wet sweat, and the hot dry dust made the afternoon seem to last forever. Finally the mountains around the valley reached out and swallowed the sun. Within an hour it was too dark to continue picking. The vines blanketed the grapes, making it difficult to see the bunches. "*Vámonos,*" said Papá, signaling to us that it was time to quit work. Papá then took out a pencil and began to figure out how much we had earned our first day. He wrote down numbers, crossed some out, wrote down some more. "*Quince,*" he **murmured**.

4. Why do they work from morning until it is too dark to see?

SE p. 150, paragraph 1

When we arrived home, we took a cold shower underneath a waterhose. We then sat down to eat dinner around some wooden crates that served as a table. Mamá had cooked a special meal for us. We had rice and tortillas with *"carne con chile,"* my favorite dish.

5. Did they have a bathroom? How do you know?

SE p. 150, paragraphs 2–3

The next morning I could hardly move. My body ached all over. I felt little control over my arms and legs. This feeling went on every morning for days, until my muscles finally got used to the work.

It was Monday, the first week of November. The grape season was over and I could now go to school. I woke up early that morning and lay in bed, looking at the stars and **savoring** the thought of not going to work and of starting sixth grade for the first time that year. Since I could not sleep, I decided to get up and join Papá and Roberto at breakfast. I sat at the table across from Roberto, but I kept my head down. I did not want to look up and face him. I knew he was sad. He was not going to school today. He was not going tomorrow, or next week, or next month. He would not go until the cotton season was over, and that was sometime in February. I rubbed my hands together and watched the dry, acid-stained skin fall to the floor in little rolls.

6. Why do you think the narrator wasn't expected to pick cotton?

SE p. 150,
paragraphs 4–6

When Papá and Roberto left for work, I felt relief. I walked to the top of a small grade next to the shack and watched the *Carcachita* disappear in the distance in a cloud of dust.

Two hours later, around eight o'clock, I stood by the side of the road waiting for school bus number twenty. When it arrived I climbed in. No one noticed me. Everyone was busy either talking or yelling. I sat in an empty seat in the back.

page break

When the bus stopped in front of the school, I felt very nervous. I looked out the bus window and saw boys and girls carrying books under their arms. I felt empty. I put my hands in my pants pockets and | walked to the principal's office. When I entered, I heard a woman's voice say: "May I help you?" I was startled. I had not heard English for months. For a few seconds I remained speechless. I looked at the lady who waited for an answer. My first instinct was to answer her in Spanish, but I held back. Finally, after struggling for English words, I managed to tell her that I wanted to enroll in the sixth grade. After answering many questions, I was led to the classroom.

7. Why was the narrator struggling with his English?

SE p. 151,
paragraphs 1–2

Mr. Lema, the sixth grade teacher, greeted me and assigned me to a desk. He then **introduced** me to the class. I was so nervous and scared at that moment when everyone's eyes were on me that I wished I were with Papá and Roberto picking cotton. After taking roll, Mr. Lema gave the class the assignment for the first hour. "The first thing we have to do this morning is finish reading the story we began yesterday," he said **enthusiastically**. He walked up to me, handed me an English book, and asked me to read. "We are on page 125," he said politely. When I heard this, I felt my blood rush to my head; I felt dizzy. "Would you like to read?" he asked hesitantly. I opened the book to page 125. My mouth was dry. My eyes began to water. I could not begin. "You can read later," Mr. Lema said understandingly.

For the rest of the reading period, I kept getting angrier and angrier with myself. I should have read, I thought to myself.

8. Why was he disappointed with himself for not reading?

SE p. 151, paragraph 3

During recess, I went into the restroom and opened my English book to page 125. I began to read in a low voice, pretending I was in class. There were many words I did not know. I closed the book and headed back to the classroom.

SE p. 152, paragraphs 1–2

Mr. Lema was sitting at his desk correcting papers. When I entered he looked up at me and smiled. I felt better. I walked up to him and asked if he could help me with the new words. "Gladly," he said.

The rest of the month, I spent my lunch hours working on English with Mr. Lema, my best friend at school.

9. What did the narrator value more than making friends?

SE p. 152, paragraphs 3–6

One Friday during lunch hour, Mr. Lema asked me to take a walk with him to the music room. "Do you like music?" he asked me as we entered the building.

"Yes, I like Mexican *corridos*," I answered. He then picked up a trumpet, blew on it, and handed it to me. The sound gave me goose bumps. I knew that sound. I had heard it in many Mexican *corridos*. "How would you like to learn to play it?" he asked.

He must have read my face, because before I could answer, he added: "I'll teach you how to play it during our lunch hours."

That day I could hardly wait to get home to tell Papá and Mamá the great news. As I got off the bus, my little brothers and sisters ran up to meet me. They were yelling and screaming. I thought they were happy to see me, but when I opened the door to our shack, I saw that everything we owned was neatly packed in cardboard boxes.

10. Predict what will happen next.

For confirmation of engagement, take 30 seconds to have students share how they would have reacted if they were Panchito.

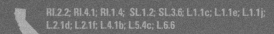

Lesson Opener

Before the lesson, choose one of the following activities to write on the board or post on the *LANGUAGE! Live* Class Wall online.

- *Describe a relationship you have had with a teacher. How did that teacher impact your life?*
- *All families have good and bad qualities. Write one sentence explaining something good about your family. Write one sentence explaining something bad about your family. Identify the adjectives and adverbs in each sentence.*
- *Write five questions you would ask your teacher if you were new to a school.*

Vocabulary

Objective
- Review key passage vocabulary.

Review Passage Vocabulary

Direct students to page 146 in their Student Books. Use the following questions to review the vocabulary words from "The Circuit." Have students answer each question using the vocabulary word or indicating its meaning in a complete sentence.

- When Panchito's mother *exchanges* words with Mr. Sullivan, what do they do? (When she and Mr. Sullivan exchange words, they talk.) Panchito's family picks grapes in the vineyard in *exchange* for what? (They pick grapes in exchange for money and a place to stay.)

- The garage where the family stays is *populated* by what? (The garage is populated by earthworms.) What types of regions or areas are *populated* by migrant farm workers? (Regions with many farms are populated by migrant farm workers.)

- What causes Panchito to drop to the ground and remain *motionless*? (Drinking water too fast causes him to feel ill, drop to the ground, and remain motionless.) Can farm workers remain *motionless* for long? Why or why not? (Farm workers cannot remain motionless for long because if they do not work, they will not be paid.)

- What kind of *drone* does Panchito hear as he lay on the ground? (He hears the drone of insects.) Would you expect to hear the *drone* of machines in this vineyard? Why or why not? (No, you would not expect to hear the drone of machines because if there were machines doing the work, humans would not have to.)

- Where does Roberto draw *designs*? (He draws designs in the dirt.) What kind of work might a person who draws *designs* be good at? (A person who draws designs might be good at art, fashion, or photography.)

- Panchito and his brother *instinctively* hide from the school bus. Is it likely the first time they have done so? Why or why not? (No; if they are hiding from the school bus instinctively, it has become a habit. They have hidden from many buses before.) After picking grapes for hours on end, do you think the workers can do so *instinctively*? Why or why not? (Yes, they can pick grapes instinctively because they have done it for so long that they don't have to think about it.)

- When Papá *murmurs* the amount they've earned, to whom is he mainly speaking? (When he murmurs the figure, he is speaking mainly to himself.) What does the *murmuring* tell you about Papá's feelings? (Because he is murmuring, you can guess that Papá is not happy with the number; he wishes it were larger.)

- Does Panchito *savor* the idea of going to school? Why or why not? (Yes, he savors the idea of going to school because he won't have to work in the vineyards.) What does he end up *savoring* at school itself? (He savors his language and music lessons with Mr. Lema.)

- When he *introduces* Panchito to the class, what does Mr. Lema probably say? (When he introduces Panchito, he probably says his name and welcomes him to the class.) Who *introduces* Panchito to the woman in the front office? (He has to introduce himself.)

- When Mr. Lema invites him to read aloud, does Panchito respond *enthusiastically*? Why or why not? (No, he does not respond enthusiastically; he is nervous and afraid to read aloud.) Later, when Panchito asks Mr. Lema for help, does the teacher respond *enthusiastically*? How so? (Yes, he responds enthusiastically; he is happy to help the boy with his reading.) When Panchito returns home, do you think he responds to what he sees *enthusiastically*? Why or why not? (No, it is unlikely that he would respond enthusiastically to the packed boxes because he loves school and does not want to move away.)

Objectives
- Identify verb tenses and use them to clarify meaning.
- Identify the function and purpose of linking verbs.
- Identify the function and purpose of helping verbs.

Tense Timeline: Past and Present Tense

Direct students to page 154 in their Student Books. Like nouns, verbs fall into different categories. Some verbs show action and other verbs just connect, or link, the subject of the sentence with the rest of the sentence. What are two categories for verbs? (action verbs, linking verbs) Verbs also work to signal time. We use verbs to talk about yesterday, today, and tomorrow. What do we call verbs that help us talk about yesterday? (past tense verbs) What do we call verbs that help us talk about today? (present tense verbs)

Look at the examples for present tense verbs:

- *I walk. She walks.*
- *We skip. He skips.*
- *They fade. It fades.*
- *We floss. He flosses.*
- *I carry. He carries.*
- *I write. She writes.*

Lesson 2	Grammar	
Tense Timeline: Past and Present Tenses		Answers will vary.

Read the examples of different types of verbs. Write examples in the past progressive and the present progressive for each pronoun usage (as done with *helping*).

Yesterday — Today — Tomorrow

Past Tense	Present Tense	Future
I walked. She walked. We skipped. He skipped. They faded. It faded. We flossed. He flossed. I carried. He carried. I wrote. She wrote.	I walk. She walks. We skip. He skips. They fade. It fades. We floss. He flosses. I carry. He carries. I write. She writes.	

Past Progressive	Present Progressive	Future
I was helping. You were helping. He was helping. We were helping. They were helping.	I am helping. You are helping. He is helping. We are helping. They are helping.	
It was fading. I was skipping. We were carrying.	It is fading. I am skipping. We are carrying.	
I was eating. You were eating. He was eating. We were eating. They were eating.	I am eating. You are eating. He is eating. We are eating. They are eating.	

154   Unit 4   © 2016 Voyager Sopris Learning, Inc. All rights reserved.

What do we add to *walk* in the present tense when the subject is third-person singular, like *she*? (-s) **Direct students to the word *flosses*. Explain the addition of -es when the word ends in -s, -z, -x, -ch, -tch, or -sh. Then, direct students to the word *carries* and explain that when a word ends in -y, we change the *y* to *i* and add -es.**

Look at the examples for past tense verbs:

- *I walked. She walked.*
- *We skipped. He skipped.*
- *They faded. It faded.*
- *We flossed. He flossed.*
- *I carried. He carried.*
- *She wrote. I wrote.*

What do we add to *walk* to talk about something that has already happened? (-ed)

Direct students to the word *skipped*. Tell students that, by rule, in a single-syllable word, we double an ending single consonant when it is preceded by a short vowel spelled with one letter, as in *skipped*. Direct students to the word *faded*. Explain that when a word ends in silent e, we drop the silent e and add -ed. Then, direct students to the word *carried* and explain that when a word ends in -y, we change the *y* to *i* and add -ed.

Direct students to the word *wrote*.

Remember, another way to categorize verbs is as regular or irregular verbs. *Write* is an example of an irregular verb. There's no pattern for how to make an irregular verb past tense. You just have to learn them.

Now, let's look at the bottom section of the chart.

Write the following sentences on the board.

> *He plays football.*
>
> *He is playing football.*
>
> *She writes for the newspaper.*
>
> *She is writing for the newspaper.*

Think about the difference in meaning between the verbs *plays* and *is playing* and *writes* and *is writing*.

When we want to talk about something that is happening right now, we use verb phrases like *is playing* or *is writing*. At this moment, I *am talking* and you *are listening*. The action is ongoing or progressing. How did we change the verb to show action that is happening right now? Look at the examples with the verb *help*.

Guide students through the examples, pointing out how the helping verb *be* changes as the subject changes from first person to second person to third person as well as from singular to plural. Point out the dropping of the -e in *fading*, the doubling of the -p in *skipping*, and the fact that the -y remains in *carrying*.

We add -ing to the verb and use a form of the verb *be* to describe action that is ongoing or progressing. What do we add to the verb? (-ing and a form of the verb *be*)

When the verb *be* is used as the main verb, it is a linking verb, as in this sentence: *I am restless*. We also use the verb *be* frequently as a helping verb. It helps verbs express time differently. When used alone, what kind of verb is *be*? (linking verb) When it is partnered with another verb, what kind of verb is it? (helping verb)

This new verb tense is called present progressive. The name should help you think about ongoing action or action that is progressing. What tense shows action that is ongoing or progressing? (present progressive) The trickiest thing about this tense is getting the helping verb right.

Have students generate a list of 5–10 different action verbs and write them on the board. Have partners choose a verb and complete the chart for present progressive. They will duplicate the progression of helping. Once students have finished, have volunteers read their examples of present progressive verbs.

We can also talk about an action that lasted or was ongoing in the past. Listen to this sentence: *They were playing football when it began to rain*. There is still the sense of ongoing action. It just happened in the past.

Read the examples of past progressive with me: *I was helping. You were helping. He was helping. We were helping. They were helping.* What changed to express something that has already happened? Did we use a different form of *help*? **(no)** Did we use a different form of the verb *be*? **(yes)** We use the helping verb *be* to show that the ongoing action has already happened. Work with your partner to change the present progressive verb you wrote in your charts to past progressive. **Once students have finished, have volunteers read their examples of past progressive verbs.**

There were many examples of different verb tenses in the text we read this week. **Direct students to page 155 in their Student Books and read the instructions.**

Model

Listen to the first example: *He was not going to school today.* Who is this sentence about? *He* is the answer to the *who* question. What did he do? *Was going* is the answer to the *did what* question. Although the word *not* impacts the meaning of the verb, it is not considered a part of the verb phrase, so I wouldn't underline it. The second step in the instructions is to determine the tense of the verb. Is it past, past progressive, present, or present progressive? *Was going* is the verb phrase. It is an ongoing action that happened in the past. The use of the verb *be* and -ing tells me it is past progressive. It belongs under past progressive in the chart.

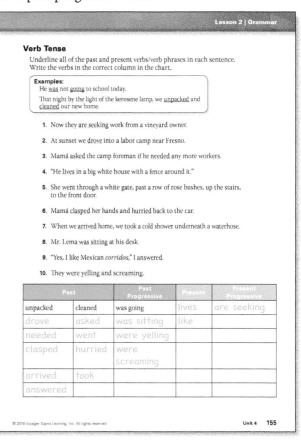

Listen as I read the second example: *That night by the light of the kerosene lamp, we unpacked and cleaned our new home.* Who or what is this sentence about? *We* is the answer to the *who* question. What did *we* do? *Unpacked* and *cleaned* answer the *did what* question, so I would underline both verbs. My second step is to determine the tense of the verbs, *unpacked* and *cleaned*. They both end with -ed, which signals the past tense. They belong under Past in the chart.

Guided Practice

Look at number one: *Now they are seeking work from a vineyard owner.* Who or what is the sentence about? **(they)** What are *they* doing? **(are seeking)** You should underline *are seeking.* What is the second step in our instructions? **(determine the verb tense and write it in the chart)** *Are seeking* is an action that is happening now and it is ongoing. What is the tense? **(present progressive)** Write it in the proper column in the chart.

Read the next sentence and guide students in underlining the verb or verb phrase and determining the tense.

Have students complete the activity. Review the answers as a class.

Linking Verb or Helping Verb

Verbs perform a variety of tasks in a sentence. Even the verb *be* can perform different jobs. It can function as a linking verb or as a helping verb. We just worked with progressive tense verbs that required a helping verb. It's important to constantly be aware of the verbs in sentences we read or write and determine how they are functioning.

Direct students to page 156 in their Student Books and read the instructions aloud.

Model

Listen to the first example: *Everyone was busy. Everyone* answers the *who* question. Now, I have to ask *what did they do?* As it turns out, they didn't do anything. In this sentence, I learn something about them. The verb *was* links the describing word *busy* to the subject, *everyone.* I underline *was* and write it in the chart under Linking Verb.

Listen to the next example: *We were hiding from the bus.* Again, I have to ask the *who* question. *We* answers the *who* question. What did *we* do? I see the verb *were*, but it's followed by *hiding.* I have an answer to the *did what* question. *Were hiding* answers the *did what* question. In this sentence, *were* is a helping verb. I underline *were hiding* and write it under the Helping Verb + Main Verb column.

Linking Verb or Helping Verb

Underline the verb or verb phrase in each sentence. Write the verb or verb phrase in the proper column in the chart.

Examples:
Everyone <u>was</u> busy.
We <u>were hiding</u> from the bus.

1. The grapes are ready for harvest.
2. I was planning to talk to my parents about my trumpet lessons.
3. It was after two o'clock.
4. I was reading to myself in the bathroom.
5. We are on page 125.
6. My mouth was dry.
7. I was so nervous and scared at that moment.
8. Boys and girls were carrying books under their arms.
9. Mr. Lema was sitting at his desk.
10. They were happy to see me.

Linking Verb	Helping Verb + Main Verb
was	were hiding
are	was planning
was	was reading
are	were carrying
was	was sitting
was	
were	

Guided Practice

Listen to the first sentence: *The grapes are ready for harvest.* What word answers the *who or what* question? **(grapes)** What do the grapes do? **(nothing)** The grapes are being described as *ready. Are* is functioning as a linking verb in this sentence. After you underline it, what should you do? **(write it in the chart under Linking Verb)**

Independent Practice

Have students complete the activity. Review the answers as a class.

Objectives

- Identify the subject and predicate of a sentence.
- Use adjectives and adverbs correctly in sentence writing.
- Produce, expand, and rearrange complete sentences for clarity and style.
- Refine word choice in sentences.

thesauruses or
online dictionaries

Masterpiece Sentences: Stage 5—Paint Your Words

Today, you're going to work through a new stage in masterpiece sentences. Like an artist who seeks to refine his or her work, stage 5 calls for you to refine your word choice. To get started with our sentences, we often choose common words. Once we have painted the predicate and subject, we can take a look at the words we have chosen. Upgrading, or choosing one or two more descriptive words, can really help to improve the sentence. A good place to start is the verb.

Write the following sentence on the board:

> *In the cool of the morning, the frisky colt ran across the lush meadow.*

Underline *ran*. Read the sentence aloud.

I'm happy with all of the words in this sentence except *ran*. That is such an overused and imprecise word. What other word could I use to paint the action more precisely? **Encourage students to brainstorm other words for *ran*.** (Possible responses: galloped, scampered, skipped, leapt, sprinted, trotted) When I'm having a hard time thinking of a better word, I use a thesaurus. It suggests other words and helps me upgrade my word choices. Dictionaries often provide a few synonyms, but a thesaurus will provide a nice long list of synonyms, related words, and antonyms, if there are any.

Direct students to page 157 in their Student Books and read the instructions. If possible, give students access to a thesaurus.

Guided Practice

Guide students in the replacement of the underlined words for the first two sentences.

Independent Practice

Have partners replace the underlined words and rewrite the remaining sentences. Have volunteers share their sentences and correct as needed.

Masterpiece Sentences: Stage 5—Paint Your Words

Rewrite the following sentences by replacing the underlined words with more descriptive words or phrases. Answers will vary.

1. After fixing the barn, the <u>tired man sat</u> in the chair on the porch.

   New sentence: After fixing the barn, the exhausted laborer slumped into the chair on the porch.

2. During lunch, the <u>nice</u> teacher <u>worked</u> with the new student.

   New sentence: During lunch, the determined teacher studied with the new student.

3. When we got there, Mamá <u>walked</u> up to the <u>house</u>.

   New sentence: When we got there, Mamá purposefully marched up to the enormous white castle.

4. <u>At sunset</u>, we <u>drove</u> into a labor camp near Fresno.

   New sentence: As night was falling, we chugged into a labor camp near Fresno.

5. After <u>lunch</u>, we <u>went</u> back to <u>work</u>.

   New sentence: After dining on my mom's best fare, we reluctantly trudged back to grape picking.

6. <u>When we arrived home</u>, we took a <u>cold</u> shower underneath a waterhose.

   New sentence: When our tired bodies finally made their way back to the garage, we took a bone-chilling shower underneath a waterhose.

7. My mouth was <u>dry</u>.

   New sentence: My mouth was as dry as a bone.

8. I <u>walked up to</u> him and <u>asked if he could help me</u> with the new words.

   New sentence: I tentatively approached him and begged him to assist me with the new words.

Masterpiece Sentences: Stages 1–5

Direct students to page 158 in their Student Books.

Now, I want you to write a sentence of your own, working through all five stages. Consider the images in your Student Book as you think about the text we read in the last lesson. Think about how you would prepare your canvas for each picture. Work with students to generate ideas for the simple subject and simple predicate of each picture. Write their ideas on the board. Spend a few minutes helping students get an idea of how to begin. (Possible responses: couple worked, people stood, the grapes were picked, worker picked, boxes sat, boxes were filled).

Choose one picture and work your way through the stages by completing the chart. Remember, your sentence is a work in progress. You have to get started before you can make improvements to it. Complete stage 1 in the writing process. Have students write their base sentence. Remind them that stage 1 can include the answer to the *to what* question, but sometimes that question cannot be answered. It depends on the verb they choose. Have volunteers share their base sentences. Make sure all students have completed stage 1 and then move to stage 2. Guide students through the process, calling on a few to share their ideas with each stage. When students get to stage 5, have them use their thesaurus if one is available. If not, have students work with their partner to brainstorm better words for their "upgrades." Have volunteers share their sentences once they have completed all five stages.

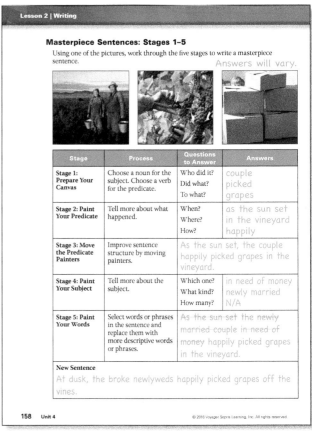

Subject and Predicate: Simple and Complete

Write the following sentence on the board without the underlines:

> <u>During the year,</u> the weary family with little to eat <u><u>moved from field to field to find work.</u></u>

Read the sentence aloud. Underline *family* once. Underline *moved* twice. Explain that this is the simple subject and the simple predicate.

I want to determine what the complete subject is. Are there any words in the sentence that "paint" the subject? What words describe the family? *The* answers the question *how many. Weary* describes the family, and *with little to eat* answers the *which one* question. I will underline the complete subject once. Now, what is the complete predicate? I know that *moved* is the verb. *During the year* tells me *when* they moved, *from field to field* tells me *where* they moved, and *to find work* tells me *why* they moved. This is all a part of the complete predicate, so I will underline it twice.

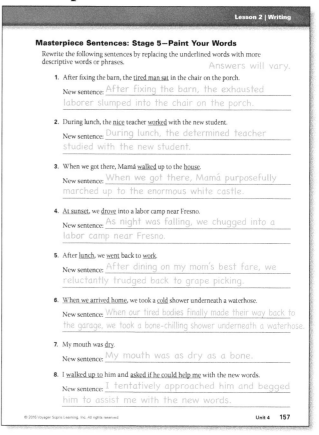

Direct students back to page 157 in their Student Books.

Look at the sentence you wrote for number 1. Underline the simple subject once and the simple predicate twice. **Have volunteers share their simple subjects and predicates.** Now, underline the complete subject once and the complete predicate twice. Look for your subject painters to help you find the complete subject and your predicate painters to help you find your complete predicate. **To ensure understanding, have volunteers share their complete subject and predicate.**

If time permits, have students repeat the process with the remaining sentences on the page.

Unit 4

Lesson 3

RL.3.6; RI.4.2; RI.6.1; RI.6.2; RI.8.2; RI.3.6; RI.5.7; RI.5.9;
RI.6.7; RI.3.10; RF.2.4a; RF.5.4a; W.5.9a; L.1.1j; L.3.4a; L.6.5a

Lesson Opener

Before the lesson, choose one of the following activities to write on the board or post on the *LANGUAGE! Live* Class Wall online.

- *What would you have done if you were Panchito and struggled to read because you didn't know the words?*
- *Describe a time when you asked for help. Who did you ask and what did you need help with?*
- *Write five sentences about the job of a teacher. Use helping verbs and the present progressive tense.*

Reading

Objectives

- Objectively summarize text.
- Identify multiple main ideas of a text.
- Determine the central idea of a text.
- Establish a purpose for rereading autobiographical text.
- Use critical thinking skills to write responses to prompts about text.
- Support written answers with text evidence.
- Explain how the values and beliefs of characters are affected by the historical and cultural setting.

Summarization

After reading text like "The Circuit," we often form opinions of the characters. For example, "Panchito's parents didn't value education." Sometimes, it is hard to keep those opinions from popping up when we talk or write about the text. When we summarize text, it is important to write an objective summary—one free from our own opinions.

Turn to your partner and summarize the text objectively. Then, switch.

Central Idea

It is important to identify the central idea of a text even if the author does not explicitly state it. A central idea is the main message the author is trying to convey and can be applied to life. It usually teaches a lesson. In *The Play of the Diary of Anne Frank*, the author wanted us to know about life in hiding during the Holocaust. The central idea was that Jewish families lost their freedom and self-worth trying to survive the Holocaust. Let's apply the concept of central idea to "The Circuit."

Generate a class discussion about four sections of the story. Have students tell you what the main idea of the story is before Panchito's family began working in the vineyard. Then, have them tell you the main idea of the story during the time Panchito and his family were picking grapes. Then, have them tell you the main idea of the story during Panchito's time at school. Finally, have them tell you the main idea of the story when Panchito returned home after being offered trumpet lessons.

Possible answers:

Pre-vineyard Work: Migrant farm workers move often to find work, often living in primitive accommodations.

Vineyard Work: Migrant farm workers work very hard at a young age for little pay.

Schooling: Schooling is difficult for migrant students because of poor attendance and lack of practice.

End of Season: Life for the families of migrant farm workers is constantly changing, making it difficult to form relationships, learn, and enjoy life.

Let's take those main ideas and determine the central idea of the whole text. Please know that, unlike a summary, your thoughts as they relate to the central idea are subjective, or based on your own feelings and ideas. That means that your thoughts are probably different from my thoughts or your classmates' thoughts. What is the central idea? **Have students share their ideas and write them on the board.** (Possible answers: Migrant workers have a difficult life. Migrant workers put money before education and fun. Because migrant workers follow the harvest, they live in poor accommodations, have limited schooling, and struggle to make ends meet. Education and learning should be coveted.)

Multiple central ideas are possible. Central ideas need be related to the text in a way that makes sense, but each of us may think the central idea is something different based on our experiences and how we interpret the text. Can there be more than one central idea? (yes) Central ideas are not explicitly stated word for word.

Reading for a Purpose: "The Circuit"

Sometimes, it is helpful to give yourself a purpose for reading. Our purpose for this read is to help us answer questions about the text. Let's read the questions about "The Circuit" to provide a purpose for rereading the text.

Direct students to page 159 in their Student Books. Have students read the prompts aloud with you.

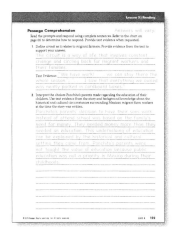

1. Define *circuit* as it relates to migrant farmers.

2. Interpret the choices Panchito's parents made regarding the education of their children. Use text evidence from the story and background knowledge about the historical and cultural circumstances surrounding Mexican migrant farm workers at the time the story was written.

3. Report the obstacles that migrant children faced when trying to get a good education.

4. Compare Panchito's point of view on education with your point of view on education.

5. Interpret the meaning of the quote "the mountains reached out and swallowed the sun."

6. Compare Panchito's point of view when he sees the packed boxes with Anne Frank's point of view when she learns they will be moving into the annex.

Now, it is time to reread the text.

Direct students to page 147 in their Student Books or have them tear out the extra copy of "The Circuit" from the back of their book.

> **Note:** To minimize flipping back and forth between the pages, a copy of each text has been included in the back of the Student Books. Encourage students to tear this out and use it when working on activities that require the use of the text.

Choose an option for reading text. Have students read the text according to the option that you chose.

Options for reading text:
- Teacher read-aloud
- Teacher-led or student-led choral read
- Paired read or independent read with bold vocabulary words read aloud

Remind students to pay special attention to text structure as it relates to time sequence. They should also be prepared to answer prompts after reading.

Passage Comprehension

We are going to check our comprehension of the passage by answering questions. Remember, questions appear in a variety of difficulty levels. Some are in the form of questions and some are in the form of prompts. Prompts are statements that require a constructed response, which can range from a list to a complete sentence to a paragraph or an essay.

Write the words *compare, define, interpret,* and *report* on the board. Have students read the words aloud with you.

Direct students to page 66 in their Student Books. It is critical to understand what the question is asking and how to answer it. Today, we will review four direction words used in prompts. You will become more familiar with these question words and learn how to respond.

Have students review the words on the board in the chart on page 66. Check for understanding by requesting an oral response to the following questions.

- If the prompt asks you to *compare*, the response requires you to . . . (state the similarities between two or more things).

- If the prompt asks you to *define*, the response requires you to . . . (tell or write the meaning or definition).

- If the prompt asks you to *interpret*, the response requires you to . . . (make sense of or assign meaning to something).

- If the prompt asks you to *report*, the response requires you to . . . (tell or write about the topic).

Direct students to pages 159 and 160 in their Student Books. Let's practice answering questions that are written as prompts that require critical thinking.

Model

Listen as I model the first one for you.

> 1. Define *circuit* as it relates to migrant farmers. Provide evidence from the text to support your answer.

How will we start our answer? According to the chart, if the prompt asks you to *define*, the response requires that you tell or write the meaning or definition.

Now, we need to turn the prompt into a question to confirm our understanding. For this prompt, we will ask ourselves basic questions using questions words like *what* and *how*. What does *circuit* mean? How does it relate to migrant farming?

One of the definitions of *circuit* in the dictionary is "a course or journey in a circle." Here is where the higher-level thinking comes in. We'll apply the definition of *circuit* and relate it to migrant workers. What are migrant workers? **(workers who travel from one area to another to find work to support their family)** I know that migrant farm workers move from area to area to pick crops based on the growing season. Therefore, I know that their life is based on a cycle. For instance, one season they pick strawberries, one season they pick grapes, one season they pick lettuce, and then maybe they pick oranges in the fourth season. I assume after the fourth season, they repeat the cycle—and return to the place they began.

My answer would be *The circuit is a way of life that involves constant change and circling back for migrant workers and their families.*

In order to be sure that my answer is plausible, I need to find text evidence. Work with your neighbor to see if our answer makes sense based on what we read. **Have volunteers share text evidence.** (Possible answers: "We have work! . . . we can stay there the whole season."; " . . . I saw that everything we owned was neatly packed in cardboard boxes.")

Passage Comprehension   Answers will vary.

Read the prompts and respond using complete sentences. Refer to the chart on page 66 to determine how to respond. Provide text evidence when requested.

1. Define *circuit* as it relates to migrant farmers. Provide evidence from the text to support your answer.

The circuit is a way of life that involves constant change and circling back for migrant workers and their families.

Text Evidence: "We have work! . . . we can stay there the whole season."; " . . . I saw that everything we owned was neatly packed in cardboard boxes."

2. Interpret the choices Panchito's parents made regarding the education of their children. Use text evidence from the story and background knowledge about the historical and cultural circumstances surrounding Mexican migrant farm workers at the time the story was written.

Panchito's parents' decision to have their sons work instead of attend school was based on the family's need for money. They needed money more than they needed an education. This undervaluing of education can be explained by the historical and cultural setting they came from. Panchito's parents were not taught the value of education because public education was not a priority in Mexico during their childhoods.

Unit 4   159

Guided Practice

2. Interpret the choices Panchito's parents made regarding the education of their children. Use text evidence from the story and background knowledge about the historical and cultural circumstances surrounding Mexican migrant farm workers at the time the story was written.

Students will need to have watched the Unit 4A Text Training video to answer this question.

Turn the prompt into a question to confirm your understanding. Tell your partner the question. (Why did Panchito's parents keep their sons from attending school to work in the field?)

In the video we watched during Lesson 1, we learned about Mexican immigration and the life of migrant farm workers. What was education in Mexico like in the early 1900s? (undervalued and difficult to come by)

Use this information to write your answer.

Write the following sentence frame on the board for students to work from.

Panchito's parents' decision to have their sons work instead of attend school was based on _____.

Have volunteers share their answers.

To be sure that your answer is plausible, you need to find text evidence. Work with your partner to find the evidence to support your answer. **Have volunteers share text evidence.**

You have just answered two questions that require critical thinking. The author wants his readers to understand the complications involved with the transient life, but also to understand where many of the thoughts and ideas of the time came from.

Independent Practice

Have students respond to the remaining questions. For students who need more assistance, provide the alternative questions and sentence starters.

Lesson 3 | Reading

Passage Comprehension (cont.)

3. Report the obstacles that migrant children faced when trying to get a good education.

A focus on earning money for the family, speaking a different language than what is used in school, and a transient lifestyle were obstacles keeping migrant children from getting a good education.

4. Compare Panchito's point of view on education with your point of view on education.

Answers will vary but should include Panchito's value and enthusiasm for education because it was a privilege rarely given to him.

5. Interpret the meaning of the quote "the mountains reached out and swallowed the sun."

"The mountains reached out and swallowed the sun" means that the sun was setting as night was falling and cooling the fields.

6. Compare Panchito's point of view when he saw the packed boxes with Anne Frank's point of view when she learned they would be moving into the annex.

Both Anne Frank and Panchito were sad and disappointed to leave their homes, but they knew that moving was necessary for the good of the family, so they did not complain.

160   Unit 4   © 2016 Voyager Sopris Learning, Inc. All rights reserved.

Alternative questions and sentence starters:

3. What kept migrant children from getting a good education?

   _____, _____, and _____ *were obstacles keeping migrant children from getting a good education.*

4. How is Panchito's point of view on education similar to your point of view on education.

   Panchito and I both _____

   _____.

5. What does the quote "the mountains reached out and swallowed the sun" mean?

   "The mountains reached out and swallowed the sun" means _____.

6. How was Panchito's point of view when he saw the packed boxes similar to Anne Frank's point of view when she learned they would be moving into the annex?

   Both Anne Frank and Panchito _____.

Lesson 4

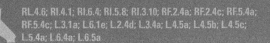
RL.4.6; RI.4.1; RI.6.4; RI.5.8; RI.3.10; RF.2.4a; RF.2.4c; RF.5.4a;
RF.5.4c; L.3.1a; L.6.1e; L.2.4d; L.3.4a; L.4.5a; L.4.5b; L.4.5c;
L.5.4a; L.6.4a; L.6.5a

Lesson Opener

Before the lesson, choose one of the following activities to write on the board or post on the *LANGUAGE! Live* Class Wall online.

- *Dress your avatar as though you were attending a new school for the first time. Explain your choices.*
- *Use linking verbs to write five sentences about why attending school is better than working in the heat.*
- *Make a list of adjectives describing Panchito. Make another list of adjectives describing Mr. Lema.*

Reading

Objectives

- Read autobiographical text with purpose and understanding.
- Answer questions to demonstrate comprehension of text.
- Identify and explain explicit details from text.
- Monitor comprehension of text during reading.
- Determine the meaning of idioms in text.
- Identify the use of personification in text.
- Identify first-person literary point of view.
- Determine the meaning of foreign words used in literature.
- Make inferences regarding the feelings and actions of characters in a story.

Close Reading of "The Circuit"

Let's reread "The Circuit." I will provide specific instructions on how to mark the text that will help with comprehension.

Have students get out a highlighter or colored pencil.

Direct students to pages 161–165 in their Student Books.

Draw a rectangle around the title "The Circuit."

Circle the paragraph that serves as an introduction. (italicized section)

Now, let's read the vocabulary words aloud.

- What's the first bold vocabulary word? (exchanged) *Exchanged* means "traded; gave one thing for another." Migrant workers *exchange* stability for money. Have partners use the word in a sentence.

- What's the next vocabulary word? (populated) *Populated* means "lived in; filled with." The bus was *populated* with well-dressed children. Have partners use the word in a sentence.

- Next word? (motionless) *Motionless* means "still; not moving." The brothers sat *motionless*, hoping the bus driver would not see them. Have partners use the word in a sentence.

- Let's continue. (drone) *Drone* means "a low, humming noise." Panchito could hear the *drone* of the bus engine in the distance. Have partners use the word in a sentence.

Highlighters or
colored pencils

- Next word? (designs) *Designs* means "patterns or drawings." The juice of the grapes made *designs* on the hands of the pickers. **Have partners use the word in a sentence.**

- Let's continue. (instinctively) *Instinctively* means "without thinking; in a natural or automatic way." Panchito and his family *instinctively* spoke in Spanish. **Have partners use the word in a sentence.**

- Next word? (murmured) *Murmured* means "spoke softly." To avoid reading aloud, Panchito *murmured* to himself. **Have partners use the word in a sentence.**

- Let's continue. (savoring) *Savoring* means "enjoying something deeply." Panchito was *savoring* the coolness of the evenings after picking grapes in the hot sun all day. **Have partners use the word in a sentence.**

- Next word? (introduced) *Introduced* means "presented one person to another person or to a group." Though it had happened many times in his life, Panchito didn't like being *introduced* to his new class. **Have partners use the word in a sentence.**

- Last word. (enthusiastically) *Enthusiastically* means "with great energy and excitement." The migrant child read *enthusiastically* before and after lunch. **Have partners use the word in a sentence.**

Talk with a partner about any vocabulary word that is still confusing for you to read consistently or to understand its meaning.

You will read "The Circuit" a section at a time. After each section, you will monitor your understanding by circling the check mark if you understand the text or the question mark if you don't understand the text. I also want you to draw a question mark over any confusing words, phrases, or sentences.

Options for reading text:
- Teacher read-aloud
- Teacher-led or student-led choral read
- Paired read or independent read with bold vocabulary words read aloud

---

Choose an option for reading text. Have students read lines 1–27 according to the option that you chose. Pay attention to the narrator's thoughts and feelings. If he is feeling happy, draw a happy face in the margin. If he is feeling scared, disappointed, sad, lonely, or frustrated, draw a sad face in the margin. If his feelings are neutral or unknown, draw a face without a mouth in the margin.

When most of the students are finished, continue with the entire class. Let's see how well you understood what you read.

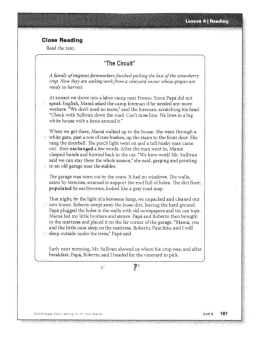

- Circle the check mark or the question mark for this section. Draw a question mark over any confusing words.

- Go to line 1. Mark the crop they picked in the summer. (**strawberry**) Write the season in the margin. (**summer**)

- On line 2, mark the crop they will pick in the fall. (**grapes**) Write the season in the margin. (**fall**)

- On the same line, mark the word that means "plantation of grapevines." (**vineyard**)

- Mark why Mamá does the talking. (**Papá did not speak English.**) Write the language they speak in the margin. (**Spanish**)

- Go to line 6. Edit the dialogue using standard English. (**Change** *no* **to** *any*.)

- On the same line, mark the synonym for *supervisor.* (**foreman**)

- On the same line, mark the body language that sometimes indicates thinking. (**scratching his head**)

- Go to line 11. Mark the synonym for *hefty.* (**husky**)

- Go to line 12. Circle *the man.* Draw an arrow to the proper noun that names the man. (**Mr. Sullivan**)

- Go to line 13. Mark the body language that sometimes indicates relief or gratefulness. (**clasped hands**)

- Number three reasons that Mamá is happy. (**1. work; 2. we can stay here the whole season; 3. old garage**)

- Go to line 17. Mark the insects that feed on wood. (**termites**)

- Go to line 18. Mark the creature that helps soil. (**earthworm**)

- Go to line 20. Mark the older brother's name with BRO. (**Roberto**)

- Go to line 24. Circle the pronoun *I.* Draw an arrow to the noun that it refers to. (**Papá**)

- In the margin, draw a quick picture of where everyone will sleep. (**drawing should show Mamá with children inside garage on mattress; Papá and two sons outside under a tree on the ground**)

- Go to line 27. Circle the pronoun *I.* Draw an arrow to the noun in the preceding paragraph that it refers to. (**Panchito**)

Have students read lines 28–58 according to the option that you chose. As you read, draw faces to document the author's feelings.

When most of the students are finished, continue with the entire class. Let's see how well you understood what you read.

- Circle the check mark or the question mark for this section. Draw a question mark over any confusing words.

- Go to line 28. Mark the temperature. (one hundred) Draw a clock to show when the temperature hit 100 degrees. (9:00 a.m.)

- Mark the figurative language that means "my mouth was dry." (my mouth felt as if I had been chewing on a handkerchief)

- Mark the proof that Roberto was used to hard work in the hot sun. (Don't drink too much; you'll get sick.)

- Go to line 34. Mark the idiom used when your eyes are fixed on something that you are watching. (eyes glued)

- Go to line 36. Mark the synonym for *improve*. (recover)

- Go to line 42. Mark the indication that signals fear or anxiety. (turn pale)

- Go to line 43. Mark the synonym for *panic*. (alarm)

- On the same line, mark the adverb that provides evidence that they have hidden from the bus in the past. (instinctively)

- Go to line 44. Circle the pronoun *I*. Who is narrating the story? Write his name in the margin. (Panchito)

- Go to line 48. Find the italicized words. Predict the meaning of the Spanish term based on context and write it in the margin. (You have to be careful.)

- Personification is an example of figurative language used to give a nonhuman object a human quality. Go to line 50. Mark the example of personification. (sun kept beating down) **Have a volunteer share what this means.**

- Go to lines 52 and 53. Mark the example of personification. (the mountains around the valley reached out and swallowed the sun)

- Go to line 58. Write the dollar amount that they earned in one day in the margin. Have a neighbor help you with the Spanish if necessary. ($15)

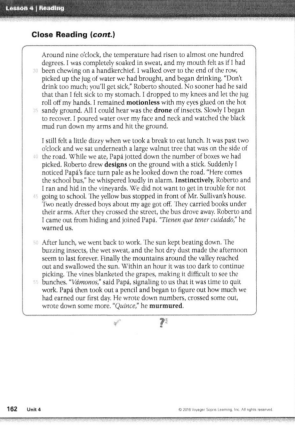

Close Reading (cont.)

Around nine o'clock, the temperature had risen to almost one hundred degrees. I was completely soaked in sweat, and my mouth felt as if I had
30 been chewing on a handkerchief. I walked over to the end of the row, picked up the jug of water we had brought, and began drinking. "Don't drink too much; you'll get sick," Roberto shouted. No sooner had he said that than I felt sick to my stomach. I dropped to my knees and let the jug roll off my hands. I remained **motionless** with my eyes glued on the hot
35 sandy ground. All I could hear was the **drone** of insects. Slowly I began to recover. I poured water over my face and neck and watched the black mud run down my arms and hit the ground.

I still felt a little dizzy when we took a break to eat lunch. It was past two o'clock and we sat underneath a large walnut tree that was on the side of
40 the road. While we ate, Papá jotted down the number of boxes we had picked. Roberto drew **designs** on the ground with a stick. Suddenly I noticed Papá's face turn pale as he looked down the road. "Here comes the school bus," he whispered loudly in alarm. **Instinctively**, Roberto and I ran and hid in the vineyards. We did not want to get in trouble for not
45 going to school. The yellow bus stopped in front of Mr. Sullivan's house. Two neatly dressed boys about my age got off. They carried books under their arms. After they crossed the street, the bus drove away. Roberto and I came out from hiding and joined Papá. "*Tienen que tener cuidado*," he warned us.

50 After lunch, we went back to work. The sun kept beating down. The buzzing insects, the wet sweat, and the hot dry dust made the afternoon seem to last forever. Finally the mountains around the valley reached out and swallowed the sun. Within an hour it was too dark to continue picking. The vines blanketed the grapes, making it difficult to see the
55 bunches. "*Vámonos*," said Papá, signaling to us that it was time to quit work. Papá then took out a pencil and began to figure out how much we had earned our first day. He wrote down numbers, crossed some out, wrote down some more. "*Quince*," he **murmured**.

162   Unit 4

Have students read lines 59–93 according to the option that you chose. As you read, draw faces to document the author's feelings.

When most of the students are finished, continue with the entire class. Let's see how well you understood what you read.

- Circle the check mark or the question mark for this section. Draw a question mark over any confusing words.

- Go to line 59. Mark the compound word whose parts define the word. (waterhose)

- Go to line 62. Find the italicized words. Predict the meaning of the Spanish term based on context and write it in the margin. (mixture of meat and spicy red peppers)

- In the second paragraph, number the phrases or sentences that describe "this feeling." (1. I could hardly move. 2. body ached all over 3. little control over my arms and legs)

- Go to line 66. Mark the reason Panchito could go to school. (grape season was over)

- Mark Panchito's grade in school. (sixth grade)

- Mark who was sad. (Roberto) Mark why he was sad. (He was not going to school today.)

- Go to line 74. Mark the crop Roberto will pick instead of going to school and write the season in the margin. (cotton; winter)

- Go to line 78. Find the italicized word. Predict the meaning of the Spanish term based on context and write it in the margin. (little, old car)

- Go to line 88. Mark the synonym for *alarmed.* (startled)

- Go to line 90. Mark the word that means "natural response." (instinct)

- Go to line 91. Mark the word that means "was able to." (managed)

Close Reading (*cont.*)

When we arrived home, we took a cold shower underneath a waterhose. We then sat down to eat dinner around some wooden crates that served as a table. Mamá had cooked a special meal for us. We had rice and tortillas with *"carne con chile,"* my favorite dish.

The next morning, I could hardly move. My body ached all over. I felt little control over my arms and legs. This feeling went on every morning for days, until my muscles finally got used to the work.

It was Monday, the first week of November. The grape season was over and I could now go to school. I woke up early that morning and lay in bed, looking at the stars and **savoring** the thought of not going to work and of starting sixth grade for the first time that year. Since I could not sleep, I decided to get up and join Papá and Roberto at breakfast. I sat at the table across from Roberto, but I kept my head down. I did not want to look up and face him. I knew he was sad. He was not going to school today. He was not going tomorrow, or next week, or next month. He would not go until the cotton season was over, and that was sometime in February. I rubbed my hands together and watched the dry, acid-stained skin fall to the floor in little rolls.

When Papá and Roberto left for work, I felt relief. I walked to the top of a small grade next to the shack and watched the *Carcachita* disappear in the distance in a cloud of dust.

Two hours later, around eight o'clock, I stood by the side of the road waiting for school bus number twenty. When it arrived I climbed in. No one noticed me. Everyone was busy either talking or yelling. I sat in an empty seat in the back.

When the bus stopped in front of the school, I felt very nervous. I looked out the bus window and saw boys and girls carrying books under their arms. I felt empty. I put my hands in my pants pockets and walked to the principal's office. When I entered, I heard a woman's voice say: "May I help you?" I was startled. I had not heard English for months. For a few seconds I remained speechless. I looked at the lady who waited for an answer. My first instinct was to answer her in Spanish, but I held back. Finally, after struggling for English words, I managed to tell her that I wanted to enroll in the sixth grade. After answering many questions, I was led to the classroom.

Unit 4 **163**

Have students read lines 94–114 according to the option that you chose. As you read, draw faces to document the author's feelings.

When most of the students are finished, continue with the entire class. Let's see how well you understood what you read.

- Circle the check mark or the question mark for this section. Draw a question mark over any confusing words.

- Go to line 96. Mark the reason Panchito was nervous and scared. **(everyone's eyes were on me)**

- Go to line 97. Mark the word that means "attendance." **(roll)**

- Go to line 103. Mark the word that means "cautiously." **(hesitantly)**

- Mark the proof that Panchito was gripped by fear. **(mouth was dry; eyes began to water; could not begin)** Write the adjective to describe a person gripped by fear in the margin. **(afraid/terrified)**

- Mark why Panchito was angry. **(I should have read.)**

- Go to lines 109 and 110. Mark the effect of speaking Spanish at home and missing months of school. **(There were many words I did not know.)**

- Go to line 113. Mark the evidence that suggests that Mr. Lema is a caring teacher. **(looked up at me and smiled)**

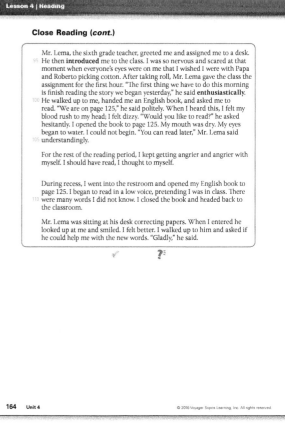

Lesson 4 | Reading

Close Reading (*cont.*)

Mr. Lema, the sixth grade teacher, greeted me and assigned me to a desk. He then **introduced** me to the class. I was so nervous and scared at that moment when everyone's eyes were on me that I wished I were with Papa and Roberto picking cotton. After taking roll, Mr. Lema gave the class the assignment for the first hour. "The first thing we have to do this morning is finish reading the story we began yesterday," he said **enthusiastically**. He walked up to me, handed me an English book, and asked me to read. "We are on page 125," he said politely. When I heard this, I felt my blood rush to my head; I felt dizzy. "Would you like to read?" he asked hesitantly. I opened the book to page 125. My mouth was dry. My eyes began to water. I could not begin. "You can read later," Mr. Lema said understandingly.

For the rest of the reading period, I kept getting angrier and angrier with myself. I should have read, I thought to myself.

During recess, I went into the restroom and opened my English book to page 125. I began to read in a low voice, pretending I was in class. There were many words I did not know. I closed the book and headed back to the classroom.

Mr. Lema was sitting at his desk correcting papers. When I entered he looked up at me and smiled. I felt better. I walked up to him and asked if he could help me with the new words. "Gladly," he said.

Have students read from line 115 to the end according to the option that you chose. As you read, draw faces to document the author's feelings.

When most of the students are finished, continue with the entire class. Let's see how well you understood what you read.

- Circle the check mark or the question mark for this section. Draw a question mark over any confusing words.

- Mark the way Panchito spent his lunch hours for the first month of school. (working on English with Mr. Lema)

- Go to line 121. Mark evidence that Panchito is excited. (goose bumps)

- Go to line 124. Mark how Mr. Lema knew Panchito wanted to learn to play the trumpet. (read my face) Write Panchito's emotion in the margin. (excitement)

- Go to line 125. Circle the pronoun *it*. Write what *it* refers to in the margin. (trumpet)

- Go to line 129. Mark the substitution for *garage*. (shack)

- Mark the evidence that the family would be moving to find another crop to pick. (everything we owned was neatly packed in cardboard boxes) Write the feeling Panchito must have felt in the margin. (disappointment)

Have partners compare text markings and correct any errors.

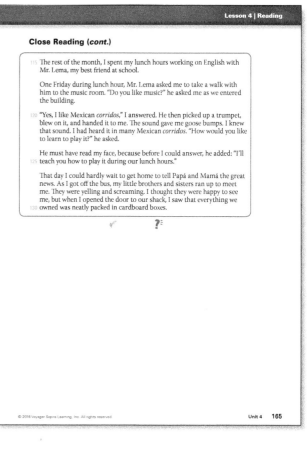

Close Reading (*cont.*)

115 The rest of the month, I spent my lunch hours working on English with Mr. Lema, my best friend at school.

One Friday during lunch hour, Mr. Lema asked me to take a walk with him to the music room. "Do you like music?" he asked me as we entered the building.

120 "Yes, I like Mexican *corridos*," I answered. He then picked up a trumpet, blew on it, and handed it to me. The sound gave me goose bumps. I knew that sound. I had heard it in many Mexican *corridos*. "How would you like to learn to play it?" he asked.

He must have read my face, because before I could answer, he added: "I'll 125 teach you how to play it during our lunch hours."

That day I could hardly wait to get home to tell Papá and Mamá the great news. As I got off the bus, my little brothers and sisters ran up to meet me. They were yelling and screaming. I thought they were happy to see me, but when I opened the door to our shack, I saw that everything we 130 owned was neatly packed in cardboard boxes.

Unit 4   165

Lesson Opener

Before the lesson, choose one of the following activities to write on the board or post on the *LANGUAGE! Live* Class Wall online.

- *Write four sentences with at least two vocabulary words in each. Show you know the meanings. (exchange, populated, motionless, drone, design, instinctively, murmur, savor, introduce, enthusiastically)*
- *Write three sentences that describe Panchito's family's work. Answer the following questions in your sentences: When do they work? Where do they work? How do they work? Combine the three sentences into one Masterpiece Sentence.*
- *What would you have done if you were Panchito and wanted to return to school but discovered you were moving?*

Vocabulary

Objective
- Review key passage vocabulary.

Recontextualize Passage Vocabulary

Direct students to page 146 in their Student Books. Use the following questions to review the vocabulary words in the excerpt of "The Circuit."

- Could you *instinctively* recite a hundred-line poem? **(no)** If someone throws something at you, do you *instinctively* duck? **(yes)** If you tie your shoes without thinking about it, how are you tying them? **(instinctively)**

- Would a person *murmur* a secret to another person in a crowded room? **(yes)** You are a fire chief. Would you *murmur* an order to another firefighter in an emergency situation? **(no)** If I ask you a question, and you mumble a response, what are you doing? **(murmuring)**

- Are frozen regions of the planet heavily *populated*? **(no)** Is your neighborhood *populated*? **(yes)** What would you call an apartment building with no vacancies? **(fully populated)**

- Is a roller coaster *motionless*? **(no)** Is a basketball player making a layup *motionless*? **(no)** If you freeze during a scary scene in a movie, what are you? **(motionless)**

- If you want a friend to meet your parent, would you *introduce* them? **(yes)** When you *introduce* two people, do you keep them from knowing each other? **(no)** If I tell a new student your name, what am I doing? **(introducing me)**

- Can the *drone* of a car engine put someone to sleep? **(yes)** Does an explosion make a *droning* sound? **(no)** If you are hearing the ongoing sound of a distant tractor, what are you hearing? **(the drone of the tractor)**

- Is a curlicue a *design*? (yes) If you paint a large Japanese dragon on your wall, what have you painted there? (a design)

- Would you *exchange* sandwiches with a friend if you liked hers but didn't like yours? (yes) Would you *exchange* a new phone for an old one that didn't work? (no) What might you do to stay in touch if a friend moved far away? (exchange letters, e-mails)

- Would an athlete receive a Most Valuable Player award *enthusiastically*? (yes) Do most students go to detention *enthusiastically*? (no) You won $500 in a contest. How do you respond when you hear the news? (enthusiastically)

- You take a bite of a food you hate. Do you *savor* it? (no) Do hardworking people *savor* vacation? (yes) Your favorite band rarely makes new music. When they put out a new song, what do you do? (savor it)

Writing

Objectives
- Use text to write coherent paragraphs in response to reading.
- Make inferences to determine a character's feelings.

Quick Write in Response to Reading

Direct students to page 166 in their Student Books and read the instructions aloud. You will write a journal entry from Panchito's point of view the night his teacher introduced him to the trumpet.

In Unit 3, we read about Anne Frank's diary. A journal is like a diary. Think about some things that Anne wrote in her diary. She shared her feelings and private thoughts that she wasn't always willing to say out loud.

How do you think you would feel if you were Panchito and you came home and saw the boxes? Think about how he would write about the day at school and what he found when he got home. His day certainly had its high points and its low points. Introduce the topic of your journal entry with a sentence that captures both your excitement and your disappointment. Use precise language and word choice, like you did in our Masterpiece Sentences. Underline any vocabulary words you include from page 146.

If students need guidance, use the sample journal entry as a guide.

Note: The example response has been broken into paragraphs. Paragraphing is desirable, and you may encourage your students to write in that manner. However, if your students aren't able to do it, it will be taught in later units.

Reading

Objectives
- Self-correct as comprehension of text deepens.
- Answer questions to demonstrate comprehension of text.
- Engage in class discussion.
- Identify the enduring understandings from a piece of text.

Revisit Passage Comprehension

Direct students back to pages 159 and 160 in their Student Books. Have students review their answers and make any necessary changes. Then, have partners share their answers and collaborate to perfect them.

Enduring Understandings

Direct students back to page 145 in their Student Books. Reread the Big Idea questions.

Is the American Dream a possibility for everyone? Explain.

What are the negative effects of a transient lifestyle?

Generate a class discussion about the questions and the answers students came up with in Lesson 1. Have them consider whether their answers have changed any after reading the text.

Use the following talking points to foster conversation. Refer to the Class Discussion Rules poster and have students use the Collegial Discussion sentence frames on page 382 of their Student Books.

- "Education, like the mass of our age's inventions, is after all, only a tool; everything depends upon the workman who uses it." This quote was written more than 100 years ago in an article called "The Simple Life." Is the same true for achieving the American Dream?

- Most people have the same goal in mind: happiness. However, the paths people take in this pursuit are widely varying. An old adage says that before you judge a man, you must walk a mile in his shoes. Would doing so change our perspective and the way we treat others?

What we read should make us think. Use our discussion and your thoughts about the text to determine what you will "walk away with." Has it made you think about a personal experience or someone you know? Has your perspective or opinion on a specific topic changed? Do you have any lingering thoughts or questions? Write these ideas as your enduring understandings. What will you take with you from this text?

Discuss the enduring understandings with the class. Then, have students write their enduring understandings from the unit. If time permits, have them post a personal response to one of the enduring understandings to the online class wall.

Remind students to consider why the author wrote the passage and whether he was successful.

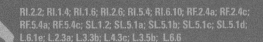

RI.2.2; RI.1.4; RI.1.6; RI.2.6; RI.5.4; RI.6.10; RF.2.4a; RF.2.4c;
RF.5.4a; RF.5.4c; SL.1.2; SL.5.1a; SL.5.1b; SL.5.1c; SL.5.1d;
L.6.1e; L.2.3a; L.3.3b; L.4.3c; L.3.5b; L.6.6

Lesson Opener

Before the lesson, choose one of the following activities to write on the board or post on the *LANGUAGE! Live* Class Wall online.

- *Imagine you are Panchito and wanted Mr. Lema to know how much he meant to you. What would you do?*
- *Describe a time when you felt like you weren't smart. What did you do about it?*
- *Write three sentences to describe Panchito's thoughts about school. Use adjectives, adverbs, and prepositional phrases in your sentences.*

Reading

Objectives

- Determine and discuss the topic of a text.
- Determine and discuss the author's purpose.
- Use text features to preview text.

Passage Introduction

Direct students to page 167 in their Student Books. Discuss the content focus for the unit.

Content Focus

enlightenment; the power of literacy

Enlightenment is education or awareness that brings change. We are about to read an excerpt from a famous autobiography about Malcolm X. Malcolm X is a well-known African American Civil Rights activist who spoke out for racial pride and justice in the 1950s and 1960s. Before becoming an activist, he was enlightened about education and the power of literacy. This means that Malcolm X increased his awareness about education and subsequently changed his path in life.

Type of Text

informational—autobiography

Informational text is divided into categories or genres. Say *genres.*
(genres)

We just finished reading "The Circuit." The author wrote about himself through short stories. What is the genre of writing? (autobiography)

We are about to read an excerpt from *The Autobiography of Malcolm X.* A journalist, Alex Haley, wrote it after interviewing Malcolm X over a period of several years.

Lesson 6 | Reading

Let's Focus: Excerpt from *The Autobiography of Malcolm X*

Content Focus	Type of Text
enlightenment; the power of literacy	informational—autobiography

Authors' Names   Malcolm X; Alex Haley

Authors' Purposes   self-expression; to teach others

Big Ideas
Consider the following quote and Big Idea questions. Write your answer for each question.

"Education is the passport to the future, for tomorrow belongs to those who prepare for it today."—Malcolm X

Is education the passport to the future? Explain.

_____

_____

Is code-switching necessary? Explain.

_____

_____

Autobiography Preview Checklist: the excerpt from *The Autobiography of Malcolm X* on pages 169–173.

- ☐ Title: What clue does it provide?
- ☐ Pictures: What additional information is added here?
- ☐ Margin Information: What vocabulary is important to understand this story?
- ☐ Features: What other text features do you notice?

Enduring Understandings
After reading the text . . .

_____

_____

_____

_____

Unit 4   **167**

He turned these interviews into an autobiography written in first person. This is considered an autobiography by most because Malcolm X edited and approved every chapter.

Author's Purpose

Who are the authors of the autobiography? (Malcolm X and Alex Haley) The author's purpose is the reason that he or she wrote the text. Authors write for different purposes. Unlike Anne Frank, who did not initially intend to have her diary published, Malcolm X wanted to tell his story to teach others about injustices and instill in them a sense of racial pride. Once he developed trust with Alex Haley, he shared his life story through a series of more than 50 interviews in two years' time.

Have students write the answers on the page.

Play the Unit 4 Text Training video, Part B found in the Teacher Resources online.

Before we read the excerpt from *The Autobiography of Malcolm X*, we will watch a short video to help build our background knowledge. **Play the Unit 4 Text Training video, Part B. Have partners discuss the main points the videographer was trying to make and what evidence was provided to support the points.**

Note: Additional Background Information regarding the Civil Rights Movement and race relations during Malcolm X's life can be found in the Teacher Resources online. Choose the Text Training tab, and then select Unit 4. The Background Information will be in the first section.

Direct students to page 167 in their Student Books. Read the quote and Big Idea questions aloud.

Big Ideas

"Education is the passport to the future, for tomorrow belongs to those who prepare for it today."

— Malcolm X

Is education the passport to the future? Explain.

Is code-switching necessary? Explain.

Offer a definition and example of code-switching.

Definition:

Code switching is the moving between variations of languages in different contexts.

Example:

In dialect, you might say "Take that sandwich out the bag." In standard English, you would say, "Take the sandwich out of the bag."

As a class, consider the two Big Idea questions.

- Encourage students with limited knowledge of the impact of an education and situations in which code-switching might occur to ask for further explanation from peers.

- Have students reflect on the Background Information for the unit and ask clarifying questions when needed.

- Provide opportunities for students to explain their ideas and answers to the Big Idea questions in light of the discussion by ensuring students follow the rules for class discussion, which can be printed in poster form from the Teacher Resources online.

- Suggest students refer to the Collegial Discussion sentence frames in the back of their books.

- Encourage speakers to link comments to the remarks of others to keep the focus of the discussion and create cohesion, even when their comments are in disagreement.

After discussing each question, have students write an answer. We'll come back to these questions after we finish reading the excerpt. You can add to your answers as you gain information and perspective.

Preview

Read the Autobiography Preview Checklist on page 167. Follow the Preview Procedure outlined below.

> ### Preview Procedure
> - Group students with partners or in triads.
> - Have students count off as 1s or 2s. The 1s will become the student leaders. If working with triads, the third students become 3s.
> - The student leaders will preview the text in addition to managing the checklist and pacing.
> - The 2s and 3s will preview the text with 1s.
> - Direct 1s to open their Student Books to page 167 and 2s and 3s to open their Student Books to page 169. This allows students to look at a few different pages at one time without turning back and forth.

If it is necessary, guide students in a short preview using the following talking points. What is the title of the text? (*The Autobiography of Malcolm X*) Describe the photograph on the title page. (a well-dressed Malcolm X speaking into a microphone) Where is Malcolm's second picture taken? (in jail) What is that type of picture called? (a mug shot) What do you see behind the text? (dictionary pages, jail bars)

Objectives

- Evaluate word knowledge.
- Determine the meaning of key passage vocabulary.

Rate Vocabulary Knowledge

Direct students to page 168 in their Student Books. We are about to read an excerpt from a book titled *The Autobiography of Malcolm X.* Before we read, let's take a look at the vocabulary words that appear in this text. Remind students that as you read each word in the first column aloud, they will write the word in the third column and then rate their knowledge of it in the fourth. Display the Vocabulary Rating Scale poster or write the information on the board. Review the meaning of each rating.

Vocabulary Rating Scale

0—I have never heard the word before.

1—I have heard the word, but I'm not sure how to use it.

2—I am familiar with the word, but I'm not sure if I know the correct meaning.

3—I know the meaning of the word and can use it correctly in a sentence.

Key Passage Vocabulary: Excerpt from *The Autobiography of Malcolm X*

Read each word. Write it in column 3. Then, circle a number to rate your knowledge of the word.

Vocabulary	Part of Speech	Write the Word	Rate the Word
acquire	(v)	acquire	0 1 2 3
functional	(adj)	functional	0 1 2 3
envy	(n)	envy	0 1 2 3
eventually	(adv)	eventually	0 1 2 3
inevitable	(adj)	inevitable	0 1 2 3
correspondence	(n)	correspondence	0 1 2 3
debate	(n)	debate	0 1 2 3
emphasis	(n)	emphasis	0 1 2 3
isolation	(n)	isolation	0 1 2 3
adjust	(v)	adjust	0 1 2 3

The points are not a grade; they are just there to help you know which words you need to focus on. By the end of this unit, you should be able to change all your ratings to a 3. That's the goal.

Read each word aloud. Have students repeat it, write it, and rate it. Then, have volunteers who rated a word *2* or *3* use the word in an oral sentence.

Preteach Vocabulary

Let's take a closer look at the words. Follow the Preteach Procedure below.

> ## Preteach Procedure
> This activity is intended to take only a short amount of time, so make it an oral exercise.
> - Introduce each word as indicated on the word card.
> - Read the definition and example sentences.
> - Ask questions to clarify and deepen understanding.
> - If time permits, allow students to share.
>
> * If your students would benefit from copying the definitions, please have them do so in the vocabulary log in the back of the Student Books using the margin definitions in the passage selections. This should be done outside of instruction time.

acquire (v)

Let's read the first word together. *Acquire.*

Definition: *Acquire* means "to gain; to earn; to come by." What word means "to gain; to earn; to come by"? (acquire)

Example 1: If you inherit your brother's bike, you have *acquired* a bike.

Example 2: To *acquire* a good job, you must have the needed skills and a positive attitude.

Example 3: You can't magically *acquire* a best friend; you have to be one first.

Question 1: If you lose a piece of jewelry, have you *acquired* it? Yes or no? (no)

Question 2: Would you want to *acquire* a bad cold? Yes or no? (no)

Pair Share: Turn to your partner and tell about an object you would like to *acquire.*

(1)

functional (adj)

Let's read the next word together. *Functional.*

Definition: *Functional* means "in working order; able to do a task or job." What means "in working order; able to do a task or job"? (functional)

Example 1: I need a new can opener; the one I own is not *functional.*

Example 2: To fill out an application, you must have a *functional* knowledge of reading and writing.

Example 3: A plug-in lantern is not *functional* at a campsite with no electricity.

Question 1: Should a brand-new computer be *functional*? Yes or no? (yes)

Question 2: When you are very sick, are you *functional*? Yes or no? (no)

Pair Share: Turn to your partner and tell why one or more items in this room are *functional.*

(2)

envy (n)

Let's read the next word together. *Envy.*

Definition: When you feel *envy*, you want what someone else has. What means "the feeling of wanting what someone else has"? (envy)

Example 1: I feel *envy* for the singing voice of many opera stars.

Example 2: *Envy* can prevent us from appreciating what we do have.

Example 3: If you forget your lunch, you might feel *envy* as you watch others eat.

Question 1: If you have two bracelets and give your friend one of them, are you feeling *envy*? Yes or no? (no)

Question 2: You wish you had your sister's new phone. Are you feeling *envy*? Yes or no? (yes)

Pair Share: Imagine that you are a superhero. Turn to your partner, tell what your superpowers are, and explain why humans should feel *envy* toward you.

eventually (adv)

Let's read the next word together. Eventually.

Definition: *Eventually* means "over time; in the end." What means "over time; in the end"? (eventually)

Example 1: Even on nights when I'm restless, I *eventually* fall asleep.

Example 2: If you argue with a true friend, you will *eventually* make up.

Example 3: When the weather is very dry, people hope that it will *eventually* rain.

Question 1: Does a large pot of water sitting on high heat *eventually* boil? Yes or no? (yes)

Question 2: If you send a text and get a response right away, did you receive it *eventually*? Yes or no? (no)

Pair Share: Turn to your partner and tell when you were waiting for someone and he or she *eventually* showed up.

inevitable (adj)

Let's read the next word together. *Inevitable.*

Definition: *Inevitable* means "to be expected; hard to keep from happening." What means "to be expected; hard to keep from happening"? (inevitable)

Example 1: That the sun will rise tomorrow is *inevitable*.

Example 2: In a good mystery story, one ending seems *inevitable*, but another one actually happens.

Example 3: If you exercise every day, it is *inevitable* that your health will improve.

Question 1: You want to start babysitting but don't know any families with kids. Is it *inevitable* that you will find a job? Yes or no? (no)

Question 2: Is it *inevitable* that you will be older tomorrow than you are today? Yes or no? (yes)

Pair Share: The electricity has gone out due to a bad storm. Turn to your partner and tell one thing that is *inevitable*.

correspondence (n)

Let's read the next word together. *Correspondence.*

Definition: The word *correspondence* refers to written messages to and from other people. What word means "written messages to and from other people"? (correspondence)

Example 1: When she grew ill, my grandmother couldn't continue our *correspondence*; I started calling her instead.

Example 2: Some people in high positions rely on assistants to keep up with their *correspondence*.

Example 3: The letters, notes, and other *correspondence* of famous people are often published and put in libraries or museums.

Question 1: Before telephones, do you imagine people relied on *correspondence* to stay in touch? Yes or no? (yes)

Question 2: If you pass a note to your neighbor in class, are you striking up a *correspondence*? Yes or no? (yes)

Pair Share: Turn to your partner and tell why someone might prefer *correspondence* (like texting) to face-to-face conversations.

debate (n)

Let's read the next word together. *Debate*.

Definition: A *debate* is a contest in which two sides argue the pros and cons of an issue. What word means "a contest in which two sides argue the pros and cons of an issue"? (debate)

Example 1: I was nervous before the *debate* because I had not studied my facts and was unsure that my arguments would be convincing.

Example 2: In a political *debate*, two or more candidates present different views on important issues.

Example 3: If you want to try out for the *debate* team, you should enjoy learning about an issue thoroughly and speaking about it persuasively.

Question 1: If you dislike competitions, would you enjoy a *debate*? Yes or no? (no)

Question 2: Is the quality of kindness important in a *debate*? Yes or no? (no)

Pair Share: It's time for a *debate*. Tell your partner what the issue is and what side you are on.

(7)

emphasis (n)

Let's read the next word together. *Emphasis*.

Definition: The word *emphasis* means "the weight, value, or importance put on something." What means "the weight, value, or importance put on something"? (emphasis)

Example 1: In school, there is an *emphasis* on learning.

Example 2: Coaches should place equal *emphasis* on winning and good sportsmanship.

Example 3: In our culture, there is sometimes too great an *emphasis* on money.

Question 1: If a child's parents are strict, do they place an *emphasis* on rules? Yes or no? (yes)

Question 2: In a car repair shop, would an *emphasis* be put on fashion? Yes or no? (no)

Pair Share: Turn to your partner and tell what quality you place the greatest *emphasis* on when choosing a partner for a class project.

(8)

isolation (n)

Let's read the next word together. *Isolation*.

Definition: The word *isolation* refers to the state of being totally alone. What word means "the state of being totally alone"? (isolation)

Example 1: Humans were not made for *isolation*; they enjoy and rely on each other.

Example 2: If a person in a hospital is very contagious, he or she might be put in *isolation* so others won't be contaminated.

Example 3: I can enjoy a short period of *isolation*, but after a few hours, I get lonely.

Question 1: You are stranded on a desert island. Are you experiencing *isolation*? Yes or no? (yes)

Question 2: You are on a crowded train. Are you experiencing *isolation*? Yes or no? (no)

Pair Share: Tell your partner why you do or do not enjoy *isolation*.

(9)

adjust (v)

Let's read the last word together. *Adjust*.

Definition: *Adjust* means "to get used to something." What means "to get used to something"? (adjust)

Example 1: If you switched schools, you would have to *adjust* to new teachers and a new schedule.

Example 2: After a few days, my adopted lizard seemed to *adjust* to his new surroundings.

Example 3: When you jump into a cold swimming pool, your body has to *adjust* to the lower temperature.

Question 1: You join a club full of strangers, but you soon make friends. Have you *adjusted*? Yes or no? (yes)

Question 2: You dig up a small tree and plant it somewhere else, but it dies. Did it *adjust*? Yes or no? (no)

Pair Share: The outfit you want to wear is dirty and wrinkled. Tell your partner how you would *adjust* to this situation.

(10)

Objectives
- Read autobiographical text.
- Monitor comprehension during text reading.

Excerpt from *The Autobiography of Malcolm X*

Direct students to pages 169–173 in their Student Books.

Now it's time to read. This text is a little more difficult than our previous texts. You will come across words that may be harder to read. Don't skip them. Try to sound them out and use the context around the words to make sense of them. If you still aren't certain, mark them and we can discuss them later.

Guiding Students Toward Independent Reading

It is important that your students read as much and as often as they can. Assign readings that meet the needs of your students, based on your observations and data. This is a good opportunity to stretch your students. If students become frustrated, scaffold the reading with paired reading, choral reading, or a read-aloud.

Options for reading text:

- Teacher read-aloud
- Teacher-led or student-led choral read
- Paired read or independent read

Choose an option for reading text. Students read according to the option that you chose. Review the purpose of the numbered squares in the text, and prompt students to stop periodically to check comprehension.

If you choose to read the text aloud or chorally, use the text below and stop to ask questions and have students answer them.

SE p. 169, paragraphs 1–2

Malcolm X was a Black Muslim minister, a militant, a social and political activist, and a hero to many. His journey toward activism began in prison, where he first learned to read with understanding and to write with precision.

It was because of my letters that I happened to stumble upon starting to **acquire** some kind of a homemade education. I became increasingly frustrated at not being able to express what I wanted to convey in letters that I wrote, especially those to Mr. Elijah Muhammad. In the street, I had been the most articulate hustler out there—I had commanded attention when I said something. But now, trying to write simple English, I not only wasn't articulate, I wasn't even **functional**. How would I sound writing in slang, the way I would say it, something such as "Look, daddy, let me pull your coat about cat, Elijah Muhammad—"

1. Why didn't Malcolm X want to write the way he spoke?

SE p. 169, paragraph 3

Many who today hear me somewhere in person or on television, or those who read something I've said, will think I went to school far beyond the eighth grade. This impression is due entirely to my prison studies.

2. Where did Malcolm X get a homemade education?

SE p. 169, paragraph 4

It had really begun back in the Charlestown Prison, when Bimbi first made me feel **envy** of his stock of knowledge. Bimbi had always taken charge of any conversations he was in, and I had tried to emulate him. But every book I picked up had few sentences which didn't contain anywhere from one to nearly all of

page break

the words that might as well | have been in Chinese. When I just skipped those words, of course, I really ended up with little idea of what the book said. So I had come to the Norfolk Prison Colony still going through only book-reading motions. Pretty soon, I would have quit even these motions, unless I had received the motivation that I did.

3. Why didn't Malcolm X understand what he read?

LE p. 170, paragraphs 1–4

I saw that the best thing I could do was get hold of a dictionary—to study, to learn some words. I was lucky enough to reason also that I should try to improve my penmanship. It was sad. I couldn't even write in a straight line. It was both ideas together that moved me to request a dictionary along with some tablets and pencils from the Norfolk Prison Colony school.

I spent two days just riffling uncertainly through the dictionary's pages. I'd never realized so many words existed! I didn't know *which* words I needed to learn. Finally, just to start some kind of action, I began copying.

In my slow, painstaking, ragged handwriting, I copied into my tablet everything printed on that first page, down to the punctuation marks.

I believe it took me a day. Then, aloud, I read back, to myself, everything I'd written on the tablet. Over and over, aloud, to myself, I read my own handwriting.

4. Malcolm X hoped to accomplish two things with his dictionary efforts. What were they?

LE p. 170, paragraph 5

I woke up the next morning, thinking about those words—immensely proud to realize that not only had I written so much at one time, but I'd written words that I never knew were in the world. Moreover, with a little effort, I also could remember what many of these words meant. I reviewed the words whose meanings I didn't remember. Funny thing, from the dictionary's first page right now, that *aardvark* springs to my mind. The dictionary had a picture of it, a long-tailed, long- | eared, burrowing African mammal, which lives off termites caught by sticking out its tongue as an anteater does for ants.

page break

LE p. 171, paragraph 1

I was so fascinated that I went on—I copied the dictionary's next page. And the same experience came when I studied that. With every succeeding page, I also learned of people and places and events from history. Actually the dictionary is like a miniature encyclopedia. Finally the dictionary's A section had filled a whole tablet—and I went on into the B's. That was the way I started copying what **eventually** became the entire dictionary. It went a lot faster after so much practice helped me to pick up handwriting speed. Between what I wrote in my tablet, and writing letters, during the rest of my time in prison I would guess I wrote a million words.

5. How would copying the dictionary help a person?

SE p. 171, paragraph 2

I suppose it was **inevitable** that as my word base broadened, I could for the first time pick up a book and read and now begin to understand what the book was saying. Anyone who has read a great deal can imagine the new world that opened. Let me tell you something: From then until I left that prison, in every free moment I had, if I was not reading in the library, I was reading on my bunk. You couldn't have gotten me out of books with a wedge. Between Mr. Muhammad's teachings, my **correspondence**, my visitors—usually Ella and Reginald—and my reading of books, months passed without my even thinking about being imprisoned. In fact, up to then, I never had been so truly free in my life.

6. What newfound ability made Malcolm X feel truly free though he was in prison?

SE p. 171, paragraph 3

page break

The Norfolk Prison Colony's library was in the school building. A variety of classes was taught there by instructors who came from such places as Harvard and Boston universities. The weekly **debates** between inmate teams were also held in the school building. You would be astonished | to know how worked up convict debaters and audiences would get over subjects like "Should Babies Be Fed Milk?"

7. How did inmates challenge the knowledge of one another?

SE p. 172, paragraphs 1–2

Available on the prison library's shelves were books on just about every general subject. Much of the big private collection that Parkhurst had willed to the prison was still in crates and boxes in the back of the library—thousands of old books. Some of them looked ancient: covers faded, old-time parchment-looking binding. Parkhurst, I've mentioned, seemed to have been principally interested in history and religion. He had the money and the special interest to have a lot of books that you wouldn't have in general circulation. Any college library would have been lucky to get that collection.

As you can imagine, especially in a prison where there was heavy **emphasis** on rehabilitation, an inmate was smiled upon if he demonstrated an unusually intense interest in books. There was a sizable number of well-read inmates, especially the popular debaters. Some were said by many to be practically walking encyclopedias. They were almost celebrities. No university would ask any student to devour literature as I did when this new world opened to me, of being able to read and *understand*.

8. What did the prison staff believe would happen to an inmate if he was interested in books?

SE p. 172,
paragraphs 3–4

I read more in my room than in the library itself. An inmate who was known to read a lot could check out more than the permitted maximum number of books. I preferred reading in the total **isolation** of my own room.

When I had progressed to really serious reading, every night at about 10:00 p.m. I would be outraged with the "lights out." It always seemed to catch me right in the middle of something engrossing.

SE p. 173, paragraph 1

Fortunately, right outside my door was a corridor light that cast a glow into my room. The glow was enough to read by, once my eyes **adjusted** to it. So when "lights out" came, I could sit on the floor where I could continue reading in that glow.

9. What did Malcolm X choose to do instead of sleep?

SE p. 173, paragraph 2

At one-hour intervals the night guards paced past every room. Each time I heard the approaching footstep, I jumped into bed and feigned sleep. And as soon as the guard passed, I got back out of bed onto the floor area of that light-glow, where I would read for another fifty-eight minutes—until the guard approached again. That went on until three or four every morning. Three or four hours of sleep a night was enough for me. Often in the years in the streets, I had slept less than that.

10. Malcolm X was used to very little sleep. Tell the difference between his reasons for staying up while on the streets and while in prison. Which reason was more beneficial?

For confirmation of engagement, take 30 seconds to have students share one thing they learned about Malcolm X.

Unit 4

Lesson 7

RI.1.2; RI.2.2; RI.3.1; RI.4.1; RI.4.2; RI.6.1; RI.6.2; RI.8.2;
RI.1.4; RI.5.4; W.5.3c; W.7.3c; W.8.2c; SL.1.2; SL.3.6; L.1.1j;
L.1.6; L.3.6; L.6.6

Lesson Opener

Before the lesson, choose one of the following activities to write on the board or post on the *LANGUAGE! Live* Class Wall online.

- *Write a summary sentence about Malcolm X's discipline.*
- *Make a list of adjectives describing Malcolm X.*
- *Write five sentences explaining what you would do if you were in total isolation without the ability to leave or talk to other people. All you have is a bed, a chair, paper, pencils, and books. Identify the adverbs and prepositional phrases.*

Vocabulary

Objective

- Review key passage vocabulary.

Review Passage Vocabulary

Direct students to page 168 in their Student Books. Use the following questions to review the vocabulary words in the excerpt from *The Autobiography of Malcolm X*. Have students answer each question using the vocabulary word or indicating its meaning in a complete sentence.

- In prison, what did Malcolm X discover that he wanted to *acquire*? (He discovered that he wanted to acquire an education.) Why did he want to *acquire* an education? (He wanted to acquire an education so he could express his ideas in letters to his teachers and friends.)

- Did Malcolm X consider the slang he knew *functional*? Why or why not? (No, he did not consider it functional because he could not use it in letters.) Did he have a *functional* grasp of basic written English? (No, he did not have a functional grasp of basic written English.)

- Why did Malcolm X feel *envy* toward his friend Bimbi? (He felt envy because Bimbi had broad knowledge and could take charge of conversations.) Did Malcolm X let this feeling of *envy* discourage him, or did he put it to good use? How? (He put the envy to good use. He used it to fuel his desire for education.)

- After he acquired a dictionary, what did Malcolm X *eventually* decide to do with it? (He eventually decided to copy it, entry by entry.) How did that project *eventually* end? (Malcolm X eventually copied the entire dictionary.)

- What *inevitable* result came from the dictionary project? (The inevitable result was that Malcolm X's word knowledge grew.) Once he knew so many words, what other *inevitable* need or desire grew in him? (Once he knew so many words, it was inevitable that he would want to read books.)

- Why was *correspondence* easier for Malcolm X once he knew the English language? (Correspondence was easier for him because he could express himself in written language.) Why might *correspondence* be so important to someone in prison? (Correspondence would be important because it is one of the few ways someone in prison can keep in touch with the outside world.)

- One prison debate topic was "Should Babies Be Fed Milk?" How would a *debate* about this issue go? (Two teams of inmates would argue the pros and cons of feeding babies milk.) Do you imagine Malcolm X was involved in the *debates*? Why or why not? (Yes, he was probably involved in the debates because he would have wanted to use and sharpen his newly acquired knowledge.)

- There was a heavy *emphasis* on what in the Norfolk Prison? (There was a heavy emphasis on learning and improving yourself.) Did Malcolm X's own personal goals match this *emphasis* or go against it? How? (His personal goals matched the emphasis; he desperately wanted to learn and improve himself.)

- Why did Malcolm X prefer *isolation*? (He preferred isolation because when he was completely alone, he could read.) Does a person who is absorbed in a book feel *isolation*? Why or why not? (No; someone who is absorbed in a book doesn't feel isolation because he or she has entered another world.)

- What had to *adjust* for Malcolm to be able to read by the soft glow under the door? (His eyes had to adjust to the low level of light for him to be able to read.) Would you say that Malcolm X *adjusted* well to life in prison? Why or why not? (Yes; he adjusted to life in prison because instead of giving up hope or getting into trouble, he made good use of his time.)

Assign online practice by opening the Tools menu, then selecting Assignments. Be sure to select the correct class from the drop-down menu.

Reading

Objectives
- Objectively summarize text.
- Identify multiple main ideas of a text.
- Determine the central idea of a text.
- Analyze texts from different cultures and the approach to a similar central idea or theme.
- Determine how to respond to prompts.
- Answer questions about text.

Summarization

It's time to summarize the autobiography about Malcolm X. When we summarize text, it is important to avoid the inclusion of your own opinions. As you summarize, don't let your opinions of Malcolm X, or his actions, or the actions of others during that particular time in history influence your summary. Keep it objective.

Turn to your partner and summarize the text objectively. Then, switch.

Central Idea

Direct students to page 174 in their Student Books. In Lesson 3, we discussed how skilled readers can identify the central idea of a text even if the author does not explicitly state it. Recall that a central idea is the main point that the author is making. When reading "The Circuit," the author wanted us to know about the difficulties of life as a migrant farmer. Let's find the central idea of the excerpt from *The Autobiography of Malcolm X*.

For "The Circuit," I led you through the process of coming up with the central idea. We broke the story into parts and determined the main idea of each part. Then, we combined those main ideas to determine the central idea, or message, of the text. We learned that central ideas can be subjective but are supported by the text. I'm going to ask you to determine the central idea of this new text with your partners. Remember, central ideas can often be applied to multiple texts and teach us a lesson.

Lesson 7 | Reading

Central Idea

Identify the main idea of each section of the excerpt from *The Autobiography of Malcolm X*. Then, use the main ideas to determine the central idea of the text.

Introduction:
Malcolm X was a prominent activist and minister because of his self-made education.

Desire to Write Articulately:
Malcolm X wasn't able to express himself articulately in letters and didn't want to use the slang he had acquired on the streets.

Dictionary Study:
He spent his days in prison copying pages of the dictionary in an effort to increase his word knowledge and improve his handwriting.

Love of Reading:
The knowledge gained from copying the dictionary and engaging in debates allowed Malcolm X to understand what he read—opening up a world of learning.

Central Idea:
With an intense desire and discipline, even people who have made mistakes can turn their lives around through education.

174   Unit 4   © 2016 Voyager Sopris Learning, Inc. All rights reserved

Have partners determine the main ideas of the sections and the central idea of the text. Review the answers as a class and determine the best answer.

Explain that central ideas need be related to the text in a way that makes sense, and they are not explicitly stated word for word. There can be more than one central idea.

How does the central idea of the excerpt from *The Autobiography of Malcolm X* compare to the central idea of "The Circuit"? Is there an underlying message about education in both texts? (Education and learning should be coveted.)

Each text was written from a different cultural perspective. What two cultures are represented? (African American and Hispanic) Each main character stopped going to school for different reasons. Which character chose to quit school? (Malcolm X) Which character was forced to skip school? (Panchito) However, both texts reveal a similar central idea. Thus, we know that multiple stories can share themes or central ideas—regardless of author, culture, or story.

Critical Understandings: Direction Words *contrast, identify, infer, summarize*

Let's review the difference between a question and prompt. In this class and in others, you are often asked questions at a variety of difficulty levels. Some are in the form of questions and some are in the form of prompts. Prompts are statements that require a constructed response, which can range from a list to a complete sentence to a paragraph or an essay. We can take prompts and turn them into questions to help understand what is being asked.

Write the words *contrast, identify, infer,* and *summarize* on the board. Have students read the words aloud with you.

Direct students to page 66 in their Student Books. It is critical to understand what the question is asking and how to answer it. Today, we will look at four direction words used in prompts.

Have students read about the four direction words in the chart with their partner.

Critical Understandings: Direction Words

Prompt	How to Respond	Model
If the prompt asks you to . . .	The response requires you to . . .	For example . . .
Analyze	break down and evaluate or draw conclusions about the information	**Analyze** the development of the text's central idea.
Assess	decide on the value, impact, or accuracy	**Assess** the level of pressure in an arranged marriage.
Compare	state the similarities between two or more things	**Compare** novels and dramas.
Contrast	state the differences between two or more things	**Contrast** a biography with an autobiography.
Create	make or produce something	**Create** a timeline of events.
Define	tell or write the meaning or definition	**Define** the unknown word using context clues.
Delineate	show or list evidence, claims, ideas, reasons, or events	**Delineate** the evidence in the text.
Describe	state detailed information about a topic	**Describe** the relationship between the plot and character development.
Determine	find out, verify, decide	**Determine** the main idea.
Distinguish	recognize or explain the differences	**Distinguish** between facts and opinions.
Evaluate	think carefully to make a judgment; form a critical opinion of	**Evaluate** the ANC's plan for change.
Explain	express understanding of an idea or concept	**Explain** how the author develops the narrator's point of view.
Identify	say or write what it is	**Identify** the character's motive.
Infer	provide a logical answer using evidence and prior knowledge	Use information from the text to **infer** the value of education.
Interpret	make sense of or assign meaning to something	**Interpret** the quote to confirm your understanding.
Paraphrase	say or write it using different words	**Paraphrase** the main idea.
Report	Tell or write about a topic	**Report** the main events of the setting.
Summarize	tell the most important ideas or concepts	**Summarize** the key details of the passage.
Tell	say or write specific information	**Tell** the date that the poem was written.
Use	apply information or a procedure	**Use** text features to identify the topic.

Chart Reading Procedure

- Group students with partners or in triads.
- Have students count off as 1s or 2s. The 1s will become the student leaders. If working with triads, the third students become 3s.
- The student leaders will read the left column (Prompt) in addition to managing the time and turn-taking if working with a triad.
- The 2s will explain the middle column of the chart (How to Respond). If working in triads, 2s and 3s will take turns explaining the middle column.
- The 1s read the model in the right column (Model), and 2s and 3s restate the model as a question.
- All students should follow along with their pencil eraser while others are explaining the chart.
- Students must work from left to right, top to bottom in order to benefit from this activity.

Check for understanding by requesting an oral response to the following questions.

- If the prompt asks you to *contrast*, the response requires you to . . . (state the differences between two or more things).

- If the prompt asks you to *identify*, the response requires you to . . . (say or write what it is).

- If the prompt asks you to *infer*, the response requires you to . . . (provide a logical answer using evidence and prior knowledge).

- If the prompt asks you to *summarize*, the response requires you to . . . (tell the most important ideas or concepts).

Direct students to page 175 in their Student Books and read the instructions aloud. Let's read some prompts about a small section of the text before we expand to the entire text.

1. Identify three positions held by Malcolm X. Provide text evidence.

2. Infer the level of Malcolm X's formal education. Provide text evidence.

3. Summarize Malcolm's motivation to learn to read and write.

4. Contrast the illiterate prisoner with the articulate street hustler.

We are going to work with the first three paragraphs of the excerpt to practice responding to prompts with these new direction words. Having a good understanding of the text from

Critical Understandings

Read the first three paragraphs of the excerpt from *The Autobiography of Malcolm X*. Read the prompts and respond using complete sentences. Refer to the chart on page 66 to determine how to respond. Provide text evidence when requested.

1. Identify three positions held by Malcolm X. Provide text evidence.
   Malcolm X held positions as a Black Muslim minister, a militant, and a social and political activist.

   Text Evidence: "Malcolm X was a Black Muslim minister, a militant, a social and political activist"

2. Infer the level of Malcolm X's formal education. Provide text evidence.
   Malcolm X's level of formal education went up to 8th grade.

   Text Evidence: Many . . . will think I went to school far beyond the eighth grade.

3. Summarize Malcolm's motivation to learn to read and write.
   Malcolm's motivation to learn to read and write came when he wanted to write a letter to his mentor while in prison.

4. Contrast the illiterate prisoner with the articulate street hustler.
   The illiterate prisoner is different from the articulate street hustler because literacy was valued in prison. In prison, Malcolm felt incompetent when he couldn't communicate with educated people outside of prison. In contrast, while on the streets, he didn't need to read and write because he used street talk to communicate with other uneducated people.

Unit 4 **175**

the beginning will help build a foundation for understanding the rest of the text and make it feel less difficult.

Have students reread the first three paragraphs of the text.

Model

Let's practice answering questions that are written as prompts. Remember to use the chart as a reference. Listen as I model the first one for you.

> 1. Identify three positions held by Malcolm X. Provide text evidence.

According to the chart, if the prompt asks you to *identify*, the response requires that you say or write what it is. Now, I will turn the prompt into a question to confirm understanding. What three positions did Malcolm X hold? What is a position? A position is like a job. Put your finger on the paragraph that provides evidence for that answer. **Check to ensure students are pointing at the introduction.**

The first sentence says, "Malcolm X was a Black Muslim minister, a militant, a social and political activist, and a hero to many." It doesn't use the word *position*, but with the exception of *hero*, they all sound like jobs or important tasks.

I will use the evidence in the text to answer the question.

My answer would be *Malcolm X held positions as a Black Muslim minister, a militant, and a social and political activist.*

Have students write the answer on the page.

Guided Practice

> 2. Infer the level of Malcolm X's formal education. Provide text evidence.

How should we respond according to the chart? (If the prompt asks you to *infer*, the response requires you provide a logical answer using evidence and prior knowledge.) Now, turn the prompt into a question to confirm your understanding. Tell your partner the question. (How long did Malcolm X attend school?)

While providing partner time, write the sentence starter on the board.

> *Malcolm X's level of formal education* _____.

Have partners answer the question and provide evidence from the text.

3. Summarize Malcolm's motivation to learn to read and write.

Turn to your partner and tell him or her how to respond according to the chart. (If the prompt asks you to *summarize*, the response requires you to tell the most important ideas or concepts.) Now, turn the prompt into a question to confirm your understanding. Tell your partner the question. (What motivated Malcolm to want to be a better reader and writer?)

While providing partner time, write the sentence starter on the board.

> *Malcolm's motivation to learn to read and write came when*
> _____.

Have partners answer the question.

4. Contrast the illiterate prisoner with the articulate street hustler.

Turn to your partner and tell him or her how to respond according to the chart. (If the prompt asks you to *contrast*, the response requires you to state the differences between two or more things.) Now, turn the prompt into a question to confirm your understanding. Tell your partner the question. (How is Malcolm the illiterate prisoner different from Malcolm the articulate street hustler?)

While providing partner time, write the sentence starters on the board.

> *The illiterate prisoner is different from the articulate street hustler because* _____.
>
> *In prison, Malcolm felt* _____.
>
> *In contrast, while on the streets* _____.

Have partners answer the question.

In the next lesson, we will work some more with these direction words.

Objectives

- Identify the function and purpose of transition words in writing.
- Use academic vocabulary to signal logical relationships.

Using Transition Words

Time and sequence transitions are used to order events in a composition that outlines a series or a process. They help demonstrate the logical order of writing and divide time order into the tenses—past, present, and future. Good writers use transitions to effectively guide their audience through the text. What are transition words? A few examples are *first, next,* and *last.* If I wanted to sequence three events, this group of transitions might be useful. If I had to tell or write about my morning routine, I could use these words.

Every day begins with the same routine. First, I turn on my coffee pot. Coffee is an essential part of my morning routine. Next, I make my breakfast. It might just be yogurt or a bowl of cereal, but eating breakfast really helps me get going. Last, I spend some time with my dog Oscar. He loves to catch a tennis ball and makes some amazing catches midair. As you can see, I save the best for last. Having a routine in the morning really helps me get to school on time.

Direct students to page 176 in their Student Books. Read through the transition families at the top of the page. Have partners use one family of transitions as they tell each other about a routine or procedure.

Circulate around the room, listening to the students use the transition families orally. If students are struggling, provide more structure for using the transition families. If necessary, work with the class to create another routine.

Direct students to the paragraph at the bottom of the page.

Lesson 7 | Writing

Using Transition Words

Examples of Transition Families			
One Another Finally	First Next At last	First of all The second A third	First Second Third
One Also Another Finally	Start by Next Then Finally	Initially Then After Later	In the spring In the summer In the fall In the winter
My first choice My second choice	First of all More important	A good An even better The best	One important Equally important
During the week On the weekend	With my friends With my family On my own	I first heard I also heard	One Another
One example Another example A third example	In the beginning As By the time Then	One good choice Another choice The best choice	Early each morning Throughout the day In the evening
To begin After that Then Next Finally	One example A better example The best example	One difference A second difference The most obvious difference	Before winter break During winter break After winter break

Read the following paragraph and circle all of the transition words and the commas.

Recycling is an important habit for several reasons. First, our landfills are overflowing with trash. Much of this trash is recyclable. Recycling paper and aluminum cans would significantly reduce the amount of trash sitting in landfills. Second, our earth's resources are not infinite. Recycling provides us with a way to maximize precious resources. Even though trees are a renewable resource, deforestation is negatively impacting our climate. In addition to positively impacting the environment, recycling can positively impact our pocketbooks. Consuming less costs less, and recycling centers actually pay for recycled paper and aluminum. For a variety of reasons, recycling is a habit worth forming.

Read the paragraph aloud without pausing at the transitions.

Recycling is an important habit for several reasons. First, our landfills are overflowing with trash. Much of this trash is recyclable. Recycling paper and aluminum cans would significantly reduce the amount of trash sitting in landfills. Second, our earth's resources are not infinite. Recycling provides us with a way to maximize precious resources. Even though trees are a renewable resource, deforestation is negatively impacting our climate. In addition to positively impacting the environment, recycling can positively impact our pocketbook. Consuming less costs less, and recycling centers actually pay for recycled paper and aluminum. For a variety of reasons, recycling is a habit worth forming.

What are the transitions used in this paragraph? (First, Second, In addition)

What kind of punctuation follows the transitions? (commas) We use commas to separate the transition word or phrase from the rest of the sentence. *In addition* is actually part of a larger introductory clause, so the comma is placed after what word? (environment) What is the final reason to recycle? (positively impact our pocketbook) We also need to use commas when we begin a sentence with a prepositional phrase. A comma is a signal to pause when we read. Commas also help keep parts of sentences together.

Unit 4

Lesson 8

RI.3.1; RI.4.1; RI.4.2; RI.6.1; RI.6.6; RI.6.10; RF.2.4c; RF.5.4c; W.5.9a

Lesson Opener

Before the lesson, choose one of the following activities to write on the board or post on the *LANGUAGE! Live* Class Wall online.

- *What would you do if you didn't go to school every day?*
- *Write the dialogue of a conversation you think Malcolm X might have had as a hustler on the street. Use the type of language he demonstrated in the text.*
- *Expand one or more of these simple sentences, using the steps in Masterpiece Sentences.*

   Malcolm read books.

   Malcolm copied words.

   Malcolm slept.

   Malcolm could not write.

Reading

Objectives

- Establish a purpose for rereading autobiographical text.
- Use critical thinking skills to write responses to prompts about text.
- Support written answers with text evidence.
- Explain how the values and beliefs of characters are affected by the historical and cultural setting.

Reading for a Purpose: Excerpt from *The Autobiography of Malcolm X*

We are going to reread the excerpt from *The Autobiography of Malcolm X*. Let's preview a few prompts to provide a purpose for rereading the text.

Direct students to pages 177 and 178 in their Student Books. Have students read the prompts aloud with you.

1. Identify the strategy that Malcolm X used to learn to read and write.

2. Infer why Malcolm X did not want to write the way he spoke.

3. Use your knowledge of the historical and cultural setting in which Malcolm X was raised to infer why he did not value education.

4. Summarize the excerpt from *The Autobiography of Malcolm X* using an IVF topic sentence strategy.

5. Contrast Malcolm as a hustler and Malcolm as a prisoner.

6. Consider Malcolm's quote "Education is the passport to the future, for tomorrow belongs to the those who prepare for it today." Contrast Malcolm's point of view regarding education with that of the pool players at the Golden Shovel in the poem "We Real Cool."

It's time to revisit the autobiography.

Choose an option for rereading text. Have students read the text according to the option that you chose.

> Choose an option for rereading text.
> - Teacher read-aloud
> - Teacher-led or student-led choral read
> - Paired read or independent read with bold vocabulary words read aloud

Direct students to page 169 in their Student Books or have them tear out the extra copy of the text from the back of their book.

Note: To minimize flipping back and forth between the pages, a copy of each text has been included in the back of the Student Books. Encourage students to tear this out and use it when working on activities that require the use of the text.

Have students read the text.

Passage Comprehension

Write the words *contrast, identify, infer,* and *summarize* on the board. Have students read the words aloud with you.

Direct students to page 66 in their Student Books. Have students quickly review the information in the chart.

Check for understanding by requesting an oral response to the following questions.

- If the prompt asks you to *contrast,* the response requires you to . . . (state the differences between two or more things).

- If the prompt asks you to *identify,* the response requires you to . . . (say or write what it is).

- If the prompt asks you to *infer,* the response requires you to . . . (provide a logical answer using evidence and prior knowledge).

- If the prompt asks you to *summarize,* the response requires you to . . . (tell the most important ideas or concepts).

Critical Understandings: Direction Words

Prompt If the prompt asks you to . . .	How to Respond The response requires you to . . .	Model For example . . .
Analyze	break down and evaluate or draw conclusions about the information	**Analyze** the development of the text's central idea.
Assess	decide on the value, impact, or accuracy	**Assess** the level of pressure in an arranged marriage.
Compare	state the similarities between two or more things	**Compare** novels and dramas.
Contrast	state the differences between two or more things	**Contrast** a biography with an autobiography.
Create	make or produce something	**Create** a timeline of events.
Define	tell or write the meaning or definition	**Define** the unknown word using context clues.
Delineate	show or list evidence, claims, ideas, reasons, or events	**Delineate** the evidence in the text.
Describe	state detailed information about a topic	**Describe** the relationship between the plot and character development.
Determine	find out, verify, decide	**Determine** the main idea.
Distinguish	recognize or explain the differences	**Distinguish** between facts and opinions.
Evaluate	think carefully to make a judgment; form a critical opinion of	**Evaluate** the ANC's plan for change.
Explain	express understanding of an idea or concept	**Explain** how the author develops the narrator's point of view.
Identify	say or write what it is	**Identify** the character's motive.
Infer	provide a logical answer using evidence and prior knowledge	Use information from the text to **infer** the value of education.
Interpret	make sense of or assign meaning to something	**Interpret** the quote to confirm your understanding.
Paraphrase	say or write it using different words	**Paraphrase** the main idea.
Report	Tell or write about a topic	**Report** the main events of the setting.
Summarize	tell the most important ideas or concepts	**Summarize** the key details of the passage.
Tell	say or write specific information	**Tell** the date that the poem was written.
Use	apply information or a procedure	**Use** text features to identify the topic.

Direct students to pages 177 and 178 in their Student Books.

Model

Let's practice answering questions that are written as prompts. Remember to use the chart on page 66 as a reference. Listen as I model the first one for you.

> 1. Identify the strategy that Malcolm X used to learn to read and write.

How should we respond according to the chart? (say or write what it is)

Let's turn the prompt into a question to confirm understanding. The question would be *What strategy did Malcolm X use to learn to read and write?*

Write the following sentence starter on the board. Have volunteers help you finish the sentence.

> *Malcolm X learned to read and write by _____.*

Malcolm X learned to read and write by copying words from the dictionary and remembering their meanings.

Guided Practice

> 2. Infer why Malcolm X did not want to write the way he spoke. Provide text evidence.

How should we respond according to the chart? (If the prompt asks you to *infer,* the response requires you provide a logical answer using evidence and prior knowledge.) Now, turn the prompt into a question to confirm your understanding. Tell your partner the question. (Why did Malcolm X not want to write the way he spoke?)

While providing partner time, write the sentence starter on the board.

> *Malcolm X wanted to write differently than he spoke because _____.*

The text says, "I became increasingly frustrated at not being able to express what I wanted to convey in letters that I wrote, especially those to Mr. Elijah Muhammad." I know from experience that when someone addresses someone as Mr., that means the person respects him. Malcolm spent most of his time on the street as a hustler, and it is likely that he didn't respect the people he dealt with. So, language wasn't

Passage Comprehension

Read the prompts and respond using complete sentences. Refer to the chart on page 66 to determine how to respond. Provide text evidence when requested.

1. Identify the strategy that Malcolm X used to learn to read and write.
   Malcolm X learned to read and write by copying words from the dictionary and remembering their meanings.

2. Infer why Malcolm X did not want to write the way he spoke. Provide text evidence.
   Malcolm X wanted to write differently than he spoke because he wanted to sound respectable to his mentor and not like a hustler from the streets without an education.

   Text Evidence: "I became increasingly frustrated at not being able to express what I wanted to convey in letters that I wrote, especially those to Mr. Elijah Muhammad."

3. Use your knowledge of the historical and cultural setting in which Malcolm X was raised to infer why he did not initially value education.
   Malcolm X did not initially value education because the education of African Americans was inferior and devalued by much of the country. The socioeconomic status of African Americans growing up in Malcolm X's neighborhood was extremely low—leading them to put making money above education.

Unit 4   177

very important to him. Now, Malcolm is writing to someone he respects. He wants to sound respectable to Muhammad and not like a hustler from the streets.

Using the text evidence and prior knowledge, answer the question.

Have partners answer the question and provide evidence from the text.

Independent Practice

Have partners respond to the remaining prompts with text evidence. For students who need more assistance, provide the alternative questions and sentence starters.

Passage Comprehension (cont.)

4. Summarize the excerpt from *The Autobiography of Malcolm X* using an IVF topic sentence strategy.

   The Autobiography of Malcolm X tells how this political activist taught himself to read and write in prison so that he would be respected by other educated people outside of prison.

5. Contrast Malcolm as a hustler and Malcolm as a prisoner.

   As a hustler, Malcolm was uneducated, spoke in slang, slept less than three hours per night, and participated in illegal activities. As a prisoner, Malcolm was different because he worked hard to become articulate in English, slept three to four hours per night, and participated in improving his education, correspondence with his mentors, and improving himself.

6. Consider Malcolm's quote "Education is the passport to the future, for tomorrow belongs to the those who prepare for it today." Contrast Malcolm's point of view regarding education with that of the pool players at the Golden Shovel in the poem "We Real Cool."

   Even though Malcolm dropped out of school around the same time as the pool players, he learned to respect education and taught himself to read and write. In contrast, the pool players seemed to disregard the importance of education and were destined for a life of sin and even an early death.

Alternative questions and sentence starters:

3. Why didn't Malcolm X initially value education?

   Malcolm X did not initially value education because _____.

4. What is the excerpt from *The Autobiography of Malcolm X* mostly about?

   _____   _____   _____

   name the item   select a verb   finish your thought

5. How is Malcolm the hustler different from Malcolm the prisoner?

   As a hustler, Malcolm was _____.

   As a prisoner, Malcolm was different because _____.

6. How did Malcolm's point of view regarding education differ from that of the pool players in the poem "We Real Cool"?

   Even though Malcolm _____.

   In contrast, the pool players _____.

Unit
4

Lesson 9

RI.2.2; RI.4.1; RI.6.4; RI.6.10; RI.7.4; RF.2.4a; RF.2.4c; RF.5.4a;
RF.5.4c; L.1.4b; L.1.4c; L.2.1c; L.2.4d; L.5.6; L.2.1e; L.3.1a;
L.4.5c; L.6.4b; L.6.6; L.7.1c; L.8.1c

Lesson Opener

Before the lesson, choose one of the following activities to write on the board or post on the *LANGUAGE! Live* Class Wall online.

- *In the autobiography, Malcolm left prison a different person. Contrast what you think you would be like before and after prison. How you would be different after spending a year in prison?*
- *Make a list of adjectives describing Malcolm before he went to prison and a list of adjectives describing Malcolm after he left prison.*
- *Write five sentences about Malcolm's routines while he was in prison. Use adverbs and prepositional phrases in your sentences.*

Reading

Objectives

- Read an autobiography with purpose and understanding.
- Answer questions to demonstrate comprehension of text.
- Identify and explain explicit details from text.
- Monitor comprehension during text reading.
- Identify words with novel meanings in text and determine the meaning.
- Identify the purpose of modifiers in text.
- Recognize misplaced modifiers and determine the better placement.
- Identify unnecessary words used for emphasis.
- Identify the use of verb moods in literature.
- Identify the meaning and purpose of conjunctive adverbs.

Close Reading of the Excerpt from *The Autobiography of Malcolm X*

Highlighters or colored pencils

Let's reread the excerpt from *The Autobiography of Malcolm X*. I will provide specific instructions on how to mark the text to help with comprehension.

Have students get out a highlighter or colored pencil.

Direct students to pages 179–183 in their Student Books.

Please mark your text according to my instructions.

Draw a rectangle around the title.

Circle the introduction.

Now, let's read the vocabulary words aloud.

- What's the first bold vocabulary word? (acquire) *Acquire* means "to gain; to earn; to come by." Malcolm X *acquired* an education while in prison. **Have partners use the word in a sentence.**

- What's the next bold vocabulary word? (functional) *Functional* means "in working order; able to do a task or job." Malcolm X did not have *functional* command of the English language. **Have partners use the word in a sentence.**

- What's the next vocabulary word? (envy) *Envy* means "the feeling of wanting what someone else has." Malcolm felt *envy* toward educated prisoners. **Have partners use the word in a sentence.**

- Let's continue. (eventually) *Eventually* means "over time; in the end." *Eventually* he learned to read and write consistently. **Have partners use the word in a sentence.**

- Next word? (inevitable) *Inevitable* means "to be expected; hard to keep from happening." Understanding what you read is *inevitable* when you expand your vocabulary. **Have partners use the word in a sentence.**

- Next word? (correspondence) *Correspondence* means "written messages to and from other people." Through *correspondence* with his mentor, Malcolm X realized that he needed to work on his English. **Have partners use the word in a sentence.**

- Let's continue. (debates) *Debates* means "contests in which two sides argue the pros and cons of an issue." Educated prisoners engaged in *debates* on many different issues. **Have partners use the word in a sentence.**

- Next word? (emphasis) *Emphasis* means "the weight, value, or importance put on something." Because there was an *emphasis* on reform, reading and writing were encouraged in prison. **Have partners use the word in a sentence.**

- Next word? (isolation) *Isolation* means "the state of being totally alone." The prisoner read in *isolation* to avoid embarrassment. **Have partners use the word in a sentence.**

- Next word? (adjusted) *Adjusted* means "got used to something." Malcolm X used reading and writing to help him *adjust* to prison life. **Have partners use the word in a sentence.**

Talk with a partner about any vocabulary word that is still confusing for you to read or understand.

As you read the excerpt, you will monitor your understanding by circling the check marks or the question marks. Please be sure to draw a question mark over any confusing words, phrases, or sentences.

Options for rereading text.
- Teacher read-aloud
- Teacher-led or student-led choral read
- Paired read or independent read with bold vocabulary words read aloud

Choose an option for reading text. Have students read lines 1–16 according to the option that you chose.

When most of the students are finished, continue with the entire class. Let's see how well you understood the first section.

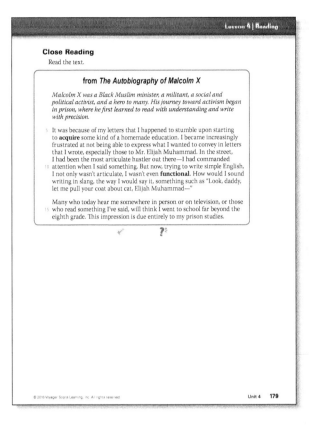

- Circle the check mark or the question mark for this text. Draw a question mark over any confusing words.

- Go to line 1. Mark the word that often refers to someone engaged in war or combat, but in this usage means "person who fights aggressively for a cause." (militant)

- Go to line 2. Mark the word that means "someone who acts on beliefs." (activist)

- On the same line, mark the word with the same root that means "process of taking action." (activism)

- Go to line 4. Mark the word that means "accuracy." (precision)

- Go to lines 6 and 7. Mark the phrase that means "progressively irritated." (increasingly frustrated)

- Mark the reason Malcolm was frustrated. (not being able to express what I wanted to convey in letters that I wrote) Draw an arrow from *letters* to who he was writing to. (Mr. Elijah Muhammad)

- Go to line 7. Circle the synonym for *tell*. (convey)

- Go to line 8. Mark the Muslim leader who mentored Malcolm X. (Mr. Elijah Muhammad)

- Go to line 9. Mark the word that means "well-spoken." (articulate)

- On the same line, mark the phrase that shows Malcolm X was respected. (commanded attention)

- Mark what Malcolm wanted to avoid in his letters. (writing in slang)

- In the second paragraph, mark the interrogative or questioning statement that doesn't have the interrogative punctuation mark. (How would I sound writing in slang, the way I would say it, something such as "Look, daddy, let me pull your coat about cat, Elijah Muhammad—")

- Go to line 13. Circle the slang used to mean "tell you." (pull your coat) Circle the slang used to mean "man." (cat) Both of these terms aren't used in a way that we typically use them today. When words are used with a new meaning, or a meaning that is unfamiliar to us, we refer to this as a *novel meaning*. We use context to determine the meaning of words with novel meanings.

- Go to line 16. Mark the word that means "opinion of others." (impression)

Have students read lines 17–41 according to the option that you chose.

When most of the students are finished, continue with the entire class. Let's see how well you understood the next section.

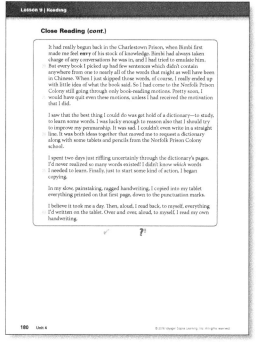

- Circle the check mark or the question mark for this text. Draw a question mark over any confusing words.

- Go to line 17. Mark the inmate that Malcolm X looked up to. **(Bimbi)**

- Mark why Malcolm envied Bimbi. **(stock of knowledge)**

- Go to lines 18 and 19. Mark the phrase that means "controlled." **(taken charge)**

- Go to line 19. Mark the word that means "mimic." **(emulate)**

- Go to lines 21 and 22. Mark the figurative language expressing that the words were difficult to understand. **(might as well have been in Chinese)**

- Go to line 24. Mark the words that mean "fake reading." **(book-reading motions)**

- Go to line 25. Mark the synonym for *inspiration.* **(motivation)**

- In the first paragraph, mark the sentence written in the conditional mood, where an outcome depends on the occurrence of something else. **(Pretty soon, I would have quit even these motions, unless I had received the motivation that I did.)**

- Go to line 29. Mark the synonym for *handwriting.* **(penmanship)**

- Number the reasons Malcolm requested a dictionary. **(1. To learn some words; 2. Improve my penmanship)**

- Go to line 31. Mark the word that means "pads of paper." **(tablets)**

- Go to line 33. Mark the word that means "flipping quickly and casually." **(riffling)**

- Go to line 37. Mark the consecutive adjectives. **(slow; painstaking; ragged)** In the margin, write the name for adjectives of equal importance that are separated by commas. **(coordinate)** Circle the compound word that means "so thorough that it hurts." **(painstaking)**

- Go to line 38. Mark what he copied on the first day. **(everything printed on that first page)**

- On the same line, mark the word that names the category that commas, periods, and apostrophes belong to. **(punctuation marks)**

- On line 39, mark the reflexive pronoun used because the subject and the object of the preposition are the same person. **(myself)**

- On line 40, mark the consecutive phrases used to modify the way he read the words. **(over and over; aloud; to myself)** In the margin, rewrite this sentence to be more clear by moving the modifiers. **(I read my handwriting aloud over and over to myself.)**

Have students read lines 42–70 according to the option that you chose.

When most of the students are finished, continue with the entire class. Let's see how well you understood the next section.

- Circle the check mark or the question mark for this text. Draw a question mark over any confusing words.

- Go to line 42. Mark the adverb that means "vastly." (**immensely**)

- Go to line 44. Mark the transition that means "also." (**moreover**) This is an example of a *conjunctive adverb*, or an adverb that is being used to join two clauses or sentences.

- On line 45, mark what Malcolm needed to remember the words and increase his vocabulary. (**a little effort**)

- On line 51, mark how Malcolm felt after copying the first page. (**fascinated**)

- Go to line 53. Mark the synonym for *next*. (**succeeding**)

- Go to line 54. Mark the synonym for *tiny*. (**miniature**)

- Mark what Malcolm learned besides words and definitions. (**people and places and events from history**)

- On line 62, mark what the dictionary helped Malcolm do when he read. (**understand**) In the margin, write what we study in this class that will help us in the same way. (**vocabulary**)

- Go to line 68. Mark Malcolm's older half-sister. (**Ella**)

- On the same line, mark Malcolm's younger brother. (**Reginald**)

- Number the four things that kept Malcolm from thinking about prison. (**1. Mr. Muhammad's teachings; 2. my correspondence; 3. my visitors; 4. my reading of books**)

- On line 70, mark the consecutive modifiers. (**truly; free**) Which one is an adjective describing Malcolm X? (**free**) Which one is an adverb describing *free*? (**truly**)

Close Reading (*cont.*)

I woke up the next morning, thinking about those words—immensely proud to realize that not only had I written so much at one time, but I'd written words that I never knew were in the world. Moreover, with
45 a little effort, I also could remember what many of these words meant. I reviewed the words whose meanings I didn't remember. Funny thing, from the dictionary's first page right now, that *aardvark* springs to my mind. The dictionary had a picture of it, a long-tailed, long-eared, burrowing African mammal, which lives off termites caught by sticking
50 out its tongue as an anteater does for ants.

I was so fascinated that I went on—I copied the dictionary's next page. And the same experience came when I studied that. With every succeeding page, I also learned of people and places and events from history. Actually the dictionary is like a miniature encyclopedia. Finally
55 the dictionary's A section had filled a whole tablet—and I went on into the B's. That was the way I started copying what **eventually** became the entire dictionary. It went a lot faster after so much practice helped me to pick up handwriting speed. Between what I wrote in my tablet, and writing letters, during the rest of my time in prison I would guess I wrote
60 a million words.

I suppose it was **inevitable** that as my word base broadened, I could for the first time pick up a book and read and now begin to understand what the book was saying. Anyone who has read a great deal can imagine the new world that opened. Let me tell you something: From then until I left
65 that prison, in every free moment I had, if I was not reading in the library, I was reading on my bunk. You couldn't have gotten me out of books with a wedge. Between Mr. Muhammad's teachings, my **correspondence**, my visitors—usually Ella and Reginald—and my reading of books, months passed without my even thinking about being imprisoned. In fact, up to
70 then, I never had been so truly free in my life.

✓   ?

Unit 4   **181**

Have students read lines 71–96 according to the option that you chose.

When most of the students are finished, continue with the entire class. Let's see how well you understood the next section.

- Circle the check mark or the question mark for this text. Draw a question mark over any confusing words.

- In the first paragraph, mark what happened in the school building. **(classes; debates)**

- Go to line 73. Mark the synonym for *convict.* **(inmate)**

- Go to line 75. Mark the substitution for *inmate.* **(convict)**

- On the same line, mark the synonym for *arguers.* **(debaters)**

- Go to line 78. Use a dollar sign to mark the millionaire that donated books. **(Parkhurst)**

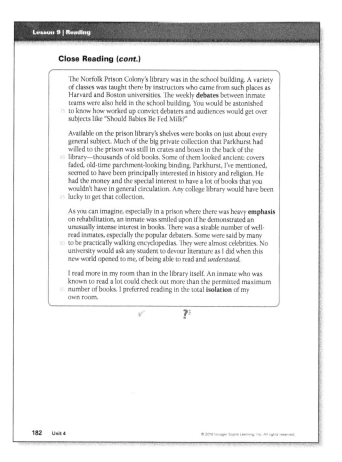

Close Reading (*cont.*)

The Norfolk Prison Colony's library was in the school building. A variety of classes was taught there by instructors who came from such places as Harvard and Boston universities. The weekly **debates** between inmate teams were also held in the school building. You would be astonished
75 to know how worked up convict debaters and audiences would get over subjects like "Should Babies Be Fed Milk?"

Available on the prison library's shelves were books on just about every general subject. Much of the big private collection that Parkhurst had willed to the prison was still in crates and boxes in the back of the
80 library—thousands of old books. Some of them looked ancient: covers faded, old-time parchment-looking binding. Parkhurst, I've mentioned, seemed to have been principally interested in history and religion. He had the money and the special interest to have a lot of books that you wouldn't have in general circulation. Any college library would have been
85 lucky to get that collection.

As you can imagine, especially in a prison where there was heavy **emphasis** on rehabilitation, an inmate was smiled upon if he demonstrated an unusually intense interest in books. There was a sizable number of well-read inmates, especially the popular debaters. Some were said by many
90 to be practically walking encyclopedias. They were almost celebrities. No university would ask any student to devour literature as I did when this new world opened to me, of being able to read and *understand.*

I read more in my room than in the library itself. An inmate who was known to read a lot could check out more than the permitted maximum
95 number of books. I preferred reading in the total **isolation** of my own room.

✓   ?

182   Unit 4   © 2016 Voyager Sopris Learning, Inc. All rights reserved.

- On line 82, mark the main topics of the majority of the books. **(history; religion)**

- Go to line 84. Mark the word that means "available to the public." **(circulation)**

- Go to line 87. Mark the word borrowed from Latin that means "make fit again." **(rehabilitation)**

- On line 88, mark the consecutive modifiers. **(unusually; intense)** Which one is an adjective describing the noun *interest*? **(intense)** Which one is an adverb describing the adjective *intense*? **(unusually)**

- Go to line 90. Mark the idiom that figuratively means "knowledgeable people." **(walking encyclopedias)**

- Go to line 91. Mark the words that literally mean "to eat books." **(devour literature)** Write the figurative meaning in the margin. **(to read a lot)**

- On line 92, mark the description of his new world. **(being able to read and understand)** The description is following the pronoun *me*, so it seems a little out of place. Draw an arrow to the word it should be following. **(world)**

- In the last sentence, mark the unnecessary adjective used for emphasis. **(own)**

Have students read from line 97 to the end according to the option that you chose.

When most of the students are finished, continue with the entire class. Let's see how well you understood the last section.

- Circle the check mark or the question mark for this text. Draw a question mark over any confusing words.

- Go to line 97. Mark the synonym for *advanced*. (progressed)

- On the same line, mark the consecutive modifiers. (really; serious) Which one is an adjective describing the noun *reading*? (serious) Which one is an adverb describing the adjective *serious*? (really)

- Go to line 99. Mark the antonym for *boring*. (engrossing)

- Go to line 100. Mark the synonym for *hallway*. (corridor)

- In the same paragraph, mark the two occurrences that were conditional on the glow of the corridor's light. (sit on the floor; continue reading) Circle the word that indicates the conditional tense. (could)

- Go to line 104. Mark the word that means *chunks of time*. (intervals)

- On the same line, mark the synonym for *walked*. (paced)

- Go to line 105. Mark the synonym for *faked*. (feigned)

- Go to line 110. Circle the pronoun *that*. Draw an arrow to the phrase that it replaces. (three to four hours of sleep)

- Mark where Malcolm was when he got less than three or four hours of sleep. (in the streets)

Have partners compare text markings and correct any errors.

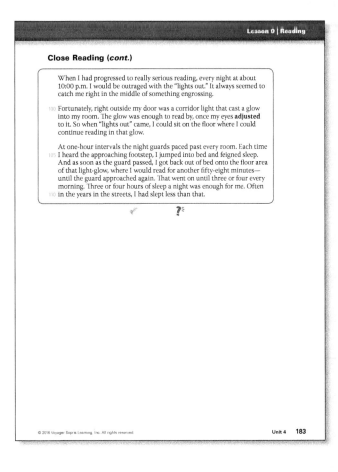

Close Reading (cont.)

When I had progressed to really serious reading, every night at about 10:00 p.m. I would be outraged with the "lights out." It always seemed to catch me right in the middle of something engrossing.

100 Fortunately, right outside my door was a corridor light that cast a glow into my room. The glow was enough to read by, once my eyes **adjusted** to it. So when "lights out" came, I could sit on the floor where I could continue reading in that glow.

At one-hour intervals the night guards paced past every room. Each time 105 I heard the approaching footstep, I jumped into bed and feigned sleep. And as soon as the guard passed, I got back out of bed onto the floor area of that light-glow, where I would read for another fifty-eight minutes— until the guard approached again. That went on until three or four every morning. Three or four hours of sleep a night was enough for me. Often 110 in the years in the streets, I had slept less than that.

Unit 4   **183**

Unit 4

Lesson 10

RI.1.4; W.2.2; W.3.2c; W.3.2d; W.5.2c; W.5.2e; W.3.5; W.5.4; W.5.5; W.3.8; W.5.9a; W.2.10; W.4.10; W.6.10; W.8.10; SL.5.1b; SL.5.1c; SL.5.1d; L.6.6

Lesson Opener

Before the lesson, choose one of the following activities to write on the board or post on the *LANGUAGE! Live* Class Wall online.

- *Write four sentences with at least two vocabulary words in each. Show you know the meanings. (acquire, functional, envy, eventually, inevitable, correspondence, debate, emphasis, isolation, adjust)*
- *Dress your avatar as though you were leaving prison and meeting your mentor in person for the first time. Explain your choices.*
- *Knowing the consequences of dropping out of school, would you drop out if given the opportunity? Why or why not?*

Vocabulary

Objective
- Review key passage vocabulary.

Recontextualize Passage Vocabulary

Direct students to page 168 in their Student Books. Use the following questions to review the vocabulary words in the excerpt from *The Autobiography of Malcolm X.*

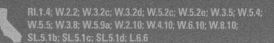

- Your phone is dead. Is it *functional*? (**no**) Is a broken umbrella *functional*? (**no**) A good night's sleep can help you feel how the next day? (**functional**)

- We both like a TV series, but we disagree which episode is best. We take turns telling why one episode is better than the other. Is this a *debate*? (**yes**) Two friends have a misunderstanding and don't speak for days. Is this a *debate*? (**no**) You are running for student council. You and your opponent express different views during an assembly. What are you having? (**a debate**)

- If I caught the flu, would you feel *envy*? (**no**) Your cousin gets a free ticket to a concert that you want to see. Do you feel *envy*? (**yes**) You enter an art contest, but someone else wins the prize. What might you feel? (**envy**)

- Does a newborn baby have to *adjust*? (**yes**) Two new people have moved into your home. Do you have to *adjust*? (**yes**) When the time changes and we lose an hour, what do we have to do? (**adjust**)

- If you wait and wait for an e-mail, and it finally comes, did it *eventually* come? (**yes**) If you were asked to do the dishes and you did them immediately, did you do them *eventually*? (**no**) You are sitting in the longest, most boring movie ever. When will it end? (**eventually**)

- If you just signed up for guitar lessons, have you *acquired* the skill? (no) If you agree to watch your baby nephew after school, have you *acquired* a new responsibility? (yes) If you get your driver's license, what has happened? (You have acquired your license.)

- You take flowers to a sick friend. Is this *correspondence*? (no) You and a former teacher exchange birthday cards. Is this *correspondence*? (yes) You write a letter to a celebrity and she answers. What is this called? (correspondence)

- In science class, is there an *emphasis* on ancient Egypt? (no) In a fitness boot camp, is there an *emphasis* on poetry? (no) The main purpose of a club you belong to is helping others. What does the club put on helping others? (an emphasis)

- Is a single fish in a fishbowl in *isolation*? (yes) Do most people graduate from high school in *isolation*? (no) You are all alone in a canoe on a quiet river. What state are you in? (a state of isolation)

- You plant a seed and forget to water it. Is it *inevitable* that it will grow? (no) Your team is evenly matched with the opposing team. Is it *inevitable* that you will lose? (no) When guests visit, you sleep on the couch. Your aunt is coming to visit. Your sleeping on the couch is what? (inevitable)

Objectives

- Write in response to text.
- Take notes on an informational text.
- Use transition words in writing.
- Orally retell key information from an informational text.
- Write a time-order paragraph.
- Use a rubric to guide and assess writing.

Six Traits of Effective Writing

Direct students back to page 30 from Unit 1 in their Student Books. Reread the Six Traits of Effective Writing.

In previous units, we have focused on sentence fluency, word choice, conventions, and organization. We have used varying sentence structures and descriptive language to keep our writing from sounding boring. We have used proper grammar, punctuation, and spelling to ensure the reader understands the text, and we have organized our paragraphs to include introductions, conclusions, and transitions.

Our focus for this unit will be ideas and content. We will make sure that our supporting details accurately support our main ideas/ topic sentences and that the supporting details are backed up with elaborations, including evidence from the text.

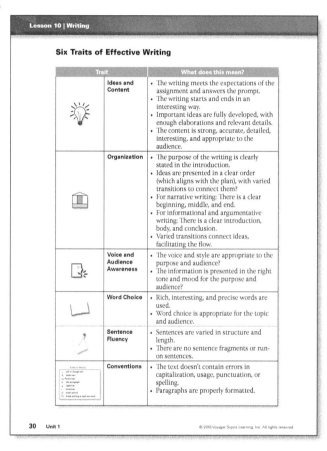

Lesson 10 | Writing

Six Traits of Effective Writing

Trait		What does this mean?
	Ideas and Content	• The writing meets the expectations of the assignment and answers the prompt. • The writing starts and ends in an interesting way. • Important ideas are fully developed, with enough elaborations and relevant details. • The content is strong, accurate, detailed, interesting, and appropriate to the audience.
	Organization	• The purpose of the writing is clearly stated in the introduction. • Ideas are presented in a clear order (which aligns with the plan), with varied transitions to connect them? • For narrative writing: There is a clear beginning, middle, and end. • For informational and argumentative writing: There is a clear introduction, body, and conclusion. • Varied transitions connect ideas, facilitating the flow.
	Voice and Audience Awareness	• The voice and style are appropriate to the purpose and audience? • The information is presented in the right tone and mood for the purpose and audience?
	Word Choice	• Rich, interesting, and precise words are used. • Word choice is appropriate for the topic and audience.
	Sentence Fluency	• Sentences are varied in structure and length. • There are no sentence fragments or run-on sentences.
	Conventions	• The text doesn't contain errors in capitalization, usage, punctuation, or spelling. • Paragraphs are properly formatted.

30   Unit 1   © 2018 Voyager Sopris Learning, Inc. All rights reserved.

Prepare to Write: Time-Order Paragraph

Direct students to page 184 in their Student Books.

Part A. Study the Prompt

Read the instructions for Part A and the prompt.

The instructions tell you to do three things after reading the prompt. What is the first thing? (Identify the topic.) Yes, you are to identify the topic. What is the topic? (Possible answers: how Malcolm X used his time in prison; the steps Malcolm X followed to improve his reading and writing skills.) **Have students write the topic on the page.**

What's the second thing you need to do? (Identify the directions.) What are the directions? (to write a paragraph; use transition words) **Have students write the directions on the page.**

What is the third thing you are asked to consider? (purpose for writing) What is the goal or purpose of this writing assignment? (explain the way Malcolm X used his time to better himself while in prison) **Have students write the purpose on the page.**

Part B. Write a Topic Sentence

Direct students to Part B. We have identified our topic, so now let's consider our opening or topic sentence. Think about the work you have been doing with sentence expansion and word order. To paint the predicate, what questions do you use? (when, where, and how) For this writing assignment, you are going to develop a topic sentence that includes the answer to a *when* and/or *where* question. Think of the prompt. We are writing about how Malcolm X used his time in prison. Determine some possible answers to the when and where questions and write them in the chart. After you have worked on your notes for the assignment, we'll come back and write the rest of the sentence. **Offer an example if necessary.**

Lesson 10 | Writing

Prepare to Write: Time-Order Paragraph

Part A. Study the Prompt   Answers will vary.

Read the prompt and identify the topic, directions, and purpose for writing.

Write a paragraph that explains how Malcolm X used his time in prison as an opportunity for personal growth. Use transition words.

Topic: routine Malcolm X developed for growth

Directions: write a paragraph; use transition words

Purpose for writing: Explain the way Malcolm X used his time to better himself while in prison.

Part B. Write a Topic Sentence (when or where + statement)

When?	Where?	Statement
while in prison	in prison	Malcolm X developed a plan to improve his ability to read and write.
during his time in prison	in jail	Malcolm X worked hard to improve his reading and writing skills.
throughout his time in prison	in the prison library	Malcolm X decided to improve his reading and writing skills.

Topic Sentence: While in prison, Malcolm X worked diligently to improve his reading and writing skills.

184   Unit 4   © 2016 Voyager Sopris Learning, Inc. All rights reserved.

Part C. Sequence Events

Direct students to Part C. Because our instructions told us to describe his routine, let's think about the steps Malcolm X followed to improve his reading and writing skills. What was the first thing he did once he realized how weak his reading skills were? (He decided to get a dictionary.) He checked out a dictionary from the prison library. Why? (He planned to look up unfamiliar words.) Have students fill in their chart as you progress through the steps. When he realized how many words were unfamiliar to him, what did he decide to do? (He decided to copy the first page of the dictionary.) What was his purpose for copying the entire page? (He thought it would help him learn the words and also help him improve his handwriting.) Did it work? (Yes, he found he could remember most of the words he had written, and he began to focus on writing more neatly.) We do the same thing when we take notes. Notes help us remember the important details about a topic. Let's go to the third step. How did Malcolm X put his notes to good use? (He read them aloud the next day and used them to help him remember the words and their meanings.) Let's move to the fourth step. He didn't just study the words he was learning; he began to use them. How did he use his new vocabulary? (He wrote articulate letters to his mentor.) What else did he do to continue growing his vocabulary? (He kept reading as much as he could.) That's our last step. He even read after "lights out." Why did he read? (to learn; engage in debates; feel free; change his life and the lives of others) He worked diligently to improve himself.

Lesson 10 | Writing

Prepare to Write: Time-Order Paragraph (*cont.*)

Part C. Sequence Events

Write the steps Malcolm X followed to improve himself and the specific purpose of each step.

Answers will vary.

2-Column Notes

Step	Purpose
• Got a dictionary	• Look up unfamiliar words when reading
• Copied a page	• Learn words • Work on handwriting
• Read the copied pages aloud the next day	• Help him remember the new words
• Wrote letters to his mentor	• Express himself articulately
• Read as much as possible	• Learn • Engage in debates • Feel free • Change his life and the lives of others

© 2016 Voyager Sopris Learning, Inc. All rights reserved. Unit 4 185

Part B. Write a Topic Sentence

Now that you have a better idea of the content of your paragraph, finish your topic sentences. Direct students to Part B and have them share ideas for a statement about what Malcolm X did while in prison. Explain that the statement should be general, not the specific steps. Write their ideas on the board and have them write three of them in their charts.

Choose a beginning when or where phrase and a statement, and then write your topic sentence on the line. Have volunteers share their topic sentences. Because topic sentences and concluding sentences work like bookends in a paragraph, let's use these thoughts to write our concluding sentence.

Part D. Write a Concluding Sentence

Direct students to Part D and read the
instructions and the words in the
chart. Starting with one of these
phrases, restate your topic sentence
and write it on the line. Have students
write a concluding sentence.

Prepare to Write: Time-Order Paragraph (*cont.*)

Part D. Write a Concluding Sentence

Develop a concluding sentence by restating the topic sentence. Choose a
word from the chart below to start your sentence. Use a comma to separate
the word or phrase from the rest of the sentence.

Answers will vary.

Concluding Words and Phrases				
As a result	Consequently	Finally	In closing	In conclusion
In summary	In the end	So	Therefore	Thus

As a result of his efforts, Malcolm X used his
time in prison to become a better reader and
more polished writer.

Write

Using your notes, you will write the body of your paragraph. I want you to use transition words from the chart on page 176 to connect one step to the next step. Have students take out a clean sheet of paper and write their paragraph. Remind them to use their notes and the transition words in the chart as they put their steps into complete sentences. Some students may need more support. Have students consult the Six Traits of Writing: Basic rubric on page 389 as they write their paragraph. If they struggle or need additional support in developing their paragraph, use the following paragraph as a model.

Exemplar Writing: Time-Order Paragraph

While in prison, Malcolm X worked diligently to strengthen his reading and writing skills. His first step was to get a dictionary from the prison library. He began to use it to look up unfamiliar words, and then he decided to begin copying the words and their definitions. He used this exercise to improve his handwriting as well as to learn as many words as possible. When he read his pages aloud the next day, he realized he remembered many of the words. In addition to his dictionary work, he wrote letters to his mentor. The letters provided an opportunity to use the new words and to continue practicing his penmanship. He also continued to read as much as possible. He checked out many books from the prison library and found a way to keep reading after "lights out." As a result of his efforts, Malcolm X used his time in prison to become a better reader and more polished writer.

Six Traits of Writing: Basic

	Ideas and Content	Organization	Voice and Audience Awareness	Word Choice	Sentence Fluency	Language Conventions
4	Focuses on the topic. Main idea (topic sentence) is clear and well supported with details and elaboration (examples, evidence, and explanations).	Topic sentence clearly states main idea. Ideas are clear and logically organized. Contains concluding sentence.	The words have a strong sense of person and purpose. Brings topic to life.	Words are specific to the content, accurate, and vivid. Word choice enhances meaning and the reader's enjoyment.	Writes complete sentences and varies sentence structure.	There are no grammar errors. There are few or no errors in spelling, capitalization, or punctuation.
3	Mostly focuses on the topic. Sentences supporting the main idea (topic sentence) may be general rather than detailed and specific.	Topic sentence states main idea. Organization mostly clear and logical. May contain concluding sentence.	The words have some sense of person and purpose.	Words are correctly used but may be somewhat general and unspecific.	Writes complete sentences and attempts to use expanded sentences.	There are no major grammar errors. There are few errors in spelling, capitalization, or punctuation.
2	Main idea (topic sentence) is unclear and/or lacks sufficient support.	Structure may not be entirely clear or logical. Paragraph may seem more like a list and/or be hard to follow.	The words have little sense of person and purpose.	Words may be used inaccurately or repetitively.	Writes mostly simple and/or awkwardly constructed sentences. May include some run-ons and fragments.	There are a few grammar errors. There are a few errors in spelling, capitalization, or punctuation.
1	Does not address prompt and/or lacks a topic sentence. Supporting details are absent or do not relate to topic.	No evident structure. Lack of organization seriously interferes with meaning.	The words have no sense of person or purpose. No sense of audience.	Extremely limited range of words. Restricted vocabulary impedes message.	Numerous run-ons and/or fragments interfere with meaning.	There are many grammar and/or spelling errors. There are many errors in capitalization and punctuation.

Writing Rubric: Basic 389

Student Handwriting:

Handwriting lessons are provided in manuscript and cursive. These explicit lessons (found online in Resources) can be taught systematically during writing lessons to strengthen legibility and fluency.

Evaluate Writing

Direct students to page 187 in their Student Books and read the information in the checklist. This checklist is a tool you can use to evaluate your writing and make sure you are using good technique. This unit's checklist is a little bit more advanced than the last unit's, so read through it carefully. As we progress through the program, we will add things we have learned that will make us better writers. Have individuals quickly assess their writing, then have partners evaluate each other's writing based on the checklist.

Note: Use Six Traits of Writing Scoring Rubric: Basic on page 564 of this book to assess students' writing. A printable version is located online in the Teacher Resources.

The Writer's Checklist

Trait	Yes	No	Did the writer . . . ?
R Ideas and Content			focus all sentences on the topic
			provide supporting details for the topic sentence
E Organization			write a topic sentence
			tell things in an order that makes sense
V			use transition words and/or phrases
			write a concluding sentence
I Voice and Audience Awareness			think about the audience and purpose for writing
S Word Choice			try to find a unique way to say things
			use words that are lively and specific to the content
E Sentence Fluency			write complete sentences
			expand some sentences by painting the subject and/or predicate
Conventions			capitalize words correctly:
E			capitalize the first word of each sentence
			capitalize proper nouns, including people's names
D			punctuate correctly:
			put a period or question mark at the end of each sentence
I			put an apostrophe before the s for a singular possessive noun
			use a comma after a long adverb phrase at the beginning of a sentence
T			use grammar correctly:
			use the correct verb tense
			make sure the verb agrees with the subject in number
			use correct spelling

Unit 4   **187**

Six Traits of Writing: Basic

Objectives

- Self-correct as comprehension of text deepens.
- Answer questions to demonstrate comprehension of text.
- Engage in class discussion.
- Identify the enduring understandings from a piece of text.

Revisit Passage Comprehension

Direct students back to pages 177 and 178 in their Student Books. Have students review their answers and make any necessary changes. Then, have partners share their answers and collaborate to perfect them.

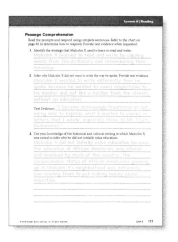

Enduring Understandings

Direct students back to page 167 in their Student Books. Reread the Big Idea questions.

Is education the passport to the future? Explain.

Is code-switching necessary? Explain.

Generate a class discussion about the questions and the answers students came up with in Lesson 6. Have them consider whether their answers have changed any after reading the text.

Use the following talking points to foster conversation. Refer to the Class Discussion Rules poster and have students use the Collegial Discussion sentence frames on page 382 of their Student Books.

- Even though Malcolm X did not have a high school diploma, he educated himself by devouring books. Other highly successful people have taught themselves to read and educated themselves, like President Abraham Lincoln and author Jack London. Through literacy and education, they changed their path in life and affected the lives of others. Education is powerful. Is it possible that the men I mentioned valued their education more because they worked so hard to achieve it? Do we value only the things we have to work hard to achieve?

- Sounding educated can be frowned upon. Why do you think that is?

What we read should make us think. Use our discussion and your thoughts about the text to determine what you will "walk away with." Has it made you think about a personal experience or someone you know? Has your perspective or opinion on a specific topic changed? Do you have any lingering thoughts or questions? Write these ideas as your enduring understandings. What will you take with you from this text?

Discuss the enduring understandings with the class. Then, have students write their enduring understandings from the unit.

Have students consider why the author wrote the passage and whether he was successful.

End-of-Unit Online Assessments

Monitor students' progress in the unit by utilizing online assessments. Students should prioritize these assessments over successive Word Training units.

- Assign Unit 4 Content Mastery quizzes to assess skills taught in this unit.
- Assign Power Pass to assess reading comprehension skills in a standardized test format.

All assessments can be assigned online by opening the Tools menu, then selecting Assignments. Be sure to select the correct class and unit from the drop-down menu.

Reteach

Based on students' performance in Content Mastery, extra practice may be needed.

- If student scores fall at 60 percent or below, reteach the content to small groups.
- If student scores fall between 61–79 percent, reinforce the skills by assigning the student reteach activity pages as homework.

Reteach lessons can be found online on the Course Reports page for each unit.

Unit 5

Unit Big Ideas

- Are suffering and normalcy relative?
- Which plays a bigger part in who we are: things we are born with or things we are surrounded by?
- At what age are our personality and belief system formed?
- To what degree is our future shaped by the people with whom we live as children?

Instructional Texts

Excerpt from *Breaking Night* by Liz Murray

Text type: informational—memoir

"From Homeless to Harvard"

Text type: informational

 Materials

- Unit 5 video (Liz Murray)
- Six Traits of Writing Scoring Rubric: Basic (print as needed)

Optional
- Online dictionary
- Progress Monitoring Across the Six Traits scales

Classroom Materials

- Highlighters or colored pencils
- Notebook paper
- Thesauruses

 Instructional Resources

- Unit 5 Reteach
- Handwriting Lessons

- Writing Project: Compare and Contrast Fiction and Nonfiction

- Progress Monitoring Across the Six Traits scales

Instructional Texts:

Excerpt from
Breaking Night

by Liz Murray

Text type: informational—memoir

"From Homeless to Harvard"

Text type: informational

LANGUAGE! Live Online

Grammar Practice

- Identify the function of linking verbs, helping verbs, and action verbs in sentences.
- Use verb tenses correctly.
- Use coordinating conjunctions to combine sentence elements.
- Use *to be* verbs correctly.

Vocabulary Practice

- Distinguish between commonly confused words and use them correctly.
- Determine the meaning of derivations of words.
- Determine the meaning of similes.

Content Mastery

- Demonstrate an understanding of . . .
  - word meaning by answering questions and using words in sentences.
  - the multiple functions of nouns.
  - coordinating conjunctions in compound sentence elements.

Word Study

- Discuss Anglo-Saxon, Greek, and Latin layers of English and the meaning of morphemes.
- Blend, read, and spell multisyllabic words with open syllables; words with prefixes pre-, re-, and super- and suffixes -er and -est; words with spellings wr-, kn-, gn-, -ch as /k/ and -ph as /f/; and contractions containing the words *had* and *have*.
- Read connected text to build fluency.

Lesson 1

Reading
- Determine and discuss the topic of a text.
- Determine and discuss the author's purpose.
- Use text features to preview text.

Vocabulary
- Evaluate word knowledge.
- Determine the meaning of key passage vocabulary.

Reading
- Read an excerpt from a memoir.
- Monitor comprehension during text reading.

Lesson 2

Vocabulary
- Review key passage vocabulary.

Grammar
- Correctly use nouns functioning as direct objects, objects of the preposition, and predicate nouns.
- Use conjunctions in compound subjects, compound predicates, and compound objects.
- Identify the meaning of coordinating conjunctions in sentences.
- Use reflexive and intensive pronouns correctly.

Writing
- Identify the structure of a sentence.
- Use adjectives and adverbs correctly in sentence writing.
- Produce, expand, and rearrange complete sentences for clarity and style.
- Write sentences with compound elements.

Lesson 6

Reading
- Determine and discuss the topic of a text.
- Determine and discuss the author's purpose.
- Use text features to preview text.

Vocabulary
- Evaluate word knowledge.
- Determine the meaning of key passage vocabulary.

Reading
- Read informational text.
- Monitor comprehension during text reading.

Lesson 7

Vocabulary
- Review key passage vocabulary.

Reading
- Determine how to respond to prompts.
- Use critical thinking skills to write responses to prompts about text.
- Support written answers with text evidence.
- Determine main ideas in informational text.
- Sequence events in a text.

Writing Project: Compare and Contrast Fiction and Nonfiction

Lesson 3

Reading

- Objectively summarize informational text.
- Determine the central idea of informational text.
- Establish a purpose for rereading a memoir.
- Determine the central idea of text.
- Use critical thinking skills to write responses to prompts about text.
- Support written answers with text evidence.
- Draw inferences from text and support with evidence.

Lesson 4

Vocabulary

- Review key passage vocabulary.

Reading

- Read with purpose and understanding.
- Answer questions to demonstrate comprehension of text.
- Monitor comprehension of text during reading.
- Determine the meaning of figurative language in text.
- Identify coordinate adjectives in text and the punctuation used to separate them.
- Identify the conditional tense in writing and understand its meaning.
- Identify stereotyping in text.
- Determine the impact of imperative verbs in text.

See p. 399 for additional lesson objectives.

Lesson 5

Vocabulary

- Review key passage vocabulary.

Writing

- Use text to write coherent paragraphs in response to reading.
- Analyze a character and how the character's traits affect the events in the text.

Reading

- Self-correct as comprehension of text deepens.
- Answer questions to demonstrate comprehension of text.
- Engage in class discussion.
- Identify the enduring understandings from a piece of text.
- Identify the influence individuals have on ideas and events.
- Identify the impact of perspective and mood.

Lesson 8

Reading

- Establish a purpose for rereading informational text.
- Monitor comprehension during text reading.
- Use critical thinking skills to write responses to prompts about text.
- Support written answers with text evidence.
- Use text evidence to support claims.
- Analyze the effect a person has on events.
- Sequence events.

Lesson 9

Vocabulary

- Review key passage vocabulary.

Reading

- Read informational text.
- Read with purpose and understanding.
- Answer questions to demonstrate comprehension of text.
- Monitor comprehension during text reading.
- Distinguish between the subjective point of view and the objective point of view.
- Identify how text is organized and how each section contributes to the whole text.

Lesson 10

Vocabulary

- Review key passage vocabulary.

Writing

- Use two texts to write coherently.
- Use a process to write.
- Compare and contrast a firsthand account and secondhand account of the same topic.
- Analyze the similarities and discrepancies between two accounts of the same topic.
- Use a rubric to guide and evaluate writing.

Reading

- Self-correct as comprehension of text deepens.
- Answer questions to demonstrate comprehension of text.
- Engage in class discussion.

See p. 449 for additional lesson objectives.

Unit
5

Lesson 1

RL.5.4; RI.1.4; RI.1.10a; RI.2.2; RI.3.1; RI.4.1; RI.5.4; RI.6.6;
RI.6.10; RF.5.4a; SL.1.2; SL.6.1b; SL.6.1c; SL.6.1d; L.1.4a;
L.3.5b; L.4.6; L.6.6

Lesson Opener

Before the lesson, choose one of the following activities to write on the board or post on the *LANGUAGE! Live* Class Wall online.

- *Describe an obstacle in your life that you overcame.*
- *Write two sentences about the importance of an education. Identify the complete subject and complete predicate.*
- *Write two sentences describing your favorite day of the week. Explain what you do on that day and why you like it. Identify the adjectives and adverbs.*

Reading

Objectives

- Determine and discuss the topic of a text.
- Determine and discuss the author's purpose.
- Use text features to preview text.

Passage Introduction

Direct students to page 189 in their Student Books. Discuss the content focus.

Content Focus

triumph

What do you think you will read about in this text? (Answers will vary.) Have you ever been faced with an obstacle that was difficult to overcome? **Provide sharing time.**

Type of Text

informational

Literature comes from the Latin root that means "letter." In order for words on a page to be considered literature, the text has to be respected, valued, and important. This consideration is subjective. What one person considers literature, another person may not. In the last unit, we read autobiographies. Turn to your neighbor and share the difference between a biography and autobiography. **Provide sharing time.** Which one provides information about a person's life but is written by someone else? (biography) What is an autobiography? (a story about a person's life told by that person) The author of "The Circuit" told his life experiences through a short story. This unit's excerpt comes from the memoir *Breaking Night*. It is written by the person it is about, just like an autobiography.

Unit
5

Lesson 1 | Reading

Let's Focus: Excerpt from *Breaking Night*

Content Focus	Type of Text
triumph	informational—memoir

Author's Name Liz Murray

Author's Purpose share information about rough childhood to inspire others to overcome obstacles

Big Ideas
Consider the following Big Idea questions. Write your answer for each question.

Are suffering and normalcy relative? Explain.

_____

_____

Which plays a bigger part in who we are: things we are born with or things we are surrounded by? Explain.

_____

_____

Narrative Preview Checklist: Excerpt from *Breaking Night* on pages 191–196.

☐ Title: What clue does it provide about the passage?

☐ Pictures: What additional information is added here?

☐ Margin Information: What vocabulary is important to understand this story?

Enduring Understandings
After reading the text . . .

_____

_____

_____

_____

_____

_____

Unit 5 **189**

However, the memoir is about a specific period of time in the author's life—not her whole life. Memoirs are informational text.

Author's Purpose

Have students glance at the text. Who is the author of this memoir? (Liz Murray) The author's purpose is the reason that he or she wrote the text. Authors write for different purposes. They write to entertain, to persuade, or to inform or teach. Knowing an author's purpose can help a reader better understand a text. Like "The Circuit," *Breaking Night* was written to inform others about the conditions and times in which the author lived. Liz Murray wrote *Breaking Night* to provide insight and motivation for others who may be faced with obstacles. She wants to help others persevere through life's obstacles. **Have students write the answers on the page.**

Play the Unit 5 Text Training video found in the Teacher Resources online.

Before we read the excerpt from *Breaking Night*, we will watch a short video to help build our background knowledge. **Play the Unit 5 Text Training video. Have partners discuss the main points the videographer was trying to make and what evidence was provided to support the points.**

Background Information

What is the title of this text? (*Breaking Night*) *Break* has many meanings. You can drop a glass and *break* it. If the pencil sharpener *breaks*, it no longer works. If you are running in the hallways, you are *breaking* the rules. When school closes over the holidays, we say it is closed for winter *break*. Can you *break* the night? Pondering the meaning of a book's title can help to focus your thoughts and increase your understanding as you begin to read.

According to the book, *breaking night* is "urban slang for staying up through the night until the sun rises." Why do you think the author used street language in her title? (Answers will vary. Guide students to realize that she lived on the streets much of her life.) Since we know that *breaking night* is defined as "staying up through the night until the light of morning comes," what do you think that term meant to Liz regarding her life? **Provide sharing time.** The title is also metaphorical. It means something more than what it says. What else could Liz Murray want to convey besides staying awake until the sun rises? (Answers will vary. Guide students to realize that she persevered through dark times until she achieved a brighter future.) Has there been a time in your life that this metaphor applies to?

Read the Big Idea questions aloud.

Big Ideas

Are suffering and normalcy relative?

Which plays a bigger part in who we are: things we are born with or things we are surrounded by?

Collegial Discussion poster

Class Discussion Rules poster

As a class, consider the two Big Idea questions.

- Encourage students with limited experiences of suffering and limited knowledge of the theory of nature vs. nurture to ask for further explanation from peers.

- Provide opportunities for students to explain their ideas and answers to the Big Idea questions in light of the discussion by ensuring students follow the rules for class discussion, which can be printed in poster form from the Teacher Resources online.

- Suggest students refer to the Collegial Discussion sentence frames in the back of their books.

- Encourage speakers to link comments to the remarks of others to keep the focus of the discussion and create cohesion, even when their comments are in disagreement.

After discussing each question, have students write an answer. We'll come back to these questions after we finish reading the text. You can add to your answers as you gain information and perspective.

Preview

Read the Preview Checklist on page 189. Follow the Preview Procedure outlined below.

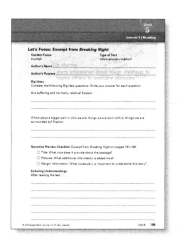

> ### Preview Procedure
> - Group students with partners or in triads.
> - Have students count off as 1s or 2s. The 1s will become the student leaders. If working with triads, the third students become 3s.
> - The student leaders will preview the text in addition to managing the checklist and pacing.
> - The 2s and 3s will preview the text with 1s.
> - Direct 1s to open their Student Books to page 189 and 2s and 3s to open their Student Books to page 191. This allows students to look at a few different pages at one time without turning back and forth.

Direct students to page 191.

If necessary, guide students in a short preview using the following talking points.

What is the title? (*Breaking Night*) Who is the author? (Liz Murray) Describe the graphic on the title page. (ID card and check) I wonder what they will have to do with the story. **Provide sharing time.**

Let's look to see what additional information the pictures provide. What is pictured on the next page? (old, yellow chair) What do you think happened to the chair? **Provide sharing time.** Describe the picture on page 193. (gumball machines with a toy spider) What is pictured on the next page? (an old building) Maybe that is somewhere they visited. Describe the picture on page 196. (ice cream truck, old black-and-white television, and French fries) Those look like things a kid would like.

Objectives

- Evaluate word knowledge.
- Determine the meaning of key passage vocabulary.

Rate Vocabulary Knowledge

Direct students to page 190 in their Student Books. Let's take a look at the vocabulary words from the excerpt from *Breaking Night*. I am going to say each word aloud. You will repeat the word and write it in the third column. Then, you will rate your knowledge of the word. Display the Vocabulary Rating Scale poster or write the information on the board. Review the meaning of each rating.

Vocabulary Rating Scale

0—I have never heard the word before.

1—I have heard the word, but I'm not sure how to use it.

2—I am familiar with the word, but I'm not sure if I know the correct meaning.

3—I know the meaning of the word and can use it correctly in a sentence.

Key Passage Vocabulary: Excerpt from *Breaking Night*

Read each word. Write the word in column 3. Then, circle a number to rate your knowledge of the word.

Vocabulary	Part of Speech	Write the Word	Knowledge Rating
anticipation	(n)	anticipation	0 1 2 3
consistency	(n)	consistency	0 1 2 3
qualify	(v)	qualify	0 1 2 3
invaluable	(adj)	invaluable	0 1 2 3
ailment	(n)	ailment	0 1 2 3
portion	(n)	portion	0 1 2 3
clamor	(v)	clamor	0 1 2 3
reassuring	(adj)	reassuring	0 1 2 3
elaborate	(adj)	elaborate	0 1 2 3
euphoric	(adj)	euphoric	0 1 2 3

190 Unit 5

Remember, the points are there to help you know which words you need to focus on. By the end of this unit, you should be able to change all your ratings to a 3. That's the goal.

Read each word aloud and have students repeat it, write it, and rate it. Then, have volunteers who rated a word *2* or *3* use the word in an oral sentence.

Preteach Vocabulary

Explain that you will now take a closer look at the words. Follow the Preteach Procedure outlined below.

Preteach Procedure

This activity is intended to take only a short amount of time, so make it an oral exercise.

- Introduce each word as indicated on the word card.
- Read the definition and example sentences.
- Ask questions to clarify and deepen understanding.
- If time permits, allow students to share.

* If your students would benefit from copying the definitions, please have them do so in the vocabulary log in the back of the Student Books using the margin definitions in the passage selections. This should be done outside of instruction time.

---

anticipation (n)

Let's read the first word together. *Anticipation.*

Definition: *Anticipation* is a feeling of excitement about something that is about to happen. What means "a feeling of excitement about something that is about to happen"? (anticipation)

Example 1: On the day before your birthday, you may feel *anticipation*.

Example 2: During the 10 minutes before a movie begins, I am filled with *anticipation*.

Example 3: *Anticipation* of the bell can keep some students from focusing on a lesson.

Question 1: Do some people feel *anticipation* before a new season of their favorite TV show? Yes or no? (yes)

Question 2: Does the thought of homework fill you with *anticipation*? Yes or no? (no)

Pair Share: Turn to your partner and describe a recent event you looked forward to with *anticipation*.

(1)

consistency (n)

Let's read the next word together. *Consistency.*

Definition: *Consistency* means something done in the same way, time after time. What means "something done in the same way, time after time"? (consistency)

Example 1: Blueberry pancakes every Saturday morning are a *consistency* at our house.

Example 2: *Consistency* in physical training is important if you want to improve your ability to play a sport.

Example 3: One *consistency* of mine is that I get up before dawn every day.

Question 1: If you often forget to floss your teeth, do you have *consistency* with flossing? Yes or no? (no)

Question 2: You text your best friend first thing every morning. Is this a *consistency*? Yes or no? (yes)

Pair Share: Turn to your partner and tell what you would like to make a *consistency* in your life.

(2)

qualify (v)

Let's read the next word together. *Qualify.*

Definition: *Qualify* means "to show that you have the right to do or have something." What word means "to show that you have the right to do or have something"? (qualify)

Example 1: If you are 65 and retired, you may *qualify* for Social Security benefits.

Example 2: Anyone who passes the driving exam *qualifies* for a driver's license.

Example 3: Students who make As and Bs *qualify* for the honor roll.

Question 1: Would anyone in this room *qualify* for a Nobel Prize in physics? Yes or no? (no)

Question 2: A person must be between 12 years of age and 15 years of age to enter a contest. Would you *qualify*? Yes or no? (Answers will vary.)

Pair Share: Turn to your partner and name a job you hope to *qualify* for someday.

(3)

invaluable (adj)

Let's read the next word together. *Invaluable.*

Definition: Something *invaluable* is extremely useful or precious and hard to replace. What word means "extremely useful or precious and hard to replace"? (invaluable)

Example 1: An *invaluable* experience is so very valuable that we can't put a price on it.

Example 2: Many people consider their vacation time *invaluable*.

Example 3: A lug wrench, a jack, and a spare tire are *invaluable* when changing a flat.

Question 1: Do many people consider their phone *invaluable*? Yes or no? (yes)

Question 2: Would a firefighter consider a water hose *invaluable*? Yes or no? (yes)

Pair Share: Turn to your partner and name something you consider *invaluable*.

(4)

ailment (n)

Let's read the next word together. *Ailment.*

Definition: An *ailment* is a sickness or something that causes pain and discomfort. What word means "a sickness or something that causes pain and discomfort"? (ailment)

Example 1: Throat strain is a common *ailment* among professional singers.

Example 2: If an *ailment* does not go away, you should see a doctor.

Example 3: Older people sometimes have back *ailments*.

Question 1: If you have a cold, are you suffering from an *ailment*? Yes or no? (yes)

Question 2: Is a soothing foot massage an example of an *ailment*? Yes or no? (no)

Pair Share: You have an idea for a TV show in which people suffer from a mysterious *ailment*. Turn to your partner and describe it.

(5)

portion (n)

Let's read the next word together. *Portion.*

Definition: A *portion* is one part of a greater whole. What means "one part of a greater whole"? (portion)

Example 1: If you only eat a *portion* of a sandwich, you have some left over.

Example 2: People who put some of their paycheck aside are saving a *portion* of it.

Example 3: In a group project, each member is responsible for a *portion* of the final product.

Question 1: If you read a *portion* of a magazine, have you read all of it? Yes or no? (no)

Question 2: Is this classroom one *portion* of the school campus? Yes or no? (yes)

Pair Share: Turn to your partner and tell what you could do with a *portion* of a dollar.

(6)

clamor (v)

Let's read the next word together. *Clamor*.

Definition: To *clamor* is to demand something in a noisy or angry way. What means "to demand something in a noisy or angry way"? (clamor)

Example 1: If you give children a very small treat, they will sometimes *clamor* for more.

Example 2: At the end of a concert, fans may *clamor* for another song.

Example 3: People who take part in political protests carry signs and *clamor* for change.

Question 1: When a teacher takes away a privilege, do students sometimes *clamor* for another chance? Yes or no? (yes)

Question 2: If a referee makes a bad call, does the crowd sometimes *clamor* for a review of the play? Yes or no? (yes)

Pair Share: Turn to your partner and pretend you are a preschooler *clamoring* for your favorite toy.

(7)

reassuring (adj)

Let's read the next word together. *Reassuring*.

Definition: If something is *reassuring*, it is comforting and causes you to feel less worried. What word means "comforting; causing one to feel less worried"? (reassuring)

Example 1: Some children find a night-light in their room *reassuring*.

Example 2: It is *reassuring* to me when a friend calls after driving home late at night.

Example 3: It can be *reassuring* for performers to have friends and family in the audience.

Question 1: You have saved money for an emergency. Is this *reassuring*? Yes or no? (yes)

Question 2: It's your first day at a new job. The boss growls at you as you enter. Is this *reassuring*? Yes or no? (no)

Pair Share: You just had a terrible basketball tryout, but the coach says something *reassuring*. Tell your partner what he or she says.

(8)

elaborate (adj)

Let's read the next word together. *Elaborate*.

Definition: *Elaborate* means "very complex; having many parts." What means "very complex; having many parts"? (elaborate)

Example 1: Marching bands perform *elaborate* routines with complicated music and marching patterns.

Example 2: An *elaborate* story is one with many characters, events, and plot twists.

Example 3: My brother came up with an *elaborate* system for catching flies, but I simply use a fly swatter.

Question 1: Do couples sometimes plan *elaborate* weddings? Yes or no? (yes)

Question 2: Is a peanut butter sandwich an *elaborate* meal? Yes or no? (no)

Pair Share: With your partner, discuss which of your backpacks has a more *elaborate* design.

(9)

euphoric (adj)

Let's read the last word together. *Euphoric*.

Definition: *Euphoric* means "feeling great happiness and excitement; overjoyed." What means "feeling great happiness and excitement; overjoyed"? (euphoric)

Example 1: Being asked to a dance can make a person feel *euphoric*.

Example 2: When a soldier returns home from a tour of duty, his or her family members are *euphoric*.

Example 3: Winning a game at the last second makes fans and players alike *euphoric*.

Question 1: You are wrongly accused of cheating. Do you feel *euphoric*? Yes or no? (no)

Question 2: After six months of no work, your uncle finds a job. Is he *euphoric*? Yes or no? (yes)

Pair Share: Imagine you are a senior in high school. Turn to your partner and tell what would make you most *euphoric* this year.

(10)

Objectives

- Read an excerpt from a memoir.
- Monitor comprehension during text reading.

Excerpt from *Breaking Night*

Direct students to page 191 in their Student Books. Now that we have previewed vocabulary, it's time to read. The structure of *Breaking Night* is descriptive.

Guiding Students Toward Independent Reading

It is important that your students read as much and as often as they can. Assign readings that meet the needs of your students, based on your observations and data. This is a good opportunity to stretch your students. If students become frustrated, scaffold the reading with paired reading, choral reading, or a read-aloud.

Options for reading text:

- Teacher read-aloud
- Teacher-led or student-led choral read
- Paired read or independent read

Choose an option for reading the text. Have students read according to the option that you chose.

Remind students to pause at the numbers and consider the questions.

If you choose to read the text aloud or chorally, use the text below and stop to ask questions and have students answer them.

SE p. 191, paragraph 1

> By the time I was almost five years old, we had become a functional, government-dependent family of four. The first of the month, the day Ma's stipend from welfare was due, held all the ritual and celebration of Christmas morning. Our collective **anticipation** of the money filled the apartment with a kind of electricity, guaranteeing that Ma and Daddy would be agreeable and upbeat for at least twenty-four hours each month. It was my parents' one **consistency**.

1. Why was the first of the month like a holiday?

SE p. 191, paragraph 2

The government gave the few hundred dollars monthly to those who, for one reason or another, were unable to work for a living—although I often saw our able-bodied neighbors crowded beside the mailboxes, eagerly watching as they were stuffed with the thin, blue envelopes. Ma, who was legally blind due to a degenerative eye disease she'd had since birth, happened to be one of SSI's legitimate recipients. I know, because I went with her the day she interviewed to **qualify**.

2. Why did they receive a welfare check?

SE p. 191, paragraphs 3–6

The woman behind the desk told her that she was so blind that if she ever drove a car, she would "probably end the life of every living thing in her path."

Then she shook Ma's hand and congratulated her both for qualifying and for her ability to successfully cross the street.

"Sign right here. You can expect your checks on the first of every month."

And we did. In fact, there was nothing our family looked forward to more than Ma's check. The mailman's arrival had a domino effect, setting the whole day, and our treasured ritual, in motion. It was my job to lean my head out of my bedroom window, which faced the front, and to call out any sighting of the mailman to Ma and Daddy.

SE p. 192, paragraphs 1–4

"Lizzy, let me know when you see *any* sign of him. Remember, look *left*."

If Ma could know a few minutes earlier that he was coming, she could grab her welfare ID out of the junk drawer, snatch her check from the mailbox, and be the first in line at the check-cashing store. The role I played in those days became an **invaluable** part of the routine.

Elbows jutting behind me, I would clutch the rusted window guard and extend my neck as far as possible into the sun, over and over again throughout the morning. The task gave me a sense of importance. When I saw the blue uniform appear over the hill—an urban Santa Claus pushing his matching cart—I could not wait to announce him. In the meantime, I'd listen to the sound of my parents waiting.

Ma in her oversize worry chair, picking out yellow stuffing.

3. What is Ma like?

SE p. 192,
paragraphs 5–7

"Damn. Damn. He's dragging his ass."

Daddy going over the details of their plans a hundred times, pacing, weaving circles in the air as though to somehow shorten the feel of his wait.

"Okay, Jeanie, we're going to stop off to buy coke, then we take care of the electric bill with Con Edison. Then we can get a half pound of bologna for the kids. And I need money for tokens."

4. Who is the "planner" in the family?

SE p. 192, paragraph 8

The moment I spotted the mailman, I could tell them the very second I knew, or I could wait just a little longer. It was the difference between having their attention and giving it away—relinquishing the one moment when I was as significant as they were, as necessary as the mailman or even the money itself. But I could never hold back; the moment I saw him round the corner I'd shout, "He's coming! I see him! He's coming!" Then we could all move on to the next stage of our day.

SE p. 193, paragraph 1

Behind the gaudy glass storefront of the check-cashing place, there was something for everyone. Children gravitated to the twenty-five-cent machines, a row of clear boxes on metal poles with toys jumbled inside. They waited impatiently for quarters to free the plastic spider on a ring, the man who expanded to ten times his size in water, or the wash-away tattoos of butterflies, comic book heroes, or pink and red hearts. Tacked up high near the register were lottery tickets for stray men with gambling **ailments** or hopeful women who allotted just a few of the family's dollars to the allure of a lucky break. Often these ladies dramatically waved the sign of the cross over themselves before scratching away with a loose dime or penny. But for many, even the smallest item was completely unaffordable until their turn in line.

5. How would this life seem to a five-year-old child?

SE p. 193, paragraph 2

Women made up that endless line; women clutching the monthly bills, women frowning, women with children. Their men (if present at all) stood off to the side, leaning coolly on the metal walls. Either they came in with the women but stood back, waiting for the check to be cashed, or they arrived beforehand, anticipating the routine, sure to shake down their wives or girlfriends for a **portion**. The women would fend them off to the best of their ability, giving up what they had to and making the most of what was left. Lisa and I became so used to the chaos that we hardly looked up at the adults **clamoring** with one another.

6. Why do you think it was mostly women in line?

SE p. 193, paragraph 3

Lisa lingered by the quarter machines, captivated by the glittery stickers. I stayed close to our parents, who were different from the other adults in that they functioned as a team, having arrived in pursuit of a shared goal. I was a participant in their giddiness, eager to make their excitement my own.

SE p. 194, paragraph 1

If I could break the joy of check day down into small segments, then nothing topped the time Ma and I spent together in line. As she waited for her turn at the counter, again I was her helper. In these urgent moments, full of anticipation, Ma relied on me most. It was my moment to shine, and I always rose to the occasion.

7. Why did Ma need Lizzy at home and at the check-cashing store?

SE p. 194, paragraphs 2–4

"Eight more ahead of us, Ma. Seven. Don't worry, the cashier's moving fast."

Her smile as I delivered the progress report belonged to me. Calling out the numbers in a **reassuring** tone determined the amount of attention she paid me. I would have traded the rest of check day for ten more people in line ahead of us, because for this guaranteed amount of time, she wasn't going anywhere. I wouldn't have to worry about Ma's habit of leaving us in the middle of things.

Once, the four of us walked over to Loews Paradise Theater on the Grand Concourse to see a discounted showing of *Alice in Wonderland*. Daddy explained on the walk over that the Concourse used to be an area of luxury, a strip of **elaborate** architecture that attracted the wealthy. But all I could see as we walked were vast, dirty brick buildings with the occasional tarnished cherubs or gargoyles over doorways, chipped and cracked but still hanging on. We sat down in a nearly empty theater.

8. Where are they now? Why are they not in line anymore?

p. 194, paragraph 5

Ma didn't stay until the end. It's not that she didn't try; she got up once, twice, three times for a "smoke." Then she got up for a final time and didn't come back. When we returned home that evening, the record player was spinning a woman's sad, throaty singing. Ma was taking a pull off her cigarette and studying her own slender, naked body in the full-length mirror.

p. 195, paragraphs 1–2

"Where were you guys?" she asked naturally, and I wondered if I might have imagined that she'd come with us at all.

But in the check line, she wasn't going anywhere. As much as she fidgeted, Ma wouldn't leave without the money. So I took the opportunity to hold her hand and to ask her questions about herself when she was my age.

9. Why did Lizzy enjoy the time with Ma in the check line more than at the theater?

p. 195, paragraphs 3–5

"I don't know, Lizzy. I was bad when I was a kid. I stole things and cut school. How many more people in front of us, pumpkin?"

Each time I faced her, Ma motioned toward the cashier, urging me to keep an eye out. Holding her attention was tricky, a balancing act between slipping in questions and showing that I was on top of things. I always assured her that we were almost there; privately, I wished she'd have to wait as long as possible, longer than anyone else.

"I don't know, Lizzy. You're a nicer kid, you never cried when you were a baby. You just made this noise like *eh, eh*. It was the cutest thing, almost polite. Lisa would scream her head off and smash everything, rip up my magazines, but you never cried. I worried you were retarded, but they said you were all right. You were always a good kid. How many more people, pumpkin?"

10. What is Lizzy like?

SE p. 195,
paragraphs 6–10

Even if I was told and retold the same stories, I never tired of asking.

"What was my first word?"

"'Mommy.' You handed me your bottle and said 'Mommy,' like you were telling me to fill 'er up. You were a riot."

"How old was I?"

"Ten months."

SE p. 196,
paragraphs 1–4

"How long have we lived in our house?"

"Years."

"How many?"

"Lizzy, move over, my turn's coming."

11. Why didn't Ma answer Lizzy's last question?

SE p. 196, paragraph 5

At home, we split off into two rooms: the living room for us kids, and next to it, the kitchen for Ma and Daddy. Unlike most times, on that first day of the month, food was abundant. Lisa and I dined on Happy Meals in front of the black-and-white TV, to the sound of spoons clanking on the nearby table, chairs being pulled in—and those elongated moments of silence when we knew what they were concentrating on. Daddy had to do it for Ma because with her bad eyesight she could never find a vein.

12. What were Lizzy's parents doing in the kitchen?

SE p. 196,
paragraphs 6–7

At last, the four of us enjoyed the second-best part of the day. We sat together, all spread around the living room, facing the flickering TV. Outside, the ice cream truck rattled its loop of tinny music and children gathered, scrambled, gathered, and scrambled again in a game of tag.

The four of us together. French-fry grease on my fingertips. Lisa chewing on a cheeseburger. Ma and Daddy, twitching and shifting just behind us, **euphoric**.

13. How much of the check do you think is left after the first day?

For confirmation of engagement, have students share how they think this kind of life affected Liz. Have volunteers share ideas with the class.

Unit 5

Lesson 2

RI.1.4; SL.3.6; L.1.1g; L.1.1i; L.1.1j; L.1.2b; L.2.1c; L.2.1f;
L.3.1a; L.3.1h; L.3.1i; L.4.2c; L.5.2a; L.6.1b; L.6.2b; L.7.1b;
L.7.2b; L.1.6; L.2.6; L.5.4c; L.6.6

Lesson Opener

Before the lesson, choose one of the following activities to write on the board or post on the *LANGUAGE! Live* Class Wall online.
- *Describe a family tradition that you look forward to.*
- *Paint the subject in the following base sentences.*
    The children ate.
    The lady relaxed.
    The men waited for the money.
- *Write five questions you would ask your mother about her childhood.*

Vocabulary

Objective
- Review key passage vocabulary.

Review Passage Vocabulary

Direct students to page 190 in their Student Books. Use the following questions to review the vocabulary words from the excerpt from *Breaking Night*. Have students answer each question using the vocabulary word or indicating its meaning in a complete sentence.

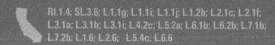

- Why does Lizzy's family feel great *anticipation* on the first of each month? (They feel great anticipation because Lizzy's mother receives a welfare check on that day.) Lizzy also feels *anticipation* about a change in her parents' behavior. Why? (She is filled with anticipation for the positive change in her parents' behavior.)

- Why does Lizzy call her parents' change in behavior a *consistency*? (She calls it a consistency because it happens every month, without fail.) Is the arrival of the welfare check a *consistency*? How so? (Yes, it is a consistency because the check comes on the first of every month.)

- Why does Lizzy's mother *qualify* for welfare? (She qualifies for welfare because she is legally blind.) Would either of Lizzy's parents *qualify* for a Parent of the Year award? Why or why not? (Neither would qualify for a Parent of the Year award because they have not shown that they deserve it; they spend all their money on drugs instead of food for the children.)

- Why does Lizzy feel *invaluable* on check day? (She feels invaluable because she plays an important role: she watches out the window and announces the coming of the mailman.) Why does she feel *invaluable* as she waits in line at the check-cashing store? (She feels invaluable there because her mother relies on her to tell how close they are to the front of the line.) Explain to students that although the prefix in- can mean "not," *invaluable* does not mean "not valuable."

- Lizzy says some of the men at the check-cashing store have "gambling ailments." Why does she use the word *ailments*? (When she says they have gambling ailments, she means that they have a gambling addiction, or illness.) What *ailments* does Lizzy's mother have? Name two. (Two of her mother's ailments are eye disease and drug addiction.)

- After women cash their checks, the men ask for a *portion*. What do the men want? (They want a part, or a portion, of the cash.) Lizzy's parents plan to use one *portion* of the money on drugs. What will they spend the other *portions* on? (They will use the other portions on the electric bill and bologna.)

- The adults in the place are *clamoring* for their checks. What are they doing? (The clamoring adults are demanding money from the clerk and each other.) Do Lizzy's parents *clamor* about the money? Why or why not? (No, they do not clamor about the money because they work as a team and have a shared goal.)

- Why does Lizzy use a *reassuring* tone with her mother as they wait in line? (She uses a reassuring tone so that her mother will stay calm and focus on Lizzy.) Why do you think her mother's stories about the past are *reassuring* to Lizzy? (They are probably reassuring to Lizzy because they make her feel like her family is normal and her mother wants to be close to her.)

- The buildings on the Grand Concourse are *elaborate*. Do they have simple or complex designs? (The elaborate buildings have complex designs.) Will Lizzy's family have an *elaborate* dinner that evening? (No, they will not have an elaborate dinner; they will have a simple meal of fast food.)

- What makes Lizzy and her sister *euphoric* on these evenings? (They feel euphoric because they have food and because the four of them are together.) What makes their parents *euphoric*? (Drugs make them euphoric.) Does Lizzy's story make you feel *euphoric*? Why or why not? (No, it doesn't make me feel euphoric; it makes me feel sad for her and her sister.)

Objectives

- Correctly use nouns functioning as direct objects, objects of the preposition, and predicate nouns.
- Use conjunctions in compound subjects, compound predicates, and compound objects.
- Identify the meaning of coordinating conjunctions in sentences.

Nouns: Multiple Functions

What are nouns? (naming words that answer *who* or *what* questions) Today's lesson focuses on the different jobs or functions that nouns can perform in sentences. Many of the questions we answer when writing Masterpiece Sentences involve nouns doing different jobs. **Write the following sentences on the board. Underline *dog* in each sentence.**

The <u>dog</u> barked.

Martha heard the <u>dog</u>.

Martha stood by the <u>dog</u>.

It was her <u>dog</u>.

The noun *dog* is in every sentence, but in each sentence, it's doing a different job. We will use Masterpiece Sentence questions to figure out the different jobs. In Stage 1, we ask *who* or *what* to generate the subject noun. Consider this sentence: *The dog barked.*

What barked? (dog) Correct, *dog* is the subject noun. What is *dog*? (the subject noun) **Write *subject noun* next to the sentence.** A sentence diagram is a graphic organizer for the sentence. It creates a picture of how the words in a sentence are connected.

Diagram the sentence. Circle *dog* on the diagram, pointing out its position on the diagram. Explain that the vertical line divides the subject and predicate.

dog | barked
The

Listen to the next sentence: *Martha heard the dog.*

Who heard? (Martha) What job is the word *Martha* doing in the sentence? (subject noun) What is the function of the word *dog* in this sentence? What did Martha hear? (dog) Yes, the dog is what's being heard. In other words, it is the *object* on which the verb is *directly* focused. In grammar terms, it is called the *direct object*. **Write *direct object* next to the sentence.** What is *dog* in this sentence? (the direct object)

Diagramming will help us see how the direct object is connected to the other words in the sentence. **Diagram the sentence.**

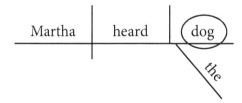

Martha | heard | dog
the

Circle *dog* and point out the different position on the diagram. Notice the difference in the two diagram patterns. The line that separates the subject noun from the predicate goes all the way through the baseline, but the line that separates the verb from the direct object stops at the horizontal line. The pattern gives a hint. It tells us this sentence has a direct object. It helps us organize the words and "see" the job each word is doing in the sentence.

Listen to the next sentence: *Martha stood by the dog.*

Who stood? **(Martha)** The noun *Martha* has the same job in this sentence. What is it? **(subject noun)** In the previous sentence, we could answer the question *What did she hear?* Can we answer the question *What did she stand?* in this sentence? **(no)** So this sentence does not have a direct object. Think about the painter questions for Stage 2: *where, when, how.* Where did she stand? **(by the dog)** *Dog* is part of a phrase, or a group of words that works together. The phrase begins with a preposition, so what kind of a phrase is it? **(a prepositional phrase)** Prepositional phrases always have a naming word or object. In this phrase, *dog* is the object of the preposition. Martha stood *by* what? **(the dog)** **Write *object of the preposition* next to the sentence.**

Diagramming the sentence will help us see how the words in this sentence are connected. **Diagram the sentence. Circle *dog* and point out the different position on the diagram.**

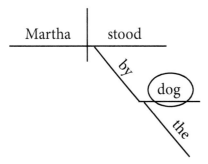

Because each sentence has words working in different jobs, the diagram patterns are different.

Listen to the last sentence: *It was her dog.*

What is the subject of this sentence? **(It)** Yes, we have a pronoun, or a word that can take the place of a noun, as the answer to the *who or what* question. What is the verb? **(was)** In this sentence, we have a different kind of verb. It is not an action verb. What kind of verb is it? **(linking verb)** A linking verb connects, or links, words in the predicate back to the subject. In this sentence, we have a noun following the verb, so we have a predicate noun. **Write *predicate noun* next to the sentence.** What is *dog*? **(predicate noun)**

Again, a diagram of this sentence will help us see how differently the words function. **Diagram the sentence. Circle *dog* and point out the different position on the diagram.**

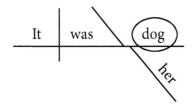

Each sentence shows us a different function for the noun. What are four jobs nouns can have in a sentence? (subject noun, direct object, object of the preposition, and predicate noun) We used our painter questions to help us figure out the jobs or functions of the words in each sentence. Our painter questions help us generate good sentences as well as analyze sentences that have already been written.

Extra practice: If students need more guided practice, use the following sentence pairs to reinforce the different functions for nouns. The underlined words are vocabulary words from previous units.

You are my underline{inspiration}. (predicate noun)
The underline{inspiration} for the book came from her life. (subject noun)

This job provides a great underline{opportunity} for advancement. (direct object)
Reading is a good underline{opportunity} to expand your vocabulary. (predicate noun)

Lee serves generous underline{portions} at her restaurant. (direct object)
The underline{portions} at the restaurant are very generous. (subject noun)

A great underline{strategy} will win the account. (subject noun)
We read through the underline{strategy} to determine if it was going to work. (object of the preposition)

Direct students to page 197 in their Student Books. Read the instructions aloud.

Model

Listen to the first example: *A milling crowd of adults surrounded me. Crowd* is the underlined noun. What surrounded me? A crowd. Because *crowd* answers the main *who* or *what* question, it is the subject noun. It goes under Subject Noun in the chart.

Listen to the next example: *I raised my head to look down the street. Head* is the underlined noun. What question does it answer? What raised? I raised, so *head* is not the subject noun. I raised what? My head. *Head* receives the action of the verb. It is the *direct* focus of the verb, so it is the direct object. It goes under Direct Object in the chart.

Nouns: Multiple Functions

Sort the underlined nouns in the following sentences according to their function. Write them in the proper column in the chart.

Examples:
A milling underline{crowd} of adults surrounded me.
I raised my underline{head} to look down the street.
The mailman had a flag on his underline{uniform}.
In our neighborhood, he was a famous underline{man}.

1. The mailman was walking toward us, his boots noisy on the underline{street}.
2. He wore a underline{flag} on his arm.
3. There were many starving underline{kids} in the streets outside our apartment.
4. underline{Dad} patiently waits for Ma to cash the check.
5. I looked out the window and saw the mailman walk around the underline{corner}.
6. The two underline{girls} watched TV and listened to their parents.
7. As Ma and I waited in line, I held tightly onto her underline{hand}.
8. The sight of the mailman started a chain underline{reaction}.
9. The welfare check is a underline{blessing} to each one of us.
10. The first of the month was my favorite underline{day}.

Subject Noun	Direct Object	Predicate Noun	Object of the Preposition
crowd	head	man	uniform
kids	flag	blessing	street
Dad	reaction	day	corner
girls			hand

Listen to the next example. *The mailman had a flag on his uniform. Uniform* is the underlined noun. What has? Mailman has, so *mailman* is the subject noun. What does he have? He has a flag, so it's not the direct object. Where is the flag? On his uniform. *Uniform* is part of a phrase that answers the *where* question. The phrase begins with *on*, and *on* is a preposition, so it is a prepositional phrase. *Uniform* is the object of the preposition because it answers the *on what* question. It goes under Object of the Preposition in the chart.

Listen to the last example: *In our neighborhood, he was a famous man. Man* is the underlined noun. I have to figure out what question it answers. The verb in this sentence is different from the other verbs. *Was* doesn't show an action. It is a linking verb. What was? *He,* so *man* cannot be the subject noun. A noun that follows a linking verb is a predicate noun, so *man* goes under Predicate Noun in the chart.

Guided Practice

Let's look at the first sentence: *The mailman was walking toward us, his boots noisy on the street.* What is the underlined noun? **(street)** Who was walking? **(mailman)** Right, so *street* is not the subject noun. Where was he walking? **(toward us)** Can we answer the *walking what* question? **(no)** So, there's no direct object. What question does *on the street* answer? **(where)** What kind of phrase is *on the street*? **(prepositional phrase)** Yes, so what is the function of *street*? **(object of the preposition)** Write it in the chart in the proper column.

Independent Practice

Read the remaining sentences and have students write their responses in the chart. Review the answers as a class.

Conjunctions

Conjunctions are words that join other words together. *And* and *or* are examples of conjunctions.

The word *and* can join two or more nouns together. For example, the subject of a sentence can name or include more than one thing. This is called a compound subject.

Write the following sentences on the board:

> *Sherry, Alaina, **and** Keisha are all members of the basketball team.*
>
> *Chocolate chips **and** flour combine with other ingredients to make great cookies.*

What's the subject? How many subjects are involved? (Sherry, Alaina, and Keisha: 3; Chocolate chips and flour: 2)

Your turn. Complete the following sentence.

> _____ **and** _____ *challenge me more than other subjects.*

The word *and* can also join two or more verbs together. For example, the predicate of a sentence can name more than one action. This is called a compound predicate.

Write the following sentence on the board:

> *Before I go to school, I have to wake up, brush my teeth, grab some breakfast, **and** check my backpack.*

What's the predicate? How many actions are taking place? (have to wake up, brush my teeth, grab some breakfast, and check my backpack: 4)

Your turn. Complete the following sentence.

*During the weekends, I like to _____ **and** _____.*

When a conjunction is used to join nouns or verbs in a subject or predicate of a sentence, we say we have a compound subject or a compound predicate.

Let's use the conjunction *or* in a compound subject and a compound predicate.

Write the following sentence on the board:

> *Either Liz **or** her sister would help Ma walk across the street.*

What's the subject? (Liz or her sister) How many subjects are named? (2)

Write the following sentence on the board:

> *Liz could go to school **or** help her mom.*

What's the predicate? (could go to school or help her mom) How many actions are named? (2)

There is another way to use conjunctions in the predicate part of a sentence that doesn't make it a compound predicate. What is the name of a noun that answers the question *What did they do it to?* (direct object) We can use conjunctions to make compound objects as well.

Write the following sentence on the board:

> *Liz will write a novel or a memoir.*

What is the verb? (will write) What is the direct object? (a novel or a memoir) There are two direct objects. Because the conjunction *or* is being used, we know that she will not do both of them. However, if the sentence was *Liz will write a novel and a memoir,* we would know that she will write both of them.

Your turn. Complete the following sentence.

*When I get home from school, I will eat _____ **and/or** _____.*

Now, let's combine some simple sentences and practice making compound subjects, compound objects, and compound predicates, using the conjunctions *and* and *or*. In the next unit, we will work on using conjunctions to join complete sentences.

Direct students to page 198 in their Student Books and read the instructions aloud.

Model

Listen to the example: *Lisa _____ Liz ate Happy Meals in the living room.*

Because I know from the story that both girls ate Happy Meals in the living room, I know the correct conjunction is *and*. It joins Lisa and Liz and means that both of them ate the Happy Meals. So, now I need to determine if this is a compound subject, compound predicate, or compound object. Because the words being joined are nouns, I know it isn't a compound predicate. The question being answered by Lisa and Liz is *Who did it*. This means that it is the subject of the sentence, not the direct object. Therefore, this is a compound subject.

Guided Practice

Listen as I read the first sentence: *We cashed the check _____ bought Happy Meals.* Who did it? **(we)** What did we do? **(cashed the check; bought Happy Meals)** Did we do both? **(yes)** Since we did both, what is the correct conjunction? **(and)** What is being compounded? **(the predicate)** There are two actions joined together with a conjunction, so we know this is a compound predicate.

Independent Practice

Have partners complete the activity. Review the answers as a class.

Reflexive and Intensive Pronouns

You have learned about subject pronouns, object pronouns, and possessive pronouns. Reflexive and intensive pronouns are two other types of pronouns.

Reflexive Pronouns

Reflexive pronouns end in *-self* or *-selves* and are used when a person or thing has already been mentioned in the sentence and needs to be referred to again. In other words, they reflect back to the subject of the sentence.

Direct students to the following chart on page 199 of their Student Books. Have students read the pronouns aloud with you.

Singular	Plural
myself, yourself, himself, herself, itself, oneself	ourselves, yourselves, themselves

Write the following sentence on the board:

Jessica emailed herself a copy of the file.

In this sentence, *Jessica* is mentioned first and needs to be referred to again with the word *herself. Herself* reflects back to the subject, *Jessica.*

Notice that if *herself* is removed from the sentence, it does not have the same meaning.

Now, let's do one together. Write the following sentence on the board:

The investigator disguised himself to work on the case.

Which word is the reflexive pronoun? (*himself*) How do we know? (*Himself* reflects back to the subject of the sentence, *the investigator.*)

Reflexive pronouns only reflect back to the subject. They should not be used as substitutes for these words.

Write the following sentences on the board:

Jessica and myself discussed the file.

Jessica and I discussed the file.

The first sentence uses a reflexive pronoun incorrectly. *Myself* is part of the subject. Reflexive pronouns can only be used to reflect back to the subject, not replace it. Therefore, the better choice in this sentence would be the subject pronoun, *I*.

Now, let's do one together. **Write the following sentence on the board:**

> *The investigator wanted to interview John and myself.*

Does this sentence correctly use a reflexive pronoun? (**no**) Why not? (Reflexive pronouns cannot replace the subject or object. They can only reflect back to the subject.) What object pronoun can we replace *myself* with to fix this sentence? (*me*)

Intensive Pronouns

Intensive pronouns have the same forms as reflexive pronouns, but they are used in a different way. Intensive pronouns emphasize, or intensify, the subject of the sentence. However, unlike reflexive pronouns, they are not necessary for the sentence to make sense.

Write the following sentence on the board:

> *You yourself are to blame for this problem.*

In this sentence, *yourself* intensifies the subject, *you*. The pronoun *yourself* could be removed and the sentence would still make sense: *You are to blame for this problem.* Intensive pronouns are often positioned right after the subject.

Now, let's do one together.

Write the following sentence on the board:

> *Instead of waiting for Mom to get home, Chris made dinner himself.*

Which word is the intensive pronoun? (*himself*) How do we know? (*Himself* intensifies the subject of the sentence, *Chris*.) Remember, *himself* could be removed, and the sentence would still make sense. *Himself* intensifies *Chris*.

Let's go over some commonly misused intensive pronouns. Remember, the correct pronoun forms are listed in your Student Book.

Write the following sentences on the board:

> *My little brother learned how to tie his shoes hisself.*
>
> *Courtney and her brother stayed home by theyselves.*

In the first sentence, *hisself* is not a standard pronoun usage. What should replace it? (*himself*) My little brother learned how to tie his shoes *himself.*

In the second sentence, *theyselves* is not a standard pronoun usage. Which is a better choice? (*themselves*) *Courtney and her brother stayed home by themselves.*

Model

Direct students to Part A on page 199 in their Student Books and read the instructions aloud.

Listen to the example: She _____ finished the job.

I know that the word she is associated with the pronoun herself, so I will write that on the blank. I see that herself is intensifying the subject she, so I think it is an intensive pronoun. It directly follows the subject, so this is another clue. I will write intensive pronoun on the line.

Guided Practice

Listen as I read the first sentence. Josefina burned _____ with the curling iron. What is the pronoun? (*herself*) *Is it reflexive or intensive?* (*reflexive*) *How do we know?* (*It reflects back to the subject, Josefina.*) Have students write their answers. Read the remaining sentences in Part A and give students time to make their choices. Have them respond chorally and correct as needed.

Independent Practice

Have students complete Part B. Review the answers as a class.

Objectives

- Identify the structure of a sentence.
- Use adjectives and adverbs correctly in sentence writing.
- Produce, expand, and rearrange complete sentences for clarity and style.
- Write sentences with compound elements.

Thesauruses or online dictionaries

Masterpiece Sentences: Stages 1–6

You have worked through the first five stages of Masterpiece Sentences, and your sentences are becoming more interesting and descriptive. In Stage 6, you will add the finishing touches. You will reread your sentence and move any sentence parts that seem awkward. You will also double-check spelling and punctuation. In the previous stages, you've been focused on expressing your ideas, but in Stage 6, you want to check for accuracy and clarity.

Direct students to page 200 in their Student Books. Read the instructions and briefly review Stages 1–5.

Stage 1

To help you get started, consider one of the Stage 1 sentences provided in your book. **Read the sentences aloud and have students determine if the sentence has a compound subject, compound predicate, or a compound object.** Choose one and decide if it already has a direct object and if not, if you want to answer the final question in Stage 1 or if you can answer the *to what* question. **Have students complete the chart for Stage 1. Have volunteers share their Stage 1 sentence.**

Write the following base sentence on the board: *The check and happiness arrived.*

Stage 2

Answer the Predicate Painter questions: *when, where, how.* **Have students add their Predicate Painters.** As they do this, add to the sentence on the board: *on the first of the month, in the mailbox, thankfully.* **Have volunteers share their Predicate Painters.**

Masterpiece Sentences

Choose one of the Stage 1 sentences and complete the chart for the remaining stages to write a masterpiece sentence.

Stage 1 Sentences:
- Mom and Dad waited. • The girls ate burgers and fries. • The girl watched and waited. *Possible Answers*

Stage	Process	Questions to Answer	Sentence
Stage 1: Prepare Your Canvas	Choose a noun for the subject. Choose a verb for the predicate. Choose a noun for the direct object. (optional)	Who or what did it? Mom and Dad What did they do? waited What did they do it to? N/A	Mon and Dad waited.
Stage 2: Paint Your Predicate	Tell more about what happened.	When? each month Where? in line How? impatiently	Mom and Dad waited in line each month impatiently.
Stage 3: Move the Predicate Painters	Create a different sentence structure.		Each month, Mom and Dad impatiently waited in line.
Stage 4: Paint Your Subject	Tell more about the subject.	Which one? Liz's What kind? irresponsible How many? N/A	Each month, Liz's irresponsible mom and dad impatiently waited in line.
Stage 5: Paint Your Words	Select words or phrases and replace them with more descriptive words or phrases.	irresponsible handicapped; codependent mom and dad mother and father in line for the funds necessary for living	
Stage 6: Finishing Touches	Move sentence parts, check spelling, and check punctuation.		Each month, Liz's handicapped mother and codependent father impatiently waited for the funds necessary for living.

Lesson 2 | Writing

© 2016 Voyager Sopris Learning, Inc. All rights reserved

200 Unit 5

Stage 3

Move the Predicate Painters. Although my sentence contains descriptors, it sounds awkward. I'm going to move them around, placing at least one at the beginning of the sentence. *Thankfully, on the first of the month, the check and happiness arrived in the mailbox.* I like that better. **Write the sentence on the board. Have students move their painters.**

Stage 4

Answer the subject painter questions: *which one, what kind, how many.* Help the reader get a more complete picture of your subject. **Have students answer the painter questions and rewrite their sentences. As students are working, add to your sentence:** *Thankfully, on the first of the month, the needed welfare check and an abundance of happiness arrived in the mailbox.* **Have volunteers share how they painted their subjects.**

Stage 5

Select at least one word or phrase to "upgrade" and make your sentence more descriptive. Try to upgrade at least one of the elements of your compounded sentence part. I will replace *arrived* with *magically appeared* and *happiness* with *euphoria.* I changed my verb to a word that I think creates a picture of how it must have been for a child. I also replaced *happiness* with *euphoria* because it is a derivative of one of the vocabulary words, which has a much greater and deeper meaning than simple happiness. I am also going to add a word. Because the euphoria was a consequence of the check, I want to make that clear. I will add the word *consequently.* Listen to my sentence and see if you agree that it creates a more positive image. *Thankfully, on the first of the month, the needed welfare check and, consequently, an abundance of euphoria, magically appeared in the mailbox.* **Have students paint their words and share their "upgrades" with the class.**

Stage 6

Apply your finishing touches. Check your spelling and punctuation, and write your final sentence in the chart. **Have partners complete Stage 6 and check each other's work. Have volunteers read their sentences aloud and indicate whether their sentence contains a compound subject, a compound object, or a compound predicate.**

Masterpiece Sentences with Compound Elements

Direct students to page 201 in their Student Books. Read the instructions aloud. You have worked through the six stages of Masterpiece Sentences, and your sentences are becoming more interesting and descriptive.

Guided Practice

Think about Liz's life or your life and the things you encounter every day at school. That is what you are going to write Masterpiece Sentences about. The structure for each sentence has been established to make sure you write sentences with compound elements. Look at the first pattern and think about who the sentence could be about. **Write their responses on the board.**

What did they do? **Write their responses on the board.**

How? **Write their responses on the board.**

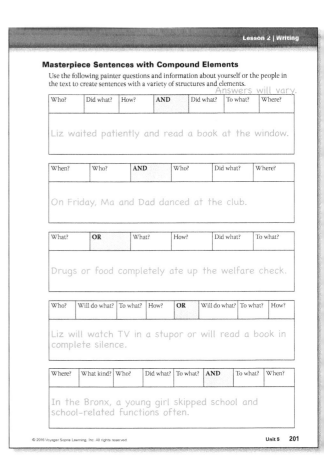

Notice the conjunction *and*. This sentence has two verbs, so whatever you've chosen for your subject noun is going to do two different actions. Look at the words on the board and see if one of those makes sense with the first verb you chose. You will need to be able to answer the *to what* question, so choose a verb that can take a direct object. **Write their responses on the board.**

Now, decide where it happened. **Write their responses on the board.**

Independent Practice

Have partners write the remaining sentences. Have volunteers share their sentences. If students struggle, continue to prompt them with questions and possible answers.

Lesson Opener

Before the lesson, choose one of the following activities to write on the board or post on the *LANGUAGE! Live* Class Wall online.

- *What would you have done with the monthly check if you were Liz Murray's parents?*
- *Describe a time when you put the needs of others before your wants and desires.*
- *Write five sentences about your plans for the future. Use a compound subject, a compound predicate, or a compound object in each sentence.*

Reading

Objectives

- Objectively summarize informational text.
- Determine the central idea of informational text.
- Establish a purpose for rereading a memoir.
- Use critical thinking skills to write responses to prompts about text.
- Support written answers with text evidence.
- Draw inferences from text and support with evidence.

Summarization

After reading text like *Breaking Night*, we often form opinions of the characters. Some of us may read this and think that Liz's parents didn't love her, but that is subjective and not a provable fact—it is an opinion. We need to keep those opinions from popping up when we talk or write about the text. When we summarize text, it is important to write an objective summary—one free from our own opinions.

Turn to your partner and summarize the text objectively. Then, switch.

Central Idea

It is important to identify the central idea of a text even if the author does not explicitly state it. A central idea is the main point that the author is making, but it is universal and can be applied to other texts and other situations.

Review the central ideas of the last three texts students have read.

- *The Play of the Diary of Anne Frank*: Jewish families lost their freedom and self-worth trying to survive the Holocaust.

- "The Circuit": Because migrant workers follow the harvest, they live in poor accommodations, have limited schooling, and struggle to make ends meet.

- *The Autobiography of Malcolm X*: With an intense desire and discipline, even people who have made mistakes can turn their lives around through education.

Let's apply the concept of central idea to *Breaking Night*.

Have partners discuss the text and determine the central idea of the text.

If necessary, model the process with the following think-aloud:

I'm thinking that children of poverty and addiction have a difficult life but may not even know it. I'm also thinking that Lizzy cherished the time with her mom in the check line when most children would be whining and complaining. It makes me realize that all children need their parents' support and approval to a certain degree. I am also thinking that her parents really did care for her . . . they just didn't always show it. I don't think her parents' intentions were to neglect her. Their actions were driven by their addiction to drugs. It makes me think that most parents love and care for their children, but sometimes selfish behaviors can make them do hurtful things.

Remember that, unlike a summary, the central idea is subjective. That means that your thoughts are probably different than my thoughts. What is the central idea? **Have partners share their central ideas.** (Children need love and affection from their parents and will do anything to get it. Children of drug addicts learn to cope. Drugs can take over a person's life and make them do terrible things like hurt the ones they love. Dysfunctional patterns of some families may be considered treasured rituals to needy children.)

Central ideas are not explicitly stated word for word, and one text may have multiple central ideas.

Reading for a Purpose: Excerpt from *Breaking Night*

After reflecting on the central idea of the text we have read, it is time to answer some more specific questions. Because critical understanding requires active participation, we are going to read the text again. This time, we will be reading for a specific purpose, which will help us pay attention to details that we may have missed the first time around.

Let's read some questions about the text to provide a purpose for rereading.

Direct students to pages 202 and 203 in their Student Books. Have students read the prompts aloud with you.

1. Infer Daddy's rationale for buying drugs before paying the electric bill.

2. Contrast Liz's relationship with Ma before and after the check was cashed.

3. Identify the family ritual on check day.

4. Consider the flashback to the theater. Infer why Liz's mom had a habit of leaving the family in the middle of things.

5. Summarize the excerpt from *Breaking Night* as it relates to a monthly circuit.

6. Compare and contrast the key details presented about Liz Murray's parents and Panchito's parents in "The Circuit."

Direct students to page 191 in their Student Books or have them tear out the extra copy of *Breaking Night* from the back of their book.

> **Note:** To minimize flipping back and forth between the pages, a copy of each text has been included in the back of the Student Books. Encourage students to tear this out and use it when working on activities that require the use of the text.

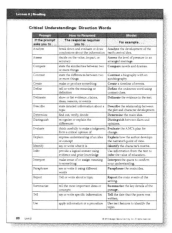

Choose an option for reading text. Have students read the text according to the option that you chose.

> Options for reading text:
> - Teacher read-aloud
> - Teacher-led or student-led choral read
> - Paired read or independent read with bold vocabulary words read aloud

Passage Comprehension

Write the words *contrast, identify, infer,* and *summarize* on the board. Have students read the words aloud with you.

Direct students to page 66 in their Student Books. It is critical to understand what the question is asking and how to answer it. Today, we will review four direction words used in prompts.

Have students review the words on the board by locating them in the chart on page 66. Check for understanding by requesting an oral response to the following questions.

- If the prompt asks you to *contrast*, the response requires you to . . . (state the differences between two or more things).

- If the prompt asks you to *identify*, the response requires you to . . . (say or write what it is).

- If the prompt asks you to *infer*, the response requires you to . . . (provide a logical answer using evidence and prior knowledge).

- If the prompt asks you to *summarize*, the response requires you to . . . (tell the most important ideas or concepts).

Direct students to pages 202 and 203 in their Student Books.

Passage Comprehension

Reread the excerpt from *Breaking Night*. Respond to each prompt using complete sentences. Refer to the chart on page 66 to determine how to respond to each prompt. Provide text evidence when requested.

1. Infer Daddy's rationale for buying drugs before paying the electric bill.
   Daddy wanted to buy drugs before paying the electric bill because drugs were more important than electricity for the family.

2. Contrast Liz's relationship with Ma before and after the check was cashed.
   Before the check was cashed, Liz and Ma had a close relationship. Liz would have Ma's attention. Ma would answer Liz's questions about her childhood. However, after the check was cashed, Liz and Ma barely had a relationship at all. Ma only cared about her relationship with drugs. She would ignore Liz and her sister.

   Text Evidence: ___ nothing topped the time Ma and I spent together in line. As she waited for her turn at the counter, again I was her helper. In these urgent moments, full of anticipation, Ma relied on me most; I would have traded the rest of check day for two more people in line ahead of us, because for this guaranteed amount of time, she wasn't going anywhere. So I took the opportunity to hold her hand and to ask her questions about herself when she was my age. At home, we split off into two rooms: the living room for us kids, and next to it, the kitchen for Ma and Daddy.

3. Identify the family ritual on check day.
   The ritual on check day started out with Lizzy on the lookout for the mailman, Ma picking the stuffing out of her worry chair, and Daddy pacing while repeating their plan to spend the money. Next, they cashed their check after waiting in a long line filled with mostly women and children. While waiting, Lizzy would cherish the time she spent monitoring the line while holding Ma's hand and asking her questions about when she was little. Once their check was cashed, her parents would buy drugs for themselves and food for the children. At home, the kids would eat their food while the parents did drugs, then they would all watch TV together feeling satisfied.

Passage Comprehension (*cont.*)

4. Consider the flashback to the theater. Infer why Liz's mom had a habit of leaving the family in the middle of things.
   Ma had a habit of leaving the family in the middle of things because the drugs made her fidgety. She didn't have the ability to sit or stand still, unless it was for important reasons—like money.

   Text Evidence: Ma didn't stay until the end. It's not that she didn't try; she got up once, twice, three times for a "smoke." Then she got up for a final time and didn't come back; But in the check line, she wasn't going anywhere. As much as she fidgeted, Ma wouldn't leave without the money.

5. Summarize the excerpt from *Breaking Night* as it relates to a monthly circuit.
   Breaking Night is about the circuit of dysfunction of a family in poverty ruled by the parents' drug addiction. The monthly circuit starts at the first of the month when the check arrives and is cashed to purchase food and drugs. As the month continues, food is much less abundant until the next check arrives.

6. Compare and contrast the key details presented about Liz Murray's parents and Panchito's parents in "The Circuit."
   Both Panchito's parents and Liz Murray's parents had limited money, looked forward to payday, and placed little value on education. Panchito's parents cared for their children and worked very hard to earn money to spend on food and necessities for their children. Liz's parents, on the other hand, did not work, used government money to buy illegal drugs, and spent the majority of their money on themselves, leaving their kids hungry.

Let's practice answering questions that are written as prompts that require critical thinking.

Model

Listen as I model the first one for you.

1. Infer Daddy's rationale for buying drugs before paying the electric bill.

According to the chart, if the prompt asks you to *infer*, the response requires that you provide a logical answer using evidence and prior knowledge. Now, I will turn the prompt into a question to confirm understanding. *Rationale* is another word for reason. So, my question would be *Why did Daddy pay for drugs before paying the electric bill?* We know from the text that Daddy was addicted to drugs. So what about our prior knowledge? I know that electricity is extremely important to most people. It is a necessity. It powers everything—the refrigerator, TV, washer and dryer, lights, air conditioning, and heat. For many people, electricity is one thing they couldn't live without. That must mean that for Daddy, drugs were more important that any of the things I mentioned. Obviously, drugs are a bigger necessity to him than electricity.

I can put part of the prompt in my answer to start my sentence.

Write the following sentence starter on the board.

Daddy wanted to buy drugs before paying the electric bill because _____.

Complete the sentence on the board.

> *Daddy wanted to buy coke before paying the electric bill because drugs were more important than electricity for the family.*

Guided Practice

2. Contrast Liz's relationship with Ma before and after the check was cashed.

How should we respond according to the chart? (If the prompt asks you to *contrast*, the response requires that you state the differences between two or more things). Now, turn the prompt into a question to confirm your understanding. First, we need to understand the question. This question has two parts related to time. What are they? (**before and after**) It is easier to understand as two separate questions. We will rephrase the question into two separate questions. What is the first question? (What was Liz's relationship with Ma before the check was cashed?) What is the next question? (What was Liz's relationship with Ma after the check was cashed?)

Write the following sentence starters on the board:

> *Before the check was cashed, Liz and Ma _____.*
>
> *However, after the check was cashed, Liz and Ma _____.*

Have students answer the questions and provide evidence from the text.

Independent Practice

Have students respond to the remaining questions. For students who need more assistance, provide the following alternative questions and sentence starters.

Alternative questions and sentence starters:

3. What is the family ritual on check day?

   The ritual on check day started out with _____.

4. Why did Liz's mom have a habit of leaving the family in the middle of things?

   Ma had a habit of leaving the family in the middle of things because _____.

5. What is *Breaking Night* mostly about? Use the words *monthly circuit* in your answer.

   Breaking Night *is about* _____.

   The monthly circuit starts _____.

   As the month continues, _____.

6. How are the key details presented about Liz Murray's parents similar to the key details presented about Panchito's parents? How are they different?

   Both Panchito's parents and Liz Murray's parents _____.

   Panchito's parents _____.

   Liz's parents, on the other hand, _____.

Unit 5

Lesson 4

RI.3.1; RI.3.3; RI.4.1; RI.6.4; RI.6.6; RI.8.6 ; RI.6.10; SL.1.2;
L.1.1b; L.2.1c; L.2.1e; L.6.1b; L.7.1c; L.7.2a; L.3.4a; L.4.5a;
L.4.5c; L.5.4a; L.6.6

Lesson Opener

Before the lesson, choose one of the following activities to write on the board or post on the *LANGUAGE! Live* Class Wall online.

- *Dress your avatar as though you were going to spend time with your parents and wanted them to notice you. Explain your choices.*
- *Write five sentences about the importance or unimportance of family. Use a compound subject, compound predicate, or compound object in each sentence.*
- *Make a list of adjectives describing Liz Murray. Make another list of adjectives describing Ma.*

Reading

Objectives

- Read with purpose and understanding.
- Answer questions to demonstrate comprehension of text.
- Monitor comprehension of text during reading.
- Determine the meaning of figurative language in text.
- Identify coordinate adjectives in text and the punctuation used to separate them.
- Identify the conditional tense in writing and understand its meaning.
- Identify stereotyping in text.
- Determine the impact of imperative verbs in text.
- Identify intensive and reflexive pronouns and distinguish between them.
- Identify the signs of a hero's tale.
- Identify misplaced modifiers in text.
- Identify allusions to known works, events, or beliefs in text.
- Distinguish between text written from an objective point of view and text written from a subjective point of view.
- Determine the meaning of ambiguous words in text using context.

Close Reading of the Excerpt from *Breaking Night*

Highlighters or colored pencils

Let's reread the excerpt from *Breaking Night*. I will provide specific instructions on how to mark the text that will help with comprehension.

Have students get out a highlighter or colored pencil.

Direct students to pages 204–209 in their Student Books.

Draw a rectangle around the title, *Breaking Night*.

Circle the word that tells you that this is one portion of a larger piece of text. (from)

Now, let's read the vocabulary words aloud.

- What's the first bold vocabulary word? (anticipation) *Anticipation* means "a feeling of excitement about something that is about to happen." We waited for our food with *anticipation*. Have partners use the word in a sentence.

- What's the next vocabulary word? (consistency) *Consistency* means "something done in the same way, time after time." Liz's parents lacked *consistency* in parenting. Have partners use the word in a sentence.

- Next word? (qualify) *Qualify* means "to show that you have the right to do or have something." She is hoping to *qualify* for the honor roll. **Have partners use the word in a sentence.**

- Let's continue. (invaluable) *Invaluable* means "extremely useful or precious and hard to replace." Time in line with her mom was *invaluable* to Lizzy. **Have partners use the word in a sentence.**

- Next word? (ailments) *Ailments* means "sicknesses; things that cause pain and discomfort." Medicine may help cure *ailments*. **Have partners use the word in a sentence.**

- Let's continue. (portion) *Portion* means "one part of a greater whole." It is wise to save a *portion* of your paycheck. **Have partners use the word in a sentence.**

- Next word? (clamoring) *Clamoring* means "demanding something in a noisy or angry way." If you are *clamoring* for a treat instead of asking politely, I will not give you one. **Have partners use the word in a sentence.**

- Let's continue. (reassuring) *Reassuring* means "comforting; causing one to feel less worry." The guide gave me a *reassuring* look just before I jumped out of the airplane. **Have partners use the word in a sentence.**

- Next word? (elaborate) *Elaborate* means "very complex; having many parts." We took apart our DVD player but couldn't put it back together because it was so *elaborate*. **Have partners use the word in a sentence.**

- Last word. (euphoric) *Euphoric* means "feeling great happiness and excitement; overjoyed." I felt *euphoric* after passing all of my tests. **Have partners use the word in a sentence.**

Talk with a partner about any vocabulary word that is still confusing for you to read consistently or to understand its meaning.

You will read the excerpt from *Breaking Night* one section at a time. After each section, you will monitor your understanding by circling the check mark if you understand the text or the question mark if you don't understand the text. I also want you to draw a question mark over any confusing words, phrases, or sentences.

> Options for reading text:
> - Teacher read-aloud
> - Teacher-led or student-led choral read
> - Paired read or independent read with bold vocabulary words read aloud

Choose an option for reading text. Have students read lines 1–20 according to the option that you chose. As you read, pay attention to the narrator's thoughts and feelings.

When most of the students are finished, continue with the entire class. Let's see how well you understood what you read.

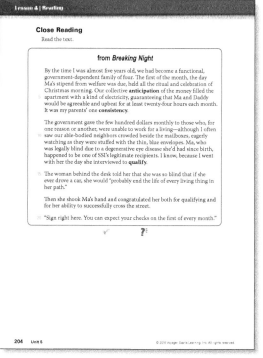

- Circle the check mark or the question mark for this section. Draw a question mark over any confusing words.

- Go to line 3. Mark the word that means "income or money." (stipend)

- Go to line 4. Mark what the first of the month is being compared to. (Christmas morning)

- Go to line 6. Mark the adjectives that describe Liz's parents on the first of every month. (agreeable; upbeat) Circle the reason for their mood and draw an arrow to connect them. (stipend from welfare was due)

- Go to line 7. Mark the pronoun *it*. Underline what *it* is referencing and draw an arrow to connect them. (Ma and Daddy would be agreeable and upbeat for at least twenty-four hours each month.) Circle the word that indicates this is cyclic, or recurring. (each)

- Go to line 9. Mark the kinds of people who were justified in getting government money. (were unable to work for a living)

- Go to line 10. Mark the kinds of people who actually received the money. (able-bodied)

- Go to line 11. Mark the two adjectives used to describe the envelopes. (thin; blue) Circle the punctuation used to separate the adjectives. (comma) **Explain that the comma is used to separate coordinate adjectives—adjectives that are equal in importance. But, if the adjectives aren't equal, they do not need a comma.**

- Go to line 12. Mark the word that means "getting steadily worse." (degenerative)

- Go to line 13. Mark the abbreviation for Supplemental Security Income. (SSI)

- On the same line, mark the synonym for *real*. (legitimate)

- Go to lines 15–17. Mark what needs to happen in order for Ma to "probably end the life of every living thing in her path." (if she ever drove a car) **Explain that this sentence is written in the subjunctive mood because it isn't based in reality. It is describing something that would happen if something else were to happen.**

- Go to lines 18 and 19. Mark the words used to indicate that the woman was stereotyping blind people. (congratulated her for her ability to cross the street)

- On line 20, mark the imperative verb that is a command from the woman. (Sign)

Have students read lines 21–51 according to the option that you chose.

When most of the students are finished, continue with the entire class. Let's see how well you understood what you read.

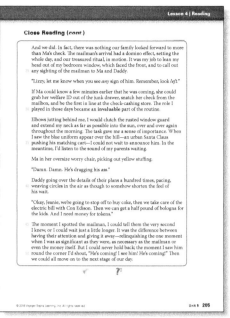

- Circle the check mark or the question mark for this section. Draw a question mark over any confusing words.

- Go to line 22. Mark the words that mean "chain of events." (domino effect)

- Go to lines 24 and 25. Mark Lizzy's job on payday. (call out any sighting of the mailman)

- Go to line 26. Mark the change in font used to show emphasis in speech or a change in inflection. (any, left)

- In the same line, mark the imperative phrases that are commands from Ma. (let me know, look left)

- Go to line 28. Mark the abbreviation for identification. (ID)

- On the same line, circle the synonym for *grab*. (snatch)

- Go to line 29. Mark the ultimate goal of Lizzy watching for the mailman. (be the first in line at the check-cashing store)

- On the same line, mark the synonym for *job*. (role)

- Number the steps of Ma's routine. (1. grab her welfare ID; 2. snatch her check; 3. be the first in line)

- Go to line 30. Mark the evidence that Lizzy is telling a hero's tale of her time with her parents. (an invaluable part of the routine)

- Go to line 33. Mark another piece of evidence that Lizzy is telling the tale of her time with her parents as though she was the hero helping them in their quest. (a sense of importance)

- Go to line 34. Mark the metaphorical description of the mailman. (urban Santa Claus)

- Go to line 37. Mark the evidence that Ma is anxious. (picking out yellow stuffing)

- Go to line 38. Mark the contraction that means "he is." (he's) In the margin, write an adverb that could be used to describe the way the mailman is moving. (slowly)

- Go to line 42. Mark the contraction that means "we are." (we're)

- On the same line, mark the street name for cocaine. (coke)

- Go to line 47. Mark the word that means "letting go." (relinquishing)

- Go to lines 48 and 49. Mark how Lizzy feels as she waits for the mailman. (as significant as they were; as necessary as the mailman or even the money itself)

- On line 49, mark the unusual pronoun used to refer to the money. (itself) Explain that this is an intensive pronoun. Intensive pronouns usually include "self" and can usually be removed from a sentence and the sentence would make sense, but authors use them for emphasis.

Have students read lines 52–77 according to the option that you chose.

When most of the students are finished, continue with the entire class. Let's see how well you understood what you read.

- Circle the check mark or the question mark for this section. Draw a question mark over any confusing words.

- Go to line 52. Mark the adjective that means "showy and tacky." (gaudy)

- Go to line 53. Mark the word that means "moved toward something" (gravitated)

- Go to line 55. Mark the adverb that means "without patience." (impatiently) Circle the suffix. (ly) Circle the prefix. (im)

- Go to lines 55–57. Because of the placement of modifiers in this sentence, it is difficult to understand. Change the way adjectives are placed and used to make a list in the margin of the six different items that could be found in the twenty-five-cent machines. (plastic spider ring, expanding man, butterfly tattoos, comic book hero tattoos, pink heart tattoos, red heart tattoos)

- Go to line 60. Mark the word that means "attraction or temptation." (allure)

- On the same line, mark the words that mean "fortunate turn of events." (lucky break)

- Go to lines 60 and 61. Mark the allusion to the Christian faith. (waved the sign of the cross over themselves) Circle the unusual pronoun used to refer to the ladies. (themselves) **Explain that this is a reflexive pronoun that also ends with** *self* **or** *selves.* Reflexive pronouns are used when a person or thing has already been mentioned in the sentence and needs to be referred to again. It cannot be removed from the sentence.

- Go to line 68. Mark the synonym for *predicting.* (anticipating)

- Go to lines 71 and 72. Mark the evidence that indicates the ritual at the check-cashing store seemed normal to Lizzy. (so used to the chaos that we hardly looked up)

- Circle the synonym for *madness.* (chaos)

- Go to line 75. Mark why Lizzy's parents were different from the other check cashers. (they functioned as a team) Mark why they worked as a team. (in pursuit of a shared goal) In the margin, write the goal. (buying drugs)

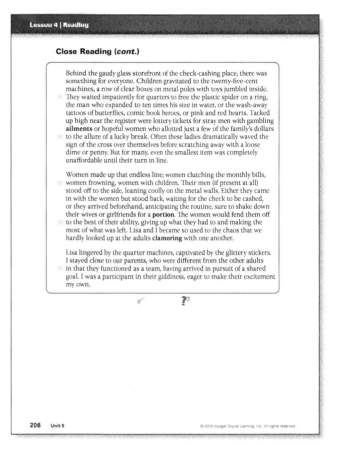

Lesson 4 | Reading

Close Reading (*cont.*)

Behind the gaudy glass storefront of the check-cashing place, there was something for everyone. Children gravitated to the twenty-five-cent machines, a row of clear boxes on metal poles with toys jumbled inside. They waited impatiently for quarters to free their plastic spider on a ring, the man who expanded to ten times his size in water, or the wash-away tattoos of butterflies, comic book heroes, or pink and red hearts. Tacked up high near the register were lottery tickets for stray men with gambling **ailments** or hopeful women who allotted just a few of the family's dollars to the allure of a lucky break. Often these ladies dramatically waved the sign of the cross over themselves before scratching away with a loose dime or penny. But for many, even the smallest item was completely unaffordable until their turn in line.

Women made up that endless line; women clutching the monthly bills, women frowning, women with children. Their men (if present at all) stood off to the side, leaning coolly on the metal walls. Either they came in with the women but stood back, waiting for the check to be cashed, or they arrived beforehand, anticipating the routine, sure to shake down their wives or girlfriends for a **portion**. The women would fend them off to the best of their ability, giving up what they had to and making the most of what was left. Lisa and I became so used to the chaos that we hardly looked up at the adults **clamoring** with one another.

Lisa lingered by the quarter machines, captivated by the glittery stickers. I stayed close to our parents, who were different from the other adults in that they functioned as a team, having arrived in pursuit of a shared goal. I was a participant in their giddiness, eager to make their excitement my own.

206   Unit 5   © 2016 Voyager Sopris Learning, Inc. All rights reserved.

Have students read lines 78–103 according to the option that you chose.

When most of the students are finished, continue with the entire class. Let's see how well you understood what you read.

- Circle the check mark or the question mark for this section. Draw a question mark over any confusing words.

- Go to line 78. Mark the word that means "separate." (break)

- Go to line 79. Mark the best part of the first of the month for Lizzy. (the time Ma and I spent together in line)

- Go to line 80. Mark the evidence that Lizzy is telling the story of her time with her parents as though she was the hero. (I was her helper.) Mark the word that indicates that this is a recurring act and Lizzy has helped before. (again)

- Go to line 81. Mark the evidence that Lizzy was dependable. (relied on me most)

- Go to line 82. Mark the phrase that means "didn't let her down." (rose to the occasion)

- Go to line 83. Mark the word that means "cashier is." (cashier's)

- Go to line 84. Find the possessive pronoun *her*. Replace it with a proper noun. (Ma's)

- On the same line, find the words *progress report*. Draw an arrow to her progress report. (Eight more ahead of us, the cashier's moving fast.)

- Go to lines 87 and 88. Mark why Lizzy liked standing in line more than French fries, TV, and money. (for this guaranteed amount of time, she wasn't going anywhere)

- Go to line 90. Mark the transition word that indicates a flashback to a previous time. (Once)

- Go to line 94. Mark the coordinate adjectives. (vast; dirty)

- Go to line 97. We have been talking about objective and subjective points of view. Circle the objective statement and underline the subjective statement. (objective: Ma didn't stay until the end.; subjective: It's not that she didn't try)

- Go to line 98. Mark the word that is obviously a code name for something else. ("smoke") What punctuation mark is used? (quotation marks) In the margin, write what she was really doing. (drugs)

- How many times did Ma leave the theater? Write the number in the margin. (four)

- Go to line 100. Mark the coordinate adjectives. (sad; throaty)

Close Reading (cont.)

If I could break the joy of check day down into small segments, then nothing topped the time Ma and I spent together in line. As she waited for her turn at the counter, again I was her helper. In these urgent moments, full of anticipation, Ma relied on me most. It was my moment to shine, and I always rose to the occasion.

"Eight more ahead of us, Ma. Seven. Don't worry, the cashier's moving fast."

Her smile as I delivered the progress report belonged to me. Calling out the numbers in a **reassuring** tone determined the amount of attention she paid me. I would have traded the rest of check day for ten more people in line ahead of us, because for this guaranteed amount of time, she wasn't going anywhere. I wouldn't have to worry about Ma's habit of leaving us in the middle of things.

Once, the four of us walked over to Loews Paradise Theater on the Grand Concourse to see a discounted showing of *Alice in Wonderland*. Daddy explained on the walk over that the Concourse used to be an area of luxury, a strip of **elaborate** architecture that attracted the wealthy. But all I could see as we walked were vast, dirty brick buildings with the occasional tarnished cherubs or gargoyles over doorways, chipped and cracked but still hanging on. We sat down in a nearly empty theater.

Ma didn't stay until the end. It's not that she didn't try; she got up once, twice, three times for a "smoke." Then she got up for a final time and didn't come back. When we returned home that evening, the record player was spinning a woman's sad, throaty singing. Ma was taking a pull off her cigarette and studying her own slender, naked body in the full-length mirror.

"Where were you guys?" she asked naturally, and I wondered if I might have imagined that she'd come with us at all.

✓   ?

Unit 5   **207**

- Go to line 103. Mark the indication that Lizzy's mom did not remember the past couple of hours. (Where were you guys?)

Have students read lines 104–130 according to the option that you chose.

When most of the students are finished, continue with the entire class. Let's see how well you understood what you read.

- Circle the check mark or the question mark for this section. Draw a question mark over any confusing words.

- Go to line 105. Mark the evidence that suggests that Ma is anxious. (fidgeted)

- Go to lines 105 and 106. Mark the indication that Lizzy didn't receive much physical contact or affection from her mom. (took the opportunity to hold her hand)

- Go to lines 108 and 109. Number two bad things that Ma did at Lizzy's age. (1. stole; 2. cut school)

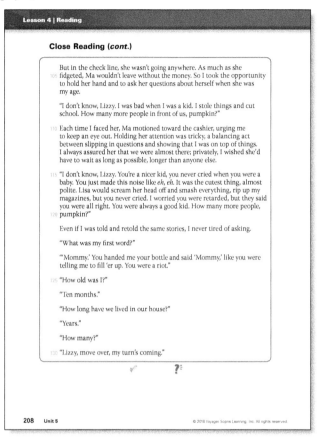

- Go to line 113. Mark the word that means "removed doubt." (assured)
- Go to line 121. Mark the word that means "repeated." (retold)
- Mark the words that mean "got bored and quit." (tired of)
- Go to line 124. Mark the evidence that Lizzy was a fun baby. (You were a riot.)
- Go to line 125. Who is talking? Write her name in the margin. (Lizzy)
- Go to line 126. Who is talking? Write her name in the margin. (Ma) **Have students continue doing this through line 130.**
- In the same set of lines, mark the answer given by Ma that could be classified as ambiguous, or left up to interpretation. (Years) In the margin, write how long you think she means.
- Go to line 130. Mark the evidence that shows that Ma can be impatient. (move over)
- Mark the word that means "turn is." (turn's)

Have students read from line 131 to the end according to the option that you chose.

When most of the students are finished, continue with the entire class. Let's see how well you understood what you read.

- Circle the check mark or the question mark for this section. Draw a question mark over any confusing words.

- Go to lines 131 and 132. Number the two rooms. (1. living room; 2. kitchen)

- Go to line 133. Mark the synonym for *plentiful.* (abundant)

- Go to line 135. Mark the word that means "long and drawn out." (elongated)

- Go to line 136. Mark who replaced Lizzy as Ma's "eyes." (Daddy)

- In the second paragraph, mark the statement written from a subjective point of view. (the four of us enjoyed the second-best part of the day)

- Go to lines 138 and 139. Underline the sentence that tells what Lizzy did with her family during the second best part of check day. (We sat together, all spread around the living room, facing the flickering TV.)

- Go to line 141. Draw a rectangle around what other children were doing at this time. (game of tag)

- Number the food that Lizzy and her sister ate. (1. French fries; 2. cheeseburger)

Have partners compare text markings and correct any errors.

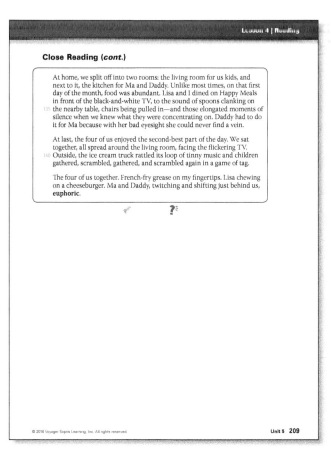

Close Reading (*cont.*)

At home, we split off into two rooms: the living room for us kids, and next to it, the kitchen for Ma and Daddy. Unlike most times, on that first day of the month, food was abundant. Lisa and I dined on Happy Meals in front of the black-and-white TV, to the sound of spoons clanking on
135 the nearby table, chairs being pulled in—and those elongated moments of silence when we knew what they were concentrating on. Daddy had to do it for Ma because with her bad eyesight she could never find a vein.

At last, the four of us enjoyed the second-best part of the day. We sat together, all spread around the living room, facing the flickering TV.
140 Outside, the ice cream truck rattled its loop of tinny music and children gathered, scrambled, gathered, and scrambled again in a game of tag.

The four of us together. French-fry grease on my fingertips. Lisa chewing on a cheeseburger. Ma and Daddy, twitching and shifting just behind us, **euphoric.**

Unit 5   **209**

Lesson Opener

Before the lesson, choose one of the following activities to write on the board or post on the *LANGUAGE! Live* Class Wall online.

- *Write four sentences with at least two vocabulary words in each. Show you know the meanings. (anticipation, consistency, qualify, invaluable, ailment, portion, clamor, reassuring, elaborate, euphoric)*
- *Write three sentences that describe check day for Liz's family. Answer the following questions in your sentences: When do they get the check? Where do they get the check? How do they get the check? Combine the three sentences into one Masterpiece Sentence.*
- *Write three sentences about what Liz Murray did on check day. Combine the sentences into one sentence with a compound predicate.*

Vocabulary

Objective
- Review key passage vocabulary.

Recontextualize Passage Vocabulary

Direct students to page 190 in their Student Books. Use the following questions to review the vocabulary words in the excerpt from *Breaking Night*.

- Do you feel *anticipation* before doing an unpleasant task you've put off for a long time? (**no**) Do fans feel *anticipation* before an important football game? (**yes**) You are receiving a phone call from a place where you've applied for a job. What do you feel before you answer the call? (**anticipation**)

- If you eat a waffle and a banana for breakfast every single morning, is this a *consistency*? (**yes**) If you dress in a different style every day, do you have fashion *consistency*? (**no**) If you clean your grandfather's house every Saturday, what do you have? (**consistency**)

- People with hot pink shoelaces are allowed to join my new club. Do you *qualify*? (**Answers may vary.**) A local radio station is looking for teen DJs. Do you *qualify*? (**yes**) If you have met the criteria to attend a youth leadership conference, what have you done? (**qualified for it**)

- You inherited your grandmother's 80-year-old wedding ring. Is it *invaluable*? (**yes**) You get a plastic toy with a fast-food meal. Is the toy *invaluable*? (**no**) You share a bedroom with three siblings. Time alone in the bedroom is what? (**invaluable**)

- I have a toothache. Is this an *ailment*? (**yes**) I have a great idea. Is this an *ailment*? (**no**) Your aunt has knee problems. What does she have? (**an ailment**)

- You watch an entire TV series in one weekend. Have you watched only a *portion* of it? (no) You and your friend babysit and split the earnings. Do you receive a *portion* of the earnings? (yes) If I bake a cake and take a big slice of it to my neighbor, what have I given her? (a portion of it)

- People outside the room are pounding on the door and want to get in. Are they *clamoring*? (yes) Several people are dozing in chairs in the library. Are they *clamoring*? (no) Some dogs are barking up a tree at some squirrels. What are the dogs doing? (clamoring)

- Is it *reassuring* when a doctor says, "This won't hurt at all"? (yes) When someone feels sad, can a hug be *reassuring*? (yes) If you think a friend is upset with you, but she smiles at you in the hallway, what is the smile? (reassuring)

- Is a plain white T-shirt *elaborate*? (no) Is a board game with a long list of rules and dozens of game pieces *elaborate*? (yes) You thought you could put together a swing set for your little brother in one morning, but you were wrong; it's way too complicated. What is the swing set? (elaborate)

- You just heard some hurtful gossip about yourself. Are you *euphoric*? (no) After trying for two months, you finally advance to the next level of a video game. Are you *euphoric*? (yes) The competition is intense, but you make the varsity team. How do you feel? (euphoric)

Objectives
- Use text to write coherent paragraphs in response to reading.
- Analyze a character and how the character's traits affect the events in the text.

Thesauruses or online dictionaries

Quick Write in Response to Reading

Direct students to page 210 in their Student Books. Read the prompt aloud. Have students consider what they learned about Liz Murray from the excerpt from *Breaking Night*. Prompt them to write notes before they begin writing their response. Encourage students to use linking words and phrases to connect ideas and to diversify their descriptive words by consulting a thesaurus.

Note: The example response is quite long because it contains multiple examples from the text. Student responses should be shorter but should include at least one example from the text to support each character trait.

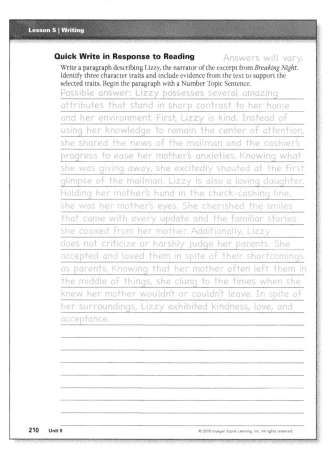

Lesson 5 | Writing

Quick Write in Response to Reading   Answers will vary.

Write a paragraph describing Lizzy, the narrator of the excerpt from *Breaking Night*. Identify three character traits and include evidence from the text to support the selected traits. Begin the paragraph with a Number Topic Sentence.

Possible answer: Lizzy possesses several amazing attributes that stand in sharp contrast to her home and her environment. First, Lizzy is kind. Instead of using her knowledge to remain the center of attention, she shared the news of the mailman and the cashier's progress to ease her mother's anxieties. Knowing what she was giving away, she excitedly shouted at the first glimpse of the mailman. Lizzy is also a loving daughter. Holding her mother's hand in the check-cashing line, she was her mother's eyes. She cherished the smiles that came with every update and the familiar stories she coaxed from her mother. Additionally, Lizzy does not criticize or harshly judge her parents. She accepted and loved them in spite of their shortcomings as parents. Knowing that her mother often left them in the middle of things, she clung to the times when she knew her mother wouldn't or couldn't leave. In spite of her surroundings, Lizzy exhibited kindness, love, and acceptance.

210   Unit 5   © 2016 Voyager Sopris Learning, Inc. All rights reserved.

Objectives

- Self-correct as comprehension of text deepens.
- Answer questions to demonstrate comprehension of text.
- Engage in class discussion.
- Identify the enduring understandings from a piece of text.
- Identify the influence individuals have on ideas and events.
- Identify the impact of perspective and mood.

Revisit Passage Comprehension

Direct students to pages 201 and 202 in their Student Books. Have students review their answers and make any necessary changes. Then, have partners share their answers and collaborate to perfect them.

Enduring Understandings

Direct students back to page 189 in their Student Books. Reread the Big Idea questions.

Are suffering and normalcy relative?

Which plays a bigger part in who we are: things we are born with or things we are surrounded by?

Generate a class discussion about the questions and the answers students came up with in Lesson 1. Have them consider whether their answers have changed any after reading the text.

Use the following talking points to foster conversation. Refer to the Class Discussion Rules poster and have students use the Collegial Discussion sentence frames on page 382 of their Student Books.

- Liz Murray tells people "As long as you are willing to work past the point when you have absolutely nothing left inside of you, that's perseverance." Sometimes, we allow ourselves to make excuses for things that seem difficult. As a teen, Murray woke up each day asking herself what she could do for herself that day to overcome her obstacles. What do you do when you feel that obstacles are too difficult to overcome? Think about talk shows. Making excuses is much easier than making changes, isn't it?

- Scientists debate about what makes a person. Is it *nature* (what we were born with) or *nurture* (how we are raised and our environment)? It is likely a combination of the two. Do you think that what is inside of you can overcome the bad or destroy the good that is around you?

What we read should make us think. Use our discussion and your thoughts about the text to determine what you will "walk away with." Has it made you think about a personal experience or someone you know? Has your perspective or opinion on a specific topic changed? Do you have any lingering thoughts or questions? Write these ideas as your enduring understandings. What will you take with you from this text?

Discuss the enduring understandings with the class. Then, have students write their enduring understandings from the unit. If time permits, have students post a personal response about their enduring understandings to the online class wall.

Remind students to consider why the author wrote the passage and whether she was successful.

The Influence of Perspective

Breaking Night is a firsthand account, which means it was written by someone who was actually there for the events. It is a nonfiction text written as a narrative by one of the characters. This method of writing changes the perspective of the story, which often greatly influences the outcome and message. What was the overall mood of the text?

Generate a class discussion about the general mood of the text. Use the following talking points to foster conversation.

1. Did the author (Liz) seem to be unhappy?

2. Did Liz seem to wish things were different?

3. Did you read the passage and think about the terrible conditions Liz was living in?

4. Did you hear resentment in the author's voice?

5. Would the story have been different if it had been written from the perspective of a social worker? What about a parent?

Unit 5

Lesson 6

RI.2.2; RI.3.1; RI.2.5; RI.2.6; RI.2.7; RI.6.6; RI.6.10; RF.5.4a;
SL.1.2; SL.6.1b; SL.6.1c; SL.6.1d; L.3.5b; L.4.6; L.6.6

Lesson Opener

Before the lesson, choose one of the following activities to write on the board or post on the *LANGUAGE! Live* Class Wall online.

- *Write two sentences about what Liz Murray will do on the day after check day. Combine the sentences into one sentence with a compound predicate.*
- *What would you eat if given the money to eat anything you wanted for an entire day? Describe the food using adjectives.*
- *Write four sentences about Liz. Use* Liz *as a subject noun, direct object, predicate noun, and an object of the preposition.*

Reading

Objectives

- Determine and discuss the topic of a text.
- Determine and discuss the author's purpose.
- Use text features to preview text.

Passage Introduction

Direct students to page 211 in their Student Books. Discuss the content focus.

Content Focus

triumph; willpower

We are about to learn more about Liz Murray. Before we begin, what questions do you have about her life after reading an excerpt from her memoir? **Record questions on the board. Revisit questions after reading the text to see if they were answered. Assign unanswered questions for further discovery if time permits.**

Type of Text

informational

Text can be literature or informational. Memoirs and autobiographies are examples of informational text. They both tell facts about a person's life. *Breaking Night* was written in first person, meaning that the narrator was a character in the story—namely Lizzy. The text we are about to read is different because it is written in third person. The narrator is not a character in the story. As a matter of fact, this text will sound less like a story and more like an essay. It may sound more professional and less conversational. *Breaking Night* and "From Homeless to Harvard" are both nonfiction. Where is the narrator in *Breaking Night*? **(inside the story)** "From Homeless to Harvard" is informational text. Will it sound more professional or more conversational? **(more professional)**

Lesson 6 | Reading

Let's Focus: "From Homeless to Harvard"

Content Focus	Type of Text
triumph; willpower	informational

Author's Name unknown

Author's Purpose inform others about the triumphant life of Liz Murray

Big Ideas
Consider the following Big Idea questions. Write your answer for each question.

At what age are our personality and belief system formed?

To what degree is our future shaped by the people whom we live with as children?

Informational Preview Checklist: "From Homeless to Harvard" on pages 213–216.
- ☐ Title: What clue does it provide?
- ☐ Pictures: What additional information is added here?
- ☐ Headings: What will you learn about in each section?
- ☐ Features: What other text features do you notice?

Enduring Understandings
After reading the text . . .

© 2016 Voyager Sopris Learning, Inc. All rights reserved.   Unit 5 **211**

Author's Purpose

Have students glance at the text. Who is the author of the text? (unknown) This text is the type of text you would read in a textbook. The information is factual, but there isn't an author's name attributed to it. It likely means that someone was paid to write this text for a publishing company but isn't necessarily considered an "author." Informational text is written to inform the reader about a subject. Because the author is not a character in the story, facts are presented in a more objective way without much emotion and in a less casual tone. Have students write the answers on the page.

Read the Big Idea questions aloud.

Big Ideas

At what age are our personality and belief system formed?

To what degree is our future shaped by the people with whom we live as children?

*llegial Discussion
ster

*ass Discussion
les poster

As a class, consider the two Big Idea questions.

- Encourage students with limited concept of personal beliefs to ask for further explanation from peers.
- Provide opportunities for students to explain their ideas and answers to the Big Idea questions in light of the discussion by ensuring students follow the rules for class discussion, which can be printed in poster form from the Teacher Resources online.
- Suggest students refer to the Collegial Discussion sentence frames in the back of their books.
- Encourage speakers to link comments to the remarks of others to keep the focus of the discussion and create cohesion, even when their comments are in disagreement.

After discussing each question, have students write an answer. We'll come back to these questions after we finish reading the text. You can add to your answers as you gain information and perspective.

Preview

Read the Preview Checklist on page 211. Follow the Preview Procedure outlined below.

Preview Procedure
- Group students with partners or in triads.
- Have students count off as 1s or 2s. The 1s will become the student leaders. If working with triads, the third students become 3s.
- The student leaders will preview the text in addition to managing the checklist and pacing.
- The 2s and 3s will preview the text with 1s.
- Direct 1s to open their Student Books to page 210 and 2s and 3s to open their Student Books to page 212. This allows students to look at a few different pages at one time without turning back and forth.

Direct students to page 213 in their Student Books.

If necessary, guide students in a short preview using the following talking points. What is the title of the text? ("From Homeless to Harvard") Describe the photo on the title page and what information it contributes. (Liz Murray on stage; she seems to enjoy speaking to audiences) Let's choral read the caption in italics. *Liz Murray inspires the audience at a speaking engagement.*

Have students predict what they will learn about Liz Murray based on the caption and the title.

Vocabulary

Objectives
- Evaluate word knowledge.
- Determine the meaning of key passage vocabulary.

Rate Vocabulary Knowledge

Direct students to page 212 in their Student Books.

We are about to read a text about the life of Liz Murray, the author of *Breaking Night.* Before we read, let's take a look at the vocabulary words that appear in this text. Remind students that as you read each word in the first column aloud, they will write the word in the third column and then rate their knowledge of it. Display the Vocabulary Rating Scale poster or write the information on the board. Review the meaning of each rating.

> ### Vocabulary Rating Scale
>
> 0—I have never heard the word before.
>
> 1—I have heard the word, but I'm not sure how to use it.
>
> 2—I am familiar with the word, but I'm not sure if I know the correct meaning.
>
> 3—I know the meaning of the word and can use it correctly in a sentence.

Lesson 6 | Vocabulary

Key Passage Vocabulary: "From Homeless to Harvard"

Read each word. Write the word in column 3. Then, circle a number to rate your knowledge of the word.

Vocabulary	Part of Speech	Write the Word	Knowledge Rating
outcome	(n)	outcome	0 1 2 3
diagnose	(v)	diagnose	0 1 2 3
conditions	(n)	conditions	0 1 2 3
alternative	(adj)	alternative	0 1 2 3
motivated	(adj)	motivated	0 1 2 3
apply	(v)	apply	0 1 2 3
opportunity	(n)	opportunity	0 1 2 3
strategy	(n)	strategy	0 1 2 3
lecture	(v)	lecture	0 1 2 3
inspiration	(n)	inspiration	0 1 2 3

The points are not a grade; they are just there to help you know which words you need to focus on. By the end of this unit, you should be able to change all your ratings to a 3. That's the goal.

Read each word aloud. Have students repeat it, write it, and rate it. Then, have volunteers who rated a word *2* or *3* use the word in an oral sentence.

Preteach Vocabulary

Let's take a closer look at the words. Follow the Preteach Procedure below.

> ### Preteach Procedure
> This activity is intended to take only a short amount of time, so make it an oral exercise.
> * Introduce each word as indicated on the word card.
> * Read the definition and example sentences.
> * Ask questions to clarify and deepen understanding.
> * If time permits, allow students to share.
>
> * If your students would benefit from copying the definitions, please have them do so in the vocabulary log in the back of the Student Books using the margin definitions in the passage selections. This should be done outside of instruction time.

outcome (n)

Let's read the first word together. *Outcome.*

Definition: An *outcome* is a result or the way something ends. What word means "a result; the way something ends"? (outcome)

Example 1: The *outcome* of the game was not what I had hoped; we lost.

Example 2: A conflict can have a positive *outcome* if you communicate clearly, calmly, and patiently.

Example 3: Artists are never sure what the exact *outcome* of a creative project might be.

Question 1: Do votes affect the *outcome* of an election? Yes or no? (yes)

Question 2: Do get-well cards change the *outcome* of an illness? Yes or no? (no)

Pair Share: You are about to complain about the service in a restaurant. Turn to your partner and name one possible *outcome*.

diagnose (v)

Let's read the next word together. *Diagnose.*

Definition: *Diagnose* means "to find out and name what is wrong with someone or something." What means "to find out and name what is wrong with someone or something"? (diagnose)

Example 1: I couldn't *diagnose* the problem with my pipes, so I called a plumber.

Example 2: After examining her, the vet *diagnosed* my cat with a flea allergy.

Example 3: It is hard to *diagnose* your own illness by looking online because you'll find so much conflicting information.

Question 1: Could a mechanic *diagnose* a problem with your car? Yes or no? (yes)

Question 2: If I say, "My computer has a virus," have I *diagnosed* it? Yes or no? (yes)

Pair Share: You return from the beach and your skin hurts. *Diagnose* the problem.

conditions (n)

Let's read the next word together. *Conditions.*

Definition: *Conditions* are all the things in the surroundings that affect how a person acts or feels. What means "all the things in the surroundings that affect how a person acts or feels"? (conditions)

Example 1: Sometimes, the *conditions* in a movie theater make me sleepy.

Example 2: Stormy *conditions* keep many people indoors.

Example 3: If you are easily distracted, you might have a hard time working in noisy *conditions*.

Question 1: Do weather *conditions* affect the clothes you choose each day? Yes or no? (yes)

Question 2: *Conditions* in your friend's home are stressful. Do you want to spend time there? Yes or no? (no)

Pair Share: Turn to your partner and describe *conditions* that make you feel peaceful and relaxed.

(3)

alternative (adj)

Let's read the next word together. *Alternative.*

Definition: *Alternative* means "different from other things of its kind." What means "different from other things of its kind"? (alternative)

Example 1: You may read this book, or you may read an *alternative* one of your choice.

Example 2: An *alternative* burger can be made with grains and beans instead of meat.

Example 3: When I drive during rush hour, I always have an *alternative* route in mind in case I run into traffic.

Question 1: Is a bicycle an *alternative* form of transportation to a bus? Yes or no? (yes)

Question 2: If you live an *alternative* lifestyle, do you live like most other people? Yes or no? (no)

Pair Share: Turn to your partner and describe a situation in which it is good to have an *alternative* plan.

(4)

motivated (adj)

Let's read the next word together. *Motivated.*

Definition: If you are *motivated*, you are focused on reaching one or more goals. What means "focused on reaching one or more goals"? (motivated)

Example 1: On days when I feel energetic and *motivated*, I get a lot done.

Example 2: Runners can stay *motivated* by picturing the finish line in their mind.

Example 3: My *motivated* cousin finished her law degree and then applied for medical school.

Question 1: Do most people feel *motivated* at the end of a long, hard day? Yes or no? (no)

Question 2: Are *motivated* athletes more likely to train regularly? Yes or no? (yes)

Pair Share: In what area of your life are you most *motivated*, and why? Tell your partner.

(5)

apply (v)

Let's read the next word together. *Apply.*

Definition: *Apply* means "to ask for something in writing or by filling out a form." What word means "to ask for something in writing or by filling out a form"? (apply)

Example 1: Before I was given this job, I had to *apply* for it.

Example 2: When you *apply* for a loan, you have to show that you will be able to pay it back.

Example 3: To win a scholarship, you must *apply* by the deadline; otherwise, you won't be considered.

Question 1: Do babies have to *apply* for the care they receive? Yes or no? (no)

Question 2: After high school, you plan to go to culinary school. Will you have to *apply*? Yes or no? (yes)

Pair Share: Turn to your partner and tell what you expect to *apply* for in the next three to five years.

(6)

opportunity (n)

Let's read the next word together. *Opportunity.*

Definition: An *opportunity* is a chance to do something you want to do. What word means "a chance to do something you want to do"? (opportunity)

Example 1: Whenever I have an *opportunity* to travel, I try to take it.

Example 2: People who see a challenge as an *opportunity* to learn usually meet the challenge successfully.

Example 3: A rainy day is a good *opportunity* to read a book or clean out a closet.

Question 1: Your friend talks constantly. Does she give you many *opportunities* to speak? Yes or no? (no)

Question 2: You want to use the computer, but your sister gets to it first. Have you missed your *opportunity*? Yes or no? (yes)

Pair Share: Turn to your partner. Name an *opportunity* you've been offered to develop a skill. Tell whether you took it, and why.

(7)

strategy (n)

Let's read the next word together. *Strategy.*

Definition: A *strategy* is a plan for doing something over time. What means "a plan for doing something over time"? (strategy)

Example 1: To win a game, you need an overall *strategy*, not just a series of good moves.

Example 2: "If at first you don't succeed, try, try again" is a good *strategy* for life.

Example 3: The city is working on a five-year *strategy* for attracting more tourists.

Question 1: If you just take your chances in a risky situation, do you have a *strategy*? Yes or no? (no)

Question 2: You drink five sodas a day but want to cut them out altogether. You decide to drink one fewer soda a day until you get to zero. Is this a *strategy*? Yes or no? (yes)

Pair Share: You are stranded on an island. What is your *strategy* for survival? Tell your partner at least two parts of it.

(8)

lecture (v)

Let's read the next word together. *Lecture.*

Definition: To *lecture* is to give an organized talk in public. What word means "to give an organized talk in public"? (lecture)

Example 1: Some teachers would rather *lecture* than lead a class discussion.

Example 2: Experts are sometimes asked to *lecture* on topics related to their work.

Example 3: It is normal for people who *lecture* on a regular basis to want some quiet time alone.

Question 1: You are asked to *lecture* for one hour on quantum physics. Are you able to do so? Yes or no? (no)

Question 2: Would a shy, self-conscious person feel comfortable *lecturing*? Yes or no? (no)

Pair Share: Turn to your partner and explain what topic you could *lecture* on and why.

(9)

inspiration (n)

Let's read the last word together. *Inspiration.*

Definition: *Inspiration* is energy to do something new or creative. What word means "energy to do something new or creative"? (inspiration)

Example 1: Everyday events can provide *inspiration* for great works of art.

Example 2: Role models give others the *inspiration* they need to reach their goals.

Example 3: Successful people stay committed to a project even after the *inspiration* wears off.

Question 1: You see a cool hairstyle and then try it on yourself. Was the first hairstyle an *inspiration*? Yes or no? (yes)

Question 2: Your friend wants to try out for the play, but you tell him he can't act. Have you given him *inspiration*? Yes or no? (no)

Pair Share: Turn to your partner and tell about a time you got the *inspiration* you needed to try something new.

(10)

Objectives
- Read informational text.
- Monitor comprehension during text reading.

"From Homeless to Harvard"

Direct students to page 213 in their Student Books.

Now that we have previewed vocabulary, it's time to read.

> **Guiding Students Toward Independent Reading**
>
> It is important that your students read as much and as often as they can. Assign readings that meet the needs of your students, based on your observations and data. This is a good opportunity to stretch your students. If students become frustrated, scaffold the reading with paired reading, choral reading, or a read-aloud.
>
> Options for reading text:
> - Teacher read-aloud
> - Teacher-led or student-led choral read
> - Paired read or independent read

Choose an option for reading text. Students read according to the option that you chose. Review the purpose of the numbered squares in the text and prompt students to stop periodically and check comprehension.

If you choose to read the text aloud or chorally, use the following text boxes and stop to ask questions and have students answer them.

SE p. 213, paragraph 1

> The winter evening is cold and windy with crisp-looking stars shining over Bronx, New York. Liz Murray, just 12 years old, doesn't want to go home because her parents are doing drugs again. She is walking the streets, alone, headed for the home of a friend. She knocks on an apartment door, hoping to spend the night on the sofa in her friend's apartment. Hopefully, her friend's parents won't mind. Maybe she'll go home to check on her mother in the morning, or maybe she'll go to school.

1. Why doesn't Liz want to go home?

p. 213, paragraph 2

What could the future hold for a child who lives like this? Could a person whose life began in a background of parental drug addiction and poverty hope to be educated at a famous university and become a public success? That **outcome** is unlikely, but Liz Murray made it possible.

Born into Poverty

p. 214, paragraphs 1–2

Liz Murray was born into a life of poverty and addiction in the Bronx in 1980. An eye disease soon left her mom legally blind. As a result of her disability, she received welfare from the government and relied on Liz to take care of her and "be her eyes." Liz was forced to do things such as watch for the mailman on the first of every month and stand in line at the check-cashing store with the other welfare recipients—while other kids her age were playing innocent games of tag and hide and seek. Once the check was cashed, her drug-addicted parents used the money for drugs and began the cycle of neglect and mistreatment of their children.

Liz remembers eating well on the first of each month. However, during the rest of the month, her parents used their support to feed their drug addictions instead of their children. Some months, after spending their welfare check on drugs, her parents only had $30 left to feed Liz and her sister.

2. Liz's parents sacrificed the well-being of their children for what?

p. 214, paragraph 3

When Liz was growing up, she lived in filthy conditions. Because of this, she was unbathed, wore unclean clothing, and often had lice. Liz was aware of the smell she gave off and the unwelcome stares from kids at school. The shame of this caused Liz to hate school and plead to stay home. Often, her mother agreed. She loved her parents and felt fortunate that they loved her back.

3. Why did Liz miss school?

Death Brings Realization

p. 214, paragraphs 4–5

Eventually, her parents separated. Liz's older sister, Lisa, went to live with their mom and her new boyfriend. Liz stayed with her father because she didn't want him to be alone. When Liz was 11, her mother was **diagnosed** with HIV and died five years later.

While her mother grew more sick, Liz's father moved to a shelter for the homeless. Liz was sent to a group home, but **conditions** at the home were so bad that she didn't stay long. Living on | the streets of New York, she found food in garbage bins and shelter in friends' homes or on subway trains.

page break

4. How did Liz's life dramatically change at age 16?

SE p. 215, paragraph 1

After her mother's death, Liz suddenly realized that she was truly on her own. Her mother had said many times, "Someday life will get better." But Liz realized her mother died before she could fix anything, so Liz resolved to change her life for the better before it was too late. She began to think seriously about her own life. She wondered if she could rise out of her background of poverty and improve her life with education. This idea pushed her forward.

5. How did Liz determine to improve her life?

Getting an Education

SE p. 215, paragraphs 2–3

At 17, Liz heard about **alternative** high schools. She researched different schools and finally found one that would accept her. Because she was intelligent and **motivated** and had taught herself to read, Liz did well in school despite her lack of previous schooling. She determined to graduate in two years instead of the usual four. Because of her willingness to study often, anywhere she could— school hallways, libraries, stairwells in apartment buildings—she did it.

During this time, she was still homeless, sleeping out on the streets sometimes and working at odd jobs to earn money. At school, her teachers encouraged her. She began to believe in herself, but she never let anyone know how she was living. Then, something happened that set the course of her life.

6. What kind of high school did Liz attend? How long did it take her to graduate?

SE p. 215, paragraph 4

A teacher chose her and a few other students to visit Boston, Massachusetts. While there, she visited Harvard University, a respected Ivy League university known for academic excellence. As she stood gazing at the campus, her teacher told her that it was possible for her to go to school at Harvard, and she believed him. Liz would later write in her memoir, *Breaking Night*, that it was a good thing he didn't tell her how hard it was to get accepted to this university. Then, she heard about a *New York Times* scholarship for needy students and **applied** for it. Applicants had to write an essay describing any hardships they had overcome to achieve academic success. Liz was one of six students who received the scholarship. She applied and was accepted to Harvard.

7. How was Liz able to go to an expensive school like Harvard?

SE p. 216, paragraph 1
Liz enrolled at Harvard in the fall of 2000 and completed several semesters of academic study. Then, in 2003, her father became sick with AIDS, and she returned to New York to take care of him.

8. Why did Liz have to leave Harvard?

A New Direction

SE p. 216, paragraph 2
Despite what appeared to be a setback in New York, Liz continued her education at Columbia University. The unexpected changes in her life also brought many exciting **opportunities.** The *New York Times* published a story about her scholarship, then the television show *20/20* told her story, and Oprah Winfrey interviewed her. Also in 2003, a television movie was made about her life.

9. Why did Liz become a subject of the media?

SE p. 216, paragraph 3
Liz's father died in 2006, having finally overcome his drug addiction. Liz returned to Harvard in May 2008 to complete her degree. She realized that her story might have the power to help others. But, even better, her experiences and her knowledge might allow her to create **strategies** to help people cope with hardships. People might use these ways to move beyond their hardships to a meaningful life.

10. What did Liz's father do before he died that would have made Liz proud?

SE p. 216, paragraph 4
Today, Liz has a company. Through workshops, she **lectures** to groups throughout the country, encouraging others to rise to their own dreams. Her sister also graduated from college and is a teacher. Whatever their dreams are, whatever background they come from, however hard they need to work, Liz Murray gives people **inspiration** to change their lives.

11. Why do you think Liz is interested in helping others?

For confirmation of engagement, have students share something positive that came from Liz Murray's troubled childhood. Have volunteers share ideas with the class.

Lesson Opener

Before the lesson, choose one of the following activities to write on the board or post on the *LANGUAGE! Live* Class Wall online.

- *Write a summary sentence about Liz Murray's determination.*
- *Write a sentence with a compound object about the obstacles Liz Murray overcame.*
- *Write two sentences about your plans for high school and college. Include a compound predicate in each sentence.*

Vocabulary

Objective

- Review key passage vocabulary.

Review Passage Vocabulary

Direct students to page 212 in their Student Books. Use the following questions to review the vocabulary words in "From Homeless to Harvard." Have students answer each question using the vocabulary word or indicating its meaning in a complete sentence.

- What was the unlikely *outcome* of Liz Murray's childhood? (The unlikely outcome was that she went to Harvard and became a successful public speaker.) Why was this *outcome* unlikely? (The outcome was unlikely because Liz had no parental support and was homeless for a time.)

- When Liz was 11, what was her mother *diagnosed* with? (Her mother was diagnosed with HIV.) When her mother used to say "Someday life will get better," was she *diagnosing* herself? How so? (No, she wasn't diagnosing herself, or naming her condition; she was just saying vague, empty words.)

- Describe the *conditions* in Liz's childhood home. (Possible response: The conditions were horrible: a dirty house, unpaid bills, no food, and ratty furniture.) What were the *conditions* of Liz's later life on the streets? (The conditions of Liz's life on the streets were worse; she found food in trash bins and slept on the subway.)

- Liz could have lived a life of poverty and homelessness. What *alternative* life did she choose instead? (Liz chose an alternative life of education and work.) She chose an *alternative* school. What might such a school be like? (An alternative school might offer different types of classes or accept students with particular backgrounds or interests.)

- Liz was a *motivated* student. What does this mean? (A motivated student like Liz wants to graduate and stays focused on that goal.) Would you describe Liz's mother as *motivated*? Why or why not? (No, her mother was not motivated; she did not focus on changing her life or take steps to do so.)

- What did Liz do to *apply* for the *New York Times* scholarship? (To apply for the scholarship, Liz wrote an essay describing hardships she had overcome.) After winning the scholarship, what did she *apply* for? How do you think she did this? (She applied for admission to Harvard, probably by filling out forms and writing another essay.)

- When Liz left Harvard to care for her father, did she lose her *opportunity* for education? (No, she did not lose her opportunity for education; she studied at Columbia instead.) Did Harvard give her another *opportunity* later on? (Yes, Harvard gave her the opportunity to complete her degree in 2008.)

- What kinds of *strategies* does Liz help others create today? (She helps others create strategies for overcoming hardships.) What are these *strategies* probably made up of? (They are probably made up of concrete goals and steps to take to reach them.)

- When Liz teaches others by *lecturing*, what is she doing? (When she is lecturing, she is giving organized talks in public.) What topics does she *lecture* on? (She lectures on overcoming hardship, staying focused on your dreams, and changing your life for the better.)

- In a sense, Liz's difficult childhood became her *inspiration*. How so? (Her difficult childhood became her inspiration because she used it to help others.) Is Liz an *inspiration* to you? Why or why not? (Possible answer: Yes; she is an inspiration to me because if she can overcome her challenges, so can I.)

Assign online practice by opening the Tools menu, then selecting Assignments. Be sure to select the correct class from the drop-down menu.

Reading

Objectives
- Determine how to respond to prompts.
- Use critical thinking skills to write responses to prompts about text.
- Support written answers with text evidence.
- Determine main ideas in informational text.
- Sequence events in a text.

Critical Understandings: Direction Words *create, delineate, determine, paraphrase*

Prompts are statements that require a constructed response, which can range from a list to a complete sentence to a paragraph or an essay. We can take prompts and turn them into questions to help us understand what is being asked.

Write the words *create, delineate, determine*, and *paraphrase* on the board. Have students read the words aloud with you.

Direct students to page 66 in their Student Books. It is critical to understand what the question is asking and how to answer it. Today, we will look at four direction words used in prompts.

Critical Understandings: Direction Words

Prompt	How to Respond	Model
If the prompt asks you to . . .	The response requires you to . . .	For example . . .
Analyze	break down and evaluate or draw conclusions about the information	**Analyze** the development of the text's central idea.
Assess	decide on the value, impact, or accuracy	**Assess** the level of pressure in an arranged marriage.
Compare	state the similarities between two or more things	**Compare** novels and dramas.
Contrast	state the differences between two or more things	**Contrast** a biography with an autobiography.
Create	make or produce something	**Create** a timeline of events.
Define	tell or write the meaning or definition	**Define** the unknown word using context clues.
Delineate	show or list evidence, claims, ideas, reasons, or events	**Delineate** the evidence in the text.
Describe	state detailed information about a topic	**Describe** the relationship between the plot and character development.
Determine	find out, verify, decide	**Determine** the main idea.
Distinguish	recognize or explain the differences	**Distinguish** between facts and opinions.
Evaluate	think carefully to make a judgment; form a critical opinion of	**Evaluate** the ANC's plan for change.
Explain	express understanding of an idea or concept	**Explain** how the author develops the narrator's point of view.
Identify	say or write what it is	**Identify** the character's motive.
Infer	provide a logical answer using evidence and prior knowledge	Use information from the text to **infer** the value of education.
Interpret	make sense of or assign meaning to something	**Interpret** the quote to confirm your understanding.
Paraphrase	say or write it using different words	**Paraphrase** the main idea.
Report	Tell or write about a topic	**Report** the main events of the setting.
Summarize	tell the most important ideas or concepts	**Summarize** the key details of the passage.
Tell	say or write specific information	**Tell** the date that the poem was written.
Use	apply information or a procedure	**Use** text features to identify the topic.

Have students read about the four direction words in the chart with their partner.

> **Chart Reading Procedure**
> - Group students with partners or in triads.
> - Have students count off as 1s or 2s. The 1s will become the student leaders. If working with triads, the third students become 3s.
> - The student leaders will read the left column (Prompt) in addition to managing the time and turn-taking if working with a triad.
> - The 2s will explain the middle column of the chart (How to Respond). If working in triads, 2s and 3s will take turns explaining the right column.
> - The 1s will read the right column of the chart (Model), and 2s will restate the model as a question.
> - Students should follow along with their pencil eraser while others are explaining the chart.
> - Students should work from left to right, top to bottom in order to benefit from this activity.
> - Attempt to give all students a chance to be a student leader as you move through the lessons.

Check for understanding by requesting an oral response to the following questions.

- If the prompt asks you to *create*, the response requires you to . . . (make or produce something).

- If the prompt asks you to *delineate*, the response requires you to . . . (show or list evidence, claims, ideas, reasons, or events).

- If the prompt asks you to *determine*, the response requires you to . . . (find out, verify, decide).

- If the prompt asks you to *paraphrase*, the response requires you to . . . (say or write it using different words).

Direct students to pages 217 and 218 in their Student Books and read the instructions aloud. Let's read some prompts about a small section of the text before we expand to the entire text.

1. Paraphrase the introduction.

2. Determine the main idea of the section Death Brings Realization.

3. Create a timeline of Liz's life from 1980 to 2000.

4. Delineate evidence of obstacles in Liz's life through high school.

We are going to focus on Liz Murray's life from birth through high school. We will practice answering prompts with these new question words.

Model

Let's practice answering questions that are written as prompts. Remember to use the chart as a reference. Listen as I model the first one for you.

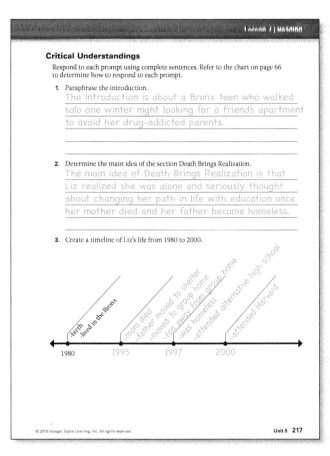

1. Paraphrase the introduction.

According to the chart, if the prompt asks you to *paraphrase*, the response requires that you say or write it using different words. Now, I will turn the prompt into a question to confirm understanding. What does the introduction say?

Let's use what we know about Masterpiece Sentences to help us with this answer. First, I will answer the masterpiece questions using words from the text.

> Who did it? Liz Murray
> When? Cold and windy winter evening
> Where? The Bronx
> What did she do? Walking the streets alone looking for a friend's apartment
> Why? Her parents are doing drugs again.

Now, I will change it to my own words, which is part of paraphrasing.

> Who did it? A Bronx teen
> When? One winter night
> What did she do? Walked solo one winter night
> Why? Looking for a friend's apartment to avoid her drug-addicted parents

Write the following sentence on the board and have students write it on the page.

The introduction is about a Bronx teen who walked solo one winter night, looking for a friend's apartment to avoid her drug-addicted parents.

Guided Practice

Let's move on to the next prompt.

2. Determine the main idea of the section Death Brings Realization.

How should we respond according to the chart? (If the prompt asks you to *determine*, the response requires that you find out, verify, or decide.)

Now, turn the prompt into a question to confirm your understanding. Tell your partner the question. (What is the section Death Brings Realization mostly about?)

While providing partner time, write the sentence starter on the board.

The main idea of Death Brings Realization is _____.

Have partners answer the question and provide evidence from the text.

3. Create a timeline of Liz's life from 1980 to 2000.

How should we respond according to the chart? (If the prompt asks you to *create*, the response requires that you make or produce something.) Now, turn the prompt into a question to confirm your understanding. Tell your partner the question. (What events occurred in Liz's life from 1980 to 2000?) For this prompt, you will make a timeline. First, determine which dates should go on the timeline. While providing partner time, write *1980, 1995, 1997,* and *2000* at the bottom of a line on the board. Model how to complete the beginning and the end of the timeline. Have students finish the timeline with your guidance as needed.

4. Delineate evidence of obstacles in Liz's life through high school.

How should we respond according to the chart? (If the prompt asks you to *delineate*, the response requires you to show or list evidence, claims, ideas, reasons, or events.) Now, turn the prompt into a question to confirm your understanding. Tell your partner the question. (What obstacles did Liz face through high school?) For this prompt, let's make a list. In order to provide a complete answer, we will have to list the obstacle and the evidence from the text. **While providing partner time, draw a T-chart on the board with *Obstacle* on the left and *Text Evidence* on the right. Discuss the first two answers before having students finish the list with their partner.**

Critical Understandings (*cont.*)

4. Delineate evidence of obstacles in Liz's life through high school.

Obstacle	Text Evidence
Parents addicted to drugs	"her drug-addicted parents"
Mom legally blind	"An eye disease soon left her mom legally blind."
Poor hygiene caused her to miss a lot of school	"Liz was unbathed, wore unclean clothing, and often had lice . . . The shame of this caused Liz to hate school and plead to stay home."
Little money for groceries	"her parents used their support to feed their drug addictions instead of their children."
Mom died of HIV	"When Liz was 11, her mother was diagnosed with HIV and died five years later."
Dad was homeless	"While her mother grew more sick, Liz's father moved to a shelter for the homeless."
Liz ran away from group home	"Liz was sent to a group home, but conditions at the home were so bad that she didn't stay long."
Homeless during high school years	"During this time, she was still homeless, sleeping out on the streets."

Lesson Opener

Before the lesson, choose one of the following activities to write on the board or post on the *LANGUAGE! Live* Class Wall online.

- *What would you do if your parents didn't care if you went to school? Would you still go? Why or why not?*
- *Write three sentences about Liz Murray's college education using compound sentence elements.*
- *Expand one or more of these simple sentences, using the steps in Masterpiece Sentences.*

  Liz slept.

  Liz moved.

  Liz ran away.

  Liz's mother died.

Reading

Objectives

- Establish a purpose for rereading informational text.
- Monitor comprehension during text reading.
- Use critical thinking skills to write responses to prompts about text.
- Support written answers with text evidence.
- Use text evidence to support claims.
- Analyze the effect a person has on events.
- Sequence events.

Reading for a Purpose: "From Homeless to Harvard"

We are going to reread "From Homeless to Harvard." Let's preview some prompts to provide a purpose for rereading the text.

Direct students to pages 219–221 in their Student Books. Have students read the prompts aloud with you.

1. Delineate the evidence that supports the claim that a child without parental supervision can become a successful adult.

2. Determine Liz's strengths that allowed her to break the cycle of poverty and addiction.

3. Paraphrase the last sentence in "From Homeless to Harvard" to explain Liz Murray's hopes for her company.

4. Create a timeline of Liz's life from 2003 to today.

5. Delineate Liz's path to a college degree.

6. Create an invitation to a speaking engagement featuring Liz Murray. Include information about the speaker as well as topics that will be covered.

It's time to revisit the text.

Choose an option for rereading text. Have students read the text according to the option that you chose.

Choose an option for rereading text.

- Teacher read-aloud
- Teacher-led or student-led choral read
- Paired read or independent read with bold vocabulary words read aloud

Direct students to page 213 in their Student Books or have them tear out the extra copy of the text from the back of their book.

Note: To minimize flipping back and forth between the pages, a copy of each text has been included in the back of the Student Books. Encourage students to tear this out and use it when working on activities that require the use of the text.

Have students read the text.

Passage Comprehension

Write the words *create*, *delineate*, *determine*, and *paraphrase* on the board. Have students read the words aloud with you.

Direct students to page 66 in their Student Books. It is critical to understand what the question is asking and how to answer it. Today, we will review four direction words used in prompts.

Have students read the chart on page 66 with their partner. Check for understanding by requesting an oral response to the following questions.

- If the prompt asks you to *create*, the response requires you to . . . (make or produce something).

- If the prompt asks you to *delineate*, the response requires you to . . . (show or list evidence, claims, ideas, reasons, or events).

- If the prompt asks you to *determine*, the response requires you to . . . (find out, verify, decide).

- If the prompt asks you to *paraphrase*, the response requires you to . . . (say or write it using different words).

Now, let's practice answering questions that are written as prompts. Remember to use the chart as a reference. Don't forget, if the direction word is confusing, try to restate the prompt by using a question word. What are question words? (who, what, where, why, when, how)

Critical Understandings: Direction Words

Prompt	How to Respond	Model
If the prompt asks you to . . .	The response requires you to . . .	For example . . .
Analyze	break down and evaluate or draw conclusions about the information	**Analyze** the development of the text's central idea.
Assess	decide on the value, impact, or accuracy	**Assess** the level of pressure in an arranged marriage.
Compare	state the similarities between two or more things	**Compare** novels and dramas.
Contrast	state the differences between two or more things	**Contrast** a biography with an autobiography.
Create	make or produce something	**Create** a timeline of events.
Define	tell or write the meaning or definition	**Define** the unknown word using context clues.
Delineate	show or list evidence, claims, ideas, reasons, or events	**Delineate** the evidence in the text.
Describe	state detailed information about a topic	**Describe** the relationship between the plot and character development.
Determine	find out, verify, decide	**Determine** the main idea.
Distinguish	recognize or explain the differences	**Distinguish** between facts and opinions.
Evaluate	think carefully to make a judgment; form a critical opinion of	**Evaluate** the ANC's plan for change.
Explain	express understanding of an idea or concept	**Explain** how the author develops the narrator's point of view.
Identify	say or write what it is	**Identify** the character's motive.
Infer	provide a logical answer using evidence and prior knowledge	Use information from the text to **infer** the value of education.
Interpret	make sense of or assign meaning to something	**Interpret** the quote to confirm your understanding.
Paraphrase	say or write it using different words	**Paraphrase** the main idea.
Report	Tell or write about a topic	**Report** the main events of the setting.
Summarize	tell the most important ideas or concepts	**Summarize** the key details of the passage.
Tell	say or write specific information	**Tell** the date that the poem was written.
Use	apply information or a procedure	**Use** text features to identify the topic.

Direct students to pages 219–221 in their Student Books.

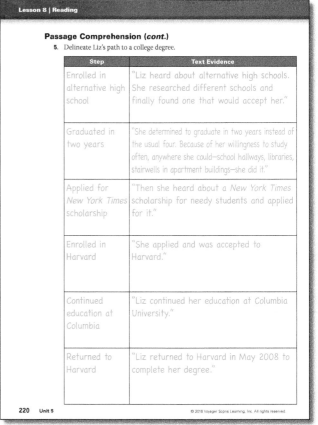

Passage Comprehension

Reread "From Homeless to Harvard." Respond to each prompt using complete sentences. Refer to the chart on page 66 to determine how to respond to each prompt.

1. Delineate the evidence that supports the claim that a child without parental supervision can become a successful adult.

   A child without parental supervision such as Liz Murray, who "is walking the streets, alone" because she "doesn't want to go home because her parents are doing drugs again," can become a successful adult. Liz proved this when she "returned to Harvard in May 2008 to complete her degree" and started her own company. Now, "through workshops, she lectures to groups throughout the country."

2. Determine Liz's strengths that allowed her to break the cycle of poverty and addiction.

   Liz possessed the strengths of intelligence, motivation, and determination. These strengths allowed her to break the cycle of poverty and addiction in her family.

3. Paraphrase the last sentence in "From Homeless to Harvard" to explain Liz Murray's hopes for her company.

   Liz Murray wants to use her story and the strategies she has learned to inspire others regardless of the lows they have been through or the highs they want to achieve.

4. Create a timeline of Liz's life from 2003 to today.

   Timeline:
   - 2003: –dad sick with AIDS; –returns to NY
   - 2006: –media attention: NYTimes, 20/20, Oprah, TV movie; –dad overcame drug addiction; –dad died
   - 2008: –returned to Harvard
   - 2010: –Breaking Night was published
   - Today: –has own company to help others

Unit 5   **219**

Passage Comprehension (*cont.*)

5. Delineate Liz's path to a college degree.

Step	Text Evidence
Enrolled in alternative high school	"Liz heard about alternative high schools. She researched different schools and finally found one that would accept her."
Graduated in two years	"She determined to graduate in two years instead of the usual four. Because of her willingness to study often, anywhere she could—school hallways, libraries, stairwells in apartment buildings—she did it."
Applied for *New York Times* scholarship	"Then she heard about a *New York Times* scholarship for needy students and applied for it."
Enrolled in Harvard	"She applied and was accepted to Harvard."
Continued education at Columbia	"Liz continued her education at Columbia University."
Returned to Harvard	"Liz returned to Harvard in May 2008 to complete her degree."

220   Unit 5

Model

Listen as I model the first one for you.

> 1. Delineate the evidence that supports the claim that a child without parental supervision can become a successful adult.

According to the chart, if the prompt asks you to *delineate*, the response requires that you show or list evidence and claims. Now, I will turn the prompt into a question to confirm understanding. What evidence supports the claim that a child without parental supervision can become a successful adult?

I need to find evidence that Liz Murray did not have parental supervision as a child. Then, I need to find evidence that she became a successful adult. The text says that Liz ". . . doesn't want

Passage Comprehension (*cont.*)

6. Create an invitation to a speaking engagement featuring Liz Murray. Include information about the speaker as well as topics that will be covered.

   Answers will vary.

Unit 5   **221**

to go home because her parents are doing drugs again. She is walking the streets, alone . . ." That is sufficient evidence that she doesn't have supervision. The evidence in the text that she became a successful adult is "Liz returned to Harvard in May 2008 to complete her degree" and "Today, Liz has a company. Through workshops, she lectures to groups throughout the country."

So my answer would be:
A child without parental supervision such as Liz Murray, who "is walking the streets, alone" because she ". . . doesn't want to go home because her parents are doing drugs again," can become a successful adult. Liz proved this when she "returned to Harvard in May 2008 to complete her degree" and started her own company in which "through workshops, she lectures to groups throughout the country."

Guided Practice

2. Determine Liz's strengths that allowed her to break the cycle of poverty and addiction.

How should we respond according to the chart? (If the prompt asks you to *determine*, the response requires that you find out, verify, or decide.) Now, turn the prompt into a question to confirm your understanding. Tell your partner the question. (What strengths does Liz have that allowed her to break the cycle of poverty and addiction?)

Have students find personality traits in the text. (intelligent; motivated; determined; willing to try hard; encouraging)

While providing partner time, write the sentence starter on the board.

> *Liz possessed the strengths of _____. These strengths allowed her to break the cycle of poverty and addiction in her family.*

Have partners answer the question and provide evidence from the text.

Independent Practice

Have partners respond to the remaining prompts with text evidence. For students who need more assistance, provide the following alternative questions and sentence starters.

Alternative questions and sentence starters:

3. What are Liz Murray's hopes for her company? Use your own words.

   Liz Murray wants _____.

4. What events occurred in Liz's life from 2003 to today?

5. What steps did Liz Murray take to earn a college degree?

6. Who is the speaker and what will be covered in the workshop?

Lesson 9

RI.1.3; RI.1.5; RI.2.2; RI.3.1; RI.4.1; RI.4.5; RI.6.4; RI.6.5;
RI.6.10; RI.7.4; RI.8.5; RF.5.4a; RF.5.4c; SL.1.2; L.4.5c; L.4.6;
L.5.4a; L.6.4a; L.6.6

Lesson Opener

Before the lesson, choose one of the following activities to write on the board or post on the *LANGUAGE! Live* Class Wall online.

- *Liz Murray overcame numerous obstacles in her life to obtain a college degree and start her own company. Liz's personality led to her success. What personality traits do you have that will help you overcome obstacles to realize your dreams?*
- *Write five sentences about how you would convince people that you have money when you really don't.*
- *Paint the predicate in the following sentences about Liz Murray's life.*

> *Liz went to college.*
> *Liz graduated from high school.*
> *Liz took care of her dad.*
> *Liz left college.*
> *Liz gives lectures.*

Reading

Objectives

- Read informational text.
- Read with purpose and understanding.
- Answer questions to demonstrate comprehension of text.
- Monitor comprehension during text reading.
- Distinguish between the subjective point of view and the objective point of view.
- Identify how text is organized and how each section contributes to the whole text.

Close Reading of "From Homeless to Harvard"

Highlighters or colored pencils

Let's reread "From Homeless to Harvard." I will provide specific instructions on how to mark the text to help with comprehension.

Have students get out a highlighter or colored pencil.

Direct students to pages 222–225 in their Student Books. Please mark your text according to my instructions.

Draw a rectangle around the title.

Circle the headings.

Now, let's read the vocabulary words aloud.

- What's the first bold vocabulary word? (outcome) *Outcome* means "result; the way something ends." You can't do the same thing and expect a different *outcome.* **Have partners use the word in a sentence.**
- What's the next bold vocabulary word? (diagnosed) *Diagnosed* means "found out and named what is wrong with someone or something." Doctors *diagnosed* my friend with cancer. **Have partners use the word in a sentence.**

- What's the next vocabulary word? (conditions) *Conditions* means "all the things in the surroundings that affect how a person acts or feels." Road *conditions* were dangerous during the storm. **Have partners use the word in a sentence.**

- Let's continue. (alternative) *Alternative* means "different from other things of its kind." *Alternative* music is increasing in popularity. **Have partners use the word in a sentence.**

- Next word? (motivated) *Motivated* means "focused on reaching one or more goals." *Motivated* people are more successful in life and school. **Have partners use the word in a sentence.**

- Next word? (applied) *Applied* means "asked for something in writing or by filling out a form." I *applied* for this job with a resume. **Have partners use the word in a sentence.**

- Let's continue. (opportunities) *Opportunities* means "chances to do something you want to do." *Opportunities* await those who are motivated. **Have partners use the word in a sentence.**

- Next word? (strategies) *Strategies* means "plans for doing something over time." Our reading *strategies* can be used in all classes. **Have partners use the word in a sentence.**

- Next word? (lectures) *Lectures* means "gives an organized talk in public." Liz *lectures* to motivate people to persevere. **Have partners use the word in a sentence.**

- Last word. (inspiration) *Inspiration* means "energy to do something new or creative." Liz provides *inspiration* to teens and adults from coast to coast. **Have partners use the word in a sentence.**

Talk with a partner about any vocabulary word that is still confusing for you to read or understand.

As you read the text, you will monitor your understanding by circling the check marks or the question marks. Please be sure to draw a question mark over any confusing words, phrases, or sentences.

Options for rereading text.
- Teacher read-aloud
- Teacher-led or student-led choral read
- Paired read or independent read with bold vocabulary words read aloud

---

Choose an option for reading text. Have students read the introduction according to the option that you chose. While reading each section, think about Liz's obstacles. Circle all the obstacles that Liz comes across in her life.

When most of the students are finished, continue with the entire class. Let's see how well you understood what you read.

- Circle the check mark or the question mark for this text. Draw a question mark over any confusing words.

- If you haven't already done so, mark Liz's obstacles. (parents doing drugs again, spend the night on sofa, hopefully her friend's parents won't mind, parental drug addiction, poverty)

- Mark words that indicate Liz is miserable on the streets. (cold and windy; alone)

- Go to line 7. Circle the words that indicate Liz's attendance at school is sporadic or unstable. (or maybe she'll go to school)

- Underline what Liz would choose to do instead of attend school. (check on her mother)

- Go to line 9. Mark the synonym for *dependence*. (addiction)

- On the same line, mark the antonym for *wealth*. (poverty)

- Go to line 11. Circle the antonym pair. (unlikely; possible)

- Mark the clause that indicates Liz Murray accomplished things on her own, without the help of others. (Liz Murray made it possible)

- Headings are used to organize text. Each section of text contributes to the overall message or purpose of the text. There is no heading for the first part of the text, but it still contributes to the whole. How does the introduction contribute to the whole text? Write your answer in the margin next to the section. (It hooks the reader by explaining a specific part of Liz's life and asks questions alluding to triumph.)

Close Reading

Read the text.

"From Homeless to Harvard"

The winter evening is cold and windy with crisp-looking stars shining over Bronx, New York. Liz Murray, just 12 years old, doesn't want to go home because her parents are doing drugs again. She is walking the streets, alone, headed for the home of a friend. She knocks on an apartment door, hoping to spend the night on the sofa in her friend's apartment. Hopefully, her friend's parents won't mind. Maybe she'll go home to check on her mother in the morning, or maybe she'll go to school.

What could the future hold for a child who lives like this? Could a person whose life began in a background of parental drug addiction and poverty hope to be educated at a famous university and become a public success? That **outcome** is unlikely, but Liz Murray made it possible.

Born into Poverty

Liz Murray was born into a life of poverty and addiction in the Bronx in 1980. An eye disease soon left her mom legally blind. As a result of her disability, she received welfare from the government and relied on Liz to take care of her and "be her eyes." Liz was forced to do things such as watch for the mailman on the first of every month and stand in line at the check-cashing store with the other welfare recipients—while other kids her age were playing innocent games of tag and hide and seek. Once the check was cashed, her drug-addicted parents used the money for drugs and began the cycle of neglect and mistreatment of their children.

Liz remembers eating well on the first of each month. However, during the rest of the month, her parents used their support to feed their drug addictions instead of their children. Some months, after spending their welfare check on drugs, her parents only had $30 left to feed Liz and her sister.

When Liz was growing up, she lived in filthy conditions. Because of this, she was unbathed, wore unclean clothing, and often had lice. Liz was aware of the smell she gave off and the unwelcome stares from kids at school. The shame of this caused Liz to hate school and plead to stay home. Often, her mother agreed. She loved her parents and felt fortunate that they loved her back.

Have students read the section Born into Poverty according to the option that you chose.

When most of the students are finished, continue with the entire class. Let's see how well you understood the next section.

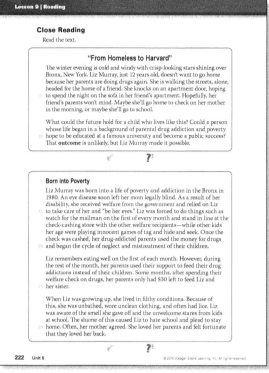

- Circle the check mark or the question mark for this text. Draw a question mark over any confusing words.

- If you haven't already done so, circle Liz's obstacles. **(poverty, addiction, mom was legally blind, received welfare, neglect, mistreatment, filthy, unbathed, unclean, lice, smell, shame)**

- Go to line 12. Mark the area in New York City. **(the Bronx)**

- Go to line 14. Mark the synonym for *impairment*. **(disability)**

- Reread lines 15–20. Mark the words used by the author that suggest he or she is not keeping his or her point of view objective, but is instead inserting opinions into this paragraph. **(forced; innocent; neglect; mistreatment)** In the margin, identify the point of view being used by the author in this paragraph. **(subjective)**

- Go to line 21. In the margin, write how many days a month Liz ate well. **(1)** Multiply that to how many times she ate well per year. Write the answer in the margin. **(12/year)**

- Go to line 22. Mark the vocabulary substitution for *welfare*. **(support)**

- Go to line 24. Mark how much her parents had to spend on food for the girls some months. **($30)** Think about how much a typical meal costs you. In the margin, estimate how many meals they could each eat that month. **(3–7 meals/ sister)**

- Go to line 26. Circle the transition phrase that tells time. **(When Liz was growing up)**

- Go to line 28. Mark the two things that Liz was aware of. **(smell she gave off; unwelcome stares)** Draw a line to the cause of these things. **(filthy conditions)**

- Go to line 29. Mark the synonym for *beg*. **(plead)**

- On the same line, mark the reason Liz did not want to attend school. **(shame)**

- On the same line, mark the word *this*. Draw an arrow from *this* to what it is referencing. **(unbathed, unclean clothing, lice)**

- On lines 30 and 31, mark how Liz felt about her parents. **(she loved them and felt fortunate that they loved her back)**

- How does the section Born into Poverty contribute to the whole text? Write your answer in the margin next to the section. **(It explains the challenges of Liz's childhood so the reader knows where she began and all she has been through.)**

Have students read the section Death Brings Realization according to the option that you chose. While reading, circle Liz's obstacles.

When most of the students are finished, continue with the entire class. Let's see how well you understood what you read.

- Circle the check mark or the question mark for this text. Draw a question mark over any confusing words.

- If you haven't already done so, circle Liz's obstacles. (parents separated, mother diagnosed with HIV, died, father was homeless, sent to a group home, conditions at the home were so bad, living on the streets)

- Go to line 32. Circle the transition word that means "after a long time." (Eventually)

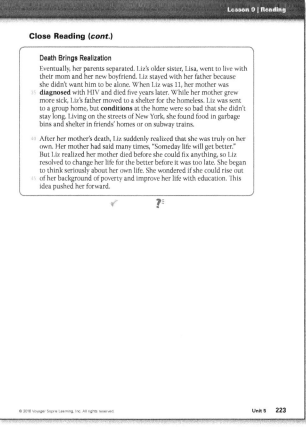

Close Reading (*cont.*)

Death Brings Realization

Eventually, her parents separated. Liz's older sister, Lisa, went to live with their mom and her new boyfriend. Liz stayed with her father because she didn't want him to be alone. When Liz was 11, her mother was
35 **diagnosed** with HIV and died five years later. While her mother grew more sick, Liz's father moved to a shelter for the homeless. Liz was sent to a group home, but **conditions** at the home were so bad that she didn't stay long. Living on the streets of New York, she found food in garbage bins and shelter in friends' homes or on subway trains.

40 After her mother's death, Liz suddenly realized that she was truly on her own. Her mother had said many times, "Someday life will get better." But Liz realized her mother died before she could fix anything, so Liz resolved to change her life for the better before it was too late. She began to think seriously about her own life. She wondered if she could rise out
45 of her background of poverty and improve her life with education. This idea pushed her forward.

✓   ?

Unit 5   **223**

- Go to line 35. Mark the disease that is associated with using dirty needles for drugs. (HIV)

- Go to line 36. Mark why Liz was sent to a group home. (her father moved to a shelter for the homeless)

- Go to line 37. Mark why she didn't stay long at the group home. (conditions at the home were so bad)

- Go to lines 38 and 39. Mark what Liz ate as a teenager. (food in garbage bins)

- Go to line 39. Mark where Liz slept as a teenager. (friends' homes, subway trains)

- Go to line 40. Circle the transition phrase that tells time. (After her mother's death)

- Mark the word that means "understood." (realized)

- Mark Liz's realization. (she was truly on her own)

- Number two things that Liz wondered. (1. if she could rise out of her background of poverty; 2. improve her life with education) Draw a star next to the means by which she hopes to improve her life. (education)

- Go to lines 45 and 46. Mark the phrase *this idea*. Draw an arrow to what it is referring to. (rise out of her background of poverty and improve her life with education)

- Mark the phrase that means "motivated her." (pushed her forward)

- How does the section Death Brings Realization contribute to the whole text? Write your answer in the margin next to the section. (It shows that a terrible time in Liz's life actually helped her put herself on the right path.)

Have students read the section Getting an Education according to the option that you chose. While reading, think about Liz's obstacles. Circle all the obstacles that Liz comes across in her life.

When most of the students are finished, continue with the entire class. Let's see how well you understood this section.

- Circle the check mark or the question mark for this text. Draw a question mark over any confusing words.

- If you haven't already done so, circle Liz's obstacles. (homeless, sleeping out on the streets, working odd jobs, father became sick with AIDS)

- Go to line 47. Circle the transition that tells time. (At 17)

- Go to line 49. Mark the incredibly difficult thing Liz was able to do. (taught herself to read)

- Go to line 53. Circle the pronoun *it*. Draw an arrow to the verb phrase that it refers to. (graduate in two years instead of the usual four)

- Go to line 57. Underline Liz's secret. (how she was living)

- Go to line 60. Circle the punctuation mark that provides a meaning cue to the words *Harvard University*. (comma after University)

- Go to line 66. Mark what Liz applied for. (scholarship for needy students)

- Go to line 67. Mark the synonym for *difficulties*. (hardships)

- Go to line 72. Mark the evidence that Liz cared deeply for her father. (she returned to New York to take care of him)

- How does the section Getting an Education contribute to the whole text? Write your answer in the margin next to the section. (It shares the path Liz took to get an education and all the obstacles that stood in her way that she ultimately overcame.)

Close Reading (*cont.*)

Getting an Education

At 17, Liz heard about **alternative** high schools. She researched different schools and finally found one that would accept her. Because she was intelligent and **motivated** and had taught herself to read, Liz did well in
50 school despite her lack of previous schooling. She determined to graduate in two years instead of the usual four. Because of her willingness to study often, anywhere she could—school hallways, libraries, stairwells in apartment buildings—she did it.

During this time, she was still homeless, sleeping out on the streets
55 sometimes and working at odd jobs to earn money. At school, her teachers encouraged her. She began to believe in herself, but she never let anyone know how she was living. Then, something happened that set the course of her life.

A teacher chose her and a few other students to visit Boston, Massachusetts.
60 While there, she visited Harvard University, a respected Ivy League university known for academic excellence. As she stood gazing at the campus, her teacher told her that it was possible for her to go to school at Harvard, and she believed him. Liz would later write in her memoir, *Breaking Night*, that it was a good thing he didn't tell her how hard it was
65 to get accepted to this university. Then, she heard about a *New York Times* scholarship for needy students and **applied** for it. Applicants had to write an essay describing any hardships they had overcome to achieve academic success. Liz was one of six students who received the scholarship. She applied and was accepted to Harvard.

70 Liz enrolled at Harvard in the fall of 2000 and completed several semesters of academic study. Then, in 2003, her father became sick with AIDS, and she returned to New York to take care of him.

✓   ?

Have students read the section A New Direction according to the option that you chose. While reading, think about Liz's obstacles. Circle all the obstacles that Liz came across in her life.

When most of the students are finished, continue with the entire class. Let's see how well you understood the last section.

- Circle the check mark or the question mark for this text. Draw a question mark over any confusing words.

- If you haven't already done so, circle Liz's obstacles. (father died)

- Go to line 74. Mark the second university Liz attended. (Columbia University) Draw an arrow to indicate the location of the university. (New York)

- Go to lines 75–78. List four media events that made her story famous. (*The New York Times*, *20/20*, Oprah, television movie)

- Go to line 79. Mark what Liz's father did before he died. (overcome his drug addiction)

- Go to line 83. Mark what Liz wants to help people do. (cope with hardships)

- In the second paragraph, mark the repeated word used to indicate that something may or may not happen. (might) What tense is this? (conditional)

- Go to line 85. Mark the transition that tells time. (Today)

- Go to lines 89 and 90. Mark what Liz gives people through her books and her lectures. (inspiration to change their lives) In the margin, write whether this statement is written from a subjective point of view or an objective point of view. (subjective)

- How does the section A New Direction contribute to the whole text? Write your answer in the margin next to the section. (It is the culmination of Liz's hard work and intended to show the reader what can happen with hard work and determination.)

- Based on the transition words marked, what informational text structure is this text written in? (sequential)

Have partners compare text markings and correct any errors.

Close Reading (*cont.*)

A New Direction

Despite what appeared to be a setback in New York, Liz continued her education at Columbia University. The unexpected changes in her
75 life also brought many exciting **opportunities**. The *New York Times* published a story about her scholarship, then the television show *20/20* told her story, and Oprah Winfrey interviewed her. Also in 2003, a television movie was made about her life.

Liz's father died in 2006, having finally overcome his drug addiction. Liz
80 returned to Harvard in May 2008 to complete her degree. She realized that her story might have the power to help others. But, even better, her experiences and her knowledge might allow her to create **strategies** to help people cope with hardships. People might use these ways to move beyond their hardships to a meaningful life.

85 Today, Liz has a company. Through workshops, she **lectures** to groups throughout the country, encouraging others to rise to their own dreams. Her sister also graduated from college and is a teacher. Whatever their dreams are, whatever background they come from, however hard they need to work, Liz Murray gives people **inspiration** to change
90 their lives.

Unit 5   225

Unit 5

Lesson 10

RI.4.6; RI.5.5; RI.5.6; RI.6.9; W.8.2b; W.8.2f; W.5.4; W.6.4;
W.5.9b; W.6.9b; W.7.9b; SL.6.1b; SL.6.1c; SL.6.1d; L.3.1h;
L.5.6; L.6.6

Lesson Opener

Before the lesson, choose one of the following activities to write on the board or post on the *LANGUAGE! Live* Class Wall online.

- *Write four sentences with at least two vocabulary words in each. Show you know the meanings. (outcome, diagnose, conditions, alternative, motivated, apply, opportunity, strategy, lecture, inspiration)*

- *Dress your avatar as though you were attending your first class at Harvard University. Explain your choices.*

- *Liz Murray attended an alternative high school and was able to graduate in two years instead of four. If you could, would you be willing to work as hard as Liz did to decrease the length of school by two years? Why or why not?*

Vocabulary

Objective

- Review key passage vocabulary.

Recontextualize Passage Vocabulary

Direct students to page 212 in their Student Books. Use the following questions to review the vocabulary words from "From Homeless to Harvard."

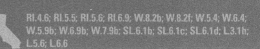

- You just saw a movie about kids who competed in ballroom dancing, and now you are interested in dancing too. Was the movie an *inspiration*? (yes) You know you should build your science fair project, but you would rather watch TV because you can't think of a good idea. Do you feel an *inspiration* to build? (no) You know the project is due tomorrow, but it is your sixth year to enter, and you can't think of something new. What do you need? (inspiration)

- You discover a nail in your bike's flat tire. Can you *diagnose* the flat tire? (yes) Should a doctor ask about symptoms before she can *diagnose* an illness? (yes) In biology, your microscope isn't working. You ask the teacher for help. What do you hope he does? (diagnose the problem)

- The coach really wants you to play basketball, but you don't like the sport and don't want to play. You sign up anyway. Are you *motivated* to have a great season? (no) A teacher needs someone to run an errand to the library, and your best friend has library the same period. Are you *motivated* to run the errand? (yes) The student with the most service hours will win a $100 gift card to the store of his or her choice. This makes many students what? (motivated)

- You drop a brick on your foot and break a toe. Is the brick the *outcome* of the event? (no) Is the broken toe? (yes) What is usually revealed in the final chapters of a book? (the outcome)

- Does a mail carrier usually *lecture* as part of his or her job? (no) Could someone *lecture* using sign language? (yes) You and a friend have been asked to give a talk to fifth-graders about life in middle school. What are you preparing to do? (lecture)

- You offer to help your older brother fix his car. Does he make you *apply* first? (no) You want to be in a movie. The director asks you to recite some lines from the script to see if you are talented. Has he asked you to *apply*? (no) You ask for a job at the corner store. The manager hands you some forms to fill out. What does she want you to do? (apply)

- The Spanish club wants to travel to Mexico City for spring break, but it has no money. Does the club need a *strategy* for raising money? (yes) You are relaxing in an inner tube in a pool. Do you have a *strategy* for floating? (no) Someday, you hope to solve the problem of world hunger. What will you need to make this happen? (a strategy)

- The bus is pulling away from the curb. Have you missed your *opportunity* to catch it? (probably) Your hand has been raised for the entire class period, but the teacher hasn't called on you. Have you had an *opportunity* to speak? (no) In an action movie, the hero jumps off a moving train when it slows down to go around a curve. He has made the most of what? (an opportunity)

- The cafeteria offers main dishes with meat and without. Does it offer *alternative* dishes? (yes) If the bowling alley is closed, you and your friends have a Plan B in mind. Do you have an *alternative* plan? (yes) You had a job as a camp counselor, but the camp got canceled. What do you need to come up with? (an alternative job)

- It's raining. Are *conditions* right for a picnic? (no) Your ride is late, and you are stuck at school. Are *conditions* right to do some homework? (yes) You're trying to sleep, but the neighbors are blasting their music. What do you hope will soon change? (the conditions)

Objectives

- Use two texts to write coherently.
- Use a process to write.
- Compare and contrast a firsthand account and secondhand account of the same topic.
- Analyze the similarities and discrepancies between two accounts of the same topic.
- Use a rubric to guide and evaluate writing.

Six Traits of Effective Writing

Direct students back to page 30 from Unit 1 in their Student Books. Reread the Six Traits of Effective Writing.

In previous units, we have focused on sentence fluency, word choice, conventions, and organization. We have used varying sentence structures and descriptive language to keep our writing from sounding boring. We have used proper grammar, punctuation, and spelling to ensure the reader understands the text, and we have organized our paragraphs to include introductions, conclusions, and transitions. We have also made sure that our supporting details accurately support our main ideas/topic sentences and that the supporting details are backed up with elaborations, including evidence from the text.

Now is the time to put them all together and make sure we are writing with all six traits.

Lesson 10 | Writing

Six Traits of Effective Writing

Trait		What does this mean?
	Ideas and Content	• The writing meets the expectations of the assignment and answers the prompt. • The writing starts and ends in an interesting way. • Important ideas are fully developed, with enough elaborations and relevant details. • The content is strong, accurate, detailed, interesting, and appropriate to the audience.
	Organization	• The purpose of the writing is clearly stated in the introduction. • Ideas are presented in a clear order (which aligns with the plan), with varied transitions to connect them? • For narrative writing: There is a clear beginning, middle, and end. • For informational and argumentative writing: There is a clear introduction, body, and conclusion. • Varied transitions connect ideas, facilitating the flow.
	Voice and Audience Awareness	• The voice and style are appropriate to the purpose and audience? • The information is presented in the right tone and mood for the purpose and audience?
	Word Choice	• Rich, interesting, and precise words are used. • Word choice is appropriate for the topic and audience.
	Sentence Fluency	• Sentences are varied in structure and length. • There are no sentence fragments or run-on sentences.
	Conventions	• The text doesn't contain errors in capitalization, usage, punctuation, or spelling. • Paragraphs are properly formatted.

30   Unit 1   © 2016 Voyager Sopris Learning, Inc. All rights reserved.

Prepare to Write: Compare and Contrast Paragraph

Direct students to page 226 in their Student Books.

Part A. Study the Prompt

Read the instructions for Part A and the prompt. Guide students through identifying the topic, summarizing the directions, and understanding the purpose for writing.

In a previous lesson, we discussed text content and organization. We talked about different ways an author can organize true information. We have two texts that give us information about Liz Murray's life, but they are organized very differently. One is a narrative with a compassionate voice, and the other is informational with very little emotion.

Part B. Write a Topic Sentence

You will need to write a topic sentence that frames this comparison. It will need to address the commonalities and the differences between the way Liz's life is portrayed in both texts. Consider using some of the terms in the chart when writing your topic sentence. We will come back to write the topic sentence after we have discussed the two text selections.

Prepare to Write: Compare and Contrast Paragraph

Part A. Study the Prompt

Read the prompt and identify the topic, directions, and purpose for writing.

Often, writers present factual information in a different way. In this unit, we read Liz Murray's firsthand account of her life as well as a secondhand account of her life written by someone else.

How is Liz's life portrayed in each text? Consider the way Liz perceives what is normal and the way Liz was treated by her parents. Write a paragraph that compares the portrayal of both topics in the excerpt from *Breaking Night* and the passage "From Homeless to Harvard." Consider how the information provided differs from one text to the other. Include examples from the texts in your comparison. Use transition words as you move from one point to another.

Topic: Liz Murray's life

Directions: Write a paragraph that compares one author's presentation of events with that of another.

Purpose for writing: Focus on the difference in information gained from the two different text structures.

Part B. Write a Topic Sentence—Compare/Contrast Statement

Compare/Contrast Words		
different	the same	unlike
in common	better	alike
differences	similar	worse

The presentation of Liz Murray's life as challenging and difficult is consistent in both texts; however, there are subtle differences regarding the severity of the situation between the two versions.

Part C. Organize Information

Draw a Venn diagram on the board, labeling it like the diagram on page 227 in the Student Book. Begin by asking students how the presentation of Liz's life is similar in both texts. Have volunteers share their thoughts. Fill in the diagram on the board and have students take notes in their Student Books. Then, have students identify the discrepancies in the way her life was portrayed in her memoir as compared to "From Homeless to Harvard." Write the differences in the correct areas of the diagram.

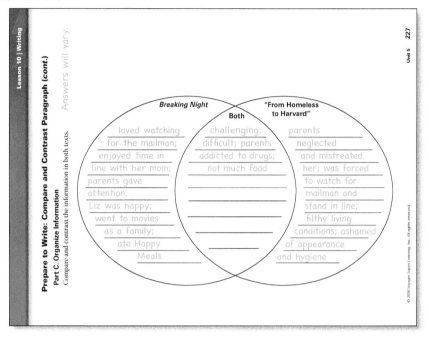

Breaking Night

loved watching for the mailman; enjoyed time in line with her mom; parents gave attention; Liz was happy; went to movies as a family; ate Happy Meals

Both

challenging; difficult; parents addicted to drugs; not much food

"From Homeless to Harvard"

parents neglected and mistreated her; was forced to watch for mailman and stand in line; filthy living conditions; ashamed of appearance and hygiene

Now that we've taken some notes and gathered our thoughts about how the texts are similar and how they are different, let's reconsider our topic sentence. Have students go back to Part B. Write the following sentence on the board:

> *The presentation of Liz Murray's life as challenging and difficult is consistent in both texts; however, there are subtle differences regarding the severity of the situation between the two versions.*

Use this sentence as a guide for your topic sentence. Your topic sentence needs two parts. One part addresses the similarities, and the other part recognizes the differences. You can decide on the order. Think of some ways to reword or restate this sentence. Have volunteers share their thoughts. Have them write their topic sentence.

Part D. Write a Concluding Sentence

Let's consider our concluding sentence. It is basically a restatement of our topic sentence. The chart contains some good words and phrases for jump-starting your concluding sentence. **Direct students to Part D on page 228 in their Student Books. Review the words in the chart, stressing the need for a comma to separate the words from the rest of the sentence. Write the following sentence on the board:**

> *In closing, though the challenges and difficulties of Liz's life are apparent in both texts, Liz Murray's presentation of events is more loving and sympathetic than the presentation from the author of "From Homeless to Harvard."*

Your concluding sentence needs to restate the fact that we learn different information about the same topic by reading the two different texts. Consider ways to restate your topic sentence. **Have volunteers share their thoughts. Have them write their concluding sentence.**

Part E. Use Transition Words to Illustrate and Compare

As you begin to put your thoughts together and write your paragraph, use transition words to help you move from one idea to the next. **Direct students to Part E. Read the words and phrases in the chart, helping students distinguish between the terms that illustrate a point and terms that help them make a contrasting point.**

Prepare to Write: Compare and Contrast Paragraph (*cont.*)

Part D. Write a Concluding Sentence

Develop a concluding sentence by restating the topic sentence. Choose a word from the chart below to start your sentence. Use a comma to separate the word or phrase from the rest of the sentence.

Answers will vary.

Concluding Words and Phrases

as a result	consequently	finally	in closing	in conclusion
in summary	in the end	so	therefore	thus

In closing, though the challenges and difficulties of Liz's life are apparent in both texts, Liz Murray's presentation of events is more loving and sympathetic than the presentation from the author of "From Homeless to Harvard."

Part E. Use Transition Words to Illustrate and Compare

Use transition words in writing to help you move from one idea to the next.

Illustrate				
for example	for instance	as an illustration	in particular	as an example
Compare/Change Direction				
in contrast	although	instead	however	on the contrary

Write

You've framed your paragraph by writing your topic sentence and concluding sentence. Now, use your Venn diagram to make your comparisons between the two texts. Use a clean sheet of notebook paper to write your paragraph.

Have students consult the Six Traits of Writing: Basic rubric on page 389 as they write their paragraph. If they struggle or need additional support in developing their paragraph, use the following paragraph as a model.

Six Traits of Writing: Basic

	Ideas and Content	Organization	Voice and Audience Awareness	Word Choice	Sentence Fluency	Language Conventions
4	Focuses on the topic. Main idea (topic sentence) is clear and well supported with details and elaboration (examples, evidence, and explanations).	Topic sentence clearly states main idea. Ideas are clear and logically organized. Contains concluding sentence.	The words have a strong sense of person and purpose. Brings topic to life.	Words are specific to the content, accurate, and vivid. Word choice enhances meaning and the reader's enjoyment.	Writes complete sentences and varies sentence structure.	There are no grammar errors. There are few or no errors in spelling, capitalization, or punctuation.
3	Mostly focuses on the topic. Sentences supporting the main idea (topic sentence) may be general rather than detailed and specific.	Topic sentence states main idea. Organization mostly clear and logical. May contain concluding sentence.	The words have some sense of person and purpose.	Words are correctly used but may be somewhat general and unspecific.	Writes complete sentences and attempts to use expanded sentences.	There are no major grammar errors. There are few errors in spelling, capitalization, or punctuation.
2	Main idea (topic sentence) is unclear and/or lacks sufficient support.	Structure may not be entirely clear or logical. Paragraph may seem more like a list and/or be hard to follow.	The words have little sense of person and purpose.	Words may be used inaccurately or repetitively.	Writes mostly simple and/or awkwardly constructed sentences. May include some run-ons and fragments.	There are a few grammar errors. There are a few errors in spelling, capitalization, or punctuation.
1	Does not address prompt and/or lacks a topic sentence. Supporting details are absent or do not relate to topic.	No evident structure. Lack of organization seriously interferes with meaning.	The words have no sense of person or purpose. No sense of audience.	Extremely limited range of words. Restricted vocabulary impedes message.	Numerous run-ons and/or fragments interfere with meaning.	There are many grammar and/or spelling errors. There are many errors in capitalization and punctuation.

Writing Rubric: Basic 389

Exemplar Writing: Compare and Contrast Paragraph

The presentation of Liz Murray's life as challenging and difficult is consistent in both texts; however, there are subtle differences regarding the severity of the situation between the two versions. In Breaking Night, *Liz Murray uses words like "treasured ritual," "joy," and "sense of importance" when she describes watching for the mailman and waiting in line at the check-cashing store. "From Homeless to Harvard," however, states that she was "forced" to participate in the happenings instead of innocently playing with other children. The reader is left to believe that Liz would rather have played with children, though there is no indication of this in* Breaking Night. *"From Homeless to Harvard" also mentions the "neglect and mistreatment" given by Liz's parents. Although Liz does say that her parents spent money on drugs instead of food in* Breaking Night, *she indicates that her parents spoke kindly to her and spent a great deal of time with her on check-cashing day. In closing, though the challenges and difficulties of Liz's life are apparent in both texts, Liz Murray's presentation of events is more loving and sympathetic than the presentation from the author of "From Homeless to Harvard."*

Student Handwriting:
Handwriting lessons are provided in manuscript and cursive. These explicit lessons (found online in Resources) can be taught systematically during writing lessons to strengthen legibility and fluency.

Evaluate Writing

Direct students to page 229 in their Student Books and read the information in the checklist.

This checklist is a tool you can use to evaluate your writing and make sure you are using good technique. This unit's checklist is a little bit more advanced than the one in the last unit, so read through it carefully. As we progress through the program, we will add things we have learned that will make us better writers. **Have individuals quickly assess their writing, then have partners evaluate each other's writing based on the checklist.**

Note: Use Six Traits of Writing Scoring Rubric: Basic on page 564 of this book to assess students' writing. A printable version is located online in the Teacher Resources.

The Writer's Checklist

Trait	Yes	No	Did the writer . . .?
Ideas and Content			focus all sentences on the topic
			provide supporting details for the topic sentence
			include examples, evidence, and/or explanations to develop the supporting detail sentences
Organization			write a topic sentence
			tell things in an order that makes sense
			use transition words and/or phrases
			write a concluding sentence
Voice and Audience Awareness			think about the audience and purpose for writing
			write in a clear and engaging way that makes the audience want to read the work; write so the reader can "hear" the writer speaking
Word Choice			try to find a unique way to say things
			use words that are lively and specific to the content
Sentence Fluency			write complete sentences
			expand some sentences by painting the subject and/or predicate
Conventions			capitalize words correctly:
			capitalize the first word of each sentence
			capitalize proper nouns, including people's names
			punctuate correctly:
			put a period or question mark at the end of each sentence
			put an apostrophe before the s for a singular possessive noun
			use a comma after a long adverb phrase at the beginning of a sentence
			use grammar correctly:
			use the correct verb tense
			make sure the verb agrees with the subject in number
			use correct spelling

R E V I S E — E D I T

Unit 5   **229**

Objectives

- Self-correct as comprehension of text deepens.
- Answer questions to demonstrate comprehension of text.
- Engage in class discussion.
- Identify the enduring understandings from a piece of text.
- Compare and contrast two portrayals of a place or historical account.
- Identify the influence individuals have on ideas and events.
- Identify the impact of perspective and mood.

Revisit Passage Comprehension

Direct students to pages 219–221 in their Student Books. Have students review their answers and make any necessary changes. Then, have partners share their answers and collaborate to perfect them.

Enduring Understandings

Direct students back to page 211 in their Student Books. Reread the Big Idea questions.

At what age are our personality and belief system formed?

To what degree is our future shaped by the people with whom we live as children?

Generate a class discussion about the questions and the answers students came up with in Lesson 6. Have them consider whether their answers have changed any after reading the text.

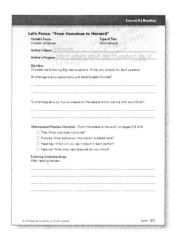

Use the following talking points to foster conversation. Refer to the Class Discussion Rules poster and have students use the Collegial Discussion sentence frames on page 382 of their Student Books.

- "I said to myself: what if I woke up, and every single day I did everything within my ability during that day to change my life. What could happen in just a month? A year?"

    — Liz Murray

- If Liz Murray had dropped out of school, become a drug addict, contracted a disease, or lived a life of poverty, would she have been justified? Is it something inside us that propels us forward, or is it something that we can generate?

What we read should make us think. Use our discussion and your thoughts about the text to determine what you will "walk away with." Has it made you think about a personal experience or someone you know? Has your perspective or opinion on a specific topic changed? Do you have any lingering thoughts or questions? Write these ideas as your enduring understandings. What will you take with you from this text?

Discuss the enduring understandings with the class. Then, have students write their enduring understandings from the unit. If time permits, have them post a personal response about one of the enduring understandings to the online class wall.

Remind students to consider why the author wrote the passage and whether he or she was successful.

The Influence of Perspective

Breaking Night and "From Homeless to Harvard" are both nonfiction texts, but one is written as a narrative by one of the characters, and the other is written through an outsider's perspective. The texts have very different moods, and the information seems to be a little biased in both.

Have partners return to the excerpt from *Breaking Night* and use the text to develop a description of the conditions at Liz's home. Then, read the following quote from "From Homeless to Harvard" aloud and have them compare the descriptions and discuss the difference in the portrayals.

> *When Liz was growing up, she lived in filthy conditions. Because of this, Liz was unbathed, wore unclean clothing, and often had lice.*

Remind students to always consider the point of view of the writer and the perspective from which the text was written. This will help them to recognize subjective information and bias.

Progress Monitoring

End-of-Unit Online Assessments
Monitor students' progress in the unit by utilizing online assessments. Students should prioritize these assessments over successive Word Training units.
- Assign Unit 5 Content Mastery quizzes to assess skills taught in this unit.
- Assign Power Pass to assess reading comprehension skills in a standardized test format.

All assessments can be assigned online by opening the Tools menu, then selecting Assignments. Be sure to select the correct class and unit from the drop-down menu.

Reteach
Based on students' performance in Content Mastery, extra practice may be needed.
- If student scores fall at 60 percent or below, reteach the content to small groups.
- If student scores fall between 61–79 percent, reinforce the skills by assigning the student reteach activity pages as homework.

Reteach lessons can be found online on the Course Reports page for each unit.

Unit Big Ideas

- What causes stereotypes and prejudices?
- What inspires people to take action?
- What is worth dying for? Do you think you could ever let it happen?
- When, and for what reasons, is violence justified?

Instructional Texts

"The Symbol of Freedom"

Text type: informational

"I Am Prepared to Die" by Nelson Mandela

Text type: informational—speech

Materials

- *Unit 6 video (Colonialism)*
- *"Nelson Mandela" audio file*
- *"Nelson Mandela" multimedia file*
- *Six Traits of Writing Scoring Rubric: Expository (print as needed)*

Optional
- *Progress Monitoring Across the Six Traits scales*

Classroom Materials

- *Highlighters or colored pencils*
- *Notebook paper*

Instructional Resources

- *Unit 6 Reteach*
- *Handwriting Lessons*

- *Unit 7 Background Information (assign as homework at the end of the unit)*

- *Writing Project: Argument*
- *Progress Monitoring Across the Six Traits scales*

Instructional Texts:

"The Symbol of Freedom"

Text type: informational

"I Am Prepared to Die"
by Nelson Mandela

Text type: informational—speech

LANGUAGE! Live Online

Grammar Practice

- Identify the function of nouns in sentences.
- Use coordinating conjunctions in compound sentences correctly.
- Distinguish between formal and informal language.
- Use verb tenses correctly.
- Identify the moods of verbs.

Vocabulary Practice

- Determine the meaning of derivations of words.
- Determine the correct usage of multiple-meaning words.
- Determine the purpose and meaning of extended similes.

Content Mastery

- Demonstrate an understanding of . . .
  - word meaning by answering questions and using words in sentences.
  - the use of the future and future progressive tenses.
  - the use of coordinating conjunctions in compound sentences.
  - the use of semicolons and commas in compound sentences.

Word Study

- Blend, read, and spell multisyllabic words with long vowels and silent -e; words with suffixes -en and -ed and prefixes anti- and sub-; and words with plural -s and possessive 's.
- Add inflectional endings to words ending in silent -e.

Lesson 1

Reading

- Determine and discuss the topic of a text.
- Determine and discuss the author's purpose.
- Use text features to preview text.

Vocabulary

- Evaluate word knowledge.
- Determine the meaning of key passage vocabulary.

Reading

- Read informational text.
- Monitor comprehension during text reading.
- Distinguish between information provided by pictures or other illustrations and information provided by the words in a text.
- Explain how graphics contribute to an understanding of the text.

Lesson 2

Vocabulary

- Review key passage vocabulary.

Grammar

- Distinguish between action, linking, and helping verbs.
- Use future and future progressive verb tenses correctly.
- Use coordinating conjunctions in compound sentences.
- Use correct punctuation when writing compound sentences.
- Use verb tense to convey various times, sequences, states, and conditions.

Writing

- Identify the structure of a sentence.
- Use conjunctions correctly in sentence writing.
- Produce, expand, and rearrange complete sentences for clarity and style.
- Write compound sentences.

Lesson 6

Reading

- Determine and discuss the author's purpose.
- Determine and discuss the topic of a text.
- Use text features to preview text.

Vocabulary

- Evaluate word knowledge.
- Determine the meaning of key passage vocabulary.

Reading

- Read a persuasive speech.
- Monitor comprehension during text reading.

Lesson 7

Vocabulary

- Review key passage vocabulary.

Reading

- Determine how to respond to prompts.
- Use critical thinking skills to write responses to prompts about text.
- Contrast ideas and concepts within a text.
- Support written answers with text evidence.
- Identify evidence used to support an argument.

Writing

- Write a thesis statement for a multiparagraph essay.
- Use correct capitalization and underlining or italics in the titles of works.

Writing Project: Argument

Lesson 3

Reading

- Establish a purpose for rereading informational text.
- Use critical thinking skills to write responses to prompts about text.
- Support written answers with text evidence.
- Determine the meaning of words and phrases in text.
- Sequence historical events.
- Draw inferences from text and support with evidence.

Lesson 4

Reading

- Read informational text with purpose and understanding.
- Answer questions to demonstrate comprehension of text.
- Identify and explain explicit details from text.
- Monitor comprehension of text during reading.
- Identify the conditional tense in writing.
- Connect pronouns to antecedents.
- Increase depth of word meaning through synonyms.
- Determine the meaning of abbreviations used in text.

Lesson 5

Vocabulary

- Review key passage vocabulary.

Writing

- Use text to write coherent paragraphs in response to reading.
- Analyze how ideas and events influence an individual and how an individual influences ideas and events.

Reading

- Self-correct as comprehension of text deepens.
- Answer questions to demonstrate comprehension of text.
- Engage in class discussion.
- Identify the enduring understandings from a piece of text.

Lesson 8

Reading

- Establish a purpose for rereading a speech.
- Monitor comprehension during text reading.
- Use critical thinking skills to write responses to prompts about text.
- Support written answers with text evidence.
- Evaluate the effectiveness of a speaker's craft and use of strategies.
- Identify evidence given in support of an argument and determine if it is sound or not.
- Contrast ideas and concepts within a text.

Lesson 9

Reading

- Read a speech with purpose and understanding.
- Answer questions to demonstrate comprehension of text.
- Identify and explain explicit details from text.
- Monitor comprehension during text reading.
- Identify the structure used to organize text and how each section contributes to the whole.
- Identify fallacies in persuasive text.
- Interpret a speaker's claims and determine the intent and validity.
- Identify the purpose of correlative conjunctions.
- Describe the relationship between a series of historical events using language that pertains to time, sequence, and cause/effect.
- Analyze in detail how a key idea is introduced, illustrated, and elaborated in a text.

Lesson 10

Vocabulary

- Review key passage vocabulary.

Writing

- Analyze the effect of media and how it changes the impact of text.
- Compare and contrast a written speech with a multimedia version.
- Use a process to write a multiparagraph essay.
- Use a rubric to guide and assess writing.

Reading

- Self-correct as comprehension of text deepens.
- Answer questions to demonstrate comprehension of text.
- Engage in class discussion.
- Identify the enduring understandings from a piece of text.

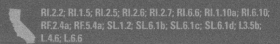

Lesson Opener

Before the lesson, choose one of the following activities to write on the board or post on the *LANGUAGE! Live* Class Wall online.

- *Tell about an issue in society that is important to you. What cause or group of people would you be willing to stand up for?*
- *Write two sentences about someone you admire. Identify the complete subject and the complete predicate.*
- *Write two sentences telling how you hope to change the world for the better someday. Identify the nouns and verbs.*

Reading

Objectives

- Determine and discuss the topic of a text.
- Determine and discuss the author's purpose.
- Use text features to preview text.

Passage Introduction

Direct students to page 231 in their Student Books. Discuss the content focus.

Content Focus

Nelson Mandela's struggle for justice in South Africa

What do you think you will read about in this text? (Answers will vary.) What do you know about South Africa or Nelson Mandela? **Provide sharing time.**

Type of Text

informational

In the last unit, we read a memoir, *Breaking Night*, narrated in first-person point of view. That means that the narrator, or person telling the story, is a character in the story. Where is the narrator? (inside the story) Next, we read an article about the author of the memoir titled "From Homeless to Harvard." It was informational. It told facts about Liz Murray's life from the third-person point of view. In third-person point of view, the narrator is outside the text. Where is the narrator in third-person point of view? (outside the text)

In this unit, we are going to read two similar texts—one written in first-person point of view and another written in third-person. The first one we will read is a nonfiction

---

Unit 6
Lesson 1 | Reading

Let's Focus: "The Symbol of Freedom"

Content Focus
Nelson Mandela's struggle for justice in South Africa

Type of Text
informational

Author's Name unknown

Author's Purpose to inform

Big Ideas
Consider the following Big Idea questions. Write your answer for each question.

What causes stereotypes and prejudices?

_____

_____

What inspires people to take action?

_____

_____

Informational Preview Checklist: "The Symbol of Freedom" on pages 233–236.
- ☐ Title: What clue does it provide about the passage?
- ☐ Pictures: What additional information is added here?
- ☐ Headings: What will you learn about in each section?
- ☐ Features: What other text features do you notice?

Enduring Understandings
After reading the text . . .

_____

_____

_____

_____

_____

Unit 6   231

article. It will give facts about Nelson Mandela from a narrator outside the text. It will be written in third-person point of view.

Author's Purpose

Have students glance at the text. Who is the author of this text? (unknown) This text is similar to one you would read in a textbook or encyclopedia. It presents factual information, but no author's name is given. Still, whoever wrote the article had a purpose in mind. An author's purpose is the reason he or she writes a text. Authors write for different reasons. They might write to entertain, to persuade, or to inform or teach. Many nonfiction texts are written to inform, or teach readers facts about a certain topic. The author of "The Symbol of Freedom" wrote the article to inform readers about a great South African leader. **Have students write the answers on the page.**

Before we read "The Symbol of Freedom," we will watch a short video to help build our background knowledge. **Play the Unit 6 Text Training video. Have partners discuss the main points the videographer was trying to make and what evidence was provided to support the points.**

Read the Big Idea questions aloud.

ay the Unit 6 Text
aining video found
the Teacher
sources online.

Big Ideas

What causes stereotypes and prejudices?

What inspires people to take action?

Illegial Discussion
ster

ass Discussion
les poster

As a class, consider the two Big Idea questions.

- Encourage students with limited knowledge of stereotypes and prejudices to ask for further explanation from peers.

- Provide opportunities for students to explain their ideas and answers to the Big Idea questions in light of the discussion by ensuring students follow the rules for class discussion, which can be printed in poster form from the Teacher Resources online.

- Suggest students refer to the Collegial Discussion sentence frames in the back of their books.

- Encourage speakers to link comments to the remarks of others to keep the focus of the discussion and create cohesion, even when their comments are in disagreement.

After discussing each question, have students write an answer. We'll come back to these questions after we finish reading the text. You can add to your answers as you gain information and perspective.

Preview

Read the Preview Checklist on page 231. Follow the Preview Procedure outlined below.

> ### Preview Procedure
> - Group students with partners or in triads.
> - Have students count off as 1s or 2s. The 1s will become the student leaders. If working with triads, the third students become 3s.
> - The student leaders will preview the text in addition to managing the checklist and pacing.
> - The 2s and 3s will preview the text with 1s.
> - Direct 1s to open their Student Books to page 231 and 2s and 3s to open their Student Books to page 233. This allows students to look at a few different pages at one time without turning back and forth.

Direct students to page 233.

If necessary, guide students in a short preview using the headings, pictures, and captions.

Vocabulary

Objectives

- Evaluate word knowledge.
- Determine the meaning of key passage vocabulary.

Rate Vocabulary Knowledge

Direct students to page 232 in their Student Books. Let's take a look at the vocabulary words from "The Symbol of Freedom." I am going to say each word aloud. You will repeat the word and write it in the third column. Then, you will rate your knowledge of the word. Display the Vocabulary Rating Scale poster or write the information on the board. Review the meaning of each rating.

Vocabulary Rating Scale

0—I have never heard the word before.

1—I have heard the word, but I'm not sure how to use it.

2—I am familiar with the word, but I'm not sure if I know the correct meaning.

3—I know the meaning of the word and can use it correctly in a sentence.

Remember, the points are there to help you know which words you need to focus on. By the end of this unit, you should be able to change all your ratings to a 3. That's the goal.

Read each word aloud and have students repeat it, write it, and rate it. Then, have volunteers who rated a word *2* or *3* use the word in an oral sentence.

Preteach Vocabulary

Explain that you will now take a closer look at the words. Follow the Preteach Procedure outlined below.

> ## Preteach Procedure
> This activity is intended to take only a short amount of time, so make it an oral exercise.
> - Introduce each word as indicated on the word card.
> - Read the definition and example sentences.
> - Ask questions to clarify and deepen understanding.
> - If time permits, allow students to share.
>
> * If your students would benefit from copying the definitions, please have them do so in the vocabulary log in the back of the Student Books using the margin definitions in the passage selections. This should be done outside of instruction time.

discrimination (n)

Let's read the first word together. *Discrimination*.

Definition: *Discrimination* is the act of treating some people worse than others for unfair reasons. What means "the act of treating some people worse than others for unfair reasons"? (discrimination)

Example 1: Not letting someone join your club because of his or her hair color would be an act of *discrimination*.

Example 2: If a restaurant owner refuses to serve people he or she doesn't like, it is *discrimination*.

Example 3: If I only handed out bubble gum to people whose names ended in a vowel, that would be *discrimination*.

Question 1: In the 1950s in the South, black people had to sit in the backs of buses. Was this *discrimination*? Yes or no? (yes)

Question 2: After a big party, your dad volunteers to give a ride home to anyone who needs one. Is this *discrimination*? Yes or no? (no)

Pair Share: Turn to your partner and describe a form of *discrimination* that takes place on the planet Oomzoom. Explain why it is *discrimination*.

(1)

resources (n)

Let's read the next word together. *Resources*.

Definition: *Resources* are things that can be sold to create wealth. What means "things that can be sold to create wealth"? (resources)

Example 1: *Resources* such as timber, fish, and coal are called "natural" because they are found in nature, not made by human beings.

Example 2: One of the most valuable *resources* in Middle Eastern countries is oil.

Example 3: Many people believe we should use or sell *resources* only as quickly as Mother Nature can replace them.

Question 1: Countries near the Mediterranean Sea are known for their relaxed way of life. Is this a *resource*? Yes or no? (no)

Question 2: Some countries have begun using wind and water to create energy. Are wind and water *resources*? Yes or no? (yes)

Pair Share: You are the ruler of your own land. Turn to your partner and tell what major *resources* you sell to other countries.

Invent (v)

Let's read the next word together. *Invent.*

Definition: *Invent* means "to make up or think of." What word means "to make up or think of"? (invent)

Example 1: Many people wonder whether a time machine will ever be *invented.*

Example 2: Democracy was first *invented* by the Greeks in about 500 BCE.

Example 3: I need to *invent* a new system for organizing my closet.

Question 1: If you copy someone else's style, have you *invented* your own? Yes or no? (no)

Question 2: In the 1900s, scientists came up with special ways for people to "speed read." Did they *invent* these methods? Yes or no? (yes)

Pair Share: Turn to your partner and tell what you wish someone would *invent* a new way to do.

(3)

access (v)

Let's read the next word together. *Access.*

Definition: *Access* means "to find a way into; to gain entry to." What word means "to find a way into; to gain entry to"? (access)

Example 1: On weekends, you have to use a security code to *access* the school building.

Example 2: If you lock yourself out of your house, you might have to *access* it through a window.

Example 3: City workers *access* drainage sewers through manholes.

Question 1: The gate to the community garden is locked, so you go home. Did you *access* the garden? Yes or no? (no)

Question 2: In one fairy tale, a prince climbs up the long hair of the princess to get inside a tower. Does he *access* the tower? Yes or no? (yes)

Pair Share: Turn to your partner and tell how a movie hero *accessed* a certain place in order to save the day.

(4)

impose (v)

Let's read the next word together. *Impose.*

Definition: *Impose* means "to force upon; to burden with." What word means "to force upon" or "to burden with"? (impose)

Example 1: Students complain when teachers *impose* rules that seem unfair.

Example 2: If a company *imposes* long work hours and low pay rates on its employees, many may quit.

Example 3: *Imposing* your strong opinions on others can actually turn people against you.

Question 1: Your brother cranks up his awful music in the car and doesn't let anyone change the station. Is he *imposing* his musical tastes on others? Yes or no? (yes)

Question 2: Your grandmother decided to stay in a hotel when she visited because she didn't want to bother anyone at your house. Did she *impose*? Yes or no? (no)

Pair Share: Do you think the city should *impose* a new tax on soft drinks? Why or why not? Tell your partner.

(5)

govern (v)

Let's read the next word together. *Govern.*

Definition: To *govern* is to rule or to direct. What means "to rule; to direct"? (govern)

Example 1: In this country, our elected leaders *govern* by making decisions and passing laws.

Example 2: When a person votes, he or she is helping decide who *governs* a city, county, state, or nation.

Example 3: In most schools, the student council can suggest ideas to the administration, but it doesn't really help *govern.*

Question 1: Your friend is the president of the honor society, but she constantly asks advice from you behind the scenes. Are you helping her *govern*? Yes or no? (yes)

Question 2: Your little sister puts all of her stuffed animals in a row and orders them to do what she says. Is she trying to *govern* them? Yes or no? (yes)

Pair Share: Turn to your partner and tell how you would *govern* a room full of preschool students.

(6)

impact (v)

Let's read the next word together. *Impact*.

Definition: *Impact* means "to have an effect on." What means "to have an effect on"? (impact)

Example 1: If you practice your solo for the musical during study hall, it might *impact* your neighbor's ability to study for a test.

Example 2: The foods you eat as a child will *impact* your eating choices as a grown-up.

Example 3: Even minor choices and small decisions can *impact* the course of a person's life.

Question 1: You thought it would be cold today, but it's hot instead. Does this *impact* your choice of clothing? Yes or no? (yes)

Question 2: You trusted a friend but then heard him say something unkind about you. Does this *impact* your feelings toward him? Yes or no? (yes)

Pair Share: Turn to your partner and describe a decision you made recently. Then, tell one thing that *impacted* your decision.

(7)

passive (adj)

Let's read the next word together. *Passive*.

Definition: *Passive* means "not taking action; letting something happen to you." What word means "not taking action; letting something happen to you"? (passive)

Example 1: I've heard that if you cross paths with a snake, you should remain *passive* and hope the snake moves on.

Example 2: If you don't care who goes first in a game, you have a *passive* attitude.

Example 3: A punching bag is *passive*; it doesn't punch you back.

Question 1: Before the fly can land on your nose, you swat it away. Are you being *passive*? Yes or no? (no)

Question 2: You are swimming in the ocean. A giant wave comes toward you. You close your eyes and relax. Are your actions *passive*? Yes or no? (yes)

Pair Share: Turn to your partner and describe a situation in which you think it is best to remain *passive*.

(8)

harmony (n)

Let's read the next word together. *Harmony*.

Definition: *Harmony* occurs when there is friendly agreement among people or when all parts of something are working together. What means "friendly agreement; the working together of all parts"? (harmony)

Example 1: In a perfectly choreographed dance, all the dancers move in *harmony*.

Example 2: Members of a community can live in *harmony* when everyone feels seen, heard, and appreciated.

Example 3: Kittens from the same litter often live in playful *harmony* with one another and their mother.

Question 1: The cheerleaders are arguing over which cheer to perform at halftime. Are they working in *harmony*? Yes or no? (no)

Question 2: Your complicated plan ended up working like a dream. Did its parts come together in perfect *harmony*? Yes or no? (yes)

Pair Share: Turn to your partner. Come up with five simple motions, and then perform them in *harmony*.

(9)

transform (v)

Let's read the last word together. *Transform*.

Definition: To *transform* is to change into something new. What word means "to change into something new"? (transform)

Example 1: Inside the cocoon, a caterpillar *transforms* into a butterfly.

Example 2: The empty lot near the park has been *transformed* into high-rise apartments.

Example 3: With a home hair-coloring kit, *transforming* your hair color is easy.

Question 1: You just got your braces off, but your teeth look exactly the same. Have they been *transformed*? Yes or no? (no)

Question 2: You drive by your grandfather's old house but don't recognize it. It's been painted bright yellow, and his vegetable garden is gone. Has it been *transformed*? Yes or no? (yes)

Pair Share: Which is easier, *transforming* your personality or *transforming* your looks? Turn to your partner and tell why.

(10)

Reading

Objectives
- Read informational text.
- Monitor comprehension during text reading.
- Distinguish between information provided by pictures or other illustrations and information provided by the words in a text.
- Explain how graphics contribute to an understanding of the text.

"The Symbol of Freedom"

Direct students to page 233 in their Student Books. Now that we have previewed vocabulary, it's time to read.

Guiding Students Toward Independent Reading

It is important that your students read as much and as often as they can. Assign readings that meet the needs of your students, based on your observations and data. This is a good opportunity to stretch your students. If students become frustrated, scaffold the reading with paired reading, choral reading, or a read-aloud.

Options for reading text:

- Teacher read-aloud
- Teacher-led or student-led choral read
- Paired read or independent read

Choose an option for reading the text. Have students read according to the option that you chose.

Remind students to pause at the numbers and consider the questions.

If you choose to read the text aloud or chorally, use the following text boxes and stop to ask questions and have students answer them.

p. 233, paragraph 1

> Nelson Mandela's lifelong fight for the cause of freedom in South Africa is a tale of inspiration and determination; it is a tale of struggle. During his 27 years in prison, he became a powerful symbol of resistance to the racial **discrimination** that has plagued South Africa, and he emerged as the first black president of South Africa in 1994.

1. Nelson Mandela was South Africa's first what?

SE p. 233, paragraphs 2–3

South Africa's landscape and environment have been described as the most enticing in the world. South Africa has a mild climate, similar to that of the San Francisco Bay. The land is fertile with plentiful mineral **resources**. In fact, South African mines are world leaders in the production of diamonds, gold, and platinum. These qualities combined to make South Africa attractive to European powers in the 17th, 18th, and 19th centuries.

South Africa had much to offer European powers looking for natural resources and economic gain. The land was colonized by the Dutch in the 1600s. During the following century, England became interested in the land and eventually defeated the Dutch. South Africa remained a colony of England until 1961.

2. Who ruled South Africa until 1961?

SE p. 234, paragraph 1

Apartheid

The political parties in control of the country consisted primarily of white men of European ancestry. These groups **invented** apartheid as a means to control the economy and the people. *Apartheid* is a Dutch word that means "separateness." Apartheid laws were aimed to keep the white, European minority in power. The laws discriminated against the black people of African ancestry, who made up more than 70 percent of the nation's population, as well as people of mixed race and Asian descent.

3. What were apartheid laws designed to do?

SE p. 234,
paragraphs 2–3

These laws touched every aspect of social life. Nonwhites could not go to white schools or hospitals or visit white beaches. They could not vote and were segregated from many jobs. To **access** designated white areas, all black Africans were required to carry "pass books" containing fingerprints, a photo, and personal information. Black Africans were forced to live in specific areas on the outskirts of South African cities and needed passports to enter the rest of the country. They were treated as visiting foreigners in their own country.

The penalties **imposed** on those who protested against the discrimination were severe. Thousands of individuals were tortured and killed. Those who were tried in court were typically sentenced to death, exile, or life in prison—like Nelson Mandela.

4. What happened to people who protested apartheid laws?

SE p. 235,
paragraphs 1–3

A Means to an End

When Mandela was 12 years old, his father died of lung disease, causing his life to abruptly change. He was adopted by a tribal chief. He lived in a palace and learned African history from elder chiefs who visited. He learned how the African people had lived in relative peace until the coming of the Europeans. According to the elders, the people of South Africa had lived as brothers, but the white man shattered this fellowship. While the black man shared his land, air, and water with the white man, the white man took all of these things for himself.

At age 16, Mandela heard a tribal leader speak with great sadness about the future of young men in South Africa. The tribal leader explained that because the land was controlled by white men, the young black men would struggle to earn a living and never have the power to **govern** themselves. This speech profoundly **impacted** Mandela and set the course for his life of activism.

After years of performing well at various schools, Mandela enrolled in law school, where he met people of all races and backgrounds. He was exposed to liberal and Africanist thought in addition to racism and discrimination. This experience served to further fuel his passion for politics. In 1944, he joined the African National Congress to become a voice for those who didn't have one.

5. What organization did Mandela join? What kind of organization was this?

SE p. 235,
paragraphs 4–5

Mandela Challenges the Apartheid Government

As more and more laws were passed to limit the progress of black South Africans, the ANC staged a campaign against apartheid laws that was structured around the theory of **passive** resistance. Mandela opened a law practice and campaigned against apartheid. Soon after, Mandela was charged with high treason, but the charges were eventually dropped. Mandela continued his important mission. The resistance to apartheid grew stronger, as did the commitment by the government to maintain white rule.

Tension with the government continued to grow. It peaked in 1960 when 69 black people were shot dead by police. The government declared a state of emergency and banned the ANC. In response, the ANC abandoned its policy of non-violence, and Mandela helped lead the armed struggle for freedom.

6. What policy did the ANC abandon in 1960? Why?

SE p. 236, paragraph 1

Imprisonment

After playing a minor role in a workers' strike and illegally leaving the country in 1961, Mandela began a five-year prison sentence. During that time, Mandela and other members of the ANC were tried for plotting to overthrow the government by violence. Mandela defended himself during his trial with words about democracy, freedom, and equality. "I have cherished the ideal of a democratic and free society in which all persons live together in **harmony** and with equal opportunities," he said. "It is an ideal for which I hope to live and to see realized. But if needs be, it is an ideal for which I am prepared to die." The verdict was life in prison.

7. For what ideal was Mandela prepared to die? What was his actual sentence?

SE p. 236, paragraph 2

Apartheid Ends

Mandela's fight did not end. During his years in prison, he became an international symbol of resistance to apartheid. In 1990, the South African government responded to international pressure and released Mandela. Talks of **transforming** the old-style government of South Africa to a new multiracial democracy began. In 1994, for the first time in South Africa's history, all races voted in democratic elections, and Mandela was elected president.

8. What landmark event took place in South Africa in 1994?

SE p. 236, paragraph 3

Nelson Mandela struggled to end apartheid in South Africa. He led the charge, became the face of resistance, and shared the hopes and dreams of many; he was the symbol of freedom. Jailed for 27 years, he emerged to become the country's first black president and play a leading role in the drive for human rights across the world.

9. Mandela was the symbol of what?

For confirmation of engagement, have partners share a fact they found interesting or inspiring. Have volunteers share facts with the class.

The Impact of Graphics

Direct students to page 233 in their Student Books. Have volunteers explain the impact of the images of South Africa. Do these images look like the Africa you had pictured in your head? (Answers will vary.) The author likely included these images because many people have negative images of the African landscape. Direct students to page 234 in their Student Books. On this page, we learned that the Africans made up the majority of the population, but didn't have the rights and privileges of the whites. Look at the chart. How does this chart help clarify and expound upon the situation in South Africa? (The discrepancies are illustrated with numbers. You can see just how poorly they were treated.) On the next page, what is the effect of seeing Mandela's prison cell? (You feel even more sorry for him when you realize he didn't have a bed or a toilet.)

Graphics and illustrations play a major role in most informational text. It is important that these "extras" are not overlooked. They often contribute greatly to what is in the text.

Lesson Opener

Before the lesson, choose one of the following activities to write on the board or post on the *LANGUAGE! Live* Class Wall online.

- *Describe your best friend. How would you feel if your friend was being unfairly treated? What would you do?*
- *The South Africa of Mandela's youth would have been considered unfair by today's standards. Write three sentences about things that are unfair. Write one sentence with a compound subject, one sentence with a compound predicate, and one sentence with a compound object.*
- *Write four sentences about* justice. *Use* justice *as the subject noun, direct object, predicate noun, and the object of the preposition.*

Vocabulary

Objective
- Review key passage vocabulary.

Review Passage Vocabulary

Direct students to page 232 in their Student Books. Use the following questions to review the vocabulary words from "The Symbol of Freedom." Have students answer each question using the vocabulary word or indicating its meaning in a complete sentence.

- Racial *discrimination* plagued South Africa. How did *discrimination* affect black people? (Discrimination caused black people to be treated unfairly.) Did Mandela support *discrimination*? (No, he fought against discrimination.)

Vocabulary Review Note: Mandela was a symbol of *resistance* against discrimination. If he *resisted* discrimination, what did he do? (He did not give in to it.)

- South Africa has plentiful *resources*. What are some of them? (South Africa's resources include minerals, diamonds, gold, and platinum.) Why did these *resources* attract Europeans in earlier times? (The resources attracted Europeans because they were valuable and could create wealth.)

Vocabulary Review Note: The Dutch first colonized South Africa, but the English *eventually* defeated the Dutch for control of the land. Did the English defeat the Dutch quickly? (No, the defeat happened over a long period of time.)

- The Europeans in control of South Africa *invented* the system of apartheid. Did apartheid exist before they *invented* it? (No; because they invented it, it was a new system.) Was the *invention* fair? (No, the system they invented was unfair.)

- Under apartheid, was it easy for black Africans to *access* non-black areas? (No, it was difficult for them to access non-black areas.) What did black Africans need in order to *access* areas reserved for whites? (To access areas reserved for whites, black Africans needed a "pass book" containing fingerprints, a photo, and other information.)

- What were *imposed* on people who protested apartheid? (Severe penalties or punishments were imposed on them.) What were some of the penalties *imposed*? (The penalties included torture, life in prison, or death.) Which of these were *imposed* on Nelson Mandela? (Imprisonment was imposed on him.)

- When he was 16, Mandela heard a tribal leader talk sadly about the future. He said that young black men would never have the power to *govern* themselves. What did he mean? (If they could not govern themselves, they could not rule or direct themselves. In other words, they could not be in charge of themselves.) Did Mandela earn the power to *govern* South Africa? (Yes, he became president and governed South Africa.)

- The tribal leader's speech *impacted* Mandela. What did it do to him? (If the speech impacted Mandela, it had an effect on him.) Would you say the *impact* was positive or negative? (The impact was positive; it inspired him to take action to create change.)

- The movement led by Mandela was based on *passive* resistance. What kind of resistance is *passive* resistance? (Passive resistance does not take action or fight back.) So, would a person involved in *passive* resistance allow him- or herself to be imprisoned or even die? Why or why not? (Yes, a person involved in passive resistance would let action be taken against him or her as a way to make a statement about not giving in.)

- While on trial, Mandela stated that he treasured the idea of a society where people lived in *harmony.* If people live in *harmony,* what do they live in? (If people live in harmony, they live in a state of peaceful agreement.) Has any society reached a state of total *harmony*? Why or why not? (No society has reached a state of total harmony because humans have competing interests and ideas about many things.)

- Mandela was imprisoned for many years and then released. Leaders began talking about *transforming* the system. If the system were *transformed,* what would happen to it? (It would change into something new.) What was South Africa's system of apartheid eventually *transformed* into? (It was transformed into a democracy.) How was Mandela's own role in South Africa *transformed* in 1994? (His role was transformed from that of resister to that of president of the new democracy.)

Objectives

- Distinguish between action, linking, and helping verbs.
- Use future and future progressive verb tenses correctly.
- Use coordinating conjunctions in compound sentences.
- Use correct punctuation when writing compound sentences.
- Use verb tense to convey various times, sequences, states, and conditions.

Action, Linking, or Helping Verbs

We already know that every sentence must contain a verb. We've worked with different kinds of verbs. Some verbs answer the *did what* question, but some verbs "link," or connect, the subject—*who* or *what*—to the rest of the sentence. Sometimes, action verbs need a little help to answer the *did what* question. **Direct students to page 237 in their Student Books and read the instructions aloud.**

Guided Practice

Listen as I read the first sentence: *He was the symbol of freedom. Who* or *what* is the sentence about? (He) Can you answer the *did what* question? (no) What is the verb? (was) Instead of "doing something," it links the subject to the rest of the sentence. Underline *was* and write it in the proper column in the chart.

Listen as I read the second sentence: *All black Africans were required to carry "pass books."* Who or what? (Africans) Did what? (were required) This sentence has two verbs working together: a helping verb and a main verb. Underline the verb phrase, and write it in the proper column in the chart.

Independent Practice

Read the remaining sentences and have students identify the verbs and the verb types. Review the answers as a class.

Lesson 2 | Grammar

Action, Linking, or Helping Verbs

Read each sentence and underline the verb or verb phrase. Write the verbs in the proper column in the chart below.

1. He was the symbol of freedom.
2. All black Africans were required to carry "pass books."
3. He learned how the African people had lived in relative peace until the coming of the Europeans.
4. He was adopted by a tribal chief.
5. South Africa remained a colony of England until 1961.
6. This group invented apartheid as a means to control the economy and the people.
7. The verdict was life in prison.
8. Thousands of individuals were tortured and killed.
9. Mandela opened a law practice and campaigned against apartheid.
10. Nelson Mandela's lifelong fight for the cause of freedom in South Africa is a tale of inspiration and determination.

Action Verb		Linking Verb	Helping Verb + Main Verb
learned	remained	was	were required
invented	opened	was	was adopted
campaigned		is	were tortured
			were killed

Unit 6   **237**

Tense Timeline: Future and Future Progressive Tenses

All verbs, regardless of their type, convey a sense of time. Another word for time is *tense*. To talk about today, we use some form of the present tense, and to talk about yesterday, we use some form of the past tense.

Write the word *fight* on the board. Have students use the word in present tense sentences with the pronouns *they* and *she*. (They fight against oppression. She fights against oppression.) Then, have them use the word in past tense sentences with the same pronouns. (They fought against oppression. She fought against oppression.) Do the same with the present progressive and the past progressive tenses. (They are fighting against oppression. She is fighting against oppression. They were fighting against oppression. She was fighting against oppression.)

Let's look at the verbs in the activity you just completed and figure out what tense they are. *Was* is a past tense verb. In fact, all of the verbs on this page are past tense except one. Which verb is not past tense? (is)

Direct students to page 238 in their Student Books. Today, we are going to add to our knowledge of verb tenses by considering how verbs reflect an action that has not happened yet. If it is going to happen tomorrow or in the future, we use the future tense. One way to create the future tense is to simply add *will* to the verb. Have students use *fight, they,* and *she* to demonstrate the future tense. (They will fight against oppression. She will fight against oppression.)

Look at the first line in the chart and read it with me: *I spoke. I speak. I will speak.* Read the next line with me: *You spoke. You speak. You will speak.* Write *will speak* in the Future tense column. Continue reading each line chorally, and have students write the future tense for each pronoun. When completed, point out that in the future tense, the verb *speak* never changes form. For first, second, third, singular, and plural, all they had to do was add the helping verb *will*. Contrast that with the challenge of using the present tense correctly. Have students look at the past tense of *speak* and note that once they put the verb in the past tense, it didn't change according to person or number either.

Work through progressive verb tenses in a similar manner, making sure students complete the chart with future progressive verbs.

Tense Timeline: Future and Future Progressive Tenses

Complete the sentences for the future and future progressive tense with the verb *speak*.

Yesterday	Today	Tomorrow

Past	Present	Future
		will + verb
I spoke.	I speak.	I will speak.
You spoke.	You speak.	You will speak.
She spoke.	She speaks.	She will speak.
We spoke.	We speak.	We will speak.
They spoke.	They speak.	They will speak.
Past Progressive	**Present Progressive**	**Future Progressive**
		will + be + -ing
I was speaking.	I am speaking.	I will be speaking.
You were speaking.	You are speaking.	You will be speaking.
She was speaking.	She is speaking.	She will be speaking.
We were speaking.	We are speaking.	We will be speaking.
They were speaking.	They are speaking.	They will be speaking.

Direct students to page 239 in their Student Books. Read the instructions for the activity.

Model

Listen as I read the first example: *The government declared a state of emergency.* My first task is to find the verb and underline it. What did the government do? It declared. *Declared* is my verb, so I've underlined it. Next, I have to change the verb to the future tense. I can look back at the chart and see that I create the future tense by adding *will* to the present tense verb. My new sentence: *The government will declare a state of emergency.* The last step is to underline the verb phrase in the new sentence: *will declare.*

Listen as I read the second example: *Mandela served a five-year prison sentence.* The first thing I have to do is find the verb, so I ask the question *Did what*? *Served* is the verb, so I've underlined it. I have to rewrite the sentence using the future progressive tense. Again, I can refer to the chart to see how I write the future progressive tense: will + be + verb + -ing. My new sentence is *Mandela will be serving a five-year prison sentence.* My last step is to underline the verb phrase in the new sentence: *will be serving.*

Guided Practice

Listen as I read the first sentence: *These laws touched every aspect of social life.* What is the first thing you need to do? (**Find the verb and underline it.**) What did these laws do? (**touched**) Remember to underline it. What tense are you going to use for the new sentence? (**future progressive**) How do you write the future progressive tense? Remember to look at the chart if you don't remember. (**will + be + verb + -ing**) The hardest part of rewriting the verb is figuring out the present tense. What is the present tense for *touched*? (**touch**) **Write it on the board.** What ending do you need to add to it? (**-ing**) What is the new sentence? (**These laws will be touching every aspect of social life.**) Make sure you remember to underline the verb phrase in the new sentence.

Verb Tenses

Underline the verb in each sentence. Rewrite the sentence, changing the tense as indicated in the parentheses. Underline the verb in the new sentence.

Examples:
The government <u>declared</u> a state of emergency. (future)
The government <u>will declare</u> a state of emergency.

Mandela <u>served</u> a five-year prison sentence. (future progressive)
Mandela <u>will be serving</u> a five-year prison sentence.

1. These laws touched every aspect of social life. (future progressive)
   These laws will be touching every aspect of social life.

2. Mandela enrolled in law school. (future)
   Mandela will enroll in law school.

3. The resistance to apartheid grew stronger. (future)
   The resistance to apartheid will grow stronger.

4. Mandela continued his important mission. (future progressive)
   Mandela will be continuing his important mission.

5. The South African government responded to international pressure and released Mandela. (future)
   The South African government will respond to international pressure and release Mandela.

Unit 6   239

Read the remaining sentences and have students change the verbs to future or future progressive tense. Review the answers as a class.

Conjunctions

Let's talk more about conjunctions. The primary function of these words is to join other words or groups of words. They can join nouns, verbs, and even sentences.

And

Use the items on your desk to complete the following sentence frame: I have _____ *and* _____ on my desk. What is the function of the conjunction *and*? (The word *and* joins two objects together.)

But

What is the function of the conjunction *but*? (The word *but* joins contrasting ideas together.) Sometimes, you need to join contrasting ideas. I wanted to go to the concert, *but* I couldn't afford the ticket. The word *but* signals a change, or contrast, in the outcome.

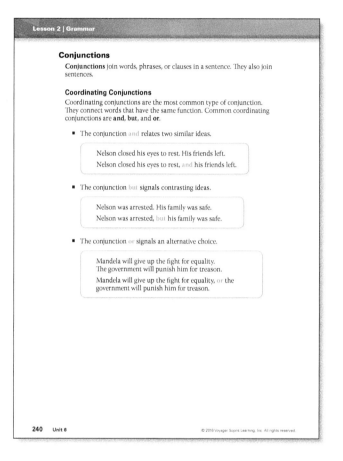

Or

If you have a choice between two things, you often use a different connecting word: I will have pizza *or* a sandwich for lunch. The word *or* signals a choice. What is the function of the conjunction *or*? (The word *or* signals a choice.)

Have students turn to page 240 in their Student Books. These three words—*and, but, or*—are conjunctions.

Consider the word *conjunction*. What do you think of when you hear the word *junction*? (Possible answers: where two roads come together, where roads or railroad track cross) *Junction* means "a place where two or more things come together or join." This is exactly what conjunctions do. In your book, you see examples of how these three conjunctions can be used in compound sentences. Review the bulleted information and each example.

Direct students to page 241 in their Student Books. Read the instructions aloud.

Model

Listen to the example: *Nelson Mandela was sentenced to life in prison, and the fight for freedom was in danger.* The first step is to find and circle the conjunction. I'm looking for one of three words: *and, but, or.* I see the conjunction *and*, so I'm going to circle it. The next step is to determine its meaning. Does it connect similar ideas, present contrasting ideas, or provide alternative choices? Nelson Mandela's prison sentence and the possible danger of the fight for freedom go together or complement each other. The conjunction is joining two similar ideas, so I would place the check mark in that column.

Guided Practice

Listen to the first sentence: *Mandela could allow the government to end his campaign, or he could continue the fight, risking imprisonment.* What is the conjunction? (or) Circle *or*. We are reading about two possible options Mandela could pursue regarding his campaign. Where does the check mark go? (Alternative Choices) He has a choice to make. Place the check mark in the Alternative Choices column.

Have students read the second sentence chorally. What is the conjunction in this sentence? (but) It's joining the hope of the government and an outcome that was very different from that hope. Where did you place the check mark? (Contrasting Ideas) The check mark goes under Contrasting Ideas because instead of the fight ending, the people continued the struggle.

Independent Practice

Have students work independently to circle the conjunctions and place the check marks in the proper columns for the remaining sentences. Review the answers as a class.

Coordinating Conjunctions

Circle the conjunction(s) in each sentence. Determine the meaning of the conjunction and place a check mark in the corresponding column.

	Similar Ideas	Contrasting Ideas	Alternative Choices
Ex: Nelson Mandela was sentenced to life in prison, and the fight for freedom was in danger.	✓		
1. Mandela could allow the government to end his campaign, or he could continue the fight, risking imprisonment.			✓
2. The government hoped to end the fight against apartheid, but the people continued the struggle against injustice.		✓	
3. Nonwhites could not go to white schools or hospitals or visit white beaches.			✓
4. The ANC abandoned its policy of non-violence, and Mandela helped lead the armed struggle for freedom.	✓		
5. The people of South Africa had lived as brothers, but the white man shattered this fellowship.		✓	
6. The white people controlled the wealth, and the black Africans lived in poverty.	✓		
7. Mandela was charged with high treason, but the charges were dropped.		✓	

Unit 6 **241**

Spotlight on Punctuation: Commas with Conjunctions

Most sentences in the previous activity have two complete thoughts joined by a conjunction. When you combine two independent thoughts or clauses, you create compound sentences. To punctuate a compound sentence correctly, you have to include commas.

However, you don't always create a compound sentence when you use a conjunction.

Write the following sentences on the board:

> *Maria and Sylvia walked to the movie theater.*
>
> *We can walk through the woods or ride our bikes to the theater.*

Read the first sentence aloud. This is not a compound sentence. I did not combine two complete thoughts. All I did was join two *whos*. This is a compound subject.

Read the second sentence aloud. Who or what? (We) Do what? (can walk or ride) This sentence contains two *do whats*. That is what is joined, not two sentences. This is a compound predicate.

Notice neither sentence has a comma.

Direct students to page 242 in their Student Books. Read the instructions aloud.

Guided Practice

Listen as I read the first sentence in the activity: *South Africa's landscape and environment have been described as the most enticing in the world.* What conjunction do you see? (and) What is it joining? (landscape and environment) Is it joining two complete thoughts? (no) What is it joining? (two *whats*) Does this sentence need a comma? (no) It does not need a comma because the conjunction is not joining two complete thoughts. This is a compound subject.

Listen as I read the second sentence: *Mandela opened a law practice and the people came to him for help.* What conjunction do you see? (and) Is it joining *practice* and *the people*? (no)

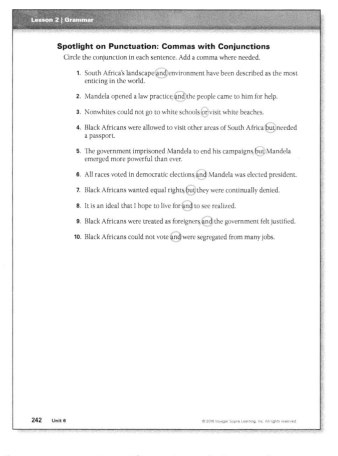

Lesson 2 | Grammar

Spotlight on Punctuation: Commas with Conjunctions

Circle the conjunction in each sentence. Add a comma where needed.

1. South Africa's landscape and environment have been described as the most enticing in the world.
2. Mandela opened a law practice and the people came to him for help.
3. Nonwhites could not go to white schools or visit white beaches.
4. Black Africans were allowed to visit other areas of South Africa but needed a passport.
5. The government imprisoned Mandela to end his campaigns but Mandela emerged more powerful than ever.
6. All races voted in democratic elections and Mandela was elected president.
7. Black Africans wanted equal rights but they were continually denied.
8. It is an ideal that I hope to live for and to see realized.
9. Black Africans were treated as foreigners and the government felt justified.
10. Black Africans could not vote and were segregated from many jobs.

242   Unit 6   © 2016 Voyager Sopris Learning, Inc. All rights reserved.

If students do not understand this, read the sentence again as if *practice* and *the people* were together as one direct object. Let's see if we have two complete thoughts. What is the first *who* or *what*? (Mandela) Did *what*? (opened) Couple that with the direct object *a law practice*, and you have a complete thought. Is there another *who* or *what* that follows the conjunction? (yes, the people) Did what? (came) Couple that with the prepositional phrase *to him*, and what do you have? (a complete thought) Listen to each part of the sentence and tell me if it is a complete thought. Mandela opened a law practice. (yes) The people came to him for help. (yes) Do we need to place a comma in front of the conjunction? (yes)

Independent Practice

Read the remaining sentences, and have students circle the conjunctions and determine if the sentence requires a comma. Review the answers as a class.

Note: Draw students' attention to number 7. Explain that the subject of each independent clause is the same; therefore, this didn't need to be a compound sentence. It could have been a sentence with a compound predicate without a comma. Have students say the sentence with a compound predicate. Explain that the second use of the subject (pronoun *they*) made it a compound sentence and thus required the use of the comma.

Writing

Objectives
- Identify the structure of a sentence.
- Use conjunctions correctly in sentence writing.
- Produce, expand, and rearrange complete sentences for clarity and style.
- Write compound sentences.

Masterpiece Sentences Using Conjunctions

Direct students to page 243 in their Student Books. Read the instructions aloud. You have worked through the six stages of Masterpiece Sentences, and your sentences are becoming more interesting and descriptive.

Guided Practice

Let's write sentences about what we learned in the text. The structure for each sentence has been established to make sure you write compound sentences. Look at the first pattern and think about who the sentence could be about. **Write their responses on the board.** (Possible answers: Nelson Mandela, South Africa, the government, the ANC) What did they do? (Possible answers: spoke, fought, treated, listened, failed) How? (Possible answers: eloquently, hard, unfairly, closely, miserably) Notice the conjunction *and*. This sentence has two complete ideas that are similar. Thus, they are connected by *and*. Who

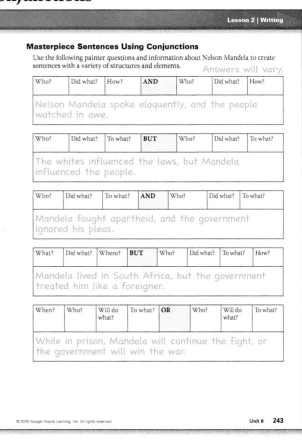

else was involved? (Answers will vary.) What did they do? (Answers will vary.) How? (Answers will vary.)

Independent Practice

Have partners write the remaining sentences. Have volunteers share their sentences. If students struggle, continue to prompt them with questions and possible answers.

Punctuation: Comma or Semicolon

Write *and*, *but*, and *or* on the board. These are the coordinating conjunctions we used to build compound sentences. Add *so* to the list on the board. Explain that *so* can also be used as a coordinating conjunction. Offer this example: *I love pizza, so I went to Freddy's Pizza Parlor for lunch.* Have partners use *so* in a compound sentence and share them with the class.

Punctuating compound sentences ensures the ideas that are being expressed are accurately understood. Punctuation marks impact meaning. Punctuation marks provide important clues for meaning. When we write compound sentences, punctuation becomes very important. If our compound sentence has a conjunction, or joining word, we use a comma before the conjunction. If we don't have a conjunction, we need to use a semicolon. A semicolon looks like a comma with a dot above it. It signals the joining or junction between two complete thoughts. Write the following sentences on the board, and point out the comma and semicolon usage.

> *I cannot sing a lick, but Mrs. Jones sings like an angel.*
>
> *I cannot sing a lick; Mrs. Jones sings like an angel.*

Direct students to page 244 in their Student Books. Read the instructions aloud.

Our first step is to decide what kind of punctuation mark is needed. How will we determine that? What does the sentence have to contain if I should use a comma? (a coordinating conjunction) If the sentence doesn't have a coordinating conjunction, what punctuation mark do I need to use? (semicolon) Then, our first step needs to be to look for a coordinating conjunction. What are the four we've used? (and, but, or, so)

Model

Listen as I read the example: *The whites were treated as native South Africans; the nonwhites were treated as foreigners.* Is a coordinating conjunction used to join these two independent clauses? (no) There is no joining word connecting the two

---

Lesson 2 | Writing

Comma or Semicolon

Read the compound sentences and decide if the sentence needs a comma or a semicolon. Fill in the blank with the proper punctuation mark.

> **Example:**
> The whites were treated as native South Africans ⨟ the nonwhites were treated as foreigners.

1. The government punished protestors ⨟ the people protested anyway.
2. Whites were allowed to live anywhere ⟋ but nonwhites were forced to live on the outskirts of South African cities.
3. Mandela was charged with high treason ⨟ the charges were dropped.
4. Mandela was sentenced to life in prison ⟋ so his fight against apartheid came to an end.
5. The struggle continued in Mandela's absence ⟋ and eventually the laws were changed.
6. New laws were passed that dictated where black Africans could live and work ⟋ so the resistance to apartheid grew stronger.
7. The government sought to limit Mandela's popularity ⨟ the people's love of him grew.
8. Mandela could see the injustice ⟋ but the government remained ignorant.
9. Mandela was jailed for 27 years ⟋ but the international fight against apartheid continued.
10. The government wished to keep the people apart ⨟ the people wished to unite.

independent clauses: *The whites were treated as native South Africans. The nonwhites were treated as foreigners.* Because there is no conjunction, I need to place a semicolon between the two clauses. It is important to remember the first criterion is that we have joined two independent clauses. If one of these clauses could not stand on its own, then we would need to consider punctuation differently.

Guided Practice

Listen as I read the first sentence: *The government punished protesters; the people protested anyway.* Is there a coordinating conjunction joining the two clauses? (no) What kind of punctuation mark do you need to use? (a semicolon) What does a semicolon look like? (a comma with a period above it)

Listen as I read the next one: *Whites were allowed to live anywhere, but nonwhites were forced to live on the outskirts of South African cities.* Insert the correct punctuation mark. After a brief pause, call on a student to share his or her choice. Clarify the correct response, if necessary.

Independent Practice

Read the remaining sentences and have students insert the proper punctuation. Review the answers as a class.

Lesson Opener

Before the lesson, choose one of the following activities to write on the board or post on the *LANGUAGE! Live* Class Wall online.

- *South Africa has a mild climate, fertile land, and rich resources. Tell how the place you live is similar to or different from South Africa.*

- *Mandela's life was forever changed when he heard a tribal elder talk sadly about the future. Write five present tense sentences about a family elder you respect. Then, write five future tense sentences about what this person has inspired you to do in the future.*

- *Write four reasons to speak out for justice in our society. Write four reasons not to. Combine the eight sentences into four sentences using conjunctions or semicolons.*

Reading

Objectives

- Establish a purpose for rereading informational text.
- Use critical thinking skills to write responses to prompts about text.
- Support written answers with text evidence.
- Determine the meaning of words and phrases in text.
- Sequence historical events.
- Draw inferences from text and support with evidence.

Reading for a Purpose: "The Symbol of Freedom"

Sometimes it is helpful to give yourself a purpose for reading.

One purpose for rereading is to find information that will help us answer questions about the text. Let's read the questions now.

Direct students to pages 245–247 in their Student Books. Have students read the prompts aloud with you.

1. Paraphrase the first paragraph.

2. Delineate the events that led to apartheid in South Africa.

3. Delineate the events in Mandela's youth that led him to join the African National Congress (ANC).

4. Create a poster persuading people to join the African National Congress (ANC).

5. Determine the meaning of the following sentence from the text:

   According to the elders, the people of South Africa had lived as brothers, but the white man shattered this fellowship.

6. Determine whether Mandela's activism was successful and the reason for this success or failure.

Direct students to page 233 in their Student Books or have them tear out the extra copy from the back of their book.

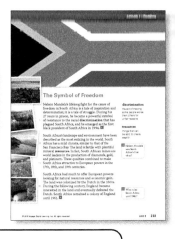

Note: To minimize flipping back and forth between the pages, a copy of each text has been included in the back of the Student Books. Encourage students to tear this out and use it when working on activities that require the use of the text.

Choose an option for reading text. Have students read the text according to the option that you chose.

> Options for reading text:
> * Teacher read-aloud
> * Teacher-led or student-led choral read
> * Paired read or independent read with bold vocabulary words read aloud

Passage Comprehension

Write the words *create, delineate, determine,* and *paraphrase* on the board. Have students read the words aloud with you.

Direct students to page 66 in their Student Books. It is critical to understand what the question is asking and how to answer it. Today, we will review four direction words used in prompts.

Have students review the words on the board in the chart on page 66. Check for understanding by requesting an oral response to the following questions.

* If the prompt asks you to *create*, the response requires you to . . . (make or produce something).
* If the prompt asks you to *delineate*, the response requires you to . . . (show or list evidence, claims, ideas, reasons, or events).
* If the prompt asks you to *determine*, the response requires you to . . . (find out, verify, or decide).
* If the prompt asks you to *paraphrase*, the response requires you to . . . (say or write in your own words what the text says).

Direct students to pages 245–247 in their Student Books.

Passage Comprehension

Reread "The Symbol of Freedom." Respond to each prompt using complete sentences. Refer to the chart on page 66 to determine how to respond to each prompt. Provide text evidence when requested.

1. Paraphrase the first paragraph.

   Mandela's effort to bring freedom to South Africa is a story of strength, motivation, and challenges. During his time in prison, and later as the nation's first black president, Mandela came to represent the struggle of his people to overcome racism.

2. Delineate the events that led to apartheid in South Africa.

   South Africa's natural resources attracted European powers. In the 1600s, the Dutch colonized South Africa. Eventually, England gained control of the land. The white men of European descent invented apartheid to control nonwhites and keep power in the hands of whites.

3. Delineate the events in Mandela's youth that led him to join the African National Congress (ANC). Write the events in the boxes.

   | Father died of lung cancer | → | Adopted by a tribal chief | → |
   | Heard one elder speak sadly about the future | → | Went to law school and was exposed to Africanist ideas | → |

   Joined the ANC

Passage Comprehension (cont.)

4. Create a poster persuading people to join the African National Congress (ANC).

   Poster should include the aim of the group to bring about political equality and serve as a voice for oppressed black South Africans.

Passage Comprehension (cont.)

5. Determine the meaning of the following sentence from the text:
   According to the elders, the people of South Africa had lived as brothers, but the white man shattered this fellowship.

   The sentence means that before the white men came, South African tribes lived peacefully together and shared the land and resources. When the white men came, they created tension among the tribes and took the land and resources for themselves. Friendly relations ended as a result.

6. Determine whether Mandela's activism was successful and the reason for this success or failure. Provide the text evidence that most strongly supports your answer.

   Mandela's activism was successful because, though he was imprisoned, the fight to end apartheid raged on in South Africa and across the globe.

   Text Evidence: While imprisoned for 27 years, Mandela became "an international symbol of resistance to apartheid." Four years after he was released, "all races voted in democratic elections, and Mandela was elected president."

Let's practice answering questions written as prompts that require critical thinking.

Model

Listen as I model the first one for you.

> 1. Paraphrase the first paragraph.

According to the chart, if the prompt asks me to *paraphrase*, I need to write what someone else has said using my own words.

Now, we need to turn the prompt into a question to confirm our understanding.

For this prompt, we will ask ourselves a basic question using the question word *what*. What is the paragraph about? The first paragraph is about "Nelson Mandela's lifelong fight for the cause of freedom in South Africa." Another question I could ask is this: What details tell more about Mandela's lifelong fight? The author states that during his 27 years in prison, he became a powerful symbol of resistance, and that he emerged as the nation's first black president.

So, how can I state the topic—Mandela's lifelong fight—plus the details—his years in prison, his presidency, and his symbolism—in my own words? Here is one way I could paraphrase this paragraph:

Mandela's effort to bring freedom to South Africa is a story of strength, motivation, and challenges. During his time in prison, and later as the nation's first black president, Mandela came to represent the struggle of his people to overcome racism.

Have students write the answer on the page.

Guided Practice

> 2. Delineate the events that led to apartheid in South Africa.

How should we respond according to the chart? (If the prompt asks me to *delineate*, I need to show or list evidence, claims, ideas, reasons, or events.) In this case, what will we be showing or listing? (events) When we tell what events led to a final event, would we do so in any old order, or would we tell the events in a certain order? (We would tell the events in chronological order.) We would tell what happened first, next, and so on, until we get to the final event—in this case, the establishment of apartheid in South Africa. Now, turn the prompt into a question to confirm your understanding. Tell your partner the question. (What events led to apartheid in South Africa?)

Guide students to find events in paragraphs 3 and 4 that led to the establishment of apartheid in South Africa.

1. *South Africa had much to offer European powers looking for natural resources and economic gain.*
2. *colonized by the Dutch in the 1600s*
3. *England . . . eventually defeated the Dutch.*
4. *The white men of European descent . . . invented apartheid to control the economy and the people.*

Now, let's use this text evidence to delineate, or outline the events. Let's paraphrase the events—put them in our own words—to make sure we understand them. Because we're describing events that happen in time, let's also use time-order words and phrases to clarify the sequence of events.

While providing partner time, write the sentence starters on the board.

South Africa's natural resources _____.

In the 1600s, the Dutch _____.

Eventually, England _____.

The white men of European descent _____.

Have partners answer the question and provide evidence from the text.

Independent Practice

Have students respond to the remaining questions. For students who need more assistance, provide the following alternative questions and sentence starters.

Alternative questions and sentence starters:

3. What events led to Mandela joining the African National Congress? In what order did they happen?

4. What was the main goal of the African National Congress? What kind of people would they have wanted to recruit? Include: goals and aims; qualities of a good member; catchy, persuasive language

5. What does the sentence "According to the elders, the people of South Africa had lived as brothers, but the white man shattered this fellowship." mean?

   The sentence means _____.

6. Was Mandela's activism successful? How? Give strong evidence from the text to support your answer.

   Mandela's activism _____.

Lesson Opener

Before the lesson, choose one of the following activities to write on the board or post on the *LANGUAGE! Live* Class Wall online.

- *Think of one strong belief you have about the world. Tell what events in your earlier life led to you having this strong belief.*
- *Use linking verbs to write five sentences telling why non-violence is a good policy.*
- *Describe how you would feel if you could not go to certain schools or beaches because of your skin color. Use conjunctions in your description.*

Reading

Objectives

- Read informational text with purpose and understanding.
- Answer questions to demonstrate comprehension of text.
- Identify and explain explicit details from text.
- Monitor comprehension of text during reading.
- Identify the conditional tense in writing.
- Connect pronouns to antecedents.
- Increase depth of word meaning through synonyms.
- Determine the meaning of abbreviations used in text.

Close Reading of "The Symbol of Freedom"

Highlighters or colored pencils

Let's reread "The Symbol of Freedom." I will provide specific instructions on how to mark the text that will help with comprehension.

Have students get out a highlighter or colored pencil.

Direct students to pages 248–252 in their Student Books. Please mark your text according to my instructions.

Draw a rectangle around the title, "The Symbol of Freedom."

Circle the headings.

Now, let's read the vocabulary words aloud.

- What's the first bold vocabulary word? (discrimination) *Discrimination* means "the act of treating some people worse than others for unfair reasons." Mandela led the struggle against *discrimination* in South Africa. Have partners use the word in a sentence.

- What's the next vocabulary word? (resources) *Resources* means "things that can be sold to create wealth." South Africa was rich in natural *resources*. Have partners use the word in a sentence.

- Next word? (invented) *Invented* means "made up or thought of." The white leaders in South Africa *invented* apartheid. Have partners use the word in a sentence.

- Let's continue. (access) *Access* means "to find a way into; to gain entry to." Under apartheid, it was difficult for nonwhites to *access* white areas. Have partners use the word in a sentence.

- Next word? (imposed) *Imposed* means "forced upon; burdened with." Harsh penalties were *imposed* on people who protested the apartheid laws. **Have partners use the word in a sentence.**

- Let's continue. (govern) *Govern* means "to rule; to direct." Tribal leaders worried that young black men would never have the chance to *govern* themselves. **Have partners use the word in a sentence.**

- Next word? (impacted) *Impacted* means "had an effect on." Hearing the tribal leaders speak sadly about the future *impacted* Nelson Mandela. **Have partners use the word in a sentence.**

- Let's continue. (passive) *Passive* means "not taking action; letting something happen to you." The ANC had a policy of *passive* resistance. They would resist the laws by not following them, but they would not resort to violence. **Have partners use the word in a sentence.**

- Next word? (harmony) *Harmony* means "friendly agreement; the working together of all parts." Mandela treasured the idea of a South African society in which all citizens lived together in *harmony*. **Have partners use the word in a sentence.**

- Last word. (transforming) *Transforming* means "changing into something new." Mandela's efforts were key in *transforming* South Africa into a democracy. **Have partners use the word in a sentence.**

Talk with a partner about any vocabulary word that is still confusing for you to read consistently or to understand its meaning.

You will reread "The Symbol of Freedom" one section at a time. After each section, you will monitor your understanding by circling the check mark if you understand the text or the question mark if you don't understand the text. I also want you to draw a question mark over any confusing words, phrases, or sentences.

Options for reading text:
- Teacher read-aloud
- Teacher-led or student-led choral read
- Paired read or independent read with bold vocabulary words read aloud

Choose an option for reading text. Have students read the introduction according to the option that you chose.

When most of the students are finished, continue with the entire class. Let's see how well you understood what you read.

- Circle the check mark or the question mark for this section. Draw a question mark over any confusing words.

- Go to line 1. Mark what Mandela fought for. (freedom in South Africa)

- Go to lines 3 and 4. Mark what Mandela became a symbol of. (resistance to the racial discrimination)

- Go back to line 2. Mark the synonym for *resistance*. (struggle)

- Go to line 5. Mark what Mandela became in 1994. (first black president of South Africa)

- Go to the second paragraph. Underline the words and phrases that describe South Africa. (most enticing in the world; mild climate; land is fertile, with plentiful mineral resources; mines are world leaders; attractive to European powers)

- Go to lines 9 and 10. Mark three examples of resources. (diamonds, gold, platinum)

- Go to line 11. Mark the synonym for *enticing*. (attractive)

- Go to lines 12 and 13. Mark the two things European powers were looking for. (natural resources and economic gain)

- Go to lines 13 and 14. Mark the two groups who ruled South Africa. (the Dutch, England)

- Go to line 15. Mark the synonym for *conquered*. (defeated)

- Go to line 16. Mark when South Africa gained freedom from England. (1961)

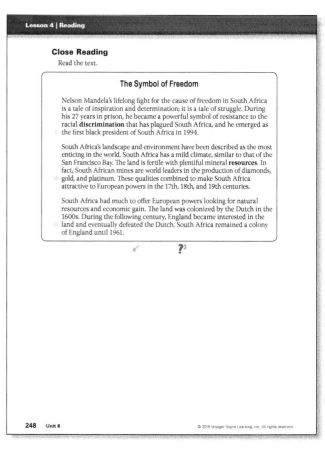

Have students read the section Apartheid according to the option that you chose.

When most of the students are finished, continue with the entire class.
Let's see how well you understood what you read.

- Circle the check mark or the question mark for this section. Draw a question mark over any confusing words.

- Go to lines 17 and 18. Mark who ruled South Africa after it gained independence. (white men of European ancestry)

- In the same line, mark the subject of the next sentence. (These groups) Draw an arrow from the subject to the noun phrase it represents. (political parties in control of the country)

- Go to line 19. If you haven't done so already, mark the two things apartheid controlled. (the economy and the people)

- Go to line 20. Mark the meaning of the Dutch word *apartheid*. ("separateness")

- Go to lines 20 and 21. Mark what the apartheid laws aimed to do. (keep the white, European minority in power)

- Go to lines 21 and 22. Mark what else the laws did. (discriminated against the black people of African ancestry) Mark the two other groups that were discriminated against. (people of mixed race and Asian descent)

- On line 22, mark the percent of the population that was black Africans. (70 percent)

- Go to line 24. Mark the subject of the first sentence. (These laws) Draw a line from the subject to the descriptive noun in the previous paragraph. (Apartheid laws)

- On the same line, mark the synonym for *affected*. (touched)

- Go to line 25. Mark three places the apartheid laws kept nonwhites from going. (white schools, hospitals, white beaches)

- Go to line 28. Mark three things "pass books" contained. (fingerprints, photo, personal information)

- Underline the part of *pass books* that tells what they allowed black Africans to do. (pass)

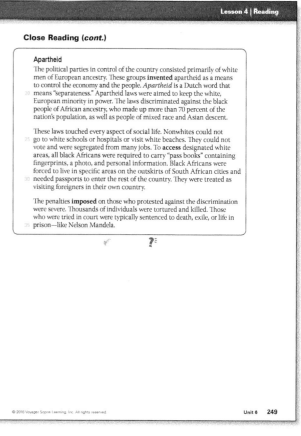

Close Reading (*cont.*)

Apartheid

The political parties in control of the country consisted primarily of white men of European ancestry. These groups **invented** apartheid as a means to control the economy and the people. *Apartheid* is a Dutch word that
20 means "separateness." Apartheid laws were aimed to keep the white, European minority in power. The laws discriminated against the black people of African ancestry, who made up more than 70 percent of the nation's population, as well as people of mixed race and Asian descent.

These laws touched every aspect of social life. Nonwhites could not
25 go to white schools or hospitals or visit white beaches. They could not vote and were segregated from many jobs. To **access** designated white areas, all black Africans were required to carry "pass books" containing fingerprints, a photo, and personal information. Black Africans were forced to live in specific areas on the outskirts of South African cities and
30 needed passports to enter the rest of the country. They were treated as visiting foreigners in their own country.

The penalties **imposed** on those who protested against the discrimination were severe. Thousands of individuals were tortured and killed. Those who were tried in court were typically sentenced to death, exile, or life in
35 prison—like Nelson Mandela.

Unit 6 249

- Go to line 29. Mark where black Africans were forced to live. **(outskirts of South African cities)**
- Go to line 30. Mark the documentation needed by all travelers to enter another country. **(passport)** Do you need a passport to visit another city in your state or another state in your country? Write your answer in the margin. **(no)**
- Go to line 32. Mark the clause that clarifies who "those" were. **(who protested against the discrimination)**
- Go to line 34. Mark the clause that clarifies who "those" were. **(who were tried in court)**
- In the same sentence, number the three possible sentences for protesters. **(1. death, 2. exile, 3. life in prison)** Mark the penalty that means "kicked out of your country and forbidden to return." **(exile)** Circle the option you would prefer.

Have students read the section A Means to an End according to the option that you chose.

When most of the students are finished, continue with the entire class. Let's see how well you understood what you read.

- Circle the check mark or the question mark for this section. Draw a question mark over any confusing words.

- Go to line 36. Mark what happened to Mandela's father. (**died of lung disease**)

- Go to line 37. Mark who adopted Mandela. (**tribal chief**)

- Go to lines 38 and 39. Mark two things Mandela learned from visiting elders. (**African history; how the African people had lived in relative peace**)

- Go to line 41. Mark a synonym for *destroyed*. (**shattered**)

- Go to lines 42 and 43. Mark the verb that tells what the black man did and the verb that tells what the white man did. (**shared; took**)

- On line 43, mark the reflexive pronoun used because the subject of the clause, *the white man,* could not be reused as the object of the preposition. (**himself**)

- Go to line 44. Mark what Mandela did at age 16. (**heard a tribal elder speak with great sadness**)

- On line 48, mark the reflexive pronoun used because the object is the same as the subject of the clause. (**themselves**)

- Go to lines 48 and 49. Mark how the elder's words affected Mandela. (**profoundly impacted Mandela and set the course for his life of activism**)

- Go to line 51. Mark the kind of school Mandela enrolled in. (**law school**) Go to the beginning of the sentence and mark when he enrolled. (**After years of performing well at various schools**)

- Go to lines 52 and 53. Mark four things Mandela was exposed to. (**liberal and Africanist thought, racism, discrimination**)

- Go to lines 53 and 54. Mark what was fueled. (**passion for politics**)

- Go to line 54. Mark what Mandela joined. (**the African National Congress**) Mark his reason for joining. (**to become a voice for those who didn't have one**)

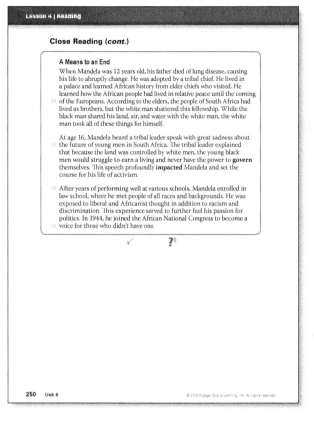

Close Reading (cont.)

A Means to an End

When Mandela was 12 years old, his father died of lung disease, causing his life to abruptly change. He was adopted by a tribal chief. He lived in a palace and learned African history from elder chiefs who visited. He learned how the African people had lived in relative peace until the coming of the Europeans. According to the elders, the people of South Africa had lived as brothers, but the white man shattered this fellowship. While the black man shared his land, air, and water with the white man, the white man took all of these things for himself.

At age 16, Mandela heard a tribal leader speak with great sadness about the future of young men in South Africa. The tribal leader explained that because the land was controlled by white men, the young black men would struggle to earn a living and never have the power to **govern** themselves. This speech profoundly **impacted** Mandela and set the course for his life of activism.

After years of performing well at various schools, Mandela enrolled in law school, where he met people of all races and backgrounds. He was exposed to liberal and Africanist thought in addition to racism and discrimination. This experience served to further fuel his passion for politics. In 1944, he joined the African National Congress to become a voice for those who didn't have one.

Have students read the section Mandela Challenges the Apartheid Government according to the option that you chose.

When most of the students are finished, continue with the entire class. Let's see how well you understood what you read.

- Circle the check mark or the question mark for this section. Draw a question mark over any confusing words.

- Go to line 57. Mark the abbreviation used to represent the African National Congress. (ANC) Mark what the ANC staged, or organized. (a campaign against apartheid laws)

- Go back to line 56. Underline when they staged the campaign. (as more and more laws were passed)

- Go to line 58. Mark the synonym for *idea*. (theory)

- In the same line, mark the phrase that means "fighting against something through non-violent means." (passive resistance)

- In the same paragraph, mark four phrases that tell what Mandela did. (opened a law practice, campaigned against apartheid, was charged with high treason, continued his important mission)

- Go to line 62. Mark the phrase that indicates something else happened at the same time. (as did)

- In the same sentence, mark the synonym for *keep up* or *preserve*. (maintain)

- Go to line 64. Mark what continued to grow. (tension)

- Go to line 65. Mark what happened in 1960. (69 black people were shot dead by police)

- Go to line 66. Mark what the government banned. (the ANC)

- Mark what the ANC did in response. (abandoned its policy of non-violence)

- Circle the word that is similar to peace. (non-violence) Draw an arrow from this word to a synonymous term in the preceding paragraph. (passive resistance)

- Go to line 67. Mark the phrase that means "a struggle with weapons." (armed struggle)

Close Reading (cont.)

Mandela Challenges the Apartheid Government

As more and more laws were passed to limit the progress of black South Africans, the ANC staged a campaign against apartheid laws that was structured around the theory of **passive** resistance. Mandela opened a law practice and campaigned against apartheid. Soon after, Mandela was 60 charged with high treason, but the charges were eventually dropped. Mandela continued his important mission. The resistance to apartheid grew stronger, as did the commitment by the government to maintain white rule.

Tension with the government continued to grow. It peaked in 1960 when 65 69 black people were shot dead by police. The government declared a state of emergency and banned the ANC. In response, the ANC abandoned its policy of non-violence, and Mandela helped lead the armed struggle for freedom.

✓   ?

Unit 6   251

Have students read the sections Imprisonment and Apartheid Ends according to the option that you chose.

When most of the students are finished, continue with the entire class. Let's see how well you understood what you read.

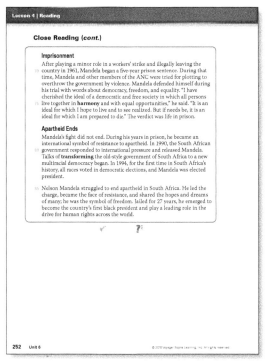

- Circle the check mark or the question mark for this section. Draw a question mark over any confusing words.

- Go to lines 69 and 70. Number the two reasons why Mandela was imprisoned. (1. playing a minor role in a workers' strike; 2. illegally leaving the country)

- Go to lines 70 and 71. Mark the phrase that answers when. (During that time) Draw a line from the phrase to the words in the previous sentence that indicate what time. (five-year prison sentence)

- Go to lines 71 and 72. Mark what Mandela and others were tried for. (plotting to overthrow the government by violence)

- Go to line 72. Mark the reflexive pronoun used because the subject of the sentence is the same as the direct object. (himself)

- Go to line 74. Mark the word that means "perfect thing or situation." (ideal) Mark the ideal Mandela dedicated his life to. (a democratic and free society)

- Go to line 76. Mark the phrase that indicates that what he is about to say is a condition that may or may not happen because it is dependent on something else. (if needs be)

- Go to line 77. Mark what Mandela was prepared to do for this ideal. (die)

- Go to line 79. Mark the word that means "around the world." (international)

- When was Mandela released from prison? Circle the year. (1990)

- Mark what caused his release. (international pressure)

- Go to line 82. Mark the adjective that describes the kind of democracy that came to South Africa. (multiracial) Circle the part of this adjective that means "many." (multi)

- In the next paragraph, mark four phrases that tell what Mandela did. (struggled to end apartheid; led the charge; became the face; shared the hopes and dreams of many)

- What was he the symbol of? Circle the word. (freedom)

- Go to line 88. Mark what Mandela became. (the country's first black president) Circle the word that is a possessive noun. (country's)

- In the final line, mark what Mandela had an effect on around the world. (human rights)

Have partners compare text markings and correct any errors.

Lesson Opener

Before the lesson, choose one of the following activities to write on the board or post on the *LANGUAGE! Live* Class Wall online.

- *Write four sentences with at least two vocabulary words in each. Show you know the meanings. (discrimination, resources, invent, access, impose, govern, impact, passive, harmony, transform)*
- *Write three sentences that describe an action the ANC took to resist apartheid. Answer the following questions in your sentences. What? When? How? Combine the three sentences into one Masterpiece Sentence.*
- *What would you have done if you were a member of the ANC, and the harder you tried to resist apartheid, the stricter the apartheid laws grew? Would you have continued using non-violence? Why or why not?*

Vocabulary

Objective

- Review key passage vocabulary.

Recontextualize Passage Vocabulary

Direct students to page 232 in their Student Books. Use the following questions to review the vocabulary words in "The Symbol of Freedom."

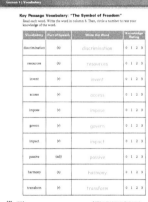

- Your friends will play basketball with anybody, regardless of how good or bad that person's skills are. Do they practice *discrimination*? (no) At one time, women were not allowed to attend universities. Today, would we consider this *discrimination*? (yes) Your little sister won't let anyone over the age of 10 in her bedroom. You consider this what? (discrimination)

- Texas is full of mosquitoes. Are mosquitoes one of its natural *resources*? (no) Texas is also rich in natural gas. Is natural gas one of its *resources*? (yes) Your aunt grows herbs and sells them at a street kiosk. Your aunt's herbs are what? (resources)

- You and your friend make up a complicated hand-slapping routine. Did you *invent* the routine? (yes) You download a photo-editing app. Did you *invent* the app? (no) Alexander Graham Bell thought of and built the first telephone. What did he do? (invented it)

- You need to get in the supply closet for some paper towels, but it's locked. Can you *access* it? (no) You run down the hall and grab paper towels from the restroom instead. Have you *accessed* the restroom? (yes) Your cousin is working backstage at a concert, and she gives you a badge that allows you into the area. You can now what? (access the backstage area)

- A late paper gets docked 10 points. You turn in a paper early. Is the penalty *imposed*? **(no)** Your older brother stayed out too late too many times, and now your mom has given both of you a 9:00 curfew. Has she *imposed* the curfew on you? **(yes)** A new law forbids skateboards on sidewalks. You skateboard everywhere you go. What will happen to you? **(the law will be imposed upon me)**

- Do the elected leaders of a nation *govern* it? **(yes)** Do the players on a team *govern* the team? **(no)** What does a coach do? **(govern the team)**

- Does stormy weather *impact* outdoor events? **(yes)** Does the explosion of a star 6,000 light-years away *impact* your daily life? **(no)** You were going to bake a cake, but you are out of eggs. Having no eggs does what? **(impacts your plan to bake a cake)**

- Your brother is not affected by tickling. When you tickle him, can he remain *passive*? **(yes)** A character on TV plays a prank on another character, and that character plays a prank right back. Was the second character *passive*? **(no)** Your puppy jumps and barks and begs for a treat. You are trying to train him not to do this, so you completely ignore him. You remain what? **(passive)**

- The family next door is constantly bickering and carrying on. Does that family live in a state of *harmony*? **(no)** The triplets agree on everything. They spend all their time together. They love each other. Do they live in *harmony*? **(yes)** You write a poem for a competition. Its last lines go like this: "If we agree to disagree, there'll be peace for you and me." What is your poem about? **(harmony)**

- Your mom is busy turning the ugly balcony into a garden oasis. Is she *transforming* the balcony? **(yes)** You lie on your bed and daydream about ways to improve your life. Are you *transforming* your life? **(no)** Your uncle takes outdated computers and cell phones and turns them into works of art. What does he do to the old hardware? **(transforms it)**

Objectives
- Use text to write coherent paragraphs in response to reading.
- Analyze how ideas and events influence an individual and how an individual influences ideas and events.

Quick Write in Response to Reading

Direct students to page 253 in their Student Books. Read the prompt. Make sure students understand the term *demise*. Encourage them to look back through the text for evidence that most strongly supports their answer before they begin writing.

Quick Write in Response to Reading   Answers will vary.

Nelson Mandela helped end apartheid in South Africa. Write an essay summarizing what apartheid was and how Mandela's activism led to its demise. Include major turning points and events in Mandela's life in sequential order.

When South Africa gained freedom from England, its white rulers created apartheid laws to keep control of the nonwhite population. The apartheid laws prevented nonwhites from entering white-only buildings and areas. Black people were forced to live on the outskirts and carry passports to enter other parts of the country.

As a child, Nelson Mandela learned that South Africa hadn't always been this way. Long ago, Africans had lived in peace. The coming of the white man had shattered this way of life. Mandela decided to devote his life to the cause of regaining his people's freedom. After attending law school, he joined the African National Congress. This group was built on the idea of passive resistance. However, the apartheid laws got tighter and tighter, and the government began using violence to put down the resistance.

The ANC eventually decided to use force too. Mandela and others were imprisoned and tried for attempting to overthrow the government. While on trial, Mandela stated that he had dedicated his life to the ideal of a peaceful, democratic South Africa and was prepared to die for it too. Mandela was imprisoned for 27 years, during which time he became a symbol of resistance and freedom. He was eventually released due to international pressure and, in 1994, became the first democratically elected black president of South Africa.

Objectives

- Self-correct as comprehension of text deepens.
- Answer questions to demonstrate comprehension of text.
- Engage in class discussion.
- Identify the enduring understandings from a piece of text.

Revisit Passage Comprehension

Direct students back to pages 245–247 in their Student Books. Have students review their answers and make any necessary changes. Then, have partners share their answers and collaborate to perfect them.

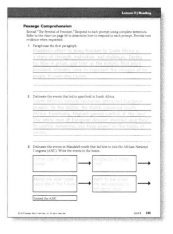

Enduring Understandings

Direct students back to page 231 in their Student Books. Reread the Big Idea questions.

What causes stereotypes and prejudices?

What inspires people to take action?

Generate a class discussion about the questions and the answers students came up with in Lesson 1. Have them consider whether their answers have changed any after reading the text.

Use the following talking points to foster conversation. Refer to the Class Discussion Rules poster and have students use the Collegial Discussion sentence frames on page 382 of their Student Books.

- Where do hatred and fear really come from? Do they come from ignorance? Do they come from experiences? Do they come from outside influences—those trying to make us think or believe in a certain way?

- Do people just wake up one day and decide to do great things? What has to happen in the weeks, months, and years before? Do people do great things just because they are told to do them? What external factors inspire people to take action? What internal factors inspire them? Can change start with one person? Can one person accomplish great things alone?

What we read should make us think. Use our discussion and your thoughts about the text to determine what you will "walk away with." Has it made you think about a personal experience or someone you know? Has your perspective or opinion on a specific topic changed? Do you have any lingering thoughts or questions? Write these ideas as your enduring understandings. What will you take with you from this text?

Discuss the enduring understandings with the class. Then, have students write their enduring understandings from the unit. If time permits, have them post a personal response about their enduring understandings to the online class wall.

Remind students to consider why the author wrote the passage and whether he or she was successful.

Unit 6

Lesson 6

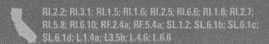
RI.2.2; RI.3.1; RI.1.5; RI.1.6; RI.2.5; RI.6.6; RI.1.8; RI.2.7;
RI.5.8; RI.6.10; RF.2.4a; RF.5.4a; SL.1.2; SL.6.1b; SL.6.1c;
SL.6.1d; L.1.4a; L.3.5b; L.4.6; L.6.6

Lesson Opener

Before the lesson, choose one of the following activities to write on the board or post on the *LANGUAGE! Live* Class Wall online.

- *Imagine you are Nelson Mandela, standing trial for trying to create change in society. What ideal, or hope for the future, would you say you are totally dedicated to? Why?*
- *Describe a time when you felt unfairly judged. What did you do about it?*
- *Write one sentence about a friend who inspires you to be a better person. Write one sentence about a teacher who has inspired you to be a better person. Combine the sentences using a conjunction to create a compound sentence.*

Reading

Objectives

- Determine and discuss the author's purpose.
- Determine and discuss the topic of a text.
- Use text features to preview text.

Passage Introduction

Direct students to page 254 in their Student Books. Discuss the content focus.

Content Focus

Nelson Mandela's trial statement

After reading about Nelson Mandela in the first half of this unit, we are now going to hear from Mandela himself. We are going to hear him describe his work for the cause of freedom in South Africa. Before we read this text, what questions do you have about what we read in the text "The Symbol of Freedom"? Record questions on the board. Revisit questions after reading the text to see if they were answered. Assign unanswered questions for further discovery if time permits.

Type of Text

informational—speech

A speech is a work of nonfiction. It is spoken by a real person, in a real situation, and includes true information. The speaker in the text we are about to read is Nelson Mandela. Who is speaking in this text? (**Nelson Mandela**) Because Mandela himself is the speaker and author of the text, what is this point of view called? (**first-person point of view**) What words convey it in the text? (*I, myself, me,* and *we*)

Lesson 6 | Reading

Let's Focus: "I Am Prepared to Die"

Content Focus	Type of Text
Nelson Mandela's trial statement	informational—speech

Author's Name Nelson Mandela

Author's Purpose to defend and persuade

Big Ideas
Consider the following Big Idea questions. Write your answer for each question.

What is worth dying for? Do you think you could ever let it happen?

_____

_____

When, and for what reasons, is violence justified?

_____

_____

Speech Preview: "I Am Prepared to Die" on pages 257–268.

- ☐ Title: What clue does it provide about the passage?
- ☐ Pictures: What additional information is added here?
- ☐ Epigraph: What do you know from reading this?

Predict what tone of voice Mandela will use in his speech.

_____

_____

Enduring Understandings
After reading the text . . .

_____

_____

_____

_____

254   Unit 6   © 2016 Voyager Sopris Learning, Inc. All rights reserved

---

Is a speech a work of fiction or nonfiction? (nonfiction) Does it include information about real events? (yes) When the speaker in a text refers to him- or herself using *I* or *me*, we say the text is written in what point of view? (first person)

Author's Purpose

This text was spoken aloud by Mandela at his trial in 1964. It was later transcribed, or written down. Like other authors' texts, Mandela's speech has a purpose. One purpose of nonfiction texts is to give information—and Mandela's speech does that. What other purpose might the speech have? Remember, he gave the speech while he was on trial. **Provide sharing time.** In addition to giving information, Mandela's speech was given to explain and defend his actions. He wanted to convince his audience—the judge—that his actions were justified, or made sense, given the circumstances.

Have students write the answers on the page.

Public Speaking Strategies

When speakers are trying to persuade an audience to take action or agree with certain ideas, they use strategies. They might speak forcefully, or they might speak softly. They might directly state their central idea, or they might lead the audience toward it indirectly. They sometimes give powerful evidence, or facts and figures. They sometimes use figurative language, or word pictures. They sometimes repeat words or phrases to make an impression or a point. They might also use aphorisms, or memorable phrases. These are all valid, or honest and effective, strategies. **Direct students to page 255 in their Student Books. Review the first six strategies listed in the chart.**

Point out the seventh strategy. In their attempt to persuade, however, speakers can also use errors in logic called fallacies. They hope by "fudging" a point, they will sway the audience's thinking.

Review the fallacies listed in the second chart.

If you pay attention while you listen to news or talk shows, you'll hear people using these fallacies all the time. As we read "I Am Prepared to Die," we'll watch to see whether Mandela uses any of the strategies or fallacies we've identified.

Direct students to page 254 in their Student Books. Read the Big Idea questions aloud.

> ## Big Ideas
>
> What is worth dying for? Do you think you could ever let it happen?
>
> When, and for what reasons, is violence justified?

As a class, consider the two Big Idea questions.

- Encourage students with limited concept of martyrdom and examples of justified violence to ask for further explanation from peers.

- Provide opportunities for students to explain their ideas and answers to the Big Idea questions in light of the discussion by ensuring students follow the rules for class discussion, which can be printed in poster form from the Teacher Resources online.

- Suggest students refer to the Collegial Discussion sentence frames in the back of their books.

- Encourage speakers to link comments to the remarks of others to keep the focus of the discussion and create cohesion, even when their comments are in disagreement.

After discussing each question, have students write an answer. We'll come back to these questions after we finish reading the text. You can add to your answers as you gain information and perspective.

Preview

Read the Preview Checklist on page 254. Follow the Preview Procedure outlined below.

Preview Procedure
- Group students with partners or in triads.
- Have students count off as 1s or 2s. The 1s will become the student leaders. If working with triads, the third students become 3s.
- The student leaders will preview the text in addition to managing the checklist and pacing.
- The 2s and 3s will preview the text with 1s.
- Direct 1s to open their Student Books to page 254 and 2s and 3s to open their Student Books to page 257. This allows students to look at a few different pages at one time without turning back and forth.

Direct students to page 257. If necessary, guide students through a preview of the pictures and captions on pages 257–268. Then, read the prediction prompt on page 254. Tell students that tone is the feeling or attitude a speaker's words express. Have students make a prediction.

Vocabulary

Objectives
- Evaluate word knowledge.
- Determine the meaning of key passage vocabulary.

Rate Vocabulary Knowledge

Direct students to page 256 in their Student Books.

Before we read the text, let's take a look at the vocabulary words that appear in this speech. Remind students that as you read each word in the first column aloud, they will write the word in the third column and then rate their knowledge of it. Display the Vocabulary Rating Scale poster or write the information on the board. Review the meaning of each rating.

Lesson 6 | Vocabulary

Key Passage Vocabulary: "I Am Prepared to Die"

Read each word. Write the word in column 3. Then, circle a number to rate your knowledge of the word.

Vocabulary	Part of Speech	Write the Word	Knowledge Rating
contribution	(n)	contribution	0 1 2 3
exploitation	(n)	exploitation	0 1 2 3
defy	(v)	defy	0 1 2 3
suspend	(v)	suspend	0 1 2 3
policy	(n)	policy	0 1 2 3
massive	(adj)	massive	0 1 2 3
prospect	(n)	prospect	0 1 2 3
legacy	(n)	legacy	0 1 2 3
hamper	(v)	hamper	0 1 2 3
irrelevant	(adj)	irrelevant	0 1 2 3

Vocabulary Rating Scale

0—I have never heard the word before.

1—I have heard the word, but I'm not sure how to use it.

2—I am familiar with the word, but I'm not sure if I know the correct meaning.

3—I know the meaning of the word and can use it correctly in a sentence.

The points are not a grade; they are just there to help you know which words you need to focus on. By the end of this unit, you should be able to change all your ratings to a 3. That's the goal.

Read each word aloud. Have students repeat it, write it, and rate it. Then, ask volunteers who rated a word *2* or *3* to use the word in an oral sentence.

Preteach Vocabulary

Let's take a closer look at the words. Follow the Preteach Procedure below.

Preteach Procedure

This activity is intended to take only a short amount of time, so make it an oral exercise.

- Introduce each word as indicated on the word card.
- Read the definition and example sentences.
- Ask questions to clarify and deepen understanding.
- If time permits, allow students to share.

* If your students would benefit from copying the definitions, please have them do so in the vocabulary log in the back of the Student Books using the margin definitions in the passage selections. This should be done outside of instruction time.

---

contribution (n)

Let's read the first word together. *Contribution.*

Definition: A *contribution* is something given in support of an effort or cause. What word means "something given in support of an effort or cause"? (contribution)

Example 1: The Nobel Peace Prize is given to people who make a significant *contribution* to world peace.

Example 2: The pet shelter is asking for *contributions* of blankets and pet food.

Example 3: Soup kitchens and food pantries rely on *contributions* of canned goods.

Question 1: Your group leader asks for ideas, but you are too shy to offer any. Have you made a *contribution*? Yes or no? (no)

Question 2: You read your friend's paper and make several suggestions for improvements. She gets an A on the paper. Did you make a *contribution*? Yes or no? (yes)

Pair Share: Turn to your partner and tell how you could make a *contribution* to world peace today.

exploitation (n)

Let's read the next word together. *Exploitation.*

Definition: *Exploitation* is the act of using someone for your own selfish gain. What word means "the act of using someone for your own selfish gain"? (exploitation)

Example 1: Companies that own factories in very poor countries and pay workers very low wages are sometimes accused of *exploitation*.

Example 2: Dating someone who is popular only to be popular yourself is a form of *exploitation*.

Example 3: You make your little brother clean your room in exchange for a nickel. He is only five, so he thinks this is a good deal. This is *exploitation*.

Question 1: You enjoy doing people's hair. You help your cousin do her hair for a big dance. Is this *exploitation*? Yes or no? (no)

Question 2: You agree to babysit your neighbors' child because you know they have good snacks and satellite TV. You put the child to bed an hour early and invite friends over. Is this *exploitation*? Yes or no? (yes)

Pair Share: You make friends with someone just so she can help you get an A in algebra, but you end up really liking her. Is this *exploitation*? Tell your partner why or why not.

defy (v)

Let's read the next word together. *Defy.*

Definition: To *defy* means "to boldly resist; to challenge." What means "to boldly resist; to challenge"? (defy)

Example 1: If you break the dress code on purpose, you are *defying* it.

Example 2: The Civil Rights movement succeeded because thousands of people were willing to take risks and *defy* laws that they believed were unfair.

Example 3: You command your dog to sit. He jumps up, even though he knows better. He is *defying* your command.

Question 1: Every time your mother asks you to do something, you say no. Are you *defying* her? Yes or no? (yes)

Question 2: Your conscience tells you to apologize for a rude comment. You do. Have you *defied* your conscience? Yes or no? (no)

Pair Share: Recently, a law was passed that banned the eating of chocolate. Will you *defy* this law? Why or why not? Tell your partner.

(3)

suspend (v)

Let's read the next word together. *Suspend.*

Definition: *Suspend* means "to put off or do away with." What means "to put off or do away with"? (suspend)

Example 1: If an athlete is hurt on the field, play will be *suspended* until he or she is checked out and taken care of.

Example 2: Community programs are sometimes *suspended* if money is short or volunteer participation is low.

Example 3: A session of Congress may be *suspended* if an agreement cannot be reached.

Question 1: Even though it's sprinkling, the parade will go on. Has the parade been *suspended*? Yes or no? (no)

Question 2: The jury cannot make a decision. They decide to go home for the night and meet again tomorrow. Have their deliberations been *suspended*? Yes or no? (yes)

Pair Share: Turn to your partner and tell about a time a game, a play, a concert, or another event you were involved in was *suspended*, and why. If you can't think of one, make something up.

(4)

policy (n)

Let's read the next word together. *Policy.*

Definition: A *policy* is a rule or a stated way of doing things. What word means "a rule; a way of doing things"? (policy)

Example 1: My *policy* in this classroom is that if you want to speak, you must raise your hand.

Example 2: It is the *policy* of many stores to give a refund for a purchase only if you have your receipt.

Example 3: Many Americans support *policies* that protect animals.

Question 1: A club you belong to can't really decide on its membership rules. Does it have a firm membership *policy*? Yes or no? (no)

Question 2: Your bus driver requires anyone who stands up while the bus is in motion to sing three rounds of "Row, Row, Row Your Boat." Is this your bus driver's *policy*? Yes or no? (yes)

Pair Share: Turn to your partner and name one school *policy* you wish you could change.

(5)

massive (adj)

Let's read the next word together. *Massive.*

Definition: If something is *massive*, it is huge or on a very large scale. What word means "huge; on a very large scale"? (massive)

Example 1: It takes a lot of money to launch a *massive* political campaign.

Example 2: Poverty is a *massive* problem that will take many creative minds to solve.

Example 3: Social media can turn a small complaint into a *massive* national movement for change.

Question 1: You see gigantic thunderclouds forming on the horizon. Are they *massive*? Yes or no? (yes)

Question 2: You notice a fleck of parsley in your teacher's teeth. Is the parsley *massive*? Yes or no? (no)

Pair Share: You are directing a science fiction movie. In one scene, people walk out their front doors and see something *massive* in the sky. Describe what they see to your partner.

(6)

prospect (n)

Let's read the next word together. *Prospect*.

Definition: A *prospect* is a possibility that something will happen soon. What word means "a possibility that something will happen soon"? (prospect)

Example 1: If you are the only person running for office, your *prospects* for winning are very good.

Example 2: After the financial crisis of 2008, many people's job *prospects* disappeared.

Example 3: Long ago, if a woman had no marriage *prospects* by the age of 25, she started to worry.

Question 1: At the basketball tryout, you miss every shot, foul five people, and yell at the volunteer referee. Are you *prospects* good for making the team? Yes or no? (no)

Question 2: You and a friend are tired of arguing. You miss being friends. Are your *prospects* good for making up? Yes or no? (yes)

Pair Share: You are an astronaut lost in space. The only way you can get back home is to solve a complicated mathematical formula. How strong are your *prospects*? Tell your partner why.

legacy (n)

Let's read the next word together. *Legacy*.

Definition: A *legacy* is something passed down from earlier people or times. What means "something passed down from earlier people or times"? (legacy)

Example 1: If a school's team always wins, that school has a *legacy* of victory and pride.

Example 2: If your grandparents died poor but left you hundreds of happy memories, you could say they left you a *legacy* of love.

Example 3: In many ways, the *legacy* of racial discrimination still haunts our society.

Question 1: You receive an invitation to a party. Is this a *legacy*? Yes or no? (no)

Question 2: For generations, women in your family have been described as strong and opinionated. Could this be considered a *legacy*? Yes or no? (yes)

Pair Share: Turn to your partner and tell what *legacy* you hope to leave behind for future generations.

hamper (v)

Let's read the next word together. *Hamper*.

Definition: To *hamper* is to make it hard for someone to do something. What word means "to make it hard for someone to do something"? (hamper)

Example 1: Windy weather can *hamper* the efforts of firefighters battling a forest fire.

Example 2: Wearing gloves can *hamper* your ability to use your smartphone.

Example 3: Travelers are sometimes *hampered* by delayed flights.

Question 1: You are on a relay team. Your teammate smoothly hands you the baton. Does the hand-off *hamper* your running? Yes or no? (no)

Question 2: Music is blaring outside your window. Does it *hamper* your ability to sleep? Yes or no? (yes)

Pair Share: Turn to your partner and tell about a time you were trying to get somewhere but were *hampered*.

(9)

irrelevant (adj)

Let's read the last word together. *Irrelevant*.

Definition: If something is *irrelevant*, it is unrelated or beside the point. What word means "unrelated; beside the point"? (irrelevant) Something that *is* related is *relevant*. Add the prefix ir- (meaning "not") and you get *irrelevant*, or not related.

Example 1: Math skills are usually *irrelevant* in a language arts classroom, but grammar skills are completely relevant.

Example 2: When a witness in a court case is shown to have lied, his or her testimony becomes *irrelevant*.

Example 3: Your teacher asks the class to write reports on weather types. You write a report on World War II. Your report is *irrelevant*.

Question 1: You know how to solve a problem, and so you speak up. Is your input *irrelevant*? Yes or no? (no)

Question 2: Your friend asks, "Does this outfit look good?" You answer, "It's Tuesday!" Is your answer *irrelevant*? Yes or no? (yes)

Pair Share: Turn to your partner and ask the first question you think of. Give each other an *irrelevant* answer.

(10)

Objectives

- Read a persuasive speech.
- Monitor comprehension during text reading.

"I Am Prepared to Die"

Direct students to page 257 in their Student Books.

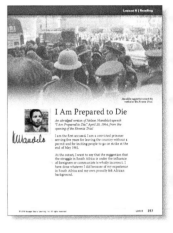

Now that we have previewed vocabulary, it's time to read. Remember, the text is written in first-person point of view. Only one person is speaking in the text.

Guiding Students Toward Independent Reading

It is important that your students read as much and as often as they can. Assign readings that meet the needs of your students, based on your observations and data. This is a good opportunity to stretch your students. If students become frustrated, scaffold the reading with paired reading, choral reading, or a read-aloud.

Options for reading text:

- Teacher read-aloud
- Teacher-led or student-led choral read
- Paired read or independent read

Choose an option for reading text. Students read according to the option that you chose. Review the purpose of the numbered squares in the text and prompt students to stop periodically and check comprehension.

If you choose to read the text aloud or chorally, use the text boxes on the following pages and stop to ask questions and have students answer them.

"Nelson Mandela" audio file

Due to the difficult nature of the text, a complete audio recording is in the online resources. If you feel students would benefit from hearing the text—as it was delivered—prior to reading, play the audio file and have students follow along in their Student Books.

p. 257,
paragraphs 1–3

An abridged version of Nelson Mandela's speech "I Am Prepared to Die," April 20, 1964, from the opening of the Rivonia Trial

I am the first accused. I am a convicted prisoner serving five years for leaving the country without a permit and for inciting people to go on strike at the end of May 1961.

At the outset, I want to say that the suggestion that the struggle in South Africa is under the influence of foreigners or communists is wholly incorrect. I have done whatever I did because of my experience in South Africa and my own proudly felt African background.

p. 258,
paragraphs 1–3

In my youth, I listened to the elders of my tribe telling stories of wars fought by our ancestors in defense of the fatherland. I hoped then that life might offer me the opportunity to serve my people and make my own humble **contribution** to their freedom struggle.

Some of the things so far told to the court are true and some are untrue. I do not, however, deny that I planned sabotage. I did not plan it in a spirit of recklessness, nor because I love violence. I planned it as a result of a calm assessment of the political situation that had arisen after many years of tyranny, **exploitation**, and oppression of my people by the whites.

I admit that I was one of the persons who helped to form Umkhonto we Sizwe. I deny that Umkhonto was responsible for a number of acts which have been charged in the indictment against us. We felt that without sabotage there would be no way open to the African people to succeed in their struggle against white supremacy. All lawful modes of expressing opposition had been closed by legislation, and we were placed in a position in which we had either to accept permanent inferiority or to **defy** the government. We chose to defy the government.

1. What does Mandela admit he helped to plan? What reasons does he give for this?

SF p. 258,
paragraphs 4–5

We first broke the law in a way which avoided violence; when this form was legislated against, and the government resorted to a show of force to crush opposition, only then did we decide to answer violence with violence. But the violence we chose was not terrorism. We who formed Umkhonto were all members of the African National Congress and had behind us the ANC tradition of non-violence.

The African National Congress was formed in 1912 to defend the rights of the African people, which had been seriously curtailed. For 37 years—that is, until 1949—it adhered strictly to a constitutional struggle. It put forward demands and resolutions; | it sent delegations to the government in the belief that African grievances could be settled through peaceful discussion. But white governments remained unmoved, and the rights of Africans became less instead of becoming greater.

page break

SE p. 259, paragraph 1

Even after 1949, the ANC remained determined to avoid violence. At this time, however, a decision was taken to protest against apartheid by peaceful, but unlawful, demonstrations. More than 8,500 people went to jail. Yet there was not a single instance of violence. I and nineteen colleagues were convicted, but our sentences were **suspended** mainly because the judge found that discipline and non-violence had been stressed throughout.

2. The ANC was determined not to use what?

SE p. 259,
paragraphs 2–3

During the defiance campaign, the Public Safety Act and the Criminal Law Amendment Act were passed. These provided harsher penalties for offenses against the laws. Despite this, the protests continued and the ANC adhered to its **policy** of non-violence.

In 1956, 156 leading members of the Congress Alliance, including myself, were arrested. When the court gave judgment some five years later, it found that the ANC did not have a policy of violence. We were acquitted.

SE p. 260, paragraph 1

In 1960, there was the shooting at Sharpeville, which resulted in the declaration of the ANC as unlawful.* My colleagues and I, after careful consideration, decided that we would not obey this decree. The African people were not part of the government and did not make the laws by which they were governed. We believed the words of the Universal Declaration of Human Rights, that "the will of the people shall be the basis of authority of the government." The ANC refused to dissolve but instead went underground.

3. What did the government declare the ANC to be? How did the ANC respond?

SE p. 260
paragraphs 2–3

The government held a referendum which led to the establishment of the republic. Africans, who constituted approximately 70 percent of the population, were not entitled to vote. I undertook to be responsible for organizing the national stay-at-home called to coincide with the declaration of the republic. The stay-at-home was to be a peaceful demonstration. Careful instructions were given to avoid any recourse to violence.

The government's answer was to introduce new and harsher laws, to mobilize its armed forces, and to send armed vehicles into the townships in a **massive** show of force. The government had decided to rule by force alone, and this decision was a milestone on the road to Umkhonto.

4. What was the government's answer to the stay-at-home strike organized by Mandela?

SE p. 260,
paragraphs 4–5

What were we, the leaders of our people, to do? We had to continue the fight. Anything else would have been surrender. Our problem was not whether to fight, but was how to continue the fight.

By this time, violence had become a feature of the South African political scene. There had been violence in 1957 when the women of Zeerust were ordered to carry passes; there was violence in 1958 with the enforcement of cattle culling in Sekhukhuneland; there was violence in 1959 when the people of Cato Manor protested against pass raids; there was violence in 1960 when the government attempted to impose Bantu authorities in Pondoland. Each disturbance pointed to the growth among Africans of the belief that violence | was the only way out. A government which uses force to maintain its rule teaches the oppressed to use force to oppose it.

page break

SE p. 261, paragraph 1

I came to the conclusion that as violence was inevitable, it would be unrealistic to continue preaching peace and non-violence. This conclusion was not easily arrived at. It was only when all channels of peaceful protest had been barred that the decision was made to embark on violent forms of struggle. I can only say that I felt morally obliged to do what I did.

5. Why did Mandela stop preaching peace and non-violence?

SE p. 261, paragraph 2

Four forms of violence are possible. There is sabotage, there is guerrilla warfare, there is terrorism, and there is open revolution. We chose to adopt the first. Sabotage did not involve loss of life, and it offered the best hope for future race relations.

SE p. 262, paragraph 1

The initial plan was based on a careful analysis of the political and economic situation of our country. We believed that South Africa depended to a large extent on foreign capital. We felt that planned destruction of power plants, and interference with rail and telephone communications, would scare away capital from the country, thus compelling the voters of the country to reconsider their position. The selection of targets is proof of this policy. Had we intended to attack life, we would have selected targets where people congregated and not empty buildings and power stations.

6. Why did the ANC decide that sabotage was the form of violence they should use?

SE p. 262, paragraphs 2–4

The whites failed to respond by suggesting change; they responded to our call by suggesting the laager. In contrast, the response of the Africans was one of encouragement. Suddenly, there was hope again. People began to speculate on how soon freedom would be obtained.

But we in Umkhonto weighed the white response with anxiety. The lines were being drawn. The whites and blacks were moving into separate camps, and the **prospects** of avoiding a civil war were made less. The white newspapers carried reports that sabotage would be punished by death.

We felt it our duty to make preparations to use force in order to defend ourselves against force. We decided, therefore, to make provision for the possibility of guerrilla warfare. All whites undergo compulsory military training, but no such training was given to Africans. It was in our view essential to build up a nucleus of trained men who would be able to provide the leadership if guerrilla warfare started.

7. What seemed inevitable, or likely to happen? How did Mandela's group prepare for this?

E p. 262, paragraph 5

At this stage, the ANC decided that I should attend the Conference of the Pan-African Freedom Movement, which was to be held in 1962. After the conference, I would take a tour of the African states with a view to whether facilities were

age break

available for the training of soldiers. My tour was successful. | Wherever I went, I met sympathy for our cause and promises of help. All Africa was united against the stand of white South Africa.

E p. 263, paragraph 1

I started to make a study of the art of war and revolution and, while abroad, underwent a course in military training. If there was to be guerrilla warfare, I wanted to be able to fight with my people. On my return, I found that there had been little alteration in the political scene save that the threat of a death penalty for sabotage had now become a fact.

8. What did Mandela learn during his tour of the African states? What did he learn on his return home?

E p. 263,
aragraphs 2–3

Another of the allegations made by the state is that the aims and objects of the ANC and the Communist Party are the same. The allegation is false. The creed of the ANC is, and always has been, the creed of freedom and fulfillment for the African people in their own land. The most important document ever adopted by the ANC is the Freedom Charter. It is by no means a blueprint for a socialist state. It calls for redistribution, but not nationalization, of land; it provides for nationalization of mines, banks, and monopoly industry because big monopolies are owned by one race only, and without such nationalization racial domination would be perpetuated. Under the Freedom Charter, nationalization would take place in an economy based on private enterprise. The realization of the Freedom Charter would open up fresh fields for a prosperous African population.

As far as the Communist Party is concerned, and if I understand its policy correctly, it stands for the establishment of a state based on the principles of Marxism. The Communist Party's main aim was to remove the capitalists and to replace them with a working-class government. The Communist Party sought to emphasize class distinctions while the ANC seeks to harmonize them. This is a vital distinction.

9. How is the ANC different from the Communist Party? (Remember, *harmony* means "all parts working together.")

SE p. 264,
paragraphs 1–2

It is true that there has often been close cooperation between the ANC and the Communist Party. But cooperation is merely proof of a common goal—in this case, the removal of white supremacy—and is not proof of a complete community of interests. The history of the world is full of similar examples. Perhaps the most striking is the cooperation between Great Britain, the United States, and the Soviet Union in the fight against Hitler. Nobody but Hitler would have dared to suggest that such cooperation turned Churchill or Roosevelt into communists.

What is more, for many decades communists were the only political group in South Africa prepared to treat Africans as human beings and their equals; who were prepared to eat with us, talk with us, and work with us. They were the only group prepared to work with the Africans for the attainment of political rights.

10. Why did the ANC choose to work with the Communist Party? Give two reasons.

SE p. 264,
paragraphs 3–5

Because of this, many Africans today tend to equate freedom with communism. They are supported in this belief by a legislature which brands all exponents of democratic government and African freedom as communists and banned many of them under the Suppression of Communism Act. Although I have never been a member of the Communist Party, I myself have been convicted under that act.

I have always regarded myself, in the first place, as an African patriot. Today, I am attracted by the idea of a classless society, an attraction which springs in part from my admiration of the structure of early African societies. The land belonged to the tribe. There were no rich or poor, and there was no exploitation.

I and many leaders of the new independent states accept the need for some form of socialism to enable our people to catch up with the advanced countries of this world and to overcome their **legacy** of extreme poverty. But this does not mean we are Marxists.

11. Why do Mandela and his colleagues think some form of socialism—redistribution of wealth—is needed?

p. 265, paragraphs 1–2

Our fight is against real and not imaginary hardships or, to use the language of the state prosecutor, "so-called hardships." Basically, we fight against two features of African life in South Africa: poverty and lack of human dignity. We do not need communists to teach us about these things.

South Africa is the richest country in Africa. But it is a land of remarkable contrasts. The whites enjoy the highest standard of living, while Africans live in poverty and misery. The complaint of Africans, however, is not only that they are poor and the whites are rich, but that the laws are designed to preserve this situation.

12. What is the main complaint of black Africans?

p. 265, paragraphs 3–5

There are two ways to break out of poverty. The first is by formal education, and the second is by the worker acquiring a greater skill at his work and thus higher wages. As far as Africans are concerned, both these avenues of advancement are deliberately curtailed by legislation.

The government has always sought to **hamper** Africans in their search for education. There is compulsory education for all white children at virtually no cost to their parents. But approximately 40 percent of African children between seven and fourteen do not attend school. For those who do, the standards are vastly different from those afforded to white children.

The other main obstacle to the advancement of the African is the industrial color bar under which all the better jobs of industry are reserved for whites. Moreover, Africans in the unskilled and semi-skilled occupations are not allowed to form trade unions. This means that they are denied the right of collective bargaining permitted to white workers.

13. How does the African government hamper blacks' opportunities for advancement?

*SE p. 266,
paragraphs 1–2*

The government answers its critics by saying that Africans in South Africa are better off than inhabitants of other countries in Africa. Even if this statement is true, it is **irrelevant**. Our complaint is not that we are poor by comparison with people in other countries, but that we are poor by comparison with the white people in our own country, and that we are prevented by legislation from altering this imbalance.

The lack of human dignity experienced by Africans is the direct result of the policy of white supremacy. White supremacy implies black inferiority. Legislation designed to preserve white supremacy entrenches this notion. Menial tasks in South Africa are invariably performed by Africans. When anything has to be carried or cleaned, the white man will look around for an African to do it for him. Because of this sort of attitude, whites tend to regard Africans as a separate breed. They do not look upon them as people with families of their own; they do not realize that we fall in love, that we want to be with our wives and children, that we want to earn enough money to support our families properly.

14. How do whites view black Africans? Why?

SE p. 266, paragraph 3

Poverty and the breakdown of family have secondary effects. Children wander the streets because they have no schools to go to, or no parents at home to see that they go, because both parents, if there be two, have to work to keep the family alive. This leads to a breakdown in moral standards, to an alarming rise in illegitimacy, and to violence. Not a day goes by without somebody being stabbed or assaulted. And violence is carried out of the townships into the white living areas. People are afraid to walk the streets after dark. Housebreakings and robberies are increasing, despite the fact that the death sentence can now be imposed for such offences. Death sentences cannot cure the festering sore.

15. What are some secondary effects of poverty?

SE p. 266, paragraph 4

page break

The only cure is to alter the conditions under which Africans are forced to live. Africans want to be paid a living wage. Africans want to perform work which they are capable of doing. We want to be allowed | to own land. We want to be part of the general population and not confined to ghettoes. We want to be allowed out after eleven o'clock at night and not to be confined to our rooms like children. We want to be allowed to travel in our own country. We want security and a stake in society.

SE p. 267, paragraphs 1–2

Above all, we want equal political rights because without them, our disabilities will be permanent. I know this sounds revolutionary to the whites in this country because the majority of voters will be Africans. This makes the white man fear democracy.

But this fear cannot be allowed to stand in the way of the only solution which will guarantee racial harmony and freedom for all. It is not true that the enfranchisement of all will result in racial domination. Political division, based on color, is entirely artificial. When it disappears, so will the domination of one color group by another. The ANC has spent half a century fighting against racialism. When it triumphs, it will not change that policy.

16. What do black South Africans want, above all? Why do white South Africans fear this?

SE p. 268, paragraph 1

Our struggle is a national one. It is a struggle of the African people, inspired by our own suffering and our own experience. It is a struggle for the right to live. During my lifetime, I have dedicated myself to this struggle. I have fought against white domination, and I have fought against black domination. I have cherished the ideal of a democratic and free society in which all persons live together in harmony and with equal opportunities. It is an ideal for which I hope to live and to see realized. But if needs be, it is an ideal for which I am prepared to die.

17. For what is Nelson Mandela prepared to die?

For confirmation of engagement, have students discuss at least two things Mandela used as reason for his actions. Have volunteers share reasons with the class.

Lesson Opener

Before the lesson, choose one of the following activities to write on the board or post on the *LANGUAGE! Live* Class Wall online.

- *Write a sentence telling why Nelson Mandela is on trial.*
- *Make a list of adjectives describing Mandela's tone of voice in the speech.*
- *Think of a group of people you feel are treated unfairly. Write three sentences in the future progressive tense telling what you will do to support that group.*

Vocabulary

Objective

- Review key passage vocabulary.

Review Passage Vocabulary

Direct students to page 256 in their Student Books. Use the following questions to review the vocabulary words in "I Am Prepared to Die." Have students answer each question using the vocabulary word or indicating its meaning in a complete sentence.

- Nelson Mandela hoped to make a *contribution* to his people's struggle for freedom. What did he hope to do? (He hoped to give something in support of the struggle.) What kind of a *contribution* did he end up making? (He made a major contribution. He gave his time, energy, and ultimately his freedom for the cause.)

- Mandela worked to end the *exploitation* of his people. What did he work to end? (He worked to end the selfish use and abuse of blacks by the whites who ran the country.) Had the *exploitation* of blacks by whites been happening for only a short while? (No, the exploitation of blacks by whites had been happening for generations.)

- Mandela and his colleagues decided to *defy* the government rather than be oppressed, or beaten down. What did they decide to do? (They decided to resist or challenge the government.) Did they plan to *defy* the government by using violence? (No, they decided to resist the government in nonviolent ways.)

Vocabulary Review Note: Remember, *govern* means "to rule; to direct." A *government* does the work of *governing.*

- After a peaceful demonstration, Mandela and some others went to jail. However, the judge *suspended* their sentences. What did the judge do? (He put off or did away with the sentences.) Why did he *suspend* the sentences? (He suspended them because he found that the demonstrations were nonviolent.)

- For Mandela's group, the ANC, non-violence was a *policy*. What was it? (Non-violence was a rule or a way of doing things.) Did the South African government share this *policy*? How so? (No, it did not share this policy. It often responded to the demonstrations with violence.)

- After a national stay-at-home day organized by the ANC, the South African government responded with a *massive* show of military force. Was it a small show of force? (No; if it was a massive show of force, it was a huge or large-scale show of force.) The stay-at-home day was organized to protest the fact that 70 percent of the population could not vote. Was a small portion of the population unable to vote? (No; a massive portion of the population was unable to vote.)

- The ANC thought the *prospects* for civil war were great. Did civil war seem inevitable? (Yes; if the prospects for war were great, war seemed inevitable.) Because war seemed inevitable, the ANC made plans to use sabotage. Sabotage uses attacks on buildings and facilities, not people. With sabotage, were the *prospects* of hurting people great? (No; with sabotage, the prospects for hurting people were small.)

Vocabulary Review Note: Remember, *inevitable* means "expected; hard to keep from happening."

- Mandela's group believed that some form of socialism—redistribution of wealth—was needed to help black people overcome their *legacy* of poverty. Where does a *legacy* come from? (A legacy comes from the past.) What *legacy* did Mandela want to hand on to his fellow South Africans? (He wanted to hand on a legacy of hope and equality.)

- Mandela accused the South African government of *hampering* blacks' search for education. Did the government help educate black people? (No, the government made it difficult for blacks to get an education.) Did the government *hamper* the education of white children? (No, the government made it easy for white children to be educated.)

- The government pointed out that blacks in South Africa were better off than blacks in other African countries. Mandela replied that this fact was *irrelevant*. Did he think it was a valid claim? (No, he thought it was unrelated or beside the point.) Mandela responded that black people in South Africa were poor by comparison with white people there. Did he think this imbalance was *irrelevant*? (No; he believed the imbalance was so important that he was willing to die to change it.)

ssign online practice y opening the Tools enu, then selecting ssignments. Be sure o select the correct lass from the drop- own menu.

Objectives

- Determine how to respond to prompts.
- Use critical thinking skills to write responses to prompts about text.
- Contrast ideas and concepts within a text.
- Support written answers with text evidence.
- Identify evidence used to support an argument.

Critical Understandings: Direction Words *analyze, assess, distinguish, evaluate*

Prompts are statements that require a constructed response, which can range from a list to a complete sentence to a paragraph or an essay. It can be helpful to take prompts and turn them into questions to help them understand what is being asked.

Write the words *analyze, assess, distinguish,* and *evaluate* on the board. Have students read the words aloud with you.

Direct students to page 66 in their Student Books. It is critical to understand what the question is asking and how to answer it. Today, we will look at four direction words used in prompts.

Lesson 8 | Reading

Critical Understandings: Direction Words

Prompt	How to Respond	Model
If the prompt asks you to . . .	The response requires you to . . .	For example . . .
Analyze	break down and evaluate or draw conclusions about the information	**Analyze** the development of the text's central idea.
Assess	decide on the value, impact, or accuracy	**Assess** the level of pressure in an arranged marriage.
Compare	state the similarities between two or more things	**Compare** novels and dramas.
Contrast	state the differences between two or more things	**Contrast** a biography with an autobiography.
Create	make or produce something	**Create** a timeline of events.
Define	tell or write the meaning or definition	**Define** the unknown word using context clues.
Delineate	show or list evidence, claims, ideas, reasons, or events	**Delineate** the evidence in the text.
Describe	state detailed information about a topic	**Describe** the relationship between the plot and character development.
Determine	find out, verify, decide	**Determine** the main idea.
Distinguish	recognize or explain the differences	**Distinguish** between facts and opinions.
Evaluate	think carefully to make a judgment; form a critical opinion of	**Evaluate** the ANC's plan for change.
Explain	express understanding of an idea or concept	**Explain** how the author develops the narrator's point of view.
Identify	say or write what it is	**Identify** the character's motive.
Infer	provide a logical answer using evidence and prior knowledge	Use information from the text to **infer** the value of education.
Interpret	make sense of or assign meaning to something	**Interpret** the quote to confirm your understanding.
Paraphrase	say or write it using different words	**Paraphrase** the main idea.
Report	Tell or write about a topic	**Report** the main events of the setting.
Summarize	tell the most important ideas or concepts	**Summarize** the key details of the passage.
Tell	say or write specific information	**Tell** the date that the poem was written.
Use	apply information or a procedure	**Use** text features to identify the topic.

Have students read about the four direction words in the chart with their partner.

Chart Reading Procedure
- Group students with partners or in triads.
- Have students count off as 1s or 2s. The 1s will become the student leaders. If working with triads, the third students become 3s.
- The student leaders will read the left column (Prompt) in addition to managing the time and turn-taking if working with a triad.
- The 2s will explain the middle column of the chart (How to Respond). If working in triads, 2s and 3s take turns explaining the middle column.
- The 1s read the model in the right column (Model), and 2s and 3s restate the model as a question.
- All students should follow along with their pencil eraser while others are explaining the chart.
- Students must work from left to right, top to bottom in order to benefit from this activity.

Check for understanding by requesting an oral response to the following questions.

- If the prompt asks you to *analyze*, the response requires you to . . . (break down and evaluate or draw conclusions about the information).

- If the prompt asks you to *assess*, the response requires you to . . . (decide on the value, impact, or accuracy).

- If the prompt asks you to *distinguish*, the response requires you to . . . (recognize or explain the differences).

- If the prompt asks you to *evaluate*, the response requires you to . . . (think carefully to make a judgment; form a critical opinion of).

Direct students to pages 269 and 270 in their Student Books and read the instructions aloud. Let's read some prompts about a small section of the text before we expand to the entire text.

1. Mandela argues that the ANC is not a communist group. His first piece of evidence is a document called the Freedom Charter. Evaluate the strength of this document as evidence.

2. Distinguish between the goals of the Communist Party and the goals of the African National Congress.

3. Analyze the attraction of many black South Africans to communism.

4. Assess the law that branded all supporters of democracy "communists."

Critical Understandings

Reread lines 183–236 of "I Am Prepared to Die." Refer to the chart on page 66 to determine how to respond to each prompt. Respond using complete sentences.

1. Mandela argues that the ANC is not a communist group. His first piece of evidence is a document called the Freedom Charter. Evaluate the strength of this document as evidence.

   The Freedom Charter was a strong piece of evidence because it called for an economy based on free enterprise. Even though it also called for some redistribution and nationalization, it did so only to create a level playing field for oppressed blacks— a playing field on which they could build their own businesses and prosper.

2. Distinguish between the goals of the Communist Party and the goals of the African National Congress.

   The Communist Party sought to establish a state based on Marxism. It wanted to do away with capitalism and emphasize class distinctions. In contrast, the ANC aimed to eliminate class distinctions and work together for the good of everyone. Although it wanted to nationalize major industries, it also wanted to encourage private enterprise.

Unit 6   269

We are going to focus on one small section of the speech.

We will practice answering prompts with these new question words. Having a good understanding of this particular section of the speech will help build a foundation for understanding the rest of the speech and make it feel less difficult.

Critical Understandings (*cont.*)

3. Analyze the attraction of many black South Africans to communism.

Many black South Africans were drawn to communism because members of the Communist Party treated them as human beings; were willing to work, eat, and talk with them; and shared some of their political aims, such as ending white supremacy. Working with the Communist Party probably made black South Africans feel respected, connected, and hopeful.

4. Assess the law that branded all supporters of democracy "communists."

The law that branded all supporters of democracy "communists" was erroneous. It was based on a misunderstanding of the aims of the ANC and other groups. It negatively impacted those who were incorrectly identified as communists by banning their activity and sometimes sending them to prison.

Read the following excerpt aloud.

Another of the allegations made by the state is that the aims and objects of the ANC and the Communist Party are the same. The allegation is false. The creed of the ANC is, and always has been, the creed of freedom and fulfillment for the African people in their own land. The most important document ever adopted by the ANC is the Freedom Charter. It is by no means a blueprint for a socialist state. It calls for redistribution, but not nationalization, of land; it provides for nationalization of mines, banks, and monopoly industry because big monopolies are owned by one race only, and without such nationalization racial domination would be perpetuated. Under the Freedom Charter, nationalization would take place in an economy based on private enterprise. The realization of the Freedom Charter would open up fresh fields for a prosperous African population.

As far as the Communist Party is concerned, and if I understand its policy correctly, it stands for the establishment of a state based on the principles of Marxism. The Communist Party's main aim was to remove the capitalists and to replace them with a working-class government. The Communist Party sought to emphasize class distinctions, while the ANC seeks to harmonize them. This is a vital distinction.

It is true that there has often been close cooperation between the ANC and the Communist Party. But cooperation is merely proof of a common goal—in this case, the removal of white supremacy—and is not proof of a complete community of interests. The history of the world is full of similar examples. Perhaps the most striking is the cooperation between Great Britain, the United States, and the Soviet Union in the fight against Hitler. Nobody but Hitler would have dared to suggest that such cooperation turned Churchill or Roosevelt into communists.

What is more, for many decades communists were the only political group in South Africa prepared to treat Africans as human beings and their equals; who were prepared to eat with us, talk with us, and work with us. They were the only group prepared to work with the Africans for the attainment of political rights.

Because of this, many Africans today tend to equate freedom with communism. They are supported in this belief by a legislature which brands all exponents of democratic government and African freedom as communists and banned many of them under the Suppression of Communism Act. Although I have never been a member of the Communist Party, I myself have been convicted under that act.

Model

Let's practice answering questions that are written as prompts. Remember to use the chart as reference. Listen as I model the first one for you.

> 1. Mandela argues that the ANC is not a communist group. His first piece of evidence is a document called the Freedom Charter. Evaluate the strength of this document as evidence.

Because the prompt is asking me to *evaluate*, I know that I need to think carefully to make a judgment or form a critical opinion of something.

Now, I will turn the prompt into a question to confirm understanding. How strong was the document as evidence that the ANC was not communist?

Write the following sentence starter on the board.

> *The Freedom Charter (was/was not) a strong piece of evidence because*
> _____.

Mandela says the Freedom Charter was "the creed of freedom and fulfillment for the African people in their own land." It was not a blueprint for a socialist state, although it did call for redistribution of wealth and the nationalization—or government ownership—of some industries, so as to keep whites only from controlling them. The Freedom Charter called for these things within an economy based on free enterprise, which is another term for capitalism. Free enterprise was what communism wanted to do away with.

Based on these facts, my answer would be *The Freedom Charter was a strong piece of evidence because it called for an economy based on free enterprise. Even though it also called for some redistribution and nationalization, it did so only to create a level playing field for oppressed blacks—a playing field on which they could build their own businesses and prosper.*

Have students write the answer on the page.

Guided Practice

Let's move on to the next prompt.

> 2. Distinguish between the goals of the Communist Party and the goals of the African National Congress.

How should we respond according to the chart? (If the prompt asks you to *distinguish*, the response requires that you recognize or explain the differences.)

Now, turn the prompt into a question to confirm your understanding. Tell your partner the question. (How were the goals of the Communist Party different from the goals of the African National Congress?)

Look in the paragraph starting "As far as the Communist Party is concerned . . ." for your answer. You can also use information from your answer to number 1.

While providing partner time, write the sentence **starters** on the board.

The Communist Party sought to _____.

In contrast, the African National Congress aimed to _____.

Have partners answer the question.

3. Analyze the attraction of many black South Africans to communism.

How should we respond according to the chart? (If the prompt asks you to *analyze*, the response requires that you break down and evaluate or draw conclusions about the information.)

Now, turn the prompt into a question to confirm your understanding. Tell your partner the question. (Why were some South Africans attracted to communism? What conclusion can you draw based on these reasons?)

While providing partner time, write the sentence starters on the board.

Many black South Africans were drawn to communism because members of the Communist Party _____, _____, and

_____.

Working with the Communist Party probably made black South Africans feel _____.

Have partners answer the question.

4. Assess the law that branded all supporters of democracy "communists."

How should we respond according to the chart? (If the prompt asks you to *assess*, the response requires you to decide on the value, impact, or accuracy.)

Now, turn the prompt into a question to confirm your understanding. Tell your partner the question. (Was the law a good one? What or whom did it impact, and how?)

While providing partner time, write the sentence starter on the board.

The law that branded all supporters of democracy "communists" was

_____.

Have partners answer the question.

Objectives
- Write a thesis statement for a multiparagraph essay.
- Use correct capitalization and underlining or italics in the titles of works.

Thesis Statements

As you have continued to build your writing skills, you have learned a variety of patterns for topic sentences. These frame the work you do at the paragraph level. But, how do you introduce a written response that is more than one paragraph in length? When a prompt calls for multiple paragraphs, you will want to start with a thesis statement. A thesis statement is like a topic sentence for the entire paper. It is an assertion of fact or opinion that is then supported in the essay with details and evidence. As well as framing the topic, it sets up the content and sequence of the paragraphs.

List the following on the board: *Subject; Specific Movie; Three Reasons; Thesis Statement.*

Imagine you were asked to write an essay about your favorite movie. What is the subject? (favorite movie) **Write it in on the board.**

> *Subject: Favorite Movie*

My favorite movie is *To Kill a Mockingbird.* **Write it on the board next to** *Specific Movie* **and underline it. Have volunteers share their favorite movies.**

> *Specific Movie:* To Kill a Mockingbird

When we write the title of a movie or a book, we italicize it if we are typing it, but we underline it if we are writing it. This is because it is difficult to italicize our handwriting. Also, pay close attention to the words that are not capitalized. Any word that is less than three letters (unless it's a main word) should be lowercase. Why isn't *To* lowercase? (the first word and last word are always capitalized)

I need to think of three reasons why I like the movie so much. This serves as a cue for the number of paragraphs I will need to write. I think the story is very powerful and the cast was great. Gregory Peck plays Atticus Finch perfectly. I also thought telling the story from Scout's perspective allowed us to experience the story with childlike innocence and recklessness. **Write the reasons on the board. Have volunteers share three reasons why a certain movie is their favorite movie.**

> *Three Reasons: powerful story, good cast, point of view*

Now, I have to write my thesis statement. I can write my thesis statement as one long sentence, or I can write it as two sentences. I've chosen to break it into two sentences. **Write the thesis statement on the board.**

> *Thesis statement: My favorite movie is* To Kill a Mockingbird. *It is a powerful story about human strengths and weaknesses, the cast is wonderfully talented, and Scout's point of view gives the story honesty and innocence.*

Have students write thesis statements about their favorite movies and share them with the class.

My thesis statement becomes my introductory paragraph, and I know I need to write a paragraph about each reason. My final paragraph will be my concluding paragraph, so I will have written a five-paragraph essay. It sounds harder than it really is. We will revisit this task in Lesson 10, where you will be prompted to write a thesis statement in response to the text excerpts that we have been reading.

Lesson Opener

Before the lesson, choose one of the following activities to write on the board or post on the *LANGUAGE! Live* Class Wall online.

- *Write a thesis statement for an essay on how you hope to change the world for the better.*
- *Write five compound sentences about prejudices. Use a conjunction in three of the sentences and use a semicolon in the other two.*
- *Expand one or more of these simple sentences, using the steps in Masterpiece Sentences.*

  Nelson Mandela went to jail.

  Nelson Mandela gave a speech.

  South Africa changed.

  Laws were unfair.

Reading

Objectives

- Establish a purpose for rereading a speech.
- Monitor comprehension during text reading.
- Use critical thinking skills to write responses to prompts about text.
- Support written answers with text evidence.
- Evaluate the effectiveness of a speaker's craft and use of strategies.
- Identify evidence given in support of an argument and determine if it is sound or not.
- Contrast ideas and concepts within a text.

Reading for a Purpose: "I Am Prepared to Die"

We are going to reread "I Am Prepared to Die." Let's preview some prompts to provide a purpose for rereading the speech.

Direct students to pages 271–274 in their Student Books. Have students read the prompts aloud with you.

1. Assess Mandela's reference to his youth as a way to begin the speech.

2. Evaluate the ANC's policy of non-violence.

3. The ANC ultimately decided to use violence. Evaluate the reasons and evidence Mandela gives for this decision. Does he support them with evidence—facts and details from real life? Are his reasons and evidence sound?

4. Distinguish between sabotage and the other three types of violence Mandela names.

5. Evaluate whether Mandela's travels around the African continent were useful.

6. Distinguish between the lives and opportunities of white South Africans and black South Africans.

7. Analyze the secondary effects of poverty.

8. Assess Mandela's willingness to die for the ideal of a free and democratic South Africa.

This speech is a difficult text. Now that we have read it once, it should be a little easier to read. Keeping these questions in mind as we read will help increase our comprehension. Let's reread the speech.

Choose an option for rereading text. Have students read the text according to the option that you chose.

> Choose an option for rereading text.
> - Teacher read-aloud
> - Teacher-led or student-led choral read
> - Paired read or independent read with bold vocabulary words read aloud

Direct students to page 257 in their Student Books or have them tear out the extra copy of the speech from the back of their book.

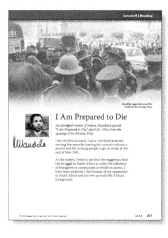

Note: To minimize flipping back and forth between the pages, a copy of each text has been included in the back of the Student Books. Encourage students to tear this out and use it when working on activities that require the use of the text.

"Nelson Mandela" audio file found in the Teacher Resources online

Have students reread the speech. Due to the difficult nature of the speech, an audio file of the complete speech—as it was delivered—can be found online in the Teacher Resources. Play the speech and have students follow along if you feel it would be beneficial.

Passage Comprehension

Write the words *analyze, assess, distinguish,* and *evaluate* on the board. Have students read the words aloud with you.

Direct students to page 66 in their Student Books. It is critical to understand what the question is asking and how to answer it. Today, we will review four direction words used in prompts.

Have students read about the words in the chart on page 66 with their partner. Check for understanding by requesting an oral response to the following questions.

- If the prompt asks you to *analyze*, the response requires you to . . . (break down and evaluate or draw conclusions about the information).

- If the prompt asks you to *assess*, the response requires you to . . . (decide on the value, impact, or accuracy).

- If the prompt asks you to *distinguish*, the response requires you to . . . (recognize or explain the differences).

- If the prompt asks you to *evaluate*, the response requires you to . . . (think carefully to make a judgment; form a critical opinion of).

Let's practice answering questions that are written as prompts. Remember to use the chart on page 66 as a reference. Don't forget, if the direction word is confusing, try to restate the prompt by using a question word.

Critical Understandings: Direction Words

Prompt	How to Respond	Model
If the prompt asks you to . . .	**The response requires you to . . .**	**For example . . .**
Analyze	break down and evaluate or draw conclusions about the information	**Analyze** the development of the text's central idea.
Assess	decide on the value, impact, or accuracy	**Assess** the level of pressure in an arranged marriage.
Compare	state the similarities between two or more things	**Compare** novels and dramas.
Contrast	state the differences between two or more things	**Contrast** a biography with an autobiography.
Create	make or produce something	**Create** a timeline of events.
Define	tell or write the meaning or definition	**Define** the unknown word using context clues.
Delineate	show or list evidence, claims, ideas, reasons, or events	**Delineate** the evidence in the text.
Describe	state detailed information about a topic	**Describe** the relationship between the plot and character development.
Determine	find out, verify, decide	**Determine** the main idea.
Distinguish	recognize or explain the differences	**Distinguish** between facts and opinions.
Evaluate	think carefully to make a judgment; form a critical opinion of	**Evaluate** the ANC's plan for change.
Explain	express understanding of an idea or concept	**Explain** how the author develops the narrator's point of view.
Identify	say or write what it is	**Identify** the character's motive.
Infer	provide a logical answer using evidence and prior knowledge	Use information from the text to **infer** the value of education.
Interpret	make sense of or assign meaning to something	**Interpret** the quote to confirm your understanding.
Paraphrase	say or write it using different words	**Paraphrase** the main idea.
Report	Tell or write about a topic	**Report** the main events of the setting.
Summarize	tell the most important ideas or concepts	**Summarize** the key details of the passage.
Tell	say or write specific information	**Tell** the date that the poem was written.
Use	apply information or a procedure	**Use** text features to identify the topic.

66 Unit 2

Direct students to pages 271–274 in their Student Books.

Model

Listen as I model the first one for you.

> 1. Assess Mandela's reference to his youth as a way to begin the speech.

Because the prompt is asking me to *assess*, I know that I need to decide on the value, impact, or accuracy of Mandela's reference to his youth. Now, I will turn the prompt into a question to confirm understanding. What is the value, impact, or accuracy of Mandela's reference to his youth at the beginning of the speech?

I can't know the accuracy of the reference, since I wasn't in Mandela's childhood tribe. But I can assess the value or impact of the reference in terms of the speech and in terms of his purpose—to persuade the judge that his actions made sense and were justified.

Passage Comprehension

Reread "I Am Prepared to Die." Use text evidence to respond to each prompt in complete sentences. Refer to the chart on page 66 to determine how to respond to each prompt.

1. Assess Mandela's reference to his youth as a way to begin the speech.
   Mandela's reference to his youth at the beginning of the speech is very effective. It impacts his audience by bringing up strong thoughts of community, history, courage, and strength. It suggests to Mandela's audience that his actions weren't just about him; they were about his people and his legacy. The reference to his youth casts Mandela in a heroic light.

2. Evaluate the ANC's policy of non-violence.
   The ANC's policy of non-violence was a good policy because it showed the South African government that the ANC was dedicated to peace. Such a policy matched the ANC's main goal: to build a society in which people of all colors lived together peacefully. Also, the ANC's non-violent actions were impossible to convict in court. Now, as he stands trial for sabotage, Mandela is able to point to more than one ruling in which the judge found the ANC innocent of violence. This gives credibility to his claim that the group was committed to non-violence from the beginning and only used violence when it became necessary.

Unit 6 **271**

Mandela says that in his youth, he "listened to the elders" of his tribe "telling stories of wars fought" by their ancestors, "in defense of the fatherland." He also says that listening to these stories caused him to hope that his own life would "give [him] the opportunity to serve [his] people and make [his] own humble contribution to their freedom struggle." These are powerful words. They speak of community, history, courage, and strength. They are noble words, and they cast Mandela's later actions in a noble light.

Some people might say these words are loaded. Using loaded terms is one of the fallacies we learned about earlier. These words are certainly powerful, but I don't think Mandela is trying to manipulate anyone. He is using language that matches his experience and his memories. We know the experience and memories are strong, because they helped determine the course of his life.

So my answer would be *Mandela's reference to his youth at the beginning of the speech is very effective. It impacts his audience by bringing up strong thoughts of community, history, courage, and strength. It suggests to Mandela's audience that his actions weren't just about him; they were about his people and his legacy. The reference to his youth casts Mandela in a heroic light.*

Have students write the answer on the page.

Guided Practice

2. Evaluate the ANC's policy of non-violence.

How will I start my answer? Tell your partner how to respond according to the chart. (If the prompt asks you to *evaluate*, the response requires you to think carefully to make a judgment; to form an opinion of.) Turn the prompt into a question to confirm understanding. (Why was the ANC's policy of non-violence a good or bad policy?) Now, answer the question. Write the following sentence starter on the board.

The ANC's policy of non-violence was a (good/bad) policy because

_____
_____
_____.

Have students answer the question. Have volunteers share their answers.

Passage Comprehension (*cont.*)

3. The ANC ultimately decided to use violence. Evaluate the reasons and evidence Mandela gives for this decision. Does he support them with evidence—facts and details from real life? Are his reasons and evidence sound?

Reason for Decision	Evidence to Support Claims	Sound?
harsher and harsher penalties	Public Safety Act, Criminal Law Amendment Act	Answers will vary.
growing violence from government	shooting at Sharpeville	Answers will vary.
exclusion of Africans from government	republic established, but Africans (70% of population) not allowed to vote	Answers will vary.
sense of helplessness; refusal to surrender	"What were we, the leaders of our people, to do?"	Answers will vary.
violence a "feature of the landscape"	examples from 1957, 1958, 1959, 1960; government that uses violence teaches oppressed to use it too	Answers will vary.

4. Distinguish between sabotage and the other three types of violence Mandela names.
The four types of violence Mandela names are sabotage, guerrilla warfare, terrorism, and open revolution. Sabotage is different from the others because it does not involve the loss of human life.

_____
_____

Passage Comprehension (*cont.*)

5. Evaluate whether Mandela's travels around the African continent were useful.
Mandela's travels around Africa were useful because on the tour, he met with other people fighting for freedom in African countries; he met "sympathy for our cause and promises of help," and he underwent military training. If the situation in South Africa turned to civil war, he would be prepared.

_____
_____
_____
_____
_____

6. Distinguish between the lives and opportunities of white South Africans and black South Africans.
The lives of white South Africans and black South Africans were very different. White South Africans were rich. There was compulsory education for all white children. Black people performed menial chores that made white people's lives easier. Black South Africans, on the other hand, were poor. They were not given an education or allowed to gain skills and advance in their work, and they were viewed as a separate, lesser breed of human.

_____
_____
_____
_____

Passage Comprehension (*cont.*)

7. Analyze the secondary effects of poverty.
The secondary effects of poverty in South Africa included children wandering the streets, a breakdown in moral standards, a rise in illegitimacy, and violence. The violence, in turn, spread to white areas. People were put to death for housebreakings and robberies. These effects tell me that black people felt desperate. They tell me that poverty leads to death.

_____
_____
_____
_____

8. Assess Mandela's willingness to die for the ideal of a free and democratic South Africa.
Mandela's willingness to die must have had a strong impact at the trial. It must have made the judge see that his motives were selfless. If Mandela led a group that chose violence, it was only because they were forced to. We know that these final words of Mandela's speech had a strong impact on his jury, too, because he wasn't sentenced to death after all; instead, he was sentenced to life in prison. The words were also a rallying cry for his supporters to carry on the fight and to not let his suffering be in vain.

_____
_____
_____

Independent Practice

Have partners respond to the remaining prompts, providing text evidence as needed to support their claims. For students who need more assistance, provide the following alternative questions and sentence starters.

Alternative questions and sentence starters:

3. Was the ANC's decision to use violence a good decision or a bad decision? Why? Complete the chart.

4. How is sabotage different from the other three types of violence Mandela names?

   The four types of violence Mandela names are _____, _____, _____, and _____.

   Sabotage is different from the others because _____.

5. Were Mandela's travels around the continent of Africa useful? Why?

   Mandela's travels around Africa (were/were not) useful because _____.

6. How were the lives and opportunities of white South Africans different from those of black South Africans?

   The lives of white and black South Africans were very different.

   White South Africans _____.

   Black South Africans, on the other hand, _____.

7. What were the secondary effects of poverty in South Africa? What conclusion can I draw about them?

   The secondary effects of poverty in South Africa included _____, _____, and _____. This tells me that _____.

8. What impact would Mandela's willingness to die have on his audience, the judge?

   Mandela's willingness to die must have had a _____ impact on his audience. It must have made the judge see that _____. We know these words had an impact on his audience because _____.

RI.1.2; RI.1.3; RI.2.2; RI.3.1; RI.3.3; RI.4.1; RI.4.3; RI.5.3;
RI.6.3; RI.7.3; RI.4.5; RI.6.4; RI.6.5; RI.6.6; RI.7.4; RI.8.6;
RI.1.8; RI.2.8; RI.3.8; RI.5.8; RI.6.8; RI.8.8; RI.6.10; W.8.9b;
SL.6.3; SL.8.3; L.5.1c; L.5.1e; L.4.5c; L.5.4a; L.5.6; L.6.6

Lesson Opener

Before the lesson, choose one of the following activities to write on the board or post on the *LANGUAGE! Live* Class Wall online.

- *Nelson Mandela spent 27 years in prison for standing up against injustice. When he was released, the changes he fought for were being made. Imagine you were locked up for 27 years, then released into a changing nation. Contrast what you might be like before and after prison.*
- *Write one compound sentence with a coordinating conjunction about Nelson Mandela and the ANC.*
- *Write five sentences about the ANC's decision to use sabotage. Identify the nouns and verbs.*

Reading

Objectives

- Read a speech with purpose and understanding.
- Answer questions to demonstrate comprehension of text.
- Identify and explain explicit details from text.
- Monitor comprehension during text reading.
- Identify the structure used to organize text and how each section contributes to the whole.
- Identify fallacies in persuasive text.
- Interpret a speaker's claims and determine the intent and validity.
- Identify the purpose of correlative conjunctions.
- Analyze in detail how a key idea is introduced, illustrated, and elaborated in a text.
- Describe the relationship between a series of historical events using language that pertains to time, sequence, and cause/effect.

Close Reading of "I Am Prepared to Die"

Highlighters or colored pencils

Let's reread "I Am Prepared to Die." I will provide specific instructions on how to mark the text to help with comprehension.

Have students get out a highlighter or colored pencil.

Direct students to pages 275–281 in their Student Books.

Draw a rectangle around the title.

Mark the word in the introduction that indicates this version of the speech has been shortened or altered. (abridged)

Now, let's read the vocabulary words aloud.

- What's the first bold vocabulary word? (contribution) *Contribution* means "something given in support of an effort or cause." Mandela made a big *contribution* to the cause of freedom in South Africa. **Have partners use the word in a sentence.**

- What's the next bold vocabulary word? (exploitation) *Exploitation* means "the act of using someone for your own selfish gain." Mandela fought against the *exploitation* of black people. **Have partners use the word in a sentence.**

- What's the next bold vocabulary word? (**defy**) *Defy* means "to boldly resist; to challenge." If you *defy* authority, there can be an unpleasant consequence. **Have partners use the word in a sentence.**

- Let's continue. (**suspended**) *Suspended* means "put off or did away with." When phone service is *suspended*, it is shut off. **Have partners use the word in a sentence.**

- Next word? (**policy**) *Policy* means "a rule; a way of doing things." The African National Congress had a *policy* of non-violence. **Have partners use the word in a sentence.**

- Next word? (**massive**) *Massive* means "huge; on a very large scale." Over time, a small social movement can become *massive*. **Have partners use the word in a sentence.**

- Next word? (**prospects**) *Prospects* means "possibilities that something will happen soon." Our *prospects* for a blizzard are small today. **Have partners use the word in a sentence.**

- Let's continue. (**legacy**) *Legacy* mean "something passed down from earlier people or times." Black South Africans inherited a *legacy* of poverty. **Have partners use the word in a sentence.**

- Next word? (**hamper**) To *hamper* means "to make it hard for someone to do something." Having a cast on your arm can *hamper* your ability to write. **Have partners use the word in a sentence.**

- Last word. (**irrelevant**) *Irrelevant* means "unrelated; beside the point." Some teachers think that the reason a student is tardy is *irrelevant*. Tardy is tardy. **Have partners use the word in a sentence.**

Talk with a partner about any vocabulary word that is still confusing for you to read or understand.

As you read the speech, you will monitor your understanding by circling the check marks or the question marks. Please be sure to draw a question mark over any confusing words, phrases, or sentences.

As we read, we will be watching for the strategies that Mandela and the authorities he speaks of use. Do they use strong, effective language? Do they use true facts that make a powerful impression? Or do they use fallacies, or logical errors? **Have students turn to page 255 of their Student Books and briefly review the strategies and fallacies.**

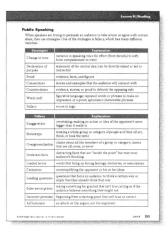

Options for rereading text.

- Teacher read-aloud

- Teacher-led or student-led choral read

- Paired read or independent read with bold vocabulary words read aloud

Direct students to page 275 in their Student Books. Choose an option for reading text. Have students read lines 1–32 according to the option that you chose.

When most of the students are finished, continue with the entire class. Let's see how well you understood what you read.

- Circle the check mark or the question mark for this section. Draw a question mark over any confusing words.

- Go to line 4. Mark the synonym for *stirring up* or *motivating*. (inciting)

- Go to lines 6 and 7. Mark the fallacy Mandela's opponents use against him. (struggle in South Africa is under the influence of foreigners or communists)

- Mandela introduces the idea of communist influence. Does he expand upon it? (no)

Expanding Instruction:
Oftentimes, writers introduce a topic or idea early on in writing but do not expand upon it or explain it till much later. This can cause great confusion for struggling readers. Draw students' attention to these occurrences while reading text, and have them be on the lookout for the expansion and explanations. This allows students to understand the author's purpose for doing so as well as increase comprehension.

- Go to line 10. Mark the time in his life Mandela is speaking of. (youth)

- Go to lines 12 and 13. Mark one verb and one verb phrase that tell what Mandela hoped to do. (serve; make my own humble contribution)

- Go to line 15. Mark the word that names a kind of violence. (sabotage)

- In the same paragraph, mark the sentence in which Mandela denies a false premise, or claim, the government has made. (I did not plan it in a spirit of recklessness, nor because I love violence.)

- Go to lines 16 and 17. Circle the two words that tell what the decision to use sabotage was a result of. (calm assessment) Remember, when a person *assesses*, he or she carefully decides on the value or impact of something.

- Go to line 18. Mark the powerful words used to describe the government actions that gave rise to the current political situation. (many years of tyranny, exploitation, and oppression)

- Go to lines 19 and 20. Mark what Mandela admits. (I was one of the persons who helped to form Umkhonto we Sizwe) Umkhonto we Sizwe was the armed wing of the African National Congress. If they were armed, what kind of resistance do you think they planned: violent or non-violent? Write your answer in the margin. (violent)

- Go to lines 20 and 21. Mark the fallacy of the government that Mandela denies. (Umkhonto was responsible for a number of acts which have been charged in the indictment against us) Circle the word that means "charges; accusations of wrongdoing." (indictment)

- Go to line 23. Mark the phrase that sums up what Mandela and his group are fighting against. (white supremacy)

- In the same line, mark the word that is sometimes used in an overgeneralization. (All) Underline the claim Mandela makes using this word. (All lawful modes of expressing opposition had been closed by legislation) If you think this is a fallacy, or overgeneralization, write *F* in the margin. If you think he is telling the truth and making a powerful point, write *P* in the margin.

- Go to lines 25 and 26. Mark the two choices the ANC felt they had. (accept permanent inferiority; defy the government) Underline the correlative conjunctions used here to indicate there is a choice. (either; or) Do you think the word *permanent* is used as a loaded term? If you think so, write *F* in the margin. If you think it is an accurate assessment, write *P*.

Expanding Instruction:
Correlative conjunctions (*either/or* and *neither/nor*) are frequently used in writing. When possible, point this out during reading so students understand the purpose of the conjunctions and when and where to use them, as well as the importance of including both words in the set.

- In the same paragraph, circle the plural pronoun used multiple times. (we) Draw an arrow from the pronoun to the noun it is representing. (Umkhonto)

- Go to line 27. Underline the way the ANC first broke the law. (in a way which avoided violence)

- Go to line 28. Underline who responded with a show of force. (the government)

- Go to line 29. Underline the powerful phrase used by Mandela to explain the need for action. (answer violence with violence)

- Go to line 30. Underline the phrase that tells who "we" are. (Umkhonto; members of the African National Congress) When Mandela uses the first-person pronoun *we* in this speech, he is referring to this group of people— members of the ANC.

Have students read lines 33–72 according to the option that you chose. In the previous section, Mandela laid out his major claims. In this section, and the following ones, Mandela will go back and retell the events that led up to the decision of the ANC to use sabotage. Each section of the speech will contribute to the whole in a way that he hopes is persuasive. As we continue reading, remember to watch for strategies Mandela uses.

When most of the students are finished, continue with the entire class. Let's see how well you understood what you read.

- Circle the check mark or the question mark for this section. Draw a question mark over any confusing words.

- Go to lines 33 and 34. Mark why the ANC was formed. (**to defend the rights of the African people**)

- Go to line 35. Mark the word that means "followed." (**adhered**) Mark the adverb used to describe the degree to which they followed the policy. (**strictly**)

- Go to lines 35 and 36. Mark two ways the ANC did its work in the early years. (**put forward demands and resolutions; sent delegations to the government**)

- Go to lines 38 and 39. Mark what happened as a result of the ANC's efforts. (**rights of Africans became less**)

- Go to line 42. Mark the new strategy the ANC decided to use. (**demonstrations**)

- On the same line, mark the result of the demonstrations. (**More than 8,500 people went to jail**)

- Go to line 45. Mark why Mandela's sentence was suspended. (**discipline and non-violence had been stressed throughout**) Mandela is showing that he and his group were committed to non-violence. Even the judge agreed. Is this a powerful point, or a misleading one? Write *P* or *F* in the margin.

- Go to line 47. Mark what the government imposed on people who demonstrated and resisted. (**harsher penalties**)

- Go to line 52. Mark the phrase that tells what the court found again. (**the ANC did not have a policy of violence**) Powerful point or fallacy? Write *P* or *F* in the margin. Circle the word that means the same as "found not guilty." (**acquitted**)

- Go to line 53. Mark what happened in 1960. (**shooting at Sharpeville**) Read aloud the footnote at the bottom of the page. Write who was responsible for the shooting in the margin. (**police**)

Close Reading (cont.)

The African National Congress was formed in 1912 to defend the rights of the African people, which had been seriously curtailed. For 37 years—that is, until 1949—it adhered strictly to a constitutional struggle. It put forward demands and resolutions; it sent delegations to the government in the belief that African grievances could be settled through peaceful discussion. But white governments remained unmoved, and the rights of Africans became less instead of becoming greater.

Even after 1949, the ANC remained determined to avoid violence. At this time, however, a decision was taken to protest against apartheid by peaceful, but unlawful, demonstrations. More than 8,500 people went to jail. Yet there was not a single instance of violence. I and nineteen colleagues were convicted, but our sentences were **suspended** mainly because the judge found that discipline and non-violence had been stressed throughout.

During the defiance campaign, the Public Safety Act and the Criminal Law Amendment Act were passed. These provided harsher penalties for offenses against the laws. Despite this, the protests continued and the ANC adhered to its **policy** of non-violence.

In 1956, 156 leading members of the Congress Alliance, including myself, were arrested. When the court gave judgment some five years later, it found that the ANC did not have a policy of violence. We were acquitted.

In 1960, there was the shooting at Sharpeville, which resulted in the declaration of the ANC as unlawful.* My colleagues and I, after careful consideration, decided that we would not obey this decree. The African people were not part of the government and did not make the laws by which they were governed. We believed the words of the Universal Declaration of Human Rights, that "the will of the people shall be the basis of authority of the government." The ANC refused to dissolve but instead went underground.

The government held a referendum which led to the establishment of the republic. Africans, who constituted approximately 70 percent of the population, were not entitled to vote. I undertook to be responsible for organizing the national stay-at-home called to coincide with the declaration of the republic. The stay-at-home was to be a peaceful demonstration. Careful instructions were given to avoid any recourse to violence.

The government's answer was to introduce new and harsher laws, to mobilize its armed forces, and to send armed vehicles into the townships in a **massive** show of force. The government had decided to rule by force alone, and this decision was a milestone on the road to Umkhonto.

*Between 5,000 and 7,000 protestors went to the police station in Sharpeville to peacefully demonstrate against the Pass laws. The police opened fire on the protestors, killing 69 people.

- Go to line 54. Mark what the government declared the ANC. (unlawful)

- Go to lines 55–57. Underline the sentence telling why the ANC would not accept the status of "unlawful." (The African people were not part of the government and did not make the laws by which they were governed.) Is this a sound and logical point? Or is it a logical error? Write *P* or *F* in the margin.

- Go to lines 58 and 59. Mark the statement that means the government should only have the power and control that the majority of the people want them to have. (the will of the people shall be the basis of authority of the government) Circle the document that this statement came from. (Universal Declaration of Human Rights)

- Go to line 60. Mark where the ANC went. (underground) This means it continued to operate in secret.

- Go to line 62. Mark who were not allowed to vote in the newly established republic. (Africans) Is Mandela making an overgeneralization, or is this a true fact? Write *P* or *F* in the margin.

- Go to line 64. What did the ANC organize in response? Mark the phrase that refers to a strike or a "don't go to work" day. (stay-at-home)

- Go to line 65. Mark the adjective that describes the strike, or stay-at-home. (peaceful)

- Go to lines 67 and 68. Mark what the government did in response. (introduce new and harsher laws, mobilize its armed forces, send armed vehicles)

- Go to lines 69 and 70. Mark how the government had decided to rule. (by force alone)

- Go to line 70 and mark the reminder that this happened before his discussion on the previous page. (the road to Umkhonto)

I have students read lines 73–101 according to the option that you chose. Remember to pay attention to Mandela's strategies.

When most of the students are finished, continue with the entire class. Let's see how well you understood what you read.

- Circle the check mark or the question mark for this section. Draw a question mark over any confusing words.

- Go to line 73. Mark the question. (What were we, the leaders of our people, to do?) Is this a leading question? Is it meant to manipulate the audience, or does it express how the ANC really felt? Write *P* or *F* in the margin.

- Go to line 75. Mark the ANC's new problem. **(how to continue the fight)**

Close Reading (cont.)

What were we, the leaders of our people, to do? We had to continue the fight. Anything else would have been surrender. Our problem was not
75 whether to fight, but was how to continue the fight.

By this time, violence had become a feature of the South African political scene. There had been violence in 1957 when the women of Zeerust were ordered to carry passes; there was violence in 1958 with the enforcement of cattle culling in Sekhukhuneland; there was violence in 1959 when the
80 people of Cato Manor protested against pass raids; there was violence in 1960 when the government attempted to impose Bantu authorities in Pondoland. Each disturbance pointed to the growth among Africans of the belief that violence was the only way out. A government which uses force to maintain its rule teaches the oppressed to use force to oppose it.

85 I came to the conclusion that as violence was inevitable, it would be unrealistic to continue preaching peace and non-violence. This conclusion was not easily arrived at. It was only when all channels of peaceful protest had been barred that the decision was made to embark on violent forms of struggle. I can only say that I felt morally obliged to do what I did.

90 Four forms of violence are possible. There is sabotage, there is guerrilla warfare, there is terrorism, and there is open revolution. We chose to adopt the first. Sabotage did not involve loss of life, and it offered the best hope for future race relations.

The initial plan was based on a careful analysis of the political and
95 economic situation of our country. We believed that South Africa depended to a large extent on foreign capital. We felt that planned destruction of power plants, and interference with rail and telephone communications, would scare away capital from the country, thus compelling the voters of the country to reconsider their position. The selection of targets is proof of
100 this policy. Had we intended to attack life, we would have selected targets where people congregated and not empty buildings and power stations.

✓   ?

- In the second paragraph, mark the years when violent events occurred. (1957, 1958, 1959, 1960) Are these facts and events irrelevant? Are they "beside the point"? Write *P* for powerful point or *F* for fallacy in the margin.

- Go to lines 83 and 84. Mark the point Mandela is trying to make by giving all the examples of violence. (**A government which uses force to maintain its rule teaches the oppressed to use force to oppose it.**)

- Go to line 85. Mark the word that means *likely to happen.* (**inevitable**) Mark what is inevitable. (**violence**)

- Go to line 89. Mark how Mandela felt about using violence. (**morally obliged**) Is he bragging or calmly admitting something? Is his tone loud and angry or soft and humble? Write a word describing his tone in the margin.

- Go to lines 90 and 91. Mark the four types of violence. (**sabotage, guerrilla warfare, terrorism, open revolution**) Underline why the ANC chose sabotage. (**did not involve loss of life**) Knowing what you know about the ANC, does this ring true? Do you trust that the claim is true? Write *P* or *F* in the margin.

- Go to line 96. Mark the word that means "money" or "wealth." (**capital**) *Capital* is money invested in companies. Foreign capital is money invested by people in other countries. If the ANC targeted power plants and telephone lines, what did they hope would happen? Mark the result. (**scare away capital from the country**)

- Go to lines 100 and 101. Mark how Mandela argues against the fallacy that the ANC was trying to kill people. (**Had we intended to attack life, we would have selected targets where people congregated**) Logical point or illogical point? Write *P* or *F* in the margin.

Have students read lines 102–138 according to the option that you chose. Continue marking strong, valid points with a *P*, and any fallacies you detect with an *F*.

When most of the students are finished, continue with the entire class. Let's see how well you understood what you read.

- Circle the check mark or the question mark for this section. Draw a question mark over any confusing words.

- Go to line 103. Mark the word used to indicate that the government would maintain control through brute, military force. (laager)

- Go to line 104. Mark how black Africans responded to the ANC's acts of sabotage. (there was hope again)

- Go to line 108. Mark what the leaders of the ANC feared. (civil war)

- Go to line 109. Mark what sabotage would now be punished with. (death)

- Go to lines 112 and 113. Mark what black Africans did not receive. (military training)

- Go back to line 110. The ANC leaders felt it was their what to be trained in warfare? (duty)

- Go to lines 116 and 117. Mark what Mandela attended in 1962. (the Conference of the Pan-African Freedom Movement)

- Go to line 120. Mark the word that means "feelings of understanding." (sympathy)

- Go to line 121. Mark what all of Africa was united against. (white South Africa) Might this be an overgeneralization? Was every single person in Africa united against white South Africa? Write *P* or *F* in the margin.

- Go to line 124. Mark the noble gesture that intends to show that Mandela is not above his people. (I wanted to be able to fight with my people)

- Go to line 125. Mark the synonym for *change*. (alteration)

- Go to line 126. Mark what Mandela found was now a fact. (death penalty for sabotage) People fighting for change had been put to death while Mandela was away. Is this an irrelevant fact, or a powerful point? Write *P* or *F* in the margin.

- Go to line 128. Mark the incorrect premise, or claim, the government has made. (the ANC and the Communist Party are the same)

Close Reading (*cont.*)

The whites failed to respond by suggesting change; they responded to our call by suggesting the laager. In contrast, the response of the Africans was one of encouragement. Suddenly, there was hope again. People began to
105 speculate on how soon freedom would be obtained.

But we in Umkhonto weighed the white response with anxiety. The lines were being drawn. The whites and blacks were moving into separate camps, and the **prospects** of avoiding a civil war were made less. The white newspapers carried reports that sabotage would be punished by death.
110 We felt it our duty to make preparations to use force in order to defend ourselves against force. We decided, therefore, to make provision for the possibility of guerrilla warfare. All whites undergo compulsory military training, but no such training was given to Africans. It was in our view essential to build up a nucleus of trained men who would be able to provide
115 the leadership if guerrilla warfare started.

At this stage, the ANC decided that I should attend the Conference of the Pan-African Freedom Movement, which was to be held 1962. After the conference, I would take a tour of the African states with a view to whether facilities were available for the training of soldiers. My tour was successful.
120 Wherever I went, I met sympathy for our cause and promises of help. All Africa was united against the stand of white South Africa.

I started to make a study of the art of war and revolution and, while abroad, underwent a course in military training. If there was to be guerrilla warfare, I wanted to be able to fight with my people. On my return, I found
125 that there had been little alteration in the political scene save that the threat of a death penalty for sabotage had now become a fact.

Another of the allegations made by the state is that the aims and objects of the ANC and the Communist Party are the same. The allegation is false. The creed of the ANC is, and always has been, the creed of freedom and
130 fulfillment for the African people in their own land. The most important document ever adopted by the ANC is the Freedom Charter. It is by no means a blueprint for a socialist state. It calls for redistribution, but not nationalization, of land; it provides for nationalization of mines, banks, and monopolies because big monopolies are owned by one race
135 only, and without such nationalization racial domination would be perpetuated. Under the Freedom Charter, nationalization would take place in an economy based on private enterprise. The realization of the Freedom Charter would open up fresh fields for a prosperous African population.

✓   ?

278   Unit 6

- Go to lines 132–134. Mark what two things the Freedom Charter calls for. (redistribution of land; nationalization of mines, banks, and monopoly industry)

- Go to line 137. Mark what the entire economy would be based on under the charter. (private enterprise)

- Go to line 138. Mark the figurative language, or word picture, Mandela uses. (fresh fields)

Have students read lines 139–172 according to the option that you chose. Mandela has concluded his account of the events that led up to sabotage and the ANC's preparation for warfare. In that section, he was admitting to the charge of sabotage but showing why it was justified. In the next section, he will address the charge that the ANC is a communist group, which was introduced in the beginning of the speech. In this section, he will illustrate and elaborate on the connection between the ANC and the Communist Party. Each section contributes to the overall speech. He is arguing against the charges, one by one.

When most of the students are finished, continue with the entire class. Let's see how well you understood what you read.

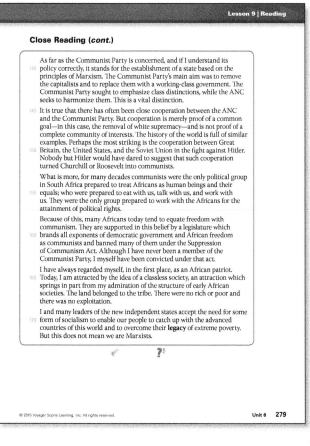

Close Reading (cont.)

140 As far as the Communist Party is concerned, and if I understand its policy correctly, it stands for the establishment of a state based on the principles of Marxism. The Communist Party's main aim was to remove the capitalists and to replace them with a working-class government. The Communist Party sought to emphasize class distinctions, while the ANC seeks to harmonize them. This is a vital distinction.

145 It is true that there has often been close cooperation between the ANC and the Communist Party. But cooperation is merely proof of a common goal—in this case, the removal of white supremacy—and is not proof of a complete community of interests. The history of the world is full of similar examples. Perhaps the most striking is the cooperation between Great

150 Britain, the United States, and the Soviet Union in the fight against Hitler. Nobody but Hitler would have dared to suggest that such cooperation turned Churchill or Roosevelt into communists.

What is more, for many decades communists were the only political group in South Africa prepared to treat Africans as human beings and their

155 equals; who were prepared to eat with us, talk with us, and work with us. They were the only group prepared to work with the Africans for the attainment of political rights.

Because of this, many Africans today tend to equate freedom with communism. They are supported in this belief by a legislature which

160 brands all exponents of democratic government and African freedom as communists and banned many of them under the Suppression of Communism Act. Although I have never been a member of the Communist Party, I myself have been convicted under that act.

I have always regarded myself, in the first place, as an African patriot.

165 Today, I am attracted by the idea of a classless society, an attraction which springs in part from my admiration of the structure of early African societies. The land belonged to the tribe. There were no rich or poor and there was no exploitation.

I and many leaders of the new independent states accept the need for some

170 form of socialism to enable our people to catch up with the advanced countries of this world and to overcome their **legacy** of extreme poverty. But this does not mean we are Marxists.

✓   ?

Unit 6   **279**

- Circle the check mark or the question mark for this section. Draw a question mark over any confusing words.

- Go to lines 139 and 140. What indirect statement is made purposefully to further separate Mandela from the Communist Party? (and if I understand its policy correctly) Is this an exaggeration of sorts; is Mandela pretending that he isn't sure what Communism is? (yes)

- Go to lines 141 and 142. Mark what the communists' aims were. (remove the capitalists)

- Go to line 143. Mark what communists seek to do that a people who are impoverished would likely not appreciate. (emphasize class distinctions)

- Go to line 144. Mark the word that means "very important." (vital)

- Go to lines 149 and 150. Mark the example Mandela uses. (the cooperation between Great Britain, the United States, and the Soviet Union in the fight against Hitler) Nobody claimed that the United States or the British were communists. Is this an irrelevant fact? Write *P* or *F* in the margin.

- Go to lines 154 and 155. Mark how communists treated black South Africans. (as human beings and their equals)

- Mark what the communists were the only group prepared to do. (work with the Africans for the attainment of political rights) Do you trust this claim, or do you think Mandela is exaggerating just to be persuasive? Is it possible that there were democratic groups who would have worked with them? Write *P* or *F* in the margin.

- Go to line 158. Mark the pronoun used as a reason. (this) Draw an arrow to connect *this* to what it represents. (only group prepared to work with Africans for the attainment of political rights)

- Go to lines 162 and 163. Mark what the South African government accused Mandela of being. (a member of the Communist Party)

- Go to line 164. Mark what Mandela views himself to be. (an African patriot) If you agree that Mandela loves his homeland above all else, write *P* in the margin. If you believe Mandela loves the Communist Party above all else, write *F*.

- Go to line 171. Mark what the ANC believes some form of socialism would accomplish. (overcome their legacy of extreme poverty) But, Mandela says this does not mean what? (we are Marxists) Is Mandela being honest, or is he fudging the truth? What do you think? Write *P* or *F*.

- Go to line 172. Mark the word used synonymously with communists. (Marxists)

- Was Mandela successful at illustrating the connection between the ANC and communism, while explaining the distinction between the two? (Answers will vary.)

Have students read lines 173–211 according to the option that you chose. In earlier sections, Mandela responded to two main charges leveled against him and the ANC—sabotage and communism. In this section, he will develop his overall argument that black South Africans are oppressed, and that his actions and the actions of the ANC are justified.

When most of the students are finished, continue with the entire class. Let's see how well you understood what you read.

Close Reading (cont.)

Our fight is against real and not imaginary hardships or, to use the language of the state prosecutor, "so-called hardships." Basically, we fight against two
175 features of African life in South Africa: poverty and lack of human dignity. We do not need communists to teach us about these things.

South Africa is the richest country in Africa. But it is a land of remarkable contrasts. The whites enjoy the highest standard of living, while Africans live in poverty and misery. The complaint of Africans, however, is not only
180 that they are poor and the whites are rich, but that the laws are designed to preserve this situation.

There are two ways to break out of poverty. The first is by formal education, and the second is by the worker acquiring a greater skill at his work and thus higher wages. As far as Africans are concerned, both these avenues of
185 advancement are deliberately curtailed by legislation.

The government has always sought to **hamper** Africans in their search for education. There is compulsory education for all white children at virtually no cost to their parents. But approximately 40 percent of African children between seven and fourteen do not attend school. For those who do, the
190 standards are vastly different from those afforded to white children.

The other main obstacle to the advancement of the African is the industrial color bar under which all the better jobs of industry are reserved for whites. Moreover, Africans in the unskilled and semi-skilled occupations are not allowed to form trade unions. This means that they are denied the right of
195 collective bargaining permitted to white workers.

The government answers its critics by saying that Africans in South Africa are better off than inhabitants of other countries in Africa. Even if this statement is true, it is **irrelevant**. Our complaint is not that we are poor by comparison with people in other countries, but that we are poor by
200 comparison with the white people in our own country, and that we are prevented by legislation from altering this imbalance.

The lack of human dignity experienced by Africans is the direct result of the policy of white supremacy. White supremacy implies black inferiority. Legislation designed to preserve white supremacy entrenches this notion.
205 Menial tasks in South Africa are invariably performed by Africans. When anything has to be carried or cleaned the white man will look around for an African to do it for him. Because of this sort of attitude, whites tend to regard Africans as a separate breed. They do not look upon them as people with families of their own; they do not realize that we fall in love, that
210 we want to be with our wives and children, that we want to earn enough money to support our families properly.

✎   **?**

- Circle the check mark or the question mark for this section. Draw a question mark over any confusing words.

- Go to line 173. Mark the word that means "troubles" or "struggles." **(hardships)** Mark a fallacy of the prosecutor that Mandela is calling out. **(so-called hardships)**

- Go to line 175. Mark two things blacks struggle against. **(poverty and lack of human dignity)** Is this an exaggeration? What do you think? Write *P* or *F*.

- Go to lines 180 and 181. Mark the main complaints of black Africans. **(they are poor and the whites are rich; the laws are designed to preserve this situation)** Overgeneralization? Are ALL whites rich and ALL blacks poor? Write *P* or *F*.

- Mark the two ways to break out of poverty. **(formal education; acquiring a greater skill at his work)**

- Go to line 185. Mark the word that means "reduced." **(curtailed)**

- Go to lines 187 and 188. Mark the word that tells how many white children attend school. **(all)** How many black children do not? **(40 percent)**

- Go to line 191. Mark the synonym for *road block*. **(obstacle)**

- Go to line 192. Mark who gets the better jobs. **(whites)**

- Go to line 194. Mark what black Africans cannot form. **(trade unions)** A trade union is a group that protects the rights of workers. Is this irrelevant? Write *P* or *F*.

- Go to lines 196 and 197. What irrelevant point does Mandela accuse the government of making? Mark it. **(Africans in South Africa are better off than inhabitants of other countries in Africa)** Circle the word that means "people who live in a place." **(inhabitants)**

- Go to line 200. Who are black South Africans poor in comparison with? Mark the phrase. **(white people in our own country)**

- Go to line 203. Mark what white supremacy implies, or suggests. (black inferiority)

- Go to line 205. Mark what many blacks have to perform. (menial tasks)

- Go to line 208. Mark what whites view black as. (separate breed)

- Go to lines 209–211. Mark what white people do not realize. (we fall in love, we want to be with our wives and children, we want to earn enough money to support our families) Is this a false assumption? What do you think? Write *P* or *F*.

Have students read line 212 to the end according to the option that you chose. In this section, Mandela wraps up his argument. These paragraphs bring all of his earlier points to a single conclusion.

When most of the students are finished, continue with the entire class. Let's see how well you understood what you read.

- Circle the check mark or the question mark for this section. Draw a question mark over any confusing words.

- Go to lines 212 and 213. Mark a secondary effect of poverty. (children wander the streets)

- Go to lines 215 and 216. Mark three more effects of poverty. (breakdown in moral standards, alarming rise in illegitimacy, violence) Circle the word used to mean "fatherless children." (illegitimacy) Do you think this is a fallacy, or do you think facts and statistics would back up what he is saying? What do you think? Write *P* or *F*.

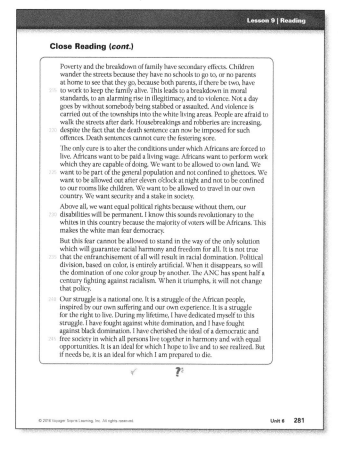

- Go to lines 217 and 218. Mark the sentence that implies that much of the violence has happened in the black neighborhoods. (**And violence is carried out of the townships into the white living areas**)

- Go to line 221. Mark the figurative language, or word picture, Mandela uses. (festering sore) Draw an arrow from this term to what is causing it. (poverty) Is this loaded language? What do you think? Write *P* or *F*.

- Go to the second paragraph. Underline the two words that Mandela repeats over and over again in this paragraph. (**Africans want; We want**) Is this effective rhetorical strategy or overgeneralization? Write *P* or *F*.

- Go to line 232. Mark what stands in the way of democracy. (fear)

- Return to the preceding line and mark why they fear democracy. (majority of voters will be Africans)

- Go to line 238. Mark what the ANC wants to do away with. (racialism)
- Mark the statement that is a loaded term meant to instill fear in the white men. (when it triumphs)
- Go to line 242. For what right are the African people fighting? Mark it. (the right to live)
- In the last paragraph, mark three verbs that tell what Mandela has done. (dedicated, fought, cherished) Is he bragging or exaggerating, or is he stating the truth? Write *P* or *F.*
- Go to lines 244 and 245. Mark the ideal Mandela cherishes, or deeply values. (a democratic and free society)
- Go to line 247. Mark the memorable phrase Mandela uses. (if needs be, it is an ideal for which I am prepared to die) This phrase has become an aphorism. Mandela is remembered for saying it. Do you think it was just dramatic talk, or did he mean it? Write *P* or *F.*

Have partners compare text markings and correct any errors.

Then, as a group, draw some conclusions about Mandela's use of rhetorical strategies to persuade his audience. Remind students that the penalty for sabotage was death, but that Mandela's sentence was life in prison instead. Discuss whether Mandela's relative "success"—his avoidance of the death penalty—was due to a use of fallacies or strong and honest arguments. Guide students to see that honest language is often far more powerful than misleading language. Invite them to keep an ear open for misleading language they might hear in their everyday lives.

Relationships Between Events

Write the following three groups of events on the board without the numbers. Explain that students will be discussing events they have learned about in both texts for this unit.

Apartheid laws were passed 2

Nelson Mandela became an international symbol of freedom and equality 4

Europeans colonized South Africa 1

Protesters of apartheid were sentenced to death, exile, or life in prison 3

Mandela imprisoned for 27 years 2

Apartheid ends 4

Mandela released from prison 3

Mandela elected president 5

The ANC begins the fight for equality 1

ANC began passive resistance campaign 1

ANC banned 3

Sharpeville shooting 2

ANC began sabotage campaign 4

ANC makes preparations to use force 6

Sabotage became punishable by death 5

Have partners describe the relationships between the historical events using time order sequence words. The lists are numbered in order. In informational texts, events and ideas can be connected in a multitude of ways. Sometimes, we talk about events in a simple chronological fashion. Other times, we talk about events in a more complex manner, such as cause and effect. It is important to understand that sometimes this is similar, but oftentimes it isn't. For instance, if I was talking about four events that happened this morning, I might say the following:

First, I woke up late. Then, I got ready for school. After getting ready, I rushed out the door, neglecting to eat breakfast. By second period, my stomach began hurting.

That is the order in which the four things happened. However, one did not necessarily cause the next one. Waking up late did not cause me to get ready for school. What did it cause? (rushing and neglecting to eat breakfast) What was the effect of doing this? (stomach hurting by second period) As you can see, there is one event in our sequence that isn't a cause or an effect, but the rest are.

Have partners describe the relationships between the same sets of events using cause and effect transition words.

Sample Answers:

Group 1: Cause and Effect: Because protesters of apartheid were sentenced to death, exile, or life in prison, Nelson Mandela became an international symbol of freedom and equality.

Group 2: Cause and Effect: Because the ANC begins the fight for equality, apartheid ends. Since apartheid ended, Mandela was elected president. The effect of Mandela being imprisoned was his release from prison, the end of apartheid, and Mandela being elected president.

Group 3: Cause and Effect: A result of the ANC's passive resistance campaign was the Sharpeville shooting. The Sharpeville shooting led the government to ban the ANC. The effect of the ban on the ANC was the ANC's sabotage campaign, which then led to the declaration that sabotage was punishable by death. Because of this declaration, the ANC made preparations to use force.

Unit 6 · Lesson 10

RI.5.1; RI.6.7; RI.8.7; W.2.2; W.3.2a; W.3.2b; W.3.2c; W.3.2d; W.8.2b; W.3.8; W.5.8; SL.6.1b; SL.6.1c; SL.6.1d; L.4.2b; L.6.6

Lesson Opener

Before the lesson, choose one of the following activities to write on the board or post on the *LANGUAGE! Live* Class Wall online.

- *Write four sentences with at least two vocabulary words in each. Show you know the meanings. (contribution, exploitation, defy, suspend, policy, massive, prospect, legacy, hamper, irrelevant)*
- *Dress your avatar as though you were disrespected by the government and treated as inferior. Explain your choices.*
- *If your friend said she would die for a slice of pizza right now, would you believe her? Why or why not?*

Vocabulary

Objective
- Review key passage vocabulary.

Recontextualize Passage Vocabulary

Direct students to page 256 in their Student Books. Use the following questions to review the vocabulary words from "I Am Prepared to Die."

- Everyone helped to get dinner on the table except you. Did you make a *contribution* to the dinner effort? (no) A friend is trying to raise money to help pay a family member's medical bills. You chip in $10. Have you made a *contribution*? (yes) Your art teacher asked each member of the class to bring an old photograph to use in a collage. You bring a photo of two-year-old you in superhero pajamas. The photo is your what? (contribution)

- You want to trade dishwashing nights with your sister so that you can go to a movie tonight. She agrees but also charges you five dollars. Are you a victim of *exploitation*? (yes) Your friend picks you up for the movie in his new car. Is this *exploitation*? (no) When people pay day laborers one-quarter the minimum wage because they know the workers are undocumented, what is it? (exploitation)

- You love working in the library on your free period. You help the librarian with whatever needs doing. Do you *defy* her requests for help? (no) The school now requires everyone—boys and girls alike—to wear floor-length skirts. Do you consider *defying* this new rule? (yes) Your coach ordered everyone to stay away from sweets. But then, your grandmother brings over a chocolate cake she made just for you. What might you end up doing? (defying the coach's orders)

- You're grounded, but your mother lets you attend the family reunion on Saturday. Has she *suspended* your grounding? (yes) After the "guilty" verdict, the judge sent the suspect straight to prison. Did he *suspend* the sentence? (no) You were supposed to have a geography test, but the teacher's computer crashed and she lost it. What does she do? (suspend the test)

- You brush your teeth three times a day, no matter what. Do you have a brush-three-times-a-day *policy*? **(yes)** There aren't any rules in my nephew's preschool classroom. The teacher just goes with the flow. Does she have classroom *policies*? **(no)** As a rule, Myrna waits five minutes before answering any text. What does Myrna have? **(a texting policy)**

- Boris has a very slight crush on Cecilia. Does he have a *massive* crush on her? **(no)** The quarterback tosses you the ball. You look up and see an enormous linebacker coming your way. Is the linebacker *massive*? **(yes)** The Battle of Antietam was the bloodiest one-day battle of the Civil War. More than 20,000 soldiers died in a single day. The casualties were what? **(massive)**

- You want to try out for the swim team, but you don't know how to swim. Are your *prospects* good for making the team? **(no)** You want it to snow so that school will be canceled, but the forecast is for sunny, warm weather. Are the *prospects* good for a snow day? **(no)** Your team is down by 12 with 15 seconds left in the game. What are growing smaller and smaller by the second? **(your prospects for winning)**

- For generations, your family has been active in local politics. Does your family have a political *legacy*? **(yes)** When your niece was born, your sister just made up a name for her. Was the name a family *legacy*? **(no)** Your rich uncle dies and leaves you a fortune. You received a part of his what? **(legacy)**

- You're late for school and trying to race out the door, but your Chihuahua Pebbles is running circles around your feet. Is she *hampering* your progress? **(yes)** At the regional spelling bee, volunteers in black-and-yellow T-shirts help contestants get where they need to be. Do the volunteers *hamper* the contestants? **(no)** Everyone in your family loves the sack race at the fall festival, but you find that putting both legs in a sack does what? **(hampers your ability to move)**

- You ask your friend what time it is, and she responds, "Yellow." Is her response *irrelevant*? **(yes)** You ask your brother to format a document for you because you don't know how. He suggests you watch and learn how. Is his suggestion *irrelevant*? **(no)** You learn that you can fly to the Bahamas for $249, but you only have $19. As far as you're concerned, the special deal is what? **(irrelevant)**

Writing

Objectives

- Analyze the effect of media and how it changes the impact of text.
- Compare and contrast a written speech with a multimedia version.
- Use a process to write a multiparagraph essay.
- Use a rubric to guide and assess writing.

Six Traits of Effective Writing

Direct students back to page 30 from Unit 1 in their Student Books. Reread the Six Traits of Effective Writing.

We have been using the six traits of effective writing. It becomes more and more important as the scope of our writing grows. Refer to the six traits as you are writing your multiparagraph essay and be sure to address all six traits in your writing.

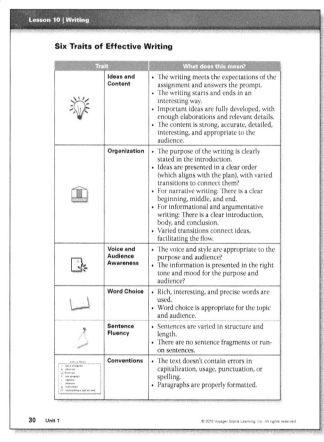

Lesson 10 | Writing

Six Traits of Effective Writing

Trait	What does this mean?
Ideas and Content	• The writing meets the expectations of the assignment and answers the prompt. • The writing starts and ends in an interesting way. • Important ideas are fully developed, with enough elaborations and relevant details. • The content is strong, accurate, detailed, interesting, and appropriate to the audience.
Organization	• The purpose of the writing is clearly stated in the introduction. • Ideas are presented in a clear order (which aligns with the plan), with varied transitions to connect them? • For narrative writing: There is a clear beginning, middle, and end. • For informational and argumentative writing: There is a clear introduction, body, and conclusion. • Varied transitions connect ideas, facilitating the flow.
Voice and Audience Awareness	• The voice and style are appropriate to the purpose and audience? • The information is presented in the right tone and mood for the purpose and audience?
Word Choice	• Rich, interesting, and precise words are used. • Word choice is appropriate for the topic and audience.
Sentence Fluency	• Sentences are varied in structure and length. • There are no sentence fragments or run-on sentences.
Conventions	• The text doesn't contain errors in capitalization, usage, punctuation, or spelling. • Paragraphs are properly formatted.

30   Unit 1

© 2016 Voyager Sopris Learning, Inc. All rights reserved.

Prepare to Write: Multiparagraph Essay

Many good stories are made into movies. I prefer to read the book first, then watch the movie. I do this because I want to create my own pictures in my head. If I watch the movie first, I am picturing the actors and the setting as it was shown in the movie, and often it is not the same as it is written. When I finish the movie, I am always amazed at how much changed from text to screen. Does this happen to you?

We have listened to the audio version of a text and identified how hearing a text can change what we "get" from the text. Right now, we are going to combine audio elements and visual elements to see if our understanding, as well as the impact, of the speech changes. We will hear Mandela's speech as it was delivered during the trial. Listen to his voice, his inflection, his tone, and his rhythm. Pay close attention to how his tone of voice and inflection change the words. You will also be watching a video montage in the background of his speech. I want you to watch carefully. It is important to figure out if the images you see affect what you hear in the speech.

y the "Nelson andela" multimedia found in the acher Resources ine.

Play the "Nelson Mandela" multimedia file, which can be found online in the Teacher Resources.

Have partners discuss the impact of the images accompanying the speech as well as the impact of hearing the speech as it was delivered.

Direct students to page 282 in their Student Books.

Part A. Study the Prompt

Read the instructions for Part A and the prompt. Point out the capitalization in the title as well as the use of quotation marks for the name of the speech. Explain that articles, short stories, poems, and speeches are not underlined or italicized, but placed in quotations. Guide students through identifying the topic, summarizing the directions, and understanding the purpose for writing.

In a previous lesson, we began talking about prompts that will require more than one paragraph in response. This prompt will require you to write a multiparagraph response. Each paragraph will have a different job, or purpose. All the paragraphs together will support the main idea you put forth in your thesis statement.

Lesson 10 | Writing

Prepare to Write: Multiparagraph Essay

Part A. Study the Prompt   Answers will vary.

Read the prompt and identify the topic, directions, and purpose for writing.

You have read the text version of Nelson Mandela's speech "I Am Prepared to Die." You have also viewed a multimedia version of excerpts from the speech. Write an essay that compares and contrasts the text and the video. In your essay, do the following:

- Analyze the impact of Mandela's words in each version.
- Evaluate the pros and cons of using each format to communicate Mandela's message.

Topic: different versions of Mandela's speech

Directions: compare and contrast the text of the speech with the multimedia version of the speech

Purpose for writing: explaining the pros and cons of each format

Part B. Write a Thesis Statement

Write at least two sentences that introduce the subject and identify the big ideas.

Mandela dedicated his life to a single message. He expressed this message in a speech he gave when standing trial for sabotage in April 1964. Both the text of the speech and the multimedia version are powerful, but in my view, the multimedia version brings Mandela's message to life more effectively.

282   Unit 6   © 2018 Voyager Sopris Learning, Inc. All rights reserved.

Part B. Write a Thesis Statement

In a little while, you will need to write a thesis statement that sums up your main ideas. You have been prompted to write at least three sentences that will serve as your introduction. The first sentence or two should introduce the topic of Mandela's speech. The next sentence or two should briefly tell how the text of the speech and the multimedia version are similar and how they are different. Before you can write this introduction though, you will need to take notes about the two versions' similarities and differences. Let's do that now.

Part C. Take Notes

Have students work with a partner to discuss the strengths and weaknesses of each version of the speech. Remind students that they can look back to the text of the speech if they need to. You may also want to play the video another time or two while students work.

Now that we've identified the similarities and differences between the two versions of the speech, let's draw a conclusion. Which version did you find more powerful? Why? Complete the sentence at the bottom of the chart.

Now that we've taken notes and drawn a conclusion, let's go back and work on our thesis statement.

Have students write their introductions. Have volunteers share what they've written. Share this example if students need more support:

Mandela dedicated his life to a single message. He expressed this message in a speech he gave when standing trial for sabotage in April 1964. Both the text of the speech and the multimedia version are powerful, but in my view, the multimedia version is more powerful because it brings Mandela's message to life more effectively.

Prepare to Write: Multiparagraph Essay (cont.)

Part C. Take Notes

Evaluate how well each version presents Mandela's argument, creates a mood, helps you understand apartheid, and persuades you to agree with Mandela.

How well did this version . . .	Text of Speech	Multimedia Version of Speech
present Mandela's claims and arguments?	Does this very well. The text includes well-supported arguments explaining why the ANC used sabotage and why the ANC is not a communist organization. It also provides facts and statistics that show how unjust apartheid was.	Does this less well. The multimedia version of the speech pulled some key phrases out of the speech and presented them through Mandela's own voice and through words on the screen. But it did not include evidence, facts, or details to support these key phrases.
create a certain tone, mood, or feeling?	Does this to a degree. The tone of the speech is very formal and objective, so the reader has a difficult time detecting a mood or feeling. However, the reader can tell Mandela is dignified and calm. This alone causes the reader to respect him.	Does this very well. The sound of Mandela's voice, along with the images of peaceful protestors being abused by police, hungry children, and poverty-stricken villages, creates a strong mood of injustice. The viewer hears the sadness and urgency in Mandela's voice and sees it on the faces of black South Africans.

Unit 6   283

Part D. Write a Conclusion

Your conclusion should restate your thesis, or main idea. It should also wrap up your writing in a memorable way. Including a quote is one good way to emphasize a key point and end on a memorable note. Write the following example on the board:

In both the text of the speech and the multimedia version, we hear Nelson Mandela say that his ideal of democracy is "an ideal for which I am prepared to die." On paper, these words communicate the message that Mandela was a man of strong principles. In the multimedia version, though, these words—and others—come to life powerfully. They take the viewer back to 1964. They make us want to stand side-by-side with this great man and help him fight for democracy. They make us want to be great people too.

Prepare to Write: Multiparagraph Essay (*cont.*)

How well did this version . . .	Text of Speech	Multimedia Version of Speech
persuade the reader or viewer to believe Mandela's message?	Does this well. Mandela's arguments, evidence, and rhetorical strategies all combine to convince the reader that Mandela means what he says. By the end of the speech, the reader fully agrees that apartheid should end and Mandela did what he did out of necessity.	Does this well. Hearing Mandela's voice helps the reader know how sincere he is and how strongly he feels about his cause. It is impossible to watch the video and conclude that Mandela is acting for selfish or self-promoting reasons.

Overall, I found the <u>multimedia version</u> more powerful because it <u>brings the words to life</u>

Part D. Write a Conclusion

Write at least two sentences that restate the thesis and summarize the key ideas.

In both the text of the speech and the multimedia version, we hear Nelson Mandela say that his ideal of democracy is "an ideal for which I am prepared to die." On paper, these words communicate the message that Mandela was a man of strong principles. In the multimedia version, though, these words—and others—come to life powerfully. They take the viewer back to 1964. They make us want to stand side-by-side with this great man and help him fight for democracy. They make us want to be great people too.

Note: Help students punctuate their quote if they choose to include one. Because the quote used in the sample comes after the linking verb *is*, no comma is used before the open quotation mark; the quotation serves as the subject complement. However, an introductory phrase such as *According to Mandela* **would** require a comma before the open quotation mark. Or, if students choose to write a complete sentence to set up the quote, they need to separate the sentence from the quote with a colon.

Part E. Write Topic Sentences

Before you begin writing your essay, take a minute to write a sentence that sums up each row in your notes chart. These sentences will be the topic sentences for the body paragraphs of your essay. Use compare and contrast words such as *both, but, better,* and *equally* as you express similarities and differences.

Have students write their topic sentences. If needed, share the following sentences as examples:

Both the text and the multimedia version of the speech communicate Mandela's claims, but the text version does this better.

When it comes to setting a tone or a mood, the multimedia version of the speech is the clear winner.

Both versions of the speech are equally persuasive.

Prepare to Write: Multiparagraph Essay (*cont.*)

Part E. Write Topic Sentences

Use your notes to write the topic sentences for each point of comparison between the two versions of the speech.

Paragraph #1

Both the text and the multimedia version of the speech communicate Mandela's claims, but the text version does this better.

Paragraph #2

When it comes to setting a tone or a mood, the multimedia version of the speech is the clear winner.

Paragraph #3

Both versions of the speech are equally persuasive.

Write

Have students write their essay on a piece of notebook sheet. Encourage them by reminding them that they've written the frames for the entire essay. Have students consult the Six Traits of Writing: Expository Rubric on page 390 as they write their paragraph. If they struggle or need additional support in developing their paragraph, use the following essay as a model.

Six Traits of Writing: Expository

	Ideas and Content	Organization	Voice and Audience Awareness	Word Choice	Sentence Fluency	Language Conventions
4	The thesis is very clear and well focused. Supporting details make the paper very easy to understand and interesting.	Ideas are very clearly organized. All parts of the essay (introduction, body, and conclusion) work together to support the thesis.	The writer's voice is distinctive and shows an interest in the topic. The writer knows who his or her audience is.	Words are used correctly and are very well chosen. They create pictures in the reader's mind.	Sentences have an easy flow and rhythm. Transitions are very smooth.	There are no grammar errors. There are few or no errors in spelling, capitalization, or punctuation.
3	The thesis is clear. Supporting details make the paper easy to understand.	Ideas are clearly organized. The paper includes all parts of an essay (introduction, body, and conclusion).	The writer's voice is natural and shows an interest in the topic. The writer knows who his or her audience is.	Words are used correctly. Some words may be a bit general.	Sentences are formed correctly and are varied in structure. Transitions are clear.	There are no major grammar errors. There are few errors in spelling, capitalization, or punctuation.
2	The thesis is not clear. The ideas are somewhat developed, but there are only a few details.	Ideas are fairly well organized. The paper includes all parts of an essay (introduction, body, and conclusion).	The writer's voice is natural, but the writer is not fully engaged in the topic. At times, the writer's viewpoint may be vague.	Most words are used correctly. A few words are too general. Some words are repeated.	Sentences are formed correctly, although they may be similar in structure. Most transitions are clear.	There are a few grammar errors. There are a few errors in spelling, capitalization, or punctuation.
1	The thesis of the paper is unclear or missing. The paper is poorly developed and/or confusing.	Ideas are not clearly organized. The paper may be missing an introduction or a conclusion.	The writer seems uninterested in the topic and unaware of his or her audience.	Most words are used incorrectly, many are too general or frequently repeated.	The sentences do not flow well and lack structure. They are short and choppy or long and confusing.	There are many grammar and/or spelling errors. There are many errors in capitalization and punctuation.

Writing Rubric: Expository

390   *Writing Rubric: Expository*

Exemplar Writing: Multiparagraph Essay

Mandela dedicated his life to a single message. He expressed this message in a speech he gave when standing trial for sabotage in April 1964. Both the text of the speech and the multimedia version are powerful, but in my view, the multimedia version brings Mandela's message to life more effectively.

Both the text and the multimedia version of the speech communicate Mandela's claims, but the text version does this better. The text includes well-supported arguments explaining why the ANC used sabotage and why the ANC is not a communist organization. It also provides facts and statistics that show how unjust apartheid was. The multimedia version of the speech, on the other hand, used only key phrases from the speech. It presented these phrases through Mandela's own voice and through words on the screen. But it did not include evidence, facts, or details to support these ideas.

When it comes to setting a tone or a mood, the multimedia version of the speech is the clear winner. On paper, the speech has a formal and objective tone, so the reader has a difficult time "feeling" Mandela's words. The video, on the other hand, evokes strong emotions. The sound of Mandela's voice, along with the images of peaceful protestors being abused by police, hungry children, and poverty-stricken villages creates a strong sense of injustice. The viewer hears the sadness and urgency in Mandela's voice and sees it on the faces of black South Africans.

Both versions of the speech are equally persuasive. In the text, Mandela's arguments, evidence, and rhetorical strategies all combine to convince the reader that Mandela means what he says. By the end of the speech, the reader fully agrees that apartheid should end and that Mandela did what he did out of necessity. Similarly, hearing Mandela's voice in the video helps the reader know how sincere he is and how strongly he feels about his cause. It is impossible to watch the video and conclude that Mandela is acting for selfish or self-promoting reasons.

In both the text of the speech and the multimedia version, we hear Nelson Mandela say that his ideal of democracy is "an ideal for which I am prepared to die." On paper, these words communicate the message that Mandela was a man of strong principles. In the multimedia video, though, these words—and others—come powerfully to life. They take the viewer back to 1964. They make us want to stand side-by-side with this great man and help him fight for democracy. They make us want to be great people too.

Student Handwriting:
Handwriting lessons are provided in manuscript and cursive. These explicit lessons (found online in Resources) can be taught systematically during writing lessons to strengthen legibility and fluency.

Evaluate Writing

Direct students to page 286 in their Student Books and read the information in the checklist.

This checklist is a tool you can use to evaluate your writing and make sure you are using good technique. This unit's checklist is a little bit more advanced than the one in the last unit, so read through it carefully. As we progress through the program, we will add things we have learned that will make us better writers. **Have individuals quickly assess their writing, then have partners evaluate each other's writing based on the checklist.**

Note: Use Six Traits of Writing Scoring Rubric: Expository on page 565 of this book to assess students' writing. A printable version is located online in the Teacher Resources.

The Writer's Checklist

Trait	Yes	No	Did the writer . . .?
Ideas and Content			clearly state the topic of the composition
			focus each paragraph on the topic
			include examples, evidence, and/or explanations to develop each paragraph
Organization			Paragraph Level:
			tell things in an order that makes sense
			Report Level:
			write an introductory paragraph that states the topic and the plan
			use transition topic sentences to connect paragraphs
			write a concluding paragraph that restates the introductory paragraph
Voice and Audience Awareness			think about the audience and purpose for writing
			write in a clear and engaging way that makes the audience want to read the work
Word Choice			find a unique way to say things
			use words that are lively and specific to the content
Sentence Fluency			write complete sentences
			expand some sentences using the steps of Masterpiece Sentences
			use compound sentence elements and compound sentences
Conventions			capitalize words correctly:
			capitalize the first word of each sentence
			capitalize proper nouns, including people's names
			punctuate correctly:
			end sentences with a period, question mark, or exclamation mark
			use an apostrophe for possessive nouns and contractions
			use commas and/or semicolons correctly
			use grammar correctly:
			use the correct verb tense
			make sure the verb agrees with the subject in number
			use correct spelling

Letters down left side: R E V I S E E D I T

286   Unit 6   © 2016 Voyager Sopris Learning, Inc. All rights reserved.

Six Traits of Writing: Expository

Objectives

- Self-correct as comprehension of text deepens.
- Answer questions to demonstrate comprehension of text.
- Engage in class discussion.
- Identify the enduring understandings from a piece of text.

Revisit Passage Comprehension

Direct students back to pages 271–274 in their Student Books. Have students review their answers and make any necessary changes. Then, have partners share their answers and collaborate to perfect them.

Enduring Understandings

Direct students back to page 254 in their Student Books. Reread the Big Idea questions.

What is worth dying for? Do you think you could ever let it happen?

When, and for what reasons, is violence justified?

Generate a class discussion about the questions and the answers students came up with in Lesson 6. Have them consider whether their answers have changed any after reading the text.

Use the following talking points to foster conversation. Refer to the Class Discussion Rules poster and have students use the Collegial Discussion sentence frames on page 382 of their Student Books.

- Mandela professed his willingness to die for a cause. If he had been sentenced to death, then he would have been referred to as a martyr. Are there causes worth dying for?

- Ultimately, Mandela believed the ANC was compelled to use violence. But they did it only as a last resort. Was this a good approach? Why or why not? How did the ANC's efforts to use non-violence for so long come in handy during his trial speech? What generalizations can you make about using non-violence and/or violence in a struggle for basic human rights?

What we read should make us think. Use our discussion and your thoughts about the text to determine what you will "walk away with." Has it made you think about a personal experience or someone you know? Has your perspective or opinion on a specific topic changed? Do you have any lingering thoughts or questions? Write these ideas as your enduring understandings. What will you take with you from this text?

Discuss the enduring understandings with the class. Then, have students write their enduring understandings from the unit. If time permits, have them post a personal response to one of the enduring understandings to the online class wall.

Remind students to consider why Mandela delivered the speech and whether he was successful.

End-of-Unit Online Assessments

Monitor students' progress in the unit by utilizing online assessments. Students should prioritize these assessments over successive Word Training units.

- Assign Unit 6 Content Mastery quizzes to assess skills taught in this unit.
- Assign Power Pass to assess reading comprehension skills in a standardized test format.

All assessments can be assigned online by opening the Tools menu, then selecting Assignments. Be sure to select the correct class and unit from the drop-down menu.

Reteach

Based on students' performance in Content Mastery, extra practice may be needed.

- If student scores fall at 60 percent or below, reteach the content to small groups.
- If student scores fall between 61–79 percent, reinforce the skills by assigning the student reteach activity pages as homework.

Reteach lessons can be found online on the Course Reports page for each unit.

Comprehension Building

Background knowledge is a key component of reading comprehension. It is important for students to develop knowledge of a topic prior to class discussion and reading of complex text.

Print Unit 7 Background Information from the online Resources and assign as homework for students to read. Encourage students to come to class prepared for discussion.

Additional Resources

Posters

Reading

Posters can also be printed from the Teacher Resources online.

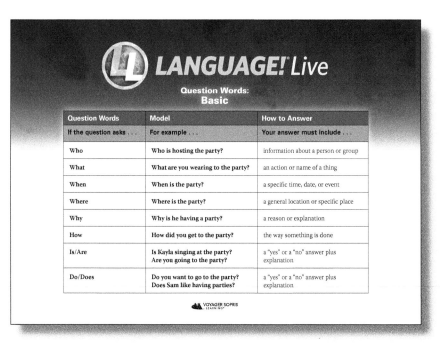

LANGUAGE! Live

Question Words:
Basic

Question Words	Model	How to Answer
If the question asks . . .	For example . . .	Your answer must include . . .
Who	Who is hosting the party?	information about a person or group
What	What are you wearing to the party?	an action or name of a thing
When	When is the party?	a specific time, date, or event
Where	Where is the party?	a general location or specific place
Why	Why is he having a party?	a reason or explanation
How	How did you get to the party?	the way something is done
Is/Are	Is Kayla singing at the party? Are you going to the party?	a "yes" or a "no" answer plus explanation
Do/Does	Do you want to go to the party? Does Sam like having parties?	a "yes" or a "no" answer plus explanation

VOYAGER SOPRIS
LEARNING

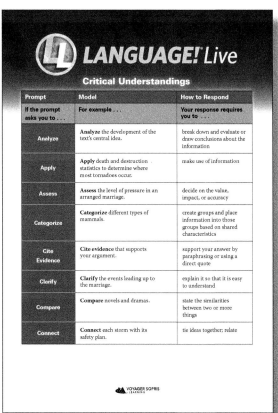

LANGUAGE! Live

Critical Understandings

Prompt	Model	How to Respond
If the prompt asks you to . . .	For example . . .	Your response requires you to . . .
Analyze	**Analyze** the development of the text's central idea.	break down and evaluate or draw conclusions about the information
Apply	**Apply** death and destruction statistics to determine where most tornadoes occur.	make use of information
Assess	**Assess** the level of pressure in an arranged marriage.	decide on the value, impact, or accuracy
Categorize	**Categorize** different types of mammals.	create groups and place information into those groups based on shared characteristics
Cite Evidence	**Cite evidence** that supports your argument.	support your answer by paraphrasing or using a direct quote
Clarify	**Clarify** the events leading up to the marriage.	explain it so that it is easy to understand
Compare	**Compare** novels and dramas.	state the similarities between two or more things
Connect	**Connect** each storm with its safety plan.	tie ideas together; relate

VOYAGER SOPRIS
LEARNING

Reading

Posters can also be printed from the Teacher Resources online.

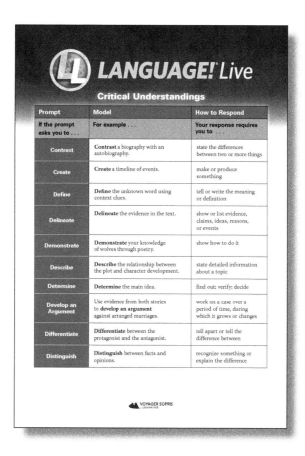

LANGUAGE! Live
Critical Understandings

Prompt	Model	How to Respond
If the prompt asks you to . . .	For example . . .	Your response requires you to . . .
Contrast	**Contrast** a biography with an autobiography.	state the differences between two or more things
Create	**Create** a timeline of events.	make or produce something
Define	**Define** the unknown word using context clues.	tell or write the meaning or definition
Delineate	**Delineate** the evidence in the text.	show or list evidence, claims, ideas, reasons, or events
Demonstrate	**Demonstrate** your knowledge of wolves through poetry.	show how to do it
Describe	**Describe** the relationship between the plot and character development.	state detailed information about a topic
Determine	**Determine** the main idea.	find out; verify; decide
Develop an Argument	Use evidence from both stories to **develop an argument** against arranged marriages.	work on a case over a period of time, during which it grows or changes
Differentiate	**Differentiate** between the protagonist and the antagonist.	tell apart or tell the difference between
Distinguish	**Distinguish** between facts and opinions.	recognize something or explain the difference

VOYAGER SOPRIS
LEARNING

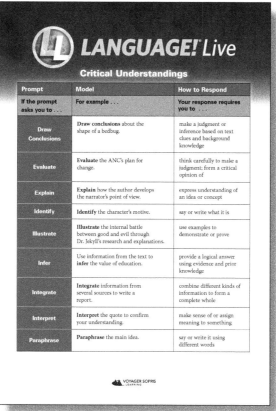

LANGUAGE! Live
Critical Understandings

Prompt	Model	How to Respond
If the prompt asks you to . . .	For example . . .	Your response requires you to . . .
Draw Conclusions	**Draw conclusions** about the shape of a bedbug.	make a judgment or inference based on text clues and background knowledge
Evaluate	**Evaluate** the ANC's plan for change.	think carefully to make a judgment; form a critical opinion of
Explain	**Explain** how the author develops the narrator's point of view.	express understanding of an idea or concept
Identify	**Identify** the character's motive.	say or write what it is
Illustrate	**Illustrate** the internal battle between good and evil through Dr. Jekyll's research and explanations.	use examples to demonstrate or prove
Infer	Use information from the text to **infer** the value of education.	provide a logical answer using evidence and prior knowledge
Integrate	**Integrate** information from several sources to write a report.	combine different kinds of information to form a complete whole
Interpret	**Interpret** the quote to confirm your understanding.	make sense of or assign meaning to something
Paraphrase	**Paraphrase** the main idea.	say or write it using different words

VOYAGER SOPRIS
LEARNING

Posters

Reading

Posters can also be printed from the Teacher Resources online.

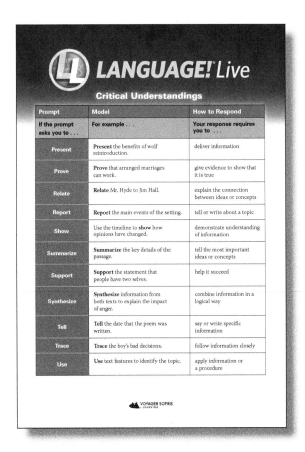

Vocabulary

Posters can also be printed from the Teacher Resources online.

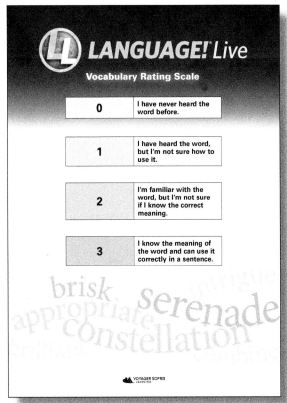

Grammar

Posters can also be printed from the Teacher Resources online.

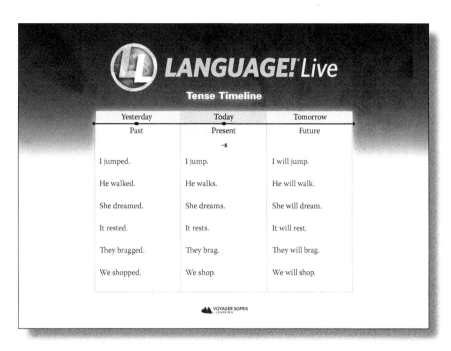

Tense Timeline

Yesterday	Today	Tomorrow
Past	Present	Future
	-s	
I jumped.	I jump.	I will jump.
He walked.	He walks.	He will walk.
She dreamed.	She dreams.	She will dream.
It rested.	It rests.	It will rest.
They bragged.	They brag.	They will brag.
We shopped.	We shop.	We will shop.

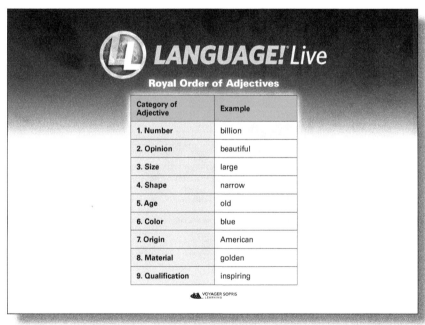

Royal Order of Adjectives

Category of Adjective	Example
1. Number	billion
2. Opinion	beautiful
3. Size	large
4. Shape	narrow
5. Age	old
6. Color	blue
7. Origin	American
8. Material	golden
9. Qualification	inspiring

Posters

Grammar

Posters can also be printed from the Teacher Resources online.

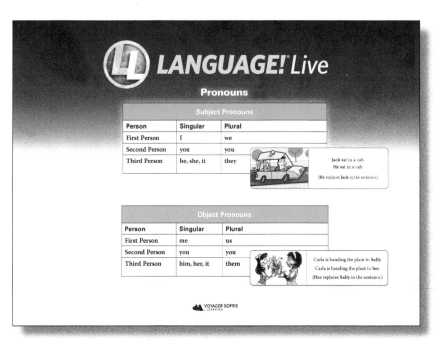

LANGUAGE! Live

Pronouns

Subject Pronouns

Person	Singular	Plural
First Person	I	we
Second Person	you	you
Third Person	he, she, it	they

Jack sat in a cab.
He sat in a cab.
(He replaces Jack in the sentence.)

Object Pronouns

Person	Singular	Plural
First Person	me	us
Second Person	you	you
Third Person	him, her, it	them

Carla is handing the plant to Sally.
Carla is handing the plant to her.
(Her replaces Sally in the sentence.)

VOYAGER SOPRIS LEARNING

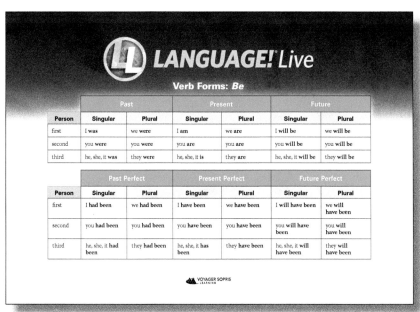

LANGUAGE! Live

Verb Forms: *Be*

Person	Past		Present		Future	
	Singular	Plural	Singular	Plural	Singular	Plural
first	I was	we were	I am	we are	I will be	we will be
second	you were	you were	you are	you are	you will be	you will be
third	he, she, it was	they were	he, she, it is	they are	he, she, it will be	they will be

Person	Past Perfect		Present Perfect		Future Perfect	
	Singular	Plural	Singular	Plural	Singular	Plural
first	I had been	we had been	I have been	we have been	I will have been	we will have been
second	you had been	you had been	you have been	you have been	you will have been	you will have been
third	he, she, it had been	they had been	he, she, it has been	they have been	he, she, it will have been	they will have been

VOYAGER SOPRIS LEARNING

Writing

Posters can also be printed from the Teacher Resources online.

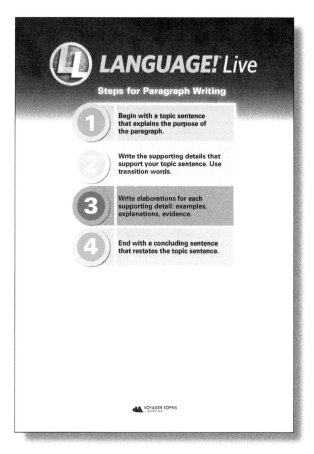

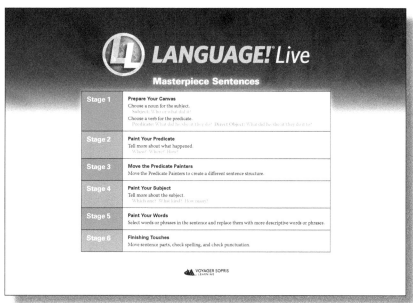

Posters

Writing

Posters can also be printed from the Teacher Resources online.

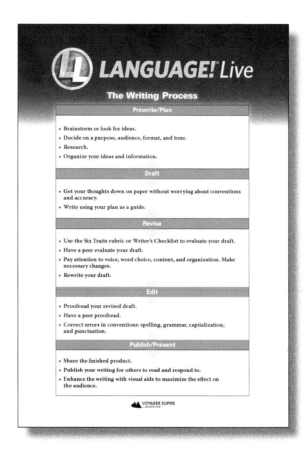

LANGUAGE! Live

The Writing Process

Prewrite/Plan

- Brainstorm or look for ideas.
- Decide on a purpose, audience, format, and tone.
- Research.
- Organize your ideas and information.

Draft

- Get your thoughts down on paper without worrying about conventions and accuracy.
- Write using your plan as a guide.

Revise

- Use the Six Traits rubric or Writer's Checklist to evaluate your draft.
- Have a peer evaluate your draft.
- Pay attention to voice, word choice, content, and organization. Make necessary changes.
- Rewrite your draft.

Edit

- Proofread your revised draft.
- Have a peer proofread.
- Correct errors in conventions: spelling, grammar, capitalization, and punctuation.

Publish/Present

- Share the finished product.
- Publish your writing for others to read and respond to.
- Enhance the writing with visual aids to maximize the effect on the audience.

VOYAGER SOPRIS LEARNING

LANGUAGE! Live

Elements of Formal Writing

Formal writing . . .

- is clear and direct.
- is grammatically correct.
- uses polite language.
- does not use slang.
- is free of strong emotion.
- gives support and evidence for general ideas.
- is free of contractions.
- is free of text message jargon, abbreviations, or "cutesy" elements.

VOYAGER SOPRIS LEARNING

Speaking and Listening

Posters can also be printed from the Teacher Resources online.

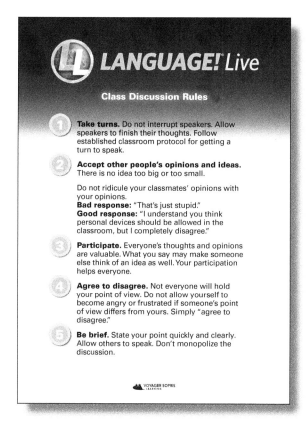

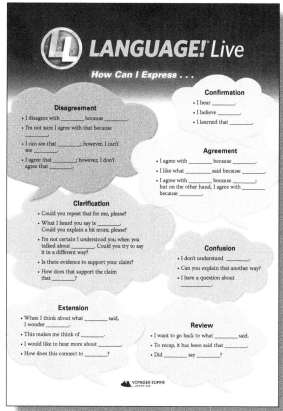

Six Traits of Writing: Basic

	Ideas and Content	Organization	Voice and Audience Awareness	Word Choice	Sentence Fluency	Language Conventions
4	Focuses on the topic. Main idea (topic sentence) is clear and well supported with details and elaboration (examples, evidence, and explanations).	Topic sentence clearly states main idea. Ideas are clear and logically organized. Contains concluding sentence.	The words have a strong sense of person and purpose. Brings topic to life.	Words are specific to the content, accurate, and vivid. Word choice enhances meaning and the reader's enjoyment.	Writes complete sentences and varies sentence structure.	*Capitalization & Punctuation* No errors. Indents paragraphs. *Grammar/Usage* 0–1 error *Spelling* 0–1 error
3	Mostly focuses on the topic. Sentences supporting the main idea (topic sentence) may be general rather than detailed and specific.	Topic sentence states main idea. Organization mostly clear and logical. May contain concluding sentence.	The words have some sense of person and purpose.	Words are correctly used but may be somewhat general and unspecific.	Writes complete sentences and attempts to use expanded sentences.	*Capitalization & Punctuation* 1 error. Indents paragraphs. *Grammar/Usage* 2 errors *Spelling* 2 errors
2	Main idea (topic sentence) is unclear and/or lacks sufficient support.	Structure may not be entirely clear or logical. Paragraph may seem more like a list and/or be hard to follow.	The words have little sense of person and purpose.	Words may be used inaccurately or repetitively.	Writes mostly simple and/or awkwardly constructed sentences. May include some run-ons and fragments.	*Capitalization & Punctuation* 2 errors. May not indent paragraphs. *Grammar/Usage* 3 errors *Spelling* 3 errors
1	Does not address prompt and/or lacks a topic sentence. Supporting details are absent or do not relate to topic.	No evident structure. Lack of organization seriously interferes with meaning.	The words have no sense of person or purpose. No sense of audience.	Extremely limited range of words. Restricted vocabulary impedes message.	Numerous run-ons and/or fragments interfere with meaning.	*Capitalization & Punctuation* 3+ errors. May not indent paragraphs. *Grammar/Usage* 4+ errors interfere with meaning *Spelling* 4+ errors
Value						

Comments _____

Six Traits of Writing: Expository

	Ideas and Content	Organization	Voice and Audience Awareness	Word Choice	Sentence Fluency	Language Conventions
4	The paper is very clear and well focused. Supporting details make the paper very easy to understand and interesting.	Ideas are very clearly organized. All parts of the essay (introduction, body, and conclusion) work together to support the thesis.	The writer's voice is distinctive and shows an interest in the topic. The writer knows who his or her audience is.	Words are used correctly and are very well chosen. They create pictures in the reader's mind.	Sentences have an easy flow and rhythm. Transitions are very smooth.	*Capitalization & Punctuation* No errors. Indents paragraphs. *Grammar/Usage* 0–1 error *Spelling* 0–1 error
3	The paper is clear and well focused. Supporting details make the paper easy to understand.	Ideas are clearly organized. The paper includes all parts of an essay (introduction, body, and conclusion).	The writer's voice is natural and shows an interest in the topic. The writer knows who his or her audience is.	Words are used correctly. Some words may be a bit general.	Sentences are formed correctly and are varied in structure. Transitions are clear.	*Capitalization & Punctuation* 1 error. Indents paragraphs. *Grammar/Usage* 2 errors *Spelling* 2 errors
2	The paper has a clear thesis. The ideas are somewhat developed, but there are only a few details.	Ideas are fairly well organized. The paper includes all parts of an essay (introduction, body, and conclusion).	The writer's voice is natural, but the writer is not fully engaged in the topic. At times, the writer's viewpoint may be vague.	Most words are used correctly. A few words are too general. Some words are repeated.	Sentences are formed correctly, although they may be similar in structure. Most transitions are clear.	*Capitalization & Punctuation* 2 errors. May not indent paragraphs. *Grammar/Usage* 3 errors *Spelling* 3 errors
1	The thesis of the paper is unclear or missing. The paper is poorly developed and/or confusing.	Ideas are not clearly organized. The paper may be missing an introduction or a conclusion.	The writer seems uninterested in the topic and unaware of his or her audience.	Most words are used incorrectly, many are too general or frequently repeated.	The sentences do not flow well and lack structure. They are short and choppy or long and confusing.	*Capitalization & Punctuation* 3+ errors. May not indent paragraphs. *Grammar/Usage* 4+ errors interfere with meaning *Spelling* 4+ errors
Value						

Comments _____

Writing Rubric: Fiction

Six Traits of Writing: Fiction

	Ideas and Content	Organization	Voice and Audience Awareness	Word Choice	Sentence Fluency	Language Conventions
4	Clear plot events, as well as a readily identifiable conflict/problem and setting. The climax and resolution are clear. Rich details and sensory description make characters come to life. No irrelevant material.	Beginning grabs reader's attention. Logically sequenced plot. Story transitions link events. Conclusion caps off story and does not leave the reader hanging.	Strong sense of person and purpose behind the words. Brings story to life.	Words are specific, accurate, and vivid. Word choice enhances meaning and reader's enjoyment.	Writes complete sentences with varied sentence patterns and beginnings	*Capitalization & Punctuation* No errors. Indents paragraphs. *Grammar/Usage 0–1 error* *Spelling 0–1 error*
3	Identifiable plot events. Conflict/problem may not be entirely clear. The climax or resolution may not be clear. Some details/sensory description. Characters present but may not be fully developed. Setting may be missing. Limited irrelevant material.	Beginning interests reader. Plot somewhat logically sequenced but may lack one story element such as climax or satisfying conclusion. Story transitions link some events.	Some sense of person and purpose behind the words.	Words are correctly used but may be somewhat general and unspecific.	Writes complete sentences with some expansion. Limited variety.	*Capitalization & Punctuation* 1 error. Indents paragraphs. *Grammar/Usage 2 errors* *Spelling 2 errors*
2	Limited plot and/or the conflict/problem is not clear. The setting, climax, and/or resolution may not be apparent. There are insufficient details and description. Characterization is weak. Too repetitious or too much irrelevant material.	Beginning does not capture reader's interest. Plot under-developed and two or more story elements (setting, initiating event, climax, resolution) missing. Story transitions missing.	Little sense of person and purpose behind the words.	Word choice limited. Words may be used inaccurately or repetitively.	Writes mostly simple and/or awkwardly constructed sentences. May include some run-ons and fragments.	*Capitalization & Punctuation* 2 errors. May not indent paragraphs. *Grammar/Usage 3 errors* *Spelling 3 errors*
1	Does not address the prompt OR the plot, conflict/problem are not discernible. Description, details, and characterization are missing.	Text has evident structure. Lack of organization seriously interferes with meaning.	No sense of person or purpose behind the words.	Extremely limited range of words. Restricted vocabulary impedes message.	Numerous run-ons and/or sentence fragments interfere with meaning.	*Capitalization & Punctuation* 3+ errors. May not indent paragraphs. *Grammar/Usage 4+ errors* interfere with meaning *Spelling 4+ errors*
Value						
Comments						

	Ideas and Content	Organization	Voice and Audience Awareness	Word Choice	Sentence Fluency	Language Conventions
4	Clearly states a position on the issue. Fully develops main ideas with evidence, examples, and explanations that are compelling. No irrelevant information.	Introduction clearly states position. Ideas logically sequenced. Transition sentences link ideas. Conclusion ties essay together and gives reader something to think about. Follows required format.	Strong sense of person and purpose behind the words. Brings issue to life.	Words are specific, accurate, and vivid. Word choice enhances meaning and reader's enjoyment.	Writes complete sentences with varied sentence patterns and beginnings	*Capitalization & Punctuation* No errors. Indents paragraphs. *Grammar/Usage* 0–1 error *Spelling* 0–1 error
3	States a position on the issue. Develops main ideas adequately with some evidence, examples, and explanations. Limited irrelevant information.	Introduction states position. Ideas mostly logically sequenced. Some linkage among ideas. Conclusion ties essay together. Follows required format.	Some sense of person and purpose behind the words. Sense of commitment to the issue. Text may be too casual for the purpose.	Words are correctly used but may be somewhat general and unspecific.	Writes complete sentences with some expansion. Limited variety.	*Capitalization & Punctuation* 1 error. Indents paragraphs. *Grammar/Usage* 2 errors *Spelling* 2 errors
2	Does not state a clear position on the issue and/or does not support main ideas with sufficient evidence, examples, and explanations. May be too repetitious or too much irrelevant information.	Introduction may not state a position. Ideas not logically sequenced. Transition sentences missing. Conclusion may be missing. Does not follow required format.	Little sense of person and purpose behind the words. Very little engagement with reader. Text may be too casual for the purpose.	Word choice limited. Words may be used inaccurately or repetitively.	Writes mostly simple and/or awkwardly constructed sentences. May include some run-ons and fragments.	*Capitalization & Punctuation* 2 errors. May not indent paragraphs. *Grammar/Usage* 3 errors *Spelling* 3 errors
1	Does not address the prompt OR does not develop a position. Elaboration lacking or unrelated to the issue.	Text has no evident structure. Lack of organization seriously interferes with meaning.	No sense of person or purpose behind the words. No sense of audience.	Extremely limited range of words. Restricted vocabulary impedes message.	Numerous run-ons and/or sentence fragments interfere with meaning.	*Capitalization & Punctuation* 3+ errors. May not indent paragraphs. *Grammar/Usage* 4+ errors interfere with meaning *Spelling* 4+ errors
Value						

Comments _____

	Ideas and Content	Organization	Voice and Audience Awareness	Word Choice	Sentence Fluency	Language Conventions
4	States thesis clearly. Develops main ideas fully with elaborations. Direct quotations from text support ideas. All information pertinent to thesis.	Introduction contains thesis statement and purpose behind the words. cites title, author of work. Ideas logically sequenced. Transition sentences link ideas. Conclusion offers some evaluation of the work.	Strong sense of person and purpose behind the words. Brings topic to life.	Words are specific, accurate, and vivid. Word choice enhances meaning and reader's enjoyment.	Writes complete sentences with varied sentence patterns and beginnings	*Capitalization & Punctuation* No errors. Indents paragraphs. *Grammar/Usage* 0–1 error *Spelling* 0–1 error
3	States thesis clearly. Develops main ideas with some elaboration. May lack direct quotations from text to support ideas. Limited amount of irrelevant information.	Introduction contains thesis statement and cites title, author of work. Ideas mostly logically sequenced. Some linkage of main ideas. Formulaic conclusion may not offer evaluation of the work.	Some sense of person and purpose behind the words. Sense of commitment to the issue. Text may be too casual for purpose.	Words are correctly used but may be somewhat general and unspecific.	Writes complete sentences with some expansion. Limited variety.	*Capitalization & Punctuation* 1 error. Indents paragraphs. *Grammar/Usage* 2 errors *Spelling* 2 errors
2	Does not state thesis clearly and/or minimal development of main ideas. No direct quotations to support ideas. Too repetitious or too much irrelevant information.	Introduction may not have clear thesis. Ideas not logically sequenced. Transitions may be missing. May lack conclusion, or conclusion in formulaic with no evaluation of the work.	Little sense of person and purpose behind the words. Very little engagement with the reader. Text may be too casual for purpose.	Word choice limited. Words may be used inaccurately or repetitively.	Writes mostly simple and/or awkwardly constructed sentences. May include some run-ons and fragments.	*Capitalization & Punctuation* 2 errors. May not indent paragraphs. *Grammar/Usage* 3 errors *Spelling* 3 errors
1	Does not address the prompt OR does not develop a thesis. Elaboration lacking or unrelated to a thesis.	No evident structure. Lack of organization seriously interferes with meaning.	No sense of person or purpose behind the words. No sense of audience.	Extremely limited range of words. Restricted vocabulary impedes message.	Numerous run-ons and/or sentence fragments interfere with meaning.	*Capitalization & Punctuation* 3+ errors. May not indent paragraphs. *Grammar/Usage* 4+ errors interfere with meaning *Spelling* 4+ errors
Value						

Comments _____

Student Name: _____

My Progress in Writing Process
Ideas and Content

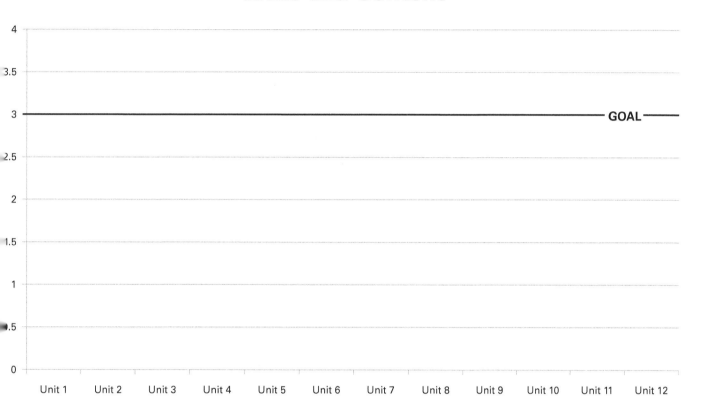

Student Name: _____

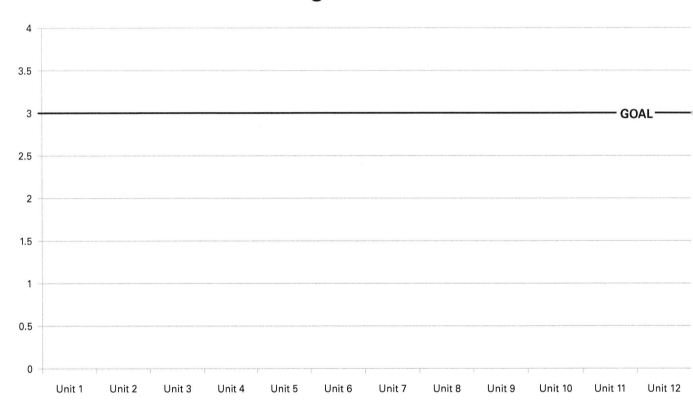

My Progress in Writing Process Organization

Student Name: _____

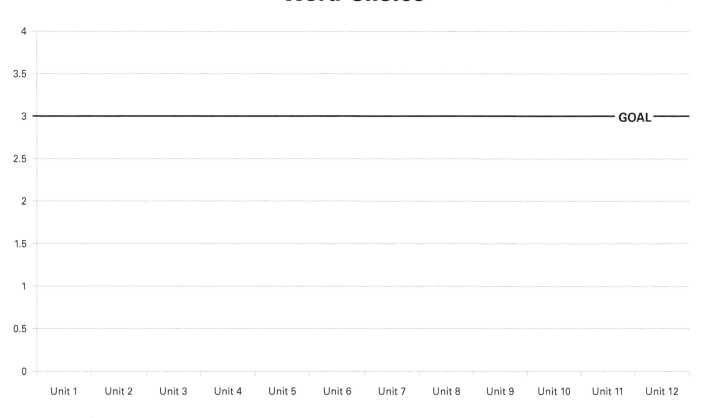

**My Progress in Writing Process
Word Choice**

Student Name: _____

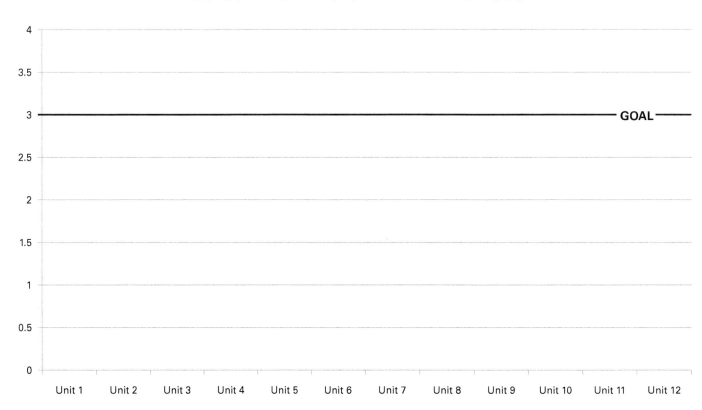

**My Progress in Writing Process
Voice and Audience Awareness**

Student Name: _____

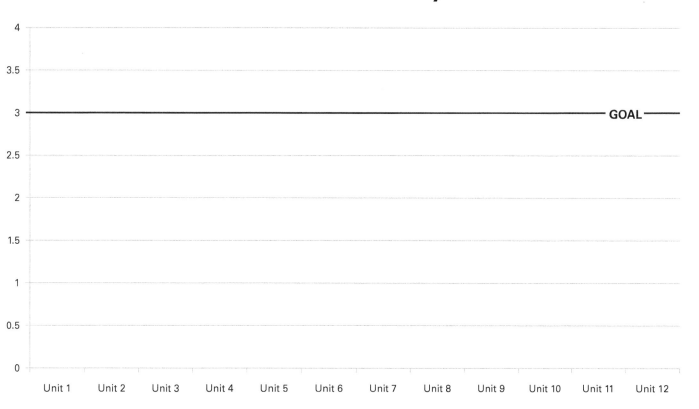

My Progress in Writing Process
Sentence Fluency

Student Name: _____

My Progress in Writing Process Conventions

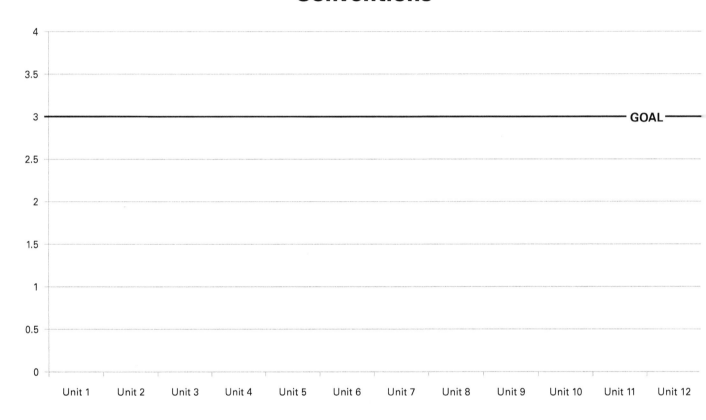

Sight Words

The following sight words are introduced by Unit and cumulatively reviewed online in Word Training and reinforced in Text Training.

Unit 1	Unit 2	Unit 3	Unit 4	Unit 5	Unit 6
hour	break	someone	ago	status	important
night	wear	news	behind	symbol	traffic
friend	hear	open	weight	energy	prove
though	buy	fiction	custom	plastic	afford
walk	loud	watch	building	bridge	guide
cover	listen	son	vision	carry	pause
special	student	river	color	young	mountains
family	talk	aunt	area	touch	toward
near	idea	able	piece	whole	table
wild	spread	refer	usual	early	money
four	truth	tower	heard	column	voice
perfect	vary	menu	during	several	cried
gone	engine	poor	honor	iron	guard
tomorrow	laugh	abroad	honest	course	guess
women	oil	against	half	certain	guest

Unit 7	Unit 8	Unit 9	Unit 10	Unit 11	Unit 12
spirit	steady	system	interesting	fragile	achieve
scene	period	ability	similar	opposite	practical
strength	distinct	information	article	science	structure
mighty	powerful	citizen	capture	official	optional
purpose	convince	mobile	creature	relief	dilemma
angle	popular	imagine	opinion	equation	surface
field	brilliant	focused	finally	government	material
notice	known	among	general	distance	instrument
figure	island	heavy	region	heart	paragraph
minutes	machine	circle	believe	probably	represent
ocean	brought	measure	exercise	length	clothes
nothing	thousand	ready	develop	present	either
busy	beautiful	captain	journal	colleague	character
business	beauty	curtain	journey	courage	education
villain	debt	language	guarantee	nuisance	extraordinary

Vocabulary

The following words are passage vocabulary explicitly taught in Text Training.

abruptly	U3	cherish	U8	diagnose	U5	govern	U6
access	U6	circumstance	U12	discrimination	U6	grudge	U11
acknowledgment	U11	clamor	U5	distinct	U9	habitat	U7
acquire	U4	collapse	U12	distracted	U10	hamper	U6
acute	U12	commit	U1	divert	U11	harmony	U6
adjust	U4	compel	U7	donor	U12	healthy	U2
advantage	U7	competition	U7	drastically	U12	hesitation	U3
ailment	U5	compromise	U7	drone	U4	hoist	U11
allergy	U2	concentrate	U3	economy	U7	identify	U1
allow	U2	conditions	U5	elaborate	U5	ignorant	U7
alter	U7	conflict	U9	eligible	U11	image	U9
alternative	U5	consist	U1	embarrass	U2	immobile	U8
anticipation	U5	consistency	U5	emphasis	U4	impact	U6
appalling	U10	conspicuous	U3	encounter	U7	implement	U9
apparent	U8	consultation	U10	enforce	U10	implicated	U8
apply	U5	consume	U12	enhance	U10	impose	U6
appropriate	U10	contradict	U10	enthusiastically	U4	incident	U9
ascent	U7	contribution	U6	envy	U4	increase	U10
aspect	U7	controversial	U9	euphoric	U5	indicate	U3
assess	U11	converse	U8	eventually	U4	individuality	U10
assume	U12	convict	U1	evidence	U1	inevitable	U4
attend	U9	correspondence	U4	exaggeration	U10	inferno	U12
automatically	U12	counsel	U8	exalted	U12	inhibition	U9
avoid	U1	course	U8	exchange	U4	innocence	U1
aware	U1	dazed	U1	experimental	U12	insecurity	U7
awkward	U3	debate	U4	exploitation	U6	inspiration	U5
balance	U2	declare	U1	falter	U3	instinctively	U4
ban	U10	decline	U7	fashion	U11	interrupt	U12
barren	U1	decorous	U11	fiber	U1	interval	U3
beckon	U8	defy	U6	formula	U9	introduce	U4
(on) behalf	U12	delicately	U11	frail	U2	invaluable	U5
cancel	U2	deny	U3	friction	U12	invent	U6
casual	U3	dependable	U3	fruition	U11	involved	U9
cease	U11	deserve	U3	functional	U4	irrelevant	U6
challenge	U9	design	U4	furnished	U2	isolation	U4
charge	U2	devise	U8	garment	U3	justification	U11

juvenile	U1	preserve	U1	stifle	U10
lacking	U12	previously	U9	stoop	U2
latch	U2	primitive	U12	straight	U2
lecture	U5	principle	U10	strategy	U5
legacy	U6	priority	U10	strict	U3
leisure	U3	procession	U11	suede	U2
lonely	U2	promotion	U7	survey	U10
lurk	U2	prone (to)	U9	suspect	U1
maintain	U8	prospect	U6	suspend	U6
massive	U6	punch	U2	tenacity	U12
media	U9	pursue	U7	trace	U1
motionless	U4	qualify	U5	transform	U6
motivated	U5	rashness	U8	transport	U9
murmur	U4	reaction	U9	truancy	U10
mutinous	U11	reassuring	U5	unique	U1
obstacle	U12	recklessly	U11	urge	U9
obtain	U9	reconsider	U8	vainly	U7
omission	U8	regretfully	U11	valid	U10
opportunity	U5	regulations	U3	vast	U1
ornery	U3	release	U2	vengeance	U7
outcome	U5	relocation	U7	verdict	U12
passive	U6	research	U9	warped	U11
peculiar	U3	resemblance	U3	wince	U12
penalty	U8	reside	U8	witness	U1
perish	U8	resist	U10		
permit	U2	resolve	U8		
persistence	U7	resources	U6		
policy	U6	restore	U8		
populated	U4	restrain	U7		
portion	U5	restrictive	U10		
possession	U3	retort	U11		
precious	U11	savor	U4		
prefer	U10	seldom	U8		
preliminaries	U11	sin	U2		
premises	U1	sought	U8		
presentable	U2	standard	U9		

Contrastive Analysis

The Contrastive Analysis charts have been developed to assist teachers in understanding the difficulties English language learners may encounter when acquiring English. The charts identify predictable areas of difficulty for native speakers of a particular language who are learning English. Specifically, these charts highlight major differences in phonology and grammar between students' first languages and English.

Differentiated Instruction

These charts on pages 582–591 and 594–601 are not intended to be a complete description of each language, nor are they all-inclusive. Rather, these charts describe the most frequent phonological and grammatical divergences between the two languages. Although first-language knowledge is only one of many factors that may influence the acquisition of English, teachers need to know how those divergences may influence students' English learning.

Most native speakers of English master pronunciations when they first learn to speak, but English learners require direct, explicit instruction of English verbs and consonants.

The information contained in these charts provides guidance for teachers to differentiate instruction for English learners. The *LANGUAGE! Live* curriculum is particularly helpful for English learners because it makes no assumptions about what students may or may not know about English.

Explicit instruction in grammar, reading, writing, and vocabulary provides students with the knowledge and understanding necessary to code-switch between their home language and the English used in schools. This knowledge is critical for students to participate fully in their own education and, later, join the workforce.

Ethnic and Regional Dialects of Native-Born Americans

All spoken languages diverge into varying dialects or vernaculars. Most native-born Americans switch with ease from Academic English to a less formal version of English—one of many ethnic and regional dialects spoken in the United States. The following are three primary characteristics of ethnic and regional dialects:

1. The divergences between Academic English and the English spoken by an ethnic or regional group are not random; rather they are rule-governed. That is, primary linguistic differences in dialects are predictable and consistent. Various dialects may share features.

2. Not all speakers within an ethnic or regional group speak a dialect; a dialect is associated with a group of speakers because it is uniquely associated with a particular ethnic or regional group.

3. Each dialect has subsets. For example, dialects spoken by particular groups of African Americans, Hispanic Americans, or Native Americans in the United States will differ in various communities.

How to Use the Contrastive Analysis

Transfer Between Languages

Many common, persistent mistakes made by students learning a foreign language can be traced to the "pull of the mother tongue." English learners use the knowledge of their first language or home language to learn English. This knowledge of their first/home language influences their acquisition of English in a process called *transfer*.

- Where two languages are similar, **positive** transfer occurs.

- Where two languages are different, **negative** transfer occurs.

English has more closed syllables and more consonant clusters before and after vowels within syllables than many other languages, including Spanish, Italian, African languages, and Pacific Islander languages. Only a few languages, such as Polish, have more consonants in clusters within syllables. Therefore, students learning English may have trouble pronouncing consonant blends or may tend to drop consonants at the ends of words. A feature of African-American dialect is systematic deletion of some consonants at the ends of words.

The vowel system of English is simpler than many Asian languages that have tonal vowels—distinctive vowels that are high, medium, or low in tone, or that are contoured to slide up or down. On the other hand, English has many more vowels than some languages such as Spanish, Italian, Hawaiian, and Swahili.

Each language system has its own inventory of vowels and consonants (and sometimes other sounds such as clicks), and students learning any language benefit from direct teaching of the speech sound inventory in that language.

The results of transfer can affect many linguistic areas, including phonology, morphology, semantics, and syntax. Each of these areas is thoroughly covered in the *LANGUAGE! Live* curriculum.

Phonology

Transferrable Skills After reviewing a student's online recording at the end of each Word Training unit, check the Contrastive Analysis chart to determine whether the sound transfers from the student's primary language into English. If the sound transfers from the student's primary language to English but the student did not perform well, have the student repeat the unit, providing support as needed.

Nontransferrable Skills After reviewing a student's online recording at the end of each Word Training unit, check the Contrastive Analysis chart to determine whether the sound transfers from the student's primary language into English. If it does NOT, reteach the lessons one-on-one, ensuring the student uses the mirror during pronunciation and views sagittal videos for clarity. Focus on articulation.

Additional Practice and Time If the skill does NOT transfer from the student's primary language into English, the student will require more time and practice mastering the sound and spellings. Allow time for one-on-one support, and work collaboratively with other support staff involved with the student to ensure instruction and focus are aligned.

Language and Usage

Transferrable Skills After reviewing a student's Content Mastery scores (Content Mastery should be administered at the end of each Text Training unit), check the Contrastive Analysis chart to determine whether the grammar skill transfers from the student's primary language to English. If the skill transfers from the student's primary language to English but the student did not perform well, assign Reteach activities.

Nontransferrable Skills After reviewing a student's Content Mastery scores, check the Contrastive Analysis chart to determine whether the grammar skill transfers from the student's primary language to English. If it does NOT, reassign the corresponding online Practice activities and reteach the skill using the corresponding Reteach lesson. A proactive approach can also be taken by preteaching upcoming grammar skills in small groups prior to the whole group lesson.

Additional Practice and Time If the skill does NOT transfer from the student's primary language into English, the student will require more time and practice to master it. Provide sentence frames and ample structured opportunities to use the skill in spoken English. Oral exchanges are critical in mastering these skills. Allow time for one-on-one support, and work collaboratively with other support staff involved with the student to ensure instruction and focus are aligned.

Phonology Contrastive Analysis

Vowels

	Spanish	Vietnamese	Cantonese/Mandarin	Russian	African American English
/ē/ as in eagle, Pete, bee, team		merges with /ĭ/ **seat/sit; ween/win**	merges with /ĭ/ **seat/sit; ween/win**	replaces with /ĭ/ **fit (feet)** has difficulty holding a vowel sound before a voiced consonant	
/ĭ/ as in itch	replaces with /ē/ **team (Tim); cheap (chip); sheen (shin)** merges with /ī/ **lit/light; spit/spite** merges with /ă/, /ĕ/, /ŏ/, and /ŭ/ **din/den/Dan/don/done**	merges with /ē/ **seat/sit; ween/win**	merges with /ē/ **seat/sit; ween/win**	has difficulty holding a vowel sound before a voiced consonant	
/ā/ as in acorn, cake, rain, play	merges with /ă/ **nape/nap; bake/back**	merges with /ĕ/ **made/med; wait/wet; mane/men**	merges with /ĕ/ **made/med; wait/wet; mane/men**	replaces with /ĕ/ **bet (bait)** has difficulty holding a vowel sound before a voiced consonant	
/ĕ/ as in echo	merges with /ă/, /ĭ/, /ŏ/, and /ŭ/ **din/den/Dan/don/done**	merges with /ā/ **made/med; wait/wet; mane/men** merges with /ā/ **head/had; leg/lag**	merges with /ā/ and /ĕ/ **made/med; wait/wet; mane/men**	has difficulty holding a vowel sound before a voiced consonant	when before /m/ or /n/, replaces with /ĭ/ **tin (ten); Jim (gem)**

Sound	merges with…	merges with (din/den)	merges with /ĕ/ head/had; leg/lag	replaces with /ŭ/ or /ĕ/ pun (pan); lend (land)	replaces with /ĕ/ met (mat)	has difficulty holding a vowel sound before a voiced consonant
/ă/ as in apple	merges with /ā/ **nape/nap; bake/back**	merges with /ĕ/, /ĭ/, /ŏ/, and /ŭ/ **din/den/Dan/don/done**	merges with /ĕ/ **head/had; leg/lag**	replaces with /ŭ/ or /ĕ/ **pun (pan); lend (land)**	replaces with /ĕ/ **met (mat)**	has difficulty holding a vowel sound before a voiced consonant
/ī/ as in ice, bike, cry	merges with /ī/ **lit/light; spit/spite**					has difficulty holding a vowel sound before a voiced consonant
/ŏ/ as in octopus	merges with /ō/ and /aw/ **boat/bot/bought**	merges with /ă/, /ĕ/, /ĭ/, and /ŭ/ **din/den/Dan/don/done**				has difficulty holding a vowel sound before a voiced consonant
/ŭ/ as in up	merges with /ă/, /ĕ/, /ĭ/, and /ŏ/ **din/den/Dan/don/done**					has difficulty holding a vowel sound before a voiced consonant
/aw/ as in law, audio, fall	merges with /ŏ/ and /ō/ **boat/bot/bought**					has difficulty holding a vowel sound before a voiced consonant
/ō/ as in open, rope, snow, boat	merges with /ŏ/ and /aw/ **boat/bot/bought**					has difficulty holding a vowel sound before a voiced consonant

	Spanish	Vietnamese	Cantonese/ Mandarin	Russian	African American English
Vowels (cont.)					
/o͝o/ as in book, put	merges with /ū/ **fool/full**	merges with /ū/ **pool/pull**	merges with /ū/ **pool/pull**	has difficulty holding a vowel sound before a voiced consonant	
/ū/ as in rule, moon	merges with /o͝o/ **fool/full**	merges with /o͝o/ **pool/pull**	merges with /o͝o/ **pool/pull**	merges with /o͝o/ **pool/pull** has difficulty holding a vowel sound before a voiced consonant	
/yū/ as in unicorn, cube				has difficulty holding a vowel sound before a voiced consonant	
/oi/ as in boy, foil				has difficulty holding a vowel sound before a voiced consonant	
/ou/ as in cow, ouch				has difficulty holding a vowel sound before a voiced consonant	
/er/ as in fern, shirt, urn				when preceded by /w/, replaces with a variety of other sounds	

/ar/ as in star				in word-final position, replaces with /ŭ/ or schwa **holla (holler)**
/or/ as in sport				
Consonants				
/p/ as in pig	in word-initial position, replaces with /b/, /d/, or /g/ **bun/done/gun (pun)**	in word-final position, is not fully articulated **bee (beep)**; in word-initial position, replaces with /b/ or /f/ **back (pack); fool (pool)**	in word-final position, is not fully articulated **bee (beep)**	replaces with /b/ **bants (pants)**	
/b/ as in bat	in word-final position, replaces with /p/, /t/, or /k/ **pup/putt/puck (pub)**	in word-final position, replaces with voiceless sounds **lap (lab)**	in word-final position, replaces with voiceless sounds **lap (lab)**	replaces with /p/ **lap (lab)**	in word-final position, voiced stop becomes voiceless **wep (web)**
/t/ as in tack, stopped	in word-initial position, replaces with /b/, /d/, or /g/ **bag/dag/gag (tag)**	in word-final position, is not fully articulated **ben (bent)**	in word-final position, is not fully articulated **ben (bent)**	replaces with /d/ **down (town)**	
/d/ as in dog, hummed	in word-final position, replaces with /p/, /t/, or /k/ **hap/hat/hack (had)**	in word-final position, replaces with voiceless sounds **hat (had)**	in word-final position, replaces with voiceless sounds **hat (had)**	replaces with /t/ **lit (lid)**	in word-final position, voiced stop becomes voiceless **hat (had)**

	Spanish	Vietnamese	Cantonese/Mandarin	Russian	African American English
Consonants (cont.)					
/k/ as in cup, kite, duck	in word-initial position, replaces with /b/, /d/, or /g/ **bot/dot/got (cot)**	in word-final position may not be fully articulated **tall (talk)**	in word-final position may not be fully articulated **tall (talk)**	replaces with /g/ **gap (cap)**	
/g/ as in goat	in word-final position, replaces with /p/, /t/, or /k/ **whip/wit/wick (wig)**	in word-final position, replaces with voiceless sounds **pick (pig)**	in word-final position, replaces with voiceless sounds **pick (pig)**	replaces with /k/ **back (bag)**	in word-final position, voiced stop becomes voiceless **sak (sag)**
/m/ as in man	in word-final position, replaces with /n/, /nk/, or /ng/ **dane/dank/dang (dame)**		in word-final position, replaces with /n/ or /ng/ **bean/bing (beam)**		
/n/ as in nest, knife, gnu	in word-final position, replaces with /m/, /nk/, or /ng/ **dame/dank/dang (dane)**		in word-initial position, merges with /l/ **knife/life; lap/nap** in word-final position, replaces with /m/ or /ng/ **king/keem (keen)**		

Phoneme					
/ng/ as in sing	in word-final position, replaces with /n/, /nk/, or /m/ **dane/dank/dame (dang)**	in word-final position, replaces with /m/ or /n/ **fame/fain (fang)**		replaces with /n/ or /g/ **brin/brig (bring)**	in word-final position (inflectional ending), replaces with /n/ **jumpin' (jumping)** in single-syllable words when preceded by /i/, replaces with /a/ /ng/ **sang (sing); brang (bring)**
/f/ as in fish, sniff		in word-final position, omits **lie (life)**			
/v/ as in valentine, serve	in word-initial position or word-medial position, replaces with /b/ **berry (very); nerbous (nervous)** in word-final position, replaces with /f/ **luff (love)**	in word-final position, omits **lu (love)**	in word-initial or word-medial position, replaces with /w/ or /f/ **falue (value); inwest (invest)** in word-final position, replaces with /f/ **luff (love)**	in word-initial position or word-medial position, replaces with /b/ **berry (very); nerbous (nervous)** in word-final position, replaces with /f/ **luff (love)**	
/th/ as in thumb	replaces with /t/ **wit (with); tin (thin)**	in word-final position, omits **fay (faith)** replaces with /t/ **welty (wealthy)**	replaces with /t/, /f/, or /s/ **pat/paff/pass (path); tank, fank, sank (thank)**	replaces with /s/ **pass (path); sank (thank)**	in word-medial and word-final position, replaces with /f/ **worf (worth); aufor (author)**

Consonants (cont.)

	Spanish	Vietnamese	Cantonese/Mandarin	Russian	African American English
/th/ as in feather	replaces with /d/ **wedder (weather); doze (those)**	in word-final position, omits **lo (loathe)** replaces with /d/ or /z/ **fodder (father); zat (that)**	replaces with /d/ or /z/ **fodder (father); zat (that)**	replaces with /z/ **fozzer (father); zat (that)**	in word-initial position, replaces with /d/ **dis (this); dat (that)** in word-medial and word-final position, replaces with /v/ **whever (whether); bave (bathe)**
/s/ as in sun, dress, cell		in word-final position, omits **pack (packs)**			
/z/ as in zebra, runs, fuzz	replaces with /s/ **crasy (crazy); fance (fans)**	in word-final position, omits **boy (boys)**	replaces with /s/ **crasy (crazy); fance (fans)**	replaces with other sounds	
/sh/ as in shoes	replaces with /ch/ **chip (ship); witch (wish)**	in word-final position, omits **ca (cash)**			
/zh/ as in pleasure	replaces with /sh/ **garash (garage); mesher (measure)**	in word-final position, omits **colla (collage)**	replaces with /sh/ **garash (garage); mesher (measure)**		
/j/ as in jam, badge, gel	in word-medial and word-final position, replaces with /ch/ **dotcher (dodger); etch (edge)**		replaces with /ch/ or another voiceless sound **etch (edge); basher (badger); chump (jump)**	replaces with /d/ or /z/ **ed (edge); bazzer (badger); dump (jump)**	

Sound				
/ch/ as in chin, patch		replaces with /s/ **pash (patch)**	replaces with /sh/ **sheep (cheap); wish (witch)**	
/y/ as in yo-yo	in word-initial position, replaces with /j/ **jess (yes)**		in word-initial position, omits **or (your)**	
/wh/ as in wheel				replaces with /v/ **ven (when)**
/w/ as in window				replaces with /v/ **vant (want)**
/h/ as in hat	in word-initial position, omits **appy (happy)**			
/l/ as in leaf, bell		replaces with /r/ **rife (life)**; in word-initial position, merges with /n/ **knife/life; lap/nap**		in word-final position, pronounces as a separate syllable **poo-el (pool)**; in word-medial or word-final position, omits **sef (self); tee (tell)**

Phonology Contrastive Analysis (cont.)

Consonants (cont.)

	Spanish	Vietnamese	Cantonese/Mandarin	Russian	African American English
/r/ as in rabbit, wren	replaces with trilled (rolled) /r/		in word-initial position, replaces with /l/ or /w/ **lace (race); wed (red)** in word-final position, replaces with /l/ **kale (care)**		

Blends

	Spanish	Vietnamese	Cantonese/Mandarin	Russian	African American English
Omitting Consonants	in word-medial or word-final position, omits one or more consonants **ness (nest); res (rests); frenly (friendly)**	in word-initial or word-final position, omits one or more consonants **ness (nest)**	in word-initial or word-final position, omits one or more consonants **ness (nest)**		
Inserting Consonants			in word-initial or word-final position, inserts a vowel sound between two consonants **sipoil (spoil)**	in word-initial or word-medial position, inserts a vowel sound between two consonants **sipoil (spoil)**	

Replacing or Separating Consonants	with /s/ + consonant in word-initial position, replaces prior to the /s/ **estop (stop):** **esports (sports)**		in word-initial position, replaces /r/ with /l/ **flee (free)**	pronounces component sounds separately rather than the fused sound

Language and Usage Contrastive Analysis

Before English language learners develop the ability to code-switch between their home language and academic English, they first must learn the rules that govern the English language. Regardless of language background, some elements of the English language prove difficult for learners of all age groups and levels of intelligence.

Difficulties with English

Common Grammatical Mistakes

- Subject-verb disagreement (subject of a sentence disagrees with the verb of the sentence in terms of number or person)

    She smile when she see me in the hallway.

- Noun-number disagreement (a noun is in disagreement with its determiner in terms of number)

    There are many book in the library. I want some pencil. Can you hand me those notebook.

- Misuse of determiners (the determiners—articles, demonstratives, possessive pronouns—are improperly used with the nouns they modify)

    I am going to cafeteria. I am reading the information about the Costa Rica.

    We are walking to that school. These is the correct answer.

    She is changing his shirt. The car has lost air in their tires.

Vocabulary and Word Use Complications

- Derivations

    English has more than 100 common prefixes and suffixes. Virtually any content word (noun, verb, and adjective) is susceptible of being derived, so the possibilities are limitless.

    - *soft* (adjective), *soften* (verb), *softly* (adverb), *softer/softest* (comparative and superlative adjectives), *softener* (noun);
    - *colony* (noun) *colonial* (adjective), *colonialism* (noun), *colonize* (verb), *colonization* (noun);
    - *play* (verb), *playful* (adjective), *playfully* (adverb), *player* (noun), *replay* (verb)

- Clipping

  Usually done in speech, English speakers often shorten (or clip) words. Many clipped words have made their way into common spoken language such as *gym*, *exam*, *lab*, *info*, *bro*, *cab*, *math*, etc.

- Borrowings

  At least half of English common words come from non-Anglo-Saxon origins. This makes spelling and usage generalizations difficult. Examples of borrowed words include *canyon* from Spanish, *kindergarten* from German, *pizza* from Italian, *shampoo* from an Indian language, *rendezvous* from French.

- Acronyms

  An acronym is a word formed from the initial letters of other words. In English, an acronym is usually spelled out when talking about it; however, it is possible to read the letters together if the resulting word complies with the English phonetic system. So *FEMA*, *radar*, and *AIDS* are pronounced like any other word but *UFO*, *AA*, and *UCLA* are spelled out.

- Blending

  A blend results from combining two words, usually the beginning of one and the ending of the other, although this may vary. Some well-known blends in English are *smog* (smoke + fog), *Spanglish* (Spanish + English), *cankles* (calves + ankles), *spork* (spoon + fork), and *brunch* (breakfast + lunch).

Nouns

Spanish	Vietnamese	Cantonese/Mandarin	Russian	African American English
confuses count and noncount nouns **the moneys** or **the stuffs**	omits -s **I have three dog.**	omits plural marker -s **I have three dog.**		omits possessive 's in nouns **The boy hat.**
uses prepositions to describe possessives **Please drive me to the house of my friend.**	uses prepositions to describe possessives **I went with the friend of my brother.**			pluralizes nouns ending in voiceless consonants by adding /ĭz/ or by deleting the final consonant **tasez** or **tas'** (tasks); **nesez** or **nes'** (nests)
uses incorrect pluralization of irregular nouns **The other childs are at the zoo.**	avoids using 's **my father car**			deletes the ending sound(s) in nouns of measure **dolla** (dollars)

Articles

Spanish	Vietnamese	Cantonese/Mandarin	Russian	African American English
overuses articles **The English is difficult to learn. The football is popular in the America.**	omits articles **She has cat. She wants dog not cat.**	omits articles **She has cat. She wants dog not cat.**	omits articles **She has cat. She wants dog not cat.**	
uses *one* in place of article *a/an* **My dad is one doctor.**	uses *one* in place of article *a/an* **My dad is one doctor.**			

uses pronouns with the inappropriate gender **He is my girlfriend.**	omits pronouns in clauses **If don't move now, we will get hurt.**	confuses subject and object pronouns **Him looked at you.**	uses inappropriate gender, particularly with neutral nouns **The house is dark; she is scary.**	replaces the possessive form *whose* with *who* **I don't know who car that is.**
omits subject pronouns **Mom isn't here. Is at restaurant.**	overuses pronouns with nouns **This job, it very hard.**	uses the wrong number for pronouns **I saw many stars in the sky. It was twinkling.**		
omits the pronoun *one* **I saw two cars, and I like the red.**	avoids pronouns and repeats nouns **Lin visits her grandma every Sunday, and Lin cleans her house.**	omits pronouns in clauses **If don't move now, we will get hurt.**		
uses indefinite pronouns incorrectly when used with negation **I do not want some.**		confuses possessive forms **The book is my.**		
uses *one* or *an* in place of indefinite pronouns with plural nouns **Will you give me one cookies.**				
uses relative pronouns incorrectly **The teacher which spoke Spanish no longer works here. The book who was read was romantic.**	confuses possessive forms **The book is my.**			

Language and Usage Contrastive Analysis

Spanish	Vietnamese	Cantonese/Mandarin	Russian	African American English
Pronouns (cont.)				
Uses articles in place of possessive pronouns *She washes the hair every day.*				
Verbs				
has difficulty pronouncing final consonant clusters in general; speakers tend to pronounce -ed in all past tense verbs as a separate syllable or to delete -ed entirely from past tense verbs with singular forms ending in /d/ or /t/ *I talk-ed in class.* (I talked in class.) *I wan- a puppy.* (I wanted a puppy.)	omits -s in present tense, third person agreement *He like pizza.*	omits -s in present tense, third person agreement *He like pizza.*	uses helping verbs *do, have, will,* and *be* in incorrect contexts and incorrect tenses	omits -s in present tense, third person agreement *He like pizza.*
omits helping verbs in negative statements *Sue no coming to school.*	omits tense markers *I study English yesterday.*	has problems with irregular subject-verb agreement *Tom and Sue has a new car.*	omits helping verbs in negative statements *Sue no coming to school.*	omits the linking verb *He hungry.*

uses the past progressive tense for recurring action in the past **When I was young, I was talking a lot.**	avoids the present-perfect tense **Marcos live here for three months.**	omits tense markers **I study English yesterday.**	uses negative pronouns *none, nobody,* and *no one* incorrectly	overgeneralizes the singular past tense *was* to both singular and plural subjects **They was there. We was there.**
confuses transitive and intransitive verbs **The child throws. The child thrown the ball.**	omits the linking verb **He hungry.**	uses the present tense for the future tense **I go next week.**		does not conjugate the infinitive form of *be* **I be thinking about going to the dance.**
omits the helping verb in the passive voice **The book opened.**	omits helping verbs in negative statements **Sue no coming to school.**			Deletion of a form of *be* in the present progressive contraction usage **I listenin' to music. He liftin' weights.**
uses *have* instead of *be* **I have happy. He has right.**		omits the main verb **Talk in class not good.**		uses *been* with the present perfect tense **I been knowin' you forever.**
uses the negative word before the verb phrase **I not have found the book.**		omits the linking verb **He hungry.**		uses variations of the verb *be* to show habitual action **He always be lying.**
uses double negatives **I didn't see nobody.**		omits the helping verb in the passive voice **The book opened.**		Uses *had* to indicate past tense **He had told me that he wanted to go.**

Language and Usage Contrastive Analysis

Spanish	Vietnamese	Cantonese/Mandarin	Russian	African American English
		Verbs (cont.)		
omits *do/does/did* and incorrectly uses *no* in place of *not* **I no understand.**		confuses transitive and intransitive verbs **The child throws. The child thrown the ball.**		uses improper subject-verb agreement with *do* and *have* **He do that just to bother me. You has to come with me.**
Uses negative word following pronouns, adjectives, adverbs in short responses **here no** not **not here**		orders inverted interrogative verb phrases incorrectly **Has seen Simon the movie?**		Uses nonstandard irregular verbs in past and past perfect tenses **We seen that.**
orders inverted interrogative verb phrases incorrectly **Has seen Simon the movie?**				mispronounces past tense -ed, either adding a syllable or deleting -ed **pickted** (picked)
omits *do/does/did* from questions **When John leave?**				Uses of double negatives **I didn't hear nobody.**
uses the simple present tense in place of present progressive **Look, it snows!**				replaces *no, never,* and *neither* with *any, ever,* and *either* after a negative word or word part **I don't want that one, neither.**

uses the simple present tense in place of future tense *We see each other tomorrow.*		uses negative inversion in sentences *Don't nobody like that girl.*
uses the simple present tense in place of past perfect tense *I live here since 1995.*		omits contracted forms *He goin' to the movie.*
uses a subject in imperative mood *Come you here.*		deletes -s from regular verbs or adds to irregular verbs in third-person singular verbs *He walk.* (He walks.); *I goes to the mall.* (I go to the mall.)
		uses *gots* instead of *have* *I gots to go.* (I have to go.)

Adjectives		
places adjectives after nouns *I saw a car red.*	places adjectives after nouns *I saw a car red.*	difficulty with irregular comparatives and superlatives (*bad, good, far*)
avoids comparatives and superlatives *I am more old than Bill, but Ted is the most old.*		confuses present participles and past participles *The book is bored.* not *The book is boring.*

Spanish	Vietnamese	Cantonese/Mandarin	Russian	African American English
Adjectives (cont.)				
confuses present participles and past participles *The book is bored.* not *The book is boring.*				
adds -s to adjectives when describing plural nouns *Look at the beautifuls flowers.*				
Adverbs				
places adverbs of frequency incorrectly in sentences *Often they have visited Costa Rica.*		Places adverbs before verbs *He quickly ran.* not *He ran quickly.*		
places the adverbial phrase before the direct object *My mom cleans very well the house.*				

English preposition use is idiomatic in nature and may be difficult for all English language learners. **talk on the phone; pick up your room; stand by your man**	English preposition use is idiomatic in nature and may be difficult for all English language learners. **talk on the phone; pick up your room; stand by your man**	English preposition use is idiomatic in nature and may be difficult for all English language learners. **talk on the phone; pick up your room; stand by your man**	English preposition use is idiomatic in nature and may be difficult for all English language learners. **talk on the phone; pick up your room; stand by your man**
uses a preposition with an indirect object **He gave to Maria the book.**		omits prepositions **I like come school.**	
avoids the coloquial use of prepositions at the end of a sentence **For what did they come?**			
follows a preposition with an infinitve verb **After to eat breakfast, we go to school.**			

Research and Evidence of Effectiveness

Alliance for Excellent Education (2010). *Issue brief – There's a crisis in America's high schools.* Alliance for Excellent Education: Washington, DC. Retrievable from: http://www.all4ed.org/about_the_crisis

Archer, A. L., Gleason, M. M., & Vachon, V. (2003). Decoding and fluency: Foundation skills for older struggling readers. *Learning Disability Quarterly, 26*(2), 89–101.

August, D., & Shanahan, T. (Eds.) (2006). Developing Literacy in Second-Language Learners: Report of the National Literacy Panel on Language-Minority Children and Youth. Mahwah, NJ: Lawrence Erlbaum.

Balfanz, R., & Herzog, L. (2006). *Keeping middle grades students on track to graduation. Part A: Early identification.* Paper presented at the Annual Meeting of the American Educational Research Association, San Francisco, CA.

Bhattacharya, A., & Ehri, L. (2004). Graphosyllabic analysis helps adolescent struggling readers read and spell words. *Journal of Learning Disabilities, 37*(4), 331–348.

Biancarosa, C., & Snow, C. E. (2006). Reading next—A vision for action and research in middle and high school literacy: A report to Carnegie Corporation of New York (2nd ed.). Washington, DC: Alliance for Excellent Education.

Boardman, A. G., Roberts, G., Vaughn, S., Wexler, J., Murray, C. S., & Kosanovich, M. (2008). *Effective Instruction for Adolescent Struggling Readers: A Practice Brief.* Portsmouth, NH: RMC Research Corporation, Center on Instruction. Retrievable from: http://www.centeroninstruction.org/files/Adol%20Struggling%20Readers%20Practice%20Brief.pdf

Byrd, M. (2001). Technology helps increase reading scores. *Media & Methods, 37*(3), 12–15.

Calhoon, M. B. (2005). Effects of a peer-mediated phonological skill and reading comprehension program on reading skill acquisition of middle school students with reading disabilities. *Journal of Learning Disabilities, 38*(5), 424–433.

Calhoon, M. B., & Petscher Y. (2013). Individual and group sensitivity to remedial reading program design: Examining reading gains across three middle school reading projects. *Reading and Writing, 26*(4), 565–592.

Calhoon, M. B., Sandow, A., & Hunter, C. V. (2010). Reorganizing the instructional reading components: Could there be a better way to design remedial reading programs to maximize middle school students with reading disabilities' response to treatment? *Annals of Dyslexia, 60*, 57–85.

Carnegie Council on Advancing Adolescent Literacy. (2010). Time to act: An agenda for advancing adolescent literacy for college and career success. New York, NY: Carnegie Corporation of New York.

Cheung, A. C., & Slavin, R. E. (2011). *The effectiveness of education technology for enhancing reading achievement: A meta-analysis.* Best Evidence Encyclopedia, John Hopkins University School of Education's Center for Data-Driven Reform in Education and the Institute of Education Sciences, U.S. Department of Education. Retrievable from: http://www.bestevidence.org

Curtis, M. (2004). Adolescents who struggle with word identification: Research and practice. In T. Jetton & J. Dole (Eds.), *Adolescent Literacy Research and Practice* (pp. 119–134). New York: Guilford.

Curtis, M., & Longo, A. M. (1999). *When Adolescents Can't Read: Methods and Materials that Work.* Cambridge, MA: Brookline Books.

Denson, K. (2008). *Passport Reading Journeys Effectiveness with Ninth Grade Students Identified for Reading Improvement Instruction in an Urban High School.* Dallas, TX: Voyager Expanded Learning, Inc.. Retrievable from: http://www.voyagerlearning.com

Deshler, D. D., Palincsar, A. S., Biancarosa, G., & Nair, M. (2007). *Informed Choices for Struggling Adolescent Readers: A Researched-Based Guide to Instructional Programs and Practices.* Newark, DE: International Reading Association.

Ehri, L. (2004). Teaching phonemic awareness and phonics: An explanation of the National Reading Panel meta-analysis. In P. McCardle & L. Chhabra, (Eds.), *The Voice of Evidence in Reading Research* (pp. 153–186). Baltimore, MD: Brookes Publishing Company.

Fletcher, J. M., Lyon, G. R., Barnes, M., Stuebing, K. K., Francis, D. J., Olson, R. K., et al. (2002). Classification of learning disabilities: An evidenced-based evaluation. In R. Bradley, L. Danielson, & D. P. Hallahan (Eds.). *Identification of Learning Disabilities: Research to Practice* (pp. 185–250). Mahwah, NJ: Erlbaum.

Fletcher, J. M., Lyon, G. R., Fuchs, L. S., & Barnes, M. A. (2007). *Learning Disabilities: From Identification to Intervention.* New York, NY: Guilford.

Foorman, B. R., Francis, D. J., Fletcher, J. M., Schatschneider, C., & Mehta, P. (1998). The role of instruction in learning to read: Preventing reading failure in at-risk children. *Journal of Educational Psychology, 90*(1), 37–55.

Foorman, B. R., & Torgesen, J. K. (2001). Critical elements of classroom and small group instruction promote reading success in all children. *Learning Disabilities Research & Practice 16*(4), 203–212.

Guskey, T. R. (1997). *Implementing Mastery Learning.* Belmont, CA: Wadsworth Publishing.

Hall, T. E., Hughes, C. A., & Filbert, M. (2000). Computer assisted instruction in reading for students with learning disabilities: A research synthesis. *Education and Treatment of Children, 23*(3), 173–193.

Hook, P. E., Macaruso, P., & Jones, S. (2001). Efficacy of fast forward training on facilitating acquisition of reading skills by children with reading difficulties—A longitudinal study. *Annals of Dyslexia, 51,* 75–96.

Kamil, M. L., Borman, G. D., Dole, J., Kral, C. C., Salinger, T., & Torgesen, J. (2008). *Improving Adolescent Literacy: Effective Classroom and Intervention Practices: A Practice Guide* (NCEE #2008-4027). Washington, DC: National Center for Education Evaluation and Regional Assistance, Institute of Education Sciences, U.S. Department of Education.

Kluger, A., & Adler, S. (1993). Person- versus computer-mediated feedback. *Computers in Human Behavior, 9*(1), 1–16.

Kulik, J. A. (1994). Meta-analytic studies of findings on computer-based instruction. In E. L. Baker & H. F. O'Neil, Jr. (Eds.), *Technology Assessment in Education and Training.* Hillsdale, NJ: Lawrence Erlbaum.

Lee, C. D., & Spratley, A. (2010). *Reading in the Disciplines: The Challenges of Adolescent Literacy.* New York, NY: Carnegie Corporation of New York. Retrievable from: http://carnegie.org/fileadmin/Media/Publications/PDF/tta_Lee.pdf

Research and Evidence of Effectiveness

Lovett, M. W., Lacerenza, L., De Palma, M., & Frijters, J.C. (2012) Evaluating the efficacy of remediation for struggling readers in high school. *Journal of Learning Disabilities, 45*(2), 151–169.

Lyon, G. R. (1995). Toward a definition of dyslexia. *Annals of Dyslexia, 45*, 3–27.

MacArthur, C. A., Ferretti, R. P., Okolo, C. M., & Cavalier, A. R. (2001). Technology applications for students with literacy problems: A critical review. *The Elementary School Journal, 101*, 273–301.

Moats, L. C. (2010). *Speech to Print: Language Essentials for Teachers*. Baltimore: Paul Brookes.

Morris, R. D., Lovett, M. W., Wolf, M., Sevcik, R. A., Steinbach, K. A., Frijters, J. C., & Shapiro, M. B. (2012) Multiple-component remediation for developmental reading disabilities: IQ, socioeconomic status, and race as factors in remedial outcome. *Journal of Learning Disabilities, 45*(2), 99–127.

Nagy, W. E., & Anderson, R. C. (1984). How many words are there in printed English? *Reading Research Quarterly, 19*, 304–330.

National Association of State Boards of Education. (2005). *Reading at Risk: How States Can Respond to the Crisis in Adolescent Literacy*. Alexandria, VA: Author. Retrievable from http://www.centeroninstruction.org/files/Reading_At_Risk_Full_Report.pdf

National Center for Education Statistics. (2009). *The Nation's Report Card: Reading 2009* (NCES 2010–458). Washington, DC: Institute of Education Sciences, U.S. Department of Education.

National Institute for Literacy. (2007). *What Content Area Teachers Should Know About Adolescent Literacy*. Jessup, MD: EdPubs. Retrievable from: http://lincs.ed.gov/publications/pdf/adolescent_literacy07.pdf

National Joint Committee on Learning Disabilities. (2008). *Adolescent Literacy and Older Students with Learning Disabilities* [Technical Report]. Retrieved from: www.asha.org/policy

National Longitudinal Transition Study II. (2003). *National Center for Special Education Research at the Institute of Education Sciences*. Washington, DC: U.S. Department of Education.

National Reading Panel. (2000). *Teaching Children to Read: An Evidence-Based Assessment of the Scientific Research Literature on Reading and Its Implications for Reading Instruction*. National Institute of Child Health and Human Development, Washington, DC.

Niemiec, C. P., & Ryan, R. M. (2009). Autonomy, competence, and relatedness in the classroom: Applying self-determination theory to educational practice. *Theory and Research in Education 7*(2), 133-144.

Reed, D. K., & Vaughn, S. (2010). Reading interventions for older students. In T. A. Glover & S. Vaughn (Eds.), *Response to Intervention: Empowering All Students to Learn, a Critical Account of the Science and Practice* (pp. 143–186). New York: Guilford Press.

Scammacca, N., Roberts, G., Vaughn, S., Edmonds, M., Wexler, J., Reutebuch, C. K., et al. (2007). *Reading Interventions for Adolescent Struggling Readers: A Meta-Analysis with Implications for Practice*. Portsmouth, NH: RMC Research Corporation, Center on Instruction.

Scarborough, H. S., and Brady, S. A. (2002). Toward a common terminology for talking about speech and reading: A glossary of the "phon" words and some related terms. *Journal of Literacy Research, 34*(3), 299–334.

Schacter, J. (1999). *The Impact of Educational Technology on Student Achievement: What the Most Current Research Has to Say.* Milken Exchange on Educational Technology, Santa Monica, CA. Retrievable from: http://www.eric.ed.gov/PDFS/ED430537.pdf

Schatschneider, C., Buck, J., Torgesen, J., Wagner, R., Hassler, L., Hecht, S., et al. (2004). A Multivariate Study of Individual Differences in Performance on the Reading Portion of the Florida Comprehensive Assessment Test:A Preliminary Report. Technical report #5, Florida Center for Reading Research.

Shankweiler, D., Lundquist, E., Katz, L., Stuebing, K. K., Fletcher, J. M., Brady, S., et al. (1999). Comprehension and decoding: Patterns of association in children with reading difficulties. *Scientific Studies of Reading, 3*, 69–94.

Slavin, R. E., Cheung, A., Groff, C., & Lake, C. (2008). Effective reading programs for middle and high schools: A best-evidence synthesis. *Reading Research Quarterly, 43*(3), 290– 322.

Snow, C. E., & Biancarosa, G. (2003). *Adolescent Literacy and the Achievement Gap: What Do We Know and Where Do We Go from Here?* New York: Carnegie Corporation of New York.

Soe, K., Koki, S., & Chang, J. M. (2000). *Effect of Computer-Assisted Instruction (CAI) on Reading Achievement: A Meta-Analysis.* Pacific Resources for Education and Learning: Honolulu, HI. Retrievable from: http://www.prel.org/products/products/effect-cai.htm

Tillman, P. S. (2010). *Computer-Assisted Instruction (CAI) and Reading Acquisition: A Synthesis of the Literature.* Retrievable from: http://teach.valdosta.edu/are/TillmanPLRFinal.pdf

Torgesen, A. W., Alexander, R. K., Wagner, C. A., Rashotte, K., Conway, T., & Rose, E. (2001). Intensive remedial instruction for children with severe reading disabilities: Immediate and long-term outcomes from two instructional approaches. *Journal of Learning Disabilities, 34*, 33–58.

Torgesen, J. K. (2004). Avoiding the devastating downward spiral: The evidence that early intervention prevents reading failure. *American Educator, 28*, 6–19.

Torgesen, J. K., Wagner, R. K., Rashotte, C. A., Herron, J., & Lindamood, P. (2010). Computer-assisted instruction to prevent early reading difficulties in students at risk for dyslexia: Outcomes from two instructional approaches. *Annals of Dyslexia, 60*(1), 40–56. doi:10.1007/s11881-009-0032-y

Tsesmeli, S. N., & Seymour, P. H. K. (2009). The effects of training of morphological structure on spelling derived words by dyslexic adolescents. *British Journal of Psychology, 100*, 565–592.

Vadasy, P. F., Sanders, E. A., & Tudor, S. (2007). Effectiveness of paraeducator supplemented individual instruction: Beyond basic decoding skill. *Journal of Learning Disabilities, 40*(6), 508–524.

Vaughn, S., Gersten, R., & Chard, D. J. (2000). The underlying message in LD intervention research: Findings from research syntheses. *Exceptional Children, 67*(1), 99–114.

Vellutino, F. R., Tunmer, W. E., Jaccard, J. J., & Chen, R. (2007). Components of reading ability: Multivariate evidence for a convergent skills model of reading development. *Scientific Studies of Reading, 11*(1), 3–32.

Index

Index

reading, 30, 51, 62, 109, 146, 195, 244, 251, 307, 337–338, 344–345, 397, 427–428, 433, 480–481, 518–519, 526
writing, 58, 59, 136, 238, 273, 299, 392, 474–475, 476
guided reading. *See* close reading

handwriting, 75, 156, 275, 349, 447, 520, 550
headings
identifying, 43, 63, 434, 456, 482
reviewing, 62, 436
helping verbs. *See* verbs
how (question word), 101, 102, 103, 107, 108, 136, 183, 187, 306, 382, 390, 431
how many (question words), 183, 187, 188, 301, 391

identify (prompt), 335, 336, 337, 341, 343, 344, 394, 395
idioms, using, 36, 115, 243, 244, 312, 351. *See also* figurative language
illustrations. *See* pictures/illustrations
imagery, 139, 140
imperative verbs, 401, 402. *See also* verbs
incorrect premise, 535. *See also* false premise/assumption
independent clauses, 473, 474, 475–476. *See also* clauses
independent practice
grammar, 19, 20, 21, 54, 55, 57, 99, 100, 102, 104, 184, 186, 298, 384, 386, 389, 468, 471, 472, 474
reading, 30, 51, 62, 109, 146, 195, 251, 308, 345, 398, 433, 481, 527
writing, 25, 59, 137, 239, 273, 299, 392, 475, 476
independent reading, 12, 27, 32, 48, 60, 64, 88, 111, 130, 143, 149, 170, 192, 197, 218, 254, 287, 304, 310, 327, 342, 347, 373, 395, 400, 418, 430, 435, 461, 478, 483, 502, 523, 529
infer (prompt), 335, 336, 337, 341, 343, 344, 394, 395, 396
inference, making, 194, 255
inflection (voice), 38, 181, 402, 444, 545

inflectional endings, 97. *See also* suffixes
Informational Preview Checklist, 43
informational text, 41, 212, 280, 320, 366–367, 412, 413, 440, 454, 465, 495–496
initiating event, 92, 93, 169
intensive pronouns, 388–389, 402
intent. *See* author's purpose
interpret (prompt), 243, 245, 248, 249, 303, 305, 307
interrogative statement, 348
irony, 200, 274
irregular spellings, 97, 296
irregular verbs, 56, 100, 296. *See also* verbs, linking verbs
irrelevant fact, 535, 536, 538
IVF topic sentence. *See* topic sentences

journal, 317–318. *See also* diary

key details, 237

language
author's choice of, 92
body language, 261, 311
descriptive, 153, 270, 272, 299, 355, 448
figurative, 112, 201, 205, 264, 312, 349, 351, 496, 529, 536, 539
literal use of, 36, 264, 351
misleading (*See* fallacies)
precise versus imprecise, 299, 317
on the street, 367
upgrading, 299, 300
leading question, 534
lesson openers, 4, 16, 26, 31, 37, 41, 52, 60, 63, 69, 80, 94, 106, 110, 118, 123, 134, 142, 147, 152, 162, 180, 191, 196, 206, 211, 236, 247, 253, 269, 280, 293, 302, 309, 316, 320, 332, 341, 346, 353, 366, 379, 393, 399, 407, 412, 422, 429, 434, 441, 454, 466, 477, 482, 490, 495, 512, 522, 528, 542
letter writing, 39

Index

linking verbs. *See* verbs
literal language, 36, 264, 351
literary text. *See* text type
literature. *See* text type; *specific kinds of literature*
loaded term, 525, 531, 540
logical errors. *See* fallacies
logic errors, 533. *See also* fallacies

main idea, 70, 237–239, 302–303, 334, 355, 427, 443, 545, 547. *See also* central idea; reading, Big Ideas; topic sentences
Masterpiece Sentences, 22–25, 57, 105, 136–137, 153, 187–188, 189, 270, 299–300, 317, 381, 390–392, 426, 474–475
melody, 139, 141
memoir, 367, 412, 454
memorable phrases. *See* aphorisms
metaphors, 367, 402. *See also* figurative language
meter, 139
misleading language. *See* fallacies
modeling
    grammar, 18, 19, 20, 21, 54, 55, 56, 99, 104, 184, 186, 297, 298, 383–384, 386, 389, 470, 472
    reading, 11, 29, 51, 87–88, 108, 145, 169–170, 194, 244, 250–251, 306, 337, 344, 396–397, 426–427, 432–433, 480, 518, 525
    writing, 25, 58, 59, 238, 273, 475–476
mood. *See also* tense
    conditional mood, 349
    identifying, 401, 411, 450
    in poetry, 139, 140
    subjunctive mood, 401
moral, 81, 150, 153, 539
movie, 40, 210, 545. *See also* video
multiparagraph essay, 521, 544, 545–550
multiple-meaning words, 211–212

naming words, 103, 382. *See also* nouns
narrative, 132, 411, 444, 450
Narrative Preview Checklist, 6, 82, 164

narrator, 4, 80, 107, 132–133, 137, 149, 150, 162–163, 281, 311, 401, 412, 454. *See also* characters
natural speaking, 199
nonexamples, 103
nonfiction, 41, 280, 411, 412, 450, 454–455, 495–496. *See also* text type
nonstandard words, 112, 113, 151
note taking, 71–72, 546
nouns. *See also* pronouns
    abstract nouns, 96
    adjectives as (*See* adjectives)
    common nouns, 17–18, 53, 96, 311
    concrete nouns, 96
    function of, 17, 266, 381–384
    identifying, 17–18, 34
    noun phrases, 265, 485
    possessive nouns, 53–55, 97
    predicate noun, 382, 383, 384
    prepositional phrases, 102–104, 136, 153, 187, 340, 382, 384, 473
    proper nouns, 17–18, 53, 96, 311
    singular versus plural, 18, 53, 59, 97
    subject noun, 381, 382, 383, 384
novel, 4, 162–163, 240, 280. *See also* fiction
novel meanings, words with, 348
number topic sentences. *See* topic sentences

objective point of view, 195, 302, 334, 393, 404, 437, 440. *See also* point of view
object of the preposition, 382, 383, 384, 487
object pronouns, 98, 137, 388
one-syllable words, 139, 296
online assessment. *See* assessment, end-of-unit
opposites, 112. *See also* antonyms
overgeneralization, 531, 533, 535, 538, 539

Index